The Other Lands of Israel

Imaginations of the Land in *2 Baruch*

By

Liv Ingeborg Lied

BRILL

LEIDEN • BOSTON
2008

This book is printed on acid-free paper.

Library of Congress Cataloging-in-Publication Data

Lied, Liv Ingeborg.
  The other lands of Israel : imaginations of the Land in 2 Baruch / by Liv Ingeborg Lied.
       p. cm. -- (Supplements to the Journal for the study of Judaism, ISSN 0169-9717 ; v. 129)
  Includes bibliographical references and index.
  ISBN 978-90-04-16556-4 (hardback : alk. paper) 1. Land tenure--Religious aspects--Judaism. 2. Sacred space--Palestine. 3. Syriac Apocalypse of Baruch--Criticism, interpretation, etc. I. Title. II. Series.

  BM538.L33L54 2008
  229'.913--dc22

                                                                      2008031293

ISSN: 1384-2161
ISBN: 978 90 04 16556 4

Copyright 2008 by Koninklijke Brill NV, Leiden, The Netherlands.
Koninklijke Brill NV incorporates the imprints Brill, Hotei Publishing,
IDC Publishers, Martinus Nijhoff Publishers and VSP.

PRINTED IN THE NETHERLANDS

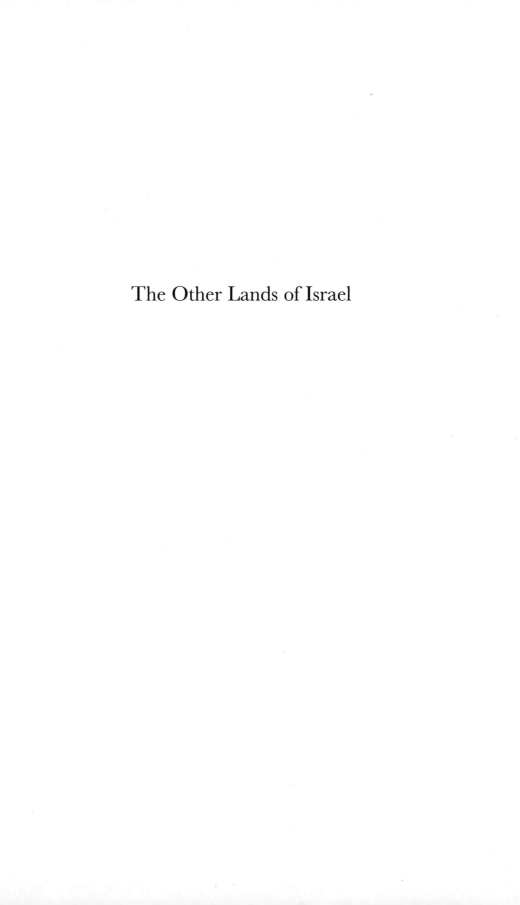

The Other Lands of Israel

Supplements

to the

Journal for the Study of Judaism

Editor

John J. Collins
The Divinity School, Yale University

Associate Editors

Florentino García Martínez
Qumran Institute, University of Groningen

Hindy Najman
Department of Near and Middle Eastern Civilizations
University of Toronto

Advisory Board

J. DUHAIME – A. HILHORST – P.W. VAN DER HORST

A. KLOSTERGAARD PETERSEN – M.A. KNIBB – J.T.A.G.M. VAN RUITEN

J.SIEVERS – G. STEMBERGER – E.J.C. TIGCHELAAR – J. TROMP

VOLUME 129

For Jørgen, Henning and Eystein

CONTENTS

ACKNOWLEDGMENTS

This book is based on my doctoral thesis at the University of Bergen, Norway, which was submitted in 2006. The study was conducted within the creative and open atmosphere of the Department of the History of Religions, and with the financial support of the Faculty of Arts. I am deeply grateful to my supervisor Einar Thomassen, who provided my course of study with the perfect balance of guidance and freedom, trusting my decisions, whilst keeping me in the loop.

I am grateful to committee members Matthias Henze, Halvor Moxnes and Lisbeth Mikaelsson for their assistance and helpful suggestions concerning changes to the thesis before publication. I am also grateful to Halvor Moxnes for introducing me to theoretical approaches to space in the late 1990's.

I thank John J. Collins, Edward W. Soja, George J. Brooke, Turid Karlsen Seim, Jorunn Økland, Samuel Rubenson, Troels Engberg-Pedersen, Torleif Elgvin, and Hugo Lundhaug for their invaluable response and support. My warmest thanks go to Ingvild Sælid Gilhus for her generosity and to Dag Ø. Endsjø for his help and encouragement.

Thanks also to the faculty at the Department of Religions and Theology at the University of Manchester and at the Department of Biblical Studies at the University of Sheffield for their input at early stages of this work.

I have benefited greatly from my participation in the project *Metamorphoses: Resurrection, Taxonomies and Transformative Practices in Early Christianity* at the Centre for Advanced Study at the University of Oslo, the PhD program *Project for the Study of Ancient Christianity*, the RCN-funded project *Det kristne menneske: Konstruksjon av kristen identitet i antikken*, and the NorFa-network *Nordic Network in Qumran Studies*. The people involved in these projects helped to open my eyes and sharpen my sight.

Special thanks go to my family: my parents, my brother and my parents-in-law. Most of all, I am forever grateful for the support of my dear sons Henning and Jørgen and of my beloved husband Eystein. This study is dedicated to the three of you.

Asker, 30.04.08
Liv Ingeborg Lied

ABBREVIATIONS

ABD	*The Anchor Bible Dictionary*. Edited by D.N. Freedman. 6 vols. New York, 1992.
ABR	*Australian Biblical Review*
ABRL	Anchor Bible Reference Library
AGJU	Arbeiten zur Geschichte des antiken Judentums und des Urchristentums
AJSL	*American Journal of Semitic Languages and Literatures*
ALGHJ	Arbeiten zur Literatur und Geschichte des hellenistischen Judentums
AnBib	Analecta biblica
ANRW	*Aufstieg und Niedergang der römishcen Welt*
ArBib	The Aramaic Bible
ArtB	*The Art Bulletin*
ARW	*Archiv für Religionswissenschaft*
ATD	Das Alte Testament deutsch
ATANT	Abhandlungen zur Theologie des Alten und Neuen Testaments
AusBR	*Australian Biblical Review*
AUSS	*Andrews University Seminary Studies*
BEATAJ	Beiträge zur Erforschung des Alten Testaments und des antiken Judentums
BHT	Beiträge zur historischen Theologie
Bib	*Biblica. Commentarii editi cura Pontificii Instituti Biblici*
BibInt	*Biblical Interpretation Series*
BibOr	Biblica et orientalia
BMI	*The Bible and its Modern Interpreters*
BRev	*Bible Review*
BSem	*The Biblical Seminar*
BWANT	Beiträge zur Wissenschaft vom Alten und Neuen Testament
BZAW	Beihäfte zur Zeitschrift für die alttestamentliche Wissenschaft
BZNW	Beihäfte zur Zeitschrift für die neutestamentliche Wissenschaft
CBET	Contributions to Biblical Exegesis and Theology
CBQ	*The Catholic Biblical Quarterly*
CBQMS	The Catholic Biblical Quarterly Monograph Series
ConBNT	Coniectanea neotestamentica or Coniectanea biblica: New Testament Series
CRINT	Compendia Rerum Iudaicarum Ad Novum Testamentum
CSJH	Chicago Studies in the History of Judaism.
CWS	The Classics of Western Spirituality. New York, 1978–

DDD	*Dictionary of Deities and Demons in the Bible*
DSD	*Dead Sea Discoveries*
EBib	Etudes bibliques
EPRO	Etudes préliminaires aux religions orientales dans l'empire romain.
ErJb	*Eranos-Jahrbuch*
FBE	Forum for bibelsk eksegese
FRLANT	Forschungen zur Religion und Literatur des Alten und Neuen Testaments
GCS	Die griechischen-christlichen Schriftsteller der ersten [drei] Jahrhunderte
GTA	Göttinger theologischer Arbeiten
HDR	Harvard Dissertations in Religion
HO	Handbuch der Orientalistik
HR	*History of Religions*
HSM	Harvard Semitic Monographs
HTR	*Harvard Theological Review*
HUCA	*Hebrew Union College Annual*
Int	*Interpretation*
JAAR	*Journal of the American Academy of Religion*
JBL	*Journal of Biblical Literature*
JbPT	Jahrbuch für protestantische Theologie
JE	Singer, I., Alder C. et al, eds. *The Jewish Encyclopedia: A Descriptive Record of the History, Literature, and Customs of the Jewish People from the Earliest Time to the Present Day.* 12 vols. New York: Funk and Wagnalls, 1901–1905. Repr. 1925.
JJS	*Journal of Jewish Studies*
JR	*The Journal of Religion*
JSem	*Journal for Semitics*
JSJ	*Journal for the Study of Judaism in the Persian, Hellenistic, and Roman Period*
JSJSup	*Supplements to Journal for the Study of Judaism*
JSNTSup	Journal for the Study of the New Testament: Supplement Series
JSP	*Journal for the Study of Pseudepigrapha*
JSPSup	*Journal for the Study of the Pseudepigrapha: Supplement Series*
JSS	*Journal of Semitic Studies*
JTS	*Journal of Theological Studies*
JudCh	*Judaica et christiana*
LCL	Loeb Classical Library
LD	*Lectio divina*
LNTS	Library of New Testament Studies
LSTS	Library of Second Temple Studies
MdB	*Le monde de la Bible*
NEchtB	*Neue Echter Bibel*
Neot	*Neotestamentica*
NovT	*Novum Testamentum*
NovTSup	Supplements to Novum Testamentum

NTS	*New Testament Studies*
NTT	*Norsk Teologisk Tidsskrift*
OBT	Overtures to Biblical Theology
OCT	Oxford Classical Texts/Scriptorum classicorum biblitotheca oxoniensis
OECT	Oxford Early Christian texts. Edited by H. Chadwick. Oxford, 1970–
OTP	*Old Testament Pseudepigrapha*. Edited by J.H. Charlesworth. 2 vols. Garden City, NY: Doubleday, 1983, 1985.
OTS	Old Testament Studies
PVTG	Pseudepigrapha Veteris Testamenti Graece
RB	*Revue biblique*
RBL	*Review of Biblical Literature*
RechBib	Recherches Bibliques
RevScRel	*Revue des sciences religieuses*
RHPR	*Revue d'histoire et de philosophie religieuses*
REJ	*Revue des études juives*
SB	Sources bibliques
SBLDS	Society of Biblical Literature Dissertation Series
SBLEJL	Society of Biblical Literature Early Judaism and Its Literature
SBLSP	Society of Biblical Literature Seminar Papers
SBS	Stuttgarter Bibelstudien
SBT	Studies in Biblical Theology
SC	Sources chrètiennes. Paris, 1943–
SJLA	Studies in Judaism in Late Antiquity
SNTSMS	Society for New Testament Studies Monograph Series
SPSHS	Scholars Press Studies in the Humanities
SR	*Studies in Religion*
SSN	Studia semitica neerlandica
ST	*Studia theologica*
STDJ	Studies on the Texts of the Desert of Judah
StPB	Studia Post-Biblica
SVTP	Studia in Veteris Testamenti pseudepigrapha
TDNT	*Theological Dictionary of the New Testament*. Edited by G. Kittel and G. Friedrich. Translated by G.W. Bromiley. 10 vols. Grand Rapids, Mich.: Eerdmans, 1964–1967.
TGUOS	Transactions of the Glasgow University Oriental Society
TSK	*Theologische Studien und Kritiken*
TU	Texte und Untersuchungen
TUGAL	Texte und Untersuchungen zur Geschichte der altchristlichen Literatur
UUA	Uppsala Universitets Årsskrift
VT	*Vetus Testamentum*
VTSup	Supplements to Vetus Testamentum
WCJS	*Proceedings of the World Congress of Jewish Studies*
WMANT	Wissenschaftliche Monographien zum Alten und Neuen Testament

WUNT   Wissenschaftliche Untersuchungen zum Neuen Testament
ZAW   *Zeitschrift für alttestamentliche Wissenschaft*
ZDPW   *Zeitschrift des deutschen Palästina-Vereins*

TRANSLITERATION OF THE SYRIAC

ʾĀlaph	ʾ	Semkath	s
Bēth	b	ʿĒ	ʿ
Gāmal	g	Pē	p
Dālath	d	Çādhē	ç
Hē	h	Qōph	q
Waw	w	Rēš	r
Zain	z	Šīn	š
Ḥēth	ḥ	Taw	t
Ṭēth	ṭ	Pṭāḥā	a
Yūdh	y	Zqāpā	ā
Kāph	k	Rbāçā	e
Lāmadh	l	Ḥbāçā	i
Mīm	m	ʿçāçā	u
Nūn	n		

The transliteration of the Syriac follows the system of T.H. Robinson, *Paradigms and Exercises in Syriac Grammar* (4th ed; Oxford: Clarendon Press, 1962).

CHAPTER ONE

2 BARUCH AND THE LAND

This study will explore the conception of Israel's Land as a redemptive category in the second century C.E. pseudepigraphon *2 Baruch*. According to the current scholarly consensus, the Land had either been rejected or become of minor importance to *2 Baruch*. In this study I will discuss the presuppositions behind this consensus with regard to the spatial epistemology it assumes.

2 Baruch: *Destruction and Consolation*

2 Baruch is commonly described as a Jewish apocalyptical and eschatological text composed in Palestine in response to the destruction of the Second Temple (70 C.E.). *2 Baruch* presents itself as "The Apocalypse of Baruch son of Neriah." The text thus invokes the authority of the famous scribe of the prophet Jeremiah, and sets the plot of its frame narrative in the last part of Baruch's life at the very end of the First Temple period. It is generally acknowledged, however, that *2 Baruch* uses this narrative background to discuss the reactions to the destruction of the Second Temple and the subsequent annihilation of the centre of Jewish power and worship in the first centuries C.E.

 2 Baruch consists of several ordered series of narrations, prayers and laments, apocalyptic visions or revelatory dialogues with their respective interpretations, followed by public addresses and speeches. In addition, the last ten chapters of *2 Baruch* (78–87) include an epistle, the so-called *Epistola Baruch*. The plot of the frame narrative, as well as the ongoing dialogue between God and Baruch, provides *2 Baruch* with a unified structure. The dialogue between God and Baruch ensures Baruch's gradual acceptance of the current catastrophe and gives him a growing understanding of God's plan for the redemption of Israel. The ongoing dialogue between God and Baruch gradually convinces Baruch that the crisis is part of God's master plan: the destruction of Jerusalem and its temple, and the dispersion of the wicked tribes signal that the end of the world is approaching. Due to the universal extent

of godlessness, the entire corruptible world will be destroyed. God tells
Baruch not to grieve over the current situation of Israel, since the catas-
trophes he is witnessing are all necessary steps towards Israel's final
redemption. Those who remain obedient to God and his Law will outlive the afflictions of the corruptible world and will achieve redemption,
first in the Messianic era and then in the incorruptible other world
together with the righteous among the resurrected dead. Consoled by
the words of God, Baruch urges the small group of followers who are
with him to study and live according to the Law and to keep up their
hopes for that other world. As long as Israel obeys the commandments,
God will eventually keep his promises in accordance with the covenant
of the patriarchs. During the last days of his life, Baruch prepares his
followers for the coming judgement and the subsequent redemption of
the righteous, and he writes letters[1] to the dispersed tribes, urging them
to return to righteousness and thus take part in the coming bliss.

Consoling Baruch: The Covenant, the Other World, and the Land

The preceding summary outline of *2 Baruch* suggested the centrality of
the Law, the covenant and the notion of the two worlds to the text. Several scholars have rightfully suggested that obedience to the Law and
the commandments is the main message of *2 Baruch*, since a life lived
according to the Law will secure resistance to affliction in the corruptible world, a positive outcome to God's judgement and subsequently
redemption in the other world.[2] In *2 Baruch*, obedience to the Law is
intimately connected to covenantal faithfulness.[3] Israel is both obliged

---

[1] One of them is presented as the *Epistola Baruch* (78–87), the other is just mentioned
briefly (77:19).

[2] Cf., e.g., *2 Bar.* 15; 77. Cf. R.H. Charles, *The Apocalypse of Baruch, Translated from
the Syriac, Chapters I–LXXVII from the Sixth Cent. MS in the Ambrosian Library of Milan, and
Chapters LXXVIII–LXXXVII—the Epistle of Baruch—from a New and Critical Text Based on
Ten MSS and Published Herewith. Edited, with Introduction, Notes, and Indices* (London: Black,
1896), 26; A.F.J. Klijn, "Recent Developments in the Study of the Syriac Apocalypse of
Baruch," *JSOP* 4 (1989): 7; C. Münchow, *Ethik und Eschatologie. Ein Beitrag zum Verständnis
der frühjüdischen Apokalyptik mit einem Ausblick auf das Neuen Testament* (Göttingen: Vandenhoeck & Ruprecht, *1981*), 100; M. Leuenberger, "Ort und Funktion der Wolkenvision
und ihrer Deutung in der Syrischen *Baruchapokalypse*," *JSJ* 36 (2005): 206–246 at 226;
229; 231.

[3] Cf., e.g., G.W. Hansen, *Abraham in Galatians: Epistolary and Rhetorical Contexts*
(JSNTSup 29; Sheffield: JSOT Press, 1989), 162–163; 179; H. Moxnes, *Theology in Conflict: Studies in Paul's Understanding of God in Romans* (NovTSup 53; Leiden: Brill, 1980),
164–169.

and blessed by the covenantal relationship God established with the patriarchs Abraham and Moses. In particular, *2 Baruch* attests to the dynamic of the Mosaic covenant, since it applies the common scheme of blessings and curses related to faithfulness and adultery respectively. As long as Israel fulfils her duties—to live according to the Law—God will bless his people, make it prosperous and allow it to live in the space that he promised to it: the Land. However, if any of the twelve tribes of the people turns wicked and thus breaks out of the marriage-like contract with God,[4] God will disperse it and remove his presence. To *2 Baruch*, the dynamic of promise and fulfilment is pivotal to the making of future hope. It is the main source of Israel's motivation and reassurance during her time of hardship in the corruptible world.

A clear eschatological orientation dominates *2 Baruch*, both in the evaluation of the history of Israel in the past, in the frustration over the turmoil of the imminent end-time and in the anticipation of future reward. The eschatology of the work is complex and manifold, and includes both the idea of a temporary Messianic era and the notion of an everlasting other word. The notion of the other world, however, dominates the description of future salvation.

The idea of the two worlds, one corruptible and transient, the other incorruptible and everlasting, plays an important role in the eschatological rhetoric that runs through the text. The existence of the other world is a main argument in *2 Baruch*'s insistence on Israel's future reward. According to *2 Bar.* 14–15, the other world was created for the sake of Israel. The other world has in fact been promised to Israel by God.[5] And at some point in the future, the other world will indeed belong to Israel. However, although that world already exists and can be seen by a select number of visionaries (4:3–6), it is generally hidden from humankind, remaining a future hope as long as the present world lingers on. The contrast between the two worlds provides a fundamental dividing line between the present order of wickedness and the future order of righteousness. However, throughout the period of end-time destruction, the corruptible world is slowly dying. And after the

---

[4] I refer to Israel as 'she', in other words as a feminine entity. I do this to underscore Israel's marriage-like relationship to God through the covenant. Cf. K.L. Gaca, *The Making of Fornication: Eros, Ethics, and Political Reform in Greek Philosophy and Early Christianity* (Hellenistic Culture and Society 40; Berkeley: University of California Press, 2003), 158; 173 ff.

[5] Cf. 14:13; 21:25; 83:5. Cf. *4 Ezra* 6:55–59 for the same idea.

day of resurrection and judgement, the other world will finally become a reality to those who are proven faithful (49–51).

According to G.B. Sayler's study *Have the Promises Failed? A Literary Analysis of 2 Baruch*,[6] and F.J. Murphy's 1985 monograph *The Structure and Meaning of Second Baruch*[7] a key issue of *2 Baruch* is the gradual consolation of Baruch and his followers, and thus implicitly of *2 Baruch*'s audience. Sayler says: "The author of 2 Baruch responds to the events of 70 C.E. by composing a story—a story in which Baruch and then his community move from grief to consolation."[8] Murphy adds that *2 Baruch*'s increased focus on the covenant, the Law, and what he designates 'the two-world concept' serve as vehicles of consolation and hope in the text:

> He [the author] adapted the two-world concept to his own purposes by dwelling on the ontological difference between the two aeons, and then by locating the Temple and Jerusalem firmly in the present, passing aeon. He thereby relativized the importance of the fall of Zion. In this process, he made a strong case for the centrality of the covenant and its Law in the life, past and present, of the community. He adapted the covenantal idea by substituting eschatological reward for earthly prosperity as the blessing that went with the covenant. In so doing he not only criticised a certain type of mourning for the fall of Jerusalem, but also discouraged hope in a restored city, proposed by some as a reward promised for covenant fidelity.[9]

The study of Murphy provides an important insight into a central assertion of *2 Baruch*. Those who are faithful to the Law will be rewarded by the fulfilment of the promises of the covenant and will take part in the future bliss of the other world. Those who reject the Law, on the other hand, will face punishment and will be destroyed together with the corruptible world. In other words, *2 Baruch*'s line of reasoning presupposes both the covenantal promises, among which the promise of the Land as redemptive space is traditionally prominent, and an explicit rejection of the corruptible world. In this tension between an apparent this-worldly promise and an explicit preference for the other world the construction of covenantal space unfolds in *2 Baruch*. This tension between the

---

[6] G.B. Sayler, *Have the Promises Failed? A Literary Analysis of 2 Baruch* (SBLDS; Chico, Calif.: Scholars Press, 1984), 20; 68; 85–86.

[7] F.J. Murphy, *The Structure and Meaning of Second Baruch* (SBLDS 78; Atlanta: Scholars Press, 1985), 8–9.

[8] Sayler, *Promises*, 38.

[9] Murphy, *Structure and Meaning*, 9.

promise of the Land and the fulfilment of promises in the other world has not been granted sufficient attention, and therefore a closer look at *2 Baruch*'s conception of the Land is warranted.

Grasping Space and Grasping Land

In 1974 W.D. Davies published the monograph *The Gospel and the Land: Early Christianity and Jewish Territorial Doctrine*,[10] a work which was eventually to become a standard work in the studies of the Land-theme[11] in Jewish and Christian sources.[12] In his discussion of the Land-theme in the texts of the so-called Apocrypha and Pseudepigrapha, Davies suggested that the interest in the Land had decreased in those texts, compared to biblical texts and rabbinic sources.[13] In his 1982 follow-up work *The Territorial Dimension of Judaism*,[14] Davies explained the reduced attention to the Land-theme by the increased focus on universal and cosmological entities:

---

[10] W.D. Davies, *The Gospel and the Land: Early Christianity and Jewish Territorial Doctrine* (BSem 25; Berkeley, LA: University of California Press, 1974; Repr., Sheffield: JSOT Press, 1994).

[11] I apply this term to grasp the wider, yet related, field of conceptions and traditions associated with the Land. I do not suggest that the Land-theme is monolithic, but rather a repertoire of conventional concepts and models (Cf. Habel, *The Land is Mine*).

[12] Other early contributors were G. von Rad, *The Problem of the Hexateuch and Other Essays* (Trans. E.W.T. Dicken; New York: McGraw-Hill, 1966); W.P. Eckert and M. Sohr Levinson, eds., *Jüdische Volk, gelobtes Land* (München: Kaiser, 1970); P. Diepold, *Israel's Land* (BWANT 95; Stuttgart: Kohlhammer, 1972). Several books have appeared since then, many of them excellent. Cf. W. Brueggemann, *The Land: Place as Gift, Promise, and Challenge in Biblical Faith* (2nd ed.; OBT; Minneapolis: Fortress Press, 2002 (1st ed 1977)); M. Weinfeld, "Inheritance of the Land—Privilege versus Obligation: The Concept of the 'Promise of the Land' in the Sources of the First and Second Temple Periods," (in Hebrew) *Zion* 49 (1984): 115–137; D. Mendels, *The Land of Israel as a Political Concept in Hasmonean Literature: Recourse to History in 2. Century BC Claims to the Holy Land* (Tübingen: J.C.B. Mohr, 1987); S. Japhet, *The Ideology of the Book of Chronicles and Its Place in Biblical Thought* (BEATAJ 9; Frankfurt am Main: Verlag Peter Lang, 1989); R.L. Wilken, *The Land Called Holy: Palestine in Christian History and Thought* (New Haven: Yale University Press, 1992); N.C. Habel, *The Land is Mine: Six Biblical Land Ideologies* (OBT; Minneapolis: Fortress Press, 1995); J. Joosten, *People and Land in the Holiness Code: An Exegetical Study of the Ideational Framework of the Law in Leviticus 17–26* (VTSup 67; Leiden: E.J. Brill, 1996); S. Kunin, *God's Place in the World: Sacred Space and Sacred Place in Judaism* (London: Cassell, 1998).

[13] Davies, *Gospel and Land*, 49; 156.

[14] W.D. Davies, *The Territorial Dimension of Judaism* (Berkeley: University of California Press, 1982).

> The promise of The Land, cherished as we have seen it to be, must be
> considered in the framework of such speculation, which could not but
> have depressed the doctrine of The Land to a less central position than
> it would otherwise have occupied. The flames of the end, feeding on a
> cosmos afire, would tend to diminish interest in The Land as such.[15]

According to Davies, the importance of the Land was suppressed by
the turning of eschatology towards universal concerns and cosmological structures. Davies undoubtedly points out a tendency which is evident in many apocryphal and pseudepigraphal texts. On the other
hand, though, it is possible that the relationship between the Land-
theme and the universal and cosmological concerns of contemporaneous eschatology was rather more complex than indicated by the above
quote. Indeed, Davies himself showed sensitivity towards the twists and
turns of the texts and in fact raised the possibility of several alternative
interpretations of the Land-theme within the above-mentioned confines of the general tendencies of eschatology.[16] There is a need, however, to further explore the function of the Land-theme within specific
texts belonging to the fuzzily defined group of Apocrypha and Pseudepigrapha, as well as to discuss both the relevance of the Land-theme
and the development of the conception of Israel's Land within these
texts.[17]

Rejecting the Land: A History of Research into the Land-theme

This study intends to look more closely at the Land-theme in *2 Baruch*.
To what extent is Davies right in his conclusions with regard to the
Land-theme in *2 Baruch*? How have scholars so far approached the
notion of Israel's Land in *2 Baruch*? And how have they viewed the
connection between the Land and the other world?

To my knowledge, no study has so far devoted itself solely to
2 Baruch's approach to the Land. D.J. Harrington's article "The 'Holy
Land' in *Pseudo-Philo*, *4 Ezra*, and *2 Baruch*," is the only study that explicitly discusses *2 Baruch*'s Land,[18] but, as the title of this article indicates,

---

[15] Davies, *Territorial Dimension*, 90–91.

[16] Cf. Davies, *Gospel and Land*, 75–158.

[17] A small number of studies have made the Land-theme within the Pseudepigrapha
their main concern. Prominent among them is B. Halpern-Amaru, *Rewriting the Bible:
Land and Covenant in Postbiblical Jewish Literature* (Valley Forge, Penn.: Trinity Press International, 1994).

[18] D.J. Harrington, "'The Holy Land' in *Pseudo-Philo*, *4 Ezra*, and *2 Baruch*," in *Ema-*

Harrington divides the focus of his article equally between *2 Baruch*, *4 Ezra* and Pseudo-Philo's *Liber Antiquitatum Biblicarum* (*L.A.B.*). Apart from Harrington's article, *2 Baruch*'s conceptions of the Land have most-ly been mentioned in the context of larger studies. The most exten-sive contributions have been made by Sayler and Murphy, and most recently by M.F. Whitters.[19] Yet other scholars have discussed the geog-raphy in the text in ways that have had bearings on their understanding of the Land. P.-M. Bogaert is prominent among these.[20]

Sayler discussed *2 Baruch*'s use of the Land-theme under the head-ing "The Loss of the Land."[21] She suggested that the loss of the Land presents a threat to the survival of Israel, since it questions God's will-ingness to keep the promises that he made to the patriarchs. Sayler argued that *2 Baruch* on several occasions recalls a geography that trig-gers allusions to the covenants God made with Abraham and Moses. Her point is that *2 Baruch*'s use of this geography is meant to assure the audience that the covenants with Abraham and Moses remain valid. Sayler's conclusion is that covenant faithfulness guarantees future bliss, and that knowledge of Israel's past is the basis upon which the commu-nity's redemption depends.[22] Implicitly, she thus understands the Land as belonging to a bygone period in the corruptible world and does not discuss how the covenant and its promises play a role in shaping future redemptive spaces.

In his 1985 study, Murphy discussed the role of Zion and the two-world concept in *2 Baruch* at length. Murphy's book is undoubtedly one of the most important contributions to the understanding of space in *2 Baruch*. The role of the Land in that text is not, however, a major focus of his study. Murphy suggests that the purpose of *2 Baruch* is to reduce the importance of the corruptible world and to promote a hope for the other world. He states that the rejection of the present world implies a denial of the Land since a focus on the Land is incompatible

---

nuel: Studies on Hebrew Bible, Septuagint, and the Dead Sea Scrolls in Honor of Emanuel Tov (eds. S.M. Paul et al.; VTSup; London: Brill, 2003), 661–672.

[19] M. Whitters, *The Epistle of Second Baruch: A Study of Form and Message* (LSTS 42; Sheffield: Sheffield Academic Press, 2003). In addition, some scholars have made small remarks about the status of the Land in *2 Baruch*. Among them is A.F.J. Klijn, "The Sources and Redaction of the Syriac Apocalypse of Baruch," *JSJ* 1 (1970): 65–76.

[20] P.-M. Bogaert, *Apocalypse de Baruch. Introduction, traduction du Syriac et commentaire* (2 vols; SC 144–145; Paris: Les editions du cerf, 1969).

[21] Sayler, *Promises*, 74–79; 86; 89.

[22] Sayler, *Promises*, 35.

with the interest in the eschatological other world.[23] Nevertheless, Murphy acknowledges the tension between the focus on the covenant and the insistence of the other world within the eschatology of the work. He says: "The author in no way wishes to deny scripture-based hope. However, in relocating the point of application of the promise from the earthly to the heavenly sphere, he has eschewed the literal interpretation of Isaiah."[24] Hence, Murphy places the Land of *2 Baruch* firmly in the corruptible world, and considers it lost when Israel enters the other world. Although Murphy acknowledges that the hopes and promises connected to the Land-theme continue somehow to influence *2 Baruch*'s description of the other world, he does not attempt to discuss how they influence the presentation of the other world.

Whitters also comments on *2 Baruch*'s Land in *The Epistle of Baruch: A Study of Form and Message*. Whitters generally agrees with Murphy. Just like Murphy, Whitters on the one hand acknowledges the importance of the Law, the covenant and its promises in *2 Baruch*, while he on the other hand insists that "the temple of Jerusalem and the Holy Land are no longer in sight."[25] Both scholars thus claim that the Land has become superfluous to the eschatological vision of *2 Baruch*.[26]

The approaches of Sayler, Murphy and Whitters are typical of one group of scholarly interpretations of the Land in *2 Baruch*.[27] These scholars either reject the importance of the Land, since they consider it to be simply part of the corruptible world, or they avoid discussing the tension between the covenantal promises and the eschatological other world of *2 Baruch*.[28]

Another group of scholars tends to treat the Land in *2 Baruch* as a reflection of the 'real,' geo-physical region of Palestine. P.-M. Bogaert

---

[23] Murphy, *Structure and Meaning*, 28; 124–125.

[24] Murphy, *Structure and Meaning*, 88.

[25] Whitters, *Epistle*, 64, 113, 124, 138–139.

[26] It should be noted that Whitters make the geography of *2 Baruch* an issue as a literary device, and in this manner his contribution to our understanding of *2 Baruch*'s spaces is important. Cf. Whitters, *Epistle*, 35; 39: 64–65; 138–140.

[27] Cf., e.g., Klijn, "Sources and Redaction," 76.

[28] Bogaert, *Apocalypse de Baruch I*, 320–321; Sayler, *Promises*, 79, 88. The study of W. Harnisch, *Verhängnis und Verheissung der Geschichte: Untersuchungen zum Zeit- und Geschichtsverständnis im 4. Buch Esra und in der syr. Baruchapokalypse* (FRLANT 97; Göttingen: Vandenhoeck and Ruprecht, 1969), is first and foremost a study of the time concept in *2 Baruch* and *4 Ezra*. As several scholars have already suggested, Harnisch's study of *2 Baruch* is weakened by the fact that he allows concerns of *4 Ezra* to influence his interpretation of *2 Baruch*.

commented on the spatial structures of *2 Baruch* in his 1969 introduction to *2 Baruch*. Under the heading "Le cadre géographique de
l'Apocalypse de Baruch et la patrie de son auteur," Bogaert claims
that the geography of *2 Baruch* first and foremost discloses the real
whereabouts of the author.[29] These conclusions are influenced by two
assumptions. First, Bogaert claims that the geography of *2 Baruch* is not
a typical apocalyptic geography and insists that it is unparalleled in
contemporary sources. Second, according to Bogaert, the geography of
the text is too insignificant to be the object of a figurative interpretation.[30]

These two assumptions are however questionable. Bogaert's study
confines itself strictly to the three sites mentioned by name in the text:
Hebron and the oak of Mambre, the grotto of the Kidron valley, and
Jerusalem with its temple. His study is therefore not an exhaustive study
of *2 Baruch*'s geography, as the heading of the chapter might indicate.
In fact, Bogaert's presentation is limited to the *toponomy* of the text. It is
possible that *2 Baruch* is the sole apocalyptic text that highlights the three
settings of Hebron, Kidron, and Jerusalem. However, if we include
the wider geographical framework of the text, his first assumption is
no longer valid. As the studies of Sayler, Murphy, and Whitters have
shown, the cosmological and geographical axes in the text are far
from insignificant. *2 Baruch* shares both the cosmological axis and the
geographical axis of the most important contemporaneous apocalypses.
If we accept that the geography of *2 Baruch* is much more than a
toponomy, this also appears to invalidate Bogaert's second assumption.

Moreover, it is questionable whether the conclusions Bogaert draws
in his presentation are justifiable and fruitful for the study of the geography of *2 Baruch*. As mentioned above, the main aim of Bogaert's discussion is to assess the historical and geographical reliability of the text
and to argue that the actual provenance of the author must be Palestine. In other words, Bogaert claims that *2 Baruch* describes the 'real'
geo-physical Palestine and consequently attempts to reconcile its apparent geographic discrepancies with a historical geography.[31] Bogaert's
arguments for a 'real' geography are in fact weakened by some of his
own reflections in the chapter. He notes, for instance, that "Babylon"
must be rendered "Rome," he sees Hebron (47:1), the oak (6:1 and

---

[29] Bogaert, *Apocalypse de Baruch* I, 320–334.
[30] Bogaert, *Apocalypse de Baruch* I, 320–321.
[31] Bogaert, *Apocalypse de Baruch* I, 330; 324.

77:18), and the tree in 55:1 as interchangeable, and he also accepts that
2 Baruch may present a 'geographic mélange.'[32] We should of course
neither discount the interest displayed by *2 Baruch* in the landscapes of
Palestine, nor deny that it *may* be an indication of the text's provenance.
However, the hypothesis that *2 Baruch* reflects the geo-historical Palestine in a one-to-one fashion is problematic and Bogaert fails to provide
a convincing argument for his interpretation.[33]

In his 2003 article, Harrington says that he will discuss the occur-
rences of the expression "holy land" in *2 Baruch*, *4 Ezra* and *L.A.B.*[34]
However, his study of *2 Baruch* encounters some problems. Although
Harrington says that he will study the expression, or the motif, of the
holy land in the text, it soon becomes evident that he looked at selected
passages of *2 Baruch* in which the Land is prominent, and not just 63:10;
71:1 and 84:4 where the motif and expression "holy land" (*ar'ā qadištā*)[35]
appears.[36] His study is not a discussion of an expression or a specific
motif, but rather a more general study of *2 Baruch*'s presentation of the
Land.

---

[32] Bogaert, *Apocalypse de Baruch* I, 321; 336–339.

[33] Cf. Sayler's critique in *Promises*, 115. R. Nir has also made a similar claim in her
2003 book *The Destruction of Jerusalem and the Idea of Redemption in the* Syriac Apocalypse
of Baruch (SBLEJL 20. Atlanta: Society of Biblical Literature, 2003). She claims that
rabbinic sources written in Palestine are closer to an essential Judaism, since they are
in fact written "on the soil of the land of Israel" (Nir, *Destruction*, 7; 27). She thus gives
the localisation itself explanatory powers. In the following study I will in general use
Nir's analysis with caution, since her study encounters serious methodological problems
(Cf. M. Henze, review of R. Nir, *The Destruction of Jerusalem and the Idea of Redemption in the
Syriac Apocalypse. RBL* (June 2004). Online: http://www.bookreviews.org/bookdetail.asp
?TitleId=3410; F.J. Murphy, review of R. Nir, *The Destruction of Jerusalem and the Idea
of Redemption in the* Syriac Apocalypse of Baruch, *CBQ* 66 (2004): 326–327; L.I. Lied,
review of R. Nir, *The Destruction of Jerusalem and the Idea of Redemption in the Syriac Apocalypse
of Baruch. JSS* 50 no. 2 (2005): 403–405).

[34] Harrington, "Holy Land," 661.

[35] *2 Baruch* is transmitted in its entirety only in Syriac. Syriac is an Aramaic dialect
with its own distinct script, and the language of the Syrian Orthodox Church. I provide
a transliteration for the Syriac text (West Syriac vowel system) to make it more available
to the readers of the book. The transliteration is in accordance with the system of
T.H. Robinson, *Paradigms and Exercises in Syriac Grammar* (4th ed; Oxford: Clarendon
Press, 1962). I note the root of the word in brackets when this is relevant to the study.
When the analysis focuses solely on the root-meaning of a word, or the point of the
discussion is the appearance of forms of a specific root, I note the root only.

[36] Of the four passages Harrington discusses (29:2; 40:2; 63:10 and 71:1), only two
call the Land "the holy land" (63:10; 71:1), and he does not mention the final reference
in *2 Baruch*, in 84:4.

Harrington's study assumes that any description of the Land in *2 Baruch* is a description of the holy land. Harrington further suggests a connection between the motif of the Holy Land in the three selected ancient texts and 'the land of Israel,' in terms of a modern day social and geopolitical reality.[37] Thus, the argument of Harrington's 2003 article presupposes that all descriptions of the Land in *2 Baruch* are descriptions of one particular geographical area.

This outline of previous interpretations of the Land-concept in *2 Baruch* shows that two general tendencies dominate. The first group of scholars consider the Land and the other world to be mutually exclusive, in the way that Davies proposed. The other group of scholars tend to treat the description of the Land in *2 Baruch* as a projection of a 'real', geo-historical, region onto text.

Readdressing *2 Baruch*'s Land: Question and Purposes of the Study

Inspired by Davies's sensitivity to the manifold tendencies of the ancient texts, this study will address the conclusions of previous research on the Land-concept in *2 Baruch*. Instead of taking for granted that references to the Land are non-existent or sparse because the other world has taken the place of the Land as a redemptive category, this study will attempt to reformulate the nature of that connection. The study will discuss whether a part of the creativity of spatial thinking found in texts such as *2 Baruch* has been overlooked by earlier interpreters due to the two convictions described above: that textual geography reflects 'real' geography, and, that the Land and the other world can not be reconciled.

The question being asked in the present study is: does *2 Baruch* reject Israel's Land as a redemptive category, or is the Land-concept rather transformed so as to identify this central covenantal space with the other world as the place of redemption?

The purpose of the present study is threefold. Firstly, the study will propose a change of spatial epistemology that hopefully will both supplement and challenge earlier interpretations of the Land-concept in *2 Baruch*.

---

[37] Harrington, "Holy Land," 661. Cf. further Z. Kallai, *Historical Geography of the Bible: The Tribal Territories of Israel* (Jerusalem: The Magnes Press, 1986); G. Galil and M. Weinfeld, eds., *Studies in Historical Geography and Biblical Historiography* (Leiden: E.J. Brill, 2000).

Secondly, this study aims to shed light on the aspect of space in an apocalyptic text.[38] Although apocalyptic texts apply spatial imagery and spatial language to a relatively high degree, previous research has paid more attention to the aspect of time than the aspect of space in these texts.[39]

Thirdly, it is my intention to shed light on the creativity involved in the construction of redemptive spaces in an eschatological and apocalyptical text such as *2 Baruch*. I wish to broaden our view with regard to the vitality of the Land-theme in the centuries after the fall of the Second Temple. This is a field of study which has hitherto not attracted the attention it deserves.[40]

Land as Imagined Space: Critical Spatial Theory and the Linguistic Turn

This work on the Land in *2 Baruch* is a study of an imagined space[41] in an ancient text. I will discuss how the Land is constructed in *2 Baruch*, and how the Land-theme becomes part of the rhetorical argumenta-

---

[38] The discussion of the concept and genre Apocalypse/Apocalyptic is long-standing. Cf. among others J.J. Collins, *Apocalypse: The Morphology of a Genre* (Semeia 14; Missoula: Scholars Press, 1979); A.F. Segal, "Heavenly Ascent in Hellenistic Judaism, Early Christianity and Their Environment," (ANRW 23.2:1333–1394; Part 2; *Principat*, 23.2; ed. W. Haase; New York: de Gruyter, 1980); C. Rowland, *The Open Heaven: A Study of Apocalyptic in Judaism and Early Christianity* (London: SPCK, 1982); Collins, *Apocalyptic Imagination*; M. Dean-Otting, *Heavenly Journeys: A Study of the Motif in Hellenistic Jewish Literature* (Judentum und Umwelt 8; Frankfurt am Main: Peter Lang, 1984); M. Himmelfarb, *Ascent to Heaven in Jewish and Christian Apocalypses* (New York: Oxford University Press, 1993); L.L. Grabbe and R.D. Haak, eds., *Knowing the End from the Beginning: The Prophetic, the Apocalyptic and their Relationships* (JSPSup 46; London: Academic Press, 2003).

[39] One exception is K.C. Bautch, *A Study of the Geography of 1 Enoch 17–19: 'No One Has Seen What I Have Seen'* (JSJSup 81; Leiden: Brill, 2003).

[40] Cf. however, the important studies of J.Z. Smith, *Map is not Territory: Studies in the History of Religions* (SJLA 23; Leiden: Brill, 1978), 109–112; R.S. Sarason, "The Significance of the Land of Israel in the Mishnah," in *The Land of Israel: Jewish Perspectives* (ed. L.A. Hoffman; Center for the Study of Judaism and Christianity in Antiquity 6; Notre Dame, Indiana: University of Notre Dame Press, 1986), 109–137; S. Rosenberg, "The Link to the Land of Israel in Jewish Thought: A Clash of Perspectives," in *The Land of Israel: Jewish Perspectives* (ed. L.A. Hoffman; Center for the Study of Judaism and Christianity in Antiquity 6; Notre Dame, Indiana: University of Notre Dame Press, 1986), 139–169; Z. Gurevitch, "The Double Site of Israel," in *Grasping Land: Space and Place in Contemporary Israeli Discourse and Experience* (ed. E. Ben-Ari and Y. Bilu; Albany, NY: State University of New York Press, 1997), 203–216; I.M. Gafni, *Land, Center and Diaspora: Jewish Constructs in Late Antiquity* (JSPSup 21; Sheffield: Sheffield Academic Press, 1997).

[41] I apply the term 'imagined space' to express that I see the Land in *2 Baruch* as a creative conception and a mental image in text.

tion of this text. In other words, this is a study of the space-making enterprise of *2 Baruch*.

Critical Spatial Theory and the Linguistic Turn

The present study is informed by the field of Critical Spatial Theory and inspired by the application of this theoretical perspective by scholars of biblical and religious studies. Recent decades have seen a rise of theoretical interest in the human conception of space and place. This field of theoretical debate has primarily developed in the social sciences, but contributions have also come from other academic disciplines such as philosophy, architecture, and geography. Among the contributors who have sparked the interest in space and spatiality in the humanities are H. Lefebvre and E.W. Soja as well as M. Foucault, J.Z. Smith, D. Harvey and D. Massey.[42]

In the field of biblical and religious studies, the works of the French philosopher Lefebvre[43] and the American geographer Soja[44] have held a special position, probably due to the investment in their works by the

---

[42] Cf. M. Foucault's essay "Des Espaces Autres," (1967), published in English as "Of Other Spaces," (trans. J. Miskowiec) *Diacritics 16* (1986): 22–27; M. Foucault, *Power/Knowledge: Selected Interviews and Other Writings 1972–1977* (ed. C. Gordon; trans. C. Gordon et al; Brighton: Harvester Press, 1980), 63–77; M. Foucault, "Other Spaces: the Principles of Heterotopia," *Lotus 48/49* (1986), 9–17; J.Z. Smith, *To Take Place. Toward Theory in Ritual* (Chicago: University of Chicago Press, 1987); D. Harvey, *The Condition of Postmodernity: An Enquiry into the Origins of Cultural Change* (Oxford: Blackwell, 1989); D. Massey, *Space, Place and Gender* (Cambridge: Polity Press, 1994). Cf. further M.M. Bakhtin, *Dialogic Imagination: Four Essays* (ed. M. Holquist; trans. C. Emerson and M. Holquist; Austin: University of Texas Press, 1981); B.M. Bokser, "Approaching Sacred Space," *HTR* 78 (1985): 279–299; E.S. Casey, *Getting Back into Place: Toward a Renewed Understanding of the Place-World* (Studies in Continental Thought; Bloomington, Ind.: Indiana University Press, 1993); T. Cresswell, *In Place, Out of Place. Geography, Ideology and Transgression* (Minneapolis: University of Minnesota Press, 1996); E.S. Casey, *The Fate of Place: A Philosophical History* (Berkeley: University of California Press, 1997).

[43] Henri Lefebvre's *La production de l'espace* was published as early as 1974 (H. Lefebvre, *La Production de l'espace* (Paris: Anthropos, 1974). It was however mostly unknown to wider circles of scholars until it was translated into English in 1991 (H. Lefebvre, *The Production of Space* (trans. D. Nicholson-Smith; Oxford: Blackwell, 1991)).

[44] Cf. E.W. Soja, *Postmodern Geographies. The Reassertion of Space in Critical Social Theory* (London/New York: Verso, 1989); E.W. Soja, *Thirdspace: Journeys to Los Angeles and Other Real-and-Imagined Places* (Oxford: Blackwell, 1996); E.W. Soja, "Thirdspace: Expanding the Scope of the Geographical Imagination," in *Architecturally Speaking: Practices of Art, Architecture and the Everyday* (ed. Alan Read; London: Routledge, 2000); E.W. Soja, *Postmetropolis: Critical Studies of Cities and Religions* (Oxford: Blackwell, 2000).

scholars affiliated with the productive SBL-forum *Construction of Ancient Space Seminar*.[45]

One of the aims of the works of Lefebvre and his follower Soja[46] was to propose a change of spatial epistemology. In reaction to a typical modern, 'Western,' notion of space as a given and passively-existing materiality, they deny that space is neutral. They hold that humans create and shape space by their practices. Consequently, scholars should not regard space as an empty box, a stage or a mere background, but rather study space as a cultural and social construct.[47]

The main contribution of Lefebvre and Soja is their focus on lived experience and social praxis, in the widest sense, as the decisive aspect of human spatiality. In the monograph *Thirdspace: Journeys to Los Angeles and Other Real-and-Imagined Places*, Soja describes space as being material-and-mental.[48] In other words, Soja studies space as the comprehensive recombination of material perceptions ('Firstspace') and mental conceptions of space ('Secondspace') *in* lived experience ('Thirdspace').[49] He holds praxis[50] as the aspect of human spatiality in which new

---

[45] Cf. www.case.edu / affil / GAIR / Constructions / Constructions.html. Cf. among others J.L. Berquist, "Critical Spatiality and the Uses of Theory," n.p. Online: http:// www.cwru.edu/affil/GAIR/papers/2002papers/berquist.html;. J.L. Berquist, "Critical Spatiality and the Construction of Ancient Worlds," in *'Imagining' Biblical Worlds. Studies in Spatial, Social and Historical Constructs in Honor of James W. Flanagan* (ed. D.M. Gunn and P.M. McNutt; Sheffield: Sheffield Academic Press, 2002), 64–80; C.V. Camp, "Storied Space, or, Ben Sira 'Tells' a Temple," in *'Imagining' Biblical Worlds: Studies in Spatial, Social and Historical Constructs in Honor of James H. Flanagan* (eds. D.M. Gunn and P.M. McNutt; London: Sheffield Academic Press, 2002), 64–80. Cf. also E. Struthers Malbon, *Narrative Space and Mythic Meaning in Mark* (New York: Harper & Row, 1986); H. Moxnes, "Kingdom takes Place: Transformations of Place and Power in the Kingdom of God in the Gospel of Luke," in *Social Scientific Models for Interpreting the Bible: Essays by the Context Group in Honor of Bruce J. Malina* (ed. J.J. Pilch; Bint.S 53; Boston: Brill, 2001); H. Moxnes, *Putting Jesus in His Place: A Radical Vision of Household and Kingdom* (Louisville, Ky.: Westminster John Knox Press, 2003).

[46] Soja openly explores and pays homage to the works of Lefebvre, while expanding and altering his perspective to some extent (Soja, "Expanding the Scope," 19–20). For the reader of Soja's 1996 monograph, the thoughts of Lefebvre and Soja sometimes seem to blend.

[47] Soja, "Expanding the Scope," 13. Another aim has been to invoke a 'spatial turn' in the social sciences and the humanities, making 'space' a central interpretative category in these disciplines, alongside 'time' and 'society' (Soja, "Expanding the Scope," 13–17).

[48] Soja, *Thirdspace*, 11. Soja applies the term 'real-*and*-imagined'.

[49] Soja, *Thirdspace*, 62; Cf. Soja, "Expanding the Scope," 21–22.

[50] Soja defines 'praxis' as 'the transformation of knowledge into action' ("Expanding the Scope," 15).

and different spaces are potentially shaped and created. This makes the continuous construction and reconstruction of 'other spaces' possible.[51]

It may well be the potential of the category 'other spaces' that has triggered interest in the works of Soja and his predecessor Lefebvre among scholars in biblical and religious studies. The understanding of space as a phenomenon defined by lived experience allows for a large creative and critical potential, an openness towards dissimilar lived realities and innovative cultural and social inventions that has proved helpful to studies of space in ancient texts.[52]

However, problems may also emerge when scholars apply spatial theories developed in the social sciences to discuss the spatiality of ancient texts. As pointed out by, among others, E.A. Clark in her monograph *History, Theory, Text: Historians and the Linguistic Turn*, studies of ancient texts differ from studies of contemporary social processes in ways crucial to spatial analysis.[53] Scholars of biblical and religious studies engage with ancient texts that are often highly literary, theological, and philosophical works, and none of the ideas expressed in these works can possibly be untouched by language. These texts neither passively reflect social realities of antiquity, nor do they transparently bring us into contact with the once real world of that time.

To scholars of the spatiality of ancient texts, this means that the spaces described in these texts are not one-to-one references to any geo-historical spaces, but representations of spaces, produced and expressed in language. These texts suggest how space was negotiated and imagined, how space was an integral part of the stories told and the rhetoric that promoted the point of view of the work, and of those who pro-

---

[51] Soja, *Thirdspace*, 5; Soja, "Expanding the Scope," 22–30.

[52] Cf. further the works of H.K. Bhabha, "The Third Space: Interview with Homi Bhabha," in *Identity, Community, Culture, Difference* (ed. J. Rutherford; London: Lawrence and Wishart, 1990); G. Rose, *Feminism and Geography* (Cambridge: Polity Press, 1993); G. Ward, introduction to *The Postmodern God: a Theological Reader* (Malden, Mass.: Blackwell, 1997), xv–xlvii.

[53] E.A. Clark, *History, Theory, Text: Historians and the Linguistic Turn* (Cambridge, Mass.: Harvard University Press, 2004). Cf. also J. Duncan and D. Ley, eds., *Place, Culture, Representation* (London: Routledge, 1993); J. Økland, *Women in their Place: Paul and the Corinthian Discourse of Gender and Sanctuary Space* (JSNTSup 269; London: T&T Clark, 2004); A.S. Jacobs, *Remains of the Jews: The Holy Land and Christian Empire in Late Antiquity* (Stanford: Stanford University Press, 2004); K.J. Wenell, *Jesus and Land: Sacred and Social Space in Second Temple Judaism* (LNTSSup 334; London: T&T Clark, 2007) and Moxnes, *Putting Jesus in His Place.*

duced and engaged with it. Texts like these lend themselves to ideological and rhetorical analysis. They do not map 'real' places of the world
of late antiquity.

The Imagined, Other, Lands of *2 Baruch*

In recent years, a series of books and articles have been published in the
fields of biblical and religious studies that attest to the awareness among
scholars of the explanatory effect of, and the challenges relating to,
spatial analysis.[54] The notion of the Land has not, however, been given
much attention in these discussions,[55] and, to my knowledge, *2 Baruch*'s
conception of the Land has not yet been studied in the light of a spatial
epistemology that gives priority to praxis.

The present study will apply some of the main insights of Lefebvre's
and Soja's theoretical grids to study the narrative geography of *2 Baruch*.
The study is in other words *an intra-textual spatial analysis* of *2 Baruch*'s
imaginations of the Land.[56]

In accordance with the suggestions of Lefebvre and Soja, the point of
departure of this study is that in order to identify the Land in *2 Baruch*
we must look for descriptions of Israel's law-abiding, social, practices
and how these practices are said to transform space. The study holds
that it is the collective righteous praxis of Israel, blessed as it is by
God's presence, that transforms a given area into the Land. The praxis-
aspect (Soja's 'Thirdspace') is considered essential to the identification

---

[54] Cf., e.g., J. Lieu, *Christian Identity in the Jewish and Graeco-Roman World* (Oxford:
Oxford University Press, 2004) 220–230; Økland, *Women in their Place*; Wenell, *Jesus and
Land*.

[55] Exceptions are Smith, *Map*, 109–112; J.W. Flanagan, "Mapping the Biblical World:
Perceptions of Space in Ancient Southwestern Asia," in *Mappa Mundi: Mapping Cul-
ture/Mapping the World* (Working Group Papers in the Humanities 9; Windsor, Ont.:
Humanities Research Group, University of Windsor), 1–18; W. Brueggemann, *The Land*
(2nd ed), xxii, and Wenell, *Jesus and Land*.

[56] The present study is an exegetical study. It is not a study of the contemporaneous
spatial *discourse* in which *2 Baruch* took part. I do not deny that *2 Baruch*'s construction
of Land and geography have been part of a spatial discourse (in a Foucauldian sense
of the term) of Late Antiquity. Nor do I deny that this discourse may have created,
negotiated, or transformed 'reality' for those who acted according to it. However, due
to the general lack of sources for post 70 C.E. Palestine and our meagre knowledge
about the provenance and discursive context of *2 Baruch*, we do not have access to the
conceived realities *2 Baruch* may have produced for those who read or listened to the
text.

of the Land, whereas the location of the Land (Soja's 'Firstspace') and the imagery applied to describe the Land (Soja's 'Secondspace') may vary.

Unlike other studies, which have given priority to the territorial aspect or the location, of the Land, this study maintains that *2 Baruch*'s descriptions of the locations of the Land are fuzzy and fluid, and that locations may be rejected and replaced. This does not mean that the Land is not considered to have a location. The Land is always located and, therefore, always has a territory associated with it, but since praxis is given priority, no single geographical spot is, *per se*, considered to be the Land. The status 'Land' is not inherent to a territory, but dependent on the transformative ability of righteous praxis.

Likewise, no single set of imagery dominates the description of the location of the Land. *2 Baruch* applies a set of established concepts —imageries, motifs, and metaphors commonly associated with the Land-theme in authoritative accounts—that describe the chosen location. *2 Baruch* thus transmits various well-known imageries of cognitive authority to describe the Land, and draws from this reservoir, or menu, of conventional concepts, but uses these concepts selectively in each description to fit differing temporal contexts and functions attributed to the Land. To a learned audience, the descriptions of the Land would be recognisable by the way in which the text triggers allusions to well known stories, maps and spaces.

Inspired by the approaches of Lefebvre and Soja, this study will consequently interpret the Land as a comprehensive, socially constructed, space. The Land is always localised and is always presented by familiar terms and imageries, but it is also always more than a location, or a territory, and more than the allusions and connotations associated with the Land-theme. The Land is the spatial outcome of the creative recombination of location and conventional concepts through Israel's collective righteous practices.

The Land: The Space of Redemption in Israel's History

Two questions must be addressed at this point: who is 'Israel' in *2 Baruch*, and in what sense is the Land a redemptive category, as initially indicated? Firstly, Sayler has pointed out that *2 Baruch* does not apply the term 'Israel' exclusively to a fixed, ethnic group. Rather, *2 Baruch* uses the term first and foremost to describe those who are righteous and hence faithful to the covenant at any given time. This means that 'Israel' is more of a moral category than a set group of tribes.[57] As we shall see in the following analysis, 'Israel' is also a highly flexible category with regard to the size of the group it denominates. In some passages 'Israel' refers to all twelve tribes, but the term can also designate the two tribes of the Kingdom of Judah, as well as the righteous remnant of the end-time.[58]

In line with *2 Baruch*'s usage of the term, the following study will apply the term 'Israel' as a designation of the group which remains faithful. It may refer to a changing number of tribes or people, which over the course of time becomes more and more marginalised, but it always designates the righteous, those who maintain the covenantal relationship between God and his people.[59]

Secondly, in accordance with my suggestion of the eschatological orientation of *2 Baruch*, I regard the presentation of history and spatiality in the text as eschatological formations, and I will study the Land-concept in the context of these formations.

One cannot say that *2 Baruch describes* the past and *invents* the future. The writing of history is just as much a creative business as is the imagining of future times. Just like the future, the past and the present are constructed, to adhere to the overall imagined goal of history: they display how that history brings about Israel's final redemption according to the plan of God. Likewise, each period in the history of Israel has its corresponding spaces. *2 Baruch*'s eschatology is not only about the end of time. It also concerns the end of space.

I identify three main periods in this eschatological history of Israel, each period having spaces that correspond to and supplement them:[60]

---

[57] Sayler, *Promises*, 20. Cf. also Leuenberger, "Ort und Funktion," 221; 239. As discussed in Chapter Five, *2 Baruch* never completely loses sight of the idea of the original twelve tribes of Israel.

[58] Note, however, that *2 Baruch* is not always consistent. 62:3 probably refers to the ten tribes by the term 'Israel'.

[59] For the sake of clarity, it should be noted that I always apply the term 'Israel' to a group of people, and never to a piece of land and of course never to the modern day state of Israel.

[60] I separate *2 Baruch*'s description of history into three periods. The separation serves analytical purposes. The first period is prominent in *2 Bar.* 1–3; 5–8 (the narrative frame) and in some apocalyptic sections (61; 63; 66) as well as in 84:8 an 85:1–2. The second period, the end-time, is also found in the frame story as well as in context of various apocalyptic accounts, particularly in 9–13; 27–28; 34; 43; 46–47; 48:31–37; 69–70; 76–77; 78:4; 80; 84:1–7; 85:3. The third period is detected, e.g., in 28–30; 36:4–37:1; 39:7–40:4; 48:48–51:16; 71–75; 85:4–5. I will return to the history that precedes the reign of David and Solomon in Chapters Two, Five, Six and Seven of this study.

1. The period of the First Temple: from the inauguration to the fall of the temple
2. The end-time: from the fall of the temple to the onset of the Messianic reign
3. The time of redemption: from the establishment of Messianic reign to the final actualisation of the other world as a place belonging to Israel

The period of the First Temple deals with the decline of righteousness. It is introduced by the glorious reign of David and Solomon and ends with the fall of Jerusalem and its temple in the days of Baruch. During this first period, the forces of wickedness expand on earth, and leave less and less space for the righteous. The end-time is characterised as a period of abnormality and perversions. Similarly, during the end-time the spaces of the corruptible world become abnormal and due to universal godlessness, the entire Creation[61] is in a process of dying. The time of redemption both includes the Messianic era that restores and transforms the world and descriptions of resurrection, judgement and actualisation of the other world as a place belonging to Israel. The Messianic era has one foot in each world and is thus a liminal space. Finally, the ultimate salvation takes place when Israel enters the other world and God's promises to Israel are fulfiled.

The present work will study the Land as an integral part of *2 Baruch*'s eschatological geography, and the imaginations of the Land will be understood within the contexts of the space and time in which they appear.[62] On the one hand, this study sees *2 Baruch*'s Land as changing throughout the presentation of Israel's history. The changes can be detected in the various ways that locations and conventional concepts relating to the Land-theme are recombined through Israel's space-transforming actions. The following study is therefore concerned with

---

[61] I will apply the terms 'world', 'earth' and 'Creation' in the following way in this study: 'world' includes aspects of time, space and world order. Time and space cannot be separated. Together they form a 'time-space,' and era or an age, a condition. 'Earth' refers to the physical ground, the material surface, the habitat of man and animals. 'Creation' (with a capital C, to distinguish it from God's creative act) is used for the material world God created during creation week. It includes among other things the earth, the created heavens and the waters.

[62] For the notion that time and space supplement each other, cf. R. Kieffer, *Le Monde symbolique de Saint Jean* (LD 137; Paris: Les Éditions du cerf, 1989), 11–32; Moxnes, *Jesus in His Place*, 19.

identifying this creative, locative, enterprise of *2 Baruch* and to study how it takes shape within the text. On the other hand, the Land is seen as a constant place of redemption, either here and now or as a future promise. Since 'Israel' is defined as the group that lives righteously, and the spatial epistemology of the present study gives priority to her praxis, the Land is interpreted as a place of righteousness and thus a good place for Israel. Although the imagination of the Land may vary, the Land is always 'covenantal space', the space set apart for those who live according to the covenant, here and now, or in the future, and therefore first and foremost to be approached as a redemptive category.[63]

Following Sayler and Murphy, I find it fruitful to view the spatial creativity of *2 Baruch* within the context of an overarching rhetoric of consolation. As a consequence of the fall of Jerusalem and its temple and of the dispossession of Palestine, *2 Baruch* presents alternative spaces to promote hope. *2 Baruch* claims the continuance of covenantal space, instead of contemplating the loss of space in the corruptible world any further and urges its readers to look for other spaces, other Lands.

The Transmission, Composition and Provenance of 2 Baruch

The following section will provide a short overview of the history of research on *2 Baruch*. The overview is highly selective, and only discusses elements of importance to the present study.[64] I will focus primarily on the status of the witnesses to the text, as well as the composition and the provenance of *2 Baruch*.

---

[63] In several texts of late antiquity we find a profound relationship between geography/cosmology and anthropology, in the sense that the moral status of a group corresponds to the quality of its space. Good people live in a good place, while the wicked live in a wicked place. In other words, there may be reason to believe that neutral territories do not exist in these texts: these accounts map moral spaces (Cf. J.G. Gammie, "Spatial and Ethical Dualism in Jewish Wisdom and Apocalyptic Literature," *JBL* 93 (1974): 356–385 at 360–362; T.E. Fretheim, "The Plagues as Ecological Signs of Historical Disaster," *JBL* 110 (1991): 385–396; Moxnes, "Kingdom takes Place," 178). At a more general level, there is a close connection between geography/cosmology and anthropology in several texts of late antiquity. The term *'almā*, "world," for instance, is clearly not just a physical space. In addition to a notion of time, it includes both physical space *and* social order.

[64] Cf. Bogaert, *Apocalypse de Baruch I*, and Whitters, *Epistle*, for more exhaustive accounts.

Witnesses to 2 Baruch*: Manuscripts and Translations*

In 1855 a complete Syriac witness to *2 Baruch* was discovered in an ancient copy of a Syriac Bible in the *Bibliotheca Ambrosiana* in Milan by its curator, Professor A.M. Ceriani.[65] The Syriac manuscript probably dates from the sixth or the seventh century and still is the only complete witness to *2 Baruch*.[66] The manuscript, often referred to as the *Ambrosianus*,[67] is in fact the earliest extant, whole copy of the Syriac Bible. In addition to the common biblical books, that Bible included *2 Baruch*, *4 Ezra* and the sixth book of Josephus's *Jewish War*. The *Epistola Baruch* is found twice in the *Ambrosianus*, both as a supplement to the so-called Apocalypse (chapters 1–77) of *2 Baruch* and as an independent

---

[65] Ceriani published a Latin translation of the manuscript in 1866, and the Syriac text based on the *Ambrosianus* manuscript in 1871. The extant Syriac text was published again by M. Kmosko, "Apocalypsis Baruch filii Neriae, translatus de graeco in syriacum," in vol. 2 of *Patrologia syriaca* (ed. R. Graffin; Paris: Firmin-Didot et Socli, 1894–1926), 1068–1207 and by S. Dedering, "Apocalypse of Baruch," part IV, fasc. iii of *The Old Testament in Syriac, According to the Peshitta Version* (ed. S.P. Brock; Leiden: E.J. Brill, 1973). It has been translated into English by R.H. Charles, *The Apocalypse of Baruch* (London: Black, 1896), and a second time by him in, "The Apocalypse of Baruch Translated from the Syriac," in vol. 2 of *The Apocrypha and Pseudepigrapha of the Old Testament in English, with Introductions and Critical and Explanatory Notes to the Several Books, Edited in Conjunction with Many Scholars* (2 vols.; ed. R.H. Charles; Oxford: Clarendon, 1913), 470–526 and by A.F.J. Klijn, "2 (Syriac Apocalypse of) Baruch," in vol. 1 of *OTP* (ed. J.H. Charlesworth; Garden City, NY: Doubleday, 1983). Two German versions appeared; in 1900 by V. Ryssel, "Die Apokalypsen des Baruch. Die syrische Baruchapokalypse," in vol. 2 of *Die Apokryphen und Pseudepigraphen des Alten Testaments* (2 vols; ed. E. Kautzsch; Tübingen: Wissenschaftliche Buchgesellschaft, 1900), 402–457; and in 1924 by B. Violet, *Die Apokalypsen des Esra und des Baruch in Deutscher Gestalt* (GCS 32; Leipzig: J.C. Hinrichs'sche Buchhandlung, 1924). In 1969 P. Bogaert provided a French version, *Apocalypse de Baruch*. *2 Baruch* also exists in translation into other European languages.

[66] The manuscript is written in the Syriac Estrangela script, and organised into three columns (Bogaert, *Apocalypse de Baruch I*, 34). Bogaert suggests that the *Ambrosianus* is of West Syrian origin, due to the similarities between the *Ambrosianus* and the West Syrian Buchanan Bible (Bogaert, *Apocalypse de Baruch I*, 37). We do not know where the Syriac manuscript was recorded, although both Antioch and the Edessa-area are interesting suggestions. Neither do we know the full history of transmission of the *Ambrosianus*, but it is known that the manuscript once belonged to a monastery in the desert of Sketis in Egypt. For further details, cf. Bogaert, *Apocalypse de Baruch I*, 37; W. Wright, *Catalogue of the Syriac Manuscripts in the British Museum* (3 vols. London: The British Museum, 1870–1872), 258–269; C. Moss, *Catalogue of Syriac Printed Books and Related Literature in the British Museum* (Gorgias Historical Catalogues 2; Gorgias Press, forthcomming), and W. Baars, "Neue Textzeugen der syrischen Baruchapokalypse," *VT* 13 (1963): 476–478.

[67] *Ambrosianus* B21 Inf fols. 257a–265b.

entity located near the canonical book of Baruch.[68] This double rendering of the *Epistola Baruch* in the *Ambrosianus* probably attests to the fact
that the *Epistola Baruch* circulated both as an integrated part of *2 Baruch*
and separate from the Apocalypse proper.[69] The *Epistola Baruch* was an
autonomous part of several Syriac Bibles and therefore also has its own
history of transmission.[70]

Some factors complicate the use of the *Ambrosianus* manuscript as
a witness to *2 Baruch*. Although the *Ambrosianus* is the only whole Syriac witness to *2 Baruch*, *2 Bar.* 44:9–15 and 72:1–73:2 are also known
from three West Syrian lectionary manuscripts, stemming from the thirteenth and the fifteenth centuries.[71] Studies suggest that these lectionar-
ies did probably not have the *Ambrosianus* as a *Vorlage*.[72] That may indicate that other Syriac versions of *2 Baruch* circulated at least as late as
the fifteenth century.[73] The 1974 find of an Arabic version of *2 Baruch* in
the Library of the Monastery of St. Catherine by Mount Sinai also confirms the existence of other Syriac witnesses to the text.[74] This tenth or
eleventh century Arabic witness to *2 Bar.* 3–86 (Apocalypse and Epistle)
is translated from a Syriac manuscript, which had close affinities with
the *Ambrosianus* but was not identical with it.[75] These, or this, alternative
Syriac witnesses have however been lost.[76]

---

[68] Bogaert, *Apocalypse de Baruch I*, 33.

[69] Bogaert, *Apocalypse de Baruch I*, 67–72; Whitters, *Epistle*, 3–7.

[70] The Epistle is recorded in maybe as many as forty surviving manuscripts (Baars,
"Neue Textzeugen," 476), dating from the sixth to the seventeenth century (Bogaert
says thirty eight manuscripts (*Apocalypse de Baruch I*, 43)), while Charles say ten (*Apocalypse
of Baruch*, xxiii). The following study will not focus on the distinct history of the Epistle
in its Christian context, but primarily concentrate on the manuscript that witness both
parts of *2 Baruch*.

[71] The lectionary manuscripts are of West Syrian provenance. We know that they
were kept for some time in the Egyptian Monastery where the *Ambrosianus* was also
kept, while the *Ambrosianus* was still in Egypt. Today, two manuscripts are kept in the
British Museum, MS Add. 14,686 (dated 1255), MS Add. 14,687 (dated 1256), The third
manuscript (MS 77, A Konath Library in Kerala), is dated 1423.

[72] Bogaert, *Apocalypse de Baruch I*, 38–39.

[73] Or, possibly, that those who produced the lectionary manuscripts knew these
sections of *2 Baruch* by heart.

[74] Baars detected the so-called 'Arabic Manuscript of Mount Sinai' as nr 589 at the
Aziz Suryal Atiya handlist (F. Leemhuis, A.F.J. Klijn and G.H.J. van Gelder, *The Arabic
Text of the Apocalypse of Baruch: Edited and Translated with a Parallel Translation of the Syriac
Text* (Leiden: E.J. Brill, 1986)).

[75] Leemhuis, Klijn and van Gelder, *The Arabic Text*, vii. For further details, cf. P.S. van
Koningsveld, "An Arabic Manuscript of the Apocalypse of Baruch," *JSJ* 6 (1975): 205–
207.

[76] Some scholars suggest that the *Ambrosianus* is not the oldest translation into Syriac,

Moreover, Syriac is not the original language of *2 Baruch*. Probably, *2 Baruch* was first composed in Greek.[77] The subheading of the *Ambrosianus* witness to *2 Baruch* reads: "Translated from the Greek into Syriac." In addition, the Syriac translation of *2 Baruch* sometimes imitates Greek constructions, whilst some clearly erroneous translations also show that there was a Greek *Vorlage*.[78] A fragment of a fourth or fifth century Greek manuscript containing 12.1–13.2 and 13.11–14.3 appeared within the rich finds of the Egyptian town of Oxyrhynchus in the early twentieth century.[79] The find of the fragment was important because it showed that the *Ambrosianus* provides a close rendering of at least this version of the Greek text.

Any study of *2 Baruch* has to rely on the Syriac version offered by the *Ambrosianus*. The small Greek fragment which witnesses an earlier Greek version of *2 Baruch* can provide some help and the other surviving manuscripts can serve as indicators of possible alternative readings of the Syriac.[80] However, we do not know who copied or translated

---

but a reworked version of an older Syriac translation (Bogaert, *Apocalypse de Baruch I*, 38–39).

[77] Charles suggested that the original language of *2 Baruch* was Hebrew (*Apocalypse of Baruch*, xliv–liii). In the early years of research this hypothesis was commonly accepted, and still is defended by many (Violet, *Die Apokalypsen*, lxvii–lxxiii; G. Stemberger, *Der Leib der Auferstehung. Studien zur Anthropologie und Eschatologie des palästinischen Judentums im neutestamentlichen Zeitalter (ca. 170 v.Cr – 100n. Chr)* (AnBib 56; Rome: Biblical Institute Press, 1972), 85; F. Zimmermann, "Translation and Mistranslation in the Apocalypse of Baruch," in *Studies and Essays in Honor of Abraham A. Neuman* (ed. M. Ben-Horin, B.D. Weinryb and Z. Zeitlin; Leiden: E.J. Brill, 1962), 580–587; Harnisch, *Verhängnis*, 15; Klijn, "2 Baruch," 616; Harrington, "Holy Land," 662). Other scholars hold that the original language is Greek and reject Charles's list of arguments (Cf., e.g., Bogaert, *Apocalypse de Baruch I*, 353–380).

[78] One example is *2 Bar.* 3:7 where the Syriac translation has *taçbitā*, "ornament," in a context where "cosmos" would be much more meaningful (Cf. Charles, *Apocalypse of Baruch*, xliii).

[79] Pap.Oxyrh. 403. B.P. Grenfell and A.S. Hunt, "Apocalypse of Baruch xii–xiv," in *The Oxyrhynchus Papyri III* (London, 1903), 4–7. Cf. M. Black and A.-M. Denis, *Apocalypsis henochi graece: fragmenta pseudepigraphorum quae supersunt graeca* (PVTG 3; Leiden: Brill, 1970), 118–120; Charles, "Apocalypse of Baruch," 487–490; Bogaert, *Apocalypse de Baruch I*, 40.

[80] I have followed the edition of Dedering for the text of *2 Bar.* 1–77 and the edition of Kmosko for the text of the *Epistola Baruch* (78–87) (Dedering's publication of *2 Baruch* does not include the *Epistola Baruch*. The publication of the Epistle is still forthcoming). I have also regularly consulted Ceriani's photolithographic edition of the *Ambrosianus* and the surviving Greek witnesses to *2 Bar.* 12:1–13:2 and 13:11–14:3. I have actively conferred and discussed the translations of Charles (1896), Violet, Bogaert, Klijn and Ryssel (V. Ryssel, "Die syrische Baruchapokalypse," in *Die Apokryphen und Pseupdepigraphen des Alten testaments* II (ed. E. Kautzsch; 2 vols; Tübingen: W. Rothstein, 1900), 404–446).

2 Baruch, nor how much the text was altered in the transmission process. The uncertain status of the *Ambrosianus* urges us to raise questions as to whom and to what context the Syriac manuscript may in fact bear witness. It remains a fact that the *Ambrosianus* first and foremost is Christian material, produced by Syriac speaking Christians in the 6th or 7th century, and that *2 Baruch* is known to us solely in the language, and possibly also the concepts, of the Syrian church.[81] Still, the *Ambrosianus* is a well preserved manuscript with no lacunas and relatively few scribal errors.[82] Also, none of the other available manuscripts show any marked disagreement with the *Ambrosianus* version.[83] Although we have to form arguments on the basis of language with caution, the main concerns of the text should be clear from the available witnesses.

The Unity of 2 Baruch

In the early days of study, several scholars regarded *2 Baruch* as a composite text. Charles suggested that *2 Baruch* was the work of multiple authors and redactors and their use of differing sources and traditions.[84] He concluded that arbitrary ideas and conflicting moods and emphases within the text could only be intelligible if "the composite nature of the book" was realised and the elements isolated in line with their respective characteristics and dates.[85]

Charles's approach was soon criticised by C. Clemen. His critique was quoted by a series of scholars in the late nineteenth and early twentieth century.[86] Throughout the early and mid twentieth century the majority of scholars considered it more likely that *2 Baruch* had a single creative author, who relied on several sources to construct his text. These scholars dealt with *2 Baruch* as one literary composition, which

---

[81] Cf. the contributions of Kraft ("Pseudepigrapha in Christianity," and "Pseudepigrapha in Christianity Revisited").

[82] Cf. Dedering, "Apocalypse of Baruch", 45–50.

[83] Baars, "Neue Textzeugen," 478. Texts such as the *Epistle of Barnabas* and the *Syriac Apocalypse of Daniel* apply motifs from *2 Baruch*. These texts show that at least some parts of *2 Baruch* have been relatively stable.

[84] Charles, *Apocalypse of Baruch*, x. Charles follows among others R. Kabisch, "Die Quellen der Apocalypse Baruchs," *JPT* 18 (1892): 66–107.

[85] Charles, *Apocalypse of Baruch*, liii–lxv.

[86] C. Clemen, "Die Zusammensetzung des Buches Henoch, der Apokalypse des Baruch und des vierten Buches Esra," *TSK* 71 (1898): 211–246. For an overview, cf. Klijn, "Sources and Redaction," 65–70.

had to be read and analysed accordingly.[87] Until 1969, however, most commentators had treated the Apocalypse (1–77) and the *Epistola Baruch* (78–87) as two separate units. Then Bogaert argued that the *Epistola Baruch* should be studied as an integrated part of a coherent *2 Baruch*.[88] A majority of scholars has subsequently accepted this addition.[89]

The scholarly consensus on the unity of composition following Bogaert's publication was complemented by a series of studies in the 60s, 70s and 80s that ordered the text into episodes.[90] These studies suggested that *2 Baruch*, like *4 Ezra*, was divided into seven parts. Even though each commentator defined the seven parts slightly differently, there was a high degree of overlap. These scholars thus regarded *2 Baruch* as one literary work with a coherent structure of ordered episodes.

Today most scholars regard *2 Baruch* as a manifold, but nevertheless united work. In recent years this consensus has been bolstered by scholars who have questioned the strictness of the episodes in the text. Rather than discussing demarcation lines, these scholars have highlighted the dynamic relation between the sections of *2 Baruch*, noting the thematic development of the composition.[91]

It is beyond the scope of this study to discuss the composition of *2 Baruch* further, and although I acknowledge that the structure of *2 Baruch* can still be disputed, I will not challenge the fundamental current consensus. My study of the Land in *2 Baruch* above all presupposes that *2 Baruch* is a unified work. Moreover, as I have suggested above, I identify three periods of time in the text. Since these periods are not confined to the proposed episodes of *2 Baruch*, I read across these suggested episodes of the text. I prefer to read the text in accordance with

---

[87] Violet, *Die Apokalypsen*, lxxiv; Bogaert, *Apocalypse de Baruch I*, 88. Cf. Harnisch, *Verhängnis*, 14.

[88] Bogaert, *Apocalypse de Baruch I*, 67–78. Cf. also the perspective of Whitters, *Epistle*, vii.

[89] Sayler's study is an exception (*Promises*, 1; 98–102).

[90] Bogaert, *Apocalypse de Baruch I*, 62; Sayler, *Promises*, 161–162; Murphy, *Structure and Meaning*, 11–13; A.L. Thompson, *Responsibility For Evil in the Theodicy of IV Ezra* (Missoula, MT: Scholars Press, 1977), 123–124, and recently, Whitters, *Epistle*, 42 and Leuenberger, "Ort und Funktion," 210–211. Note, however, that a division into seven parts was suggested already by Ceriani.

[91] M. Henze, "From Jeremiah to Baruch: Pseudepigraphy in the *Syriac Apocalypse of Baruch*," in *Biblical Traditions in Transmission: Essays in Honour of Michael A. Knibb* (eds. C. Hempel and J. Lieu; Leiden: E.J. Brill, 2006), 157–177 at 163; Leuenberger, "Ort und Funktion", 214; 216; 242.

a threefold time-space division that helps develop what I regard as the main theme of the text: the redemption of Israel.

The Date and Provenance of 2 Baruch

Although any authorial intention or original context of the production of *2 Baruch* cannot be established, most scholars today consider *2 Baruch* to be a Jewish apocalyptic and eschatological work written in Palestine in the period after the fall of the Second Temple (70 C.E.).[92] The general scholarly agreement believes that *2 Baruch* was written in the period between 70 and 132 C.E.[93] Some scholars prefer a late first century date,[94] while others suggest that *2 Baruch* was composed in the early second century.[95] Similarly, Palestine has been suggested by most scholars as the likely location of an originating group or person(s).[96] *2 Baruch* itself does not, however, give any clear indications as to where it was written.[97] Although the geography of the *narrative* focus on the heartland of Palestine, this is not necessarily proof that the text originates in this area. Moreover, since first and second century C.E. Palestine must be considered a very diverse and highly regionalised area and not a single unit, Palestine is not itself a precise place of origin. Accordingly,

---

[92] Cf. J.R. Davila, *The Provenance of the Pseudepigrapha: Jewish, Christian or Other?* (JSJ-Sup; Leiden: E.J. Brill, 2005). The debate of the provenance of the Pseudepigrapha is a longstanding one. Cf. among others R.A. Kraft, "The Pseudepigrapha in Christianity," in *Tracing the Threads: Studies in the Vitality of the Jewish Pseudepigrapha*, (SBLEJL 6; ed. J.C. Reeves; Atlanta: Scholars Press, 1994), 55–86; R.A. Kraft, "The Pseudepigrapha and Christianity Revisited: Setting the Stage and Framing Some Central Questions," *JSJ* 32 (2001): 371–385; M. de Jonge, *Pseudepigrapha of the Old Testament as Part of Christian Literature: The Case of the Testaments of the Twelve Patriarchs and the Greek Life of Adam and Eve* (SVTP 18; Leiden: E.J. Brill, 2003).

[93] Charles records the debate until 1896 (*Apocalypse of Baruch*, xxxiii–xliii), where the relation to *4 Ezra* was central to the discussion. Most scholars agree, except for R. Kabisch, "Die Quellen der Apokalypse Baruchs," *JbPT* 18 (1892): 66–107; and E. de Faye, *Les apocalypses juives. Essai de critique littéraire et théologique* (Lausanne: G. Bridel, 1892), who both suggest that *2 Baruch* was written prior to year 70. Bogaert gives a comprehensive overview of the debate until 1969 (*Apocalypse de Baruch I*, 270–295). Cf. also Harnisch, *Verhängnis*, 11; Murphy, *Structure and Meaning*, 2; Nir, *Destruction*, 1; Sayler, *Promises*, 103–110.

[94] Charles, *Apocalypse of Baruch*, xvi; Bogaert, *Apocalypse de Baruch I*, 294–295; Sayler, *Promises*, 103.

[95] Violet, *Die Apokalypsen*, xci; Klijn, "2 Baruch," 617.

[96] Violet, *Die Apokalypsen*, xc–xci; Bogaert, *Apocalypse de Baruch I*, 23, 334; Harnisch, *Verhängnis*, 15; Klijn, "2 Baruch," 617; Murphy, *Structure and Meaning*, 2; Nir, *Destruction*, 4–7.

[97] Murphy, *Structure and Meaning*, 2.

several areas and cities within Palestine have been suggested, among them Jerusalem and Javneh.[98]

While there is a tentative agreement on both the date and geographical provenance of *2 Baruch*, the question of the milieu of origin has sparked a far more lively debate. While Charles found "a hidden hostility to Christianity" in *2 Baruch*,[99] Nir on the contrary identified *2 Baruch* as a work of Christian provenance.[100] And while scholars like Rosenthal, Violet and Bogaert located the author within the most profiled rabbinic circles,[101] other scholars identified *2 Baruch* as the work of an unknown group.[102] To complete this complex picture, scholars have also identified the text as an orthodox Jewish, Pharisaic, work.[103] These marked differences of opinion are perhaps best explained in light of two considerations. Firstly, *2 Baruch* does not present a uniform 'world view' and contains ideologies and tendencies that where discussed in several milieus.[104] Secondly, it is difficult to identify any clearly defined groups or parties in the period in which *2 Baruch* originates.[105] The last decades of research have pointed out the considerable overlap between groups or 'religions' which earlier were considered as distinct social and ideo-

---

[98] F. Rosenthal, *Vier apokryphische Bücher aus der Zeit und Schule R. Akiba's: Assumptio Mosis, Das vierte Buch Esra, Die Apokalypse Baruch, Das Buch Tobi* (Leipzig, Otto Schulze, 1885), 72; Violet, *Die Apokalypsen*, xci; Bogaert, *Apocalypse de Baruch I*, 334.

[99] Charles, *Apocalypse of Baruch*, xvi, lxxx.

[100] Nir, *Destruction*, 5. Cf. Th. Zahn, *Die Offenbarung des Johannes* (vol. 18 of *Kommentar zum Neuen Testament*; ed. Th. Zahn; Leipzig: A. Deichertsche Verlagsbuchhandlung, 1924), 143. The standpoint of Zahn has been criticised by Bogaert (*Apocalypse de Baruch I*, 446. Cf. also Henze, review of R. Nir). *2 Baruch* has several affinities with Christian texts, and these similarities are of course interesting (e.g., the description of the resurrection in 1 Cor 15 and *2 Bar.* 50–51). The differences are however just as present (e.g., the description of Adam in the same passages). Cf. Charles's list (*Apocalypse of Baruch*, lxxvi–lxxix) and Sayler's discussion (*Promises*, 142–146). There are no *specific* Christian terms or ideas in *2 Baruch*, like for instance references to baptism or Eucharist, which could prove the Christian provenance of the text (cf. Nir, *Destruction*, 15 versus 199). That does not rule out the possibility that the text we have may be a Christian work or rendering, but it tells us that no one really tried to stamp it as Christian.

[101] Rosenthal, *Vier apokrüphische Bücher*, 72; Charles, *Apocalypse of Baruch*, lxxxi; Violet, *Die Apokalypsen*, xci; Bogaert, *Apocalypse de Baruch I*, 334, 438–444.

[102] Sayler, *Promises*, 117–118.

[103] Charles, *Apocalypse of Baruch*, viii; L. Ginzberg, "Apocalypse of Baruch (Syriac)," in *JE* 2 (ed. I. Singer, A. Cyrus et.al.; 12 vols.; New York: Funk and Wagnalls, 1901–1905. Repr. 1925), 551–556.

[104] Klijn, "Sources and Redaction," 75–76; Murphy, *Structure and Meaning*, 139.

[105] Sayler, *Promises*, 6; 118. Cf. J. Neusner, *Judaism: The Evidence of the Mishnah* (Chicago: University of Chicago Press, 1981), 5–14; 25–44.

logical entities.[106] This wide ranging debate has challenged the use of labels such as 'Christian' versus 'Jewish', as well as 'Hellenistic Jew' versus 'Rabbinic Jew'. As part of the same trend, scholars point to the heterogeneity of rabbinic culture. According to Murphy, for instance, there were many groups which could be called 'rabbinic' at the time. The polarity between 'marginal' and 'central' in the description of Jewish ideological tendencies of the time has also been the issue of a wide-ranging debate. Indeed, scholars are often increasingly accepting the phenomenon of Apocalypticism as part of a 'mainstream Judaism' of the first centuries C.E.[107]

2 Baruch's unclear historical provenance is further reflected in its relationship to other texts. It is evident that *2 Baruch* quotes, refers, and alludes actively to biblical texts. At the very least, Isaiah, Jeremiah, and Deuteronomy appear to be prominent. It is not entirely clear what version(s) of the Bible those who produced *2 Baruch* knew, however. Bogaert argues that they were at least familiar with the Septuagint, which is probable.[108]

---

[106] Cf. J. Neusner, E.S. Frerichs and C. McCracken-Flesher, eds., *'To See Ourselves as Others See Us': Christians, Jews, 'Others' in Late Antiquity* (SPSHS; Chico, Calif.: Scholars Press, 1985).

[107] Cf. among others J. Neusner, *Ancient Judaism and Modern Category Formation: 'Judaism,' 'Midrash,' 'Messianism,' and Canon in the Past Quarter-Century* (Lanham, Md: University Press of America, 1986); J.D.G. Dunn, *The Parting of the Ways: Between Christianity and Judaism and Their Significance for the Character of Christianity* (London: SCM, 1991); E.P. Sanders, *Judaism: Practice and Belief, 63 BCE – 66 CE* (London: SCM, 1992); J.Z. Smith, *Imagining Religion: From Babylon to Jonestown* (Chicago Studies in the History of Judaism; Chicago: University of Chicago Press, 1982), 1–18; G. Boccaccini, *Beyond the Essene Hypothesis: The Parting of the Ways Between Qumran and Enochic Judaism* (Grand Rapids, Mich.: Eerdmans, 1998); Davila, *Provenance*, 10–73. Cf. further Harnisch, *Verhängnis*, 9–15; Murphy, *Structure and Meaning*, 139–140; A.J. Saldarini, "Apocalyptic and Rabbinic Literature," *CBQ* 37 (1975): 358; W.A. Meeks, *The First Urban Christians: the Social World of the Apostle Paul* (New Haven, Conn.: Yale University Press, 1983), 33; E.S. Frerichs et. al., *'To see ourselves'*; D. Boyarin, *Carnal Israel: Reading Sex in Talmudic Culture* (NH 25; Berkeley, Calif.: University of California Press, 1993), 3–5; 24; 47; 77.

[108] Bogaert, *Apocalypse de Baruch I*, 356–362. In addition, it is probable that those who produced the *Ambrosianus* version of *2 Baruch* also read or listened to recitals of other biblical books and stories in Syriac. *2 Bar.* 4:2, for instance, follows the Syriac version of Isa 49:16. In that particular passage the Syriac version stands alone against the Massoretic, the Septuagint and the Vulgate (Charles, *Apocalypse of Baruch*, 6). If nothing else is mentioned, passages from The Syriac Bible are taken from *The Old Testament in Syriac: According to the Peshitta Version*. (Edited on behalf of the International Organization for the Study of the Old Testament by the Peshitta Institute. Leiden: E.J. Brill, 1972–). English Bible passages are from the NRSV translation of the Bible.

As this discussion of the provenance of *2 Baruch* has suggested, *2 Baruch* has affinities with several milieus and consequently attests to ideas that occur in a wide range of other texts. The contemporary texts *4 Ezra*, *Liber antiquitatum biblicarum (Pseudo-Philo)*, and *4 Baruch (Paraleipomena Jeremiou)* are probably all important to our reading of *2 Baruch*. Texts like the *Testament of Abraham*, the *Targum Jonathan to Isaiah* and 1 Corinthians also share some notions with *2 Baruch*. Questions of dependency, however, remain far from clear.

This study will assume that *2 Baruch* most probably originated within an unidentifiable Jewish milieu[109] somewhere in Palestine, between 70 and 132 C.E. It is impossible to confirm further details of origin. However, some further proposals about the context of *2 Baruch* may still be suggested. It is likely that *2 Baruch* originates within a setting of educated Jews who were also familiar with a wider spectrum of contemporary trends. In the absence of the temple and its cult, these Jews advocated a law-abiding lifestyle. They saw themselves as marginalised in the present world, probably due to Roman mastery and possibly also because of the dominance of other Jewish groups, but still regarded their knowledge as superior to that of their contemporary surroundings. Those who produced *2 Baruch* attempted to persuade others who were acquainted with a similar, traditional repertoire of stories, imageries, and metaphors to return to what they envisioned as the correct lifestyle.

A Short Presentation of the Book

This book is divided into eight chapters, including the conclusion. Chapters Two and Three discuss the period of the First Temple, as presented by *2 Baruch*. Chapter Two deals with Baruch's concern for the fall of the temple, the destruction of Jerusalem and the dispossession of Palestine,[110] and studies the consequences of destruction and dispersion

---

[109] Cf. Davila's informative discussion of the term 'common Judaism' (Davila, *Provenance*, 15–21). Following the lead of J.Z. Smith (*Imagining Religion*, 1–18; 135–141), Davila chooses to deal with a polythetic definition of 'Judaism'. He says: "Rather than attempting to find an essence common to every member, it is based on a broad grouping of characteristics and properties. A member of the class being defined must have many of these characteristics, but no single characteristic is necessarily possessed by every member" (Davila, *Provenance*, 19). In this study I apply the terms 'Jewish' and 'Judaism' in accordance with Davila's definition of the terms.

[110] Note that the term 'Palestine' has a strict local meaning throughout this study. In the remaining parts of the book it denotes a location in a narrative geography and is

on the further existence of Israel. Chapter Three studies *2 Baruch*'s construction of the Land of the past. It attempts to shed light on the importance of kingship and the inauguration of the temple to the existence of the Land, and discusses the effects of apostasy on the extent of the Land.

The two subsequent chapters, Chapters Four and Five, concern the spaces of the end-time. Chapter Four explores how *2 Baruch* imagines an alternative spatial building in the Kidron valley where Israel can survive through the end-time and secure future redemption. Chapter Five studies the consequence of Baruch's move to Hebron.

The last two chapters, Chapters Six and Seven, have the time of redemption as their topic. Chapter Six studies the Land in the Messianic era and focuses on the function and place of the Land in liminal space. Chapter Seven finally discusses how Israel takes possession of the other world and attempts to answer the main question of this study: does *2 Baruch* reject Israel's Land as a redemptive space belonging to the corruptible world only, or does it transform the Land to unite the central space of the covenant with the other world as the ultimate space of redemption?

The conclusion summarises the study. It establishes how the Land functions within *2 Baruch*'s history of consolation and redemption. The conclusion further discusses the fruitfulness of a praxis epistemology, attempting to show how this epistemological shift provides an opportunity to recontextualise the Land-concept in texts stemming from the first centuries C.E.

---

applied in its local sense only. I apply the term 'Palestine' to refer to *descriptions in texts* of the area south of the Lebanon and north of the Negev, west of the Dead Sea and east of the Mediterranean Ocean. The term is also attested in several texts dating from the first centuries C.E. (e.g., Josephus and the Mishnah).

CHAPTER TWO

QUESTIONING SURVIVAL: THE LAND IN
THE CONTEXT OF DESTRUCTION

The destruction of Jerusalem and its temple forms the backdrop of the narrative sections, visions, and discussions of *2 Baruch*. In agreement with a majority of scholars, I regard the destruction of the temple and the surrounding city as the main discursive problem of the text. Several studies have already dealt extensively with the destruction-theme in *2 Baruch*. Scholars like Nir, Charles, Bogaert, and Whitters have all devoted chapters or sections to the topic.[1] Moreover, several articles have made the destruction their main focus.[2]

Nevertheless, the attention that the dispossession of the Land has received in this context is rather sparse. To my knowledge, Sayler and Murphy are the only scholars who have explicitly addressed the issue.[3] However, in the introductory part of *2 Baruch*, the loss of the Land is important. In these paragraphs, an anxious Baruch asks God about the future fate of Israel, after the destruction:

> But one thing I will say in your presence, Lord: What, then, will there be after these things? For if you destroy your city, and you hand over your land to those who hate us, how shall the name of Israel again be remembered? Or how shall one speak of your glories? Or to whom

---

[1] Charles, *Apocalypse of Baruch*, 6–7; 13–14; Bogaert, *Apocalypse de Baruch I*, 127–176; Whitters, *Epistle*, 49–50; 64–65; 137–143; Nir, *Destruction*, 19–100.

[2] Among them, P.-M. Bogaert, "La ruine Jérusalem et les apocalypses juives après 70," in *Apocalypses et théologie de l'espérance. Congrès de Toulouse 1975* (ed. L. Monloubou; LD 95; Paris: Latour-Maubourg, 1977), 123–141; P.-M. Bogaert, "Les réactions juives après la ruine de Jérusalem. L'apocalypse de Baruch," *Le monde de la Bible* 29 (1983): 19–20; P.F. Esler, "God's Honor and Rome's Triumph. Responses to the Fall of Jerusalem in 70 CE in Three Jewish Apocalypses," *Modelling Early Christianity. Social-Scientific Studies of the New Testament in Its Context* (ed. P.F. Esler; London: Routledge, 1995), 239–258; R. Kirschner, "Apocalyptic Responses to the Destruction of 70," *HTR* 78 (1985): 27–46; A.B. Kolenkow, "The Fall of the Temple and the Coming of the End: The Spectrum and Process of Apocalyptic Argumentation in *2 Baruch* and Other Authors," *SBLSP* 21 (1982): 243–250; M.E. Stone, "Reactions to Destructions of the Second Temple," *JSJ* 12 (1981): 195–204.

[3] Sayler, *Promises*, 74–79; 86; Murphy, *Structure and Meaning*, 81–83. Cf. Whitters, *Epistle*, 137–140; 168 and Leuenberger, "Ort und Funktion," 207; 212.

will that which is in your Law be explained? Or shall cosmos return to its nature and the world again go back to primeval silence? And shall the multitude of souls be taken away and human nature not again be named? And where is all that which you said to Moses regarding us (3:4–9)?

The present chapter will be devoted to an examination of this passage and the vital role it implies for the Land.[4] The passage will be studied in light of *2 Baruch*'s destruction story in *2 Bar.* 1–9. There are three parts to this chapter. The first part addresses the question: how are the temple, the city and the Land connected in *2 Baruch*, and what is the role of righteous praxis to this connection? The second part discusses the role of the Land as Israel's place of survival in the corruptible world (3:4–6): How does the fall of Jerusalem and the temple affect the Land as an environment of survival? The third part focuses on the cosmic role of the Land (3:7–9): what was the function of the Land within the corruptible world before the destruction of the temple? How does the fall of Jerusalem and its temple change the condition of the corruptible world, and how does the fact that Jerusalem comes into foreign hands affect the landscapes of the corruptible world?

Note that this chapter will focus on the concerns of Baruch in 3:4–9 with regard to the Land and focus on reflections and notions implied by his questions to God. The answers God offers Baruch are not topics of my present discussion, but the issue of later chapters.

2 Bar. *1–9: The Fall of Zion*

To grasp the role and the function of the Land at the time of the destruction of Jerusalem and its temple, it is essential to take a closer look at *2 Baruch*'s versions of the fall in 1:1–9:2. This passage constitutes the opening section of *2 Baruch* and a central part of the frame narrative of the text.

According to 1:1, God's word came to Baruch in the twenty-fifth year of "King Jeconiah of Judah."[5] God informs Baruch that the destruction

---

[4] Leuenberger addresses these questions Baruch's 'Grundfrage' in *2 Baruch* ("Ort und Funktion," 213).

[5] This dating refers to the twenty-fifth year of King Jehoiachin/Jechonias (2 Kgs 24:8; 2 Chr 36:9 (LXX); Josephus, *J.W.* 6.2.1; Cf. Bogaert, *Apocalypse de Baruch I*, 7–9; Klijn, "2 Baruch," 621). The date is in accordance with 2 Kgs 24:8. It must be assumed

of the temple is imminent and instructs Baruch, along with Jeremiah and "all those who are like you (pl.)"[6]—the remaining righteous—to leave Jerusalem (2:1; 4:7; 5:2, 5). Baruch, Jeremiah (2:1) and their group of followers then leave the city for the Kidron valley to lament and fast (5:5–7).

The next day the army of the Chaldeans surrounds Jerusalem (6:1).[7] As Baruch sits lamenting under an oak tree outside the city, a strong wind[8] lifts him up and carries him above Jerusalem's wall (6:2–4). From this viewpoint Baruch sees four angels standing at the four corners of the city carrying torches.[9] Suddenly, a fifth angel comes down from heaven and instructs the other angels to wait (6:5).[10] Baruch observes how the angel descends into the Holy of Holies and takes away the holy objects and furniture from this innermost part of the sanctuary, including all the holy vessels of the tabernacle (6:6–7).[11] The angel then

---

that the dating of *2 Bar.* 1:1 is meant to refer to the destruction of Jerusalem and its temple in 587 B.C.E. (although the dating in 1:1 would refer to the date 592 BCE). Note further that *2 Bar.* 1–8 mentions both the reigns of King Jeconiah (1:1; 6:1) and the fate of King Zedekiah (8:3; 2 Kgs 24:17–25:7; 2 Chr 36:11) in the description of the destruction, and that according to *2 Baruch*, the siege and destruction of Jerusalem lasted one day (6:1). *2 Baruch* makes a concentrated description of the siege and destruction process described as lasting two years in, e.g., 2 Kgs 24–25 and 2 Chr 36 (Cf. Charles, *Apocalypse of Baruch*, 2; Bogaert, *Apocalypse de Baruch* I, 281–288 and II, 7; 26; Klijn, "2 Baruch," 621; Murphy, *Structure and Meaning*, 93).

[6] The expression "all those who are like you" is common in *2 Baruch* and *4 Ezra*. Cf. *2 Bar.* 13:5; 21:24; 57:1; 59:1; 66:7; *4 Ezra* 4:36; 8:51 (Cf. Charles, *Apocalypse of Baruch*, 3; Bogaert, *Apocalypse de Baruch II*, 11).

[7] Cf. *4 Bar.* 1:1–3; 4:1.

[8] The Syriac word *ruḥā* may mean "wind," "spirit," or "breath," bringing a wide field of allusions to mind (Cf. Charles, *Apocalypse of Baruch*, 10; Bogaert, *Apocalypse de Baruch II*, 21). Cf., e.g., Rev 7:1–3.

[9] *4 Bar.* 3:2; Rev 7:1; *Pesiq. Rab.* 26:6.

[10] Rev 7:2. In *4 Bar.* 3:4 and *Liv. Pro.* 2:11 Jeremiah fills the role of *2 Baruch*'s fifth angel.

[11] Cf. the parallel account of *2 Bar.* 80:1–4. According to 6:7, the angel removes the veil, the holy ephod, the mercy seat, the two tables, the holy raiment of the priests, the altar of incense, the forty-eight precious stones of the priests' clothes and the vessels of the tabernacle. Lists like these were quite common: cf. 2 Macc 2:4–5; *Aris. Ex.* 86–97; Heb 9:1–5. *2 Bar.* 6:7 has been thoroughly discussed by Nir (*Destruction*, 43–77). Cf. further Charles, *Apocalypse of Baruch*, 10–11; 168; Bogaert, *Apocalypse de Baruch II*, 22–24; Klijn, "Sources and Redaction," 71. Cf. discussions of the widespread tradition of the hiding of temple vessels: C.R. Koester, *The Dwelling of God: The Tabernacle in the Old Testament, Intertestamental Jewish Literature and the New Testament* (CBQ Monograph Series 22; Washington DC: The Catholic Biblical Association of America, 1989), 53; P.R. Ackroyd, "The Temple Vessels—A Continuity Theme," *VTSup* 23 (1972): 166–181; I. Kalimi, and D.J. Purvis, "The Hiding of the Temple Vessels in Jewish and Samaritan

commands the earth (*ar'ā*),[12] to swallow up the holy objects and protect them until they may be restored.[13] The ground then "opened its mouth and swallowed them up" (6:10).

With the holy objects safely guarded in the ground, the angel instructs the four torch bearing angels to demolish the walls of Zion. 7:1 gives the following reason for this instruction: "Overthrow, then, and destroy its walls to their foundations, so that the enemies will not boast and say: 'We have destroyed the wall[14] of Zion and set on fire the place of the mighty God.'" After the angels had broken the corners of the wall,[15] a voice was heard from the middle of the temple[16] saying: "'Enter, enemies, and come, adversaries, for he who guarded the house has abandoned it'" (8:2).[17]

When Baruch has been brought back to the spot where he originally has been standing (7:2)[18] and has walked away (8:3),[19] the Chaldean army enters Jerusalem and seizes "the house and all that is around it" (8:4).[20] The Chaldeans kill some of the inhabitants, carry away others, and bring King Zedekiah to Babylon (8:5). Baruch, Jeremiah, and their followers, however, are not captured. They mourn and fast for seven days (9:1).[21]

Literature," *CBQ* 56 (1994): 679–685; M.F. Collins, "The Hidden Vessels in Samaritan Traditions," *JSJ* 3 (1972): 97–119.

[12] The Syriac word *ar'ā* may be translated both "earth" and "land." Violet, Bogaert and Harrington suggest the translation "land" (Violet, *Apokalypsen*, 211; Bogaert, *Apocalypse de Baruch II*, 24 and I, 361–362; Harrington, "Holy Land," 671). Cf. further Jer 22:29; 2 Macc 2:4–5; *4 Bar.* 3:10; *4 Ezra* 7:62. Cf. also J.T. Milik, "Notes d'épigraphie et de topographie palestiennes," *RB* 66 (1959), 550–575.

[13] 2 Macc 2:4–8; *Liv. Pro.* 2:11; *L.A.B.* 26; *4 Bar.* 3:18–19; *Apoc. Dan.* 8 (Cf. M. Henze, *The Syriac Apocalypse of Daniel: Introduction, Text and Commentary* (Tübingen: Mohr Siebeck, 2001), 70–71; Nir, *Destruction*, 66–77).

[14] *šawrā*, "wall," is first mentioned in the plural, then in the singular.

[15] Cf. *4 Bar.* 4:2; *Apoc. Abr.* 27:3 and possibly Rev 7:1–3; 9:13–15 (Cf. Bogaert, *Apocalypse de Baruch II*, 21–22). Note that *2 Baruch* does not mention the burning of the temple, only the destruction of the wall.

[16] Cf. Ezek 9–11; Josephus, *J.W.* 6.293–300; Tacitus, *Hist.* 5.13.

[17] Cf. *2 Bar.* 10:18; Ezek 11:22–23; *Liv. Pro.* 2:12; *Pesiq. Rab.* 26. Cf. Nir, *Destruction*, 79–82 for a more elaborate discussion of rabbinic references.

[18] Cf. Charles, *Apocalypse of Baruch*, 12; Violet, *Apokalypsen*, 212. Cf. *3 Bar.* 17:2.

[19] Note, then, that Baruch does not witness the destruction of Jerusalem by the enemies (Cf. 3:1–3; 5:1). He sees only the destruction carried out by the angels (Cf. 5:2).

[20] The expression may refer to the temple compounds, or to the surrounding city.

[21] Cf. *4 Bar.* 2:2–5. According to Jer 37:11–16, however, Jeremiah was taken captive.

Grasping Spatial Overlap: 'Zion' and 'the region of Zion'

2 Bar. 1–9 presents an apparent paradox that needs some attention in the present discussion. Whereas 3:4–9, cited initially, describes Baruch's worries about the loss of the city and the Land, *2 Baruch*'s account of the destruction in 5:1–9:2 emphasises the fall of the temple and the city and does not mention the Land explicitly. The fact that 5:1–9:2 does not mention the Land is probably the reason why previous studies only rarely have focused on the loss of the Land in the context of the destruction. However, since 3:4–9 makes the Land-loss a crucial part of Baruch's worries at the eve of destruction, the relationship between the temple, the city, and the Land needs to be studied.

The Ambiguous Term 'Zion' and the Temple-City Pair

Several scholars have noted that *2 Baruch*'s use of the term 'Zion' (*çehyun*) is far from consistent.[22] 'Zion' can refer to the temple edifice, to the city Jerusalem, and to the temple-city complex.[23] Moreover, 'Zion' may sometimes also refer to Jerusalem's inhabitants.[24] Spatial overlap between temple and city is not restricted to the term 'Zion,' though. The notions of the city and the temple tend to merge in other contexts as well. The temple cult is for instance in all probability implied in 3:6: "Or how shall one speak of your glories?" In this sentence, Baruch asks God how Israel shall be able to serve God and keep his acts in remembrance after the destruction of the city and the loss of the Land.[25] In other words, Baruch asks God how Israel can serve God when the temple has fallen, but he does that without mentioning the temple explicitly.[26] Likewise, the wall described in 7:1–2 and 8:1 may belong both to the city and to the temple.[27]

2 Baruch is far from unique in this regard. Sayler notes: "The practice of using the terms ['Jerusalem', 'Zion', 'the city' and 'the Tem-

---

[22] Cf. Sayler, *Promises*, 16; Murphy, *Structure and Meaning*, 71; Davies, *Gospel and Land*, 132; Klijn, "Recent Developments," 9; Whitters, *Epistle*, 137–138.

[23] Cf. *2 Bar.* 5:1–2; 7:1; 10:3; 11:1–2; 32:2; 40:1; 61:2; 64:4; 77:9; 80:7.

[24] Cf. *Apoc. Dan.* 11, where Jerusalem is carried away into captivity.

[25] Cf. *2 Bar.* 64:6.

[26] *2 Bar.* 3:6 attests to the notions of God's glory, his name, and possibly also his glorious deeds. Cf. 5:2; 63:8–10; 64:6.

[27] Cf. Neh 2:8. Cf. Klijn, "Recent Developments," 9.

ple'] interchangeably was common in this time period."[28] The phenomenon can clearly be seen in biblical texts,[29] as well as in texts
like *4 Ezra*,[30] Josephus' *Jewish Antiquities*[31] and in the Mishnah.[32] Hence,
2 Baruch attests to commonly held ideas about the relationship of the
temple and Jerusalem. The notion of the temple may be implicit in the
notion of the city and vice versa.[33] The temple and the city tend to
overlap, to be spatially fluid, and the terms applied to describe them
oscillate between related meanings.

'The region of Zion': The Land as a Temple Environment

As we have now seen, *2 Baruch* lets the temple and the city overlap
and allows the term 'Zion' (*çehyun*) to refer either to the city or to the
temple, or to the combination of both. One question now needs to be
answered: how does the Land relate to the temple-city pair?

Like *2 Bar.* 1–9, 67:1–7 presents the time of the destruction of the
temple. However, this passage does not dwell on the event of the temple
fall, but concentrates on its consequences. 67:1 addresses "Zion now"
(*hāšā lçehyun*), the time Baruch himself witnessed.[34] 67:6 demonstrates
the effect of the destruction on the Land:

> Because so far as Zion has been surrendered and Jerusalem laid waste,
> and the idols prosper in the cities of the nations, and the steam of the
> smoke of the incense of righteousness which comes from the Law has

---

[28] Sayler, *Promises*, 16. Cf. R.G. Hamerton-Kelly, "The Temple and the Origins of
Jewish Apocalyptic," *VT* 20 (1970): 1–15 at 3 and Leuenberger, "Ort und Funktion,"
213.

[29] Ps 137; Isa 51:16; Jer 3:17; Zech 2:5; 11; Amos 1:2. Cf. M. Eliade, *Patterns in
Comparative Religion* (New York: Sheed & Ward, 1958), 375–385; Davies, *Gospel and Land*,
132; 150–154; J.D. Levenson, *Sinai and Zion: An Entry into the Jewish Bible* (New Voices in
Biblical Studies; Minneapolis: Winston Press, 1985), 137; J.D. Levenson, "The Temple
and the World," *JR* 64 (1984): 275–298 at 295.

[30] Cf. Hamerton-Kelly, "Temple and Origins," 4.

[31] Josephus, *Ant.* 12.11.145–146.

[32] Cf. J. Neusner, *The Idea of Purity in Ancient Judaism* (Leiden: E.J. Brill, 1973); J. Neus-
ner, "History and Purity in First-Century Judaism," *HR* 18 (1978): 1–17; S. Safrai,
"Jerusalem in the Halakah," in *The Centrality of Jerusalem* (ed. M. Poorthuius and C.H.
Safrai; Kampen: Kok Phaors, 1996), 94–113 at 97; Whitters, *Epistle*, 137–138.

[33] Cf. Levenson, *Sinai and Zion*, 137; Cf. also L. Fisher, "The Temple Quarter," *JSS*
8 (1963): 34–41; R.J. McKelvey, *The New Temple: the Church in the New Testament* (Oxford:
Oxford University Press, 1969), 13–14.

[34] Note the possible conflation of time here. The passage may invoke the fall of the
First as well as the Second Temple.

2 been extinguished from Zion and in the region of Zion, in the whole place, behold, the smoke of impiety is in it.[35]

This passage claims that the fall of Zion and the devastation of Jerusalem have led all righteousness to be extinguished "from Zion and in the region of Zion." Instead, there is impiety in that whole place. Interestingly, this passage refers to the area affected by the destruction as "the region of Zion" (*atrāh dçehyun*) and "the whole place" (*kul duk*). What area(s) do the expressions 'the region of Zion' and 'the whole place' refer to?

The first problem we face here is that the terms used in 67:6 are ambiguous. The expression *atrāh dçehyun* may mean "the place of Zion," "the district of Zion," or "the country of Zion."[36] It may therefore point either to the place where the temple stood, or to the place that surrounds Zion, probably Jerusalem.[37] Moreover, it may also refer to the district surrounding Zion,[38] or the area where the temple stood in an even wider sense. The interpretation depends partly on how we view the relationship between 'the region of Zion' and 'the whole place' in this sentence. On the one hand, the concepts may refer to two distinct geographical areas. If this were the case, it would be reasonable to understand 'the region of Zion' as a smaller part of 'the whole place.' On the other hand, the two concepts may also be synonyms. In that case, 'the whole place' describes the same area as 'the region of Zion.' The Syriac text says literally "in the region of Zion, in the whole place" and then lets the subsequent description of impiety refer to this area as a single unit (*bāh*). The second interpretation is thus clearly the most likely one: 'the region of Zion' and 'the whole place' are synonymous expressions and refer to one and the same area.

The second problem is that the extent of the region of Zion and the whole place can not be identified as precise territories since no such information is given in the passage. Although it is important for 67:6

---

[35] Cf. Bogaert, *Apocalypse de Baruch I*, 512. Charles translates the sentence "in every place there is the smoke of impiety" (*Apocalypse of Baruch*, 110).

[36] J.P. Smith, *A Compendious Syriac Dictionary: Founded upon the Thesaurus Syriacus of R. Payne Smith* (Oxford: Oxford University Press, 1902; Repr., Eugene, Or.: Wipf and Stock, 1999), 33. Cf. Bogaert, *Apocalypse de Baruch II*, 121 and 18. There is also the possibility that it refers to the temple only, as 'the place' (Cf. *2 Bar.* 5:1; 7:1; *L.A.B.* 19:7; *T. Mos.* 1:18). This is however improbable since the temple is referred to as 'Zion' in 67:1 and 6.

[37] *4 Bar.* 1:6 may be interpreted this way.

[38] Cf. *2 Bar.* 1:4 and Bar 2:23.

to emphasise that the situation of impiety applies to the whole area, the area in question is not defined by territorial exactness. Rather, the term 'the region of Zion' points to the reciprocity between Zion and its surroundings, the city and the surrounding region, before the destruction. 'The region of Zion' applied to the area which benefited from the impact of the temple. And the other way around, 'the region of Zion' extended *only* as far as Zion's impact among its inhabitants, since the term, by implication, would exclude territories where inhabitants served other gods or behaved wickedly.

How does this analysis of 67:6 fit the descriptions of the temple, city, and Land in 1–9?[39] 1:2–4 may shed some light on this issue. This passage claims that the sins of the two tribes who still remained within Judah were even more severe than the sins of the ten tribes who were exiled a long time before the destruction.[40] 1:4 sets out the

---

[39] One initial consideration is important here: since 67:6 describes the result of the destruction, but does not dwell on the destruction process, 1:1–9:2 may on the one hand complement the description of 67:6 by presenting the actual destruction at the times of the kings Jeconiah (1:1) and Zedekiah (8:5). On the other hand, we should also regard 1:1–9:2 as an independent and parallel account of the crisis. *2 Baruch* in a sense doubles the presentation of the crisis and gives it in two versions: once in the portrayal of world history within the context of the Apocalypse of the cloud, and once in the frame story of the temple fall giving the up beat to the general discussions and considerations of *2 Baruch* (Cf. Charles, *Apocalypse of Baruch*, 110).

[40] *2 Baruch* sometimes refers to two tribes (1:2–4), and other times to two and a half tribes (62:5; 63:3 and 64:5). The discussion of the identity of the two (and a half) tribes is longstanding. Klijn argued that the nine and a half tribes were those who inhabited the country on the western side of the Jordan, whereas the two and a half tribes (i.e., Reuben, Gad and half of Manasseh) lived on the eastern side of the river (Josh 22) (Klijn, "2 Baruch," 621). This does not make sense, since the two (and a half) tribes who are left in 1:2 and 63:3 are those who are ruled by the king of Judah. Hence, 'the two (and a half) tribes' is probably a reference to the tribes who inhabited the kingdom of Judah: these may be the tribes of Judah, Benjamin and, in the case of 63:3, the half tribe of Levites (Cf. 1 Chr 12:23–40, Ezra 1:5; *Lam. Rab.* 35a; cf. Japhet, *Ideology*, 288; H. Stegemann, "'Das Land' in der Tempelrolle und in anderen Texten aus den Qumranfunden," in *Das Land Israel in biblischer Zeit. Jerusalem-Symposium 1981 der Hebräischen Universität und der Georg-August-Universität* (ed. G. Strecker; GTA 25; Göttingen: Vandenhoeck & Ruprecht, 1983), 154–171 at 163; Stone, "Reactions," 199). These tribes may also be described as two tribes (*2 Bar.* 1:2), considering the Levites as a group, alternatively as three tribes, interpreting the Levites as a tribe (Cf. 1 Kgs 11–12; *1 En.* 89:72–73; *T. Mos.* 5). It is also possible that *2 Baruch* reckons the tribes of Judah and Levi as the two tribes, and consider Benjamin as a half tribe. At the time, Benjamin was often understood as a part of Judah. Judah and Levi, on the other hand, were the two most profiled tribes in contemporary literature (Cf. *Jub.* 31:11–20; *T. Reu.* 6:5–12; *T. Sim.* 5:4–6; *T. Jud.* 21:1–5; Cf. A. Hultgård, *L'eschatologie des Testaments des douze patriarches* (2 vols; Acta Universitatis Upsaliensis. Historia religionum 6–7; Uppsala: Almqvist & Wiksell, 1977–1981) 59; 63–64). Another possibility is that the two and a half tribes are

results of the two tribes' sins: "Therefore, behold, I shall bring evil upon this *mdita* and its inhabitants." I hesitate to translate *mdita* since its meaning is not obvious in the context of 1:2–4. The Syriac word *mdita* is most commonly translated "city," but it may also mean "region," or "country."[41] In this case all these interpretations make sense.[42] In light of the preceding sentences (1:1–3), "region" or "country" is perhaps preferable, since the inhabitants of 1:4 must logically be the two tribes that inhabited Judah. The subsequent passage (2:1), however, introduces the city of Jerusalem as the context: Baruch and his followers are commanded to leave the city, since their presence shields it. This makes the translation "city" just as probable. Thus, *mdita* in 1:4, probably refers to the fluid concept of city/region/country where the remaining inhabitants of the kingdom of Judah still lived before the destruction.

Note now that the interpretative options and challenges in 1:2–4 are somewhat similar to those of 67:6. The space of 1:2–4, has the same conceptual openness and potential as 'the region of Zion' and 'the whole place' of 67:6. The connotations evoked by each passage open up the temple-city entity to its surroundings: we find the same spatial fluidity in both. Neither passage describes clearly defined territories. Instead, the contexts must be used to assess the probability of different interpretations.

It is important to note that it is righteous inhabitance and praxis that defines space in both these passages. The interpretation of the spatial extent of the term *mdita*, above, depends to a large extent on the iden-

---

the tribes of Judah, Benjamin and the half tribe of Dan. The tribe of Dan was originally allotted territory north of Judah (Josh 19:40–48). Judg 18:10, however, describe how 600 Danites encamped in the territory north of the tribal land of Manasseh. The tribe of Dan, thus, came to be identified with both tribal areas. The borders between the tribal areas were however more fluid during the first centuries C.E. Josephus, for instance, tends to blend Dan and Benjamin, when he states that Benjamin has access to the sea. Yet another possibility is that the tribe of Simeon is implied in the group along with Judah and Levi. The tribes of Judah and Simeon, as well as their territories, tend to merge (Judg 1:1–3). However, this would leave out Benjamin, and thus the tribal area where Jerusalem is located. (Cf. C.H.J. de. Geus, *The Tribes of Israel: An Investigation into some of the Presuppositions of Martin Noth's amphictyony hypothesis* (SSN18; Assen: Van Gorcum, 1976)).

[41] Smith, *Dictionary*, 252; R.P. Smith, *Thesaurus Syriacus* (2 vols. Oxford, 1879–1901; Repr., 4. Nachdruck der Ausgabe Oxford 1879–1901; Hildesheim: Georg Olms, 2006), 844. Cf. Bogaert, *Apocalypse de Baruch II*, 10. Note that the root of *mdita* is *dwn*, "to judge," "to administer" (Smith, *Thesaurus*, 844). *mdita* is thus an area which is under the administration of law.

[42] Cf. 2 Kgs 22:16; 2 Chr 34:28; Jer 19:3–4.

tification of its inhabitants. Likewise, the main concern of 67:6 is that *righteousness* is no more to be found after the destruction of the temple and the dispossession of Jerusalem and its surrounding region. The area that was once the lawful surroundings of Zion is now instead an area totally dominated by sin. The central imagery of the passage blends sacrificial terms with the language of righteousness.[43] Righteousness, in terms of the smoke of the incense sacrifice, has been extinguished from the area.[44] Instead, the smoke of illicit offerings contaminates the air.[45] The Law's righteous fragrance has been replaced by the vapor of sin. This imagery attests both to the cessation of the temple cult and to the end of righteous inhabitancy. This blend of related imageries effectively displays the central role of lawful inhabitance and cultic action to the definition of space. The cultic activities in the temple and its compounds and the striving for purity, holiness, and lawful maintenance of the country are related practices which together defined 'the region of Zion.'[46] This implies that 'the region of Zion' is defined by the moral character of its inhabitants, not by territory.

Temple, City, Land—and Righteous Practices

The above discussion has pointed out two tendencies: firstly, that there is considerable overlap between temple, city, and the surrounding region in passages of *2 Baruch*, and, secondly, that 67:6 presents the region that surrounds Zion as a fluid and flexible temple environment defined by cultic action and righteous inhabitance. This implies that there are no clear demarcation lines between the temple, the city, and 'the region of Zion', the Land, at the time of the destruction.[47] If this is indeed the case, *2 Baruch* shares notions and ideas common in Jewish texts from the first centuries CE, not only with regard to the temple-city pair,

---

[43] Note a similar blend in *Targum Song of Songs* 7:14. Cf. also *5 Apoc. Syr. Pss.* 2:11 and IQS 9:5.

[44] Cf. *2 Bar.* 35:4; Exod 30:27, 34–38; Sir 49:1. Cf. R. Nir, "The Aromatic Fragrances of Paradise in the Greek Life of Adam and Eve and the Christian Origin of the Composition," *NT* 46 (2004), 20–45; S.A. Harvey, *Scenting Salvation: Ancient Christianity and the Olfactory Imagination* (The Transformation of the Classical Heritage 2; Berkley, Calif.: University of California Press, 2006).

[45] Cf. Gen 19:28. Impiety smells; cf., e.g., *Pss. Sol.* 2:4. Cf. Endsjø, D.Ø. "Parfyme, død og udødlighet," *Chaos 39* (2003): 91–98.

[46] Cf. the description of "a land barren of faith" in *4 Ezra* 5:1. Here, action defines space in a similar manner.

[47] Cf. Habel, *The Land is Mine*, 114; Davies, *Gospel and Land*, 150–154.

but also regarding the Land.[48] At this point in *2 Baruch*'s description of world history, the temple, the city, and the Land are interdependent aspects of the same spatial entity.[49] The temple, the city, and the Land may overlap, represent each other, and be equivalent. At the time of destruction, the reference to the destiny of Jerusalem and the temple (5:1–9:2) is simultaneously a reference to destiny of the Land (3:4–9). And consequently, the fall of Jerusalem and its temple involves the loss of the Land.

Questioning Survival: Israel without Land?

I have suggested that Baruch's fears caused by the imminent destruction of Zion and the foreign intrusion into the Land concern the very existence of Israel. How does *2 Baruch* present the role of the Land with regard to the survival of Israel? And what are the implications of destruction and dispossession to the survival of Israel?

2 Bar. 3:4–6: The Vital Role of the Land to Israel's Survival

Let us start by looking at 3:4–6 again, this time in greater detail. In 3:4 Baruch asks God about the consequences of Jerusalem's destruction: "What, then, will there be after these things?" In 3:5 Baruch elaborates on his apprehension: "For if you destroy your city, and you hand over your country to those who hate us, how shall the name of Israel again be remembered?" Baruch's questions suggest that the city and the Land are essential to the continued remembrance of the name of Israel. Israel

---

[48] Cf. R.E. Clements, "Temple and Land: A Significant Aspect of Israel's Worship," *TGUOS* 19 (1963): 16–28 at 20–24; 26; Fisher, "Temple Quarter," 34; 40; R.J. Clifford, *The Cosmic Mountain in Canaan and the Old Testament* (Cambridge, Mass: Harvard University Press, 1972), 158–159; G. Vermes, *Scripture and Tradition in Judaism* (SPB 4; Leiden: E.J. Brill, 1973); J. Blenkinsopp, *Prophecy and Canon: a Contribution to the Study of Jewish Origins* (Notre Dame, Ind.: University of Notre Dame Press, 1977), 67–69; Davies, *Gospel and Land*, 94; 132; Kunin, *God's Place*, 11–27; Levenson, *Sinai and Zion*, 137; Lieu, *Christian Identity*, 218–219. Cf. Exod 15:17; Ps 78:54; Isa 11:9; 57:13. Cf. further, "the land of Zion" (*4 Ezra* 14:31; Cf. Violet, *Apokalypsen*, 197); "the land of the house of Presence" (*Targum Jonathan to Zech* 2:15; cf. P. Grelot, *What are the Targums? Selected Texts* (trans. S. Attanasio; OTS 7; Collegeville, Minn.: Liturgical Press, 1992), 105); and *Jub.* 8; 18–19. C. Sulzbach proposes that *Jub.* 8 displays "the notion of the Land as a veritable Sanctuary" (C. Sulzbach, "The Function of the Sacred Geography in the Book of Jubilees," *JSem* 14/2 (2005): 283–305). Cf. also *Apoc. Dan.* 39.

[49] Davies, *Gospel and Land*, 154; Clements, "Temple and Land," 23–24.

risks falling into oblivion if the city is destroyed and her enemies take possession of the Land.

In what sense does falling into oblivion pose a threat? To better understand this idea, the importance of 'remembrance' in the text must be noted. *2 Baruch* applies the word "remember"[50] frequently, often in conjunction with the term "forget" (root *ṭ'*).[51] Israel is, for example, commanded to remember God's actions on her behalf (48:29; 77:11; 78:3), to remember God's promises to Moses (84:2), Zion and the suffering of Jerusalem (31:4), and not to forget the Law (44:7; 48:38; 84:7–8). God, too, remembers. God remembers both the beginning and the coming end (48:7), and he remembers Israel as long as she follows the Law (84:7).[52] In contrast, Baruch is instructed to forget that which is corruptible (43:2). 44:9 adds that the present time will be forgotten due to its corruptibility and mortality.[53] Embedded in *2 Baruch*'s notion of remembrance and oblivion, there lies an existential difference between continued life and extinction. Remembrance means continued existence, while oblivion equals extinction. Thus, behind Baruch's worries about Israel's name in 3:5 lies the fear of Israel's total extinction. Indeed, Baruch questions the very possibility of Israel's existence outside, or without, Jerusalem and the Land.[54]

Survival at Risk: Israel, the People; Israel, the Assembly

3:6 says: "Or to whom will that which is in your Law be explained?"[55] This passage adds another element to Baruch's worries about the future: the possible extinction of Israel as a cultic gathering. If Israel

---

[50] *2 Baruch* applies forms of the two roots *dkr* and *'hd*, "remember."

[51] Note that *ṭ'* may imply both "to err" and "to forget" (Smith, *Dictionary*, 177–178). According to Murphy, forms of the roots *dkr* and *'hd*, "remember," occur 26 times and the term "forget" (*ṭ'*) 14 times (*Structure and Meaning*, 128).

[52] Cf. further *2 Bar.* 19:6–7; 84:8; 86:1. Cf. Isa 43:18–19; 65:17; Wis 4:19.

[53] Cf. Murphy, *Structure and Meaning*, 127–128.

[54] Cf. Murphy, *Structure and Meaning*, 82.

[55] Cf. *4 Ezra* 4:22–25 and 14:21. Murphy has pointed out an important implication of Baruch's question in 3:6: "This question seems to imply that Zion is the only place where God can truly be praised" (Murphy, *Structure and Meaning*, 82–85. Cf., e.g., 2 Chr 6:2; Pss 65:1; 99:9; 102:21; 125:1; 137:4). Murphy regards 3:1–9 primarily as a protest, based on an ideology of Temple piety. This type of piety is, according to Murphy, also pre-eminent in Psalms, Chronicles and Ezekiel, as well as in the writings of Philo, Pseudo-Philo and Josephus. Murphy refers to W. Farmer' study of the same type of piety in the Josephus's descriptions of the temple fall (*Structure and Meaning*, 82; W. Farmer, *Maccabees, Zealots and Josephus* (New York: Columbia, 1956), 84 ff.).

no longer exists, there will be no congregation where the Law can be explained.[56] Instruction in the Law was commonly related to the cultic gatherings at the temple compounds. This context of instruction is suggested, for instance, by 61:4.[57] The destruction of the temple, the city, and the Land threatens the cult, the instruction in the Law, and therefore also the congregation.

According to 8:2, God's presence is gone when the Chaldeans attack.[58] This passage states, thus, that God has left his earthly dwelling place, the Jerusalem temple. *2 Bar.* 1:1–9:2, 64:6, and 77:8–9 show that God's presence leaves the temple in reaction to sinful actions.[59] It leaves for a period of time in response to the polluting acts of King Manasseh of Judah (64:6), and it leaves for good as a reaction to the sins of the two tribes (1:1–9:2; 77:8–9). These passages show that the divine presence was not a fixed quality of the Jerusalem temple, nor was the temple a permanent location for the presence.[60] To the contrary, God's presence

---

[56] Cf. Chapter Three.

[57] Cf. *2 Bar.* 61 and the discussion in the following chapter.

[58] *2 Baruch* does not refer to the presence of God by fixed terms. Nor do we find any set ideology relating to God's presence in the text. In this respect, *2 Baruch* resembles several other contemporary texts. The concept of *Shekinah* is supposedly a later phenomenon (Davies, *Gospel and Land*, 154). It is likely that 64:6 refers to the phenomenon of divine presence in terms of "the glory of the Most High" (*tešbuḥteh damraymā*). This is probably the term *2 Baruch* associates with God's presence; his divine radiance (Levenson, "Temple and World," 289). A similar terminology of God's presence is found in other contemporary texts, e.g., *Pss. Sol.* 2:5; *Targum Neofiti to Gen* 3:24; *Targum Pseudo-Jonathan to Gen* 22:14; *Targum Jonathan to Deut* 32:10; *Targum Pseudo-Jonathan to Deut* 34:5. Cf. further 1 Kgs 8:11; Isa 6:3; Ezek 43:4; *Targum Neofiti to Gen* 49:2. It is also possible that *2 Bar.* 64:6 refers to the cessation of praise in the temple, or to the destruction of magnificence with regard to God's temple. Alternatively, God's name *and* glory constitute his presence (*2 Bar.* 5:2. Cf. 1 Kgs 8:29; Deut 12:3–4;16:6.). We may possibly also understand "from before me" (*men qdamy*) in 1:4 as a way of expressing divine presence. Moreover, God's presence is certainly somehow implied when 8:1–2 claims that a voice tells the enemy that "he" (*hu*) who guarded the house has left it (Cf. 1 Kgs 8:13; Jer 7:2). Instead of describing *2 Baruch*'s notion of divine presence as a precisely defined phenomenon, it is probably more correct to say that *2 Baruch* combines several parallel notions about God's presence in the world (Cf. G. von Rad, *Studies in Deuteronomy* (London: SCM Press, 1953), 38–43; Davies, *Gospel and Land*, 154).

[59] Cf. *2 Bar.* 77:8–9; *4 Ezra* 3:25–26.

[60] *2 Baruch* does not elaborate further on the form of God's presence in the temple, nor the exact relation between the temple and the presence. Ancient temples were in general envisioned to be the residence of the god and we should settle with the fact that the God's presence was imagined somehow to be in the temple. This does not mean, however, that God's presence is bound to one spot only, nor that it is bound to space at all (Cf. *2 Bar.* 85:3; Koester, *Dwelling*, 10). Some accounts put God's presence first and foremost in the midst of the people (Cf. *2 Bar.* 4:3; Exod 29:45–46; 1 Kgs 6:13; Zech 2:10;

demands cultic maintenance and righteous behaviour.[61] God's presence is, as it were, free to go when the tribes and their kings do not live up to their covenantal obligations.[62] Hence, Baruch's apprehension at the eve of destruction is that the destruction of the temple would damage the vital relationship between Israel, the congregation, and her God. Without the temple, Israel could not fulfil her duties as cultic gathering, and God's presence would have left her.

3:6 may also suggest that Baruch worries about the continuity of Israel as a people, since the objects of his concern are the recipients of instruction. Explanation of the Law was the task of elders and leaders.[63] The elders and leaders had to explain the Law to the community in general and to the rising generation in particular. If there were no children, no rising generation, there would consequently be no-one to instruct. Hence, Baruch possibly implies that the renewal of Israel through production of descendants could fail outside the Land.

This notion of procreating and multiplying is probably also one of the things implied in the promises to Moses, mentioned in 3:9. According to Deut 13:17–18; 30:8–10 and 16, God will multiply Israel if she lives according to the Law. This is one of the central promises to Moses, according to Deuteronomy. It is important to note that *2 Bar.* 3:6 locates instruction, Law-abiding life, and subsequently the blessings of survival and reproduction in the Land. Baruch's worries about the recipients of instruction in the future are part of his general concern about the consequences of the destruction of Zion and the foreign occupation of the Land. A central passage in Baruch's lament after the destruction of Jerusalem and the temple (10:5–19) may further clarify this topic. 10:13–16 says:

> And you, fiancés, do not enter, and do not let the virgins adorn themselves with crowns.[64] And you, wives, do not pray to bear, for the barren

---

Targum Jonathan to Zech 2:14; often in the form of the Tabernacle; Cf. *Jub.* 1:17; *Targum Onkelos to Num* 24:5–9 and *Deut* 1:2; and even among converts: *Targum Ps* 68:19), it can be said to go with the people when they leave (Exod 29:45–46), and it is often depicted as being both in heaven and on earth (*Targum Jonathan to Isa* 6:3, 33:7; 66:1).

[61] Cf. Murphy, *Structure and Meaning*, 111.

[62] Cf. Jer 7:1–7. This dynamic is quiet commonly found in texts contemporaneous with *2 Baruch*. Cf., e.g., *Targum Jonathan to Isa* 5:3–4 and *Hosea* 5:15: God removes his presence due to the sins and returns to his holy abode in the heavens.

[63] This is a central issue in *2 Baruch*, cf. in particular 32:9; 44–46; 76–77; 84:8–9; 86:1. Cf. Chapter Four, pp. 136–138.

[64] The Syriac word *ḥatnā* means "bridegroom," or "fiancé" (Smith, *Dictionary*, 164). The word refers to a man who will be or is in the process of getting married. Since

will rejoice more. And those who have no children will be glad, and those who have children will be sad. For why should they bear in pains and bury in tears? Or why should mankind again have children, or why should the seed of their nature again be named, where this mother is desolate and her children captive.

As a result of the destruction of Jerusalem and the temple, and of the dispossession of the Land, there is no longer any joy or blessing in bringing forth children. Reproduction becomes meaningless. The passage thus questions the survival prospects of Israel, since Jerusalem—the mother[65]—is desolate, and her children—the adulterous people—are taken captive.[66] Baruch's pessimistic view of the future here confirms that the survival of Israel could be understood to be heavily dependent on life in the Land.[67]

The nurturing and sustaining quality of the Land is important in this context. The sustaining quality of the Land is a well known *topos* in biblical as well as later texts.[68] In the context of Baruch's lamentation of the fall of the temple, Baruch expresses his worry about the devastating results of sin and cessation of the cult on the nurturing abilities of an area:[69]

> You, workers, do not sow again. And you, earth, why do you give the fruits of your harvest? Keep within you the sweetness of your food. And you, vine, why do you increasingly give your wine? For an offering will

---

the Syriac word *btultā* means "virgin" (Smith, *Dictionary*, 56), I choose the translation "fiancé" for the male partner. It is clear that the imagery refers to the institution and widespread symbol of the bridal chamber, but the point of the passage is that the fiancé and the virgin should not enter it to marry and beget children. This translation also brings forth the contrast between the virgins and the wives. I thus agree with Bogaert (*Apocalypse de Baruch* I, 468) and disagree with Charles (*Apocalypse of Baruch*, 17) and Klijn ("2 Baruch," 624).

[65] The notion of Jerusalem as mother was widespread in the first centuries. Cf. Isa 49:21; Matt 23:37; Gal 4:25; *4 Ezra* 10:7. Cf. Charles, *Apocalypse of Baruch*, 4, Murphy, *Structure and Meaning*, 81; Whitters, *Epistle*, 116–117.

[66] Cf. similar imagery in Isa 49:19–21; 54:1; Jer 7:34; 16:3–4; *L.A.B.* 40:5–7; Matt 24:19; Luke 23:29.

[67] Cf. Murphy, *Structure and Meaning*, 83.

[68] Cf. Deut 8–10; 32:13–15; Ps 37:11; Zech 8:12; *Sib. Or.* 5.281–283. Cf. W.H.C. Propp, "A Land of Milk and Honey—Biblical Comfort Food," *BRev* 15/3 (1999): 16–17. An important aspect of God's care for Israel is his efforts to feed his people. There are numerous stories about how God provided for Israel, often miraculously, both in the wilderness and in the Land (Cf., e.g., Ps 145:16; 4Q370; *Targum Jonathan to Deut* 32:10–13; *Targum Onkelos to Exod* 15:2; *Targum Jonathan to Isa* 5:6; *L.A.B.* 12:8–9; Cf. Murphy, *Structure and Meaning*, 82–83).

[69] Cf. Clements, "Temple and Land," 25.

not again be given from you in Zion, and the first fruits will not again be
offered. And you, heaven, keep your dew within you, and do not open
the treasuries of rain (10:9–11).

Since the two (and a half) tribes have sinned and the temple has fallen,
Baruch questions why the earth should, and whether it can, bring forth
food for Israel.[70] There is no use tilling the earth.[71] There is no-one who
can be nurtured, and no-one to bring forth an offering in the temple.
No wonder Baruch in the subsequent verses (10:13–16), quoted above,
bids virgins and their fiancés to shun the bridal chamber and the wives
to forgo bearing children.[72] There is no place where their survival can
be assured once the Land has been taken away from them.[73]

It is evident that the fall of Zion and the dispossession of the Land
could pose a threat to Israel's survival. This is, at least, the implication
of Baruch's worries in 3:4–6. There are two aspects to the threat.
First, the destruction puts an end to the fruitful relationship between
Israel's faithful cultic service and lawful management of the Land and
the beneficial presence of God in the temple. According to 8:2, God's
presence has left, and Zion has become deserted in response to impious
practices. In other words, from this point onwards, Israel must survive
in the corruptible world without the steady presence of God in the
temple and without the protection of the Land.[74] Second, nutrition and
the capacity to bring forth descendants have all been linked to living in
the Land. In fact, Baruch fears that the existence of Israel as a people
is at stake because it has been bound to life there.

In addition, Baruch's worries question the relevance of the covenant.
The failure of the covenant promises, among them the promise of the
Land, constitutes a clear risk with regard to Israel's future redemption.
Sayler has pointed out this aspect of the crisis: "The destruction of the
city and the delivering of the Land to the enemy call into question
the promises God made to Abraham and Moses. If those promises fail,

---

[70] Cf. Bar 2:29; *Jub.* 23:18; *L.A.B.* 13:10.

[71] Cf. Deut 30:10, 16–17; Ps 126:5–6; *Ketub.* 122a (Charles, *Apocalypse of Baruch*, 116–117).

[72] Cf. Jer 7:34; 16:9; 25:10–11; Bar 2:23.

[73] Cf. Deut 28:58–63; 2 Kgs 19:3. Note that it is also a command to be fruitful and increase (Gen 1:28). This is a command that that Israel cannot fulfil at this time. (Cf. W. Zimmerli, *The Old Testament and the World* (London: SPCK, 1971), 27–35).

[74] Cf. Pss 74:2; 125:1–2; *L.A.B.* 12:4, 8–9 (Cf. Murphy, *Structure and Meaning*, 82–83; Levenson, *Sinai and Zion*, 137).

then Israel has no future whatsoever".[75] Sayler's suggestion is important. The fact that the Land becomes occupied by foreigners means
that God has retracted Israel's access to covenantal space. This may
imply that the covenant has been annulled by God.[76] A crisis potentially
threatens Israel, since her survival prospects are intrinsically linked to
God's promises to her forefathers.

The Threat of Silence: Temple and Land in Creation and Destruction

In my discussions of 3:4–6 I have argued the possible vital importance
of the Land to Israel's survival in the corruptible world. However, 3:7–9
also suggests that the Land may have a cosmic role:

> Or shall cosmos[77] return to its nature and the world again go back to
> primeval silence?[78] And shall the multitude of souls be taken away and
> human nature not again be named? And where is all that which you said
> to Moses regarding us?

According to this passage, the implications of the destruction and the
dispossession of the Land (3:5) may be the total reversal of Creation, the
extinction of man, and the failure of God's promises. In the following
section I will study the ideas implied by Baruch's worries with regard to
the role of the temple and the Land in Creation: in what regards were
the temple and the Land important to the world? And, what are the
consequences of the destruction and the dispossession to the world in
general?

2 Bar. 10:9–18: The Temple in the Corruptible World

In the above discussion of the survival prospects of Israel, I suggested
that 10:9–11 and 10:13–16 displayed threats to the existence of Israel.
However, if we read 10:9–18 as one united passage, it also shows how

---

[75] Sayler, *Promises*, 75.

[76] Cf. Deut 26:18–19; 33:28; *L.A.B.* 12:4; 13:10. Cf. Bogaert, *Apocalypse de Baruch II*, 14.

[77] As mentioned in Chapter One, it is commonly assumed that the Syriac *taçbitā*,
"ornament", is a misreading of the Greek κόσμος (e.g., Charles, *Apocalypse of Baruch*, 5;
Violet, *Apokalypsen*, 207; Bogaert, *Apocalypse de Baruch II*, 13; Klijn, "2 Baruch," 621).

[78] Cf. H. Gressmann, "Vorschläge von Hugo Gressmann. Zur Esra-Apokalypse," in
Die Apokalypsen des Esra und des Baruch in deutscher Gestalt (GCS 32; By B. Violet; Leipzig:
J.C. Hinrichs'sche Buchhandlung, 1924), 337–350 at 344; Violet, (*Apokalypsen*, 207) and
Bogaert (*Apocalypse de Baruch II*, 13) for other interpretations.

2 Baruch perceives the threat of the destruction of Zion to the entire world.[79]

According to 10:2–5, Jeremiah has left Baruch and his followers at God's command to support the captives to Babylon. Baruch then returns to Mount Zion and sits down at the doorstep of the former temple and laments its fall:

> (9) You, workers, do not sow again. And you, earth, why do you give the fruits of your harvest? Keep within you the sweetness of your food. (10) And you, vine, why do you increasingly give wine? For an offering will not again be given from you in Zion and the first fruits will not again be offered. (11) And you, heaven, withhold your dew, and do not open the treasuries of rain. (12) And you, sun, withhold your rays of light, and you, moon, extinguish the multitude of your light, for why should light rise again where the light of Zion has turned dark? (13) And you, fiancés, do not enter, and do not let the virgins adorn themselves with crowns. (14) And you, wives, do not pray to bear, for the barren will rejoice more. And those who have no children will be glad, and those who have children will be sad. (15) For why should they bear in pains and bury in tears? (16) Or why should mankind again have children, or why should the seed of their nature again be named, where this mother is desolate and her children captive? (17) From now on, do not again talk about fairness, and do not discuss beauty!

Sitting on the threshold of the ruined temple, Baruch appeals to central cosmic forces. He encourages the earth to stop producing food, the heaven to retain its life giving humidity, and the sun and the moon to withhold their light. In other words, Baruch urges these cosmic entities to withdraw from their normal activities since Zion has fallen (10:9–12): once Zion has fallen, the cosmic order will be disturbed.[80]

As I indicated above, Baruch explicitly connects the food production of the Land with the temple offering in this passage. When the sanctuary is destroyed, the ground will not bring forth its fruits since there is no place to offer them.[81] Moreover, the passage probably connects the destruction of the temple to cessation of the fulfilment of Sabbath and festivals. In 10:12, the sun and the moon are requested to extinguish their light because the light of Zion has been darkened. According to

---

[79] Cf. Leuenberger, "Ort und Funktion," 238.

[80] Cf. further Bogaert, *Apocalypse de Baruch I*, 129–157; Violet, *Apokalypsen*, 214–218; Murphy, *Structure and Meaning*, 96–101. Cf. *Targum to Isa* (Codex Reuchlin) 33:9 and *Apoc. Dan.* 18 for similar imagery.

[81] These descriptions of the vine are similar to the accounts of the vine that dries up (Isa 24:7), and the failing production of the vine in Isa 5:10.

Sir 43:7, the moon designates the sacred times and the festivals. When the light of the moon fails in *2 Bar.* 10:12, there will be no way of establishing the correct time for Sabbaths and festivals. In other words, the cult fails. The order of the moon is also related to the order of the seasons and thus the fall of rain. The disorder of the moon's circuit therefore further affects the production of fruits for offering in the temple as well as the nutrition of the people.[82] In 10:13–16, Baruch extends the analogy between cosmic powers and Zion, saying that there is no reason for mankind to have children at all since mother Jerusalem is deserted and her children led away.[83] In other words, Baruch urges the basic processes of life to halt. At this point in history, Baruch bids all talk about fairness and beauty to stop (10:18). When Jerusalem and its temple, the place of fairness and beauty, do not exist any more, Baruch requests silence.[84] The lament of Baruch in 10:9–18 thus elaborates on Baruch's fears in 3:8: there is a possibility that cosmos will return to silence.

The Role of the Temple in Creation and De-creation

The scholarly debate has long recognised the crucial connection between the sanctuary, meaning both the mobile tabernacle and the temple, and the act of creation.[85] Several notions, both overlapping and

---

[82] Cf. further Jer 26:18; Joel 3:15; *1 En.* 80:4–5; *4 Ezra* 10:45–46; *b. B. Bat.* 60b. Cf. L. Ginzberg, *The Legends of the Jews VI* (7 vols; Philadelphia: Jewish Publication Society of America, 1909–1938. Repr., 1998), 269; Propp, "Milk and Honey," 16–17.

[83] *2 Baruch* probably alludes to Isa 54:1 (as does Gal 4:27). *2 Baruch* plays with the meanings of the imagery of the barren woman being Jerusalem and the women in Israel in the end-time. The subsequent comparison between Babylonia and Jerusalem in *2 Bar.* 11–12 makes this even more probable. Cf. M.C. de Boer, "Paul's Quotation of Isaiah 54.1 in Galatians 4.27," *NTS* 50 (2004): 370–389. Cf. further Hos 4.5; *4 Ezra* 16.44–46; *L.A.B.* 3.10; 32.5. Cf. Ginzberg, *Legends VI*, 275; A.B. Kolenkow, "An Introduction to 2 Baruch 53, 56–77: Structure and Substance," (PhD diss., Harvard, 1972), 51.

[84] Cf. also the image of the beautiful land in this context: Dan 11:16; 11:41; *1 En.* 89:40.

[85] J. Blenkinsopp, "The Structure of P," *CBQ* 38 (1976): 275–277; P. Kearney, "Creation and Liturgy; The P Redaction of Exod 25–40," *ZAW* 89 (1977): 375–387; Levenson, "Temple and World," 275–298; N. Lohfink, *The Theology of the Pentateuch: Themes of the Priestly Narrative and Deuteronomy* (Minneapolis: Fortress Press, 1994), 130–133; Fretheim, "Whole Earth," 233; S. Boorer, "The Earth/Land in the Priestly Material: The Preservation of the 'Good' Earth and the Promised Land of Canaan throughout the Generations," *ABR* 49 (2001): 19–33; Murphy, *Structure and Meaning*, 84. However,

contradictory in nature, find support in ancient sources.[86] Of particular
relevance to my discussion are the suggestions of J. Blenkinsopp and
M. Weinfeld, and of J. Levenson and S. Boorer, regarding the connec-
tions in biblical texts between the creation of the world, the erection
of the sanctuary, and the establishment of the sanctuary within the
Land.[87] According to Blenkinsopp, these events are described in similar or identical language.[88] These processes of creation are thus possibly linked and interdependent. Levenson suggests that 'temple building' and 'world building' are clearly connected. He proposes that the
Hebrew Bible (Gen 1:1–2 Chr 35:23) starts with the creation of the
world and ends with the command of God to build him a temple in
Jerusalem.[89] On the one hand, therefore, the creation of the world and
the erection of the temple are parallel acts of creation. On the other
hand, though, the creation process is not completed until the inauguration of the temple in Jerusalem. In other words, the inauguration of the
temple and the establishment of God's presence in it constitute the final
phase of creation.

---

according to Himmelfarb, there was probably never a general agreement on this aspect
of Zion (*Ascent to Heaven*, 11–13).

[86] The Jerusalem temple may be described as the centre of creation, as primordial
or first created, as a microcosm, and according to Levenson, both as "a cosmic
institution" and as "the world *in nuce*" (Levenson, "Temple and World," 286). Cf.
Ezek 5:5; 38:12; *1 En.* 24–25; *Jub.* 8; Josephus, *J.W.* 3.7.7. Cf. further the discussions
of M. Eliade, *The Sacred and the Profane: The Nature of Religion* (New York: Harcourt,
Brace & Company, 1959); M. Eliade, *The Myth of the Eternal Return* (trans. W.R. Trask;
Bollingen Series 46; New York: Bollingen, 1954); Clifford, *Cosmic Mountain*, 177–181;
Smith, *Take Place*, 1–23; M. Fishbane, "The Sacred Center: the Symbolic Structure
of the Bible," in *Texts and Responses: Studies Presented to Nahum N. Glatzer on the Occasion
of his 70th Birthday by his Students* (ed. M. Fishbane & P. Mendes Flohr; Leiden: Brill,
1975), 6–27; Levenson, "Temple and World," 275–298; J., Danielou, *The Presence of
God* (Baltimore: Helicon Press, 1959),19; Davies, *Gospel and Land*, 154–155; Clements,
"Temple and Land," 24–25; Smith, *Map*, 112–115; Koester, *Dwelling*, 174–175; Stone,
"Reactions," 199.

[87] Blenkinsopp, *Prophecy and Canon*, 61–69; M. Weinfeld, "Sabbat, Miqdas, Wehamlakat H," *Bet Miqra* (1977): (in Hebrew); Levenson, "Temple and World," 275–298;
Boorer, "Earth/Land," 21.

[88] Blenkinsopp, *Prophecy and Canon*, 61–69. Note that Blenkinsopp describes the establishment of the sanctuary in Shiloh (Josh 19.51), not in Jerusalem. Levenson, on the
other hand, relates this to the temple in Jerusalem ("Temple and World," 287).

[89] Levenson, "Temple and World," 295. According to Boorer, the construction of the
mobile sanctuary and its cult in Exod 25-Lev 9 parallels the creation of cosmos in Gen
1:1–2:4. Moreover, following Boorer, "the sanctuary not only parallels but completes the
creation. It is the means by which God dwells in the midst of the nation Israel, thus
allowing God to have communion with God's creation, (…)" ("Earth/Land," 21).

However, when God's presence leaves and the angels destroy the temple in *2 Baruch*, this process of creation is reversed.[90] The escape of God's presence and the destruction of the temple do not only pose a threat to the survival of Israel, these events are fatal to the cosmos, the ordered world, as well.[91] When God renounces the world and his place of dwelling is eradicated, Creation becomes void of holiness and order. The renunciation and destruction of the temple thus brings the devastation of the ordered world and casts the entire Creation into the chaotic condition of the end-time.[92] Like creation, destruction may then be perceived both as an act and as a process. It is the destruction of the world that was blessed by divine presence: it is the end of the cosmos. At the same time, the destruction starts a longer process of desolation involving a steadily increasing chaos.[93] This is a process of de-creation:[94] Creation is in a state of dying (21:22).

The cosmic threat implied by the destruction of God's dwelling place on earth becomes particularly clear in *2 Baruch*'s rhetorical use of the opposition between sound and silence.[95] 67:3 implies that the congregation became silent when Zion fell. The assembly of Israel

---

[90] Cf. Jer 4:23–26. Cf. Davies, *Gospel and Land*, 94; Boorer, "Earth/Land," 22–33; Cf. M. Fishbane, "Jeremiah 4.23–26 and Job 3.13: A Recovered Use of the Creation Pattern," *VT* 21 (1971): 151–167; Habel, *The Land is Mine*, 87; A. Wharton, "Erasure: Eliminating the Space of Late Ancient Judaism," in *From Dura to Sepphoris: Studies in Jewish Art and Society in Late Antiquity* (ed. L.I. Levine and Z. Weiss; Journal of Roman Archaeology Supplement Series 40; Portsmouth, Ri: JRA 2000), 195–214; J.R. Branham, "Sacred Space under Erasure in Ancient Synagogues and Early Churches," *ArtB* 74 (1992): 374–394.

[91] Note how Rev 7:1–3 uses the same imagery in its description of destruction of the earth (Cf. Murphy, *Structure and Meaning*, 93). Note also the possible link between the wind that lifts up Baruch in *2 Bar.* 6:3 and the wind that swept over the waters in Gen 1:2, linking the chaos of pre-creation with the chaos that results from destruction. Blenkinsopp notes that the wind appears in three contexts within P: at the creation of the world (Gen 1:2), the construction of the sanctuary (Exod 31:3; 35:31) and the commissioning of Joshua (Num 27:18; Deut 34:9). He sees this as a structural interdependence of creation, construction of the sanctuary and occupation of the Land (*Prophecy and Canon*, 63–64. Cf. Davies, *Gospel and Land*, 94).

[92] Cf. *2 Bar.* 10. In 48:7, God's remembrance last from the beginning to the end of Creation. According to 3:5, the fall of the city leads to the risk of oblivion (Cf. 44:9; 48:29). This links the fall of Zion and its surroundings to the destruction of the world: this is as far as remembrance goes. Cf. Zion's destruction—cosmic destruction and Zion as chaos control in Pss 29; 46; 74 and 93.

[93] Cf. *2 Bar.* 27–28; 69.

[94] Fishbane, "Jeremiah and Job," 151–167.

[95] The voice that was heard from the Holy of Holies is probably the voice of God (e.g., Isa 46:1–6).

could no longer praise God. 3:6 reveals the result of the failing praise: after the fall there is no-one to praise God and Israel therefore risks extinction.[96] A similar set of connotations is at work in the reference to Israel's name in 3:5. If Israel's name is not uttered, there is silence. Silence, the non-mentioning of the name, means extinction to Israel.[97] 3:7 puts the cosmic effects of the fall in similar terms: the fall of Zion may result in a return to primeval silence, the void and dark condition that existed before creation (Gen 1:1–4).[98] The fall of Zion may thus cause the entire Creation to return to nothing. 3:8 adds that that the fall may also stop human nature from being named in the future. If human nature ceases to be named, there is silence and extinction of mankind. Silence thus threatens mankind as well as the rest of God's Creation.[99] 2 Baruch's rhetorical use of the contrast between silence and sound shows that the fall of Zion not only endangers the existence of Israel, as people and congregation, but that it also threatens mankind as well as God's entire Creation.[100]

The Role of the Land in the Corruptible World

In what sense does 2 Baruch ascribe a cosmic role to the Land? In the time before the destruction of Jerusalem and its temple, the existence of the Land was vital to the cosmos for at least three reasons. Firstly, as suggested by the above discussion, the Land was the cultic environment of the temple. Israel's constant cultic attention to and service of God kept the almighty creator satisfied and kept his destructive anger at bay. At the same time, these cultic practices secured God's blessings for the soil and kept his life bringing presence from leaving the earth.[101]

---

[96] Cf. the contrast in *Hist. Rech.* 11:2–3.

[97] Cf. further *2 Bar.* 10:16 and particularly 83:13–23 and 44:8.

[98] Cf. *4 Ezra* 6:39; 7:30; *L.A.B.* 60:2. Cf. Charles, *Apocalypse of Baruch*, 5; Bogaert, *Apocalypse de Baruch II*, 13; Kolenkow, "Introduction," 68; 76–77; 79; 119 and abstract, 4.

[99] *4 Ezra* 6:39; *L.A.B.* 12:4, 9.

[100] The imagery 2 Baruch applies when describing the destruction of the walls, "Overthrow, then, and destroy its walls to their foundations" (7:1), may also imply cosmic destruction. While 2 Baruch says that the wall is levelled *with* the ground (cf. Ps 137:7; *4 Ezra* 10:27; *Sib. Or.* 3.273–275), other parallel passages suggest that Jerusalem's gates sink *into* the ground (Lam 2:9).

[101] Cf. *Hist. Rech.* 11:2–4. Cf. Clements, "Temple and Land," 21; Davies, *Gospel and Land*, 12–13; Boorer, "Earth/Land," 22; Murphy, *Structure and Meaning*, 99; Fretheim, "Whole Earth," 232.

Secondly, *2 Bar.* 14:19; 15:7 and 21:24 expresses the notion that God originally created the world for the sake of Israel.[102] In other words, God made the world in order to give Israel a place in which she could live in accordance with his Law. The Law was meant to regulate all life on earth. Thus, lawful life was originally the correct way of being in the world.[103] However, the wicked nations as well as the apostate tribes have misused Creation and trodden the earth down (13:11). This means that most parts of God's Creation were not fulfiling their purpose. In this sense, Israel's life in her Land became the very purpose of creation.[104] As long as the Land existed, there was still a place on earth that fulfiled the intention of Creation. In other words, the Land provided *a world* for Israel.[105]

Thirdly, and in relation to the above, the Land served Creation as an enclave of lawful behavior. As long as Israel behaved righteously, her behavior made the Land the only place on earth which was managed the correct way. Israel's cultic actions and righteous way of life secured the world from destruction. Her practices in the Land thus helped to maintain the cosmos. As long as this one enclave of righteousness remained, God let Creation live. The Land in this sense kept the entire Creation alive.

However, as the destruction story of *2 Bar.*1–9 shows, Baruch, Jeremiah and their followers were the only righteous people left at the time of King Jeconiah (1:1). In 2:1–2 God asks them to leave Jerusalem:

> For I have said these things to you so that you may say them to Jeremiah and to all those who are like you so that you may retire from this city. Because your works are to this city as a firm pillar and your prayers as a strong wall.

By means of their righteousness, Baruch and those like him constituted a protection to Jerusalem, which effectively prevented God from destroying it. *2 Baruch* here alludes to the *topos* of the one righteous per-

---

[102] *2 Baruch* allows for some nuances: God created the world for 'us,' i.e., the righteous (14:19; 15:7–8) and for the patriarchs (21:24). Cf. further Chapter Seven.

[103] Cf. Isa 24:4–5.

[104] Cf. Stone, "Reactions," 199. Charles notes some parallels in rabbinic literature, as for instance: "if Israel were not, the world would not exist" (*Bammidbar Rab.* 2) and "The world was created owing to the merits of Israel, and upon Israel stands the world" (*Shemoth Rab.* 28) (*Apocalypse of Baruch*, 28–29). Cf. also *Targum Esth I* 5:1.

[105] Blenkinsopp compares the command to fill the earth with the allotment of the Land: "It is also noteworthy that in P the word *'eres* stands for both the created world and the Land of promise, the usage strongly suggesting symbolic association between the two meanings" (*Prophecy and Canon*, 68). Cf. Boorer, "Earth/Land," 19–24.

son whose presence can protect everybody, which is found, for example, in the story of Sodom (Gen 18–19).[106] Like Lot and his family, Baruch and his equals were the last people there who were living according to the Law. Their obedience kept Jerusalem as a righteous enclave in an otherwise sinful world. When they left and entered the wilderness, however, no-one would shield Jerusalem any more.

This move of Baruch and his followers to the Kidron valley (5:5) has two related consequences. Firstly, Jerusalem and its temple become open to destruction. The angels destroy the temple and open up the walls for the enemy. The enemy enters the city and the temple, and kills the impious inhabitants. Secondly, the destruction of Jerusalem affects the entire Creation. When the inhabitants of Jerusalem sin, no-one lives righteously in God's Creation any longer, no-one serves God in his chosen place, and there is no Land to house faithful living.[107] The sins of the two tribes are particularly important since these tribes inhabit the immediate area that surrounds God's chosen place on earth.[108] When their impiety makes the divine presence withdraw, it affects not only the area that they themselves inhabit, but also the world in its entirety. When Jerusalem gives in, impiety breaks down the last city wall and godlessness becomes triumphant everywhere in the world.[109] As the last righteous enclave is lost, impiety becomes a worldwide praxis.

As a result of worldwide impiety and the subsequent destruction and dispossession, there is no space left on earth that can be defined as the Land. Thus, the destruction and renunciation of the temple in Jerusalem marks the end of Israel's life in the Land and the end of her life in the inhabitable world. In a sense, Israel not only loses her Land. She also loses her world, the only part of the earth inhabitable to her.

---

[106] Cf. *2 Bar.* 5:1; 14:6–7; 19:4; 85:1–2 and further Gen 18:22; Num 16:20–24; 2 Kgs 18:34; 20:6; Isa 1:9–10; 3:9; *4 Ezra* 7:112–114; *L.A.B.* 12:4; *4 Bar.* 1:1–3; *T. Naph.* 4; *Targum Pseudo-Jonathan to Deut* 28:15; *Ta'an.* 19. Cf. Charles, *Apocalypse of Baruch*, 3–4; Kolenkow, "Introduction," 128–133; Sayler, *Promises*, 91–95; Murphy, *Structure and Meaning*, 77–78; 137; Henze, "Jeremiah," 163–164.

[107] Murphy, *Structure and Meaning*, 99; Levenson, *Sinai and Zion*, 137.

[108] Cf. 2 Kgs 23:27; Jer 6:19; *Pss. Sol.* 2:8.

[109] Charles, *Apocalypse of Baruch*, 110; Murphy, *Structure and Meaning*, 112. Cf. also Rosenberg, "Link to the Land," 157.

The Encroaching Wilderness

What happens to the landscape when Jerusalem comes into foreign hands? When Baruch and his followers, the last righteous remnant, leave Jerusalem and the last part of the inhabitable world recognisable as the Land, foreigners enter. The result of foreign occupation is that Jerusalem turns barren. Devastation is the unavoidable result of Israel's dispossession.[110]

The Syriac terms used in *2 Baruch* to describe the destruction and its consequences supports this interpretation. For instance, when 8:2 describes the escape of the divine presence, it applies the Aph'el form *arpe* (root *rp'*), meaning "to leave" in the sense of deserting or renouncing something.[111] The place where the temple stood becomes a waste, like "dust" (*ḥelā*) and "earth" (*'aprā*) (35:5). Likewise, the Syriac term applied to Jerusalem in 67:6, *ḥarbā*, means "desolate," "ruined" or "ravaged."[112] However you interpret it, it is clear that Jerusalem becomes an empty wasteland.

How did the foreign occupation turn the former Land into wilderness? The *Targum Jonathan to Isa* 10:32 describes the results of the invasions of the Land by Sennacherib and Nebuchadnezzar as a devastation of the landscape. The ground became increasingly dry as the armies first drank all the water in the Jordan, and then dug wells and emptied them. The arrival of the last company is described as follows: "(...) [they were] crossing the Jordan, and the earth was sending up dust from the ground."[113] Thus, according to this Targum, the invasions of foreigners made the Land a wilderness: they trample the ground down and drink all its water.

The description in *Pss. Sol.* 2:2 runs along the same line: "Gentile foreigners went up to your place of sacrifice; they arrogantly trampled (it) with their sandals." And further: "For the gentiles insulted Jerusalem, trampling (her) down" (2:19).[114] These passages insist that the occupa-

---

[110] Cf. *Jub.* 15:34; *T. Jud.* 23; *Apoc. El. (H)* 2:52. Cf. Lieu, *Christian Identity*, 217.

[111] Smith, *Dictionary*, 547. Cf. Charles, *Apocalypse of Baruch*, 12.

[112] Smith, *Dictionary*, 155. Cf. *Targum to Isa* 33:9 (Codex Reuchlin) where Jerusalem and the sanctuary become like a desert (Grelot, *Targums*, 83).

[113] This passage is part of an addition in the margin of Codex Reuchlin. Cf. B.D. Chilton, *The Isaiah Targum: Introduction, Translation, Apparatus and Notes* (The Aramaic Bible vol. 11; Collegeville, Minn.: The Liturgical Press, 1987), 26; Grelot, *Targums*, 77–78. Cf. the use of similar imagery in Josephus, *J.W.* 4.550; *1 En.* 56:6–7.

[114] Cf. Isa 1:12; 58:13; 63:3; *Sib. Or.* 5.264–266; *Pss. Sol.* 2:2; 17:22; 3 Macc 2:18; Rev 11:1–2.

tion of Jerusalem had severe effects on the landscape: it turned from fruitful into barren under the feet of the enemy. In this regard, the dwelling of apostates and foreigners in Jerusalem was the very nature of the disaster.[115] Jerusalem was the last place to give in, but once she did, the nations had trodden the entire earth down (13:11). And as a result, the entire earth turned into wilderness (77:14).[116]

Thus, the invasion of the enemy and the dispossession of Israel made the temple mount and Jerusalem similar to their chaotic surroundings (10:7).[117] When Israel and the divine presence left, Jerusalem became like any other place on earth. There was nothing now to separate and protect it from the wilderness. It had lost its privileged position and had merged with its surroundings.

Questions and Answers in the Context of Destruction

2 Bar. 3:4–9 describes Baruch's ultimate fears and worries, and introduces the question that the remaining part of *2 Baruch* tries to answer: "What, then, will there be after these things?" (3:5). However, we should bear in mind that the passage does not provide God's answers. In other words, the passage I have discussed in this chapter presents the concerns caused by the destruction, but it does not tell us how *2 Baruch* explains the situation.

The concerns of Baruch in 3:4–9 suggested that the fall of Zion and the loss of the Land would bring disaster both to the corruptible world and to Israel's survival. It is significant therefore to note God's answers to Baruch's questions. First of all, God assures Baruch that everything is part of his master plan. God guarantees that the destruction of the temple and the invasion of Jerusalem are not the final phase of Israel's history. Thus, the destruction of Jerusalem is said to be only a temporary loss (4:1; 6:9),[118] the disaster Israel's enemies bring about is part of God's correction of his people (5:2), and the scattering of the adulterous people is done for their own chastening, as well as for

---

[115] Cf. Klijn, "Recent Developments," 9–10 and Fretheim, "Whole World," 232–233.

[116] Cf. further *2 Bar.* 3:5; 10:3; 35:1; 63:2–3; 72:4; Pap. Oxyrh. 403, 13:11–12 (Black, *Apoclaypsis henochi*, 119).

[117] Note that the surrounding earth always has been trampled on by the nations (*2 Bar.* 13:11–12).

[118] Cf. Charles, *Apocalypse of Baruch*, 2–3.

the good of the nations (1:5; 4:1).[119] Moreover, 20:1–2 suggests that the destruction of Zion has the purpose of speeding up the time set aside for the corruptible world. Hence, the fall of Zion hastens the onset of God's judgement and makes the end of the world come faster than it otherwise would do.[120] Since *2 Baruch* regards the present world as a struggle for the righteous (15:7–8), the destruction is in fact of benefit to them, since their pains will soon come to an end.[121]

As we have seen in the presentation of the destruction story in 5:1–9:2 above, Israel's enemies did not really destroy Jerusalem, its temple, or its holy artefacts. God's presence left the house before the enemy attacked (8:2–3) and God's angel made the ground protect the inventory of the Holy of Holies. Since the holy vessels were guarded by the ground, no cultic objects could be crushed, removed, or polluted by the attackers.[122] Likewise, it was angels who demolished the wall and burnt down "the place of the mighty God" (7:1). Consequently, when the enemies entered, they found an empty temple and a city inhabited only by impious inhabitants.[123] They attacked void matter.

Moreover, *2 Baruch* underlines the fact that the temple in Jerusalem was firmly fixed in the corruptible world.[124] After the fall of the temple, Jerusalem is no different from the surrounding world. 43:2 explicitly locates this area within the world of corruption: "For you [Baruch] will

---

[119] Cf. *2 Bar.* 13:10; 41:4; 42:5; *Pss. Sol.* 7:3; *t. B. Qam.* 7:3. Cf. Whitters, *Epistle*, 124; 134–143; Gafni, *Land, Center and Diaspora*, 29; 63.

[120] Cf. Hamerton-Kelly, "Temple and Origins," 11; Kirschner, "Apoclayptic," 38; 44.

[121] Murphy proposed that the ideology of temple piety is introduced in *2 Baruch* as a rhetorical device to underscore God's correction. According to Murphy, *2 Baruch* questions the importance of the temple by pointing to the next world and the heavenly temple as alternatives and the real goals. Murphy is correct in these matters. However, I think Murphy has missed two points. First, the temple is important to the corruptible world. Even through it is not vital to the future, it was central in the past. Second, Baruch uses temple ideology to describe destruction. As temple building fulfiled creation, it also starts the process of destruction in *2 Baruch*. So what Baruch fears in *2 Bar.* 3 actually happens with regard to the corruptible world. *2 Baruch* thus does not deny temple ideology as such, instead, it confirms it with regard to the corruptible world, but argues that it is now passé.

[122] Cf. *2 Bar.* 80:1–4; *4 Bar.* 3:9–10; 4:8; Josephus, *J.W.* 5.5.5; and the destruction by God in *4 Ezra* 3:27; *Lam.Rab.* 38b (Cf. Kirschner, "Apocalyptic," 44). Cf. contrasting accounts in 2 Chr 36:14; 18–19; Jer 27:16–22; Lam 2:16; Dan 5; *Apoc. Abr.* 27; *Targum Jonathan to Ezek* 37:7. Note also *Sib. Or.* 5.397–413.

[123] Note, that *2 Bar.* 61 does not dwell on the construction of the temple edifice. The passage concentrates on the inauguration; it is this act that makes the building God's dwelling on earth. Cf. 1 Macc 2:8–12 and Chapter Three, pp. 65–66).

[124] Cf. Violet, *Apokalypsen*, 207; Murphy, *Structure and Meaning*, 92; 107; Whitters, *Epistle*, 122.

go away from this place and leave these regions which are seen by you now. And you will forget that which is corruptible and you will not again remember those things which are among the mortal ones."

This overall scheme of *2 Baruch* provides some answers to the questions that I have discussed in the present chapter. Most importantly, the destruction of the temple and the dispossession of Jerusalem and the Land does not imply the extinction of Israel. It does indeed threaten the survival of Israel, but it does not annihilate her, since there still remains a righteous remnant under Baruch's leadership that survives the destruction. *2 Bar.*1–9 argues, thus, that the destruction of Jerusalem and the temple neither gives reason to doubt God and his power, nor the coming redemption of Israel, since the destruction did not destroy anything important.[125] Jerusalem and the temple was no longer God's dwelling place, and Israel, the righteous followers of Baruch, had already left the city. The fate of the corruptible world, in contrast, is sealed. The world is headed for destruction after the divine presence renounced it.

In Chapter One I suggested that a major concern of *2 Baruch* is to transform and redirect hope from this world to the next, and to create alternative spaces for Israel's redemption. *2 Baruch* is therefore not a text that continues to lament the loss of the temple and its surroundings. Instead, *2 Baruch* is a text that imagines other spaces to argue for the survival of the righteous. How, then, does *2 Baruch* substantiate the shift from temple lament to a vision offering high expectations for the other world? And what is the place of the Land in that shift? The following chapters will discuss how *2 Baruch* applies the Land-theme to imagine past, present, and future spaces of survival for the righteous in order to legitimise the eschatological redemption of Israel.

---

[125] Cf. J.E. Wright, *The Early History of Heaven* (Oxford: Oxford University Press, 1999), 83.

CHAPTER THREE

THE LANDS OF THE RIGHTEOUS KINGS

This chapter will discuss how *2 Baruch* constructs the Land of past generations, how this construction responds to the destruction of Jerusalem and its temple, affirms the survival of Israel in the present, and legitimises the claim for Israel's future redemption.

The chapter will focus on the presentation of the Land in *2 Bar.* 53–74. This section of *2 Baruch* is commonly referred to as the Apocalypse of the cloud.[1] The so-called Apocalypse of the cloud contains Baruch's vision of a great cloud (*2 Bar.* 53) and the angel Ramael's[2] interpretation of that vision (*2 Bar.* 55–74). This apocalyptic section constitutes a major part of *2 Baruch*, it contains the last long vision in the text,[3] and is crucial to the composition as a whole.[4] This is also the section where we find most of the references to Israel's life in the Land in the period before the temple fell.[5]

The first part of this chapter will discuss the effects of kingship and of the establishment of divine presence in the temple on the presentation

---

[1] Alternatively, *2 Bar.* 53–76 (Bogaert, *Apocalypse de Baruch I*, 86). German translators commonly address it as "Die Wolkenvision" (Harnisch, *Verhängnis*, 8; Münchow, *Ethik*, 97; Leuenberger, "Ort und Funktion," 206). Bogaert called it "La vision des eaux lumineuses et noires" in the French (*Apocalypse de Baruch I*, 86). Klijn has called the apocalypse "The Apocalypse of the Clouds" (pl.) ("2 Baruch," 639). There is however only one cloud. This is stressed in the Syriac text ('*nānā ḥdā*, "one cloud," *2 Bar.* 53:1. Cf. Kolenkow, "Introduction", 65–66). On the internal structure of the apocalypse, the debate over the extent of the apocalypse and the relation between the Apocalypse of the cloud and *2 Baruch* as a whole, cf. Bogaert, *Apocalypse de Baruch I*, 86–91; Kolenkow, "Introduction," 1–8; Sayler, *Promises*, 33–35; Henze, "Jeremiah," 163; Cf. also Clemen, *Zusammensetzung*, 233; Charles, *Apocalypse of Baruch*, liii; Violet, *Apokalypsen*, lxxxvi; Harnisch, *Verhängnis*, 261. I include the vision (*2 Bar.* 53) and the interpretation (55–74) in my discussion. I do not discuss Baruch's dialogue with God and the subsequent exhortation of the people in 75–76. Note that I have also excluded *2 Bar.* 54, the so-called Prayer of Baruch, in my interpretation.

[2] Cf. Bogaert, *Apocalypse de Baruch I*, 428–438 for a discussion of Ramael's identity and importance in *2 Baruch*.

[3] With exception of Baruch's mountain outlook in *2 Bar.* 76 (Cf. pp. 166–169).

[4] Cf. Leuenberger, "Ort und Funktion," 242.

[5] Cf. Chapter One. Cf. also *2 Bar.* 1–3; 10 and 84. These sections are the topic of Chapter Three.

of Land as covenantal space. The last part of the chapter discusses
how we can identify the location of the Land in the text. The central
question in this chapter is: what is the relationship between the region
of Palestine[6] and the Land in the Apocalypse of the cloud?

The Times and Spaces of the Apocalypse of the Cloud

It is important initially to outline the structure and some main issues of
the Apocalypse of the cloud, since the dynamics of this apocalyptic
section of *2 Baruch* is central to its construction of the Land in the
period before the fall of the temple. According to *2 Bar.* 52:7 and 55:1,
Baruch receives a vision and its subsequent interpretation at his place
of sojourn at Hebron.[7] In his sleep, Baruch sees a cloud ascending from
the sea. It is filled with water and lightning flashes at its top. Swiftly, the
cloud covers the whole earth before it pours down the waters (*mayā*)[8] it
contains (53:1–3). *2 Bar.* 53:4–6 continues:

> And I saw that there was not one shape to the waters that descended
> from it. For in the beginning they were very black for a time, and after
> that the waters were bright, but they were not many. And after these, I
> saw black waters again, and after these waters bright again, and again
> black and again bright. This happened twelve times, but the black were
> always more numerous than the bright.

Following these twelve showers of black (root *'km*) and bright (root *nhr*)
waters, a thirteenth shower of the blackest water ever mingles with fire
and pours down (53:7), before the lightning on top of the cloud hurls the
cloud down to earth (53:8). The lightning heals the regions where the
last waters descended, before it takes command over the entire earth.
Finally, twelve rivers ascend from the sea and surround the lightning
(53:9–10).[9]

---

[6] As pointed out in Chapter One, pp. 29–30n.110, I apply the term 'the region of
Palestine' to a region in a narrative geography.

[7] Throughout *2 Bar.* 47–77, Baruch sojourns in Hebron. Cf. Chapter Five.

[8] The Syriac word *mayā*, "waters," is always in the plural form (Smith, *Dictionary*,
268).

[9] Several scholars have discussed the use of the number twelve. *Targum Jonathan to
Isa* 66:2 may shed some new light on the issue, since this text shares some important
elements with the Apocalypse of the Cloud and *2 Baruch* in general. According to this
Targum the number twelve reflects everything that was made for the twelve tribes: the
months, the constellations of the firmament, the day and the night (Cf. further the
twelve, or thirteen, periods of *2 Bar.* 27; *Apoc. Ab.* 29).

In *2 Bar.* 55–74, Ramael interprets Baruch's vision of the twelve sets of alternating bright and black waters as partly a résumé and partly a prophecy of world history,[10] with Israel playing the leading role.[11] This part of Baruch's vision embraces history from the transgression of Adam (56:2) to the period of the Second Temple (68:5), and it interprets the history of Israel as a regular alternation of good and bad periods. All in all, six bright and six dark waters pour down on earth. The last part of the vision (53:8–12; 69–74), containing the thirteenth water (72:1) and the lightning episode, refers to events that will take place beyond world history. In the present chapter I will concentrate on the twelve periods of world history in the apocalypse and leave the last part of the vision and its interpretation for later discussion.[12]

Ramael interprets the twelve waters of world history as follows:

Black waters:

1. The transgressions of Adam

3. The wickedness of Egypt

Bright waters:

2. The righteousness of Abraham and his successors

4. The time of Moses and his generation

---

[10] I understand 'world history' as the period belonging to 'this age'/ 'this world.' It began when Adam transgressed and ended with the fall of the First/Second temple. Note that 'Israel's history' moves far beyond the end of this world.

[11] Cf. similar apocalyptic imagery in Dan 7:13; *1 En.* 89; *4 Ezra* 4: 49–50; 11–12; 14:11–12; *Sib. Or.*4.49–192; *Targum Pseudo-Jonathan to Exod* 12:42; Rev 14:14; *Apoc. Pet.* 6. Cf. Charles, *Apocalypse of Baruch*, 86–89; Bogaert, *Apocalypse de Baruch II*, 88; 99–101; Kolenkow, "Introduction" (abstract), 12 and "Introduction," 62–66; 96. 212; 402. See further *1 En.* 85–90; 91; 93; *L.A.E.* 29 for similar models of history (Cf. P. Volz, *Eschatologie der jüdischen Gemeinde im neutestamentlichen Zeitalter. Nach den Quellen der rabbinischen, apokalyptischen und apokryphen Literatur* (Tübingen: J.C.B. Mohr, 1934; Repr. Hildesheim: Georg Olms, 1966),141–142; Kolenkow, "Introduction," 2–3; 31–33; 125–126; 130; 138–139; Murphy, *Structure and Meaning*, 108–110; L.L. Grabbe, "Chronography in *4 Ezra* and *2 Baruch*," in *Society of Biblical Literature1981 Seminar Papers* (SBLSP 20; Chico, Calif.: Scholars Press, 1981), 49–63. Cf. also *T. Mos.* 2–10 for a similar ordering of history into good and bad periods (answering Murphy, *Structure and Meaning*, 109). Cf. L. Hartmann, *Prophecy Interpreted: The Formulation of Some Jewish Apocalyptic Texts and of the Eschatological Discourse in Mark 13 par* (ConBNT 1; Lund: CWK Gleerup, 1966); D.S. Russell, *The Method and Message of Jewish Apocalyptic 200 BC – 100 AD* (London: SCM Press, 1964); R. Bultmann, "History and Eschatology in the New Testament," *NTS 1* (1954), 5–16; W. Lane, "Times of Refreshment: A Study of Eschatological Periodization in Judaism and Christianity," (PhD Diss.; Cambridge Mass.: Harward University Press, 1962); A.Y. Collins, *Cosmology and Eschatology in Jewish and Christian Apocalypticisim* (JSJSupp 50; Leiden: E.J. Brill, 1996).

[12] Cf. Chapters Four, Six and Seven for a further analysis of *2 Bar.* 53:8–12 and 69–73.

5. The sins of the period of judges	6. The glorious reign of David and Solomon
7. King Jeroboam's wickedness	8. King Hezekiah's righteous reign
9. King Manasseh's evil reign	10. The purity of King Josiah
11. The destruction of Zion	12. The rebuilding of Zion

The mid section of this exposé, from the fifth, black, waters until, and including, the twelfth, bright, waters (60–68), refers to parts of history that take place within the region of Palestine, or parts of this region. These eight waters thus focus on the shifting situations and reigns in this particular area. The four periods of black waters are, first, the idolatry and the intermarriage with neighbouring peoples in the period of the judges (60:1–2),[13] second, the perversions that took place during the reign of Jeroboam (62:1–4)[14] and the exile of the nine and a half tribes (62:5–8),[15] third, the wicked reign of Manasseh (64–65),[16] and, fourth and last, the destruction of "Zion now," the exile of the two and a half tribes and the devastation of the "region of Zion" (67:1).[17] The bright waters, on the other hand, are as follows: the rule of David and Solomon (61), the reign of Hezekiah, king of Judah (63), the reign of Josiah, king of Judah (66), and lastly the building of the Second Temple (68).[18]

The Apocalypse of the cloud does not record history in any neutral manner.[19] The apocalypse leaves the bright periods very bright, and the dark periods utterly dark.[20] The purpose of the apocalypse is to reveal

---

[13] Cf. Judg 3:5.

[14] Cf. 1 Kgs 12:25–33.

[15] Cf. 2 Kgs 17:3–6.

[16] Cf. 2 Kgs 21:1–9.

[17] Cf. pp. 36–38. I assume that *2 Bar.* 64:5 is the prophecy of the exile of the two and a half tribes, not a description of the real event (Cf. 2 Kgs 21–22). *2 Bar.* 67:5 tells us that it has already happened, but relates it to the fall of the temple, as does *2 Bar.* 1:2; 8:5 and 10:5. For another opinion, see Sayler, *Promises*, 72.

[18] The thirteenth black waters and the lightning that heals the regions victim to the last waters are topic to Chapter Seven.

[19] It omits, for instance, the transgressions of both King David and King Solomon, as well as the legends of King Manasseh's repent and restoration. According to 1 Kings, neither David's nor Solomon's reigns were always righteous (Cf., e.g., 1 Kgs 11; Josephus, *Ant.* 8.7.5; Cf. further Ginzberg, *Legends VI*, 280. Cf. 2 Chr 33 for Manasseh. *2 Baruch* chooses one version of the Manasseh legend, similar to *Mart. Ascen. Isa.* 2; 5; 11 (Cf. Charles, *Apocalypse of Baruch*, 107–108; Bogaert, *Apocalypse de Baruch I*, 296–304; Sayler, *Promises*, 72; Nir, *Destruction*, 191).

[20] Kolenkow, "Introduction," 130.

the basic dynamic of world history: the fact that God punishes the wicked and rewards the righteous throughout history.[21] The elements of the story it tells must be read with this purpose in mind.

69:3–4 provides an important key to the logic of the part of the apocalypse that deals with world history: "Concerning the wickedness of the impieties which would occur before him, he foresaw six kinds. And of the good deeds the righteous would accomplish before him, he foresaw six kinds." According to 69:3–4 it is the actions of humankind, and first and foremost the acts of the twelve tribes through their kings and leaders,[22] that decide whether the period becomes dark or bright,[23] since their actions make God work on their behalf or against them in history.[24]

In the following, I will primarily discuss how *2 Baruch*'s account of the history of the twelve tribes during the period of kingship (*2 Bar.* 60–66) in the region of Palestine may help us understand the construction of Israel's Land in the Apocalypse of the cloud. I shall apply the key 69:3–4 provides in order to discuss how the changing reigns of the kings define the situation in Palestine. Both righteous actions and wicked deeds take place within this specific geographical area and result in corresponding periods of dark and bright waters. Thus, the actions of righteous and wicked kings make the high and low points of Israel's life in Palestine, in accordance with the general logic of this part of the apocalypse. Instead of presuming that the Apocalypse of the cloud describes the good and the bad periods of Israel in her Land, I shall assume that the Apocalypse of the cloud describes construction and negation of that Land within Palestine. In other words, although the changing reigns of *2 Bar.* 60–68 are all set within the same region, this does not mean that they all take place in the Land. Thus, rather than treating territory as the decisive criterion of the Land, I will study how the actions of the various kings and their subjects shape and undermine the Land within Palestine.

---

[21] Kolenkow, "Introduction" (abstract), 3, 5; "Introduction," 92; 133; 143–146; Bogaert, *Apocalypse de Baruch I*, 88; Murphy, *Structure and Meaning*, 23; Sayler, *Promises*, 14–38; Nir, *Destruction*, 183–184. Cf. also Stone, "Reactions," 196–197.

[22] Note thus that the reigns can be understood as indexes of action, and that the kings represent their subjects.

[23] Cf., e.g., *2 Bar.* 62:2, 5, 7; 63:1; 64:1–2; 69.4. Cf. Münchow, *Ethik*, 102–103; Cf. among others Murphy, *Structure and Meaning*, 22–23; 110–111, Kolenkow, "Introduction" (abstract), 2 and "Introduction," 34.

[24] Israel and humankind affect the development of world history by their actions (Cf. 56; 85:7), but God has foreseen everything beforehand.

The Bright Waters: The Reigns of the Faithful Kings

Four of the kings that once reigned over the tribes within the region of Palestine were righteous. 61:1–8, describing the sixth, bright, waters, refers to the reign of King David and King Solomon. 63:1–11 (the eight, bright, waters) describes the heroism of the righteous King Hezekiah (63), and 66:1–8 (the tenth, bright, waters) deals with the righteous and pure King Josiah.

The Inauguration of Kingship and Temple: The Reign of David and Solomon

The first kings 2 Baruch mentions are David and Solomon (61:1–8). Among all the kings of Israel, David and Solomon played the most important role in textual accounts of the first centuries C.E. Indeed, these two kings enjoy a special status in biblical texts and later accounts alike.[25] 2 Baruch attests to the continued importance of David and Solomon in exegesis, and lets their reign introduce the period of kingship in the Apocalypse of the cloud. The first task of the present discussion is to establish the role of their kingship in the presentation of the Land. 61:1–8 says:

> And the sixth bright waters you saw, that was the period in which David and Solomon were born. And at that time the building of Zion took place, and the dedication of the sanctuary, and the shedding of much blood of the nations that sinned at that time, and the many offerings that were offered at that time during the inauguration of the sanctuary. And peace and calm arose at that time. And wisdom was heard in the gathering, and richness of understanding was increased in the assembly. And the holy festivals were fulfiled in goodness and much joy. And the judgement of the rulers was then seen without deceit, and the righteousness of the commandments of the Mighty One was accomplished in truth. And the land received mercy then at that time, and because its inhabitants did not sin, it was glorified beyond all lands, and the city of Zion then ruled over all lands and regions. These are the bright waters you have seen.

This passage gives a complex account of the blissful period of David and Solomon.[26] The passage brings up two closely related topics: it

---

[25] Cf. particularly 1 Chr 29:28. Cf. D.M. Howard, "David," *ABD* 2: 41–49.

[26] Note that the passage does not distinguish between the reigns of David and Solomon or the stories connected to them. The births of the two kings are mentioned as a marker for the beginning of the good period. Their birth as such is probably not important. (Cf. Violet, *Apokalypsen*, 296; Cf. 1 Sam 16 on the election of David

describes the interplay between the establishment of a united rule and the inauguration of the temple, and then describes the effect of these actions and events to the status of the region of Palestine. Which aspects does *2 Bar.* 61 highlight to describe the situation in Palestine in the period of David's and Solomon's kingship?

2 Bar. 61:1–2: The Inauguration of the Temple

61:2 states that during the reign of David and Solomon, the temple was built and dedicated to God.[27] The passage does not dwell on building activities. Instead, it focuses on the inauguration (*ḥudātā*) of the sanctuary (*beyt maqdšā*).[28] The passage mentions the large amount of offerings that took place on this occasion,[29] and probably refers to King Solomon's sacrifices at the dedication of the temple, as described in 1 Kgs 8–9 and 2 Chr 7.[30] According to 2 Chr 7:11, the dedication ceremony concluded Solomon's building of the temple. It is therefore likely that *2 Bar.* 61:2 mentions the inauguration rituals to underscore that

---

and 2 Sam 12:24 on the birth of Solomon). Note also that *2 Bar.* 61 mentions neither David's ascension to kingship, nor his building of Jerusalem explicitly. 61:1 does however presuppose these deeds, since the following passage describes their effects.

[27] Cf. 1 Kgs 8:63; *1 En.* 91, 93; *L.A.E.* 29.

[28] *beyt maqdšā* could also be translated "house of the holy," "holy house," "holy place," i.e., the Temple.

[29] The Syriac of 61:2 is not clear. The word *ešad*, "to shed, pour out or down" could both apply to a ritual context, and to a context of violence (Smith, *Dictionary*, 30). Nor is it clear how the word *ešad* relate to the "sinful nations" (*'ame dḥṭaw*). There are at least two likely interpretations here. On the one hand, "and the shedding of much blood of the nations that sinned at that time" may mean that nations other than Israel (i.e., "nations that sinned") also made offerings at the time (Cf. 68:5; 1 Kgs 8:41–43; 2 Chr 6:32–33; Isa 2:2; Josephus, *J.W.* 5.17.15–30; *Ant.* 8.4.3; *Targum Ps* 68:32; *Targum Ps* 45:13–15. Cf. Bogaert, *Apocalypse de Baruch II*, 114–115; Murphy, *Structure and Meaning*, 113). Alternatively, Israel made sin offerings for the sinful nations as well (Gressmann in Violet, *Apokalypsen*, 348–349). On the other hand, the blood may be the blood of the nations. Their blood may have been shed due to their sinful status (Charles, *Apocalypse of Baruch*, 103; Kolenkow, "Introduction," 106). The bloodshed could refer to David's violent wars against other inhabitants of the area (2 Sam 5:17–25; 8:1–14; 1 Chr 22:8 and 28:3; Josephus, *Ant.* 7.14.2) and was necessary to clean the Land. The wicked nations are offered at or at least for the sake of the temple and for the purity of the Land that surrounds it. Both options, however, give the same general impression. Whether the nations bring sacrifice to the temple in Jerusalem or their own blood is shed for the sake of purity, the passage intends to shows that Israel's triumph is universal and their God omnipotent.

[30] Cf. 1 Kgs 8:63–65. Cf. also Josephus, *Ant.* 8.4.4 and *1 En.* 89:50.

the construction of the sanctuary in Jerusalem had been completed. The inauguration ceremony evidently marks the moment when God's presence takes up residence in the temple.[31]

2 Bar. 61:3–7: The Obedient Acts of Israel and Her Kings

2 Bar. 61:3 presents a résumé of the acts of Israel and her kings after the inauguration of the temple. Particular attention is given to their obedience to the Law (*namusā*) and their fulfilment of cultic duties.

61:6 underscores that David and Solomon reigned and judged[32] according to God's Law and that the inhabitants of their kingdom lived in agreement with God's commandments.[33] Moreover, and as implied by the previous chapter, 61:4 describes the vitality of the congregation that benefits from instruction in the Law: "And wisdom (*hekmtā*) was heard in the gathering, and richness of understanding (*sakultānutā*) was increased in the assembly." The assumption is that a people that receives instruction will become wise and intelligent. It is a general tendency in *2 Baruch* that the concepts of Law, wisdom, and understanding are connected and complement each other. This is particularly evident in 38:2–4 and 51:3–4.[34] So, when *2 Bar.* 61:4 says that the assembly

---

[31] *2 Baruch* never provides information that says otherwise. It does not mention God's place of dwelling before the inauguration of the temple. According to various biblical accounts, the Tabernacle, the tent of meeting, served as the visible sign and mediation of God's presence until the ark of the covenant (2 Sam 6:16–19; 1 Chr 16:1), and maybe also the tent of meeting (2 Chr 5:5; 1 Kgs 8:4; Ps 74:7; Lam 2:6–7; cf. *2 Bar.* 6:7), was placed at the threshing floor of Ornan (1 Chr 21:28–30; Cf. Deut 12), at Mount Moriah, first inside the tent David had put up for it (1 Chr 6:16–17; 2 Chr 1:4), and afterwards inside Solomon's temple in Jerusalem (2 Chr 5:4–5; 1 Kgs 8:4). The Tabernacle served as the main sanctuary of Israel from its building at Mt. Sinai (Exod 25–29; 35–40). It followed Israel into Palestine and was first placed in Shiloh (Josh 18:1; 1 Sam 2:22) before the ark was removed and the tent brought to Gibeon (1 Chr 16:39–40; 21:28–30; 2 Chr 1:3–6). Some sources (Ps 74:7; Lam 2:6–7) suggest that both the ark and the tabernacle was located inside the Jerusalem temple and was destroyed along with the temple in 587 B.C.E. (Cf. R.E. Friedman, "Tabernacle," *ABD* 6, 292–294. Cf. further Josephus, *Ant.* 8.101).

[32] Ruling and judging are commonly understood to be two aspects of the same activity. The king was in other words also the judge (Cf. 1 Kgs 3:28; *Sib. Or.* 3.286–287; *T. Mos.* 2:2; *Ezek. Trag.* 1.86; *Targum Ps* 110: 4–7). Cf. K. Whitelam, *The Just King: Monarchical Judicial Authority in Ancient Israel* (JSOTSup 12; Sheffield: JSOT Press, 1979), 91–136; 165; Kolenkow, "Introduction," 105.

[33] *2 Baruch* alludes to the justice, the wisdom and the rightful judgement that were traditionally ascribed to David and Solomon. Cf. 2 Sam 8:15; 1 Kgs 3:28; 4:34; 1 Chr 11–29; Ps 72:1–4; Sir 47:12. Cf Whitelam, *Just King*, 91–136.

[34] Cf. *2 Bar.* 59:7. The wisdom and riches of understanding Moses saw, here resound

shows discernment, this means that Israel lives faithfully in accordance with the Law.[35] 61:7 also confirms the faithful status of Israel by stating explicitly that during the reigns of David and Solomon the inhabitants did not sin. In sum, 61:4, 6 and 7 show that the Law ordered life in the time of David and Solomon.

61:5 says: "And the holy festivals (*'ide*) were fulfiled in goodness (*ṭābutā*) and much joy (*busāmā*)." This passage on the one hand shows that festivals were sources of joy to Israel.[36] This joy is primarily a cultic joy. Joy is a common aspect of festivals, gatherings, and meals celebrated in God's honour in the proximity of the temple.[37] The use of the Syriac word *ṭābutā*, "goodness," in the description of the festivals *may* refer to the bountifulness of the offerings in the temple which were subsequently shared among the people present.[38] The word *ṭubā*, meaning "good," or "good things," is conventionally applied to the fruits of the earth and choice produce.[39] Hence, the goodness and joy may refer to a cultic experience at the temple, first of all since the building and inauguration of the temple are the immediate requisites for the implementation of the festivals, but also because 61:4 already put the gathering (*knuštā*), or the congregations (*kenše*),[40] at the centre of its description. Thus, joy unfolds in the congregation, understood both as 'the people' and as the cultic gathering.[41]

This passage also points out that Israel fulfiled her cultic duties during the time of David and Solomon. Since the plural *'ide*, "festivals," suggests several festivals, or festivals as such, the passage probably

---

in the assembly (cf. Kolenkow, "Introduction," 105). As Murphy has pointed out, *2 Baruch* shares this collocation with Deuteronomy (e.g., Deut 4:5–7). According to Murphy, the word pair 'wisdom and understanding' appear eleven times in *2 Baruch* and commonly appears in relation to the Law (*Structure and Meaning*, 131; Cf. *2 Bar.* 4:7; 38; 44:14; 51:3. Cf. further M. Weinfeld, *Deuteronomy and the Deuteronomic School* (Oxford: Clarendon, 1972), 244.

[35] Cf. Ps 19:7; Sir 24:2. Cf. 1 Kgs 3:12 where the word pair describes Solomon. There is probably some overlap in *2 Bar.* 61 between the description of the kings and the congregation (the people).

[36] Cf. Lev 23:39; 1 Kgs 4:20; *Targum Esth* I 7:10.

[37] Cf., e.g., Deut 12:5–7, 17–18; 14:22–23; *Jub.* 49:16–21.

[38] Bogaert, *Apocalypse de Baruch II*, 115. Cf. Neh. 8:12.

[39] Smith, *Dictionary*, 168. Joy and goodness are closely related to the gift of Land in Neh 9:35–36; 10:35–37 and in Sir 47:10.

[40] The root of both words is *knš*.

[41] It was common in the first centuries to refer to Israel as an assembly and cultic gathering. Cf., e.g., *Targum Ps* 45:11; *Targum to Song of Songs* 7:12; 8:1; *Targum Esth* I 7:10. Cf. also *Targum Lam* 4:20–22.

attests to the continuing cultic service of Israel and not of one single event. And, the passage says that the festivals are "fulfiled" (root *šlm*). This Syriac word is normally applied to describe the fulfillment, or performance, of a promise or a wow.[42] This aspect again underscores how Israel fulfils her covenantal duties towards God. In this manner, the description of the practices of Israel and her kings in 61:3–6 exhibits Israel's fidelity to the covenant and, thus, her right to inhabit covenantal space.

God's Blessings: Peace, Triumph, and Mercy

What is the outcome of the inauguration of the temple and the establishment of righteous reign in Palestine? According to 61:3, the immediate effect of the inauguration of the temple, and hence the establishment of God's presence within it, is that "peace (*šlāmā*) and calm (*šaynā*) arose (root *qwm*) at that time."[43] The word pair *šlāmā* and *šaynā* are both rich in connotations. The Syriac word *šlāmā* means "safety" and "peace" and refers to the situation of man and human society.[44] The word *šaynā* means "calm" and denotes a "cultivated or inhabited land."[45] Whereas the words *šlāmā* and *šaynā* partly overlap, they may also complement each other. While *šlāmā* means safety and peace, with regard to good health and protection of man, *šaynā* seems to connote peace and tranquility with reference to the inhabited state of a territory.[46]

In the context of David and Solomon's reign several of these connotations may be at work. First, the concept of 'safety/peace and calm' may include protection from external enemies as well as from the nations that formerly possessed Palestine.[47] The reign of David and

---

[42] Smith, *Dictionary*, 581; Kolenkow, "Introduction," 105–106.

[43] Cf. 2 Sam 7:9–11; 8:15–18; Josephus, *Ant.* 7.14.2.

[44] But also "health" and "welfare" (Smith, *Dictionary*, 582).

[45] Smith, *Dictionary*, 575.

[46] The word pair has been translated in various ways: "Heil und Friede" (Violet, *Apokalypsen*, 297), "Tranquilité" and "paix" (Bogaert, *Apocalypse de Baruch I*, 508), "Rest and peace" (Klijn, "2 Baruch," 642). Cf. further 11:4; 36:3, 6; 73:1; 74:1 (Kolenkow, "Introduction," 79).

[47] Safety and peace stand out as important qualities of David's and Solomon's reign: 2 Sam 7:10–11; 1 Kgs 4:24–25. Cf. 2 Sam 8; Sir 47:12–16; *1 En.* 89:49 and *Targum Pseudo-Jonathan to Num* 23. Peace is first and foremost considered a quality of Solomon's reign. Solomon even got his name due to the peace that prevailed during his reign (Ginzberg, *Legends IV*, 125).

Solomon provided Israel with a kingdom that kept enemies out and neutralised or expelled opponents within its realm. Second, we may also understand the concept as a reference to the ordered condition of the landscapes in the period of the sixth, bright, waters. As pointed out above, *šaynā* may refer to the cultivated or inhabited status of an area. *šaynā* is in this sense the opposite of *dabrā*, "the (wild) field," and also of *ḥurbā*, "desert," or "waste place."[48] Hence, *šaynā* is the cultivated and domestic country.[49] Third, it is likely that the peace and calm could also be the result of righteous, monarchical judicial authority, described in 61:6. On the one hand, the fact that the king rules and judges with majesty assures unity and the end of opposition among his subjects. On the other hand, submission to the Law also creates peace. When kings and the leaders submit to the will of God and rule in accordance with his commandments, peace will result. In this perspective, the reign of David and Solomon brought order to the landscapes of Palestine since it ensured the correct inhabitation of the area. In this manner, the passage conceptualises the intimate interplay between people and territory. The cultivated ground secures subsistence for the people. In return, Israel's cultivation and dwelling save that area from the chaotic condition of the uncultivated regions that surround it.

Fourth, the passage probably alludes to the many biblical passages that ascribe 'rest' to the life of Israel in the presence of God within their Land. Deuteronomy describes rest as a specific attribute of future life in the Promised Land.[50] In Deuteronomy, the notion of rest in fact distinguishes the Land of Promise from other countries.[51] And finally, in light of the discussion of creation and de-creation in the previous chapter, it is possible that the inauguration may also imply the completion of the entire creation process and that the rest that followed the temple building in *2 Bar.* 61:3 may allude to the Sabbath that signaled the completion of creation in Genesis.[52] Levenson has suggested that Solomon's temple building and inauguration in 1 Kgs

---

[48] *2 Bar.* 10:8.

[49] Moreover; "solitude" and "desolation" (Smith, *Dictionary*, 83 and 134).

[50] Cf. von Rad, *Hexateuch*, 94–96; W. Zimmerli, *Man and His Hope in the Old Testament* (SBT—Second Series; Naperville, Ill.: Allenson, 1968), 74–80; Davies, *Gospel and Land*, 36.

[51] Deut 12:8–12; 25:19; 28:64–65. Cf. 2 Sam 7:10–11 and 1 Kgs 8:56.

[52] Cf. Blenkinsopp, *Prophecy and Canon*, 63. It is possible that *2 Bar.* 61 alludes to a wider set of creation imagery. Cf., e.g., Prov 8–9.

6–9 parallels the construction of the world in seven days.[53] Levenson claims that 1 Kings' account of temple construction and inauguration alludes to the Sabbath rest in the creation week of Gen 2:2.[54] With Israel safe within her Land and God's presence established in the temple, the creation process has reached its goal. If this is so, the rest of *2 Bar.* 61:3 may also imply the completion of God's creational act.

At any rate, the choice of words in *2 Bar.* 61:3–6 suggests that rest, safety, and peace occur when God dwells in the temple, when his obedient kings keep enemies out and Israel cultivates the region she inhabits in accordance with the Law.

61:7 concludes the description of the reign of David and Solomon: "And the land received mercy then at that time, and because its inhabitants did not sin, it was glorified[55] beyond all [other] lands, and the city of Zion then ruled over all lands and regions."[56] According to this passage, "the land" (*ar'ā*), and "the city of Zion" (*çehyun mdītā*) received God's blessings, in terms of triumph and mercy (root *rhm*), during the time of David and Solomon. God blesses the land and the city of Zion in return for Israel's covenantal faithfulness. In effect, the righteous practices of Israel and her kings, sanctioned by God's mercy, produce a Land glorified beyond all lands, and makes the rule of the city of Zion all-embracing. The triumph of Jerusalem is universal, and the triumph is there for everyone to see, since all nations are subject to Israel's power.[57]

---

[53] Cf. further Fishbane, "Jeremiah and Job," 152.

[54] Levenson, "Temple and World," 288–289; 292; 293. Cf. Weinfeld, "Sabbat," 188. Cf. Ps 132:8.

[55] Or, "praised" (root *šbḥ*). Cf. *Ep. Barn.* 11:9; Bogaert, *Apocalypse of Baruch II*, 115.

[56] 61:7 is not entirely clear. It is not obvious whether the righteousness of the people is the cause of the enhanced status of the city of Zion only, or whether it is the cause of God's mercy for the country as well as the new status of the city. Cf. the equivalent of *Ep.Barn.* 11:9 (Cf. F. Perles, "Notes sur les Apocryphes et les Pseudépigraphes I. Traces des Apocryphes et des Pseudépigraphes dans la Liturgie juive," *REJ 73* (1921): 173–185 at 183; Violet, *Apokalypsen*, 297; Bogaert, *Apocalypse de Baruch I*, 272–273). Cf. the slightly differing interpretations of *2 Bar.* 61.7 in Violet, *Apokalypsen*, 295; Klijn, "2 Baruch," 642. Cf. also Bogaert's rejection of them (Bogaert, *Apocalypse de Baruch II*, 115). Cf. also Deut 11:27; 15:5; 28:1; 30:16.

[57] There is an element of triumph involved in several of the aspects I have discussed above, e.g., the mention of the bloodshed in the context of the inauguration of the temple (61:2), and the wisdom and understanding of the kings and the people (61:4, 6. Cf. Deut 4:5–7; Sir 47:12–17 and 1 Kgs 4:34).

The Reigns of Hezekiah and Josiah: The Eight and Tenth, Bright, Waters

However, the description of the situation in the region of Palestine during the reign of David and Solomon is not unique. The description of their reign is paralleled by the descriptions of the reigns of the two later kings Hezekiah and Josiah. According to *2 Baruch*, both kings were exceptional in their righteousness and outshone in this respect all the other kings that succeeded David and Solomon.[58] The descriptions of their reigns constitute the two subsequent bright waters: the eight (63:1–11) and the tenth (66:1–7) of the total twelve waters of world history.

2 Bar. 63 describes the time of Hezekiah, king of Judah (63:1).[59] When the Assyrian king Sennacherib and his multitude threaten to destroy Zion, Jerusalem, and the two and a half tribes which were left at that time (63:3), Hezekiah trusts God and turns to him for help. God hears the prayers of this wise and righteous king, and sends the angel Ramael[60] to destroy Sennacherib's army. Ramael kills one hundred and eighty-five thousand chiefs, each commands a similar amount of men, in Sennacherib's hosts and burns their bodies.[61] Their clothes and arms, however, he takes as booty. In this manner Ramael makes God's miracle visible to others and sees to that God's name is mentioned throughout the entire world (63:8). Zion and Jerusalem were saved from destruction, and Israel was freed from siege (63:9).[62] The inhabitants of "the holy land" (*ar'ā qadištā*) consequently rejoiced and praised the name of God "so that it was spoken of" (63:10).

2 Bar. 66 interprets the tenth, bright, waters. That passage describes the purity of the generation of Josiah, the last king of Judah mentioned in the Apocalypse of the cloud (66:1).[63] According to 66:1 and 5, King

---

[58] Cf. 2 Kgs 18; 22, 23:25. According to 1 Kings, there were several other good kings in Judah, e.g., Asa (1 Kgs 15:9), Jehoshaphat (1 Kgs 22:41–43), Jehoash (2 Kgs 12:1–2) and Jotham (2 Kgs 15:32–35). However, none of these good kings cleansed the country completely.

[59] Cf. 2 Kgs 18–20; 22:1; 2 Chr 28:27–32:23; Isa 36–37; Sir 48:18–22.

[60] Ramael also interprets Baruch's vision (55:3; 63:7). According to Bogaert, this function is ordinarily ascribed to the angels Gabriel and Michel (*Apocalypse de Baruch II*, 117). Cf. *Targum Jonathan to Isa* 10:32 and *b. Sanh.* 95 b.

[61] Cf. various account of this number in 2 Kgs 19:35–36; Isa 37:36; 2 Macc 8:19; *Jerusalem Targum to Isa* 10:32; *Targum Jonathan to 2 Kgs* 19:35–37; *b. Sanh.* 95 b (Cf. Bogaert, *Apocalypse de Baruch II*, 118; Klijn "2 Baruch," 643).

[62] Klijn leaves out the last part of 63:9 in his English translation ("2 Baruch," 643). Cf. also Harrington, "Holy Land," 669.

[63] Cf. 2 Kgs 16:20; 21:24–23:28; 2 Chr 33:25–35:27.

Josiah submitted completely to God.[64] He purified the country from the impurities his predecessor King Manasseh had inflicted on it during his reign.[65] Josiah sanctified the temple vessels and restored the proper cult in the Jerusalem temple.[66] This pure king exalted the righteous and "all those who were wise in understanding," and he put the priests back into ministry (66:2). Moreover, King Josiah reestablished the festivals and the Sabbaths,[67] and fought all impurity. He removed all magicians, enchanters, and diviners from the country (66:2),[68] he killed the wicked, and removed the bones of the unrighteous from their graves and burned them (66:3).[69] He also burned the impure and the false prophets. Those who listened to them, he threw into the Kidron valley (66:4). The king left no-one wicked or uncircumcised "in the whole land" (*bkulāh ar'ā*) throughout his life (66:5).

How should we understand *2 Baruch*'s version of the reigns of Hezekiah and Josiah in relation to the reign of David and Solomon? Firstly, the descriptions of the reigns of Hezekiah and Josiah are both clearly based on traditional materials and biblical accounts of the two hero kings,[70] although *2 Baruch* presents its own version of the stories. A second point to be noted is that each of these righteous reigns repairs the damages caused by a preceding wicked reign.[71] Thirdly, the reigns of Hezekiah and Josiah mirror the reign of David and Solomon.[72] The differences between them aside, Hezekiah and Josiah were both Davidic kings. They continued the Davidic dynasty both by virtue of their genealogical descent[73] and by acting in their role as 'new Davids.'[74]

---

[64] According to 2 Kgs 23–25, Josiah was particularly committed to the Law. *2 Bar.* 66:1 states that Josiah was the only one to subject himself to God at this time. This does not correspond to 66:1's statement about a whole pure generation (Bogaert, *Apocalypse de Baruch II*, 120). We should probably understand it as a statement about Josiah's heroic nature and his exceptional work for his generation (Cf. Ginzberg, *Legends VI*, 280).

[65] The ninth, black, waters (*2 Bar.* 64 and 65). Cf. *Mart. Ascen. Isa.* 2:5.

[66] Cf. 2 Kgs 23:4–5; Ps 132:16–17; 148:14; Ezek 29:21.

[67] Josiah was the first to celebrate Passover since the time of the judges (2 Kgs 23:21–22; Cf. Charles, *Apocalypse of Baruch*, 109; Bogaert, *Apocalypse de Baruch II*, 120).

[68] 2 Kgs 23:24.

[69] Cf. 2 Kgs 23:16.

[70] Cf. particularly 2 Kings and 2 Chronicles, but also Pss 132 and 148. Cf. Kolenkow, "Introduction," 118; 127.

[71] Cf. Kolenkow, "Introduction," 127–128; 130.

[72] Cf. Kolenkow, "Introduction," 128.

[73] Cf. 2 Kgs 18:3; 20:5; 22:2. Cf. 2 Sam 7:16.

[74] Sir 48:15, 22. Cf. Kolenkow, "Introduction," 6. Cf. 2 Sam 7:12–17; 23:5; Ps 89:4. Cf. Guian, "Davidic Covenant," *ABD* 2, 69–72.

Still, the most important factor is that all righteous reigns are shaped according to the same pattern within the Apocalypse of the cloud. The reigns of Hezekiah and Josiah are two of a total of four bright waters that fell within the region of Palestine,[75] and the description of these reigns are all modeled to fit the idea of a bright period in that region. As mentioned above, Hezekiah and Josiah protect and reestablish the temple and its cult in Jerusalem. Moreover, Hezekiah and Josiah reign according to the Law, just like David and Solomon did. In all cases *2 Baruch* ascribes righteousness, wisdom and understanding, either to the king (63:5) or to Israel at the time (66:2). Likewise, Israel's praise and celebration resound in all three bright periods (61:5; 63:10; 66:4). Furthermore, Israel lived in safety and peace during the reigns of Hezekiah and Josiah, as she did during David's and Solomon's reign. In the case of Hezekiah, safety and peace result from the heroic defense of Jerusalem from external attackers (63:7–10). During the reign of Josiah, safety and peace benefited the righteous after the wicked elements within society had been driven out (66:4–5). Finally, Israel enjoys triumph again. During Hezekiah's reign, the remaining clothes and arms of the attackers attest to God's military triumph on Israel's behalf. The whole earth mentions God's name and admires the joy and intensity of Israel's praise (63:8, 10). Josiah's reign displays the triumph of the righteous within their realm. They rule because the wicked are brought to punishment: they are burned in the fire, stoned in the Kidron valley, killed and extinguished (66:3–5). Consequently, it makes sense to discuss the reigns of David and Solomon, Hezekiah and Josiah as equivalent: these reigns constitute bright periods of righteous kingship in Palestine.

Shaping the Land

The above discussion has established that the descriptions of the reigns of the righteous kings are all shaped according to a set model of bright periods. The bright periods of the Apocalypse of the cloud are periods when Israel fulfils her covenantal duties and consequently benefits from the blessings of God in terms of safety, peace, order, triumph, and cultic joy. The following discussion will focus on how *2 Bar.* 61, 63 and 66 describe space. It is a fact that all three reigns take place within

---

[75] The exception is the twelfth, bright, waters that describe the rebuilding of Zion (*2 Bar.* 68).

the region of Palestine. If this study had presumed that the region of Palestine per definition was the Land, I would have concluded that these three accounts were consequently descriptions of Israel's Land. However, since a praxis epistemology guides this study, it is necessary to discuss *how 2 Baruch* constructs Land within Palestine in these passages.

The Irrelevance of the Jordan River

One initial question must be raised: is the region of Palestine already presented as the Land in the time before David and Solomon's reign? To answer this question, we must compare the descriptions of the fourth, bright, waters (59:1–12) and the fifth, black, waters (60:1–2). These two waters concern the bright period of Moses and his generation and the black period of the judges.

2 Bar. 59 describes the fourth, bright, waters as the period of Moses, Aaron, Miriam, Joshua, and Caleb "and of all those who were like them."[76] This period includes the exodus from Egypt,[77] the leadership of Moses in the wilderness, and ends with the vision and death of Moses (59:3–12). It is evident that the conquest of Palestine is not explicitly mentioned. However, we could still imagine that the mention of Joshua would allude to conquest and settlement, since Joshua is renowned for leading Israel into the country on the opposite side of the Jordan.[78] However, we cannot draw that conclusion unless the context allows for it. 59:1 mentions Joshua in the context of a series of mythological figures. Aaron, the brother of Moses, and the prophetess Miriam are both mentioned probably because they were highly profiled righteous persons among the wilderness generation.[79] Joshua is mentioned together with Caleb. The passage may therefore allude to the story in Num 14:36–38 where Joshua and Caleb were the only two spies who recognised the region across the river Jordan as being good.[80] The allusions to the pair are many, but Joshua and Caleb are probably mentioned in *2 Bar.* 59 simply as two additional exemplary figures among the wilderness generation who obeyed and trusted God.[81] The inclusion of "and

---

[76] Cf. pp. 145 and 275.

[77] Cf. *2 Bar.* 58.

[78] Cf. Josh 1:2.

[79] Cf., e.g., Exod 4:14; 15:20; 16:2; *L.A.B.* 20:8.

[80] Cf. *L.A.B.* 15:5; 20:1–10. Cf. Boorer, *Earth/Land*, 25.

[81] Num 14:20–38. Cf. Nir, *Destruction*, 192. Note that the pair Joshua and Caleb may be connected both to the spying and to the conquest (Num 14:24; 25:65; 32:12; Deut

of all those who were like them" at the end of the passage supports this conclusion.[82] Thus, Joshua is mentioned as an exemplary, righteous, figure, and not as conqueror.

The fact that Moses' vision before his death takes up most of *2 Baruch*'s interpretation (59:3–12) makes it even more likely that the fourth, bright, waters do not include the conquest. The events of this period end at the eastern shore of the Jordan.

The suggestion that the fourth, bright, waters do not include the crossing of the Jordan and the conquest of Palestine makes it the more interesting to note that the fifth, black, waters (60:1–2) depict the idolatry of the tribes and their mingling with the Amorites in the days of the judges.[83] The fifth, black, waters, then, clearly find the sinful tribes west of the Jordan.[84] This indicates that the Apocalypse of the cloud mentions neither the conquest nor the first period of settlement in Palestine. Israel is indeed in the region of Palestine, but there is no bright period in that region until the reign of David and Solomon.[85] It follows from this conclusion that according to *2 Baruch* the crossing of the Jordan and the establishment of the tribes in Palestine do not produce bliss. The change of territory and the mere inhabitation of Palestine is not enough to ensure fulfilment of the covenantal promise of the Land.[86]

The Relevance of Space-defining Cultic Action: God's Presence—Israel's Cultic Obligation

What events, and what acts, create the fulfilment of the promises if conquest and mere inhabitation do not? J. Blenkinsopp has made the following remarks about the promise of the Land in P:

1:36; Josh 14:6–15; 15:13–19; Judg 1:11–15; 1 Sam 30:14; 1 Macc 2:55–56; Sir 46:7–10. Cf. M.J. Fretz, and R.I. Panitz. "Caleb," *ABD 1*, 808–810; Henze, "Jeremiah," 168).

[82] Cf. *2 Bar.* 2:1.

[83] Cf. Josh 24:14; Ps 106; *L.A.B.* 25:9–12; 26:4; 27.9; 30. According to Nir, the Amorites appear as a symbol of the sin of Idolatry (*Destruction*, 191). Cf. further Kolenkow, "Introduction," 114.

[84] Cf. Josh 24:18 and Judg 3:5.

[85] Cf. Judg 17:6. Cf. Kolenkow, "Introduction," 117–118. Brueggemann, *Land*, 67–69; G.E. Mendenhall, "Samuel's 'Broken Rib': Deuteronomy 32," in *No Famine in the Land: Studies in Honor of John L. McKenzie* (ed. J.W. Flanagan and A. Weisbrod Robinson; Missoula: Scholars Press, 1975), 63–74.

[86] The insight that Palestine is a territory with 'a past' is of course not new. On the

> To the promise of the land in the earlier sources P adds that of the divine
> presence (...). Where our structural analysis helps us at this point is in
> drawing our attention to the thematic association in P between the land
> and the divine presence in the cult as objects of the promise.[87]

Blenkinsopp points out that the promise of the Land does not only
involve the giving of a territory: it also assumes the presence of God.
Blenkinsopp's suggestion concerns P in particular. However, his suggestion is probably relevant also to texts outside the material commonly
ascribed to P, since several texts assume a connection between the fulfilment of the Land promise and the establishment of God's presence
at Zion. As other scholars have pointed out, several texts suggest this
connection between the Land promise and the cult at Mount Zion.[88]
In this light, one aspect of the description of the reign of David and
Solomon in *2 Baruch* becomes meaningful: the building of the temple
was crucial to the fulfilment of the Land promise.

I have suggested that the inauguration of the temple in *2 Bar.* 61:2
marks the point in time when God's presence settled in Zion. Except
for the time of King Manasseh, when "the glory of the Most High"
removed itself from the sanctuary,[89] we may assume that God dwelled
in the Jerusalem temple throughout the period of kingship in Palestine
(61–66). In other words, the presence of God benefited Israel from the
time of the inauguration until it departed at the time of destruction
(8:2). In the following we must identify the cultic obligations of Israel,
and then discuss the importance of her cultic practices for the shaping
of Palestine into a proper environment for God's presence and for
branding it 'Land'.

Three groups of cultic agents are mentioned in particular by *2 Baruch*:
kings, priests and other religious specialists, and the congregation of
Israel. The Apocalypse of the cloud focuses on the cultic obligations of
the kings. A. Kolenkow has suggested that this apocalyptic section of
2 Baruch paints a picture of what a good king should do: the king must

---

contrary, the insight is crucial both to Abraham-stories and to the Exodus story (Cf.
Gen 15:16; 23:3).

[87] Blenkinsopp, *Prophecy and Canon*, 61; Cf. J. Blenkinsopp, *Treasuries Old and New:
Essays in the Theology of the Pentateuch* (Grand Rapids, Mich.: Eerdmans, 2004), 159.

[88] Cf. further M. Simon, "La Prophétie de Nathan et le Temple," *Revue d'Histoire et
de Philosophie religieuses* 32 (1952): 44–58 and L. Rost, *Das kleine Credo und andere Studien
zum Alten Testament* (Heidelberg: Quelle und Meyer, 1965), 76–101, both cited by Davies,
Gospel and Land, 132. Cf. further Gen 17:8; Deut 12:10–12; *1 En.* 89:40.

[89] Cf. pp. 61–62.

care for the temple and its vessels, uphold the Sabbath, festivals and offerings, and he must honour the wise.[90] The king was responsible for keeping the house of the sanctuary, the physical building as well as the cult, clean: no false nor foreign priests should do service there (66:2; cf. 10:18), no foreign idols should be introduced into God's house (64; 66), and the temple furnishing—the vessels, the altar and the horn—should be kept without stains (66:2). Moreover, the temple had to be protected from hostile attacks by the nations (63). The cleansing acts of David, Solomon, Hezekiah and Josiah are not, however, limited to the temple compound. These kings cared for the purity of the Land as well. They freed the Land from all foreign, apostate, and intrusive elements, be it religious specialists (66:2), idols (66:2), armies (63:2–8), illicit wives, or uncircumcised inhabitants (60:1–61:2; 66:2–3). All impious and impure elements had to go (66:3).

The second group to whom *2 Baruch* pays attention is the group of priests and religious specialists. The priests were responsible for the temple service (66:2) and the offerings in particular (35:4). 10:18 suggests that their actions guarded the temple. *2 Baruch* tends to portray the priests as an important, but vulnerable link: Josiah takes care to bring the priests back in service (66:2, cf. 64:2), but according to 10:18, when the temple fell the priests were found to be false servants.

The third group is the people. *2 Baruch* describes the righteous people, Israel, as a cultic congregation. We have seen that the Apocalypse of the cloud at several occasions alludes to the function of Israel as a cultic assembly. Israel rejoices (61:5; 63:10) and praises God (63:10), she is instructed in the Law (61; 86:1), observes the Sabbath and attends and celebrates festivals with their prescribed practices (61:5; 66:4).

The cultic actions of these groups are important to the shaping of space. Let us dwell, firstly, on the space shaping role of the Sabbaths and the festivals. The main accomplishment of King Josiah in 66:1–8 was his thorough purification of Jerusalem and the sanctuary from all of the foreign and apostate elements that King Manasseh had introduced into them. The reestablishment of the festivals and the Sabbaths in this

---

[90] Kolenkow, "Introduction," 130–131. Cf. *2 Bar.* 61; 63; 66. Kolenkow stresses the kings' use of prayer. The prayers of the kings potentially could affect God's response to Israel's actions ("Introduction," 131–134). Cf. A.R. Johnson, "The Role of the King in the Jerusalem Cultus," in *The Labyrinth: Further Studies in the Relation between Myth and Ritual in the Ancient World* (ed. S.H. Hooke; London: Society for Promoting Christian Knowledge, 1935), 73–111.

manner replaced foreign cults and personnel. Two sets of allusions are probably at work when *2 Baruch* highlights the keeping of the Sabbath: firstly, the rest and refreshment that the Sabbath brings to the Land as agricultural soil, and secondly, the care that Israel takes of the Land as covenantal space by keeping the Sabbath.

One important aspect of Sabbath ideology is the concept of allowing the soil to rest: the Land, as soil, needs its Sabbaths. According to the Sabbatical cycle, the Land should rest every seventh day (Sabbath), every seventh year (Sabbatical year) and again every fifty years (Jubilee).[91] On the weekly Sabbaths, no work should be done. No-one should either till the ground, or bring its produce to the market on Sabbath. During Sabbatical years, Israel was supposed to live off what the earth brought forth without her labour. This pause would, as a result, give the Land the rest it needed to remain fruitful.[92] If, on the other hand, Israel's Sabbath observance became lax, the fruitful Land would turn into a wilderness. Israel would consequently have to abandon the area, or would have to be removed from it so that the soil could recover from the neglected Sabbaths.[93] Thus, the cultic practices of Israel had direct consequences on the productivity of the soil and the shape of the landscape.

The second issue, care for the Land as covenantal space, is intimately linked to caring for the Land as agricultural soil. Since keeping the Sabbath was part of Israel's service and obligation to God, the cyclical and repetitive Sabbath observance secured God's continuous blessings of the Land. God brought rain in due time and thus kept drought and famine away. The consequence of not keeping Sabbath would be disastrous.[94]

Hence, Israel's Sabbath observance is fundamental to ensuring that an area remains the Land. Firstly, Sabbath observance demonstrates that the Land is inhabited by Israel and no-one else, since her cultic practices determines the cycle of agriculture. Secondly, as long as Israel tills her Land in accordance with Sabbath prescriptions, the Land will receive blessings from God, remain fruitful and provide abundantly for its inhabitants. The reintroduction of Israel's holy practices during the

---

[91] Exod 35:2; 2 Chr 36:21; Neh 13:15–16; Jer 17:27; *Jub.* 2:17–33; 50:1–3.

[92] Cf. Lev 26:32–35; Neh 10:31; 13:15–18; Jer 17:27; 2 Chr 36:21; *Jub.* 2:17–33.

[93] Cf. Lev 26:32–33; *Jub.* 2:28.

[94] According to Jer 17:27, the survival of Jerusalem depends on Sabbath observance: if the inhabitants of Jerusalem work on the Sabbath, God will burn the city by fire. Observing Sabbaths was thus a prerequisite for inhabiting Jerusalem.

reign of Josiah, thus, underlines that the Land is reclaimed by Israel and her God. Sabbath observance is in this sense a way of reclaiming the Land, putting Israel's mark on it and branding it by dominating and inhabiting it.

The celebration of festivals can also be interpreted as a part of Israel's Land-defining activity. Most passages of *2 Baruch*, 66:4 included, describe festivals in general and do not specify the rituals involved.[95] 10:10, discussed in the previous chapter, is therefore exceptional in referring to the offerings of first fruits, although the reference is to its cessation: "For an offering will not again be given from you in Zion, and the first fruits will not again be offered."[96] The offering of first fruits commonly refers to the giving of the first ripe, or choicest, fruits of the harvest to God in the temple. The term can refer to the first produce of the soil in a general sense (Exod 23:16), or to more specific products like fruits (Neh 10:35), grapes (Num 13:20), and particularly to wheat, grain, or bread (Exod 34:22; Lev 23:17).[97]

What is important to the present discussion is the fact that the giving of the first fruits was understood as a thanksgiving offering.[98] One common interpretation, based on Lev 25:23–24, is that the offering of first fruits was considered a redemption of the whole harvest, since God is the real owner of the Land and the harvest therefore legitimately belongs to him.[99] Other biblical passages present other possible rationales for the thanksgiving offering. Deut 26:1–10, for instance, stresses the capacity of God to give the Land to Israel, and points to this act as the reason for the first fruit offering:

> When you have come into the land that the LORD your God is giving you as an inheritance to possess, and you possess it, and settle in it, you shall take some of the first of all the fruit of the ground, which you

---

[95] Although several suggestions have been raised: Bogaert mentions the possibility that Josiah celebrates Passover (*Apocalypse de Baruch II*, 120) and that Baruch will die (76:4) on Yom Kippur (*Apocalypse de Baruch II*, 133).

[96] Note that the goodness of the festivals in 61:5 may refer to the food of the Land (cf. Ezra 9:12; Neh 9:35–36; Ps. 65:5; Isa 1:19. Cf. Boorer, "The Earth/Land," 19–33).

[97] First fruits were offered both at Passover (Lev 23:10–14) and at Pentecost (Num 28:26). Although the identity of the festival implied in *2 Bar.* 10:10 is not of importance *per se* for my argument, Pentecost, with "the day of the first fruits" (Num 28:26), is the most probable reference of the passage.

[98] Cf. Exod 13:11; Deut 26:1–10.

[99] Exod 22:28; Lev 18:24; 25:23–24. Cf. R.O. Rigsby, "First Fruits," *ABD 2*, 796–797; Davies, *Gospel and Land*, 24; 28–29; Clements, "Temple and Land," 24; Blenkinsopp, *Prophecy and Canon*, 68.

> harvest from the land that the LORD your God is giving you, and you
> shall put it in a basket and go to the place that the LORD your God will
> choose as a dwelling for his name (Deut 26:1–2).

When bringing the first fruits to the temple, Israel was supposed to
thank God for giving her the Land in accordance with his covenant
with the patriarchs:

> (…), you shall make this response before the LORD your God: 'A wan-
> dering Aramean was my ancestor; he went down into Egypt and lived
> there as an alien, few in number, and there he became a great nation,
> mighty and populous. (…). The LORD brought us out of Egypt with a
> mighty hand and an outstretched arm, with a terrifying display of power,
> and with signs and wonders; and he brought us into this place and gave
> us this land, a land flowing with milk and honey. So now I bring the
> first of the fruit of the ground that you, O LORD, have given me (Deut.
> 26:5–10) (…)'.

How do these interpretations fit *2 Baruch*, and 10:10 in particular, with
regard to Israel's Land-shaping cultic praxis? Firstly, by offering the first
fruits, Israel acknowledges God's ownership of the Land and declares
and reaffirms this ownership. Secondly, the offering of the first fruit
reaffirms God's promise and gift of the Land to Israel.[100] When *2 Baruch*
emphasises that Israel fulfiled the festivals and offered first fruits as long
as the temple was standing, it consequently underlines the continued
renewal of God's act of giving the Land.[101] In consequence, as long as
Israel celebrates and fulfils the festivals, the area she inhabits remains
the Land. The praxis of celebrating festivals both brands an area as the
Land and re-identifies it both as the goal of Israel's wanderings and as
God's chosen gift to his people.[102]

This central cultic component of Israel's practices in the Land also
puts the concept 'the holy land' of 63:10 in perspective.[103] According
to 63:9–10, Hezekiah's victory over the armies of Sennacherib called
forth rejoicing and praise of God throughout the Land. In this context
2 Baruch calls the Land 'holy'. What is it that makes the Land holy at
the time of Hezekiah? At the first sight, it is not clear whether holiness
is perceived of as innate within territory, or whether holiness may be
derived and relational, caused by God's dwelling in the Land and thus

---

[100] Cf. Boorer, "Earth/Land," 32.
[101] Cf. Exod 13.8.
[102] Cf. Davies, *Gospel and Land*, 50.
[103] In addition, *2 Bar.* 71:1 and 84:8 refers to "the holy land." Chapters Six and Seven
will discuss these references.

indirectly determined by Israel's righteous practices. With regard to this passage, both interpretations could be possible.[104]

Some aspects in *2 Baruch* make the latter reading preferable, though. Firstly, in view of the discussions of the previous chapter, the imminent destruction of the temple is the general backdrop to *2 Baruch*. At the time of destruction, God's presence had left the world and all cultic objects had been hidden in the ground. In this manner, 1:1–9:2 highlighted how holiness abandoned the earth before the onset of destruction. In fact, it is clear from the very first chapter of *2 Baruch* that the area which was formerly the Land is doomed to destruction. This makes it improbable that the territory described in 63:10 *per se* should be holy.

Secondly, 63:10 applies the term 'the holy land' to a time when this region was ritually pure and free from foreign intruders, and when Israel gave her due praise to God in the temple. Since Israel lived lawfully and served God, God consequently dwelled in her midst and blessed the surrounding Land. The Land was holy at this time due to God's presence there, and stayed that way as long as Israel's righteous actions provided the needed ritual purity to the area. Thus, the holiness of the Land is not intrinsic. The region inhabited by Josiah's subjects *is* not holy, but *becomes* holy when Israel lives in it righteously and causes God to dwell in it. Holiness is derivative, relational and thus a function of praxis.

This notion of derivative holiness is of course not unique to *2 Baruch*. Davies says: "Note that the term 'holy land' which suggests that the Land itself was inherently 'holy' seldom occurs in the Old Testament; that is, the holiness of the Land is entirely derivative."

Davies points for instance to Ps 78:54 and Num 35:34 to substantiate this claim. The Land is holy in these passages since God dwells there, and because he has drawn near to it. According to Davies, "it is the proximity of Yahweh alone that lends holiness to a place, or ground, or land."[105] A look at other uses of the term 'holy land' mostly confirms

---

[104] Bogaert probably presumes that Palestine, as such, is the Holy Land (*Apocalypse de Baruch II*, 118–119). Kolenkow also takes it for granted that Palestine is the Holy Land ("Introduction," 12; 16; 24; 65). As pointed out in Chapter One, pp. 10–11, Harrington does not differentiate between the motif of the Holy Land in the passages he discusses and other references to the Land in the texts ("Holy Land," 662; 668). He thus treats the holiness as given.

[105] Davies, *Gospel and Land*, 29–30; Himmelfarb, *Ascent to Heaven*, 11–13; Smith, *Map*, 110; Sarason, "Significance," 121.

this.[106] Exod 3:5, for instance, applies the term to the place where God was present at Horeb. Likewise, Josh 5:13 defines a spot near Jericho as holy due to God's presence there. A third example, *T. Job* 33:5, is particularly clear, since it describes the heavenly world of God as 'the Holy Land.'[107] As we see in these cases, holiness is dependent on God's presence, and the space it defines.[108]

The notion of derivative holiness underlines the role of the Land as a temple environment defined by cultic action. This is the Land that houses God's congregation and provides first fruits and goods for the temple service. As a result, this particular area and its inhabitants are blessed by God and benefit from his presence. The Land and the temple, as well as Israel and God, depend on each other.[109] The Land and its inhabitants cannot flourish or multiply without God's blessings, but neither will God remain in his earthly dwelling place without the constant service and cultic attention of Israel in her Land.[110]

As suggested above, 61:5 described fulfilment of festivals as Israel's duty.[111] 66:4 associates the reestablishment of festivals with the reintroduction of the Sabbaths (*šabe*) and their holy practices during Josiah's

---

[106] There are ambiguous or unclear references to holy land/ground/place in Zech 2:10–13; 2 Macc 1:7; 29; Wis 12:3; *Sib. Or.* 3.266–267; *L.A.B.* 19:10; *Legat.* 42.

[107] Cf. also *Hist. Rech.* 11:1–2, where the Island of the blessed is the Holy Land.

[108] It is also possible that *2 Baruch* links holiness more directly to Israel's righteousness. In other words, the righteous, Israel, may be considered carriers of holiness. *2 Bar.* 49:2 may indicate that the righteous somehow possess an element of "splendour" or "shining" (*ziwā*) already while they live on earth (49.2). If this interpretation is correct, the holiness of the Land may derive both from the presence of God and Israel. Lev 20:22–26, for example, shows that the holiness of the Land may derive from both. According to this passage, the Land derives its holiness from Israel, which is holy to God since God himself is holy. A similar notion of 'holy land' may be present in *2 Bar.* 63:10. The holiness of Judah may derive from the presence of God and directly or indirectly from the righteous inhabitance of Israel. And, importantly, the Land stays holy as long as, but only as long as, Israel maintain her faithful practices. When God's presence leaves in reaction to Israel's sins, the country is no longer holy. Cf. further Chapter Seven.

[109] Cf. Clements, "Temple and Land," 27–28; Boorer, "Earth/Land," 31–32.

[110] Cf. Smith, *Take Place*, 104–105. According to *2 Bar.* 3–5 and 5:8, Baruch fears that God's glory may potentially be at stake at the destruction of the temple (Cf. Murphy, *Structure and Meaning*, 90; Harrington, "Holy Land," 670). Note that the destiny of Israel and God are intrinsically woven together: God has called Israel by his name (*2 Bar.* 21:21; 48:23; Deut 28:10; 2 Chr 7:14; Isa 43:1; *4 Ezra* 4:25), and if Israel's name is forgotten, this also affects God's reputation (cf. Is 43:7, 21). God's need for a people is suggested in several texts, e.g., *L.A.B.* 12:9 and *Targum Esth I* 5.

[111] Cf. *Targum Jonathan to Ezek* 16:8. Cf. Davies, *Gospel and Land*, 94.

reign.[112] Even more than 61:5, this passage emphasises the celebrations as an *obligation* on Israel.[113] The element of obligation is also present in *2 Baruch*'s descriptions of Israel's praise of God and remembrance of God's name and glorious deeds.[114] According to 67:3, discussed in Chapter Two, the fall of the temple silences Israel. As a result of the fall, no-one glorifies God's name in Zion any longer. Consequently, the rejoicing and the continuous praise of God's glories that took place while the temple was still standing must be interpreted as part of Israel's duty towards God.[115] The fulfilment of cultic duties was part of the covenantal obligations that kept Israel alive, safe and secure, shaping a Land that rightfully belonged to her as long as she kept her part of the agreement with God.[116] This cultic relation and these reciprocal actions thus secure the identity of an area as the Land belonging to Israel as covenantal space.

The Relevance of Righteous Kingship: Creating Covenantal Space

However, as the discussion above has suggested, in the context of the Apocalypse of the cloud the inauguration of the temple and the care for the cult is intimately connected to the establishment of righteous kingship.

The blending of the reigns of David and Solomon in 61:1–8 is one important example. Biblical texts and later accounts alike tend to

---

[112] Most scholars agree with Charles, who suggested the reading "festivals" (pl.) instead of "festival" (sg.) (Charles, *Apocalypse of Baruch*, 109; cf. Dedering, *Apocalypse*, 37; Bogaert, *Apocalypse de Baruch II*, 120; Kolenkow, "Introduction," 105; Klijn, "2 Baruch," 4). However, it is possible that the single festival refers to the fact stressed by 2 Chr 35:18 and 2 Kgs 23:22 that no other king in Israel had celebrated Passover like Josiah did since the days of Samuel. The festival mentioned in *2 Bar.* 66:4 may thus be the Passover (Cf. Bogaert, *Apocalypse de Baruch II*, 120).

[113] Cf. the link between Sabbath and festivals in 1 Chr 23:31; 2 Chr 2:4; Isa 1:12–14; Lam 2:6; Hos 2:11; *Jub.* 50:10–11; Cf. *Targum Ruth* 1:16. As pointed out in the previous chapter, Sabbath observance is part of the "perpetual covenant" and a sign between Israel and God, according to Exod 31:16–17 (Cf. Exod 16:28; 31; Deut 5:12; Isa 56:1–2; 58:13–14; Jer 17.19–27).

[114] There is considerable overlap between festivals, Sabbaths, and praise with regard to God's outcome of Israel's service. Festivals are explicit occasions where God's deeds are recited, since several festivals celebrate God's creation (Gen 2:2–3; Exod 20:11; *Jub.* 2:25) and redemptive work in history (Cf. Deut 5:15). Moreover, Sabbath observance may be a criterion for admission to the Temple (Levenson, "Temple and World," 292; Cf. Deut 23:2–4; Lev 19:30).

[115] Cf. *2 Bar.* 3:6; 5:1–2; 10:10; 61:5; 63:10–11.

[116] Cf. Clements, "Temple and Land," 20; Blenkinsopp, *Prophecy and Canon*, 68.

emphasise that King David united the twelve tribes of Israel under one rule at Hebron,[117] and that he marched to Jebus and transformed the city into Jerusalem, the capital of the first united monarchy.[118] David is therefore renowned for his unifying and centralising efforts. King Solomon is equally famous as temple builder and for his peaceful reign.[119] Together these two kings provided the twelve tribes of Israel with an ordered reign in Palestine, a fixed centre, and a single place of worship at the Jerusalem temple.[120] It is likely that the merging of the reigns of the two kings in the account of *2 Bar.* 61:1–8 should be understood as a way of creating a unified perspective on these crucial events in the history of Israel.[121] If this is the case, the ordering of Israel's life in Palestine and the inauguration of the temple in Jerusalem may be interpreted as a single, decisive, act.[122]

The accentuation of David and Solomon's righteous judgement and the emphasis of Israel's lawful behaviour are also important factors serving to prove the fulfilment of the Land promise. Kolenkow has suggested that the description of the period of David and Solomon in *2 Bar.* 61 is "a picture of the time as the fulfilment of what would be desired in society."[123] Although Kolenkow's suggestion is likely, it is still possible to formulate the function of this passage more precisely. In

---

[117] The tribe of Judah first makes David its king in Hebron (2 Sam 5:5; Josephus, *Ant.* 7.1.2. Hebron was probably the main city in the tribal land of Judah, both as a marketplace and as a cultic centre (Geus, *Tribes of Israel*). The extent of David's power grows as all the twelve tribes of Israel gather in Hebron and make him their king (Cf. 2 Sam 5:1–5: 1 Chr 11:1–3; Ps 133; *T. Mos.* 2:2).

[118] Cf. 2 Sam 5:6–10; 8:15; 1 Chr 11:4–9; Ps 132; 133; Josephus, *Ant.* 7.3.2; *4 Ezra* 3:23–27. Cf. A.A. Fischer, *Von Hebron nach Jerusalem* (BZAW; Berlin: Walter de Gruyter, 2004), 43–98 and 212–256; Levenson, *Sinai and Zion*, 92–96.

[119] Cf. 2 Sam 7; Ps 89, and further Sir 47:11; *1 En.* 89:41–50. Levenson, *Sinai and Zion*, 97–101.

[120] 2 Sam 7:10–14; 1 Kgs 5–6; 2 Chr 2–5; *1 En.* 93; Josephus, *Ant.* 7.4.4 and the *Testament of Solomon.*

[121] Several texts suggest a clear continuity between David's preparations for the temple building and Solomon's implementation of the temple building (1 Chr 22:2–29:22; Josephus, *Ant.* 8.4.2–3). David bought a plot for the temple, he gathered materials for it and made plans for it. The temple is sometimes also called "house of David" (*Mek. Shirah* 1:34b, according to Ginzberg, *Legends VI*, 264). Thus, several texts regard the temple building as the work of both David and Solomon.

[122] Hence, there is no clear divide between temple and palace, between the king's ruling and his cultic activities. Cf. Levenson, *Sinai and Zion*, 98. Cf. also *4 Ezra* 10:46, where Solomon builds the city and offer offerings (cf. 10:55–56).

[123] Kolenkow, "Introduction," 105; 136. The description in *2 Bar.* 61 resembles Sir 47 (Cf. Kolenkow, "Introduction," 106–107).

my view, 61:1–8 focuses on the fact that the covenanted relationship between God and Israel is intact. During their reign, Israel and her kings obeyed the Law and fulfiled their cultic duties.[124] And due to her righteousness, Israel prevails over all other nations and the area she inhabits surpasses all other regions. 61:1–8 thus describes the construction of the Land as covenantal space.[125]

So, whereas conquest, settlement and inhabitation of the region of Palestine do not fulfil the Land promise, a lawful reign and the inauguration of the temple in Jerusalem do.[126] Together, the inauguration of the temple and the establishment of righteous life in the region of Palestine were the events that made it possible for Israel and her kings to fulfil their covenantal duties and consequently attain covenantal rights.

This discussion shows that the practices of Israel and her kings are decisive for the construction of Land in the Apocalypse of the cloud. The idea is explicit in 61:7 According to that passage, God's mercy for Palestine is bound to the particularly lawful condition at the time of David and Solomon. In other words, it applies to Palestine at a special period in time. The same passage also suggests that the glory and the universal triumph at this point were, implicitly, created by Israel's righteousness. This means that Israel's righteous acts decide the character of the space she is in. Her practices decide the situation in Palestine during the rule of David and Solomon since these practices attract and keep divine presence in the temple. Consequently, the Land of David and Solomon in *2 Bar.* 61 stands forth as the first actualisation of the

---

[124] Cf. Murphy, *Structure and Meaning*, 110.

[125] It is likely that *2 Bar.* 61 alludes to Deuteronomy's description of the Mosaic covenant when it describes David and Solomon's reign in Palestine. Safety and peace, wisdom and understanding, triumph, the joy of Israel and the righteous judgement of the rulers are all qualities describing the Promised Land in Deuteronomy (Deut 4:5–6; 11:31–12:1; 12:9–12). These aspects, belonging to a future Land of Promise in the narrative of Deuteronomy, are thus actualised in *2 Bar.* 61's description of David and Solomon's reign. It is already well documented that *2 Baruch* alludes to the book of Deuteronomy, and that the text at times attest to a Deuteronomistic ideology. Cf. O.H. Steck, *Israel und das gewaltsame Geschick der Propheten: Untersuchungen zur Überlieferung des deuteronomistischen Geschichtsbildes im alten Testament, Spätjudentum und Urchristentum* (WMANT 23; Tübingen: J.C.B. Mohr, 1992),180–184; Murphy, *Structure and Meaning*, 120–133; Whitters, *Epistle*, 47.

[126] *1 En.* 93:6–7 is not clear on the issue. If the fence for the Law in 93:6 is the Land (R.H. Charles, *The Book of Enoch or 1 Enoch* (Oxford: Clarendon, 1912), 263) fulfilment comes before the building of the temple. If the fence is interpreted otherwise (Kolenkow, "Introduction," 94; E. Isaac, "1 (Ethiopic Apocalypse of) Enoch," in *Old Testament Pseudepigrapha I* (ed. J.H. Charlesworth; 2 vols; Garden City, N.Y.: Doubleday, 1983–1985), 5–89 at 74), fulfilment depends on the temple and the kingdom.

Land in *2 Baruch*'s account of the history of Israel.[127] The desired and
promised bliss of the Land becomes a reality in Israel's history when
their reign provides her with a temple and orders life in Palestine in
accordance with the Law. Likewise, when Hezekiah and Josiah carried
on the tasks of the Davidic line, promises were again fulfiled. The reigns
of Hezekiah and Josiah ensured renewed attention to cult and covenantal duties and thus repeated fulfilment of the Land promise after periods of darkness (62:1–8; 64:1–65:2).[128]

The Black Waters: Creating Antithetical Spaces in Palestine

The above presentation of the righteous kings in the Apocalypse of the
cloud clearly alludes to common Near Eastern notions of ideal kingship.[129] The ideal king of Israel was wise, he maintained justice and
ruled according to the Law.[130] His kingship assured that the subjects
would live in safety and peace and enjoy prosperity and fertility. Moreover, the ideal king understood the importance of the temple and its
cult.[131] The maintenance of the one cult in Jerusalem would ensure
the omnipotence of the king, and thus his God, and thereby guarantee order and stability in Israel. The rule, and particularly the care
for the temple cult, was then supposed to ensure the survival of the
king's subjects.[132] The reign of the good king was also thought to have
cosmological consequences. As God once created order out of chaos,

---

[127] Cf. 1 Kgs 8:54–56.

[128] Cf. also Smith, *Map*, 110.

[129] Cf. further G. Widengren, *Sakrales Königtum im Alten Testament und im Judentum*
(Franz Delitzsch-Vorlesungen 1952; Stuttgart: Kohlhammer, 1955); W. Brueggemann,
"Kingship and Chaos: A Study in Tenth Century Theology," *CBQ 33* (1971): 317–332;
W. Brueggemann, "From Dust to Kingship," *ZAW 84* (1972): 1–18; G.E. Mendenhall,
"The Monarchy," *Interpretation* 29 (1975): 155–170; D.M. Gunn, "David and the Gift of
Kingdom," *Semeia 3* (1975): 14–45; A. Laato, *A Star is Rising. The Historical Development of
the Old Testament Royal Ideology and the Rise of the Jewish Messianic Expectations* (International
Studies in Formative Christianity and Judaism; Atlanta, Georgia: Scholars Press, 1998).

[130] Cf. 1 Kgs 3:12–14; 10:9; Prov 8:11–12; 29:4; Pss 29:4; 45:4; 72:1–4. Cf. Whitelam,
Just King, 29–37.

[131] Guinan, *Davidic Covenant*, 70; Levenson, *Sinai and Zion*, 97–101; J.J.M. Roberts,
"Zion in the Theology of the Davidic-Solomonic Empire," in *Studies in the Periods of
David and Solomon and Other Essays: Papers Read at the International Symposium for Biblical
Studies, Tokyo, 5–7 December 1979* (ed. T. Ishida; Winona Lake, Ind.: Eisenbrauns, 1982),
93–108.

[132] Ps 112:1–3.

the ideal king of Israel would continuously create and maintain order in Creation and keep chaos at bay.[133] In consequence, the ideal king would provide order and harmony to his subjects as well as to the space they inhabited: his reign should secure order in society as well as in nature.[134]

However, as my initial outline of the Apocalypse of the cloud made clear, not all kings lived up to these ideals. On the contrary, the list of wicked kings, in 2 Baruch and other accounts alike, is long. W. Brueggemann has discussed the pitfalls of kingship with a particular look to the relation between the king and the Land.[135] According to Brueggemann, the king runs the risk of treating the Land as royal possession. The king must subject himself to God and his Law and cannot manage the Land in any other way.[136] If he does not abide by God's Law, his rule comes in conflict with the interest of God, the real owner of the Land,[137] and God will punish him and his subjects. A king that neglects the Law, would therefore seriously violate the space he controls and create chaos.[138]

The Wicked Kings Jeroboam and Manasseh

The seventh and the ninth, black, waters (62:1–8 and 64:1–65:2) both describe periods of wicked kingship in Palestine. The seventh waters describe the reign of king Jeroboam, whereas the ninth waters refer to the kingship of Manasseh. 2 Baruch ascribes two sets of wicked deeds to these kings and their reigns: they challenge the temple cult and they disrupt order in the region of Palestine.

---

[133] These ideals were commonplace in the ancient Near East, and they permeate biblical accounts as well as later Jewish texts (Cf. Whitelam, *Just King*, 30–34; Levenson, *Sinai and Zion*, 108–109).

[134] The king keeps the pillars of the earth steady (Ps 75:3) and controls the waves of the sea (Ps 93:4; 89:25).

[135] Brueggemann, *Land*, 69–74.

[136] Brueggemann, *Land*, 92; Kolenkow, "Introduction," 104. Cf. also 1 Sam 8:5, 19:20; *Pss.Sol.* 1:16.

[137] *2 Bar.* 3:5 says that the Land is "your land" (*ar'āk*), i.e., the Land of God. This is the only time *2 Baruch* applies this concept, and it is thus difficult to establish exactly what it implies. Although it is possible that *2 Baruch* regards the Land, whatever area the term refers to in 3:5, as inherently God's possession (Lev 25:23; Davies, *Gospel and Land*, 24–25; 28–29), it is more likely that the Land is his due to election and presence (Josh 23:3; *4 Ezra* 5:21–26).

[138] Ps 82:5; Prov 16:12.

Challenging the Cult of the Jerusalem Temple

Murphy made the following comment about *2 Baruch*'s choice of kings
in the mid part of the Apocalypse of the cloud: "Of particular interest to us is that he [the author] has chosen four kings of the Jews
[Jeroboam, Hezekiah, Manasseh and Josiah] whose actions had specific repercussion for the cult."[139] Murphy here highlights one major
issue that decides the life of Israel in Palestine during the reigns of the
four kings that succeeded David and Solomon: their treatment of the
cult in the Jerusalem temple. As I have already pointed out, two out
of four chosen kings, Hezekiah and Josiah, defended and reestablished
the temple cult in Jerusalem. These two kings were indeed particularly
famous for their reverence of the Jerusalem temple.[140] The other two
kings, Jeroboam and Manasseh, were equally infamous for neglecting
and defiling the temple and its cult.[141]

   2 Bar. 62:1–3 says:

> And the black, seventh, waters you have seen, that is the perversion of
> the idea of Jeroboam who planned to make two calves of gold, and all
> the wicked ungodliness done by the kings who succeeded him, and the
> cursed Jezebel and the worship of idols that Israel practised at that time,
> (…).

This passage describes the wicked reigns of King Jeroboam and his
successors in the Northern kingdom; that is, the kingdom of the nine

---

[139] Murphy, *Structure and Meaning*, 111. Cf. Sayler, *Promises*, 34–35; 71–72. Cf. also the
lists of 1 Macc 2.51; Sir 45; Heb 11 (Cf. Kolenkow, "Introduction," 92–93; Harnisch,
Verhängnis, 245). According to Kolenkow, early rabbinic lists of evil kings name Jeroboam
and Manasseh together with Ahab (Jezebel's husband) as the only three kings of Israel
who have no part in the world to come ("Introduction," 135. Cf. *m. Sanh.* 10; *b. Sanh*
90b; 103b). It is relatively common to see lists of kings where the kings provide examples
of righteousness and wickedness respectively (Cf. G. Brooke, "The Significance of the
Kings in 4QMMT," in *Qumran Cave IV and MMT: Special Report* (ed. Z.J. Kaspera;
Krakow: Enigma Press, 1991), 109–113; H. von Weissenberg, "Covenantal Motifs in
4QMMT," (paper read at the First Graduate Enoch Seminar, Ann Arbor, May 3rd
2006), 6–7. Cf. also H. von Weissenberg, "4QMMT—The Problem of the Epilogue,"
(PhD diss., University of Helsinki, 2006).

[140] 2 Kgs 18; 2 Chr 29–30; 32:12.

[141] Jeroboam is the first king of the Northern Kingdom (1 Kgs 11–12). According to
2 Bar. 1:2, the kings of the North were responsible for the fall of the ten tribes, in
contrast to the two tribes who according to *2 Bar.* 1:3 later compelled their kings to
sin. Likewise, King Manasseh, son of Hezekiah, is infamous for being the worst king
ever in Judah (2 Kgs 21–23). Not even Josiah's unrivalled righteousness was enough to
heal the wounds made by Manasseh (Cf. 2 Kgs 23:26–27).

and a half tribes.[142] According to 1 Kgs 11–12, King Jeroboam reigned in the Northern kingdom after the nine and a half tribes had split with the kingdom of Judah. Jeroboam set up new places of worship and made new idols and new festivals for his subjects.[143] As 62:1–3 claims, Jeroboam made two golden calves. One calf he placed in Dan, and the other in Bethel. In addition, Jeroboam established cults on several high places.[144] In the summarising words of this passage, the nine and a half tribes[145] practised idolatry at the time of Jeroboam.

King Manasseh of Judah, the wicked king of the ninth, black, waters (2 Bar. 64–65) surpassed even the evil deeds of King Jeroboam. According to 64:2–3, King Manasseh's list of wicked acts is long:

> For he did many wicked deeds, and he killed the righteous, and he perverted judgement, and he shed innocent blood, and he violently polluted married women,[146] and he overturned altars and abolished their offering and drove away the priests lest they minister in the sanctuary. And he made an image of five faces: four of them looked to the four winds, and the fifth was on the top of the image to reject the zeal of the Mighty One.

The first part of this passage deals with Manasseh's corruption of order. The remaining part of this passage, as well as the subsequent verses, focus on Manasseh's violation of the Jerusalem temple.[147] Manasseh overthrows the altars,[148] he stops the offerings and he sends away the priests. However, the crime this passage elaborates on is the erection of an image with five faces in the temple.[149] This image explicitly chal-

---

[142] 1 Kgs 11:26–14:19. Cf. 1 Kgs 14; 18:4, 13; 2 Kgs 17; 21:7–8; 23:5.

[143] 1 Kgs 12:25–33.

[144] 1 Kgs 12:28–31.

[145] In this incident, 'Israel' in all likelihood refer to the ten tribes of the Northern kingdom. This use of the term is conventional.

[146] Cf. Bogaert's discussion of the Syriac (*Apocalypse de Baruch II*, 119). Cf. also Charles's alternative translation (*Apocalypse of Baruch*, 106).

[147] Cf. Ezek 8:5, *Mart. Ascen. Isa.* 1–2, and probably *Apoc. Ab.* 25 (Cf. Ginzberg, *Legends VI*, 371–372). Foreign practices were often part of the cult of Yahweh. *2 Baruch* here argues for the purity of the cult, probably reflecting Deuteronomy's concern for cultic centralisation and purity (Cf. G. von Rad, *Das fünfte Buch Mose. Deuteronomium* (ATD 8; Göttingen: Vandenhoeck & Ruprecht, 1983), 66).

[148] Cf. Bogaert, *Apocalypse de Baruch II*, 99.

[149] Several versions of this story coexist, e.g., 2 Kgs 21:7; 2 Chr 23:7–8 (Hebrew and Peshitta versions); Ezek 8:5; *b. Sanh.* 103b. Cf. Charles, *Apocalypse of Baruch*, 106; Violet, *Apokalypsen*, 309–310; Bogaert, *Apocalypse de Baruch I*, 304–310, Kolenkow, "Introduction," 131; Klijn, "2 Baruch," 643. Cf. *4 Ezra* 13–15 for the four winds.

lenges "the zeal of the Mighty One" (64:3). The extent of Manasseh's
wickedness becomes evident in 64:6: "And the impiety of Manasseh
increased so much that the glory of the Most High removed itself (root
rḥq) from the sanctuary."[150] Manasseh's sins brought the entire temple
cult in Jerusalem to a halt.

The wicked kings Jeroboam and Manasseh are guilty of the same
crime. Both kings introduce another cult and another god. Hence, both
challenge the role of the Jerusalem temple as God's unique place on
earth. King Jeroboam does so by setting up alternative sanctuaries in
the Northern kingdom and thereby tries to displace Jerusalem as the
one and only place of worship. He thus disregards the temple and
directs his subjects away from God. Likewise, Manasseh pollutes and
perverts the Jerusalem temple to such an extent that God's presence
leaves. The two wicked kings, then, challenge the house that David and
Solomon inaugurated as a home to divine presence on earth.

Challenging Order in Palestine

The above discussion of the reigns of the righteous has shown that
Palestine, or parts of that region, enjoyed the order, peace and safety
that goes with a rule submitted to God's Law. The reigns of the kings
Jeroboam and Manasseh, however, destabilised this order.

64:2 mentions the acts that make Manasseh's reign in Judah foreign
to the Law. Manasseh kills the righteous, perverts judgement, sheds
the blood of innocent people, and pollutes married women in a violent manner.[151] So, instead of promoting wisdom (61:4) or exalting the
righteous (66:2), Manasseh kills the pious. And whereas David and
Solomon judged rightfully (61:6), Manasseh perverts judgement. Likewise, unlike his righteous predecessors who shed the blood of guilty
people,[152] Manasseh lets the blood of innocent people flow in Jeru-

---

[150] The translation is in accordance with Violet, *Apokalypsen*, 301; Bogaert, *Apocalypse
de Baruch I*, 510 and Klijn, "2 Baruch," 643. Cf. Charles, *Apocalypse of Baruch*, 107 for an
other translation. Some texts subscribe to the idea that the Shekinah left the temple for
good when Manasseh brought the idols into the temple: i.e., long before the destruction
of the temple. Cf. further *Targum Jonathan to Isa* 66:1; *b. Sanh.* 103b (Ginzberg, *Legends VI*,
372). In *2 Baruch*, God's presence clearly leaves in 64:6, but is probably assumed to have
returned during Josiah's reign, since it leaves again before the invaders enter the temple
in 8:3–5.

[151] 2 Kgs 21:16; *b. Sanh* 103b; *Mart. Ascen. Isa.* 2:5.

[152] *2 Bar.* 61:2; 63:8; 66:3.

salem.[153] Lastly, Manasseh disrupts order even further by polluting married women. It is not entirely clear why 64:2 mentions this, but Manasseh was infamous for having sex both with his sister and his mother.[154] Illicit, violent sex may serve as a sign of disorder,[155] or the point of the reference may be the illegitimate offspring that would result from such a union.

62:2 mentions the wicked deeds of Jeroboam and his successors in more general terms. 62:3 adds a reference to one legendary wicked figure: the cursed Queen Jezebel, wife of King Ahab of the Northern kingdom.[156] According to 1 Kgs 16:31, Jezebel was a Phoenician princess. Her influence on the reign of her husband made him stray from righteous praxis.[157] The distortions brought about by Queen Jezebel were many. First of all, she was a foreigner and thus personalised the temptation of taking foreign wives.[158] Moreover, she made the king mingle with other nations and their gods. And according to 1 Kgs 18:4, Jezebel killed God's prophets. She disturbed the proper relationship between God and king, both by killing God's messengers and by making the king serve other gods. Another aspect of Jezebel's misdeeds was her interference in her husband's reign. Since she was of foreign decent, she broke the command of Deut 17:14–15, saying that Israel should never allow a foreigner to be their ruler.[159] 1 Kgs 21 elaborates in particular on the so-called vineyard incident. Jezebel arranged for the death of a man who refused to sell his vineyard to the king, since it was not the man's right to sell his ancestral inheritance. Jezebel thus treats the country her husband rules as a royal possession, and disregards that it is the possession of God.[160] The wicked deeds of Jezebel certainly excelled the wickedness of most others.[161]

---

[153] 2 Kgs 21:16. Manasseh killed the prophet Isaiah (*Mart. Ascen. Isa.* 1:8; 5:14; *Targum Jonathan to Isa* 66:1 and 2 Kgs 21:16).

[154] Cf. *Mart. Ascen. Isa.* 2:5; *b Sanh.* 103b. Cf. Bogaert, *Apocalypse de Baruch* II, 119; Ginzberg, *Legends VI*, 276; Kolenkow, "Introduction," 135.

[155] Cf. the rape of the Levite's concubine in Judg 19–20 (Cf. Whitelam, *Just King*, 33).

[156] 1 Kgs 16:29–31.

[157] 1 Kgs 21:25, 29. Cf. Brueggemann, *Land*, 88.

[158] Cf. Brueggemann, *Land*, 72; 74–75; Kolenkow, "Introduction," 117–118; 135.

[159] Cf. Brueggemann, *Land*, 71; 88–89.

[160] Cf. Brueggemann, *Land*, 87–92.

[161] Note that Jezebel's body was not properly buried. It remained lying on the ground and was eaten by dogs. Her body polluted the Land. Cf. 1 Kgs 21:17–19, 23; 22:23; 2 Kgs 9:7, 10; 36–37. Cf. Bogaert, *Apocalypse de Baruch II*, 115).

This closer look at the stories related to queen Jezebel displays that
the wickedness of the seventh and the ninth dark waters of the Apocalypse of the cloud are described by means of similar or identical acts.
2 Baruch's description of these black waters applies literary commonplaces to signal that they present periods of wickedness.[162] Both periods see the perversion of righteous judgement and the introduction of
foreign elements into the reign.[163] Likewise, both include the killing of
innocent, righteous people, and of prophets in particular.[164] And, they
also allude to the possible production of illicit offspring.[165]

De-creating Covenantal Space

As the previous discussion has shown, the reign of David and Solomon,
as well as the reigns of Hezekiah and Josiah, transformed the region
of Palestine, or parts of that region, into the Land. The black waters,
however, challenges this status of the area. It is intriguing to note that
the black waters include wicked acts which have a negative impact on
the status of Palestine as covenantal space.

The space transforming impact of wicked acts is evident on several
levels. Firstly, wickedness leads to the transformation of landscapes. 62:4
says explicitly that a result of a wicked reign is the withholding of
rain (62:4).[166] Since God withholds rain when the tribes sin, wickedness
leads to drought. During the reigns of the wicked kings the landscapes
of Palestine therefore look entirely different than the landscapes that
benefited Israel during righteous reigns.

Secondly, wickedness makes empty spaces. When lush landscapes
turn arid, people die by famine. Wickedness, and particularly idolatry,
therefore indirectly leads to the death of the country's inhabitants by
famine.[167] When women in addition eat their children due to famine

---

[162] Cf. further A.C. Tunyogi, *The Rebellions of Israel* (Richmond, Virg.: John Knox,
1969).
[163] Kolenkow has described mingling with the nations and their impurities as a titular
sin ("Introduction," 109–118). Cf. Ps 106:34–38.
[164] Cf. Kolenkow, "Introduction," 127.
[165] Cf. Lam 4–5; *T. Jud.* 23.
[166] Cf. Deut 11:10–17: 14–17; 28:1, 12; 30:10; 1 Kgs 17:1; Zech 14:17; *L.A.B.* 23:12; *Odes
Sol.* 11:13–18; *Jub.* 12:3. Cf. Davies, *Gospel and Land*, 13.
[167] Cf. Deut 4:25; 28:58; 1 Kgs 17; 2 Kgs 18:27, 31–32; *2 Bar.* 70:8; *4 Ezra* 16:21, 22; *Jub.*
23:18; *Fragmentary Targum to Deut* 32:23–24; *Targum Jonathan to Deut* 32:23–24; Mark 13:8.
Cf. Fretheim, "Plagues," 385–396.

and drought (62:4), there is even less people to populate the area.[168] Those who were left in the wicked area were sent into exile (62:5), or alternatively threatened by a prophecy that they would eventually be led into captivity (64:5). This means that wicked inhabitants will be killed or sent out of the space they inhabit and subsequently leave that place empty.[169]

Thirdly, introduction of foreign practices makes space foreign. The main problem of Queen Jezebel, discussed above, was her foreign descent and upbringing. She therefore led King Ahab astray and harmed the relationship between God and the king. Kingship, initially an institution of the nations (Deut 17:14), could easily introduce foreign habits into Israel. If a foreigner ruled, the region he ruled would turn foreign. Idolatry, in particular, makes the area of the idolatrous tribes foreign to Israel and her God.[170] Idolatry causes God's presence to go away from that area and leave its inhabitants to other gods.[171] That would make the wicked tribes like the other, sinful nations and imply that their territories are no different from the countries of the nations. In other words, introduction of foreign practice makes space foreign to Israel and her God and consequently returns that space to the surrounding wicked world. When wicked kings introduce foreign, wicked, institutions they consequently deconstruct Land.

The consequence of the wicked reign of king Jeroboam and his successors in the Northern kingdom (62:1–8) was the disqualification of the nine and a half tribes as well as the space they inhabited. When these tribes and their kings sinned, they were no longer part of righteous Israel. And consequently, due to their wickedness, their part of Palestine no longer qualified as the Land. The Northern kingdom became dry, empty and an integrated part of the wicked world.

The evil reign of King Manasseh brought wickedness also to the two and a half tribes in Judah (64:1–65:2). Although the two tribes had not yet been led into captivity and would eventually continue their wicked

---

[168] The offspring may be fetuses or children (Cf. 1 Kgs 13–14 for the context of the story). Cf. also 2 Kgs 6:28–29; Lam 4:10; *Lam. Rab.* 41b. Cf. Kirschner, "Apocalyptic," 40; H.D. Cohen, "The Destruction: From Scripture to Midrash," *Prooftexts* 2 (1982), 22. Note that Lam 2:20 and *Targum Lam* 2:20 both connect eating of infants and killing of priests and prophets.

[169] Cf. Ezek 14.

[170] Cf. Josh 23.

[171] Cf. Deut 12; 1 Kgs 12:28–33 and 2 Kgs 21:7. Cf. 2 Chr 33:7–8. 1 Kgs 11, for instance, points out that the idolatry of Solomon eventually led to the loss of the ten tribes and their inheritance, the northern part of the kingdom.

lifestyle until the fall of the temple (1:3), they were already doomed
during the reign of Manasseh by the prophecy of their captivity (64:5).
The wickedness of Manasseh's reign and the unfaithfulness of the two
and a half tribes created an antithetical space in Judah. 2 Kgs 21:7–8
describes how promises failed during the reign of Manasseh:

> The carved image of Ashera that he made he set in the house of which
> the LORD said to David and to his son Solomon, 'In this house, and in
> Jerusalem, which I have chosen out of all the tribes of Israel, I will put
> my name for ever; I will not cause the feet of Israel to wander any more
> out of the land that I gave to the ancestors, if only they will be careful
> to do according to all that I have commanded them, and according to
> all the law that my servant Moses commanded them.' But they did not
> listen; Manasseh misled them to do more evil than the nations had done
> that the LORD destroyed before the people of Israel.

This passage points out how Manasseh turns the situation in Jerusalem
upside down. He made the city the opposite of the city God had
envisioned it to be.[172] In accordance with the dynamic of the Mosaic
covenant, thus, God withdraws his blessings from the wicked tribes and
their kings when they disregard their cultic duties and transgress the
commandments of God. The result of wickedness is the destruction
and loss of covenantal space.

Antithetical Spaces in Palestine

In light of a spatial epistemology that focuses on praxis rather than
territory, the alternating righteous and wicked reigns in the region
of Palestine constitute two different spaces. Although *2 Bar.* 61–66 in
its entirety describes Israel's history in Palestine, only 61:1–8; 63:1–11
and 66:1–8, the periods of bright waters, describe the region as the
location of the Land. Israel transforms the region of Palestine, or parts
of Palestine, into the Land in these bright periods only. The two black
periods also take place in Palestine, but the space ascribed to these
periods is not the Land, but its antithesis.

As I have already suggested, 69:2–4 claims that Israel's acts decide
the run of history, since Israel's alternating righteous and wicked acts
provoke God's blessings or curses respectively. Thus, the Apocalypse of
the cloud applies the logic of the Mosaic covenant to argue, as well as

---

[172] Cf. further 2 Chr 33:7–9; 2 Kgs 21:13–14. Cf. also Sayler, *Promises*, 94.

to deny, Israel's right to the Land. As suggested in Chapter One, the Mosaic covenant presupposes that God allows Israel to live in the Land on the condition that she lives in accordance with his Law. As a logical consequence of that presupposition, those among Israel who break his commandments are no longer entitled to live there. The practices of Israel, often described through the acts of her kings, do not only decide the course of history, they also decide the nature of the space she lives in.

The above outline of the dynamics of the Apocalypse of the cloud shows that the promise of the Land is actualised in limited periods of time. It is identifiable in righteous periods only. Fulfilment of promise both unfolds and fails in Palestine in accordance with Israel's actions. In terms of a praxis epistemology, the tribes and their kings actively create and de-create Land throughout their history in Palestine.

The Territory Issue: Palestine—Judah—Jerusalem

The conclusions I have now drawn concerning the Land in the Apocalypse of the cloud open up a new field of discussion. I have argued that the crossing of the Jordan and the conquest of Palestine are irrelevant to the description of the Land in this section of *2 Baruch*. Instead, the Apocalypse of the cloud focuses on the Land-shaping acts of Israel and her kings. Moreover, I have suggested that *2 Baruch* describes two radically different spaces in the region of Palestine. The Land is one of them, and the chaotic antithesis to the Land is the other. In other words, this region is the Land only when Israel inhabits it righteously. In light of these proposals, the location of the Land needs some further attention. How do we locate the Land, and what is the importance of territory to the construction of Land within this section of *2 Baruch*?

Locating the Land: Topography, Geography and Borders

As the first step in this part of the study, I will consider what geographical and topographical information *2 Baruch* in general provides its reader with. Next, I will discuss the territorial information provided by the Apocalypse of the cloud. I have so far suggested in a quite loose manner that the region of Palestine is the location where Israel's Land, as well as its spatial antithesis, takes place. 'Palestine' is however no precise local term. What area does *2 Baruch* envisage when it describes the

territory Israel transforms into Land? And, can we identify any exact
or steady location of the Land in *2 Baruch*?

Basically, *2 Baruch* uses the Syriac word *ar'ā* "land," "country,"
"earth," "ground" to conceptualise any country.[173] Thus, the Syriac
word *ar'ā* does not alone tell us anything about the Land of Israel,
neither its territorial aspect nor any other aspect. It is always the context that decides what country *2 Baruch* describes. *2 Baruch* describes the
Land belonging to Israel by means of the following terms: "the land"
(*ar'ā*),[174] alternatively as "this land" (*hāde ar'ā*),[175] "your land" (*ar'āk*),[176]
"our land" (*ar'an*)[177] and "the holy land" (*ar'ā qadištā*).[178] These expressions provide us with information about fundamental characteristics
and ownership, but the identity of the area implied is still unknown.

How do we identify the areas *2 Baruch* talks about in terms of the
Land? Firstly, as the above discussion has shown, the region roughly
defined as Palestine, or parts of it, is identified as the Land in important periods of Israel's past history. *2 Baruch* mentions select towns and
landscapes in the region and provides some topographical information.
Zion,[179] Jerusalem[180] and the nearby Kidron valley[181] are all named sites
in the text. Likewise, *2 Baruch* mentions the city of Hebron (47:1–2).[182]
Descriptions of the elevated temple mount (43:2) within a city of walls
and fortifications,[183] descending into the brook of Kidron, as well as the
elevations and mountains of the Hebron area (76:3), all bring to mind
the well known topography of these parts of Palestine.[184] A closer look at
2 Baruch displays that these place names identify two stereotype areas in
the heartland of Palestine: the Jerusalem area and the surroundings of

---

[173] Smith, *Dictionary*, 30; Smith, *Thesaurus*, 397–399.

[174] *2 Bar.* 61:7; 66:2; 66:5; 77:9.

[175] *2 Bar.* 29:2.

[176] *2 Bar.* 3:5.

[177] *2 Bar.* 85:3.

[178] *2 Bar.* 63:10; 71:1; 84:8.

[179] Note that 'Zion' may refer either to the temple mount or the city Jerusalem, or to
both (Cf. pp. 35–36).

[180] References to Zion and Jerusalem are numerous in *2 Baruch*, but appear particularly in *2 Bar.* 1–9 and 61–68.

[181] Cf. *2 Bar.* 5:5; 21:1; 66:4. The Kidron valley lies east of Jerusalem, between the
city and the hill known as the Mount of Olives (Levenson, *Sinai and Zion*, 92). "Kidron"
probably means "dark," "not clear," "turbid" (W.H. Mare, "Kidron," ABD *IV*, 37).

[182] Cf. Chapter Five, pp. 150–154.

[183] *2 Bar.* 2:1; 5:3; 6:3–4; 7:1; 80:1.

[184] It is possible that *2 Baruch* regards the Jerusalem area and the Hebron area as two
separate regions. Cf. further Chapter Five, pp. 153–154.

Hebron. These references would clearly trigger the memory, the imagined landscapes, of some central areas of the Land of past generations.

Secondly, in some passages *2 Baruch* presents a notion of the Land as a coherent whole and as a Land set apart from the wicked world. The first notion is clearly present in 66:5 where King Josiah purifies "the whole country." This passage conveys the idea of a coherent and complete entity, even though the territorial extent of this entity is not defined. The second notion is evident in 61:7. As I have pointed out in the above discussion, the Land under David and Solomon's rule is considered to have been different from the rest of the world at that time since it was loved by God.[185] However, although *2 Baruch* identifies certain sites and landscapes as belonging to the Land, and defines the Land as a coherent entity set apart, we are still ignorant about its precise size and territorial extent.

So, *2 Baruch* neither mentions exact borders nor specifies the extent of the territory when it describes the Land. Neither can we identify "the land" (*ar'ā*) as corresponding to any precise territorial entity. *2 Baruch* does not name or map territory, nor does it tell us which areas it includes or excludes by its terms. This means that *2 Baruch* never defines Land in terms of a bordered, well defined territory. Consequently, we cannot at this point identify any exact location of the Land in *2 Baruch*. If this interpretation is correct, does territorial exactness play no part in *2 Baruch*, or is the extent of the territory not a primary issue in the text? Is Land better identified by other factors than territorial extent?

The Land of David and Solomon: Mapping Righteousness and Wickedness

The description of the kingdom of David and Solomon is in agreement with this general assumption: there is no information in *2 Bar*.61 to provide us with any clearly defined territorial borders of their Land. The only explicit geographical reference in the paragraph is "the city of Zion" (61:7).

Still, the immediate context of the passage provides us with hints that allow for a tentative localisation of David and Solomon's kingdom. We have already seen that the preceding waters (60:1–2) locate Israel west of the Jordan, since this was the area were the Amorites lived (60:1). Likewise, 61:1–8 clearly finds Israel in Palestine, and adds a fixed

---

[185] Cf. further the discussion of 10:10 in Chapter Two, pp. 47–49.

centre, Jerusalem and its temple (61:2, 7). In addition, and as I pointed out above, 61:7 articulates a notion of a Land set apart at the time of David and Solomon. This is the Land God loved due to the faithfulness of the inhabitants (61:7). So, since 61:1–8 does not map territory, but still defines the Land spatially, we must study *how* the Apocalypse of the cloud maps the kingdom of David and Solomon.

How can we identify the extent of the Land under David and Solomon's reign? The above discussion of the wicked reigns showed that the wicked period that succeeded the time of David and Solomon, the time of Jeroboam (62:1–8), led to the break between the nine and a half tribes in the North and the two and a half tribes in Judah. We may infer that the Land suggested by 61:7 most probably refers to the Land of the united monarchy. The passage maps Israel at its most powerful: the time when Israel was still a unified, righteous, people, and their kingdom included all the tribal lands of the twelve tribes of Israel.[186] This would indicate that David and Solomon ruled over all of Palestine as well as the tribal lands of the tribes Manasseh, Gad and Ruben east of the Jordan. The Land of David and Solomon in 61:1–8 is thus in all likelihood the Land of the united monarchy with the city of Zion at its centre and the united, righteous, people of Israel as its subjects.

However, *2 Bar.* 61 never identifies the territory of the Land, except for the reference to the city of Zion. How can this missing geographical interest of the passage be accounted for? We must look closer at what it is that 61:1–8 maps, given that it is not territorial extent. Let us look at the first part of 61:7 once more: "And the land received mercy then at that time, and because the inhabitants did not sin, it was glorified beyond all other lands, (…)." I have already suggested that God's mercy for the Land cannot be considered a stable fact, since it depends on the faithfulness of the inhabitants. So, although I have now established that the Land set apart under David and Solomon's reign probably refers to the extent of all twelve tribal lands, it still is the inhabitance of faithful tribes that determines the map of the Land. This definition of Land

---

[186] During David and Solomon's reign, the Land is commonly identified as the Land of the twelve tribes both by 2 Samuel, 1 Kings and 2 Chronicles (Cf. 2 Sam 24:5–7; 1 Kgs 4:7–19). Note however, that only eleven of the tribes had tribal areas assigned to them. The Levites had their own towns and fields within other tribal territories, and were supposed to have their inheritance "in God" (Cf. Num 8:14; 35:1–8; Deut 18:1–2; Josh 21).

is not based on the idea of a permanent territory. On the contrary, it refers to the dwelling in it of righteous inhabitants.

In addition to a Land set apart, 61:7 provides the reign of David and Solomon with a potentially universal power sphere. At the time of their reign, the city of Zion ruled over "all lands and regions" (*'al kul ar'ātā watrawātā*).[187] Does this expression refer to territory? 'All lands and regions' may of course refer to all known lands or to the lands and kingdoms it traditionally was important to dominate.[188] However, the territorial implication of 'all lands and regions' cannot be confirmed by the text, and territory is therefore probably not the central criterion.[189] The most likely interpretation follows from the idea, suggested above, that the triumph of the city of Zion in 61:7 was created by the righteousness of her inhabitants. The reward for righteousness was the subordination of other nations, which were not righteous. The main point of the description is thus to prove the triumph of the righteous over the wicked. This idea appears several times in the Apocalypse of the cloud. 63:8 highlights how God's name was mentioned in the entire world during the reign of Hezekiah after Ramael slaughtered Sennacherib's armies.[190] The bloodshed at the inauguration of the temple in 61:2, as well as the respect the nations show the rebuilt temple in 68:6, also display how the righteous dominate the wicked. Likewise, the reference to the relief experienced by the wicked nations at the destruction of Jerusalem confirms that Israel's power had been felt among them: "'She is suppressed who for a long time suppressed (others), and she is subjected who used to subject (others)'" (67:2). Hence, 'all nations and regions' refer to the world of the wicked, and not to a precise geographical area. The divide between righteousness and wickedness is therefore the most relevant criterion for spatial division.

---

[187] Several biblical accounts ascribe a similar double scope to the reigns of David and Solomon (1 Kgs 4:24–25).

[188] Cf. *Targum Jonathan to Ezek* 16:13.

[189] 2 Samuel, 1 Kings and 2 Chronicles identify the larger power sphere of David and Solomon with the Land promised to Abraham in Gen 15:17–18. The Land of Promise embraced all land from the river of Egypt to the river of Euphrates, and the more or less equivalent power sphere of David and Solomon extended from Lebo-hamath in the North to "wadi of Egypt" in the South (1 Kgs 8:65), and from the Euphrates to Gaza (1 Kgs 4:24). It is possible that *2 Bar.* 61:7 may refer to the region implied by God's promise to Abraham, but this cannot be confirmed and the otherworldly perspective of *2 Bar.* 57 makes the suggestion less likely cf. pp. 274–277.

[190] Cf. *2 Bar.* 61:2, 7–8; 63:8–10; 68:6.

Consequently, 61:1–8 ascribes both a core Land of righteousness and
a potentially universal subordination of all wickedness to the reign of
David and Solomon. The divide between the Land set apart and the
rest of the world does not follow territorial lines, but the moral status of
its inhabitants.[191]

Why is this emphasis relevant to the study of the Land in the Apocalypse of the cloud? It may at first look insignificant to discuss how
the apocalypse maps the extent of David and Solomon's reign, since
the region of Palestine is anyhow more or less identical to the area the
twelve faithful tribes of Israel inhabited.[192] In other words, even though
I would claim that *2 Bar.* 61 maps faithful tribes instead of territory, that
would still not challenge a definition of the Land that gives priority to
territory. This is why I will bring the discussion further to include a
study of the location of the Land during the kingships of Hezekiah and
Josiah. A study of these reigns will point out the paradox a mapping of
territory brings about.

Judah: The Holy Land of the Two and a Half Tribes

Due to the wicked reign of king Jeroboam and his successors in the
Northern kingdom, the nine and a half tribes were exiled by "Sal-
banasar, the king of the Assyrians" (62:5–6). The description of the captivity in 62:5 is the last reference to the affairs of the Northern kingdom.
The Apocalypse of the cloud never refers to that kingdom again and is
also tacit about the tribal lands of the nine and a half tribes. From other
parts of *2 Baruch*, however, we learn that the nine and a half/ten tribes
remain in captivity.[193] According to 1:2 and 77:22 they are already long
gone at the time of the destruction of the temple. The nine and a half
tribes have thus left their tribal lands in the North for good.

The tribal lands of the southern tribes, however, were still not affected by the wickedness of the seventh, black, waters. The two and
a half tribes continued their righteous practices and their service in
the Jerusalem temple during this period. This is confirmed by the
description of the righteous reign of King Hezekiah (63:1–11). These

---

[191] Cf. similar tendencies in 2 Sam 24:5–7; 1 Kgs 4:7–19; 8:65; 2 Chr 7:8; Josephus, *Ant.*
7.2.2; *Targum Ps* 110:3, and the territorial alternative in 1 Kgs 4:21, 24; 1 Chr 13:5. Cf.
also Ginzberg, *Legends VI,* 254.

[192] With the exception of the tribal lands east of the Jordan.

[193] *2 Bar.* 1:2; 77:19–78:1.

tribes thus continued to uphold life in the Land. And due to the triumphs of Hezekiah, the Holy Land rejoiced (63:10).

However, what is the territorial reference of the Holy Land during Hezekiah's reign? Is the assumed territory under Hezekiah's command equivalent to the implied territorial extent of David and Solomon's kingdom, or is the Land under Hezekiah's rule considerably smaller? As could be expected in context of the Apocalypse of the cloud, 63:1–11 does not describe the exact territorial extent of Hezekiah's kingdom. The passage does however tell us that Hezekiah was king of Judah (63:1). Since the two and a half tribes were his subjects (63:3), and not just the one tribe of Judah, we can be quite sure that "Judah" (*ihudā*) in this case refers to the Kingdom of Judah. The core territory of the Kingdom of Judah is commonly described as the elevated area between "Geba and Beer-Sheba" (2 Kgs 23:8). This indicates that the area Hezekiah had under his command was this area in the south of Palestine.[194]

However, the crux of the matter is the description of the relation between the two and a half tribes and Judah in *2 Bar.*63. 63:9–10 says: "For Zion was saved and Jerusalem exulted, and Israel was freed from siege. And all those who where in the holy land rejoiced and praised the name of the Mighty One so that it was spoken of." But who is Israel, the people who is freed from siege, in this passage? According to 63:3, the subjects of Hezekiah—"his people" (*'ameh*)—are equivalent to the two and a half tribes. The two and the half tribes are logically the ones who were threatened in 63:3 and subsequently freed from siege in 63:9. In 63:9, thus, the term 'Israel' probably applies to the two and a half tribes.[195] They are the righteous subjects of Hezekiah and those who inhabit Judah. When 63:9 then tells us that "those who were in the holy land rejoiced," it refers to the two and a half tribes—Israel—in Judah. The term 'the holy land' then refers to the area inhabited by faithful and righteous tribes. In this passage, thus, Judah is 'the holy land.'[196]

---

[194] Cf. also Jer 17:25–26.

[195] The term can possibly be applied for the ten tribes (cf. 62:3), but this is not probable in context of 62:4–63:10. 2 Kgs 17:3–6 confirms that the ten tribes remained in captivity.

[196] Several texts regard Judah as prominent. Cf. 2 Kgs 19:29–34; Isa 37:30–32; Zech 2:12; 2 Macc 1:1–7; 1QM XII, 13; XIX, 5; *T. Mos.* 2:3–5; 4:6. Cf. H. Stegemann, "'Das Land' in der Tempelrolle und in anderen Texten aus den Qumranfunden," in *Das Land Israel in biblischer Zeit: Jerusalem-Symposium 1981 der Hebräischen Universität und der Georg-August-Universität* (ed. G. Strecker; GTA 25; Göttingen: Vandenhoeck & Ruprecht, 1983),

Consequently, during the righteous reign of Hezekiah 'the holy land,' the Land belonging to Israel, applies to a much smaller territory than during the kingship of David and Solomon. Whereas the tribal lands of the twelve tribes constituted the territory of David and Solomon's Land, the tribal lands of the two and a half tribes compose the territory of Hezekiah's Land. However, although the extent of the Land was obviously heavily reduced by the disqualification of the Northern kingdom, Judah continued to qualify as the Land due to the righteousness of its inhabitants.

The Kidron Valley and 'the whole land'

2 Bar. 66:1 presents King Josiah as a king of Judah, like King Hezekiah before him. 66:1–8 asserts that Josiah purified the country from idols, that he expelled religious specialists foreign to Israel and that no-one un-circumcised or wicked could inhabit "the whole land" (kulāh arʿā). But, what geographical entity is 'the whole land' in this context?[197]

Like 2 Bar. 61 and 63 before it, 66:1–8 does not provide any explicit territorial information. However, in contrast to the passages discussed above, 66:1–8 does not mention the tribal identity of the inhabitants of Josiah's kingdom either. We could imagine that the two and a half tribes were Josiah's subjects, since Josiah after all is king of Judah. However, as I have already pointed out, the two and a half tribes were doomed during the reign of Manasseh due to their wickedness.[198] Although the two and a half tribes were not yet exiled, the prophecy of their coming exile was explicitly stressed during the reign of Manasseh in 64:5. Their wicked status may be the reason why these tribes are not mentioned during the reign of the righteous Josiah, in contrast to the description of the reign of his righteous predecessor, King Hezekiah.[199] Due to this

---

154–171 at 163; Davies, *Territorial Dimension*, 62; L.I. Lied, "Frå Palestina til himmelen: Forestillingane om Landet i Testamentet til Moses," (Masters thesis, University of Bergen, 2000), 51–56. Note further that we may ascribe universal aspirations to King Hezekiah as well (63:8–10). Cf. also the fluidity of core land and power sphere, and the middle position of Samaria in the biblical accounts of Hezekiah and Josiah (2 Kgs 14:23–29; 23:17–20).

[197] Note that 2 Kgs 22–23 provides Josiah's kingship with a clear centre in Jerusalem, a kingdom in Judah, and a power sphere that comprises Samaria and the North as well.

[198] 2 Kgs 21:12–14; 2 Chr 33:7–8. Cf. 2 Bar. 1:3.

[199] 2 Bar. 1:2 holds the two and a half tribes responsible for the destruction of the temple. When the temple falls, there is only a small remnant left (2:1; 5:5).

status of the two and half tribes we cannot identify with certainty the extent of the Land under Josiah's rule by reference to tribal lands.

Josiah's kingdom is not void of inhabitants, but they are identified by other characteristics than tribal affiliation. 66:2 describes the righteous, the wise in understanding, and the priests, and 66:5 includes the faithful and circumcised[200] as its inhabitants. Thus, even more than before, the inhabitants of Josiah's Land are identified by their righteousness, their faithful status and function as cultic assembly.

The Kidron Valley: Outside and Beyond

To help us identify the location and extent of Josiah's Land, however, 66:4 in fact refers explicitly to a well known landscape in Judah. In contrast to the generally fluid description of inhabitants and geographical extent in 66:1–8, this passage mentions the Kidron valley (*naḥlā dqedrun*). What is the function of the Kidron valley in this passage? 66:3–4 says:

> And not only did he kill the wicked that were living, but also the bones of the dead they brought out of the graves and burned in the fire. (…), and the polluted [ones] he burned in the fire, and the lying prophets which deceived the people he also burned in the fire, and the people who obeyed them when they were living, he brought to the Kidron valley, and heaped stones upon them.

In this passage, the Kidron valley functions as a place of punishment and execution. It is not clear whether the passage locates only the stoning of those who listened to false prophets there, or whether the fire that burns the polluted ones is there as well.[201] Both options are possible. The depictions of King Josiah's acts in 2 Kgs 23:4, 6 and 12 probably resound in 66:4's reference to the Kidron valley. According to 2 Kgs 23, Josiah destroyed and burned impure vessels, idols, and altars in the valley. Likewise, the righteous kings Asa and Hezekiah of Judah both burned or threw away idols, altars, and other unclean objects in the Kidron gorge.[202] In those accounts, the Kidron valley stands forth as a dump particularly fit for extinguishing impure cultic objects. In the case of *2 Bar.* 66, however, the Kidron receives wicked people doomed to punishment and destruction, not impure objects for annihilation. It

---

[200] Or, "no uncircumcised or accused inhabitant."
[201] Cf. the reference to tormenting fire in *2 Bar.* 44:15; 59:2; 64:7. According to the *Targum Ruth* 1:17 burning by fire and stoning are two out of four death penalties. The other two are execution by sword and hanging on wood.
[202] 1 Kgs 15:13; 2 Chr 29:16; 30:14.

is possible that 66:4 combines acts that 2 Kings held apart. 2 Kgs 23:15 and 20 say that King Josiah burned the bones of the wicked dead on the altars of the high places of the Northern kingdom to defile these foreign sanctuaries, whereas the ashes of the Asherah image he burned in the Kidron valley he spread upon the graves of common people as an act of disgrace (23:7). These graves of common people could have been in the caves of the Kidron valley, since the Kidron valley was also known as a burial site.[203] It is thus possible that 66:3–4 connect all these acts of King Josiah to the Kidron valley, or that *2 Baruch* extends the function of the valley to apply also to people, not only to objects.[204] At any rate, in 66:3–4 the Kidron valley serves as a fitting locale for Josiah's disposal of impure and sinful subjects.

The role of the Kidron valley with regard to the extent of Josiah's Land, however, is not yet clear. The Kidron valley is mentioned two more times in *2 Baruch*, in 5:5 and 21:1–2. In both cases the Kidron valley is first and foremost conceived as a place outside Jerusalem. According to 5:5, Baruch brings the nobles of the people to the Kidron valley when God asks him to leave the city (2:1). The Kidron valley thus becomes a prototype outside-space in *2 Baruch*.[205] In this manner, *2 Baruch* attests to a common understanding of this valley. 2 Sam 15:23 and 1 Kgs 2:37 both present the Kidron valley as being outside Jerusalem and as the closest part of the wilderness east of Jerusalem. The valley is where the wilderness starts. Moreover, the topography of the site and the surrounding landscape adds to the impression of the reader of *2 Baruch* that the Kidron is a place outside and different from Jerusalem. The Kidron is a gorge, and thus commonly conceived of as a topographical opposite to the elevated area of the city and its temple. This topographical aspect to the Kidron valley highlights its role as a landscape conventionally connected to death and punishment, as opposed to the idealised view of Jerusalem with its temple on high.[206]

---

[203] Note that the Kidron valley was associated with the graves of the prophets Isaiah, Haggai and Zechariah (*Liv. Pro.* 1:9, 15:6). It is also possible that the royal necropolis and the graveyard of the priests were placed there. This is, however, uncertain (D.R.A. Hare, "The Lives of the Prophets," in vol. 2 of *OTP* (ed. J.H. Charlesworth; 2 vols; Garden City, NY: Doubleday, 1985), 379–399 at 386; Mare, *Kidron*, 38; Bogaert, *Apocalypse de Baruch I*, 328–330). *b. Meg.* 17b–18a describes the Kidron valley as unclean (cf. Davies, *Gospel and Land*, 135–137).

[204] Notice the resemblances with the description of Jer 7:30–8:3 of the Valley of Hinnom. The Kidron valley joins with the Valley of Hinnom south of Jerusalem.

[205] Cf. *4 Bar.* 1:8; 4:4 who states that Baruch is located outside the city.

[206] Note that there are other, more positive, connotations to the Kidron valley as well.

Consequently, when King Josiah locates the sinful and impure elements in the Kidron valley he in effect locates them in a place outside and opposite Jerusalem. In this manner, Josiah cleanses his Land, as David and Hezekiah did before him.

Josiah's Land: Mapping the Remnant

But, how can the reference of the Kidron valley help us define the extent and location of Josiah's Land? As the prototypical opposite to Jerusalem and as the place where the wilderness outside Jerusalem starts, it is possible that the Kidron valley in fact serves as a border to the Land.[207] This interpretation is legitimate if the group of people mentioned in 66:2 may be identified as Land-definers. If this is the case, the size of Israel and the extent of the Land have again been reduced.

Let us look at 66:2 more carefully:

> And he purified the land from idols, and he sanctified all the vessels which had been polluted, the offerings he restored to the altar, and he raised the horn of the holy,[208] and he exalted the righteous, and he praised all those who were wise in understanding, and he brought the priests to their ministry, and blotted out and removed[209] the enchanters, magicians, and diviners from the land.

Firstly, as I have already argued, the presentation of Josiah's reign places a clear focus on the cult and the temple in Jerusalem. 66:2 deals first and foremost with Josiah's reestablishment of the Jerusalem sanctuary and the spatial focus of the passage is accordingly the temple. Secondly, the above discussion has shown that the extent of Josiah's Land is not at all clear, nor does the passage refer to landholding tribes which could indicate a territorial foundation for Josiah's kingdom.

Still, the group of people 66:2 does in fact mention, may give us a lead. The last part of the passage is most precise. It states that

---

The Kidron valley may be connected to the lush garden of the King (2 Kgs 25:4; Neh 3:15; maybe John 18:1 (Cf. Mare, *Kidron*, 37)). The valley is also the place of the Gihon, the water supply (Mare, *Kidron*, 37). Cf. further *Liv. Pro.* 1:2–10.

[207] *3 Baruch* refers to Baruch's location by the Kidron River. This may allude to the river as a border line. However, *3 Baruch* does not say on which shore Baruch is located.

[208] Cf. Violet, *Apokalypsen*, 302; Bogaert, *Apocalypse de Baruch I*, 511.

[209] *ṭā* may mean "to blot out," "efface," and "to cancel," while *bar* in the Aphʿel form means "to remove," "transfer," and "transplant" (Smith, *Dictionary*, 409 and 399). Thus, Josiah probably both killed and transported these religious specialists away from the Land.

the true priests came back into office and that they replaced religious specialists who were foreign to the cult of Israel's God.[210] This confirms the temple focus in the passage. The first part of the passage concerns "the righteous" and "those wise in understanding,"[211] in other words, the cultic assembly of Israel that still served God in the temple. 66:3–5 further suggests that this is the group that lives in covenantal space. 66:4 points out that Josiah reestablished the Sabbath. The Sabbath is the sign of the Mosaic covenant (Exod 31:12–18).[212] And 66:5 in fact defines the extent of the Land by referring to circumcision: "he [King Josiah] left no uncircumcised or accused inhabitant in the whole land all the days of his life." Thus, 'the whole land' turns into the Land of the circumcised in Josiah's day (66:5).[213] Since circumcision is the sign of the Abrahamic covenant (Gen 17:11), the Land of Josiah becomes the Land of those who remain faithful to the covenant of Abraham.

It is therefore possible that *2 Bar.* 66 presents only the temple and its immediate surroundings in Jerusalem as the extent of the Land in the days of Josiah. The sins of the two and a half tribes during the reign of Manasseh led to the rejection of their tribal lands, and there is only a faithful remnant left in Jerusalem. If this is the case, the Kidron valley does not only constitute the eastern border of Jerusalem: it is simultaneously the territorial border of Josiah's Land. The borders of the city Jerusalem and the Land of Josiah would in this case be identical.[214] Consequently, like 61:1–8 an 63:1–11 before it, 66:1–8 maps faithful inhabitants, and thereby points out the ultimate territorial stronghold of Israel in Palestine before the fall of the temple: Jerusalem. This understanding of Jerusalem and its temple in the tenth, bright, waters is relevant, since the eleventh, black, waters that follow (67:1–9) are dedicated the destruction of the temple and the city of Jerusalem.

Seen from this angle, the Apocalypse of the cloud tells a story of Israel's decline in Palestine. The reign of David and Solomon is generally renowned as a definite highpoint in Israel's life, with regard to power as well as extent. Accordingly, the Apocalypse of the cloud

---

[210] Cf. *T. Jud.* 23:1.

[211] This may be one group or two groups of people. It is most likely, however, that *2 Bar.* 66 describes the same group as both righteous and wise.

[212] Cf. Ezek 20:12; *Jub.* 2:17, 21.

[213] Cf. Isa 52:1; *Jub.* 15:28; 1 Macc 2:45–48; Cf. Kolenkow, "Introduction," 131.

[214] The Kidron valley is the eastern border, but by implication this border separates Jerusalem from the surroundings.

describes their Land as the largest and most powerful. The righteous kingdoms that succeeded the reign of David and Solomon have in contrast seen a steady deterioration. The number of faithful tribes has decreased and the extent of the Land these righteous subjects inhabit has diminished accordingly. The Apocalypse of the cloud first rejects the Northern kingdom. Then, the two and a half tribes and their areas are rejected during the reign of Manasseh. The two and a half tribes are possibly still present in Judah during the reign of Josiah, but since they are no longer faithful, they no longer inhabit the Land. During the time of Josiah there is thus only a faithful remnant left in Jerusalem.

The Lands of the Righteous Kings: Territory or Praxis?

This chapter has suggested that the inauguration of the temple and the introduction of righteous kingship shaped the Land as covenantal space within the region of Palestine. So, what is the relationship between the region of Palestine and the Land in the Apocalypse of the cloud, and why is the nature of this relationship relevant to the survival of Israel when the temple falls and the end-time is imminent? This chapter has pointed out two related tendencies which are both important to our understanding of the Land in 2 Baruch.

First, it is fruitful to assume that Land is shaped by Israel's practices. From the perspective of a praxis epistemology, we cannot understand the Land in the Apocalypse of the cloud as a passive territory which just lies there and waits to be populated. On the contrary, the tribes actively create and de-create Land depending on their faithfulness towards God and his covenant. The region of Palestine first becomes Land when David and Solomon provide Israel with an ordered reign and establish a house for divine presence among the inhabitants of the area. These institutions are, however, vulnerable. When wicked kings seize power and make their subjects turn to sin, God removes his presence and his blessings and leaves their territories to chaos. This conclusion shows that the Land cannot be seen as a territorial phenomenon only, as a territorial epistemology would presume. Although the Land always 'takes place', the regions of Palestine, Judah, and Jerusalem become Land only when Israel's actions comply with the demands of the covenant. Moreover, as the above study has suggested, the Apocalypse of the cloud first and foremost maps presence and practices, not territory. With few exceptions, it does not describe landscapes or territorial borders. When it describes the extent and location of the Land it always focuses on the righteous acts of Israel and the population of righteous tribes.

Second, the Apocalypse of the cloud describes three versions of the Land, or three Lands. The Apocalypse of the cloud tailors the righteous reigns according to the same pattern and continuously stresses that law-abiding practices and cultic service create Land. Still, the decreasing number of righteous tribes and the subsequent rejection of tribal areas during the course of Israel's history lead to the identification of three different territorial entities as Land: Palestine, Judah, and Jerusalem. All three areas share the temple as their centre, but since the extent of the area they cover varies considerably, each location creates a different atmosphere for the description of the Land. Although territory may not decide the definition of the Land, the territorial aspect is therefore still important in the description of it. The territory of David and Solomon's reign covers a wide area and shows that Israel is at the peak of worldly power. The territory of Hezekiah's Land still includes traditionally important territory, but the reduction of power is striking. Josiah's Land limits itself to Jerusalem. This central city remains on Israel's hands and the temple still stands, but the bliss that characterised the Land of former righteous kings no longer prevails. Jerusalem seems more like a last protected enclave[215] than a centre of worldwide power.

Land Construction and Eschatological Rhetoric

These descriptions of the Lands of the righteous kings in the Apocalypse of the cloud show how *2 Baruch* constructs the Lands of the past generations. How does this construction of the past become relevant to the remnant at the time of the fall of the temple, discussed in the previous chapter? Three aspects suggest that the construction and reshaping of the Land of the past in the Apocalypse of the cloud serve the need of an eschatological rhetoric. Firstly, the descriptions of Israel's life in the Land display what there potentially is to lose at the fall of the temple and the dispossession of Jerusalem. Israel is in danger of losing the spaces that provided triumph, mercy, protection, joy, as well we survival during the course of history. There is, in other words, due cause to Baruch's worries, discussed in the previous chapter.

---

[215] Cf. Smith, *Map*, 109.

Secondly, the Apocalypse of the cloud offers an explanation for Israel's loss of the temple, Jerusalem, and the Land. The scheme of alternating black and bright periods shows that Israel is herself responsible for the destruction and dispossession, since history proves that God responds to her failing fulfilment of covenantal duties. At the same time, the apocalypse also explains how she can regain the loss and achieve blessing: Israel has to stay righteous and live according to the Law.

A third aspect is crucial to the current discussion. I have suggested that Jerusalem and its temple became the *only* explicit geographical reference at the time of King Josiah. But, as pointed out in Chapter Two, the inhabitants of Jerusalem caused the city to be lost to the enemy when they turned impious. Baruch witnesses how Israel loses Jerusalem, the last area recognisable as Israel's Land in the Apocalypse of the cloud. However, since the design of the space Israel inhabited in the past was, implicitly, shaped by her practices, the design of future spaces will also be shaped by her actions. The varying territorial extent of the Land in the Apocalypse of the cloud implies that Israel is not necessarily dependent on a defined region to survive. The Land-concept is in other words not intrinsically dependent on the region of Palestine. This observation is important as the remnant group, Baruch and his followers, leaves Jerusalem at the eve of the destruction of the temple and enters the Kidron valley as the end-time sets in.

The following two chapters of this study will discuss how *2 Baruch* constructs alternative spaces for Israel in the aftermath of the destruction.

CHAPTER FOUR

THE CITY OF THE PILLAR AND THE WALL: LANDSCAPES OF THE END-TIME

The temple has fallen. Jerusalem, and the Lands of past generations, have been lost. The consequences are devastating to the present world. Since the last enclave of righteousness in an otherwise wicked world is now gone and no-one is attending to the cult that maintains cosmos, godlessness is universal and Creation is necessarily heading towards chaos and final destruction.

The previous chapters showed the important role the Land played in the history of Israel prior to the destruction of the temple. However, *2 Baruch* stresses the necessity of the destruction, and explains that it is part of God's overall plan for Israel's redemption. There are other spaces waiting for Israel in the future, first and foremost in the other world. As we already know, redemption will not come immediately, but has been postponed in time and in place to an eschatological future, to the Messianic reign and to the other world. *2 Baruch* thus allows for a period of chaos between the fall of the temple and the establishment of the Messianic reign, which will be the beginning of redemption. This period is the end-time.

In this chapter I will examine the spaces of the end-time, since the end of time is also an end of space. I will first address *2 Baruch's* general descriptions of the landscapes of the end-time in order to isolate the most important rhetorical devices of the text. I will then look at the function of the Kidron valley for the righteous remnant during the end-time, and in particular the description of the community of the righteous as a fortified city within the valley in 2:1–2. The main questions the chapter poses are: how does *2 Baruch* envisage the remnant's marginal existence outside the temple centred Land, and how does *2 Baruch* construct space during the end-time to promote the future redemption and life of Israel?

Reversals and Mega-events in the Universal Wilderness

What is the end-time, and what characterises its spatiality? As I suggested in Chapter Two, *2 Baruch* links the beginning of the end-time with the removal of the divine presence and the destruction of Jerusalem and its temple. In the wake of the fall of the temple, the world enters a process of destruction that will not end until the corruptible world is destroyed.[1] In the Apocalypse of the cloud, a thirteenth water follows the twelve waters of world history (69:1–5), discussed in Chapter Three. We can identify this thirteenth water as the end-time:

> For the last waters you have seen which were blacker than all those preceding them, those which came after the twelfth, those which were brought together; they concern the whole world. (…) Therefore, these were neither black waters with black, nor bright waters with bright. For that was the end (*šulāmā*).

This passage gives a rather typical description of the end-time, pointing out some of its important features: the end-time is beyond world history, it is a period of compressed and intense terror and it affects the entire world.[2]

How does *2 Baruch* describe the end-time's corresponding spaces? As the previous chapters pointed out, there is an important link between wickedness and devastation.[3] The mechanism works as follows: ungodliness produces wilderness or, in other words, moral disaster brings ecological as well as cosmic disaster.[4] So, whereas Creation originally attested to the greatness of its creator, mankind's mistaken action has turned it into a chaos. Creation will therefore necessarily be destroyed. And, given that the act of creation was commonly understood as an ordering event, the time of disorder at the end is therefore a process of de-creation. This very process of destruction characterizes the end-time and its spaces.

In the context of Baruch's lamentation at the fall of Zion in 10:6–8 we find the following call:

---

[1] For discussions of the term 'end-time,' cf. Henze, *Syriac Apocalypse of Daniel*, 70–71; 75; M.E. Stone, *Fourth Ezra: A Commentary on the Book of Fourth Ezra* (Hermeneia; Minneapolis: Fortress Press, 1990), 103–105; J.J. Collins, "Apocalyptic Eschatology as the Transcendence of Death," *CBQ* 36 (1974): 21–48 at 26.

[2] Cf. also *2 Bar.* 27:13.

[3] Cf. Jer 12:10; 50:12; Mic 7:13.

[4] Cf. Münchow, *Ethik*, 102; Himmelfarb, *Ascent to Heaven*, 73–79; Boorer, "Earth/Land," 26; Fretheim, "Whole Earth," 232–233; Blenkinsopp, *Treasures*, 49.

Blessed is he who was not born, or he who was born and died. But we, the living ones, woe to us! We saw the afflictions of Zion and that which happened to Jerusalem. I call the sirens from the sea, and you, liliths, from the desert and demons and jackals from the forest. Wake up, and gird your loins for mourning, and take up lamentation with me, and mourn with me!

In this passage, Baruch calls demons, phantoms and beasts from the sea, the desert and the forest.[5] Baruch summons these forces of chaos to share in the lamentation over the destruction of Zion and Jerusalem.[6] This description of the inauguration of the end-time reveals some basic characteristics of its landscapes. 10:8 attests to a perceived demarcation between inhabited parts of the earth, and landscapes of wilderness such as forest, sea and desert.[7] The forces of chaos are called from their normal habitats where man does *not* live to the part of the earth where humans *do* live.[8] Thus, the passage describes how Baruch summons creatures of chaos from the surrounding wilderness and asks them to join him in the lament over the loss of the last part of Creation which still was inhabitable: the Land where Israel once lived (10:7). In a sense, Baruch invites the forces of chaos to break down the borders of that remaining Land. Forest demons, sirens from the sea and the liliths of the desert intrude from the landscapes of the surrounding wilderness, adding the former Land to their habitat. From this point onwards Creation is all wilderness.[9]

Note that the term 'wilderness' comprises several different landscapes. As 10:8 suggests, the term includes waters in various forms, forests and arid landscapes such as deserts.[10] This means that wilderness can be arid, densely forested, and flooded at the same time (cf. 77:14). The common denominator of all the landscapes on earth that con-

---

[5] These beasts and demons are commonly connected to various landscapes of the wilderness. Cf. Isa 34:12–15; *4 Ezra* 5:6–8. Cf. Charles, *Apocalypse of Baruch*, 15–16; Bogaert, *Apocalypse de Baruch II*, 28–31, and Violet for an alternative interpretation (*Apokalypsen*, 215). Beasts and demons are also associated with foreign kingdoms (Cf. *Targum Jonathan to Deut* 32:23–24).

[6] Sea and desert are both areas of chaos and death. The sea and its monsters were commonly seen as the main agents of chaos (Cf. 2 Sam 23:3–4; Ps 46:3; Cf. Levenson, *Sinai and Zion*, 109). According to F. Stolz, sea is also associated with desert ("Sea," *DDD*, 740–742).

[7] Cf. *4 Ezra* 4:13–21.

[8] Cf. further *1 En.* 89:55–57; *T. Mos.* 3:4; *Apoc. El. (H)* 4:26–27.

[9] Cf. further Smith, *Map*, 109.

[10] Cf. Jer 2:6; 26:18; *1 En.* 28:1; 77:4.

stitute the wilderness is that they are not inhabited. The wilderness
is the uninhabitable world. We must, however, add some important
nuances to this definition. Firstly, since acts of wickedness cause devastation, wilderness is a flexible and expanding space. Throughout world
history it has steadily grown at the expense of the inhabitable world.
Secondly, and consequently, the constitutive aspect of the inhabitable
world is its inhabitance by righteous, law-abiding people, not mankind
as such. The contrast between the wilderness and the inhabitable world
is therefore also a contrast between the spaces of wicked and righteous
people.

Thus, the main thrust in *2 Baruch*'s description of end-time geography
is the presentation of the entire world as a wilderness. As pointed
out in the previous chapters, Jerusalem, as the last place to give in,
merges with her surroundings and also becomes part of the worldwide
wilderness. This is thus the final transformation from order into chaos.
The world has now become totally uninhabitable.

In the following discussion I will continue to study how *2 Baruch*
describes the spaces of the end-time. Two intertwined tendencies distinguish *2 Baruch*'s descriptions. Firstly, *2 Baruch* makes the end-time into
a mega-event, and describes its corresponding spaces accordingly. Secondly, the spaces of the end-time are characterised by so-called eschatological reversals. As we shall see, these two tendencies are often closely
connected. Moreover, *2 Baruch* concentrates on two spatial levels: the
first is a particular focus on Jerusalem and its temple; the second is a
universal level focusing on the entire world.

Identifying the Mega-event: Exile in the Wilderness of the Wicked

As I pointed out in the introductory chapter of this study, it is generally acknowledged that *2 Baruch* models the destruction of the Second
Temple in 70 c.e. on the fall of the First Temple in 587 b.c.e. Although
the figures and the events described by the text belong to the age of
the fall of the First Temple, it is evident that its focus is the current crisis that has befallen Israel after the destruction of the Second Temple.
The event that *2 Baruch* describes can thus be approached as an interplay of the two crises. By blending these two scenarios, *2 Baruch* melts
historical layers into one, and makes the two destructions of Jerusalem
and its temple happen simultaneously. This adds to the intensity of the
destruction. C. Sulzbach has identified this relatively common rhetorical move as "the phenomenon of a collapsing of events into one mega-

event."[11] However, *2 Baruch* does not only create the narrative of the frame story by means of this rhetorical device, we also find the same phenomenon at work in the presentation of the end-time. As I pointed out above, 69:1 describes the end-time as an accumulated and intensified version of past evil events applicable to the whole world. Thus, *2 Baruch* piles crisis upon crisis to explain the impact of the ultimate calamity.

Landscapes of Exile and Oppression: Fusion of Exiles

2 Baruch identifies the terror of the end-time as an exilic experience. In the end-time divine presence has retracted from the earth, the wicked are triumphant everywhere and oppress Israel (e.g., 67:2). During the end-time the entire world therefore becomes a place of exile and oppression to Israel.[12] In *2 Baruch*'s sketch of the last exile,[13] former places of deportation blend into the description of the exile of the end-time.

8:4–5 describes the deportation of the two wicked tribes after the destruction of the temple. Basing the description of the end-time on the story of the crisis of 587 B.C.E., the geographical point of departure is the deportation from Jerusalem to Babylon:

> And it happened after these things that the army of the Chaldeans entered and seized the house and all that surrounds it. And they led the people away captive and killed some. And they bound King Zedekiah and sent him to the king of Babylon (8:4–5).

This version of the uprooting of the two and a half tribes to Babylon introduces *2 Baruch*'s account of the ultimate exile.[14] Starting from the narrative frame, *2 Baruch* expands its version of the story, merging the

---

[11] C. Sulzbach, personal communication. Cf. further Soja, *Postmodern*, 2–3. This relatively common rhetoric tool is used to describe the result of the temple fall in *2 Baruch*, *4 Ezra*, and in somewhat later rabbinic literature (Cf. Bogaert, *Apocalypse de Baruch I*, 103).

[12] Cf. *2 Bar.* 27:13.

[13] I understand 'exile' first and foremost as the experience of being away from God's presence (in one version or another) and the community of the righteous, and not necessarily as being away from Palestine. Note that *2 Bar.* 1.4 describes how destruction brings the people and Jerusalem "away from before my presence" (1.4). Cf. Violet, *Apokalypsen*, 204. Cf. further 2 Kgs 17:20, 23; 23:27; 24:3; Jer 32:31.

[14] Compare 2 Kgs 25. 2 Chr 36, *Bar* 1, *4 Bar.* 3; 5:19; 6:20.

exile in Egypt with the deportation to Babylon.[15] Whereas Jer 43:6–
7 states that Jeremiah left for Egypt, *2 Bar.* 10:2 and 33:1–3 claim that
he followed the captives to Babylon.[16] Moreover, when *2 Baruch* speaks
explicitly about the turmoil of the end in apocalyptic sequences,[17] a
special role is ascribed to Egypt and the Egyptians.[18] The Egyptians are
described as extraordinarily cruel oppressors in a number of contemporary texts. The wickedness of Egypt in *2 Bar.* 58:1 is paralleled by the
descriptions of their cruelty in *L.A.B.* 9:1, in *1 En.* 89:15–22 and *Jub.*
46:11–16.[19] The Egyptians are therefore exceptionally fit for the role of
oppressors in the end-time. The darkness (*heṣukā*) connected to Egypt in
59:2, is also a distinguishing mark of the end.[20] In fact, 75:7–8 likens the
present, corruptible, world with Egypt. Egypt thus becomes the main
symbol of a place of exile and wickedness: the first exile informs the
last.[21]

2 Baruch also blends the exile in Babylon with the uprooting and
the oppression of the people by the Romans.[22] "Now" (*hāšā*) in 67:1

---

[15] Cf. *4 Bar.* 6:23–25; *Targum Jonathan to Isa* 10:32. It is quite common to blend
different historic enemies. For instance, Edom blends with Rome in *Targum Lam* 4:22.

[16] The suggestion that Jeremiah went to Babylon (*2 Bar.* 10:2–4; 33:1–2) is found
in several texts (cf. 4Q385a, *4 Bar.* 3:11; *Pesiq. Rab.* 26:18, 2 Macc 2:1–4; cf. Henze,
"Jeremiah"). Possibly, Jeremiah was only supposed to support the captives and then
come back (Cf. *Pesiq. Rab.* 6:6). However, since Baruch has the leading role in *2 Baruch*,
this is not probable. Jeremiah's return would compromise Baruch's leading position.
Note also that *2 Baruch*'s localisation of Baruch in the Kidron valley may be understood
according to the similar logic. Canonical Jeremiah locates Baruch in Egypt, while later
rabbinic sources locate him in Babylon. So, Baruch stays in the region of Palestine,
unlike the canonical Baruch-figure who goes to Babylon, according to Bar 1:1–4.
2 Baruch sends Jeremiah instead and lets Baruch send a letter to the tribes in Babylon.
(Cf. Bogaert, *Apocalypse de Baruch I*, 103).

[17] Cf. *2 Bar.* 22–30; 35–40; 53–74.

[18] Cf. Ezek 19:4–9; Bar 1:1–4; *4 Bar.* 4:5 (Babylon, though earlier than in the parallel
sequence in *2 Bar*), *Pesiq. Rab.* 26:6 (according to Klijn, "2 Baruch," 823). The description of idolatry in 5:1 may also allude to Egypt, since Egypt was particularly infamous
for idolatry (Isa 19:1; *Liv. Pro.* 2:8, and as a motif in *Joseph and Aseneth* and in the *Apocalypse of Abraham*). It is, however, also possible that the remark refers to the exile of the
ten tribes by the Assyrians (62:1–8). Or, both interpretations may be implied. Note also
the merging of Egypt with Assyria in Isa 19:23–25.

[19] Egypt is also the most articulate foreign land, a land of slavery and oppression,
where Israel is orphan and helpless like a baby (according to *Targum Jonathan to Ezek*
16:4). Egypt is envisioned as a prison in *Targum Ps* 68:7.

[20] *2 Bar.* 46:3, 77:13–14. Cf. Isa 8:22–9:2; 10:24–26; 11:16; *L.A.B.* 19:12–13; *Sib. Or.*
5.477; *Targum Onkelos to Exod* 12:41–42.

[21] Egypt is explicitly equated with the world of the end-time in *Targum Onkelos to Exod*
12:41–42.

[22] Compare *Sib. Or.* 5.143; Rev 14:8; 16:19; 18:2 (Russell, *Method and Message*, 211).

may refer both to the time of Baruch—the time of the First Temple—
and to the here and now of the second destruction (67:1, 7). Likewise,
scholars generally acknowledge that Rome is being referred to as the
fourth and ultimate wicked oppressor in the Apocalypse of the vine and
the cedar (39:5), pointing far beyond the time and place of the frame
story. Consequently, in the various accounts of the Babylonian exile
in *2 Baruch*, the author blends the exile in Egypt with the dispersion
effected by the Romans.[23]

Through this procedure of merging former exiles, *2 Baruch* highlights
how the end-time exile exceeds all of its predecessors. The ultimate
exile encompasses all former exiles in its intensity. Indeed, the last exile
is even harsher than the summary of the former would imply. In a
blending of former oppressors, the author of *2 Baruch* creates a fusion
of time and place befitting of a final exile of universal extent. Places
are merged through shared connotations and interwoven allusions in
the repeating history of Israel, making the final exile into a mega-event.
Thus the final exile will be felt all around the world, in a manner which
far exceeds the effect of former events of oppression.

The universal proportions of the last exilic oppression underscore the
intensity of the ultimate exile. The universal nature of this final crisis is
expressed in various ways throughout *2 Baruch*. As was shown above, the
author expresses himself through highly apocalyptic imagery (e.g., 53:2–
3). Moreover, in 78:4, in the context of the *Epistola Baruch*, the same idea
is stated when Baruch argues for the unity of the people, even in exile:
"Indeed, I know, behold, all twelve tribes are bound by one chain, in
as much as we are born from one father?"[24] This remark on the shared
situation of the twelve tribes does *not* refer to a common location. On
the contrary, the scattering of the tribes has been emphasised, and the
scattering is also the explicit motivation for the writing of the Epistle
(77; 1:4). Whereas two tribes, or two and a half, are captives in Babylon
(1:2; 64:5; 77:17), ten tribes, alternatively nine and a half, are sojourning
in an unspecified place of dispersion, maybe in Assyria.[25] In addition,
a remnant is left in the Kidron valley outside Jerusalem.[26] Baruch's

---

[23] Another possible reference is Assyria (Cf. 5:1; 62:1–7).

[24] Cf. *T. Mos.* 3:5–7. According to Bogaert and Whitters, the passage could refer
to a common captivity, but also to the common observance of the Law (Bogaert,
Apocalypse de Baruch I, 333; Whitters, *Epistle*, 55. Cf. further Violet, *Apokalypsen*, 350; Klijn,
"2 Baruch," 648).

[25] Cf. *2 Bar.* 62:7. At least east of the river Euphrates (77:22).

[26] Cf. *2 Bar.* 5:5; 10:5; 31–34; 44:1; 77:6.

statement suggests a common experience, which embraces all of the tribes in dispersion. It points out the contrast between the common ancestor of the past and the diffusion of his descendants in the end-time. This statement on the one hand sets a universal exile up against a particular and local home, and on the other hand, shows a fusion of locations, as it embraces and annuls the particularity associated with the various places of exile throughout history. As a result, it makes the exile of the end-time the universal, all embracing exilic experience of Israel.

End-Time Reversals

A second literary device also characterises *2 Baruch*'s descriptions of the end-time: the reversal of Creation, including all of its structures and institutions.[27] When describing the general atmosphere of the end, *2 Baruch* stresses its inverted nature, for instance in the description of the very last black waters in the Apocalypse of the cloud:

> And the insolent will rule over the honourable, and the unworthy will raise themselves over the glorious. And many will be delivered to the few, those who are nothing will rule over the strong, the poor will have abundances beyond the rich, and the impious will exalt themselves over heroes. The wise will be silent, and the foolish will speak (70:3–4).

This imagery of reversal shows the flavour of *2 Baruch*'s end-time: every ideal is turned upside down.[28] How then, does the reversed imagery of the end apply to the landscapes of the end-time? In the previous chapter I discussed *2 Baruch*'s idea that the world was originally created for Israel, and the notion that Creation should benefit those who lived in it righteously. When the end-time sets in, however, Creation does not benefit Israel, but suffers under the triumph of Israel's enemies. So, just as the end of time is an era of exile and oppression for Israel, the world is a place of happiness for the wicked.[29] Thus, the carefree world of the wicked is a feature of the emerging picture of the reversed world of end-time.

---

[27] This is a common rhetorical move (also outside Jewish-Christian circles). Cf., e.g., Isa 64:10. Cf. Whitters, *Epistle*, 93–96.

[28] Cf. *2 Bar.* 48:33–35; 51:13; 70:3–6; 83:9–23 in addition to *T. Mos.* 6 and *Apoc. El. (H)* 2:29–38.

[29] Cf. *Jub.* 23:19. Cf. Kolenkow, "Introduction," 108.

Jerusalem, Harlot and Lonely Mother: The Impulse of Babylon and Sodom

The phenomenon of eschatological reversals sheds light on *2 Baruch*'s description of post-destruction Jerusalem, the most important spot in the universal, exilic wilderness. *2 Bar.* 10:16, discussed in Chapter Two, describes Jerusalem as the lonely mother. The mother sees the dispersal of her offspring and mourns over her great loss.[30] 11:1–2 extends this motif by comparing Jerusalem's misery to the current joy of Babylon:

> Now I, Baruch, say this to you, O Babylon: If you had lived in prosperity and Zion dwelt in her glory, it would have been a great sorrow to us that you had been equal to Zion. But now, behold, the grief is infinite and the lamentation immeasurable, because, behold, you are prosperous and Zion is desolate (*ḥarbā*).

This passage clearly displays the reversal of Jerusalem's position.[31] She, who once was Babylon's superior, has been destroyed, whereas Babylon has assumed the position Jerusalem once had in the world (cf. 67:2–6). This switch or roles turns the common connotations of these well-known biblical cities around. The joy that should belong to life in Jerusalem has been replaced by grief and lawlessness during the end-time. The honoured mother Jerusalem of the past is now addressed in a language of sorrow.[32] In addition, this common rhetorical device of comparing Jerusalem to Babylon, the harlot, creates an ambiguous picture of the city. The motif of Babylon as a harlot in a sense contradicts the concept of Jerusalem as a mother.[33] Still, both motifs attest to the notion of eschatological reversal and strengthen its intensity. The honoured Jerusalem has turned into the harlot-mother of the end-time.

---

[30] Cf. *2 Bar.* 3:1, 3; 67:1–9.

[31] The notion of Jerusalem as mother is widespread. So is the notion of Jerusalem as the lonely, the old, or unwilling, mother (Cf. Isa 49:21; 51:16; 54:1; Jer 50:12; Lam 4:22; Hos 4:5; *4 Ezra* 4:17–29; 5:50; 10:7; Matt 23:27; Gal 4:25). Cf. Charles, *Apocalypse of Baruch*, 4; Bogaert, *Apocalypse de Baruch II*, 12; Murphy, *Structure and Meaning*, 81; Whitters, *Epistle*, 116–117 and particularly Rosenberg, "Link to the Land," 141–146.

[32] Cf. Jer 50:12–13.

[33] Cf. Rev 14:8; 17:5; Cf. also Gaca, *Fornication*, 170–176. It is hard to tell whether *2 Bar.* 3:1–3 sees the evil deeds taking place in Jerusalem as the *acts* of the mother or as an *assault* on the mother (cf. 77:9–10), and consequently whether the description is modelled on the whore motif of Ezekiel, or the victim motif of *4 Ezra* 2 and 10. Both may be hinted at, since *bištā* (3:1, 3) can be translated both "evil" and "misfortune" (Smith, *Dictionary*, 43). However, the results are the same: Jerusalem is brought to justice and is punished by destruction. Cf. further Harrington, "Holy Land," 671.

By way of allusions, *2 Bar.* 14 also compares Jerusalem to Sodom.
As Sayler has pointed out, Baruch's discussion with God over the destiny of Jerusalem in 14:6–8 can be read as an allusion to the story of
Abraham's discussion with God about the destruction of Sodom and
Gomorrah in Gen 18–19.[34] Baruch repeats the main argument of Abraham's haggling with God in the Genesis story: Jerusalem should have
been saved by the righteous few living there. However, since God has
commanded Baruch and his followers—the last righteous inhabitants
of Jerusalem—to leave the city (2:1), Jerusalem faces the same destiny as Sodom and Gomorrah. In other words, Baruch's argumentation in 14:6–8 shows that *2 Baruch* views Jerusalem as the Sodom and
Gomorrah of the end-time.[35] The transgressions of Jerusalem's inhabitants have thus turned God against the city and led to its destruction.[36]

Thus, by referring to Babylon, Sodom, and Gomorrah, *2 Baruch*
triggers the connotations associated with these well known biblical cities
to create a reversed picture of Jerusalem in the end-time.[37]

Landscapes of Death

Originally, Creation was intended for the living. However, due to the
universal triumph of godlessness, *2 Baruch* presents the world of the end-
time as a dying world and a realm of the dead.[38] The text describes the
mechanisms of the end-time world as a process of dying, and interprets
the period in terms of decay and degeneration:

> For the youth of the world has passed away, and the strength of Creation
> is sufficiently exhausted, and the advent of the times decrease rapidly and
> passes by, and the pitcher is near the well, and the ship to the port, and
> the course of the journey to the city and life to the completion (85:10).

From Baruch's point of view, the direction of the world is clear: "From
now, therefore, everything is in a state of dying (*kyānā māyutā*)" (21:22).[39]

---

[34] Sayler, *Promises*, 91–95.
[35] Cf. Isa 1:8–10; CD II; *T. Naph.* 4:1; *T. Benj.* 9:1; Rev 11:8; Jude 7. God's judgement
of Sodom and Gomorrah appears as a central motif in descriptions of the state of
the wicked after the final judgement (*Gk. Apoc. Ezra* 7:13). Allusions to Sodom and
Gomorrah are also found in descriptions of the sufferings in hell (*T. Isaac* 5:27).
[36] Cf. the link between whoredom and death in Hos 4.
[37] Note also that the destruction of Jerusalem is made into yet another mega-event.
This is the ultimate destruction of a sinful city.
[38] Cf. *2 Bar.* 10:9–12; 21:22–23; 43:2–3; 51:16.
[39] Cf. *2 Bar.* 19:5; 44:10–14. Cf. Hos 4:2–3.

Through the use of contrastive imagery of life and death, *2 Baruch* points out how the degenerative process accelerates and leads the world towards total destruction.[40]

In this world of death and deterioration, Baruch claims that the end-time is better for the dead than for the living. For example, Baruch would rather be dead than see Jerusalem destroyed (3:2). He claims that the dead are generally more happy than the living (11:4–7) and he envies those who were not even born (10:6).[41] These statements of course underscore the intensity of the end-time afflictions, but they also display how abnormal the world has become. The world serves the dead instead of the living and the wicked instead of the righteous.

These descriptions of the dying world of the end-time stand in stark contrast to what was the expressed purpose of Creation. The world, which was once created for the living, for Israel and the patriarchs, is now the realm of the wicked and the dead.[42] The purpose, as well as the course of the world, has been turned upside down.

Making Landscapes of End-Time

The above outline shows that the spaces of the end-time are confusing and paradoxical spaces. The dying world has its own logic of reversals and compiled evil events. By turning the end-time into a mega-event, *2 Baruch* unites specific experiences in the history of Israel to highlight the ultimate character of the end. Likewise, when the world is turned upside down, it becomes clear that time beyond history adheres to deviant rules. The prime spatial expression of this process is the universal wilderness. The dying, godless, world has thus become a gigantic, chaotic, landscape.[43] It is safe to say that *2 Baruch*'s wilderness is portrayed as a typical anti-place or a non-place. The end-time wilderness is both beyond world history and beyond the inhabitable world. This means that it is situated outside the limitations of ordinary time and space. The general void of divine presence creates exile everywhere, regardless of and despite any former spatial distinctions. Death, whoring, barrenness, sorrow, and utter chaos dominate entirely.

---

[40] Cf. *2 Bar.* 3:7; 14:14; 70:6–10.
[41] Cf. further *2 Bar.* 48:41 and 52:2–4. Cf *Apoc. El. (H)* 2:5, 37.
[42] *2 Bar.* 14:19; 15:7; 21:24. Cf. *4 Ezra* 6:59; 7:10; 8:1; *T. Mos.* 1:13.
[43] It is a common strategy in the first centuries CE to describe end-time reversals in terms of transformation of landscapes. Cf., e.g., *4 Ezra* 6:18–24; *Targum Jonathan to Isa* 10:33.

These are the circumstances in which the remnant has to survive. This marginalised group of righteous people is the sole law-abiding community on earth. They are thus essentially different from their surroundings. How can they survive?

Gathering in the Kidron Valley: The Paradoxes of the Wilderness

To *2 Baruch* it is of pivotal importance that the remnant survives through the hardships of the end-time. Of all the places in the chaotic wilderness of the end, *2 Baruch* chooses to situate this last group of righteous people, the followers of Baruch, in the Kidron valley (*2 Bar.* 5–6). As Chapter Three of this study pointed out, the Kidron valley was in no way a fitting place of sojourn for righteous people. 66:4 describes the valley of Kidron as a place of punishment, a dump for illicit cultic objects, as well as a graveyard. In addition, its topography marks it as dark and lowly, in contrast to the lofty and glorious city of Jerusalem. The Kidron valley is thus hopelessly outside and below Jerusalem in both the moral and topographical sense of the words. Still, when the end-time is imminent, just before Zion falls, this is exactly where Baruch leads his followers. How can we explain this location of the remnant in light of the logic of reversals outlined above?

2 Bar. 2:1, discussed in Chapter Two, gives us a first lead. This passage states that Baruch and his group have to leave Jerusalem, since their presence there shields the city. As we have now seen, the remnant left to enable God to demolish Jerusalem, just as he previously destroyed Sodom and Gomorrah. And just like Lot and his family in the Genesis account, Baruch and his followers obediently leave Jerusalem to enable God's righteous punishment of the wicked city. Their move to the Kidron valley can thus be seen as a crossing of the borders of Jerusalem into the city's immediate surrounding to the east.[44]

This explanation is, however, only partially satisfactory. Probably, the mechanism of reversal, described above, is also evident in *2 Baruch*'s choice of location for the righteous followers of Baruch. Jerusalem has become a Sodom and Gomorrah of the end-time, and consequently stands in stark contrast to the idealised Jerusalem of past times. At this point in history it is therefore first of all Jerusalem that provides

---

[44] Cf. pp. 103–105.

an unfitting environment for the righteous, not the Kidron valley! To escape the inevitable destruction of the wicked city, the righteous turn to its spatial opposite: the valley of Kidron. This move to the Kidron valley makes this place of impurity and death a place of escape during the end-time.

The remaining part of this chapter will discuss how *2 Baruch* constructs a space for the righteous in the Kidron valley. The discussion has to consider two issues. On the one hand, the location that Baruch and his followers enter into is part of the end-time wilderness and thus both outside history and outside the inhabitable world. Although still in Palestine, and even located in Judah, they are outside Jerusalem and thus also outside the territory of the Land of King Josiah. As I mentioned above, Baruch claims that the experience of exile encompasses all the tribes, including the remnant (78:4; 85:3). There is thus no doubt that *2 Baruch* considers their stay in the Kidron valley to be an exilic situation.[45]

On the other hand, though, the move to the Kidron valley in fact saved the righteous. When the enemies finally entered Jerusalem, they killed some inhabitants and took others as prisoners (9:5). God could allow this to happen since the righteous had left the city and could not be harmed by the enemy. The remaining residents were impious and deserved to be punished. To some extent, the remaining inhabitants were 'empty shelves', just like the temple building and the impure city.[46] Their destruction did not threaten Israel's eschatological survival. Consequently, when the enemy attacked, Jerusalem provided no shelter to her inhabitants any more, whereas the Kidron valley offered protection to its righteous newcomers. The Kidron valley is therefore portrayed as a highly ambiguous place. It somehow offers its sojourners protection, while still being an exilic wilderness. How can we understand the space the righteous construct in the Kidron valley? And what is the role of the Kidron location in that spatial building?

Baruch and His Followers in the Wilderness: Praxis in the Kidron Valley

2 Baruch's description of the stay in the Kidron valley concentrates on two different, but related, settings. One describes Baruch's solitary

---

[45] Cf. Whitters, *Epistle*, 52.
[46] Cf. pp. 56–58. Note, however, that God has not forgotten the tribes completely. *2 Baruch* in general attests to hope for the dispersed tribes. Cf. pp. 170–175; 260–262.

actions in different landscapes of the wilderness, whilst the other depicts
the gathering of the followers in the Kidron valley and Baruch's instructions of them. How does Baruch use the wilderness locations, and what
do Baruch's actions in these locations tell us about the functions of the
wilderness? Also, what is the role of the Kidron valley as a gathering
place for the righteous?

   2 Baruch provides a detailed description of Baruch's movements in
the Kidron valley and its immediate surroundings.[47] The text presents
two different types of spatial contexts for his actions. Firstly, on three
occasions Baruch leaves his followers and retreats to a suitable place to
prepare for communication with God. He enters a cave in the Kidron
valley in 21:1 and unspecified locations in 12:5 and 32:8 to fast for seven
days and sanctify himself before the divine encounters. These episodes
of solitary fasting and lamentation are preceded by two depictions of
joint fasting and grief in the Kidron valley.[48] Secondly, after fulfiling
the prescribed seven days of preparation, Baruch either leaves the
people and sits down by an oak (6:1), or he ascends the desolate Mount
Zion to receive visions and in various ways communicate with God.[49]
After these episodes of communication, Baruch returns to gather his
followers in the Kidron valley.

   How should we interpret *2 Baruch*'s use of these locations? *2 Baruch*
locates all ritualised preparations in the Kidron valley. 21:1–2 describes
it as follows:

> I went from there and sat in the valley of Kidron in a cave of the earth
> and sanctified my soul there, and I ate no bread, but I was not hungry;
> I drank no water, but I was not thirsty. And I was there until the seventh
> day as he had commanded me.

Here, Baruch is said to be sanctifying himself before communicating
with God. Among his acts of sanctification *2 Baruch* mentions weeping

---

[47] The idea that important biblical figures head for the wilderness is a common
place. Cf., e.g., Abraham in 2 Chr 3:1; *Jub.* 18:7–13; Josephus, *Ant.* 1.8.3; David in 2 Sam
15; 16; 20; *L.A.B.* 59; 61; Elijah in 1 Kgs 19; Isaiah in *Mart. Ascen. Isa.* 1–2. Cf. Bogaert,
Apocalypse de Baruch I, 328–330.

[48] Moreover, in *2 Bar.* 5:7 Baruch fasts and laments there together with his followers, and in 9:1–2 he fasts in the company of Jeremiah. The location of Baruch's and
Jeremiah's fast in 9:1–2 may also be the desolate Mount Zion (Cf. 10:5). According to *4 Bar.* 2–4, Baruch and Jeremiah lament both at Mount Zion and outside
Jerusalem.

[49] *2 Bar.* 10:5; 13:1; 21:2; 34:1–35:1. Cf. Pap.Oxyrh. 403, 13:1 (Black, *Apocalypsis Henochi*,
119). Baruch's journey to Hebron (47:1–2; 55:1–2) is the topic of the next chapter.

(35:1) fasting (12:5; 20:5; 21:1–2; 47:2)[50] and prohibitions on talking (20:5; 21:1–2).[51] *2 Baruch* chooses the low-lying Kidron valley, and even caves in this sunken landscape, possibly a grave,[52] as settings for these acts of sanctification. Not only are Baruch's actions set in the wilderness, with the death and chaos connotations that go with that landscape; *2 Baruch* strengthens the atmosphere of death and chaos by placing him in a cave (*m'artā*) in the Kidron valley. He sits in the lowliest parts of the topographical continuum. Thus, during the seven days Baruch prepares for his encounters with God, he is situated as close as you can get to the interior of the earth, traditionally perceived as the realm of the dead.[53]

In sharp contrast to these locations, *2 Baruch* sets Baruch's visions and communication with God on Mount Zion and under an oak.[54] Both mountains and oaks were tall and lofty landmarks in the landscape. They stand up above ground level and stretch towards heaven. Moreover, and probably because of their geophysical appearance, oaks[55] and mountains[56] were commonly associated with visions, encounters and other forms of communication between cosmic spheres. When Baruch ascends Mount Zion he literally removes himself from the ordinary level of human affairs and climbs as high as he can to meet with God and to see clearly. Likewise, when he sits down by the oak, com-

---

[50] Fasting was a regular part of rituals of atonement, penance and mourning (Cf. Lev 16:29; 1 Sam 14:24; Ps 35:13). Fasting may also be connected to divination (Exod 24:28; *2 Bar.* 5:7; *Mart. Ascen. Isa.* 2:7–11). Cf. J. Muddiman, "Fast, Fasting," *ABD* 2,773–776. In Jewish liturgy seven days of fast was prescribed (Cf. Bogaert, *Apocalypse de Baruch I*, 26; Charles, *Apocalypse of Baruch*, 9; Whitters, *Epistle*, 37–38).

[51] Cf. *Hist. Rech.* 1:1; 8:3; Matt 4:2.

[52] A cave in the Kidron valley is by implication a grave, since the caves of that valley were commonly used as burial places. Cf. Chapter Three, pp. 103–104, and Bogaert, *Apocalypse de Baruch I*, 328.

[53] Cf. *4 Bar.* 4; *Hist. Rech.* 2:1.

[54] Cf. Whitters, *Epistle*, 40.

[55] Oaks could be understood as visionary trees, or as 'oracle oaks,' often with broader connotations to communication and meeting (Cf. Deut 11:30; Judg 9:37; 1 Kgs 13:14–16; *QG* 4, 1; *Gen Rab.* 47. Bogaert, *Apocalypse de Baruch I*, 325–326; S. Sandmel, *Philo's Place in Judaism: a Study of Conceptions of Abraham in Jewish Literature* (Oxford: Oxford University Press, 1971), 179; T. Stordalen, *Echoes of Eden: Genesis 2–3 and Symbolism of the Eden Garden in Biblical Hebrew Literature* (CBET 25; Leuven: Peeters, 2000), 123. Cf. also Stordalen's semantic considerations regarding oaks and terebinths as tall trees (*Eden*, 42).

[56] Mountains were particularly fit for communication with the upper spheres (Cf., e.g., *2 Bar.* 22:1; Gen 28:10–22; Ezek 40:1–4; *L.A.B.* 15:6). Cf. Clifford, *Cosmic Mountain*, 98–192; Clements, "Temple and Land," 20–21; Levenson, *Sinai and Zion*, 94; 125.

monly considered as a visionary tree, he ensures an outstanding clarity
of mind, a necessity for a visionary.[57]

Clear Visions in Obscure Landscapes

What are the implications of Baruch's use of landscapes during the end-
time? First, *2 Baruch* plays on the contrast between the Kidron valley
and Mount Zion, or alternatively the oak, to underscore the importance of Baruch's encounters with God. Baruch descends as low as he
can get for his preparations, and afterwards ascends the mountain to
receive visions and gain knowledge. The text's contrast between the
cave in the valley and the top of Mount Zion shows how important
it was to ensure that Baruch received the visions and vital information about Israel's future destiny from God. Similarly, *2 Baruch* locates
Baruch under a lofty oak to signal that important information will be
transmitted to the seer.

Possibly, *2 Baruch*'s general choice of a wilderness setting for Baruch's
visions supports this idea. Several contemporaneous texts suggest that
the wilderness was particularly fit for revelations. This idea was in
fact rather widespread.[58] As a landscape void of human habitation
and the antithesis to the city, the wilderness is seen as suitable for
hosting exceptional and rare meetings. It presents the ultimate setting for communication between God and man.[59] Within this context,
2 Baruch builds up a complex picture of Baruch's place of visions. Not
only does Baruch enter the wilderness to see clearly, he also climbs
the deserted Mount Zion and sits by the oak to further promote the
clarity of the visions and dreams granted to him by God. It is also
possible that *2 Baruch* uses the contrast between the Kidron valley and
Mount Zion to hint at the future destiny of Israel as presented in the
visions. There is a huge contrast between the here and now of Israel

---

[57] Imagery of light and darkness is used to describe the places where Baruch receives
visions (Cf. 21:3; 34:1). Baruch climbs Mount Zion to receive more light (*nuhārā*).

[58] To mention one example, *4 Ezra* 10:51–54.

[59] Diepold, *Israel's Land*, 114–115; D.J. Harrington, "Interpreting Israel's History: The
Testament of Moses as a Rewriting of Deut 31–34 [Summary of G. Reese, *Die Geschichte
Israels in der Auffassung des frühen Judentums*, chapter 3]," in *Studies on the Testament of Moses:
Seminar Papers* (ed. G.W.E. Nickelsburg; Septuagint and Cognate Studies 4; Cambridge,
Mass.: Society of Biblical Literature, 1973), 59–70 at 69; T.L. Burden, *The Kerygma of the
Wilderness Traditions in the Hebrew Bible* (AUSS 7; Theology and Religion 163; New York:
Peter Lang Publishing Inc., 1994), 4; 230–231.

in the end-time—the dark and low Kidron valley—and what will come in the future according to Baruch's visions. The Mount Zion setting may suggest a return to Mount Zion, the place of Baruch's revelations, and even an ascent into the other world, the most important future destination according to Baruch's visions.

The Ritual Use of Landscapes

The topographical preferences of *2 Baruch* also provide ritual allusions. The contrast between Baruch's preparations in the low lying Kidron valley and his various acts of communication with God on Mount Zion and under the oak underscores the special nature of Baruch's encounters with God. *2 Baruch* makes a point out of the seclusion of Baruch when he communicates with God. There are no examples of Baruch communicating with God in populated locations. Baruch is said to "(go) outside" (root *npq*) (6:1, 47:1), to "go away" (root *'zl*) (8:3, 32:8, 43:2), and "to leave" (root *šbq*) (34:1), and it is explicitly mentioned that "nobody was with [him]; [he] was alone" (77:18, cf. 20:6; 32:7). Baruch meets with God alone and in a highly ritualised manner.

As a general rule, *2 Baruch* describes the actions of Baruch as twofold. First, Baruch separates from the people to prepare for communicating with God by fasting and other forms of sanctification. As a second step, he contacts God through prayers (48:1) or lamentations (10:5, 35:1–4), and he is answered through visions, dreams and following interpretations.[60]

Furthermore, *2 Baruch* distinguishes between the common efforts of the community of the righteous in lamenting, praying and fasting on the one hand and the acts of Baruch himself on the other. The valley of Kidron houses the shared actions of the group of the righteous. Throughout *2 Baruch*, the Kidron valley is the location for shared fasting, lamentation and appeals to God by the righteous remnant. As described in 5:5–6:

> And I went away and led Jeremiah and Adu and Seraiah and Jabish and Gedaliah and all the honourable of the people with me. And I brought them to the valley of Kidron and told them all what had been said to me. And they raised their voices and they lamented. And we sat there and fasted until the evening.

---

[60] Cf. Job 2:20; Ezra 9:3–5; Isa 3:24–26; Tob 3:10; 2 Macc 13:12; *4 Ezra* 5:19–20; 6:35; 9:3–5, 26–27; 12:50–51; *4 Bar.* 4:7; *T. Mos.* 9:6–7.

In this passage the righteous are said to raise their voices, to lament and to fast in the Kidron valley. Here, as well as in 31–33 and 43:3, the remnant assembles, it raises its voice in a lament to God and ends the sequence of acts by fasting.[61]

Taking the activities ascribed to the community in the Kidron valley together with Baruch's solitary activities, it seems likely that *2 Baruch* is alluding to the basic layout of well attested rituals of grief, repentance and atonement, since the actions of Baruch in relation to his followers reflect the basic scheme of such rituals.[62] *4 Bar.* 2:3 describes the equivalent acts of Jeremiah, and also sets Jeremiah's actions in a ritual context: "[Baruch said this] because whenever the people sinned, Jeremiah sprinkled dust on his head and would pray for the people until the sin was forgiven them."[63] Equally, Deut 9:18 explains why Moses is fasting: "And I lay prostrate before the LORD, as before, for forty days and forty nights: I neither ate bread, nor drank water, because of all the sin which you had committed, provoking the LORD by doing what was evil in his sight." Thus, when Baruch fasts, weeps and prays, he follows a familiar pattern of divine intermediaries atoning for the sins of the people in the mythical history of Israel.[64] Possibly, the separation between the acts of Baruch and the community may also allude to the rituals of the Day of Atonement. According to the regulations of Lev 16, the high priest[65] should purify the sanctuary once every year, be it the Jerusalem temple or the mobile sanctuary, to free the sanctuary from pollution. According to Lev 16:17, the ritual acts of the high priest

---

[61] *2 Bar.* 31–33 omits the fasting.

[62] Cf. *1 En.* 13:7–10 for an equivalent scene in the wilderness. Ezra 9:3–10:12; Neh 8:18–9:4; Isa 5:13; 15:1–6, 3 Macc 5:51; 6:17 and *T. Mos.* 3:4–5 attest to similar relations between an intermediary and his respondents in rituals of grieve and lamentation. Baruch's praxis in the wilderness may be read as a temple critique since it takes up aspects of the cult, particularly the communication aspect. There is possibly also some liturgical use of the wilderness in *2 Baruch*, for instance the seven days of fast in 9:1. Note also that Baruch probably was thought to be either a priest or a Levite (Cf. Bogaert, *Apocalypse de Baruch I*, 108–110; Whitters, *Epistle*, 129). And who are the men mentioned by name in 5:5? Jeremiah is probably Jeremiah the prophet (a Levite, according to Neh 12:1, 12), Seraiah is Seraiah the Levite (Neh 12:1), Jabish is unknown according to Klijn ("2 Baruch," 622), Gedaliah is mentioned in Jer 38:1 and 40:14 (Cf. Bogaert, *Apocalypse de Baruch II*, 19–21; Charles, *Apocalypse of Baruch*, 8–9; Violet, *Apokalypsen*, 209).

[63] 'To sprinkle dust on one's head' is a common parallel to rending garments, weeping and fasting.

[64] Cf., e.g., *Hist. Rech.* 8–9. Cf. Murphy, *Structure and Meaning*, 72–77; Whitters, *Epistle*, 129.

[65] Or Aaron, according to Lev 16.

are a solitary task. He enters the holy of holies alone, while the community stays away from the sanctuary, fasting and resting (16:29–31). As we have seen, *2 Baruch* underscores the contrast between the actions Baruch performs alone on Mount Zion and the communal acts in the Kidron valley during the rites of atonement, complying with the demands Lev 16 makes of the high priest and the laity.

At the onset of the end-time, nothing is more appropriate than atoning for the wicked tribes, considering the recent dispersion of the tribes on account of their sins. To secure the future of the tribes after the end-time, atonement and reconciliation are necessary. *2 Baruch* thus uses the various landscapes of the wilderness to highlight the function of the ritualised actions of Baruch and his followers.

The Kidron Valley: Place of Instruction

In addition, the valley of Kidron plays a crucial role as a place of instruction.[66] Baruch re-enters the Kidron valley after his periods of seclusion to inform his followers about the content of his visions and the key points of his newly achieved wisdom. Baruch preaches and teaches his followers, and urges them to follow God's Law and commandments (32:1; 44:2–3) and to look to the other world (31:5; 44:5–15).

It is important that *2 Baruch* primarily describes the Kidron valley as a place of gathering and instruction, and not as a place of dwelling. Both 31:1–2 and 44:1 imply that the followers arrive from an anonymous nearby location to receive instruction.[67] But *2 Baruch* does not focus on where they actually dwell. This does not mean that the followers of Baruch could not dwell in the Kidron valley. They may of course dwell somewhere else in the valley, and they probably do (31:1–3), but that is not the concern of *2 Baruch*. It is the role of the valley as place of instruction that matters in the text. The importance of the group comes above all from its role as Baruch's audience and recipients of his transmitted knowledge.

A likely explanation is that *2 Baruch* envisions a larger group of anonymous followers, called Baruch's people (*'amy*, "my people") in 44:1, while a smaller assembly of elders and leaders represent them to receive instruction.[68] This is suggested both in 31:1–2 and in the continuation

---

[66] *2 Bar.* 31:1–34:1; 43:1–47:1.
[67] Cf. further 47:1.
[68] Cf., e.g., Deut 5:23; 27:1; 29:10; 31:28; Josh 24:1; 1 Kgs 8:1. The Syriac word

of 44:1: "And I, Baruch, went from there and came to my people and
called my first-born son and Gedaliah, my friend,[69] and seven of the
elders (*sābe*) of the people (...)."[70] If this interpretation is correct, it is
this group of community leaders, representing Israel, and its function
of responding to Baruch *in his acts of instruction* that first and foremost
defines the presence of Baruch's followers in the Kidron valley.

The Paradoxical Kidron Valley

In light of these three functions of the Kidron valley, it becomes clear
that Baruch and his followers stay in the wilderness first and foremost
to secure the *future* redemption of Israel. Baruch receives visions and
communicates with God on Mount Zion to gain crucial knowledge
about future events. He becomes Israel's intermediary, and together
with his followers he atones for the transgressions of the tribes. After
each episode of communication, Baruch instructs his followers. This
instruction is vital to their survival, since knowledge of the Law and the
importance of living by it are what will ultimately save Israel.

Thus, *2 Baruch* reshapes the web of meanings attached to Mount Zion
and the Kidron valley in the end-time. On the one hand, since both
places are part of the wilderness of the end-time, Mount Zion and the
Kidron valley share common traits. They are uninhabitable, chaotic
and connote death. When Baruch sits in the cave of the earth as well as
when he climbs the deserted temple mount,[71] he balances on the very
edge of the geography accessible to man.[72] In the cave Baruch dwells as
close as he can get to the interior of the earth, traditionally perceived

---

sābā describes any elderly person, or "the elders of Israel" (Smith, *Dictionary*, 357). Cf.
Charles, *Apocalypse of Baruch*, 70; Murphy, *Structure and Meaning*, 131.

[69] Cf. Charles, *Apocalypse of Baruch*, 70; Klijn, "2 Baruch," 634 for another interpretation.

[70] In accordance with the description of steering bodies in cities in Josephus, *Ant.*
4.18.14, Bogaert has proposed that the group in *2 Baruch* consisting of seven elders and
two additional persons, the friend Gedaliah and Baruch's firstborn son, represents the
legitimate steering body of the community in the Kidron valley (Bogaert, *Apocalypse
de Baruch II*, 70; Whitters, *Epistle*, 43). In addition, as Murphy has pointed out, the
structure and organisation of the followers of Baruch may allude to the organisation of
the people under Moses (Murphy, *Structure and Meaning*, 131). Cf. further Josephus, *Ant.*
4.8.14, for the role of the elders as judges.

[71] Cf. *3 Baruch*, where the Slavonic witness places Baruch at Zion, whereas the Greek
witness uses the valley of Kidron as setting for the following apocalypse.

[72] Cf. *1En.* 13:7–8.

as the realm of the dead. The hidden and forbidden geography of the dead in the cave of Kidron is paralleled by the remains of the concealed and equally forbidden inner courts of the former temple at Mount Zion (35:1–4). As the most holy place of former days, the desolate condition of Zion in the end-time also demonstrates the reversal that has taken place and the all-embracing character of wilderness. Zion is 'in dust and ashes', expressions alluding both to rituals of sorrow, and to death:

> Because at the place where now I am prostrate, the high priests used to offer holy sacrifices, and to place thereon the steam of the incense of fragrant spices. Now, however, our pride has become dust, and our soul's desire has become ashes (35:4–5).

Thus, Mount Zion and the Kidron valley in this sense resemble each other as chaotic, forbidden and set apart spaces.[73]

On the other hand, however, the Kidron valley remains a topographical, and therefore connotational, contrast to Mount Zion during the end-time, but now the two places contradict each other within a landscape defined by a reversed logic. In the same way that Mount Zion once was the axis of communication between God and man through the rituals enacted in the temple there, it becomes, paradoxically, once again the main axis of communication after the destruction of the temple. This time, however, not because it is the location of the temple and its rituals, but as the foremost mountain of wilderness. As wilderness, and as mountain, and as the last spot the wilderness embraced, it is particularly apt to help Baruch receive his visions.

But why does the remnant stay in the Kidron valley? In accordance with end-time's affinity with death, the Kidron valley's continued association with the dead and with impure objects is exactly what attracts the righteous. Just as Baruch's clarity of mind is enhanced through the fact that Mount Zion is both wilderness and a mountain, the death allusions of the Kidron valley are doubled during the end-time. The Kidron valley is both a wilderness and a graveyard. These allusions to the valley as a place of the dead fit the purpose of the rituals that take place there. The righteous receive instruction and perform atonement in the Kidron valley. In other words, they atone for the transgressions of the tribes that caused the death-like situation of the end-time, and

---

[73] The oak in the Kidron valley also brings to mind connotations of death. Oaks were often connected to holy graves (Cf. *Liv. Pro.* 1:1; 5:2; 10:8; 18:5). I will discuss this topic and the tree of 55:1 in the next chapter.

they try to learn how to find a way out of death. There is thus hope
that they will rise again from this temporary death in non-space and
transcend the dying world.[74]

The Pillar and the Wall: Baruch and His Group as Space of Survival

The preceding discussion showed that the dark and sunken Kidron
valley harbours Baruch's followers, the righteous remnant of the end-
time, and that the escape to this death-like space is what rescued the
remnant when the enemy entered Jerusalem. I have suggested that the
main purpose of the stay is to secure the future redemption of Israel. To
guarantee that redemption, it is vital that Baruch receives clear visions,
that he atones for the tribes together with his followers and that he
instructs them, so that the group of followers continues to live according
to the Law. Now, to fulfil the aim of future redemption, *2 Baruch* must
also secure the present survival of the group. Since the temple, the city
and the Land no longer exist as an accessible place for Israel during the
end-time, the remnant no longer benefits from the protection that its
righteous practices gave it there. The protection that *2 Baruch* ascribes
to them in the Kidron valley must therefore be based on other aspects
of their praxis and must become another spatial construction. How
can the Kidron valley protect the righteous and secure their survival?
What spatial construction can assure their present protection as well as
promote their future survival?

The Importance of Law, Leadership, and Life

The importance of the Law and the continuity of Law-abiding praxis
are undoubtedly two of the central concerns of *2 Baruch*.[75] *2 Baruch*'s
focus on the Law is generally acknowledged and highlighted in studies of the text.[76] Of specific interest to earlier studies has been the role
of the Law after the temple fall and the dispossession of the Land.
Scholars have pointed out that *2 Baruch*, like several other contemporary texts, puts the Law at the heart of Israel's life after the destruction.

---

[74] Cf. examples of the extensive dangers associated with the wilderness in *2 Bar.* 10:7;
77:14; Dan 4:23–26; *L.A.B.* 15:5–6.
[75] Cf. *2 Bar.* 14; 21:12–26; 31–32; 42; 75–76; 82–85.
[76] Cf. Chapter One, pp. 2–5. Cf. Münchow, *Ethik*, 100.

2 Bar. 85:3 clearly supports this view: "(...), and we have also left the land, and Zion has been taken away from us, and now we have nothing except the Mighty One and his law."[77] As this passage makes clear, *2 Baruch* highlights the role of the Law in Israel's survival during the end-time. The Law, as well as God,[78] are Israel's only hopes during that period. This observation is important since it shows that *2 Baruch*, unlike some other earlier and contemporaneous texts, considers the Law independent of any given geographical area.[79] Thus, *2 Baruch* takes sides in an ongoing debate of the first centuries C.E. as to the universality of the Law and the validity of the Law outside the former Land.[80] *2 Baruch* disconnects the Law from its geographical dependence and highlights its significance for Israel also in the wilderness.[81]

Whitters has also suggested that the Law takes the place of the Land, or alternatively the temple, during this period.[82] This suggestion points to an intriguing aspect of the text by highlighting the importance of the Law within the new situation, but in relation to *2 Baruch*'s spatiality we need to add some nuances to the proposal: does the Law make space, or is the Law space? I would suggest that a more precise formulation would be to regard Law-abiding *praxis* as the constitutive element of *2 Baruch*'s construction of space in the wilderness. In my view, the Law

---

[77] Cf. *C. Ap.* 2:38. Cf. Charles, *Apocalypse of Baruch*, 158; Whitters, *Epistle*, 47.

[78] *2 Baruch* states clearly that God's presence has left the earth and retracted to heaven after the destruction of the temple (cf. pp. 32–34; 57). Still, divine presence may be represented on earth by the Law and relate to the assembly Israel rather than a particular spot (the temple). This creates a dynamic understanding of God's presence and a mobile, dynamic understanding of sacred space. These notions of divine presence were the topic of debate at the time of *2 Baruch*. Cf. Murphy, *Structure and Meaning*, 92; 96; 108; Kirschner, *Apocalyptic*, 43; Whitters, *Epistle*, 136. Cf. also Chapter Six.

[79] Cf. Davies, *Gospel and Land*, 57–58.

[80] Cf., e.g., 1 Macc 1:44, where the laws Antiochus introduces are "alien to the land" (Cf. Lieu, *Christian Identity*, 217). The shift from temple to Torah is a transformation common to rabbinic literature and apocalyptic writings (Cf. *T. Levi* 13:3–8; *4 Ezra* 9:31–32; 14:22; *2 Bar.* 48:22–24; 85:3, 14). Cf. Klijn, "Recent Developments," 9–10; Murphy, *Structure and Meaning*, 83; 132; Laato, *Star*, 358; Whitters, *Epistle*, 122; 138–140; 144; Lieu, *Christian Identity*, 225. Cf. in particular M. Desjardins, "Law in *2 Baruch* and *4 Ezra*," *SR* 14 (1985): 25–37; M. Hirshman, "Rabbinic Universalism in the Second and Third Centuries," *HTR* 93 (2000): 101–115.

[81] Of course, the origin of the Law is heavily associated with a wilderness location and with Mount Sinai in particular (Cf. *4 Ezra* 3:16; *Targum Onkelos to Deut* 1:1–2; *Targum Ps* 68:16–18). Cf. Bogaert, *Apoclaypse de Baruch I*, 389; G. Delling, "Von Morija zum Sinai (Pseudo-Philo Liber Anitquitatum Biblicarum 32.1–10)," *JSJ* 2 (1971): 14–15; Fretheim, "Whole Earth," 230; Hirshman, "Rabbinic Universalism," 101–115; Whitters, *Epistle*, 136.

[82] Cf. Whitters, *Epistle*, 140. Cf. also Davies, *Gospel and Land*, 354.

itself is not a spatial entity.[83] Lawful praxis, on the other hand, constitutes space. The Law is indeed at the heart of Israel's life during
the end-time, but it creates space only when it dictates praxis. Israel's
choice of and adherence to righteousness are thus vital to the ability of
the Law to define space. Two of the central claims of *2 Baruch* support
this view. Firstly, Israel does not only need the Law to survive through
the end-time, she also needs leaders to guide her according to the Law.
And secondly, the notion of praxis is implied by *2 Baruch*'s insistence that
the Law, though instruction, is life.

The Importance of Leadership and Instruction

On several occasions *2 Baruch* points out the importance of leadership
and instruction.[84] *2 Baruch* regards leadership and the wise man's teach-
ing of the Law as vital to the survival of Israel.[85] The above discussion
of the function of the Kidron valley sheds light on the role Baruch plays
in the end-time. I have suggested that he performs atonement, receives
crucial information through visions and instructs his followers in accordance with his newly gained knowledge. A particularly rich description of the figure of Baruch is given by J.E. Wright.[86] Wright describes
Baruch as a Torah-sage, a divinely inspired interpreter of the Law and
an apocalyptic seer. Wright concludes that *2 Baruch* describes Baruch as
the perfect community leader of the first centuries c.e.[87]

2 Baruch suggests that there have always been leaders in Israel.[88] In
addition to the kings David, Solomon, Hezekiah and Josiah, Israel benefited from helpers, prophets and pious men (85:1–3). *2 Baruch* mentions
or alludes to Abraham and Moses several times as important leaders

---

[83] I am not denying that other texts may ascribe spatial qualities to the Law. Cf. Lieu
regarding *T. Levi* 13:3–8 (*Christian Identity*, 225).

[84] Chapter Three pointed out the importance of the king's ability to rule and judge
according to the Law, and Chapter Two showed the devastating consequences of the
practices of false priests.

[85] Cf. Kolenkow, "Interpretation," 107–109; Sayler, *Promises*, 74; 79–86; Whitters,
Epistle, 115–119; 142–143.

[86] J.E. Wright, *Baruch ben Neriah: From Biblical Scribe to Apocalyptic Seer* (Colombia, SC:
University of South Carolina Press, 2003).

[87] Wright, *Baruch ben Neriah*, 38–39; 40–69; 82; 89–92; 111–112; 124. According to
Wright, Baruch—the inspired interpreter and community leader—becomes the same
kind of leader as the Teacher of Righteousness, Jesus, and Paul (*Baruch ben Neriah*, 93–
97).

[88] Cf. *Jerusalem Targum to Gen* 49:8–12 and *Targum Onkelos to Gen* 49:10.

for Israel in their respective generations (57; 59; 84). And as we have already seen, God sends Jeremiah to help the captives in Babylon (10:2; 33:2), while Baruch, the perfect community leader, cares for the remnant that remains. A central aspect of Baruch's ideal leadership is his ability to pass his leadership on to his successors. 44:1–3 explains that Baruch will transmit his duties as leader to his first-born son, his friend Gedaliah and the council of elders. Thus, when Baruch dies or goes away, there will be other leaders to admonish and instruct the people. Moreover, in the eschatological future, *2 Baruch* imagines the Messiah, the ultimate leader of Israel, to guard and direct the people towards the other world. This effort to establish a line of leaders in the history of Israel shows how *2 Baruch* tries to legitimise the claim of 46:4 that Israel will never be in want of a leader to protect and instruct her.

2 Baruch argues the necessity of someone administering the Law.[89] In fact, *2 Baruch* intimately links the Law, its interpreters and their interpretations: Israel needs the Law, but she also needs someone to instruct her and judge her by it in order to survive.[90] Why is this connection important to my approach to space? 85:1 describes the function of helpers, prophets and pious men within the Land:

> Further, know that in the times of former generations, our fathers had righteous helpers, prophets and pious men. But then we were also in our land, and they helped us when we sinned, and they prayed for us to him who created us, because they trusted their works, and the Mighty One heard their prayers and absolved us.

This passage shows that these men were of vital importance to Israel within the Land.[91] The existence of righteous leaders who could intervene and interpret the Law protected all inhabitants of the Land. These high-profile individuals were the ones who kept Israel's covenantal relationship to God intact and consequently secured Israel's continued stay in the Land.[92]

Now, righteous leaders, possibly with exception of the prophets, also create space outside the former Land. An excellent description of the importance of Baruch's leadership is given in 46:1–3. The complaint

---

[89] Cf. in particular *2 Bar.* 44–46.

[90] Cf. in particular 15:5–6; 77:13–16.

[91] According to *b. B. Bat.* 91a, the merits of the fathers will not benefit a man who leaves the Land for another (Charles, *Apocalypse of Baruch*, 52). According to that text the effects of their actions are confined to the Land.

[92] Cf. *2 Bar.* 2:1; 61; 63; 66.

of Baruch's followers in this passage suggests what would be at stake
should Baruch leave them:

> Did the Mighty One humiliate us to such a degree that he will take you
> away from us quickly? And truly we will be in the darkness, and there
> will be no light to the people who are left. For where shall we again
> investigate the law, or who (*manu*) will distinguish for us between life and
> death?

This passage suggests that if Baruch leaves his followers they will be left
in darkness (*ḥeṡukā*), without any light (*nuhrā*). The loss of the leader is
here described using the same vocabulary that depicted the fall of Zion
in 10:12 as an extinction of light. Thus, without the light of the leader
and his practices, the world would turn chaotic—dark—to his followers
just as it did when the temple fell.[93] Moreover, this passage also displays
that the role of the leader can be put in terms of a "where," *aykā*. If he
leaves the group, there will be no place for the group to investigate the
Law. It is his practices that create that place for Israel.

   We thus see that *2 Baruch* indeed upholds the importance of the Law
within the community of Israel in the end-time. However, the Law
primarily constitutes space through the leader's practice of instructing
his followers in the Law. It is Baruch's instruction and ruling according
to the Law that upholds the Law-defined space.

Law, Instruction, and Life

46:1–3 also illustrates that the important relation between the concepts of Law and life in *2 Baruch* goes though instruction. The passage
describes investigation of the Law as a procedure that separates life
from death, and keeps the dangerous merging of the two at bay. The
passage thus even links life itself to considerations about where and by
whom the Law should be explained.

   This connection between Law, life and instruction appears several
times in *2 Baruch*. We need to look at some details in order to grasp
the nature of this connection in the text. 38:2 states that Law itself
is life: "Your law is life, and your wisdom is the (right) direction."[94]
Other passages, however, such as 45:2 and 76:5 claim that *instruction*
in the Law leads to life.[95] 76:5 describes God's command to Baruch

---

[93] Cf. *2 Bar.* 77:13–14. Cf. 1 Sam 16:11; 2 Sam 7:7–8; *L.A.B.* 59:2–3.
[94] Cf. also *2 Bar.* 19:1.
[95] Cf. further *2 Bar.* 15:5; 44:2–3; 84:1.

to instruct the people during the last forty days of his life on earth: "Thus, go now during these days and instruct (root *ylp*) the people as much as you can so that they will learn and not die in the last time, but learn and live (root *ḥy'*) in the last times." The message of 45:2 is very similar. This time it is Baruch who urges his successors to admonish the people: "You, therefore, instruct (root *rt'*) the people as much as you can, for that task is ours. For when you teach (root *ylp*) them, you make them live." It is clear from these examples that the concept of the Law is deeply intertwined with the concept of life. However, there is not necessarily a synonymous relationship between the two, as has been suggested.[96] 38:2, cited above, certainly says that Law is life, but it adds that wisdom, thoroughly identified with the Law in *2 Baruch*, is 'the right direction'. So even this passage can be construed as an insistence on instruction. Although *2 Baruch* is not unambiguous in this matter, the main impression is that the praxis of instruction links Law and life: instruction in the Law gives life and leads to life.

Two important issues still remain to be discussed. Firstly, although *2 Baruch* suggests that obedience to the Law assures survival here and now, it is none the less clear that instruction in the Law above all guarantees *future* life. In other words, the praxis of giving instruction in the Law here and now leads not only to temporary survival in the present; it assures life in the eschatological future. *2 Baruch* in a sense postpones real life, or puts life on hold through the age of death. Instruction keeps the people going, but they will not yet be able to enjoy the fruits of their loyalty fully until a future time and place.

Secondly, 46:3 implies that instruction in the Law is also a space-making praxis. The followers of Baruch fear that Baruch's death, or disappearance, will create a spatial void: There will be nowhere to investigate the Law and thus nowhere to secure present survival and future life. The potential loss of the leader and his instruction is therefore both a loss of space and a loss of life, since his practices were constitutive to the space of present protection and the space of future life.[97]

This discussion shows that the Law as such does not take the place of the Land. It is the continued Law-abiding praxis of the group and the

---

[96] Cf. S. Burkes, "'Life' Redefined: Wisdom and Law in Fourth Ezra and Second Baruch," *CBQ* 63 (2001): 55–71. Cf. further Murphy, *Structure and Meaning*, 106–107; Fretheim, "Whole Earth," 230.

[97] Cf. Kolenkow, "Introduction," 108; Whitters, *Epistle*, 48.

instruction of the community leader that ensure continued protection and survival after the destruction of Zion, both in the present and in the future. And importantly, these practices of the leader and his followers are also the factors that constitute a space for the righteous during the end-time.

The Works of the Righteous: A Firm Pillar and a Strong Wall

The above discussion has proposed that Baruch's leadership involves the same strategies and acts that the leaders of the Land once pursued. Baruch performs atonement, and instructs and judges the people, just like his predecessors. Likewise, we have seen that lawful practices and instruction are what constitutes life, both within the former Land and outside it in the Kidron valley. The important role of practice in defining space gives rise to two questions: how does 2 Baruch describe the space obedience and instruction create, and how does this praxis inform our understanding of the Kidron valley as an end-time location of the righteous?

2:1–2 says:

> For I have said these things to you so that you may say them to Jeremiah and to all those who are like you (pl.) so that you may retire from this city. Because your works are to this city as (ak) a firm pillar and your prayers as (ak) a strong wall.

According to 2:2, the works of the righteous community ('bādaykun, "your (pl.) works") are as (ak) a firm pillar ('amudā šārirā) of the city, and their prayers (çlawtekun, "your (pl.) prayers") like a strong wall (šurā ḥayltānā). In other words, the works and prayers of Baruch, Jeremiah, and the remaining righteous kept the city standing and hindered enemies from entering it. This passage probably relies on Jer 1:18–19's description of Jeremiah as a pillar and a wall against the wicked in Judah:

> And I for my part have made you today a fortified city, an iron pillar, and a bronze wall, against the whole land—against the kings of Judah, its princes, its priests, and the people of the land. They will fight against you; but they shall not prevail against you, for I am with you, says the LORD, to deliver you.

In this passage the prophet Jeremiah is made into a fortified city, an iron pillar and a bronze wall to protect him from the attacks of the wicked forces in Judah and to secure his deliverance in spite of the difficult task that lies ahead of him.[98] *2 Bar.* 2:1–2 combines the notion of the single city-protecting righteous man with the motif of the fortified city in Jer 1:18.[99] What is the outcome of this recombination?

According to *2 Bar.* 2:1–2 it is not Baruch, nor Jeremiah, alone who is a pillar and a wall. It is the good works and the prayers of the group of remaining pious people that become a pillar and a wall. In other words, *2 Baruch* makes the actions of a community, not the figure of a single man, into a structure that supports the city.[100] As we already saw in the previous chapter, the entire group must therefore leave the city before God can destroy it. However, due to its strong allusive connection to Jer 1:18–19, this characterisation of the group does not only define its role in Jerusalem, it probably also applies to its structure in the wilderness; it refers to its resistance against wicked attacks in the wilderness. When Baruch's group leaves Jerusalem for the wilderness, Jerusalem collapses. In other words, the fortifying structure has abandoned Jerusalem and escaped to the Kidron valley. The followers of Baruch, like Jeremiah before them, become a fortified city in the wilderness in order to protect themselves from the wickedness of the end-time. This is the city God protects throughout the end-time, not Jerusalem (Jer 1:19).

Now, the previous chapters showed how the distinctions between the temple, the city and the Land are blurred in *2 Baruch*. At the time of the fall of Zion, temple, city, and Land can be viewed as aspects of each other. The temple, the city and the Land were interchangeable. To leave the city on the eve of destruction is thus simultaneously to abandon the temple and the Land. Given this interpretation, the community of righteous in the Kidron valley can certainly be seen as a fortified city, but a fortified city containing the integrated aspects of temple and Land. This city is end-time's mirror image of what Jerusalem was to the righteous before wickedness transformed it into Sodom and Babylon. From this point onwards, it is the community-based fortified city in the Kidron valley that protects the righteous and assures their survival throughout the last wicked times.

As I have pointed out, this end-time city is based on the good works and prayers of Baruch, Jeremiah and the community (2:2). In other words, the spatial structure that protects Israel during the end-time is

---

[98] Cf. also Jer 15:20.

[99] Cf. also Bogaert, *Apocalypse de Baruch I*, 359–360.

[100] Cf. *4 Bar.* 1:2, where Jeremiah and Baruch together become like a pillar and a wall. Cf. further *Pesiq. Rab.* 26. Cf. Bogaert, *Apocalypse de Baruch I*, 224.

clearly based on the practices of the group. This city, with its inherent
Land and temple aspects, is constituted by the righteousness of its
constitutive members.[101] How do we approach the component parts of
this spatial building?

Multivalent Allusions

The question we need to address now is: what allusions are at work
in the construction of the end-time city in the Kidron valley? First,
it is evident from the preceding conclusions that the Land, the city
and the temple are one general source of allusions and connotations.
The end-time city construction continues and recycles the aspects of
protection and survival earlier attributed to the Land and its institutions.[102] Likewise, the end-time city reinterprets the functions associated
with Jerusalem and its temple. This can, for instance, be seen from the
way 2 Baruch describes the gatherings taking place in the Kidron valley
as occasions of instruction. Instruction was in general associated with
the Jerusalem temple or related institutions.[103] During pilgrimages to
Jerusalem and its temple, instruction was a natural part of the activities
of the gathering (Deut 31:12). In addition, it is possible that 2 Baruch
alludes to the interrelated topography of the temple and the Land,
alternatively between the mobile sanctuary and the camp of the Exodus story (or both), implied by the rituals of the Day of Atonement,
discussed above.[104] As the place where the community fasts and waits,
the Kidron valley becomes the equivalent to the Land, alternatively the
camp.

Furthermore, and of particular interest, there are allusions triggered
by the reference to the pillar and the wall (2 Bar. 2:2). Clearly, pillars
and walls were parts of a city's structure and, as we saw above, 2:2
definitely alludes to the city-sustaining function of the pillar and the

---

[101] Descriptions of communities in spatial terms were quite common in the first
centuries CE (Cf. particularly Davies, Gospel and Land, 178–179; 182).

[102] Of course, protection of the righteous in the end-time is a topos (Davies, Territorial
Aspects, 55–61; 65). Both biblical and pseudepigraphical accounts are primed with
references to the protecting qualities the wilderness has for Israel (Exod 13–15; Deut
1:30–31; Jer 31:2; 4 Ezra 1:15–23; 5, 41;13:16–93; L.A.B. 10:7; Pss. Sol. 17:17), as well as for
individuals or groups of opponents of ungodly regimes in Jerusalem (1 Macc 2; 2 Macc
7; T. Mos. 9; Apoc. El. (H) 4:24–26).

[103] Cf. Isa 2:3; Lam 2:9; Sir 24.

[104] The description of Lev 16 is set in the wilderness in context of the Exodus story,
but applies equally to the temple and the Land.

wall. Likewise, the wall was presented as the most important defensive structure of Jerusalem and its temple in 7:1–8:1.[105] The destruction of that city/temple wall meant the destruction of the city and its sanctuary at that time. The establishment of a wall in 2:2 thus indicates the survival of the community as a strong and secure spatial entity.[106]

Moreover, the mention of the pillar may also have evoked other associations. Pairs of pillars were commonly found in shrines in the ancient Middle East. The two gigantic bronze pillars of the Solomonic temple, Jachin and Boaz, were of particular importance to the structure of the Jerusalem sanctuary. They marked the entrance to the forecourt of the interior space of the temple, and thus also the entrance to the earthly dwelling of God. These two pillars were thus of cultic as well as cosmological importance.[107] In addition, the two pillars had a function in royal ideology. The king courted under the pillars. It was the place of ruling and judging.[108]

2 Kgs 23:2–3, like 2 Bar. 2:2, mentions the location of a single pillar and describes it as the place of the renewal of the covenant after the high priest Hilkiah had found the book of the Law in the temple during the reign of Josiah:

> The king went up to the house of the LORD (…); he read in their hearing all the words of the book of the covenant that had been found in the house of the LORD. The king stood by the pillar and made a covenant before the LORD, to follow the LORD, keeping his commandments, his decrees, and his statutes, with all his heart and all his soul, to perform the words of this covenant that were written in this book. All the people joined in the covenant.

We thus see that the mention of the pillar in 2 Bar. 2:2 may have evoked particular allusions both to the connection between Israel and God, and to the stabilising and preserving function of the pillar(s) of the former Jerusalem temple.

---

[105] Note the temple-city blend implied in 7:1–8:1 (pp. 35–36). Cf. Neh 2:8. Note how 2 Kgs 25 and 1 En. 90:28–29 make special notice of the walls and the pillars in connection with the fall.

[106] Cf. Ezra 9:9; Sir 48:17; 4 Bar. 1:2.

[107] Cf. 1 Kgs 7:15–22; 41–42; Jer 52; 17:20–23. Cf. Levenson, "Temple and World," 285; Stordalen, Eden, 120–122; C.L. Meyers, "Jachin and Boaz in Religious and Political Perspective," CBQ 45 (1983): 167–178; E. Bloch-Smith, "'Who is the King of Glory?' Solomon's Temple and Its Symbolism," in Scripture and Other Artifacts: Essays on the Bible and Archeology in Honor of Philip J. King (ed. M.D. Coogan et al; Louisville, KY: Westminster/John Knox, 1994), 18–31.

[108] Stordalen, Eden, 120–122; Clifford, Cosmic Mountain, 178.

The second field of allusions related to the end-time city is the camp-space of the Exodus-story. In important respects, the city construction of the end resembles the community that settled in camps in the wilderness under the leadership of Moses. One link is of course provided by the wilderness landscapes. Like the camp, the end-time city takes place in an uninhabitable area. And like its Exodus model, it is a spatial construction that promotes the survival of Israel outside the Land and independently of the temple. Moreover, as Murphy has pointed out, Baruch, like Moses before him, assembles a group of elders and leaders around him to instruct them on behalf of the entire people. These groups primarily function as Baruch's and Moses' immediate surroundings and as audiences for their messages.[109] There is no fixed location for either group, and neither is defined by a relation to a specific spot. The groups are mobile entities under a Law-abiding leadership.

A third and explicit field of reference is exilic space. As the above discussion of the ultimate exile has shown, Baruch considers the stay of the remnant in the Kidron valley to be an exile. This idea is clearly expressed in 85:3. This passage claims that the remnant has actually left the Land, even though the context shows that Baruch and his followers are still well within the confines of Palestine. Several scholars have commented on this apparent contradiction. Charles suggested that the contradiction showed that *2 Baruch* came from different sources. According to Charles, the description of the location of the remnant as an exile proves that the *Epistola Baruch*, where 85:3 appears, was written in Babylon, while other sections of *2 Baruch* are written in Palestine.[110] As Charles's multiple source theory is rejected by the great majority of scholars, the contradiction remains unsolved by this suggestion. Violet, on the other hand, proposes that the discrepancy in the assessment of the remnant's location points to the real location of the author of *2 Baruch*, namely Javneh.[111] Bogaert, however, rejects this argument since Javneh is also a town in Palestine and therefore cannot be a place of exile.[112] Instead, he suggests that the situation of the remnant

---

[109] *2 Bar.* 84:1–7 makes this link between the wilderness generation and the generation of the end-time explicit, saying that the experiences and the actions of the two generations are the same. Cf. Chapter Seven, pp. 303–304.

[110] Charles, *Apocalypse of Baruch*, 155–156. Charles refers to the geo-historical region of Palestine.

[111] Violet, *Apokalypsen*, xci; Bogaert, *Apocalypse de Baruch I*, 333–334.

[112] Although Bogaert denies Violet's argumentation here, he agrees on other grounds

is equivalent to the situation of the exiled tribes, and that the remnant thus experiences a spiritual and moral exile.[113] Whitters' interpretation concurs with Bogaert's understanding of the passage:

> The point of the former reference (85:2) is to mark Baruch's solidarity with the audience. Baruch is saying that the people of Palestine live the same disenfranchised life as those of the Diaspora, that is, that they live without the temple and its sacrifices, and that only the Law can safeguard them now. Thus, the Jews of Palestine were themselves living in a spiritual and moral exile.[114]

Whitters makes a good point when he claims that *2 Baruch* highlights Baruch's solidarity with his audience. Moreover, the situation of the remnant *does* match the life of the dispersed tribes. However, there is no need to limit the interpretation of the remnant's experience to "a spiritual and moral exile" as Bogaert and Whitters do. In this part of the narrative Palestine *is* a place of exile comparable to the other places of exile. There is no reason to make an exception for this area just because it is part of Palestine.[115] Indeed, no exceptions are made for any part of the earth at this point. So, although the remnant is staying within the borders of Palestine, and even in the heartland of Judah, this is an exile for the remnant. It is probably not a coincidence that *2 Baruch* describes the former Land in these terms. It both underscores the reversed nature of creation and highlights the character of the end-time as a mega-event: even Jerusalem, the last location of former generations' Land has been lost. And since God's presence has been withdrawn from the world, the entire world has now become a place of exile.

Overall, *2 Baruch* plays on multivalent allusions to present the end-time city in the Kidron valley. The end-time city can be described both in terms of exile, camp and Land-space. This paradoxical merging of allusions makes the city fit for the time context it appears in. We can either call it a blessed exile, an alternative Land, or equally well a mixture of camp and Land in foreign territory. And as we shall see

---

that *2 Baruch* is most probably written in Javneh (Bogaert, *Apocalypse de Baruch I*, 331–334).

[113] Bogaert, *Apocalypse de Baruch* I, 334: "L'exil de l'auteur de ce texte est donc spirituel et moral."

[114] Whitters, *Epistle*, 52. Just like Charles, Bogaert and Whitters refer to the geo-historical Palestine.

[115] Note how Bogaert's rejection of Javneh is based on a territorial epistemology.

in the following chapter, *2 Baruch* uses this paradoxical spatiality of the end-time to the utmost extent.

The Wilderness Location: Community in Non-Place

As shown by the above discussion of the nature of the end-time wilderness, the wilderness is an anti-place, or a non-place. It is void of divine presence, and it is outside history and beyond the inhabitable world. The Kidron valley, as a distinct part of that wilderness, is a place of death, impurity, and punishment. The place where *2 Baruch* locates its end-time city is thus utterly chaotic. Is the Kidron the valley part of the remnant's end-time city? Or put another way, do the righteous practices of the community transform the Kidron valley into an ordered space of city dwelling?

The Kidron valley no doubt is the place where the end-time city is *set*. That is where the group receives instruction, and it is where the remnant atones, enjoys protection and consequently survives. However, the Kidron valley is not necessarily described as a part of the end-time space of the remnant. Three arguments support this view. Firstly, the fact that the remnant moves to and gathers in the Kidron valley does not change the character of the valley. It remains, as we have seen, a wilderness and a place of impurity and death despite the remnant's entry. Certainly, the end-time reversals apply to the Kidron valley in the sense that it becomes the setting of the righteous after their move from Jerusalem, but these reversals do not change the basic character of the landscape. Instead, the righteous are attracted by what is already there. The presence of the righteous does not therefore transform the landscape. As I have suggested, the life-generating consequences of their actions are postponed in time and space. They have no bearing on the corruptible world here and now.

Secondly, as I have also pointed out in the previous discussion, *2 Baruch* does not present the end-time city in the Kidron valley as a place of permanent dwelling. Although *2 Baruch* does not necessarily deny that the remnant sojourn there, the concern of the text is clearly the activities of instruction and atonement. It is thus primarily a place of gathering, not a place of ordered habitation. So, we see once again that the gathering in the Kidron valley points beyond itself to the future.

Thirdly, *2 Baruch* stresses the essential difference between the remnant and the end-time landscapes of the corruptible world. While the remnant is righteous and thus survives, the surroundings are wicked and thus dead. No matter where they went, no earthly location could possibly respond to their righteous praxis. At this time in history, the remnant is totally foreign to the world.[116]

But if the Kidron valley plays no part in the end-time city construction, what then is its territorial basis? My proposal is that the community of righteous followers of Baruch itself constitute the 'territory' of the end-time city. In my view, we should read *2 Bar.* 2:2 quite literally and ascribe the function of territory to the community.[117] In other words: *2 Baruch* maps people, a social space. It maps the continued existence of the remnant as the outcome of the joint prayers and works of Baruch, Jeremiah and those like them.[118] The pillar and the wall they build by their actions to uphold and protect themselves is the real space of survival in the chaotic end-time landscapes.

The Kidron Valley and the City of the End-Time

In the universal, godless wilderness of the end-time, *2 Baruch* maps the community of the righteous remnant as the space that can rescue Israel through the last, wicked period of the dying world. The remnant itself becomes the end-time city enclave. Works and prayers defend the righteous from the surrounding wickedness and ultimately save them. This city of the end-time is not, however, a glorious place of dwelling. Although it secures the survival of the last righteous group, it is not a place of abundant life and blessing. Rather, the description of the end-time city draws on allusions to contrasting places like the camp, Land

---

[116] Cf. Josephus, *Ant.* 4.6.8.

[117] Cf. further B. Gärtner, *The Temple and Community in Qumran and the New Testament: A Comparative Study in the Temple Symbolism of the Qumran texts and the New Testament* (SNTSMS 1; Cambridge: Cambridge University Press, 1965); L. Gaston, *No Stone on Another: Studies in the Significance of the Fall of Jerusalem in the Synoptic Gospels* (NovTSup 23; Leiden: E.J. Brill, 1970); J. Økland, "The Language of Gates and Entering: On Sacred Space in the Temple Scroll," in *New Directions in Qumran Studies: Proceedings of the Bristol Colloquium on the Dead Sea scrolls, 8–10th September 2003* (eds. J.G. Campbell, W.J. Lyons and L.K. Pietersen; LSTS 52; London: T&T Clark International, 2005), 149–165 at 152; 165; L.I. Lied, "Another Look at the Land of Damascus: The Spaces of the *Damascus Document* in the Light of Edward W. Soja's Thirdspace Approach," in *New Directions in Qumran Studies: Proceedings of the Bristol Colloquium on the Dead Sea Scrolls, 8–10 September 2003* (ed. J.G, Campbell, W.J. Lyons and L.K. Pietersen; LSTS 52; London, T&T Clark, 2005), 101–125 at 108–110. Cf. Murphy, *Structure and Meaning*, 114; Whitters, *Epistle*, 48.

[118] *2 Bar.* 86.1 suggests that the place of fast and instruction is first and foremost "in your assemblies," i.e., in the gathering of the people, not in a given locality.

and exilic space and is portrayed as a marginal spatial building totally dependent on the atonement and instruction of Baruch.[119]

Given that it is not a part of the end-time city, what then is the role of the Kidron valley? The answer again lies in the nature of the remnant's actions in the valley. The righteous atone for the past transgressions of the twelve tribes, and learn to secure future redemption. In other words, their actions are directed towards the past and the future, not towards the present. The remnant does not perform cultic duties, it does not till the ground, nor does it produce descendants: no acts uphold life in the present. This is because, as 10:6–17 points out, it is not meaningful to maintain life in this world when the temple has been destroyed and the Land has been lost. As Baruch points out in 10:6–8, death is preferable to life during the end-time, as there is no light, no joy or beauty, nor descendants to Israel (10:11–16). Although alive enough to survive until the coming of the Messiah, the remnant is dead to this world and its processes, since any real association with the corruptible world would surely lead to complete destruction.

The setting of the city amongst the impurity and death of the Kidron valley becomes meaningful in this perspective. The chaotic, sunken Kidron valley can accommodate the remnant's death-like situation. A place of the dead needs no ordering care, and a place of ritual impurity does not demand cultic observance. The Kidron valley can therefore harbour the efforts of the remnant to repair the past and create the future, without demanding any share in their cosmos-maintaining actions. The remnant can be dead to this world and still produce future spaces by their righteous practices. Just as the corruptible world is totally alien to the remnant, the remnant and its acts can remain alien to the dying, corruptible world and still prepare for future life.

---

[119] This spatial construction shares some traits with other Land-like protective spaces of the end-time, described in other texts. The Land of Damascus in the *Damascus Document* (e.g., CD VI–VIII) resembles *2 Baruch*'s end-time city (Cf. Lied, "Damascus," 101–125. It is noteworthy that CD VIII.20–21 identifies those who went to Damascus with Jeremiah and Baruch, as well as Elishah and Gehazi. Cf. also the Holy Land at the Island in *Hist. Rech.* 8–11, as well as the description of how Aseneth becomes like a walled mother-city for those who take refuge in God's name (*Jos. Asen.* 16:16)). Cf. further Eph 2:21.

CHAPTER FIVE

'HERE WITH ME': THE LAST DAYS OF BARUCH

The previous chapter has shown that the righteous remnant survives in the Kidron valley. Still, although the escape to the Kidron valley saved the remnant during the destruction of Jerusalem, and although it enhanced the survival prospects of the remnant in the sense that it enabled the remnant to be dead and foreign to the order of the corruptible world, it was the social space of the city of the pillar and the wall, constituted by the practices of the righteous remnant, that safeguarded the community. Hence, in order to argue the rescue of the remnant from the hardships of the end-time *2 Baruch* envisions the righteous community and its practices in spatial terms. The remnant and its righteous works are therefore themselves the main factors of end-time survival.

A central issue in the previous chapter was *2 Baruch*'s stress on Baruch's leadership. In the end-time, the acts of Baruch, the perfect community leader, were vital to the survival of the remnant. He atoned for the tribes, he instructed his followers and he comforted them with regard to their future prospects. Indeed, as that chapter pointed out, the leader and his acts were foundational to the space of the community. Since the leader distinguished for them light from darkness and life from death by his investigation of the Law, his presence among them was decisive for the continued existence of a protective spatial enclave.

2 Bar. 43 introduces an important shift in *2 Baruch*. In that passage God announces to Baruch that Baruch will leave Mount Zion and that he will die, or otherwise leave the earth. Baruch obediently follows God's command. He leaves Mount Zion for good and goes to Hebron. In Hebron he prepares for his ultimate departure from earth. In light of the conclusion of the previous chapter, this prospect challenges the very basis of the remnant's spatial foundation and existence. If the leader in fact leaves the remnant, what will there be?

In the present chapter I will discuss how *2 Baruch* envisions the effect of Baruch's imminent departure from earth on the space of the remnant. The remnant is still in the wilderness of the end-time, but Baruch's move from Mount Zion to Hebron affects the description of the

space of the remnant. How does Baruch's move to Hebron change
the description of the space of the remnant during the last days of
Baruch's life on earth? How does 2 Baruch picture the remnant's space
after Baruch has left them?

The Last Days and Deeds of Baruch

Announcing Baruch's departure from the wicked world,[1] God says:

> You, then, Baruch, strengthen your heart for that which has been said
> to you, and trust the things which have been shown to you, because for
> you there are many eternal consolations. For you will go away from this
> place and leave these regions which are seen by you now. And you will
> forget that which is corruptible and you will not again remember those
> things which are among the mortal ones. Go therefore and command
> your people and come to this place, and afterwards fast seven days, and
> then I will come to you and speak with you (43:1–3).

This passage proclaims Baruch's imminent departure from this world.
According to 43:2, he will leave the place *(atrā hānā)* and regions *(atra-
wātā ayleyn)* he dwells in, and leave behind everything that belongs to
the corruptible world. In fact, 2 Baruch already hinted at Baruch's near
departure in 3:1–3:[2]

> And I said: O Lord, my Lord! Have I come to this world to see the evils
> of my mother? No, my Lord. If I have found mercy in your eyes, take
> first my spirit, that I may go to my fathers and not see the destruction of
> my mother. For both these two matters are pressing to me: I cannot resist
> you, but my soul also cannot see the evils of my mother.

This passage shows that Baruch is torn between life on earth and resting with the fathers already before the destruction of Jerusalem. However, the announcement of the approaching departure becomes explicit

---

[1] *2 Baruch*'s descriptions of Baruch's departure from the earth are not unanimous.
He may die (e.g., 78:5; 84:1), or maybe his departure is better described as a rapture
(13:3; 76:2. Himmelfarb has defined 'rapture' in the following manner: "Ascent to
heaven at the initiative of God" (*Ascent to Heaven*, 5; Cf. also A.W. Zweip, *The Ascension
of the Messiah in Lukan Christology* (Leiden: Brill, 1997), 74–75)). Probably, *2 Baruch* is
intentionally unclear on the issue, maybe to imitate other exemplary figures (Cf. *4 Ezra*
14:9; *L.A.B.* 48:1–2; *2 En.* 36; 64; *Targum Pseudo-Jonathan to Deut* 32; 34:5). In any case,
Baruch will depart and be taken up (43:2; 46:7; 48:30). Cf. further Charles, *Apocalypse
of Baruch*, 68–69; 73; Bogaert, *Apocalypse de Baruch I*, 113–119; II, 78; Whitters, *Epistle*,
44–45.
[2] As well as in 13:3.

only in 43:2. Then Baruch's preparation for his farewell becomes a central issue in the frame narrative. 44:1–2 describes Baruch's immediate response to God's command:

> And I, Baruch, went from there and came to my people and called my first-born son and Gedaliah, my friend, and seven of the elders of the people and said to them:[3] Behold, I will go to my fathers in accordance with the way of the whole earth. You, however, do not withdraw from the way of the law, but protect and guard the people who are left so that they do not renounce the commandments of the Mighty One.

Baruch informs the representatives of Israel about his coming departure and commands them to continue the instruction of the people when he himself is gone. However, Baruch's tasks on earth are still not completed. The remaining parts of the text, in fact a large bulk of *2 Baruch*, describe Baruch's visions and their interpretation (53–75), his prayers and dialogues with God (48–52), his continuing instruction of the people in form of public speeches (77) and letters (78–87) during the last days of his life on earth. In this manner, *2 Baruch* employs the prospect of Baruch's immanent departure to highlight the importance of the message he presents. This testament imagery of the text, thus, frames his instruction during the end-time as his last words to Israel.[4] Moreover, since Baruch's last days in this world coincide with the imminent destruction of the corruptible world during the end-time, his acts and whereabouts at this point bear particular significance. Baruch goes to spend his last days at Hebron, and in the meantime the death of the entire world draws nearer. In this regard, the Hebron reference both serves as a fitting setting for Baruch's last deeds and as a hint about the end of the world of corruption. The coming departure of Baruch in

---

[3] Cf. also the discussion of this passage in Chapter Four, pp. 129–130.

[4] The genre Testament is discussed by e.g., M. de Jonge, *The Testaments of the Twelve Patriarchs: A Study of Their Text, Composition and Origin* (Van Gorcum's Theologische Bibliotheek 25; Assen: Van Gorcum & comp., 1953); E von Nordheim, *Das Testament als Literaturgattung im Judentum der hellenistisch-römischen Zeit: Die Lehre der Alten, vol. I* (ALGHJ 131; Leiden: E.J. Brill, 1980); D. Dimant, "The Testament as a Literary Form in Early Jewish Pseudepigraphic Literature," *WCJS* 8 (1982): 79–83; J.J. Collins, "Testaments," in *Jewish Writings of the Second Temple Period: Apocrypha, Pseudepigrapha, Qumran Sectarian Writings, Philo, Josephus: The Literature of the Jewish People in the Period of the Second Temple and the Talmud, Vol. 2* (ed. M.E. Stone; CRINT 2; Assen: Van Gorcum, 1984), 325–356; A.B. Kolenkow, "The Literary Genre 'Testament,'" in *Early Judaism and Its Modern Interpreters* (ed. R.A. Kraft and G.W.E. Nickelsburg; BMI 2; Atlanta: Scholars Press, 1986), 259–267. Cf. also Harnisch, *Verhängnis*, 208–222; Sayler, *Promises*, 95–98; Whitters, *Epistle*, 44–48; 165–168.

the frame narrative therefore also serves as an interpretative clue to his visions and dialogues.[5] These are his last words, and last words demand attention.

Of particular interest to the following discussion are the locations of Baruch's solitary acts of sanctification, communication, visions and letter writing as well as his public instruction and dialogue with his followers after he has moved to Hebron. According to 47:1, Baruch first goes to Hebron, he appears before God in 48:1, in 55:1 he sits down there under a tree, he ascends a mountain in 76:3, and in 77:18 he sits down under an oak again. These are the locations of his secluded actions. The locality of his public instruction and dialogue in 77:1–15 is vaguer and need further attention. What is the relationship between the location of Baruch's solitary acts at Hebron and the space of the remnant? And how does the set of connotations associated with Hebron and its surroundings reshape the space of Baruch's followers?

Locating Baruch and His Followers

2 Bar. 43:1–3, cited above, does not only say that Baruch will leave the world, it simultaneously announces a shift in the earthly location of his last time on earth. God commands him to leave Mount Zion, the place of his divine encounters up to that time, to instruct his followers (44:1–46:7), and to go "to this place" (*latrā hānā*).[6] Baruch thus leaves Mount Zion and journeys to Hebron. 47:1–2 describes Baruch's arrival there:

> When I went away and dismissed them, I left from there and said to them: Behold, I will go to Hebron, for to that place (*ltamān*) the Mighty One has sent me. And I arrived at that place which was told me there (*tamān*), and I sat down there and fasted seven days.[7]

This passage tells us how Baruch acts according to God's command (43:3). He leaves "from there" (*men tamān*) (47:1)—Mount Zion—and arrives at "that place" (*lhaw atrā*) (47:2)—at Hebron—sits down and fasts the appointed period of seven days before he again prays to God either

---

[5] Cf. e.g., Whitters, *Epistle*, 45.
[6] Scholars have disagreed about the interpretation of "this place" (43:3), the relationship between 43 and 47, and whether Baruch goes to Hebron or not. Bogaert has argued convincingly that Baruch goes to Hebron (*Apocalypse de Baruch II*, 85–86). This interpretation makes good sense out of the details of the Syriac.
[7] I agree with Bogaert (*Apocalypse de Baruch I*, 292–293), and disagree with the translations of Charles (*Apocalypse of Baruch*, 73–74) and Klijn ("2 Baruch," 635).

in an unidentified spot (48:1), from a mountain top (76:3), from under a tree (55:1) or under an oak (77:18).

These topographical references indicate that Baruch uses the landscapes surrounding Hebron just like he earlier used the landscapes in the Jerusalem area.[8] Just like he entered a cave (21:1–2) and other unidentified locales in the Kidron valley (12:5; 32:8) to sanctify himself before he ascended Mount Zion or sat down under an oak,[9] he now fasts in Hebron before he ascends a mountain and sits down under trees again to receive God's revelations. In other words, whereas Baruch leaves the Jerusalem area and moves to Hebron, 2 Baruch treats the topography of these two places in equivalent terms.

What does 2 Baruch tell us about the location of Baruch's followers after Baruch has gone to Hebron? Do they go to Hebron as well? 2 Baruch does not identify any exact location of the remnant after 2 Bar. 47. In fact, 47:1–2 indicates that Baruch undertakes his journey to Hebron by himself. He dismisses his followers after instructing them, announces his departure and then goes. It therefore seems likely that Baruch's followers remain behind, possibly in the vicinity of Jerusalem and the Kidron valley.

Does this mean that Baruch abandons his followers? Baruch's departure to Hebron could be understood as an abandonment of the group.[10] However, if that were the case, it would run counter to a central issue of the text: the concern of the leader for his followers. In fact, 2 Baruch repeatedly shows that Baruch does not leave the group when he goes to Hebron.[11] Moreover, as I just pointed out, Baruch's move to Hebron resembles the episodes of the text where Baruch alone sanctified himself and then communicated with God at Mount Zion. He leaves the gathering of the people in both instances, but he clearly does not abandon his followers; the opposite is the case. According to 34:1, for example, Baruch promises not to leave his followers, and confirms that promise by ascending Mount Zion to provide more knowledge for the group. Baruch's ascension to Mount Zion is thus interpreted as a way of proving his fidelity to his followers and is not to be understood as an aban-

---

[8] Cf. Chapter Four.

[9] Cf. 2 Bar. 6; 10:5; 13:1; 21:3; 34:1.

[10] The outcry of Baruch's followers in 46:1–7 can be interpreted that way. However, the reason for their outburst may just as well be the immanent death of Baruch. Note that they fear his departure in 33–34 as well. Baruch then swears he will not leave him, and then ascends Mount Zion.

[11] Cf. 2 Bar. 10:1–5; 32:8–34:1; 46:1–7; 77:1–6, 11–17.

donment of them. The character of his actions in the two settings further supports this view. The move to Hebron and his solitary actions in the Kidron valley and at Mount Zion do not run counter to his role as leader. It is instead a part of what he does *as* leader of the group.

In fact, Baruch's presence is essential to the identification of the space of the group after Baruch's move to Hebron. 77:1–5 shows this:

> And I Baruch went from there and came to the people and I gathered them from the greatest to the smallest. And I said to them: hear, children of Israel, see how many remain of the twelve tribes of Israel. For to you and your fathers the Lord gave the law above all peoples. And because your brothers transgressed the commandments of the Most High, he demanded vengeance upon you and upon them. And he did not spare the former, and even the latter he placed in captivity, and he did not leave a remnant of them.[12] And behold, you are here with me.

77.5 provides the most important identification of the localisation of Baruch's followers: They are "here with me" (*hārkā 'amy*),[13] in other words, in a 'here' defined by the presence of Baruch among them. Baruch's followers continue to be in Baruch's presence, as his audience and as recipients of his instruction also when he goes to Hebron. The geographical distance between Hebron and the Kidron valley is therefore not of primary importance, since the location of the group is not defined by territorial belonging, but rather by their dependence on Baruch.[14] The group waits patiently for Baruch, whether he leaves them for Mount Zion, an oak, or for another mountain and oak in the Hebron area. The group clearly expects him to return to them. We are thus facing a similar spatial construction as the one identified in the previous chapter. The space of the Baruch group is a space

---

[12] I understand "the former" (*qadāmye*), as the nine and a half tribes (Cf. 62:5–8; 78:1. 1:2 says "ten tribes"), and "the latter" (*aḥrāye*) as the two and a half tribes (Cf. 63–64; 77:17. 1:2 says "two tribes"). Cf. Charles, *Apocalypse of Baruch*, 119–120, and Klijn, "2 Baruch," 646–647 for an alternative translation.

[13] *'itaykun hārkā 'amy*. Alternatively, "you are here, my people." Both translations of *amy* ("my people" or "with me") are possible (cf. Kmosko, *Liber Apocalypseos*, 1202–1203; Bogaert, *Apocalypse de Baruch II*, 134). Bogaert claims that the author of 2 Baruch would never dare to call the remnant "my people." Thus, he rejects this translation (Bogaert, *Apocalypse de Baruch II*, 134). Note, however, that 43.3 may also be translated "your people" (*amāk*). Still, "with me" is preferable in 77:5 since it stresses the fact that Baruch never left his followers. This is an important topic throughout 2 Baruch (cf. 33:1–34:1; 46:1–7).

[14] The distance between Hebron and Jerusalem was anyhow not considered as wide. Josephus, for instance, says the following about Hebron: "another city (...) in the hill country not far from Jerusalem" (*J.W.* 4.9.9). Cf. also Klausner, *Messianic Idea*, 330–331.

which first and foremost is based on the existence of the community and its dependence on a leader. Baruch's followers are clearly still in the wilderness,[15] be it in the Kidron valley[16] or not, but they exist independently of it as an autonomous spatial building 'here with me'.

So, what is the importance of Baruch's move to the Hebron area to the spatial construction 'here with me'? The above outline has shown that *2 Baruch* continues to map the community under Baruch's leadership and their practices as constitutive to this end-time space. Baruch and his followers atone and receive instruction in order to survive the end-time and regain the life promised in the other world. However, on the level of connotations the remnant's end-time space is clearly changed by Baruch's move to Hebron. In other words, his move to Hebron provides the space of the remnant with a new field of allusions and connotations which subsequently changes the character of this spatial construction.

What allusions and connotations are triggered by *2 Baruch*'s reference to Hebron? Why does *2 Baruch* choose the Hebron area as the location of the last days of Baruch's life?[17] As I have pointed out above, *2 Bar.* 43 on the one hand announces Baruch's coming departure from earth. Baruch will leave this corruptible world for the other, incorruptible world. On the other hand, Baruch is not only going to leave this world. He will also leave the ruins of Zion for a mountain and an oak at Hebron, and the cave of the Kidron valley for a similar place at Hebron. Consequently, when 43:2 states that Baruch shall "go away from this place and leave these regions" the text *both* predicts that Baruch will leave this world, *and* presents God's command to Baruch to leave the ruins of Zion. When he journeys to the Hebron area, Baruch leaves his 'mother' to go to his fathers, abandoning mother Jerusalem for the famous gravesite of the patriarchs in Hebron (3:1–2).[18] Thus, we can interpret the scene on two related levels: Baruch leaves the vicinity of one city for the vicinity of another, *and* he chooses death, or rapture,

---

[15] Cf. *2 Bar.* 76:5; 77:1; 77:13–18.

[16] Cf. Bogaert, *Apocalypse de Baruch II*, 134.

[17] Whitters suggests that changes of physical location in the frame narrative signal literary division in *2 Baruch* and that the movements of Baruch and his followers in the landscape introduce new episodes of the narrative. Whitters observes that the move to Hebron in *2 Bar.* 47 introduces a new episode of the frame narrative (Whitters, *Epistle*, 39–40).

[18] This is where the fathers rest in the earth (*2 Bar.* 11:4; 21:24–25; 85:9). For the expression "go to my fathers," cf. 44:2; 11:4; 85:9; Gen 15:15.

instead of continued marginal existence on earth.[19] Moreover, according to 43:2, Baruch shall forget "that which is corruptible" and not remember "those things that are among the mortal ones". It is plausible that this passage has the corruptible world in general as its topic, but it probably also implies a final denial of the earthly temple and of Jerusalem.[20] When Baruch leaves these spaces behind, the temple lies in ruins and Jerusalem is destroyed. *2 Baruch* puts no hope in their restoration. Instead, he redirects hope to the other world—and to the Hebron location.[21]

The Mountain and the Oak:
Readdressing the Wilderness of the End-Time

The following part of the chapter will discuss the functions of the merging allusions to death and hope triggered by the Hebron-reference and provide some suggestions as to their transforming effect on the character of the spatial construction 'here with me'. I will concentrate on the ambiguous connotations to the oak and the tree (55:1; 77:18) and to Baruch's mountain sojourn (76:1–5).

The Trees of the Hebron Area: The Life and Death of Abraham

Hebron and its surrounding area have probably been well known to *2 Baruch*'s audience as an important location of the stories of Abraham. The name Hebron would therefore bring a complex set of connotations to mind. In the Genesis account, the Hebron area is a place where Abraham dwelled (Gen 13:8; 14:13; 18:1), it is the place of the covenant

---

[19] Charles, *Apocalypse of Baruch*, 4–5; Bogaert, *Apocalypse de Baruch I*, 323. Cf. *4 Ezra* 10:5–9.

[20] Cf., e.g., *2 Bar.* 21:19; 44:9 (Cf. Charles, *Apocalypse of Baruch*, 40–41).

[21] Cf. further Sayler, *Promises*, 95; Whitters, *Epistle*, 39–41. Note that Hebron was a contested city and that its status must have been ambiguous. Whereas Hebron was called a city of Judah by Josh 21:11; 1 Chr 6:55 and 2 Sam 2:1, Hebron was considered a part of Idumea in the 2nd century C.E. (Whitters, *Epistle*, 122). Note further that the fields and villages surrounding Hebron belong to Caleb and his descendants, and not to Judah. It is set a part from the rest of Judah by several biblical sources (Num 14:24; 32:12; Deut 1:36; Josh 14:6–15; 15:1–19; Judg 1:11–15; 1 Sam 30:14. Cf. Sir 46:7–10; Cf. M.J. Fretz and R.I. Panitz, "Caleb," *ABD 1*, 808–810; Henze, "Jeremiah," 168–169). Note also that several of these sources describe Hebron as a Levitical city. In that sense it is set apart from tribal ownership, and thus beyond the land of the tribe of Judah.

with the patriarch (13:14–18; 15:17–21),[22] it serves as a place of worship (13:18), it is the only part of Canaan Abraham owned (23), and it is the place of Abraham's grave (23:19–20; 25:8–10).[23] In other words, Hebron is intrinsically involved both with the life and the death of Abraham.

The allusions to the Abraham stories triggered by the reference to Hebron become even more evident when 2 Baruch locates Baruch under a tree in 55:1 and under an oak in 77:18. 55:1 introduces the interpretation part of the Apocalypse of the cloud like this: "I sat down there under a tree (ṯeyt 'ilānā) to rest in the shadow of its branches (bṭelālā dsawke)." While sitting in the shadow of that tree, the angel Ramael helps Baruch understand the vision he received in 53:1–12. 77:18 refers to an oak as the place where Baruch sits down to write letters to the dispersed tribes: "And it happened on the twenty-first day of the ninth month[24] that I, Baruch, came and sat down under an oak (baluṭā) in the shadow of the branches (bṭelālā dsawke), and nobody was with me; I was alone." Although only 77:18 says explicitly that the tree is an oak, the clear resemblance between the two descriptions of the trees and the identical location of the two at Hebron, makes it likely that both passages bring the same tree to mind.

With some exceptions,[25] most scholars have in fact identified the oak of 77:18 with the famous Mamre oaks.[26] Gen 13:18 says: "So Abram moved his tent, and came and settled by the oaks of Mamre, which are at Hebron;[27] and there he built an altar to the LORD." In all likelihood,

---

[22] Or the place Abraham settles immediately after the making of the covenant.

[23] Cf. alternative versions in Jub. 12–23; L.A.B. 7–8.

[24] Cf. Bogaert (Apocalypse de Baruch II, 133; 137) concerning the date.

[25] Charles, Apocalypse of Baruch, 10. Charles locates the oak outside the Kidron valley (Cf. 6:1). This interpretation is possible, but the context of 77:18 talks in favour of Hebron. It is not surprising that 2 Baruch mentions different oaks. Firstly, oaks are impressive trees, and they were relatively frequent in the Levant. Secondly, both biblical and later texts describe several famous oaks (Cf. the oak of Moreh (Gen 12:6; Deut 11:30), oaks of Bashan (Ezek 27:6), the oak of Rogel (Liv. Pro. 1:1), an oak in Shiloh (5:2; 18:5) and Deborah's oak near Bethel (10:8). Cf. also other unspecified oaks in 4 Ezra 14:1). Note also that the pillars of the Jerusalem temple, discussed in the previous chapter, may be equated to trees, i.e., they may be vegetation-like pillars. Note that rulers courted under trees (Judg 4:5; 1 Sam 14:2; 22:6). 2 Kgs 23:3 also suggests that the king courted under the pillars (Cf. Stordalen, Eden, 120–122).

[26] Bogaert, Apocalypse de Baruch I, 323–324; II, 134; Whitters, Epistle, 40; 165–167. Klausner has even suggested that the oak of 6.1 may be the one in Hebron (Klausner, Messianic Idea, 330).

[27] The place names Hebron (Kiriath-arba), Mamre, Machpelah and Ramat el-Khalil tend to overlap in different sources (Cf. Gen 23:2; Neh 11:25; 1QapGen XXI, 19). E. Mader suggests that the field "Ardat" ("Arpad"/ "Arbad") in 4 Ezra 9:26 could

therefore, 55:1 and 77:18 associate Baruch's trees with the oaks in the vicinity of Hebron.[28]

The Oak and the Cave: The Death of Abraham

One aspect of *2 Baruch*'s description needs some attention before we continue the discussion. Whereas the Genesis account describes plural oaks,[29] and does not necessarily equate the oaks at Mamre with the trees that surround Abraham's grave, *2 Baruch* describes single trees and does not seem to differentiate between the various allusions to Abraham's life and death. In what manners can the trees of *2 Bar.* 55:1 and 77:18 recall the life as well as the death of Abraham?

According to Gen 23:17–19, Abraham bought a field east of Mamre to bury his wife Sarah. The Machpelah cave at the end of Ephron's field was considered the ideal burial place (23:6): the field lies in the vicinity of the city, it is lush and filled with trees (23:4, 17). When Abraham later dies, the Machpelah cave becomes his burial place as well (Gen 25:8–10).[30] Gen 48:29–32 adds that Isaac and Rebecca, as well as Jacob and Leah, were also buried there.[31] Later exegetes add that several other biblical figures have the Machpelah cave as their gravesite. The *Testaments of the Twelve Patriarchs*, for instance, claims that the twelve sons of Jacob rest there.[32] This means that to the audiences

---

also be a reference to Hebron (*Die Ergebnisse der Ausgrabungen im heiligen Bezirk Râmet El-Halîl in Südpalestina 1926–1928* (Freiburg im Breisgau: Erich Wewel, 1957), 278). Bogaert rejects this interpretation (Bogaert, *Apocalypse de Baruch I*, 323).

[28] Baruch is clearly not *in* the city or an inhabited area. He chooses a place of solitude. This is common in *2 Baruch* and also what Abraham does in the Genesis account. Note that Abraham is often associated with the wilderness. He does not only leave his native land, he also leaves city life (Cf. LXX Gen 12:9; *Abr.* 87. Cf. Sandmel, *Philo's Place*, 115–116; 141. On the other hand, Philo also considers Abraham a city dweller (Sandmel, *Philo's Place*, 125). Note that David may also be presented as a wilderness dweller (1 Sam 20; *L.A.B.* 59).

[29] Cf. Gen 13:18; 14:13; 18:1. Genesis mentions both oaks and terebinths. There is often no clear distinction between the species oak and terebinth, and they may be interchangeable (Cf. Isa 6:13 and *Targum Jonathan to Isa* 6:13; Cf. Violet, *Apokalypsen*, 264; I. Jacob and W. Jacob, "Flora," *ABD* 2, 803–817 at 806; 808).

[30] Cf. *Jub.* 19:5; 23:7; *T. Ab.* 20:11; *T. Jac.* 6:12–13; Josephus, *Ant.* 1.14.1; 1.17.1.

[31] Gen 50; *T. Jac.* 6:12–13; *Jub.* 45:15; Josephus, *Ant.* 1.22.1. Cf. the special circumstances of the death of Joseph (*T. Jos.* 20).

[32] *T. Reu.* 7:1–2; *T. Sim.* 8:2; *T. Levi* 19:5; *T. Jud.* 26:4; *T. Iss.* 7:8; *T. Zeb.* 10:6; *T. Dan* 7:2; *T. Naph.* 9:1; *T. Gad* 8:4; *T. Ash.* 8:1–2; *T. Jos.* 20:6; *T. Benj.* 12:4. Cf. *Jub.* 45:5–10 and Josephus, *Ant.* 2.8.1–2. Cf. also the burial of Ezekiel and Jonah in caves equivalent to the Machpelah cave (*Liv. Pro.* 3:3 and 10:9).

of the first centuries C.E. the Machpelah cave in the Hebron area was the final resting place for the earthly remains both of the patriarchs and of a number of other biblical figures. It must thus have been perceived as the family grave and burial site *par excellence* of the people of Israel.[33]

How does *2 Baruch* allude to the death and grave of Abraham? We shall once more look at the tree in *2 Bar.* 55:1 and the oak in 77:18. Trees, and particularly oaks, were in general associated with holy graves in the first centuries C.E.[34] Both biblical texts and later literature give several examples of graves placed underneath oaks and other trees.[35] According to Gen 23:17, the Machpelah cave, where Abraham was buried, lies in a field with many trees. Although this Genesis passage confirms the relationship between those trees and the grave of the patriarch, it does not specify the species of these trees and it is questionable whether Genesis considers them identical with the oaks of Mamre, the setting of Abraham's life at Hebron.[36]

The *Testament of Abraham*, however, both relates death explicitly to these various trees and blends the image of the trees with the image of a singular oak of Mamre. The *Testament of Abraham* locates Abraham in a field by the oak of Mamre (2:1) and by the trees of Mamre (16:7) when he receives his two death announcements.[37] The archangel Michael first searches for Abraham "at the oak of Mamre" to tell him about his imminent death, but finds him in the nearby field (2:1). The second time, Death in person approaches Abraham (16:7):

> Now the righteous Abraham (had) come out of his room and (was) seated under the trees of Mamre, holding his chin in his hand and waiting for the arrival of the archangel Michael. And behold a sweet odor came to him and a radiance of light. And Abraham turned around and saw Death coming toward him in great glory and youthful beauty.[38]

---

[33] Cf. *Targum Ruth* 1:17. Cf. Bogaert, *Apocalypse de Baruch II*, 84; L.I. Lied, "Døde, jordiske bein i Guds himmel? Det lova landet og dødens geografi," *Chaos* 39 (2003): 71–90 at 74–77.

[34] Jeremias, *Heiligengräber*, 120. Groves of oaks were often considered holy (Jacob and Jacob, "Flora," 806). Oaks were also connected to holy sites and often marked the location were a visionary received visions (*Jub.* 13:2–3; *4 Ezra* 14:1; *2 Bar.* 6:1; 55:1).

[35] Gen 35:8; *Jub.* 32:30; *Liv. Pro.* 1:1; 5:2; 10:8; 18:5.

[36] These trees are probably not identical in the Genesis account (Gen 13:18; 18:1; 23:17).

[37] Cf. The Greek Testament of Abraham, Recension A, according to J.A. Robinson, *Texts and Studies. No. 2. The Testament of Abraham* (Contributions to Biblical and Patristic Literature; Cambridge: University Press, 1892), 78 and 97.

[38] Translation by E.P. Sanders, "Testaments of the Three Patriarchs," in vol. 1 of

These passages of the *Testament of Abraham* identify Abraham's dwelling place as being at the oak and the trees of Mamre. *T. Ab.* 20:12 adds a description of the location of Abraham's grave: "And they buried him in the promised land at the oak of Mamre." Thus, according to this account, Abraham did not only live at the oak of Mamre. He is buried by that oak as well. In the *Testament of Abraham*, the oak, or the trees, of Mamre serves simultaneously as setting for Abraham's last deeds, his final cosmic journey, Abraham's will and finally his death and burial. In other words, the *Testament of Abraham* lets 'the oak of Mamre' represent both the 'oaks of Mamre' of the Genesis account *and* the trees of the Machpelah field.[39]

To the exegetes of the first centuries C.E. the variety of oaks and trees of the Abraham stories apparently tended to blend into a singular, undifferentiated 'oak of Mamre'.[40] In fact, the LXX and the Syriac version of Gen 18:1 both render the plural oaks of the Hebrew versions with a singular oak.[41] The singular oak of Mamre thus combines the connotations related to the several oaks and trees mentioned in the Abraham story of Genesis, including the connotations to the grave of Abraham.

The reference to the oak in *2 Bar.* 77:18 and the tree in 55:1 is then probably to this undifferentiated 'oak of Mamre' of the later tradition. The reference to the tree and the oak would then possibly both connote scenes from Abraham's life *and* allude to the signpost of the most important gravesite of the forefathers and foremothers of Israel. The connotations that go with *2 Baruch*'s tree references thus strengthen the testament imagery that was noted above. Under the branches of the tree in 55:1 Baruch receives the lengthy interpretation of his last major vision. And under the branches of the oak in 77:18 Baruch also writes letters to the twelve tribes, as his final act on earth (77:18–19).[42] The

---

OTP (ed. J.H. Charlesworth; 2 vols; Garden City, NY: Doubleday, 1983), 869–918 at 892.

[39] It is possible that *Jub.* 19:1 also suggests this when it says that Abraham dwells "opposite Hebron": in Gen 23:19, the Machpelah cave faces Hebron.

[40] According to Ginzberg, the Oak of Abraham was "a subject for popular fancy" in the first centuries C.E. (*Legends V*, 235). Cf. Josephus, *Ant.* 1.10.4; 1.11.2; *J.W.* 4.9.7; *QG* 4, 74 and further Sandmel, *Philo's Place*, 65; Stordalen, *Eden*, 105–107; 123.

[41] Cf. Y.L. Arbeitman, "Mamre," *ABD* 4, 492–493 at 492. Cf. also *Jub.* 14:10; Josephus, *Ant.* 1.11.2; *QG* 4,1; *T. Ab.* 1:2; 2:1; 20:12. *T. Ab.* 16:7, though, keeps the plural.

[42] According to *4 Bar.* 6:19, Baruch gets papyrus and ink from "the marketplace of the gentiles" to write a letter to the people in Babylon. Hebron was famous for its great market (Bogaert, *Apocalypse de Baruch II*, 137).

oak in the Hebron area is thus Baruch's final place of sojourn in the corruptible world, just like it once was a central place of sojourn and the final resting place of Abraham.

Abraham the Stranger, Abraham the Landowner

The choice of Hebron as location in the last half of *2 Baruch* also has wider implications. The shift of Baruch's location from the Jerusalem area to Hebron evokes additional sets of connotations with important bearings on space definition. In the following, I shall focus on the ambiguous role of the Hebron area. It can be considered both as an alternative stronghold within Palestine and as a place that highlights the role of Israel as strangers to the world.

Several accounts ascribe the making of God's covenant with Abraham to Hebron, or more specifically to the oaks of Mamre.[43] The Hebron setting of *2 Baruch* thus probably alludes to the establishment of God's everlasting covenant with Abraham. Again, the oak of 77:18 becomes the centre of our attention. According to Whitters, that oak is "an emblem of the original covenant with Abraham."[44] The place where Baruch writes letters to instruct the tribes and to encourage them to keep up hope is thus the very place where God's covenant with Abraham was set up. Baruch's location under the oak thus evokes the promises of the Abraham covenant.

According to Genesis, the only piece of land Abraham actually owned lies in the Hebron area.[45] As noted above, Abraham bought a field from the Hittite Ephron in Machpelah for the price of four hundred shekels (Gen 23:16–17). The Genesis account underscores the fact that Abraham actually purchased the field. Although the Hittites offered to give Abraham the field for free, Abraham insisted to pay for the piece of land "in the presence of all who went in at the gate of his city" (23:18). The field thus became Abraham's rightful possession,

---

[43] Gen 13:8–18; 14:13; 15:17–21; 18:1; *Jub.* 13–14. Note that God promises Abraham the Land in a number of places, among them Haran (Gen 12:1–3), Shechem (12:6–7) in the Bethel area (13:3–14) and in Mamre (15:17–21), or already in Mesopotamia (15:7; Josh 24:3; Neh 9:7; Heb 11:8; Acts 7:2–3; *Abr.* 162–167 (Cf. Moxnes, *Theology in Conflict*, 195–196)).

[44] Whitters, *Epistle*, 166–167. Cf. R. Rendtorff, *The Covenant Formula: An Exegetical and Theological Investigation* (trans. M. Kohl; OTS; Edinburgh: T&T Clark, 1998), 14–15.

[45] Cf. Davies, *Gospel and Land*, 15–24 for a discussion of Abraham's Land in the Pentateuch.

firstly, because he paid a decent price for it, and, secondly, because the transaction between the Hittites and Abraham took place in the presence of numerous witnesses (23:8–16).[46]

As Abraham's possession, the field of Machpelah is significant. Although Gen 15:18–19 states that the entire Canaan had already been promised to Abraham's seed, Abraham's own relation to Canaan is complex. On the one hand, Genesis says that Abraham remained a stranger in the land of Canaan (e.g., Gen 23:3). Canaan, identified as the Land of Promise remains a *future* gift throughout Abraham's own life time.[47] It was never fully acquired by him (Gen 12:7–8).[48] On the other hand, other passages seem to suggest that God gave the Land to Abraham *as well as* to his descendants (e.g., Gen 13:14–17). Later exegetes tend to maintain this ambivalence in the Genesis narrative. They either interpret Abraham's possession of Canaan as implied in the promise directed to future generations, or they suggest that Abraham actually owned that country in his own lifetime. Or, they transmit both versions. Sulzbach has pointed out that *Jub.* 13 implies Abraham's ownership of the region. Although *Jub.* 13 is clearly a rewriting of Gen 12–13, it leaves out the description of the presence of the Canaanites in the Land (Gen 12:6). Sulzbach proposes that "the author at this point in the text deliberately did not want to compromise Abraham's presence in the land with that of the Canaanites."[49] This observation is important, since *Jub.* 13 is the passage where God promises Abraham the Land. By not mentioning the presence of the Canaanites, *Jub.* 13 stresses Abraham's rights to the Land.[50] The *Genesis Apocryphon* makes a similar interpretation. Whereas Gen 13:17 only *suggests* that Abraham

---

[46] Cf. Gen 25:10; *Jub.* 19:1–9; Josephus, *Ant.* 1.14. Cf. Davies, *Gospel and Land*, 22. Some later sources also say that Abraham owned Miriam's well (Ginzberg, *Legends III*, 52). Cf. also Jacob's purchase of land close to the city Shechem in Gen 33:18–20. According to Josephus, *Ant.* 7.13.4, David bought the threshing floor from Aranuah for fifty shekels to build an altar to God. This is the place where Solomon later builds the temple.

[47] Note that according to Josephus, Canaan is equivalent to Judea in this context (*Ant.* 1.7.1).

[48] Although a future promise in a sense also determines the here and now. Since God guarantees the fulfilment of promise, it is already fulfiled (Cf. Moxnes, *Theology in Conflict*, 181–182). Alternatively, the purchase starts the fulfilment process (cf. Blenkinsopp, *Prophecy and Canon*, 61).

[49] Sulzbach, "Function," 295–296.

[50] Cf. also *Jub.* 12:29; 14:7–8; 19:3–9.

passed through the land he has just been promised (13:14–16),[51] the *Genesis Apocryphon* describes the implementation of God's promise and presents Abraham's journey throughout that land in great detail (1Qap-Gen XXI:15–20).[52] Both texts, therefore, highlight the interpretation of Canaan as Abraham's Land in his own life time.[53]

Other accounts, however, make a point of Abraham's position as a stranger in Canaan. Abraham dwells there, but does not own Canaan.[54] He thus has to *buy* a place to bury his wife. *Jub.* 19:9 says, for instance, that he begs for a piece of land to bury his wife, even though he knew that the country was his by promise. Josephus also suggests this, saying: "Now Abram dwelt near the oak called Ogyges, the place belongs to Canaan" (*Ant.* 1.10.4). Philo implies it as well in his allegorical interpretation of Abraham's relation to the land of Canaan in Gen 17:8, saying that the mind of the virtuous man is a sojourner in its corporeal place rather than an inhabitant.[55] Acts 7:5 plays out the ambivalence involved: "He did not give him any of it as a heritage, not even a foot's length, but promised to give it to him as his possession and to his descendants after him, even though he had no child." In these accounts Canaan is not actualised as Abraham's possession.[56] However, it continues to be potentially his, due to the everlasting promise to his descendants.

Thus, these various interpreters have disagreed on the exact relationship between Abraham and Canaan. Consequently, it is not clear whether Abraham bought the Machpelah field *although* he already owned the area, or whether he acquired it *because* the ownership applied to his descendants only. However, most interpretations agree that at

---

[51] Gen 13:17: "Rise up, walk through the length and the breadth of the land, for I will give it to you."

[52] Cf. also Tob 14:7; *Gen Rab.* 58:6 (Ginzberg, *Legends V*, 256).

[53] Abraham's Land is at any rate no clear-cut, well defined territorial entity. The definitions may have been fluid and flexible, fitting different contexts (Cf. Moxnes, *Theology in Conflict*, 121; 142). There is possibly a tension in the sources of the Pentateuch between a definition of the Machpelah cave, the Hebron area, Canaan and the greater region as Abraham's Land (Davies, *Gospel and Land*, 18–20). According to Davies, Gen 15:1, 19 and 17:1–14 describe only the Hebron area as the Land of Promise. Deut 4:14; 11:31 and 12:10 makes Canaan the Land of Promise (Davies, *Gospel and Land*, 20). Finally, the variant versions of the Land from the river of Egypt to Euphrates are well known (Gen 15:17–21; Sir 44:19–21). It is quite possible that there never existed such a thing as a clear cut version of Abraham's Land.

[54] *L.A.B.* 7:4; 8:1–2; Josephus, *Ant.* 1, 7.1.

[55] Cf. *Her.* 267. Cf. Sandmel, *Philo's Place*, 150; Ginzberg, *Legends I*, 288–289; V, 256.

[56] Cf. Heb 11:8–9.

any rate this particular field in the Hebron area was in Abraham's possession. In this perspective, the special status of the Machpelah field becomes clearer: The Machpelah field belonged to Abraham both by promise and by acquisition. Abraham bought the field and made it his property, although the area was promised as the possession of his seed. The field of Machpelah was thus the first 'real estate' of Israel. It became the very first part of Palestine the people of Israel owned, long before the conquest under the command of Joshua.[57]

2 Baruch's Hebron: Everlasting Possession and Transitory Dwelling Place

When *2 Baruch* locates Baruch at Hebron, Baruch therefore dwells in the only area Abraham possessed by promise and by purchase.[58] Three factors are important for my study in this context. Firstly, Hebron is an alternative stronghold in Palestine. After Jerusalem fell, there is still Hebron, the only part of Palestine Israel owned before Joshua's conquest and before David conquered Jerusalem.[59] The possession of Abraham is there independently and in spite of Israel's failing dominance of Jerusalem. In this regard, Baruch dwells at the hereditary estate of Israel.[60] When Baruch sits down under the oak in 55:1 and 77:18 he therefore claims this alternative stronghold of Israel.

Secondly, since Hebron was the first stronghold of Israel in Palestine, it will also be her last stronghold in the area. When Baruch leaves Jerusalem for Hebron in *2 Bar.* 47, this does therefore not only signal his imminent departure. It also signals that Baruch enters his last location within the region of Palestine. There is no other place to turn to neither in Palestine, nor anywhere else in the corruptible world.

Thirdly, the choice of the Hebron setting underlines the position of Baruch and his followers as strangers both to the situation in Jerusalem and to the corruptible world. When Baruch leaves the neighbourhood of Jerusalem, there is no longer any hope that Israel will control her

---

[57] Cf. Ginzberg, *Legends I*, 288–290, for various interpretations of the transaction with regard to the Land promise.

[58] Cf. the purchase in Jer 32:6–15 as "a right of redemption by purchase." Cf. Davies, *Gospel and Land*, 43–44; Sayler, *Promises*, 77.

[59] Note that David bought the site of the temple in 2 Sam 24:15–25. *2 Baruch* thus locates Baruch in two of the places noble men of Israel had bought.

[60] Cf. Lied, "Døde, jordiske bein," 75–76.

former Land. The evacuation of the Jerusalem area thus implies that Israel has surrendered the former centre of the Land to the occupants. This puts Baruch and his followers in the same position as Abraham and his family. They are strangers in that country, as well as in the corruptible world.[61]

From what has been said above, we see that Hebron has connotations of an everlasting possession and a transitory dwelling place. Hebron was never a permanent dwelling place for Abraham during his lifetime. Abraham dwelled in Hebron for some periods, but he never settled down there. On the contrary, Abraham lived in a tent.[62] He could potentially pull up his tent pegs and leave on short notice. And he did. Abraham continued to wander around in Canaan throughout his life.[63] In death, on the other hand, Abraham, or alternatively his bodily remains, rests in Hebron. He continuously rests there under the oak, awaiting future resurrection. And by God's promise to Abraham, by his purchase and by his burial there, this particular site continues to be his.

2 Baruch probably uses this tension between the role of Hebron as eternal possession and temporary dwelling place to point out the future hope of Israel. Baruch's relocation to Hebron is his last and decisive journey within the wilderness of Palestine. Baruch witnessed the final loss of Jerusalem standing at the oak by the Kidron valley (6:1).[64] He then left that oak and went to sit down under the oak where Abraham was promised the Land at Hebron (Gen 12:6–7). The move to Hebron thus signals the beginning of the end of Israel's sojourn in Palestine. At the same time, this move alludes to a hope of a new life and a regained chance of possessing what God once promised Abraham as his everlasting property. Israel has indeed lost Palestine, Jerusalem and the temple, but she has not lost the promise of the future Land.

---

[61] Several texts note that Israel is a stranger to Jerusalem, to her former Land and to the entire world in the end-time (Cf. Lev 25:23; Ps 39:13; Jer 14:8; *4 Ezra* 16:40; *Targum Jonathan to Ezek* 16:1–3; John 17:16). Cf. Clements, "Temple and Land," 23; Lieu, *Christian Identity*, 230–238.

[62] Gen 13:18; 18:1; Heb 11:9. Cf. A. Alt, *The God of the Fathers: Essays on Old Testament History and Religion* (trans. R.A. Wilson; Oxford, Blackwell, 1966), 48; 65; Davies, *Gospel and Land*, 18. *T. Ab.* 3:1; 4, however, provides Abraham with a nice house where he even has his own room (19:1) in addition to a tent (1:2).

[63] Gen 13:2; 20:1; 22:19; *Jub.* 13:5, 15; 1QapGen XXI, 7.

[64] Cf. Sayler, *Promises*, 75–76.

Baruch's Mountain Sojourn

A similar blending of death and hope allusions can be found in 76:1–5. Forty days before Baruch's death, God commands Baruch to climb a mountain:

> And he answered and said to me: since the revelation of this vision has been explained to you as you prayed for, hear the word of the Most High, so that you know that which is prepared to happen to you after these things. For you will depart from earth, but then not to death, but to be kept until that time. Ascend therefore to the top of this mountain, and all regions of this earth (*kulhun atrawātā darʿā hāde*) will pass before you, and the form of the world, and the top of the mountains, and the depth of the valleys and the depths of the seas, and the numbers of the rivers, that you may see what you leave and to where you go. This then will happen after forty days. Thus, go now during these days and instruct the people as much as you can so that they will learn and not die in the last time, but learn and live in the last times (76:1–5).

This passage describes Baruch's view from the mountain top, forty days before he departs from earth.[65] From the mountaintop, Baruch sees both what he will soon leave behind and where he will go (76:3). He sees a selection of landscapes which summarises the main forms of this present world.[66] Both wilderness and the inhabitable parts of the world pass before his eyes, he sees the highest and the lowest points of the earth, and he sees the waters. In addition, he sees the "the form," "the archetype," or "the image"[67] of the (inhabitable) world[68] (*dmutāh dtibeyl*). Probably, this means that Baruch is granted a look at the other world, the perfect, incorruptible model of the present world and the place where he will finally go.[69] God then urges Baruch to instruct the

---

[65] Cf. Bogaert and Whitters have suggested that Baruch ascends the mountain at Yom Kippur (Bogaert, *Apocalypse de Baruch I*, 163–176; II, 133; Whitters, *Epistle*, 37; 50). The forty days could allude to the forty days (and forty nights) of Moses in Deut 9:24–29: Moses prays for the people so that God should not destroy them. The forty days may also allude to the context Deut 9:24–29 gives them: with an appeal to the covenant, Moses assures the people that they will not die in the wilderness (Cf. *Jub.* 50:4; Davies, *Gospel and Land*, 21–22). In addition, the forty days may recall the forty days in the history of David in *L.A.B.* 61 (1 Sam 17:16).

[66] Alternatively, "all the regions of this land" (Cf. Charles, *Apocalypse of Baruch*, 118 and Sayler, *Promises*, 97–98, versus Klijn, "2 Baruch," 646 and Bogaert, *Apocalypse de Baruch I*, 517).

[67] Smith, *Dictionary*, 94; Smith, *Thesaurus*, 914–915.

[68] Smith, *Dictionary*, 602; Smith, *Thesaurus*, 4378–4379.

[69] The interpretation of this passage is not straightforward. Possibly, Baruch sees the shape of the present world, and not of the other world. But if this is the case, what he

people as much as he can during his remaining forty days on earth. His instruction is of vital importance for the survival of Israel during the end-time: a people learned in the Law will live to see the other world. Baruch then comes down from the mountain and gathers his followers (77:1).[70]

The Ascension of Moses

76:1–5 contains both a note on the imminent ascension of Baruch, a command to climb the mountain, and a command to instruct the followers. These elements bring familiar farewell scenes to mind, in particular the farewell and ascension of Moses.[71] Deut 32:44–52 and 34:1–8 both describe the last days of Moses. The sequence in *2 Bar.* 76 particularly recalls Deut 32:44–52.[72] In that passage, Moses instructs the people (32:44–47), is told by God that he will soon die (32:48–49), and climbs a mountain (32:50). *2 Bar.* 76 and Deut 32:44–52 not only share the same sequence of acts. *2 Bar.* 76 also relates the purpose of Baruch's instructions to the people to the equivalent instruction given by Moses. Deut 32:46–47 describes how Moses admonishes the people:

> 'Take to heart all the words that I am giving in witness against you today; give them as a command to your children, so that they may diligently observe all the words of this law. This is no trifling matter for you, but rather your very life; through it you may live long in the land that you are crossing over the Jordan to possess'.

Moses thus instructs the people to live according to the Law and to teach their children to keep the commandments. This is a matter of life and death. If they keep the Law, they will live. More specifically, they will live in the country they are about to enter. The purpose of Moses'

---

sees does not correspond to what God says he will see, i.e., both what he leaves and where he will go.

[70] Whitters, *Epistle*, 40.

[71] There are other possible allusions at work as well: cf. the ascension of Elijah (1 Kgs 17–19; 2 Kgs 1–2); of Phineas (*L.A.B.* 48), the assumption of Enoch (*2 En.* 36; 64) and of Jesus (Matt 4) in addition to the outlook of Abraham in Gen 13:14–18 (Cf. Bogaert, *Apocalypse de Baruch II*, 132). Notice that Gen 13:14–18 and *Jub.* 13:19–21 do not identify the view point. Both accounts say, however, that Abraham dwells near Bethel. 1QapGen XXI, 7–13, on the other hand, states explicitly that Abraham ascends Ramat Hazor, north of Bethel. This account draws on both Gen 13:14 and 15:17–19 in the description of Abrahams view from Mount Hazor (Cf. *Apoc.Ab.* 12 where Abraham sees 'all things' from mount Horeb). Cf. also *Targum Ps* 68:16–18.

[72] Cf. Sayler, *Promises*, 97–98; Murphy, *Structure and Meaning*, 129.

instruction is thus to ensure the people's survival in the time after his death.[73]

The parallel between Deut 32:46–47 and *2 Bar.* 76 is clear with regard to the purpose of instruction.[74] Instruction in the Law is in both cases the means that will ensure life for Israel. In the text from Deuteronomy, life according to the Law will secure life at the opposite shore of the Jordan, while *2 Baruch* states that a law-abiding life will ensure life in the other, incorruptible world.[75] Moreover, both texts place the instruction within a farewell scene. That context makes the message of the two biblical heroes of uttermost importance. Since Moses and Baruch both know that they will soon leave the earth, the Law is promoted as the most important guide for the people after their departures (77:15–16). The two scenes thus share important characteristics. *2 Baruch* probably applies the Deuteronomy model to appropriate the authority contained in the last words and acts of Moses.[76]

Mountain Views: Mount Nebo and the Elevations at Hebron

The spatial elements of the two scenes are of particular interest for our discussion. Both the geographical locations of the mountain scenes in the respective texts and the geographical range of the visions of Moses and Baruch deserve attention: where are the two scenes in the respective texts set? And what do Baruch and Moses see?

According to Deut 32:49 and 34:1, Moses ascends Mount Nebo. Mount Nebo lies "in the land of Moab, across from Jericho" (32:49) on the eastern shore of the Jordan.[77]

---

[73] The traditions concerning the death of Moses are diverse. Many texts make a point out of the miraculous character of his death and his tomb. Some texts also question whether Moses actually died, since his grave cannot be precisely located (Cf. *L.A.B.* 19; *T. Mos.* 1:15; 10:12; 11:8; *Mos.* 2, 291; Josephus, *Ant.* 4. 8.48).

[74] Murphy, *Structure and Meaning*, 130. Note that *2 Bar.* 76 presents a different order than Deut 32:44–52. Baruch does not die on the mountain as Moses (maybe) does. Baruch comes down again to instruct the people during the last forty days of his life. It is possible that *2 Bar.* 76 recalls a series of events related to Moses, above all the Mount Sinai/Horeb scene. This underlines the importance of the instruction (Cf. Exod 19–20; 24:18; 34:28; Deut 9:9; *4 Ezra* 14:23, 42–44). Cf. Bogaert, *Apocalypse de Baruch II*, 133; Whitters, *Epistle*, 166.

[75] *2 Bar.* 45:2. Cf. *L.A.B.* 19:9.

[76] Cf. Cf. Klijn, "Recent Developments," 8; Wright, *Baruch ben Neriah*, 87; Whitters, *Epistle*, 163–168; Henze, "Jeremiah," 164–165.

[77] Cf. *Targum Pseudo-Jonathan to Deut* 34:1. Num 27:12 states that Moses climbs a mountain "of the Abarim range." Both *L.A.B.* 19:8–10 and Josephus, *Ant.* 4.8.48 say

The mountain Baruch climbs in *2 Bar.* 76 is not named and located in a similar way. This fact has caused speculation about the identification of the mountain. Some scholars have noted the similarities with the Mount Nebo scene in Deuteronomy and proposed that Baruch's mountain could be Mount Nebo as well.[78] Others have suggested that the mountain has to be a mountain in the Hebron area, since the context described in the frame story advocates this location.[79] Bogaert even suggests that the mountain can be Ramat el Khalil, the so-called 'Mountain of Judah' north of Hebron.[80] There is no further information in *2 Baruch* to confirm or rule out this suggestion. Still, the proposal points out that the landscapes of the Hebron area may serve as a fitting equivalent to Mount Nebo. The audience of *2 Baruch* has probably been familiar with the mountains and elevations of the Hebron area. Josephus, for instance, presents Hebron in this manner: "another city (…) in the hill country not far from Jerusalem" (*J.W.* 4.9.9).

These two suggestions are not necessarily irreconcilable. On the one hand, the location of the *2 Bar.* 76 scene probably implies a mountain in the Hebron area. This is likely, firstly because the context of the passage suggests this (47:1–2; 77:18), and secondly, because the elevated landscapes of the Hebron area would fit the reader's imagination of a mountain scenery.[81] On the other hand, *2 Baruch* clearly likens that mountain to Mount Nebo. The Moses typology and the equivalence of the mountains make the location and acts of Baruch meaningful. So, when Baruch ascends the mountain, he does it in the Hebron area, but by means of allusion he also climbs Mount Nebo. The allusions

---

that he ascends Mount Abarim. These texts probably all refer to the same mountain, since Nebo is a peak in the Abarim mountain range (Cf. Ginzberg, *Legends III*, 443). *T. Mos.* 1:4–5, however, locates the farewell scene in "Amman across the Jordan" (*Amman trans Jordanem*), i.e., slightly north of Moab.

[78] Charles, *Apocalypse of Baruch*, 188.

[79] Whitters, *Epistle*, 166.

[80] According to Bogaert, this is the most elevated place in the south of Palestine (Bogaert, *Apocalypse de Baruch, II*, 132–133). Bogaert refers to Mader (*Mambre*, 272–273).

[81] Note that Abraham's places of dwelling are also generally associated with the elevated parts of Palestine. Gen 13 describes the separation of the family of Lot and the family of Abraham. Lot decided to settle among the cities in the plain (13:11), while Abraham dwelled with his family in the elevated areas of the land of Canaan (13:12). Josephus maintains the distinction between the highland and the plain in *Ant* I.8.3 (Cf. *L.A.B.* 8:2; *Jub.* 13:16–22; *Apoc. Ab.* 13:8).

to the authoritative Nebo scene inform the audience how it should understand Baruch's mountain experience.[82]

Does this typology remain meaningful when we consider what Moses and Baruch see from their mountain lookout point? According to Deut 32:49, Moses sees "the land of Canaan, which I am giving to the Israelites for a possession." Deut 34:1–3 elaborates further on what Moses saw: "…and the LORD showed him the whole land: Gilead as far as Dan, all Naphtali, the land of Ephraim and Manasseh, all the land of Judah as far as the Western Sea, the Negeb, and the Plain— that is, the valley of Jericho, the city of palm trees—as far as Zoar." On Mount Nebo Moses thus sees the entirety of the Land God had promised Israel (Deut 34:4).[83]

In comparison, what does Baruch see? As already mentioned, Baruch is granted a view that spans the deepest and the lowest points on earth, earth and water, as well as the habitable and inhabitable parts of the world. In fact, Baruch sees the entire corruptible world. In addition, he sees the incorruptible world, where he will eventually go. Thus, while Moses sees the whole Land (Deut 34:1–4), Baruch sees the whole corruptible world as well as the incorruptible world.[84]

Are there points of connection between these two descriptions? An important feature of the story about the death of Moses is that he was denied entrance into the Land of Promise (Deut 34:4). Due to the wicked acts of the people in the wilderness, Moses is not let into that land (Deut 32:50–52). Instead he dies in Moab, just before Israel crosses the Jordan (Deut 34:5–6). Thus, God denies him entrance to the Promised Land because of the sins of the people, and when he dies, Moses leaves it behind. In the case of Baruch, the lawlessness of the tribes and all humankind is the underlying reason for his rapture from this world and the explicit reason why he left the Jerusalem area (43:1– 3). As pointed out in previous chapters, the entire corruptible world has to be evacuated due to the general state of lawlessness during the end-time. Baruch will depart first (76:2) and later the righteous will follow

---

[82] Several accounts demonstrate the tendency of letting different mountains merge or overlap (Cf. Bautch, *Study of the Geography*, 287–288).

[83] Cf. Ginzberg, *Legends III*, 443. Cf. *Targum Pseudo-Jonathan to Deut* 34:1–15.

[84] Note that *2 Bar.* 59 grants Moses a similar vision of 'all things'. Cf. further *Ezek. Trag.* 1.87–89; *Apoc.Ab.* 12:10; 21:3–5. Note that some later texts also say that Moses sees the whole world, but they do not explicitly state where he has this vision. Other texts claim that historical revelations were given to Moses on Mount Nebo (Cf. Ginzberg, *Legends VI*, 151).

him (14:13–14; 30; 50–51). This will happen even though this world was
initially promised to them (14:19; 15:7–8). Thus, both Moses and Baruch
are granted a look at what they will leave behind at their death: the
land of Canaan in Deuteronomy and the corruptible world according
to *2 Baruch*.

Thus, by means of allusions to this well known Deuteronomy scene,
2 Baruch makes the wilderness of the Hebron area equivalent to the
wilderness of Moab. Baruch climbs a mountain, as Moses did, and
Baruch sees what he will soon leave behind, as Moses did. Neither of
them is allowed to possess the spaces which had been promised Israel in
the earthly context. So, although Baruch sojourns in the region west of
the river Jordan and thus in a sense lives in the land into which Moses
was not allowed to enter, Baruch is still not in the Land of Promise.
Instead, he is 'on the wrong shore of the Jordan'. The allusions to the
Deuteronomy scenes thus turn the evaluation of Palestine upside down
and make the reader expect that the wilderness of Palestine will soon
be left behind and that the entry into the Land of Promise is yet to
come. This conclusion then agrees with the conclusions of Chapter
Four. Baruch and his followers are in the wilderness of Palestine, but
not yet in the Land.

Note, however, that *2 Bar.* 76 adds an important element to its Deuteronomy model, and thus changes its pattern somewhat. Baruch does
not only see what he will leave behind. He also sees the place he, and
subsequently Israel, will enter: the other world. *2 Baruch* in this manner
further withdraws God's promise of the Land from Palestine. At the
same time, *2 Baruch* redirects hope to the other world. And, as we shall
see in Chapter Seven of this study, for *2 Baruch* promises belong to that
other world.

Death and Hope 'here with me'

How is Baruch's stay at the mountain and under the oak relevant to the
spatial construction 'here with me'? As I suggested in the introductory
part of the chapter, the space of the remnant depends on the presence
of Baruch. The remnant is in a 'here' defined by the presence of
Baruch. The instruction Baruch transmits to the remnant 'here with
me' depends on the knowledge he receives on the mountain and under
the oak. Since he is the leader and teacher of the group, the allusions
connected to the mountain and the oak also influence the space of
the remnant. In other words, these allusions expand and transform the

conception of the remnant's end-time space. So, although the remnant may still be in the Kidron valley and their practices in the end-time city remain the same, Baruch's move to Hebron alters the connotations that go with that place fundamentally.

The above discussion has pointed out that the description of the last days of Baruch's life on earth alludes heavily to hope. *2 Baruch's* use of the mountain scene and the oak at Hebron re-actualises God's promises to Moses and Abraham and applies them to the situation of Baruch and his followers.[85] By way of allusion, they will soon escape the wilderness and enter the Land of Promise, just like the Exodus-generation did. And although they have lost Palestine, the everlasting promise to Abraham will not fail them.

Now, how do these allusions transform the space of the followers 'here with me', that is, here with Baruch? The wilderness space of the community under Baruch's leadership is no longer only a marginal space of protection, atonement and instruction; it turns into a space of hope. Although still in a wilderness setting, the spatial building of the remnant now includes the optimistic potential implied by the Moses and Abraham stories and transforms into a very promising place.

The Place of the Remnant: The Re-gathering of the Tribes

An important hope of Baruch, and thus a central issue of *2 Baruch*, is that all the twelve tribes may assemble again.[86] That can only take place, however, if the tribes return to righteousness. According to 76:5, God repeats to Baruch the necessity of instruction to reach that goal. Baruch acts according to God's command and addresses his followers 'here with me' (77:5). In addition, Baruch now expands the scope of his instruction to include not only his righteous followers, but also the twelve tribes in dispersion.[87] Sitting under the oak (77:18), he writes two letters to the dispersed tribes, one to the two and a half tribes and another to the nine and a half tribes (77:11–87:1).[88] The *Epistola Baruch* (78–87) is identified as that letter to the nine and a half tribes. By means

---

[85] Cf. Sayler, *Promises*, 79.

[86] Cf. Klijn, "Recent Developments," 9–10.

[87] Cf. Whitters, *Epistle*, 42–46.

[88] The letter to the two and a half tribes in Babylon (77:17) is either lost, or most probably never existed. We know the letter to the nine and a half tribes only (78–87). Note that the two and a half tribes have Jeremiah as their leader (10:2–5; 33:2). The

of his speech to the followers and the letters to the dispersed tribes Baruch thus carries out God's command to instruct the people as much as he can during his last forty days on earth.

The following section will focus on the space of the future return. Where are the dispersed tribes? What are the obstacles that prevent reassembly? Why does Baruch address the tribes from a Hebron location? And where will the tribes assemble again after Baruch himself is dead?

The Sojourn of the Dispersed Tribes: Babylon and beyond the River

2 Bar. 77 divides the twelve tribes of Israel into three groups: The nine and a half tribes (77:4, 17, 22), the two and a half tribes (77:4, 12, 17, 19) and the remnant, which is identical with the followers of Baruch (77:1, 5–6, 11).[89] The three groups dwell in three different locations. The remnant is 'here with me', in the presence of Baruch. The two other groups, however, live far away from them. *2 Baruch* says explicitly that the two and a half tribes are in Babylon.[90] The nine and a half tribes, on the other hand, are never precisely located by *2 Baruch*. According to 62:6, they have been carried away into captivity by the king of the Assyrians (Cf. 1:2). They may therefore be in Assyria, although *2 Baruch* does not confirm that in these passages.

The Nine and a Half Tribes: Far Away and Close to the End

Although the location of the nine and a half tribes is not precisely defined, the location of these tribes turns into a device for assessing the range of Israel's scattering when *2 Baruch* picks up this topic again in 77:17–78:1. According to 77:17–19, Baruch calls three men to carry the letter to the two and a half tribes in Babylon.[91] He then summons an eagle to carry the other letter to the nine and a half tribes:

> And I called an eagle and said these words to him: the Most High has created you so that you should fly higher than all birds. And now go and do not rest in any place, do not enter a nest, do not stay upon any tree

---

nine and a half tribes do not have a leader and therefore need the guidance the letter of Baruch can give them.

[89] Charles, *Apocalypse of Baruch*, 119–120. Cf. similar divisions in *T. Mos.* 2:4–3:9.

[90] *2 Bar.* 8:5; 10:2; 64:5; 77:17–19; 80:4–5; 85:7.

[91] Cf. Bogaert, *Apocalypse de Baruch II*, 138.

until you have flown over the breadth of the many waters of the river Euphrates and have come to the people that live there and cast down to them this letter (77:20–22).

So, where are the nine and a half tribes? According to 77:22 they are beyond the river Euphrates (Cf. 78:1). This can of course allude to the Assyrian captivity, but once more the exact location is probably not the main issue.[92] Instead, the allusive description of the location first and foremost suggests that these tribes are far away.[93]

Indeed, several aspects of the description underscores that the nine and a half tribes reside in a very distant place. The first part of 77:20–22 describes how Baruch summons an eagle to carry the letter. Baruch rhetorically appeals to the eagle's superior flying capabilities. The eagle flies higher, and it can cover wider distances than other birds.[94] In the following sentence we understand why this is a central point: The addressees of the letter live far away and in an inaccessible place. Only an eagle may be able to reach the nine and a half tribes in their distant location. The reference to the eagle thus points out to the reader that the ten tribes are in a location far away from Baruch. Two additional references in the passage support this interpretation. First, the tribes are beyond the river Euphrates. Whitters has pointed out that the Euphrates can serve as a metonym for a region far away.[95] The nine and a half tribes are even beyond this river. Second, the nine and a half tribes are in the East. They are east of Palestine and they are even east of the Euphrates. This implies that they dwell at the margins of the earth.[96] Some scholars have suggested that 77:18–78:1 alludes to the place called "Arzareth."[97] *4 Ezra* 13:40–45 tells the story about the captivation of the ten tribes by the Assyrian king and the decision of the ten tribes to move to an even more distant region where mankind had never lived (*4 Ezra* 13:41):

---

[92] It could also refer to Babylon, but 80:4–5 shows clearly that the two and a half tribes and the nine and a half tribes are not in the same place.

[93] Cf. Whitters, *Epistle*, 48–49.

[94] The oak and the eagle are the most excellent among trees and birds. According to *4 Bar.* 7:3 the eagle is "the chosen from all the birds of heaven." Notice that the eagle of *4 Bar.* 7 flies to Jeremiah in Babylon. Cf. Charles, *Apocalypse of Baruch*, 122; Bogaert, *Apocalypse de Baruch II*, 137–140; Whitters, *Epistle*, 47, 50. Cf. also *T. Mos.* 10:8; *L.A.B.* 48:1; *4 Bar.* 7.

[95] Whitters, *Epistle*, 50. Cf. Isa 8:9.

[96] Cf. *T. Job* 52:10.

[97] Charles, *Apocalypse of Baruch*, 119–121; Whitters, *Epistle*, 50–51.

> And they went in by the narrow passages of the Euphrates River. For at that time the Most High performed wonders for them, and stopped the springs of the river until they had passed over. To that region there was a long way to go, a journey of a year and a half: and that country is called Arzareth (*4 Ezra* 13:44–45).[98]

According to this account the ten tribes move further east into the distant land of Arzareth beyond the Euphrates.[99] *4 Ezra* thus locates the ten tribes in a very remote area.

2 Baruch similarly describes the location of the nine and a half tribes in a faraway place, whether it is equivalent with Arzareth or not.[100]

Whitters has suggested that the location of the nine and a half tribes beyond the Euphrates is an idealised location, and I find his proposal likely.[101] It has been more important to point out the distance between Baruch's dwelling at Hebron and the place of the nine and a half tribes east of the River, than to point out exactly where they were. The nine and a half tribes are first and foremost far away.[102]

Another series of passages in *2 Baruch* suggest that the dispersed tribes are spread out among several nations of the world. 1:4 says: "And I shall scatter this people among the nations that they may do good for the nations."[103] The idea of a widespread dispersion is also present in 67:5 and in 72:4–6. The latter passage, for instance, suggests that the people of Israel have lived among a number of nations. These passages do not refer to particular places of exile. Instead, they express the idea of dispersion as a universal phenomenon.[104] On the one hand, this idea turns the exile of the tribes into a positive force in history. The tribes of Israel were not only meant to help the gentiles to a better way of

---

[98] Translation by Stone (*Fourth Ezra*, 393).

[99] "Arzareth" probably means "another land" (Stone, *4 Ezra*, 405; Whitters, *Epistle*, 50, Lied, "Damascus," 124–125). Cf. Deut 29:28; Josephus, *Ant.* 11.5.2. Notice that this place is not identical with Assyria. It lies further east.

[100] This concept of the distant place also has its temporal counterpart. The regions beyond the Euphrates were considered close to the end (*4 Ezra* 13:46; Rev 16:12; Isa 8:7. Cf. Whitters, *Epistle*, 48; 50).

[101] Whitters, *Epistle*, 51.

[102] Cf. Deut 30:4.

[103] Cf. *2 Bar.* 41:4; 42:5. The theme of the blessing of the nations appears in several texts (*Jub.* 12:23; Sir 44:21; *T. Benj.* 10:5–6; Rom 4; Gal 3; Acts 3:25; 13:26, 32, 47). Cf. Davies, *Gospel and Land*, 177; Ginzberg, *Legends VI*, 98; J.S. Siker, *Disinheriting the Jews: Abraham in Early Christian Controversy* (Louisville, Ky.: Westminster/John Knox Press, 1991), 20–21.

[104] Deut 30:3; Isa 11:11–12; Jer 29:14; Ezek 37:21; 2 Macc 2:18; *T. Levi* 15:1; *T. Ash.* 7:3.

life. In return, the exile also had a chastening effect on Israel (78:4, 6).[105] On the other hand, the idea of the universal exile implied in these passages underscores the great geographical span Baruch must overcome to reach the addressees of his instruction in *2 Bar.* 77.[106] The dispersed tribes are thus not only in a remote region and close to the end of the world. They are also all over the world.[107]

These various descriptions of the dispersion of the tribes and Baruch's effort to reach and instruct them show that *2 Baruch* first and foremost stresses the difficulties and the obstacles Baruch has to overcome to help the tribes back on the right track. His instruction must reach the very outposts of the earth and it must resound universally to have any effect.

The Gathering of the Tribes

So, where will the tribes return to, if Baruch in fact manages to convince them to embrace righteousness? Once again, 77:5–6 deserves our attention: "And behold, you are here with me. If therefore you will make straight your ways, you will not leave as your brothers did, but they will come to you." This passage assures that the remnant ("you") will not be taken away, that is, from Baruch, as long as it keeps the commandments. Instead, if the remnant lives according to the Law, the dispersed brothers will return to it. The passage thus reveals the anticipation that the tribes and the remnant could assemble again.

It is evident that 77:5–6 uses some widespread ideas. Several sources of the first centuries C.E. express hope for a future gathering of the tribes.[108] *2 Baruch*'s main argument for the future re-gathering is the notion that the tribes ideally belong together. Therefore, they will one day be assembled again. *2 Baruch* expresses this idea through some common sets of imagery. Firstly, *2 Baruch* refers to the tribes as "brothers" (e.g., 78:2; 85:6). The brothers of Israel descended from one father (84:4) and lived in their mother city (3:1–3). Unfortunately, the family unit has split up, and the brothers have left 'mother Jerusalem'

---

[105] Cf. *2 Bar.* 13:10; *Pss. Sol.* 9.

[106] Cf. Whitters, *Epistle*, 36; 40; 48–49.

[107] The idea that the dispersed tribes must be gathered from the most remote parts of the earth is a *topos*. Cf. Isa 43; Jer 31:10; *Pss. Sol.* 11:2–3.

[108] Cf. for instance *4 Ezra* 13:12; 14:46–50; *4 Bar.* 6–8; *Mek. to Exod* 14:15 (cf. Charles, *Apocalypse of Baruch*, 128–130; Cf. Whitters, *Epistle*, 49).

(*2 Bar.* 3:1–3).[109] Secondly, *2 Baruch* underscores the ties that bind the tribes together. The tribes share the same history and the geographical belonging stressed by that history (e.g., 84:4; 85:1–3). Even more importantly, they have the same rights and obligations toward the covenant, the promises and the Law.[110] Moreover, Baruch several times appeals to the experience the twelve tribes all share during the end-time. They are all captives (78:4), they are all in the wilderness (77:13–14), and they are all strangers and homeless in this world.[111]

Mapping People: The Remnant as Place of Assembly

One aspect of 77:5–6, however, is not that clear or commonplace: *Where* will the tribes assemble? Does the passage imply any particular territorial location for the return? The discussion of the previous chapter showed that the followers of Baruch gathered in the Kidron Valley. That chapter argued that the Kidron valley was the setting of instruction and atonement and probably important to the survival of the remnant at the onset of the end-time, although it was foreign to the spatial construction of the end-time city (2:1–2). In the discussion of the present chapter I have pointed out that the move to Hebron was Baruch's solitary act and that *2 Baruch* did not specify the location of the remnant after 47:1. The remnant was first and foremost Baruch's audience and its space was defined by his presence. However, I also suggested that the remnant might possibly stay behind in the Kidron valley, since *2 Baruch* does not suggest any change in the location of the group.

We can, however, attempt to identify the geographical location of the group somewhat more closely, looking once more at the 'here' of 77:5. First of all, we can be quite certain that Baruch's followers are still in the wilderness. The entire story of the end-time, also after Baruch moves to Hebron, is set in wilderness locations. Moreover, another passage, 80:5–7, also suggests that the remnant remains in the proximity of Mount Zion. 80:5 describes the situation of the remnant like this: "And we have been left here (*hārkā*), being very few." In this passage "here" refers to the area "the inhabitants of Zion (*'umrāh çehyun*)

---

[109] Cf. Violet, *Apokalypsen*, 350; Bogaert, *Apocalypse de Baruch I*, 142; 333; Whitters, *Epistle*, 55. Cf. Bar 5:5.

[110] Cf. Whitters, *Epistle*, 55.

[111] Cf. the above discussion and Chapter Four. Whitters, *Epistle*, 47.

used to control" (80:7).[112] As Chapter Three of this study showed, that place could therefore be Palestine, Judah or Jerusalem, depending on the period the passage refers to. Still, it is most probably a reference to the Jerusalem area, since that area was the last region that fell.

Now, does this mean that *2 Baruch* envisions a return of the dispersed tribes to the Jerusalem area, and even to Palestine? Evidently, 77:5–6 tells us that the dispersed tribes will return to the remnant. That could indicate that the passage alludes to the commonly held view that the tribes will once return to their Promised Land.[113] This idea of a return to the Promised Land is attested widely, as for example in Deut 30:4–5:

> Even if you are exiled to the ends of the world, from there the LORD your God will gather you, and from there he will bring you back. The LORD your God will bring you into the land that your ancestors possessed, and you will possess it; he will make you more prosperous and numerous than your ancestors.

2 Baruch certainly draws on the notion of the promised return of the tribes from dispersion to the Land.[114] That could indicate that the tribes would return to Jerusalem and to Palestine.

However, an interpretation of 77:5–6 that looks first and foremost to territory is problematic for several reasons. Firstly, the above interpretation focuses only on the territorial aspect of the place. In other words, it underscores the geographical location of the remnant as the decisive factor for the return of the dispersed tribes. As we have already seen, *2 Baruch* is never explicit on the location of the remnant. Instead, 77:5–6 keeps the location imprecise by making vague allusions and unspecified references to a possible future place of gathering. It is therefore justifiable to question whether we should allow the territorial aspect to determine our interpretation.

Secondly, we must consider other references to re-gathering in *2 Baruch*. 1:4–5 says: "And I shall scatter this people among the gentiles that they may do good to the gentiles. And my people will be chastened, and the time (*zabnā*) will come that they will look for that which can make their times prosperous." This passage suggests that the time spent

---

[112] Alternatively, "the habitation of Zion." In both cases, the area referred to is the same.

[113] Isa 11; 49; Jer 23:1–8; 29:14; 32:42–44; Ezek 37:21; Amos 9:11–15; 2 Macc 2:18; Bar 4:36–37; 5:5; Tob 7:7; *Pss. Sol.* 11.

[114] Cf. Leuenberger, "Ort und Funktion," 225.

in dispersion will prepare the tribes for the coming prosperous *times*. Thus, some future time is implied as the 'space' of the gathering.[115] If we look closer at 78:6–7, we see that it expresses a similar hope:

> Therefore, if you consider the things you have suffered now for your good so that you may not at the end be condemned and tormented, you shall receive everlasting hope, above all if you remove from your minds the foul error for which you went away from here. For if you do these things in this manner, he will continually remember you. He who always promised on our behalf to those who were better than us that he will not forever forget or forsake our seed, but with much love gather together (root *knš*) again all those who were dispersed (root *bdr*).

As in the previous passage, 78:6–7 does not say explicitly where the tribes will assemble. The passage argues for the future reunion of the tribes on basis of the polarity between righteousness and life in the Land, on the one hand, and vengeance and dispersion on the other: Those who went away "from here" (*men hārkā*) to dispersion will assemble again, supposedly in the same 'here,'[116] if they resume a life in accordance with the Law. However, as the previous chapters have also shown us, living in the Land is not just a matter of being in a specific spot. Righteous praxis transforms a given region to the Land. The return of the tribes is thus first and foremost dependent of their conversion to righteousness, and not on dwelling within a given territory. By implication however, this passage alludes to the promises to the patriarchs. The explicit promises the passage refers to, however, are everlasting hope, God's remembrance, and re-gathering under God's mercy. The passage does not tell us where this will happen. So, neither 1:5, nor 78:6–7 suggests any specific geographical locale for the gathering of the tribes. They mention the gathering as something that primarily will take place in a future age. The Land promise is indeed hinted at, but *2 Baruch* ascribes gathering either to a future time or to the other world.

Thirdly, my previous discussions in this chapter showed that *2 Baruch* gives a rather paradoxical description of the 'here' of 77:5–6. The members of the remnant that dwell 'here' experience that they are no longer in the Land (85:3). They find themselves in the wilderness (77:14)

---

[115] Charles suggested that 1.5 refers to the future Messianic kingdom on earth (*Apocalypse of Baruch*, 3). This is possible, but the protective Messianic reign of *2 Baruch* seems to be only for the few. Cf. Chapter Six, pp. 200–206.

[116] Cf. further Charles, *Apocalypse of Baruch*, 119–120; Bogaert, *Apocalypse of Baruch II*, 134.

and in captivity (78:4). They are strangers to their place of sojourn, like Abraham was. And they are, by way of allusion to the Nebo-scene, at the wrong shore of the Jordan.[117] The locality of the 'here' of 77:5–6 is therefore not identical with the Land. At this point in the narrative rather the opposite is the case.

These factors make it less likely that 77:5–6 would imply that the tribes will return to Palestine. But still, something draws them towards this 'here': this is the remnant. It should be noted that the concept 'here' is relative to the followers of Baruch, not to territory. On a general level the existence of a 'here' depends logically on the location of a subject, in this case the remnant group. 'Here' leaves the territory unspecified. Thus, 77:5–6 does not map territory; rather, it maps people. The passage focuses on the whereabouts of the remnant, and place comes into existence by the fact that the remnant stays there. The geographical unspecified 'here' becomes meaningful only in its relation to the remnant. 'Here' is therefore above all the place where the remnant is, under the leadership of Baruch. 77:5 and 80:5–7 may imply that the 'here' of the remnant could be a location close to Mount Zion, potentially confirming the Kidron valley hypothesis.[118] Still, it remains a fact that 2 Baruch does not locate the remnant territorially, but rather addresses space as depending on the presence of the group under Baruch's leadership. I am therefore not denying that the remnant may be in the Kidron valley. I am however arguing that territory is not the constitutive aspect of their present sojourn.

This clarification is important because it underscores how the redemption of Israel, as well as a possible future assembly of the dispersed tribes, may be independent of the region of Palestine, as well as the end-time wilderness and the corruptible world in general. The space of redemption depends on the community of the remnant, just like the end-time city of the previous chapter. Of all the twelve tribes of Israel, only Baruch's own followers are left as a faithful remnant.[119] His followers atone for all the tribes and gain wisdom through Baruch's instruction. As long as they keep the commandments and live according to the Law, God will not send them away. Instead, the tribes of

---

[117] Regardless of the shore they are on: this is the wrong one.

[118] Cf. 4 Bar. 3:16; 6:2. Ginzberg, Legends IV, 319; 322.

[119] I.e., God did not spare a remnant of "them" (77:4), the wicked tribes, but he did spare "you" (77:5). Note that the remnant is therefore essentially different from the twelve tribes at this stage.

Israel will come back to them. *2 Baruch* thus uses the allusions triggered by the notion of return to transform the remnant into the place of return.[120]

Out of This World: The Departure of Baruch and the Space of the Remnant

One important issue still remains to be clarified: what happens to the space of the remnant when Baruch dies? As I have pointed out several times, 'here with me' depends on the presence of Baruch with the group. But as we know, Baruch's departure is imminent. He will soon abandon the group.

From 'here with me' to 'come to you'

77:6 distinguishes between 'here with me,' the place of the remnant in the present, and 'come to you' (*neton lwātkun*, i.e., "they will come to you") as the place of the future return. The presence of Baruch is not fundamental to that spatial building, the remnant alone is. Thus, the remnant becomes that autonomous future place of return.

How has Baruch assured the survival of the remnant as a spatial option for return after his death? And where will that return take place? Firstly, Baruch has transmitted all his knowledge to his followers. His instruction, and particularly the *Epistola Baruch*, constitutes Baruch's testament.[121] As I pointed out initially, as long as the remnant stays faithful and the tribes return to righteousness, his instructions in the Law will help them survive even though he dies.

Secondly, Baruch's location at the oak and the mountain does not only influence the place 'here with me', it also has implications for the future gathering in the place of the remnant. In the above discussion I have pointed out that Hebron plays a role in biblical narratives as a place of gathering in the sense that it is the national burial site

---

[120] The expressions "return to you," "return to the law," "return to God" and "return to the land" (or the cities) are probably part of the same semantic field. They enter into metonymical relationships. This means that there is a spatial dimension to these utterances, although not necessarily implying a given spot, but rather the space and condition of righteousness in a broader sense. This notion is part of a Deuteronomistic ideology of repentance and return (cf. G. Braulik, *Deuteronomium II 16,18–34,12* (NEchtB 28; Würzburg: Echter verlag, 1992), 16–34; 45; 218–219; Cf. Weissenberg, "Covenantal Motifs," 15–17). Cf. Deut 4:30; 30:1–10; Jer 31:16–22; 4QMMT 105–108.

[121] Whitters, *Epistle*, 165–168; Henze, "Jeremiah," 169.

of Israel. In addition, a Hebron location may also add authority to
Baruch's request to the tribes to reassemble. As I have already men-
tioned, the oak at Hebron was the location of the Abraham covenant.
That covenant should assure the future assembly (78:7). In addition,
Hebron is the gathering place of the tribes of Israel in the stories of
King David. 1 Chr 11:3–5 says:

> So all the elders of Israel came to the king at Hebron, and David
> made a covenant with them at Hebron before the LORD. And they
> anointed David king over Israel, according to the word of the LORD by
> Samuel. David and all Israel marched to Jerusalem, that is, Jebus where
> the Jebusites were, the inhabitants of the land. The inhabitants of Jebus
> said to David, 'You will not come in here.' Nevertheless, David took the
> stronghold of Zion, now the city of David.

In this account Hebron is the city where David established his rule at
God's command.[122] Hebron is the site where David consolidated the
twelve tribes of Israel and founded his kingdom.[123] It is noteworthy that
David and the tribes subsequently walk on from Hebron to Jerusalem
to establish their capital.[124] Just like Baruch's stay at Hebron, the stay
of David in Hebron was not permanent. In this regard, Hebron is a
place of transition that points to the building of the city Jerusalem.[125]
Israel's stay at Hebron under David's command transformed the war
ridden people into a powerful and motivated army (1 Chr 10:1–11:47).
Hebron has thus probably connoted gathering, consolidation and transformation, and in this manner developed the allusions to the Abraham
covenant.

Allusions to David's Hebron would further brighten the image 2 Baruch creates of Hebron. When Baruch preaches a future gathering
of the tribes, he potentially alludes to David's consolidation of the
tribes. Baruch has to strengthen the people for their last efforts in this
world before the righteous eventually will inherit the world to come. If
2 Baruch has David's Hebron in mind it refers to an equivalent transitory
stay there and suggests a similar glorious goal for the journey. In the
David stories, the gathering in Hebron enables the tribes to go and

---

[122] Cf. 2 Sam 2:1; 5:1–5; Ps 132:11–12.
[123] 2 Sam 5:1–4; 1 Chr 11:2–3.
[124] 2 Chr 11:4–5.
[125] 4 Ezra 3:23.

take possession of Jerusalem.[126] In the *2 Baruch* equivalent, the stay of the remnant 'here with Baruch' would prepare the tribes to go take possession of the heavenly Jerusalem.[127]

Thirdly, these allusions to a re-gathering of Israel should probably also be read in connection with Hebron's role as a place that allows for contact between the earth and the heavenly realms. In the previous chapter I argued that *2 Baruch* locates Baruch's communication with God at spots that suit the purpose of interaction. Baruch moves from the ruins at the temple mount in Jerusalem to the oak and the mountain in the vicinity of Hebron. I suggested that these wilderness locations could accommodate these extraordinary encounters between Baruch and God, and that the mountain and the oak, in their respective ways, would help Baruch see clearly and understand God's words. On the basis of the discussion of the present chapter we can add one more aspect to Hebron as a place of contact. I have already established that the frame narrative of *2 Bar.* 47–77 is set in the vicinity of Hebron. In other words, both the Apocalypse of the cloud and the following mountain scene are set at Hebron. A main theme in this final sequence of *2 Baruch* is the resurrection and life in the other world (e.g., 49–50; 73–75). The message of the speeches that follow Baruch's communication with God thus coincides with the announcement and preparation for Baruch's death/rapture in the frame story.[128] In this manner, Baruch's departure from earth forecasts Israel's future departure: the righteous will make the same journey as he did. Where Baruch goes at the end of the forty days period (76:4), Israel will finally go at the very end of this world. *2 Baruch* thus uses Baruch's departure as a paradigm for the subsequent evacuation of the righteous.[129]

There is also the possibility, that *2 Baruch* connects the oak imagery even more thoroughly with the future re-gathering and resurrection of Israel. *Targum Jonathan to Isa* 6:13 says:

---

[126] Davies, *Gospel and Land*, 19. Cf. in particular R.E. Clements, *Abraham and David: Genesis XV and Its Meaning for Israelite Tradition* (SBT; Second Series 5; London: SCM, 1967).

[127] Cf. 2 Sam 5:1–5; 7:12, 16; 23:5; Ps 89:4; *L.A.B.* 62:9.

[128] Note, for instance, that *1 En.* 20:7–8 describes the angel "Remiel" (Isaac, "1 (Ethiopic Apocalypse of) Enoch," 24 n. g) possibly the angel Ramael (*2 Bar.* 55.3), who interprets Baruch's vision of the cloud, as the angel in charge of those who rise.

[129] Murphy, *Structure and Meaning*, 56, 129. *2 Baruch* mentions Baruch's death in most of the eschatological predictions (Whitters, *Epistle*, 46).

> (...) and they will again be for scorching like the terebinth or the oak,
> which when their leaves drop off appear dried up, and even then they
> are green enough to retain from them the seed. So the exiles of Israel
> will be gathered and they will return to their land.[130]

We find a similar use of these ideas in *Targum Esth I* 7:10, now specifically connected to the remnant:

> For it is written: 'A Tenth of them shall remain, and they shall again be
> delivered to thinning like the oak tree and the terebinth whose residue
> leaves resembles dried out things, and up to that time they are moist
> because their seed subsists: thus the exiled community of Israel shall
> return to its land, for its plant is the holy seed, (...).'[131]

So, the move to the oak at Hebron introduces the new orientation
towards the incorruptible other world. As we have already seen, the
geographical shift in the frame narrative of *2 Baruch* parallels the shift of
interest in the composition of the text. At this point, the focus of *2 Baruch*
changes from the destruction of the temple to the coming assumption
of Baruch, the future gathering and the imminent end of the world.[132]
2 Baruch thus advocates a change of focus from temple lamentation to
hope for the other world. The Hebron location gives authenticity and
adds hope to Baruch's instruction. It points forward to the coming life
in the other world. According to *2 Bar.* 46–47, Baruch goes to Hebron
knowing that he will soon leave that place again. However much it
is his last move on earth, it is not his final place of destiny. Rather,
Baruch will depart from earth, and this departure foreshadows the
future departure of Israel. In this regard, Hebron points both to a new
era and another world.[133] Thus, Baruch's departure from earth does
not become the catastrophe the remnant feared it would be. Just like
the fall of the temple, the departure of Baruch is part of God's plan.
The worries of his followers are therefore groundless.[134] His departure
signifies hope, rather than destruction.

Fourthly, Israel will never be in want of leaders (46:4). As the previous
chapter showed, Baruch summons his son, his friend and the elders in

---

[130] Translated by Chilton, *The Isaiah Targum*, 15.

[131] Translated by Grelot, *Targums*, 137.

[132] Cf. Murphy, *Structure and Meaning*, 28; 141–142.

[133] Whitters, *Epistle*, 40; 46.

[134] Note how the discussion between Baruch and his followers concerning the departure of Baruch resembles the discussion between Baruch and God concerning the fall
of the temple.

Israel to continue the instruction of the people after he himself is gone. However, that does not exclude the possibility that *2 Baruch* presents Baruch as the forerunner of the Messiah. Several contemporary texts deal with the concept of a forerunner and a Messianic figure. John the Baptist, for instance, functions as the antecedent of Jesus.[135] In fact, when Baruch departs from earth, the Messianic era is imminent. The Messianic era will assure that the remnant lives through the last shakings of the present world and departs to the other world.

Consequently, by means of Baruch's leadership during the end-time and the hope and promises implied by his locations, the faithful remnant will itself be able to serve as a place of return for the future ingathering of the dispersed tribes. The tribes can return to them, if they embrace righteousness. In this manner, the righteousness of the remnant creates a place for the tribes to return to, although not in their present locality in the wilderness, but rather in the future other world.

---

[135] Cf. Laato, *Star*, 367; Klausner, *Messianic Idea*, 343; J.H. Charlesworth, "From Jewish Messianology to Christian Christology: Some Caveats and Perspectives," in *Judaism and Their Messiahs at the Turn of the Christian Era* (ed J. Neusner, W.S. Green and E.S. Frerichs; Cambridge: Cambridge University Press, 1987), 225–264 at 246–247; J.J. Collins, *The Scepter and the Star: The Messiahs of the Dead Sea Scrolls and Other Ancient Literature* (ABRL; New York: Doubleday, 1995), 116–118; J. Zimmermann, *Messianische Texte aus Qumran: köngliche, priesterliche und prophetiche Messiasvorstellungen in den Schriftfunden von Qumran* (WUNT 104; Tübingen: Mohr Siebeck, 1998), 455–458. Several texts also link the fate of the Messiah-figure and the group of righteous (Cf. *1 En.* 37–71 (The Similitudes); Cf. J.J. Collins, *The Apocalyptic Imagination: An Introduction to the Jewish Matrix of Christianity* (New York: Crossroad, 1984), 152–153; Himmelfarb, *Ascent to Heaven*, 61).

CHAPTER SIX

THE MESSIANIC LAND: TRANSFORMING
THE REMNANT AND THE WORLD

At the end of the end-time, the manifestation of the Messiah and his reign saves the remnant and overcomes the evil forces of the wicked world. Thus, although Baruch has departed from earth and left his followers in the wilderness, Israel will not be in want of a leader. On the contrary, the leadership of Baruch will be replaced by that of the Messiah. During the Messianic era moreover, Israel will finally leave the wilderness and become the triumphant master of the world.

2 Baruch describes the Messianic era three times, in each of the major sections of apocalyptic revelation in the text (*2 Bar.* 22–30; 35–40; 53–74). These sections present three different, though equivalent, versions of the Messianic age. The three versions share one important trait: they describe a temporary Messianic era. All three versions agree that the Messianic era brings the end-time to halt and restores the world to Israel. Hence, the coming of the Messiah finally terminates Israel's suffering in the corruptible world and introduces the ultimate period of bliss in the history of Israel. Yet, the Messianic era is not the final location of Israel's redemption in either of the three apocalyptic sections of *2 Baruch*. Instead, the Messianic era will be succeeded by resurrection and the actualisation of the other world, once the Messiah has fulfiled his tasks. *2 Baruch's* descriptions of the Messianic era are particularly intriguing, given the fact that only a handful of texts dating from the first centuries C.E. describe the Messianic age as a temporary phenomenon in this manner.[1]

---

[1] Cf. *4 Ezra* 7:26–31; 11:1–12:39; *1 En.* 91:12–17; *Sib. Or.* 3.652–808; Rev 19–20 and 1 Cor 15:20–28. Possibly also *Apoc. Ab.* 31:1–2; 1 Thess 4:13–18; 2 Thess 1:5–12 and *Ep. Barn.* 15. Cf. H.A. Wilcke, *Das Problem eines messianischen Zwichenreichs bei Paulus* (ATANT 51; Zürich/Stuttgart: Zwingli Verlag, 1967), 13–19. There is also a close relationship between the Messianic ideas of *2 Baruch* and some rabbinic texts (Cf. Klausner, *Messianic Idea*, 331; Charlesworth, *Jewish Messianology*, 225–264; A. Laato, *Star*, 366–368). *2 Baruch* and *4 Ezra*, in particular, share several traits. However, it should also be noted that the accounts of *2 Baruch* and *4 Ezra* are not identical. Both texts describe protection in the Land, Messianic pangs, annihilation of the wicked empire and the coming of a paradisiacal other world. However, commentators have in a varying

The following discussion will isolate three central aspects of *2 Baruch*'s descriptions of the Messianic era. These aspects are common to all three versions and attest to important functions ascribed to the period. The first aspect is protection: God (29:1), the Messiah (40), or the Holy Land (71:1) will protect the remnant from the turbulence of the end-time and final destruction. The second aspect concerns the recapitulation of time and space that takes place during the Messianic era: the Messianic era sums up the times and the spaces of the present world. The third aspect of the study is transformation, since each of the apocalyptic sections makes the transformation of the righteous and their spaces a central characteristic of the Messianic age.

The spatiality of the Messianic era is a particular focus of this chapter and an interest that runs through the following discussion of the three aspects. The spatiality of the Messianic era is particularly interesting to this study for two reasons: First, the reign takes part both in the present, corruptible world and in the other, incorruptible world, and yet it is not fully a part of any of them.[2] What implication does this temporary, liminal character of the era have for its spatiality, and what is the function of that spatiality in the context of the general redemptive scheme of *2 Baruch*? Second, *2 Baruch* makes the Land part of its description of the Messianic reign: What is the role of the Land within a temporary, liminal Messianic era?

Three Versions of the Messianic Era

As suggested above, the three descriptions of the Messianic era appear in three different apocalyptic sections of *2 Baruch*. The first description (*2 Bar.* 29–30) occurs in the context of a revelatory dialogue between

---

degree taken the differences between *2 Baruch* and *4 Ezra* into consideration, and when they are overlooked, *4 Ezra*'s version has been allowed to overshadow *2 Baruch*. Cf. further Charles, *Apocalypse of Baruch*, lxvii–lxxvi; C.C. Torrey, "The Messiah Son of Ephraim," *JBL* 66 (1947): 253–277; P. Grelot, "Le Messie dans les Apocryphes de l'Ancien Testament, état de la question," in *La Venue du Messie: Messianisme et eschatologie* (ed. E. Massaux; Recherches Bibliques 6; Bruges: Descleé de Brouwer, 1962), 19–50 at 28–31; Klausner, *Messianic Idea*, 350; Bogaert, *Apocalypse de Baruch I*, 414–419; Harnisch, *Verhängnis*, 302–318; Münchow, *Ethik*, 99–103; Charlesworth, *Jewish Messianology*, 245–246; Laato, *Star*, 360–361.

[2] Cf. Klausner, *Messianic Idea*, 408–419; Bogaert, *Apocalypse de Baruch I*, 413–414; 416; Münchow, *Ethik*, 103; Laato, *Star*, 393.

God and Baruch (22–30).[3] The second description appears in the so called Apocalypse of the vine and the cedar (36:6–37:1/39:7–40:4), and the third in the Apocalypse of the cloud (53:9–11/70:9–74:2).[4] I will present each version of the Messianic era in its context before I compare them, stressing some central features of each description. Note also that I study the vision and interpretation parts of the apocalyptic sections together, since they in each case depend on one another.[5]

The Revelatory Dialogue of Afflictions and Messianic Abundance (2 Bar. 29–30)

The first presentation of the Messianic era appears within a longer dialogue between God and Baruch that focuses on the end-time and the final redemption of Israel (24:1–25:4). Baruch asks God about the duration of the time of suffering at the end of this world (26:1). God answers him that the time of tribulation will be divided into twelve parts (*mnawān (mnātā)*) bringing diverse afflictions for mankind,[6] with the twelfth part as a mixture of the preceding eleven (27:1–15).[7] While most of those who live on earth during that last period do not realise that this is the end, the few who are wise will understand that the end of time has come.[8] Baruch then asks God whether the coming turmoil will

---

[3] I am grateful to M. Henze for his suggestions regarding the composition of *2 Baruch*. Henze proposed that *2 Bar.* 22–30 (in continuation of 13–20) presents a revelatory dialogue.

[4] The composition and names of the apocalyptic sections of *2 Baruch* are debated Cf. among others Harnisch, *Verhängnis*, 8; Bogaert, *Apocalypse de Baruch I*, 482; 486; 501; Münchow, *Ethik*, 97; Sayler, *Promises*, 90; Klijn, "2 Baruch," 630; 632; 639; Whitters, *Epistle*, 36; Leuenberger, "Ort und Funktion," 219–220.

[5] I have not included the subsequent public addresses, nor the continuing discussions between God and Baruch (31–34; 41–43; 75–77) in my interpretation. A more thorough study could include these, but I have chosen a narrow focus on the passages that discusses the Messianic era explicitly.

[6] Similar lists of afflictions are found, e.g., in *4 Ezra* 5:1–12; 6:21–24; *Jub.* 23:13, 16–25; Matt 24.

[7] This list of twelve parts differs from the twelve periods of world history in the Apocalypse of the cloud, since it concerns only the time of troubles that precede the coming of the Messiah. Cf. further Charles, *Apocalypse of Baruch*, 49; Bogaert, *Apocalypse de Baruch II*, 59–62. Cf. *Apoc. Ab.* 29; *4 Ezra* 14:11–12.

[8] Probably since they are acquainted with the calculation of time; two parts, weeks of seven weeks (28:2). Cf. Violet, *Apokalypsen*, 243; L. Gry, "La date de la fin des temps selon les révélations ou les calculs du Pseudo-Philon et de Baruch (Apocalypse syriaque)," *RB* 48 (1939): 336–356 at 345–356; Klausner, *Messianic Idea*, 333–334; Bogaert, *Apocalypse de Baruch I*, 288–295 and II, 59–62; A.Y. Collins, "Numerical Symbolism in Jewish and Early Christian Apocalyptic Literature," *ANRW* 21.2 (1984): 1224–1249;

affect the whole earth (ar'ā), or whether only one place (atrā)[9] or one of
its parts (mnawātā) will experience the afflictions (28:7).[10] God responds
that the afflictions will affect the entire earth and that all will notice
it. At that time, God will protect only those found "in this land" (bhāde
ar'ā).[11]

When everything designed to happen "in those parts" (bhāleyn mnawātā) has taken place, the Messiah (mšīḥā) will "begin to be revealed"
(nšare dnetgle, root gl').[12] Then, the two primordial monsters Leviathan
and Behemoth will come from their places of dwelling and become
nourishment to those who are left (29:4). Likewise, the regained fertility
of the earth will provide for the remnant with its abundance (29:5–7).[13]
Even manna will once more descend from above to feed "those who
have arrived at the consummation of time" (29:8, cf. 27:15).

When the tasks of the Messiah have been completed and he leaves
in glory, probably to return to heaven,[14] "those who have fallen asleep
in hope of him"[15] will rise. The treasuries (awçre) containing the souls
of the righteous will be opened,[16] and the righteous will come out and

---

Klijn, "Sources and Redaction," 74; Laato, *Star*, 365–366 Henze, *Syriac Apocalypse of
Daniel*, 75. Cf. Dan 9:24–27; 12:10; Matt 24:15; Aristob., fragm. 5; *Apoc. Dan.* 13.

[9] *atrā* may mean "place," but also "region" or "land" here (Smith, *Dictionary*, 33).
The reference is not exact, but the idea is clearly to contrast a particular effect to a
universal one.

[10] Violet suggests that the Roman Empire is "the whole earth" here (*Apokalypsen*,
244).

[11] Note the play on the word *ar'ā* here. *2 Bar.* 28–29 apllies the word both in the
meaning "earth" and the meaning "land." The special role of the one land here stands
in contrast to the earth in its entirety.

[12] Cf. further Bogaert, *Apocalypse de Baruch II*, 63. Charles proposes that the phrase is
corrupt (*Apocalypse of Baruch*, 52).

[13] Cf. *Sib. Or.* 3.619–623.

[14] Bogaert suggests that the Messiah dies as a prelude to the general resurrection
(*Apocalypse de Baruch II*, 65; Cf. *4 Ezra* 7:29). However, *2 Bar.* 30:1 does not say that the
Messiah dies, only that he will return (root *hpk*), probably to God and his heavenly
sphere (cf. *2 Bar.* 73:1; Klausner, *Messianic Idea*, 343; Collins, "Afterlife," 130). In other
words, the Messiah returns to where he comes from (Cf. *4 Ezra* 12:32; 14:9; Cf. Charles,
Apocalypse of Baruch, 52; 56; Violet, *Apokalypsen*, 246; Bogaert, *Apocalypse de Baruch I*, 414;
Leuenberger, "Ort und Funktion," 219). The idea that the Messiah does not die is also
found in the Talmudic versions of the Messiah ben David (Klausner, *Messianic Idea*, 343;
A.J. Ferch, "The Two Aeons and the Messiah in Pseudo-Philo, *4 Ezra* and *2 Baruch*,"
AUSS 15 (1977): 135–152 at 150).

[15] *aylyen dadmeku bsabreh*. Possibly, this is not a general resurrection. It may concern
only those who died righteous (Cf. *2 Bar.* 14:12–13; 25:4; 44:11; Ps 16. Cf. Charles,
Apocalypse of Baruch, 56; Bogaert, *Apocalypse de Baruch II*, 65).

[16] Cf. *2 Bar.* 21:23; 24:1; *4 Ezra* 4:35–43; 7:32, 80, 95; *L.A.B.* 21:9; 32:13. Cf. further
Violet, *Apokalypsen*, 360.

be seen together "in one gathering, of one mind."[17] "And the first will rejoice and the last will not grieve,"[18] for they know that the end of time has come (30:1–4). The souls of the impious, however, will wither even more when they see this.[19] They realise that their torment and destruction have arrived (30:5).[20]

The Apocalypse of the Vine and the Cedar (2 Bar. 35–40)

The second apocalyptic section of *2 Baruch*, the Apocalypse of the vine and the cedar, follows after Baruch has instructed his followers about his previous dialogue with God (31–33). Baruch climbs the deserted temple mount and weeps at the ruins of the Holy of Holies. He falls asleep there and sees a new vision:[21] On a plain (*pqaʿtā*)[22] surrounded by mountains and rocks a forest (*ʿābā*) grows and occupies "much space" (*atrā sagiʾā*) (36:2). A vine (*gpetā*)[23] rises over against it[24] and from under it a fountain (*mabuʿā*) comes forth peacefully.[25] The fountain is then stirred

---

[17] *bḥad kensā. dahdā tarʿitā*. The assembly is "of one mind" (or: "opinion," (...) "belief" (Smith, *Dictionary*, 621)). In other words, the assembly is united.

[18] This passage describes the righteous souls only (Cf. 51:12–13; *4 Ezra* 13:16–18). In other words, this is not a resurrection of all Israel or a universal resurrection of mankind (50–51). "The first" ("the ancients," "of old"; Smith, *Dictionary*, 490) may either refer to the patriarchs (85:1–4), the angels (51:12–13), or other dignified figures (*4 Ezra* 6:25–26), while "the last" probably are those who arrived at the end of time, i.e., the remnant (29:8; cf. 1 Thess 4:15; Cf. Charles, *Apocalypse of Baruch*, 55–56; Bogaert, *Apocalypse de Baruch II*, 66). Violet suggests that "the last" refer to the nine and a half tribes (*Apokalypsen*, 247), but this is unlikely since *2 Bar.* 30 does not mention the ingathering.

[19] Cf. *2 Bar.* 51:5; *4 Ezra* 7:87. The wicked are probably the ones who see the gathering in 30:2.

[20] Cf. *4 Ezra* 13:16–20.

[21] Cf. *2 Bar.* 52:8.

[22] *pqaʿtā* may mean "plain," or "broad valley" (Smith, *Dictionary*, 456; Cf. Bogaert, *Apocalypse de Baruch II*, 71).

[23] Note that the Syriac word *gpetā*, "vine," is feminine, and that the vine/Messiah is described by feminine forms of the words throughout this apocalyptic section. Thus, It would be correct to translate 36:6, for instance, into English like this: "she comes with the fountain to a place not far from the cedar" (36:6).

[24] *Men lqubleh* may mean both "over against it" and "opposite it" (Smith, *Dictionary*, 492).

[25] It is not clear whether *men lqubleh* ("over against it") should imply that the vine grows in a location positioned above the forest (for instance, in the mountains) as a contrast to the fountain that flows under the forest, or whether the vine just grows opposite the forest on the same plain. Both options are possible. Cf. the allusions to cosmic geography evoked by mountains and subterranean springs in *1 En.* 13 and *T. Levi* 2 (Clifford, *Cosmic Mountain*, 186–189).

up into great waves and overthrows the forest and its surrounding mountains (36:3–5). Only a single cedar (*arzā*) remains.[26] When this last cedar has also been uprooted, nothing is left of the forest, and even its former location cannot be known any more (36:6). The vine then arrives,[27] accompanied by the fountain, in a place not far from the cedar. The fallen cedar is brought there and the vine passes judgement over it:

> Are you not the cedar which was left of the forest of wickedness? Through you wickedness continued and was passed on during all these years, but never goodness. And you kept conquering what was not yours, and what was yours you never loved. And you kept extending your power to those who were living far from you and those who were brought near you, you retained in your nets of impiety, and you exalted yourself all the time like someone who could not be uprooted. But now your time has hastened and your moment has arrived. Therefore, go also you, cedar, follow the forest which went before you and become dust with it, and let your ashes be mixed together. And now, sleep in distress and rest in pain until your last time will come, in which you will come again to be tormented even more (36:7–11).

Finally, Baruch sees the cedar burning, whereas the vine and all that surrounds it, "the plain full of flowers that do not fade," grows (37:1).[28] Baruch wakes up, rises and asks God for the explanation of the vision.[29]

In 39–40 God explains Baruch's vision.[30] According to 39:3–6, four successive kingdoms (*malkutā*) will rule the world, the one worse than the other.[31] The fourth and last kingdom, which is like the trees on the

---

[26] Vegetation and plant metaphors were commonly used to describe peoples and nations (Cf. Stordalen, *Eden*, 86–94). The cedar, the last wicked ruler, can be interpreted as the last Roman Caesar (Laato, *Star*, 368). Rulers are often described as trees: cf. Ezek 17; 19; Dan 4. Cf. further G., Widengren, *The King and the Tree of Life in Ancient Near Eastern Religion* (King and Saviour 4; Uppsala Universitets Årsskrift 4; Uppsala/Wiesbaden: Lundquistska Bokhandeln/Harrassowitz, 1951), 42–58. On the imagery of this apocalypse, cf. also Ezek 17:3–10; Isa 10:34.

[27] Or, "is coming," "begins to come" (Charles, *Apocalypse of Baruch*, 62). The coming of the Messiah may thus again be envisioned as a process more than an event.

[28] There are several possible ways of translating 37:1. Cf. Charles (*Apocalypse of Baruch*, 63) on the one hand and Klijn ("2 Baruch," 634) on the other. Cf. further the discussion below.

[29] Cf. similar imagery in Ps 29:5; 37:35–36; Isa 10:33–11:1; Ezek 17; 31; *1 En.* 27: 1–2; *4 Ezra* 4:13–15; 11:36–42; 1QapGen XIX, 14–15; CD II, 19–21, 6Q8 II, 1–3.

[30] Klausner suggested that the interpretation did not agree with the vision (*Messianic Idea*, 338–339). I will return to this below.

[31] The imagery of the four evil kingdoms is an apocalyptic commonplace (Dan 7; cf. 4Q553, fragments 1, 6 and 8) probably referring to Babylon, Persia, Greece and

plain and which exalts itself like the cedars of Lebanon (39:6; cf. 36:2, 5), is the harshest and most evil of them all.[32] When the time is ripe, however, the dominion (*rišītā*) of the Messiah, which is like the fountain and the vine (39:7; cf. 36:3), will be revealed. The Messiah (the vine),[33] will bring the last ruler of the fourth kingdom (the cedar) up to Mount Zion and judge him for all his wicked deeds, as well as the evil works of his host (cf. 36:7–11). The Messiah will then kill him and protect (root *gn*) the remnant, "who will be found in the place that I have chosen"[34] (40:2). The dominion of the Messiah "will last forever until the world of corruption has ended and until the times aforesaid have been fulfilled" (40:3).[35]

The Apocalypse of the Cloud (2 Bar. 53 and 70–74)

The Apocalypse of the cloud offers *2 Baruch*'s last version of the Messianic era. After an outline of Israel's history in the world (56–69),[36] the apocalypse turns to the events that take place *after* the fulfilment of world history.[37] *2 Bar.* 53:7–11 describes Baruch's vision of this phase:

> And it happened at the end of the cloud that, behold, it caused black waters to rain and they were even darker than all those waters that had been before. And fire was mixed into it. And where those waters descended, they caused desolation and destruction. And after these things I saw that lightning, which I had seen at the top of the cloud, it seized it and caused it to descend to the earth. Now that lightning shone even more, so as to give light to the whole earth.[38] And it healed those regions where the last waters had descended and had brought about destruction. And it took hold of the whole earth and had dominion over

---

Rome. Cf. further Charles, *Apocalypse of Baruch*, 64; Klausner, *Messianic Idea*, 338–339; Bogaert, *Apocalypse de Baruch II*, 73; Collins, *Cosmology*, 77–78.

[32] Dan 7:23; *4 Ezra* 12:10–30; *Apoc. El. (H)* 3:66. The forth kingdom is commonly identified as the Roman Empire (Cf. Charles, *Apocalypse of Baruch*, 61; 64; Harnisch, *Verhängnis*, 258; Klijn, "2 Baruch," 633; Klijn, "Sources and Redaction," 73; Laato, *Star*, 368).

[33] Cf. John 15:1.

[34] *Wnagen ʿal šarkeh dʿamy haw dmeštkaḥ batrā dagbit* (40:2).

[35] Both Volz (*Eschatologie*, 73) and Wilcke (*Problem*, 43) claim that *2 Bar.* 40 describes an everlasting kingdom. 40:3 says that the kingdom of the Messiah will last until the world ends. In other words, it does not outlive the corruptible world.

[36] Cf. Chapters Two and Three.

[37] Cf. the notion of the passing cloud in 82:9.

[38] It is common to see meteorological phenomena related to judgement: e.g., the Messiah as lightning, and the last dark waters that overflow the earth (Cf. Dan 7:13; *1 En.* 43:9–22; Matt 24:27.).

it. And after these things I saw, behold, twelve rivers ascending from the sea, and they gathered around the lightning and became subject to it. And because of my fear I woke up.[39]

In the explanation of this vision (70–74), Baruch's interpreter, the angel Ramael, describes two phases: first, the destructive, fire-mingled black waters that bring an end to the corrupted world (70:1–9);[40] second, the last bright waters that make bliss unfold for the righteous (72:1–74:4). According to 70:1–9, impious people will die in wars and earthquakes, or they will burn in fire and perish by famine in the confusion of the end-time. At the very end, all remaining inhabitants of the world will be delivered into the hands of the Messiah. In other words, no one will escape: "For the whole earth will devour its inhabitants" (70:10). There is one exception to this universal destruction, however. 71:1 says: "And the holy land will have mercy on its own and will protect its sojourners at that time."[41]

These last black waters of the end-time are followed by the final bright waters of the Messianic reign (72:1).[42] During this period, the Messiah will call all nations to judgement. He will spare those nations who have known Israel but not trodden her down, whereas those who have ruled over Israel he will kill (72:2–6). 73:1–74:4 describes the blissful last events of the bright waters:[43]

> And it will happen after he has brought down everything that is in the world ('almā)[44] and he has sat down in everlasting peace on the throne of the kingdom,[45] then joy will be revealed and rest will appear.[46] And then

---

[39] The fear the visionary experiences is a common topic. Cf. Gen 28:16–17; 41:7–8; Dan 2:1; 4:5; 7:28; *1 En.* 83:6–7; 90:41–42; *2 En.* 1:6–7; *4 Ezra* 12:3–5; 13:14; *Ezek. Trag.* 1:82.

[40] Cf. Chapter Four, pp. 112–114.

[41] The translation "sojourner" is preferable to "inhabitant" in light of the terminology of 29:2 and 40:2: "those who are found" (*ayleyn dmeštakḥin*). This is not a stable population.

[42] Charles emended the text to "the last bright lightning," to make the interpretation fit the vision in 53 (*Apocalypse of Baruch*, 114).

[43] The Syriac lectionary manuscript containing *2 Bar.* 72:1–73:2 (ms. 14, 687) omits some words and changes the spelling of others (Cf. further Baars, "Short Notes," 478). The changes are minor and not crucial to my reading of the passage. I will however note all relevant divergences.

[44] Ms. 14, 687, folio 175a–176a omits *lkul* and *b'ālmā* (73:1).

[45] Ms. 14, 687, folio 175a–176a omits *dmalkuteh* (73:1).

[46] Ms (*Ambrosianus*): *bbwsm'*: "in joy." Rendered by Ceriani, and accepted by Charles (*Apocalypse of Baruch*, 115), Ryssel ("Apokalypsen des Baruch," 439), Kmosko (*Liber apocalypseos*, 1186) and Violet (*Apokalypsen*, 311).

healing will descend in dew,[47] and sickness will be put away, and anxiety and sadness and lamentation will pass away from among men, and joy will proceed through the whole earth (ar'ā).[48] And no one will die again untimely, nor will any adversity interrupt the calm. And judgements, and accusations, and controversies, and vengeances, and blood, and desires, and envy, and hate and all similar things will go to condemnation when uprooted. For these are the things that filled the world with evil, and because of them the life of man has been very troubled. And beasts will come from the forest and they will serve men, and asps and dragons will go out from their caves to be slaves of an infant.[49] And women will not again be in pain whenever they bear, nor will they be tormented when they give forth the fruit of the womb. And it will happen in those days: reapers will not be weary by labour, nor will farmers toil. For of themselves the products will grow quickly, while they work on them in full rest. Because that time is the end of that which is corruptible, and the beginning of that which is not corruptible. Therefore, these things which were said beforehand will happen in it. Therefore, it is far away from evil and near to those who do not die.

This complex passage (73:1–74:1) describes the process of transition that takes place at Messianic times in terms of unfolding bliss. As stated by 74:2, this is the era that comprises both the end of the corruptible world *and* the beginning of the incorruptible world.

2 Baruch's *Three Versions of the Messianic Era: Similarities and Differences*

2 Baruch's three versions of the Messianic era evidently differ on some points.[50] Firstly, they stress diverse characteristics of the Messiah-figure corresponding to his differing tasks in each context. Whereas the Messiah of *2 Bar.* 29–30 is relatively passive,[51] the Messiah of the two other

---

[47] MS: *ṭelālā*, "shade"/ "protection"/ "dew." Rendered by Ceriani and accepted by Charles (*Apocalypse of Baruch*, 115), Ryssel ("Apokalypsen des Baruch," 439) and Kmosko (*Liber apocalypseos*, 1186). The rendering is feasible, firstly because the spelling of the Syriac word for "dew" was not fixed, and secondly because of the parallel in 29.7 (*ṭalā*) in a similar context. Compare the Hebrew and Syriac versions of Isa 26:19 where the same confusion appears. Cf. also the Syriac *Odes Sol.* 11:14, where *ṭelālā* most probably must be rendered "dew."

[48] Or: "land."

[49] Alternatively "infants" (pl.) (Ryssel, "Apokalypsen des Baruch," 440; Violet, *Apokalypsen*, 312). This is not clear in the manuscript.

[50] Cf. Charles, *Apocalypse of Baruch*, liii–lxi; Bogaert, *Apocalypse de Baruch*, 415.

[51] Cf. Charles, *Apocalypse of Baruch*, 61–62; Charlesworth, *Jewish Messianology*, 247; Laato, *Star*, 368. Cf. *1 En.* 90:37–39; *4 Ezra* 7:28–29. Note however, that the chaos monsters Leviathan and Behemoth are somehow controlled by the Messiah. Chaos

apocalyptic sections plays a more active role.[52] He intervenes in history and brings rulers to judgement and punishment (40:1–4; 72:1–5). He protects the remnant (40:2) and ascends the throne as king and judge (73:1).[53] Secondly, the three versions of the Messianic era differ in focus. Whereas *2 Bar.* 29–30 stresses the regained fertility of the earth and the rise of the dead, the Apocalypse of the vine and the cedar pays attention to the judgement and punishment of the wicked. The Apocalypse of the cloud, where we find the last and most extensive description of the Messianic era, divides its attention between these topics. Thirdly, the diverse imageries of the apocalyptic sections display creativity typical of contemporary literature. In the Apocalypse of the vine and the cedar, for instance, the story of the four kingdoms appears, while the other two sections employ a twelve period scheme, either to the end-time or to world history as a whole. It was pointed out in Chapter Three that the cloud is the main metaphor of the Apocalypse of the cloud. And whereas *2 Bar.* 29–30 describes the effect of the Messianic reign on earth in food categories, flora and vegetation constitute the central imagery of the Apocalypse of the vine and the cedar.[54]

However, the three descriptions of the Messianic era also share crucial elements. Despite the diversity of imagery, all versions present the Messianic era by means of conventional apocalyptic language and imagery. And within each of the three apocalypses the Messianic age has a similar function with regard to the history of the world: It brings the end-time to a halt, and serves as a grand finale to the present world. Likewise, all three versions ascribe similar functions to the Messianic era in the history of Israel. In each case, the Messianic reign protects Israel during the final turmoil of the end-time, it stages judgement and

---

monsters normally belong to myths of the warrior Messiah (*3 En.* 45:5). This indicates that the Messiah is active.

[52] Cf. Charles, *Apocalypse of Baruch*, 52; 61–62; 65; 87; 115; Klausner, *Messianic Idea*, 331; Klijn, "2 Baruch," 633; Charlesworth, *Jewish Messianology*, 247; Laato, *Star*, 368. Cf. Isa 11.4; *1 En.* 37–70, particularly 46:3–6; 62:2; *Pss. Sol.* 17–18; *4 Ezra* 12:32–34; 13:32–50.

[53] Note how the Messiah has two important aspects of divine leadership ascribed to him in this apocalypse: the he is warrior and judge (Cf. Grelot, "Messie," 22–32; Whitelam, *Just King*, 164).

[54] Similar imagery is found in a series of texts: 1QH XVI, 4–11; 1QapGen XIV, 19; *Gen Rab.* 14 (Cf. further E. Eshel, "The Dream Vision in the Noah Story of the Genesis Apocryphon and Related Texts" (paper read at the 4th annual symposium of the Nordic Network in Qumran Studies, Copenhagen, August 25, 2006)). According to Klausner, the Messianic ideas of *2 Baruch* are similar to ideas found in the oldest parts of the Talmud and the Mishnah. He points to *Ketub.* 111b and *Sipre Deut* 315 (Klausner, *Messianic Idea*, 331).

punishment, and it assures survival and renewed joy. In addition, all
three reigns are temporary.[55] Although the Messianic era, in all three
versions, puts an end to the chaos of the end-time, it constitutes the
final goal of Israel in none of them. Instead, the Messianic reign prepares Israel for life in the other world.[56]

In the following discussion I will treat *2 Baruch*'s three versions of
the Messianic era as parallel descriptions of the same era. The three
variants have central features in common; enough to assume that they
were meant to supplement and elaborate on each other.[57] *2 Baruch* tells
more or less the same story three times, using familiar imagery and
apocalyptic commonplaces. I will therefore use the three versions of the
Messianic era to shed light upon each other. Still, I do not consider the
three versions as identical accounts. Each version of the Messianic era
is part of an autonomous apocalyptic account and must be understood
in its given context.

Establishing a Beginning and an End to the Messianic Era

One more aspect must be established: What events mark the beginning
and the end of the Messianic era? The identification of the beginning
of the Messianic era was an area of speculation in the first centuries C.E.
Several phenomena were imagined to signal the coming of the Messiah,
but there was no general agreement as to the exact nature of the signs.[58]
Several commentators have noticed that the birth pangs of the Messiah
signal the coming of the Messianic era in *2 Baruch*.[59] The hardships and
tribulations of the end-time are simultaneously signs of the imminence
of the Messiah.[60] Thus, the Messianic pangs are identical to the domes-

---

[55] Cf. Charles, *Apocalypse of Baruch*, 66; Klausner, *Messianic Idea*, 229; 339; 408–419.

[56] Cf. Bogaert, *Apocalypse de Baruch* I, 416.

[57] Cf. Bogaert, *Apocalypse de Baruch* I, 416; Klijn, "Sources and Redaction," 72. Cf.
Leuenberger, "Ort und Funktion," 218–219, for a slightly different view.

[58] The unsettled status of the matter is possibly reflected in *2 Baruch*, as well as in
4 Ezra and a selection of other contemporary texts. According to Laato, the beginning
of the Messianic age was one among seven things hidden from human sight (*Star*,
282). According to Klausner, the fall of the temple was an act of punishment, but
simultaneously "'the birth pangs of Messiah.' It was clear to them that end was near"
(*Messianic Idea*, 331).

[59] Even though the coming of the Messiah is described in terms of pangs, *2 Baruch*'s
Messiah is possibly pre-existent (Cf. *2 Bar.* 29:3; 30:1; *1 En.* 37–71; *4 Ezra* 7:28; 12:32;
13:32; 13:26. Cf. Laato, *Star*, 362–363; 367).

[60] Cf. Charles, *Apocalypse of Baruch*, 49; Violet, *Apokalypsen*, 245; Klausner, *Messianic
Idea*, 331; Ferch, "Two Aeons," 147; Sayler, *Promises*, 59; Laato, *Star*, 366; 368; 384–385.

tic turmoil and worldwide catastrophe, the suffering of the righteous as well as ecological disaster of the end-time. Alternatively, as pointed out by A. Laato, the beginning of the Messianic era was sometimes identified as the end of the Roman Empire.[61] To the Apocalypse of the vine and the cedar, this is a fitting description. The beginning of the Messianic era in that section is simultaneously the end of a wicked reign. In other words, whether the beginning of the Messianic era is described as the deliverance of the Messiah in terms of pangs, or is described as the termination of the wicked kingdom, the effect as regards the temporal scheme is the same: there is an overlap between the last phase of the end-time and the beginning of the Messianic age.[62]

The period of Messianic dominion, or his reign proper, begins once the Messiah has come into power. However, as we know by now, the Messianic era of *2 Baruch* is a transitory phase: it will come to an end. What elements mark its end? As to the end of the Messianic era, *2 Baruch* differs from *4 Ezra*. Whereas *4 Ezra* defines a fixed time limit for Messianic reign[63] and explicitly states that the death of the Messiah and the return to a seven days primal silence means the end of the era as the well as of the world (7:28–29),[64] no such clarity exists in *2 Baruch*. The Apocalypse of the vine and the cedar does not say how the Messianic reign will end, but simply states that it will do so when the world of corruption ends (40:3). In the context of the revelatory dialogue of 22–30 the reign probably ends when the Messiah returns to heaven (30:1). However, this passage neither describes any abrupt end to the Messianic reign, nor does it mention the death of the Messiah. The Apocalypse of the cloud stresses continuity even more. According to 74:2, the Messianic era is both part of the present world and the other world. Thus, neither does *2 Baruch* define one single factor that clearly

---

Cf. further Isa 8:23–9:6; 1QM I, 11–12; *4 Ezra* 13:29–23; Mark 13; Matt 24; Luke 21; *m. Soṭah* 9:15; *b. Sanh.* 97a. It may also be described as the birth pains of the resurrection (*4 Ezra* 4:40–43).

[61] Laato, *Star*, 382–383.

[62] Cf. Klijn, "Recent Developments," 11; Klijn, "Sources and Redaction," 74. Cf. further 55:7.

[63] According to the Latin and Arab (1) manuscripts, the reign of the Messiah in *4 Ezra* will last four hundred years (cf. *b. Sanh.* 99a). However, the Syriac manuscript says thirty years, whereas the Arab (2) says a thousand years (according to B.M. Metzger, "The Fourth Book of Ezra: A New Translation and Introduction," in vol. 1 of *OTP* (ed. J.H. Charlesworth; 2 vols. Garden City, N.Y.: Doubleday, 1983), 516–559 at 537; Cf. Wilcke, *Problem*, 42–43; Laato, *Star*, 383).

[64] Cf. *4 Ezra* 12:34 where the day of judgement marks the end of the reign.

ends one world and introduces the other, nor are the various apocalyptic sections explicit with regard to how the end comes about. Instead, a series of events brings the end of the wicked world: the manifestation of the Messiah, the Messianic judgement and enthronement, alternatively his return to the other world in 30:1, all set the transformation in motion.[65] The end of the corruptible world is therefore better described as an ongoing process than as an event. In this manner, 2 Baruch's Messianic era bridges the gap between worlds.[66] Nevertheless, in spite of the fluid borders between the worlds in 2 Baruch's Messianic era, two factors can still be singled out as the means of transition that will finally bring the Messianic age to its consummation: resurrection and judgement. Resurrection, God's judgement, as well as the subsequent transformations, will finally bring Israel to redemption in the other world (30:1–5; 37:1; 50–51; 74:2–75:8).[67]

The following study will discuss the web of events that together shape the spatiality of the temporary Messianic era. I will study how the Messianic reign overcomes the wicked world and protects, transforms, and prepares the marginalised remnant for its resurrection to the other world.

The Protective Land

The preceding chapters have shown that protection is an important function of the Land in 2 Baruch throughout world history. In the final phase of the end-time, when chaos and suffering intensify and the Messianic era is imminent, 2 Baruch highlights the role of the Land as shelter for the remnant. Each apocalyptic sequence includes a reference to this role of the Land:

> For at that time I will protect (*magen*, root *gn*) only those who are found in those days in this land (29:2).[68]

> And afterwards he [the Messiah] will kill him [the last ruler] and protect (*nagen*, root *gn*) the remnant of my people who will be found in the place I have chosen (40:2).

---

[65] Cf. *Jub.* 23:29–31.

[66] Cf. Klijn for a slightly different view ("Sources and Redaction," 74–75).

[67] Cf. Charles, *Apocalypse of Baruch*, 40–41; Bogaert, *Apocalypse de Baruch I*, 419–420; Klijn, "Sources and Redaction," 76; Stemberger, *Leib der Auferstehung*, 96; Murphy, *Structure and Meaning*, 66–67.

[68] Cf. Dedering concerning the indications of time (ms.: *zbn'* and *ywmt'*) in this

And the holy land will have mercy on its own and will protect (*tgen*, root
gn) its inhabitants at that time (71:1).

These three descriptions stress that protection depends on being present in a particular place or area at a certain time, and that this protection is limited to those present there at that time. Hence, in all three
passages space becomes crucial for survival at the culmination of the
present world. Moreover, all three passages agree that the world of corruption is what the sojourners need protection *from*. In other words, it
is evident that 29:2, 40:2 and 71:1 all argue for the protection of the
sojourners in a particular place, and that they see this place as crucial
to protection from the destruction of the corruptible world.

However, in order to understand *2 Baruch*'s presentation of the protective Land in these three passages, we need to discuss some aspects
of this description. First of all, what are the locations of the respective
places of protection in the three passages? Second, is it the location *per
se* that protects the sojourners, or is it the practices of the righteous
in that location that make the place protect them? And, importantly,
what function does this protective space have in the continuance of the
Messianic era once wickedness has been overcome?

Locating "this land," "the holy land," and "the place I have chosen"

2 Bar. 40:1–4 provides the most explicit answer as to the location of the
place of protection. According to 40:2, the Messiah will protect those
who are found "in the place I have chosen" (*batrā dagbit*). This expression commonly denotes Jerusalem (Zech 2:12), or more specifically the
location of the temple (Deut 26:2). In the context of *2 Bar.* 40, it is relevant to interpret 'the place I have chosen' as Mount Zion: 40:1 says that
the last wicked ruler will be brought to Mount Zion where the Messiah will rebuke him and afterwards kill him. And as we have already
seen, this is also the place where the Messiah will protect the remnant
until the world of corruption ends. Thus, the place of protection in the
Apocalypse of the vine and the cedar is likely to be Mount Zion.

29:2 and 71:1 are not as explicit about the location of their place
of protection. Charles suggested that the place of protection in 29:2

---

sentence (*Vetus Testamentum*, 15). However, the photolithographic reproduction of the
Ambrosianus seems clear, and Kmosko makes no remarks to this sentence (*Liber Apocalypseos*, 1126).

had to be Palestine.[69] 'This land' may of course refer to the region of Palestine in the narrative, but as I have argued in previous chapters, the term 'this land' may also refer to smaller areas. In addition to Palestine (61), it may refer to Judah (63), as well as to Jerusalem (66). Thus, the suggestion of Charles is imprecise. In fact, we cannot establish what region 'this land' is, based on that reference only. In a similar manner, 71:1 states that 'the holy land' protects its inhabitants. As Chapter Three showed, holiness is not an inherent quality of a territory.[70] So, when 71:1 mentions 'the holy land,' the territorial reference is not given. In result, the location of 'the holy land' is just as undetermined as the location of 'this land' in 29:2.[71]

However, the description of Mount Zion in 40:2 may shed at least some light on 71:1. We have seen that 40:1–4 describes a judgement scene. Similarly, the main task of the Messiah in 72:2–6 is to judge all nations, and subsequently to kill those who oppressed Israel, but spare the others. This scene is equivalent to the judgement scene in 40:2, set on Mount Zion. The separation between the righteous and the wicked in 72:2–6 therefore probably implies the same location as the scene in 40:2. The fact that judgement is typically related to Mount Zion in biblical literature supports this hypothesis.[72] It is thus probable that the Holy Land of 71:1 *is* Mount Zion, or at least, it *focuses* on Mount Zion.

The location of 'this land' in 29:2 is however still uncertain. As we have seen in previous chapters, it has been helpful to identify the sojourners (29:2; 40:2) or inhabitants (71:1) of an area to establish the identity of a locality. The identification of the sojourners may thus hopefully shed light on the location of 'this land' in 29:2, and also substantiate the assumption that 'the holy land' is Mount Zion (71:1). A central point in all three versions of the protective Land is that protection is for the few. There is no mention of a return of the tribes

---

[69] I.e., the geo-historical region of Palestine (Charles, *Apocalypse of Baruch*, lvi; 61. Cf. further Klausner, *Messianic Idea*, 342; Ferch, "Two Aeons," 145; 150).

[70] Cf. Chapter Three, pp. 80–83.

[71] Cf. *4 Ezra* 13:48. Kolenkow says that "*2 Baruch* commonly uses 'holy' in relation to land (...)" ("Introduction," 24). She further suggests that *2 Baruch* applies the term 'holy' to define an area of salvation, safety and protection (Kolenkow, "Introduction," 12; 16; 65). On the term 'holy land' in Messianic times, cf. further L. Gry, "La Mort du Messie en IV Esdras, VII, 29 [III, v. 4]," in *Mémorial Lagrange: Cinquantenaire de l'École biblique et archéologique française de Jérusalem, 15 novembre 1890 – 15 novembre 1940* (ed. L.-H. Vincent; Paris: J. Gabalda, 1940), 133–139.

[72] Cf. 1 Kgs 7:7; *2 Bar.* 61:6.

from exile in either of the descriptions of the Messianic era.[73] All three
versions suggest that the number of survivors is limited.[74] According to
29:1–2, those present in the Land, and only they, survive, while the rest
of the inhabitants on earth suffer and die. Likewise, while the earth in
general devours its inhabitants, those present in 'the holy land' escape
(70:10–71:1). It is therefore plausible that the sojourners that benefit
from protection in 29:2 and 71:1 are the same as those referred to in
40:2. Again, 40:2 is the most explicit of the passages with regard to the
identity of its sojourners. It says that the sojourners are 'the rest of my
people,' in other words the few members of the people who remained
righteous. In light of this consideration and 2 Baruch's general concern
for the survival of the righteous few, it is quite clear that the group
in question is the remnant. The identification of the sojourners of the
protective space as the remnant implies that 'this land' and 'the holy
land' are first and foremost the area the pious remnant inhabits.

So, given the overlap between the three versions of the Messianic
era, it is probable that the implied location of the protective Land is
Mount Zion, still accepting that the references are vague and keeping
in mind that the spatial definition depends on the inhabitants. This
is the place where God, the Messiah, or alternatively the Holy Land,
protects the remnant. In this first, introductory stage of the Messianic
reign, the remnant has returned to the place it inhabited at the time of
the destruction of Zion and the onset of the end-time. In other words,
the remnant has returned to Mount Zion.

2 Bar. 40:1–4: The Return of the Remnant to Mount Zion

Chapters Four and Five have demonstrated that during the end-time
2 Baruch reserved the location on Mount Zion for Baruch's encounters
with God. Baruch's followers were never allowed to go with him. They
were deprived of any connection to Mount Zion and the Zion centred
Land they had before the fall of the temple. The followers waited in
the lowlands of the Kidron valley, Jerusalem's topographical opposite,
as a patient audience for the instruction Baruch would give them. The
Baruch group was still in the wilderness, outside Jerusalem, and outside
the inhabited world.

---

[73] Cf. my discussion of 53:11 at p. 238. Ferch suggests that there may be returnees
during the Messianic era ("Two Aeons," 150).

[74] Cf. 2 Bar. 41:1; 75:5; 4 Ezra 7:47; 13:16–20; 47–50.

Now, while the previous chapter found the remnant—the followers
of Baruch—in the wilderness, the descriptions of the Messianic age
assume that the remnant is once again present at Mount Zion. Hence,
the manifestation of the Messianic era not only involves a shift in time,
it also implies a radical shift in the location of the remnant.

One question must be answered in this context: does *2 Baruch* describe an eschatological return of the remnant to Mount Zion? Although all three versions of the Messianic reign presuppose a return,
2 Baruch does not treat the return to Mount Zion as an independent
topic. Nevertheless, the Apocalypse of the vine and the cedar includes
a note on the return of the remnant in its description of the judgement
scene at Mount Zion:

> The last ruler at that time will be taken captive alive, whereas the
> multitude of his people will be brought to destruction. He will be bound
> and they will bring him up to Mount Zion. And my Messiah will rebuke
> him for all his impieties, and he will gather and set before him all the
> works of his multitude. And afterwards he will kill him and protect the
> remnant of my people who will be found in the place I have chosen
> (40:1–2).

This passage describes the capture, the judgement and the killing of
the last, wicked ruler as the central accomplishments of the Messiah.
When these acts have been accomplished, the Messiah will protect
his remnant in the chosen place. However, 40:1 also says: "He will
be bound and they will bring him up (*nasqunāyy*, root *slq*) to Mount
Zion." It is not entirely clear who 'they'[75] are. It is plausible, though,
that the ones who carry him up to Mount Zion are protagonists of the
Messiah. The identity of his assistants may of course be anonymous,
but since all humankind is suppressed by the power of the Messiah,
and the remnant is mentioned explicitly in 40:2, it seems logical that
the assistants are the remnant.[76] If this interpretation is correct, it is the
remnant that brings the wicked ruler to Mount Zion.

The most interesting aspect of 40:1, however, is its description of the
transfer of the ruler to Mount Zion. *nasqunāyy*, translated above with

---

[75] The plural agent is implied by the form *nasqunāyy*.

[76] In the vision equivalent of 36:6–7, the identity of the agent is also obscure and
depends on how we interpret the fountain in the vision context. According to 37:6–7,
the vine is the Messiah, and a look to 39:7 shows that the fountain and the vine together
constitute the Messianic reign. Within the vision of 36:1–11 the fountain may probably
refer to the supporters of the Messiah (Cf. further Charlesworth, *Jewish Messianology*,
247).

"they will bring him up" does not only imply that the last ruler is brought to judgement. Since the following sentences suggest that the Messiah protects the remnant at Mount Zion (40:2–3), 40:1 in all like-lihood includes also the move of the remnant from the Kidron valley to Mount Zion.[77] Thus, the remnant brings the last ruler to judgement and at the same time abandons the place where they sojourned during the end-time.[78] Possibly, *2 Baruch* also envisioned this move as an ascent. Forms of the root *slq* also mean "to go up," "to ascend," "to rise up," and is commonly used to describe ascent to heaven and ascent to the temple.

At any rate, the description of the return to Mount Zion in 40:1–4 marks a definite change in the remnant's spatial context both in the sense that the remnant is once more granted access to Mount Zion, and in the sense that it is again located in the inhabitable world. So, whereas the Baruch group experienced that it was outside the Land in the end-time (85:3), the manifestation of the Messianic reign brings them back to the Land at the very culmination of the corruptible world.[79]

Praxis and Protection

I have now established that the stay at Mount Zion is crucial to the protection of the remnant in all three apocalyptic sections of *2 Baruch*. In sharp contrast to *2 Baruch*'s construction of spaces of survival during the end-time, a specific location is again central to the survival of Israel, as it was before the fall of Zion.[80] The previous two chapters showed that the spaces of the remnant were defined by the spatial structures righteousness, leadership, and instruction could provide in the chaotic wilderness. The spaces of the end-time were paradoxical, mobile and temporary. At the onset of the Messianic period, then, the remnant is re-introduced into the territory Israel once inhabited, and this setting provides protection: Israel has returned to her Land.

---

[77] Cf. Smith, *Dictionary*, 379; Smith, *Thesaurus*, 2646–2651. In the vision equivalent, forms of the root *qrb*, "to come near," is applied. In Paʿel: "to bring near" (Smith, *Dictionary*, 517).

[78] Cf. *Targum Song of Songs* 8:1–2. Cf. also *4 Ezra* 13:36.

[79] The fact that the remnant stayed in the Kidron valley up to this point is probably relevant. The Kidron valley was also associated with final judgement (Mare, *Kidron*, 38). Some accounts include the Kidron valley in the eschatological Jerusalem (J. Høgen-haven, "Geography and Ideology in the Copper Scroll" (paper read at the 4th annual symposium of the Nordic Network in Qumran Studies, Copenhagen, 25 August 2006)).

[80] Cf. Chapter Two.

Charles, and several scholars after him, have suggested that 2 Baruch attests to the common idea of a special blessing attached to residing in Palestine. Indeed, the idea of a special protection within the Land is evident in, for example, Joel 2:32; 4 Ezra 12:31–34; 13:48–49.[81] However, as the above discussion has shown, it is not obvious that it is the region of Palestine in its entirety that protects Israel in 29:2, 40:2 and 71:1. It is more probable that Mount Zion is the location of the Land in these passages.[82] Nor is it clear whether protection is a function of a territory *per se*, or a result of the re-introduction of the righteous in that area. The following discussion will focus on this issue: in what sense are the protective qualities of a place dependent on Israel's practices? What makes one land stand out from the rest of the earth as 'this land,' 'the holy land' and 'the place I have chosen' in the Messianic era? And why does that land protect its sojourners, while the earth kills its inhabitants? Can this be explained only as a function of a given territory? To determine this, a closer look at the relevant passages is called for.

29:2 and 40:2 agree that 'this land,' or 'the place I have chosen,' is where protection will take place. However, both passages also agree that protection will be provided by an agent. According to 29:2, God himself protects the remnant,[83] whereas the Messiah is the protective agent of 40:2. It is their power that ensures the remnant protection. On the one hand, therefore, the protection these passages describe resembles the protection Baruch provided for his group in the wilderness through his leadership during the end-time. These passages in this sense belong to a series of protective scenarios involving varying protective agents.[84]

On the other hand, the descriptions of protection given in 29:2 and 40:2 differ from the presentation of Baruch's protective activity on some crucial points. Firstly, the protective agents of these passages, God and the Messiah, are all-powerful and their act of protection manifests itself while the corruptible world comes to an end. Secondly, the Syriac vocabulary 2 Baruch uses to describe the protective activity of God and of the Messiah shows that this protection is different from that described in other episodes. 29:2, 40:2 and 71:1 apply forms of the

---

[81] And possibly in 4 Ezra 6:25; 9:7–8; b.Pesaḥ. 113b (Cf. Charles, *Apocalypse of Baruch*, 49; 51–52; 114; Charles, "Apocalypse of Baruch," 497; Violet, *Apokalypsen*, 244; Davies, *Gospel and Land*, 51–52; Sayler, *Promises*, 59–60).

[82] Cf. Joel 2:32.

[83] Cf. Ps 16:1; 4 Ezra 7:122; *Apoc. Ab.* 29:17.

[84] Cf. Chapters Four and Five.

root *gn*, translated in its forms *magen* (29:2), *nagen* (40:2) and *tgen* (71:1) with "protect," as the keyword in their descriptions of the protective place of the Messianic age.[85] It is therefore interesting to note the web of meaning related to this root. The root-sense of *gn* is "to lie down or upon." In the Aph'el, *agen* or *magen* get the meaning "to make descend," or "rest upon."[86] In Syriac Bible manuscripts the word is sometimes applied to describe the protective movement of God's hand, as for instance in Exod 33:21–22 where God protects Moses at Sinai.[87] However, forms of the root *gn* is most frequently used in descriptions of God's protection and defence of Jerusalem and its inhabitants. Variants of this usage can be found in 2 Kgs 19:34; Isa 31:5; Jer 17:17; Zech 9:15 and 12:8.[88] In other words, *2 Baruch*'s use of *gn* to describe protection in the three variant descriptions of the protective Land carries with it special allusions to God's protection of Jerusalem. In addition, *gn* not only implies protection. It also connotes presence: God makes his presence rest on the Land of the Messianic era. Davies noted this aspect in his discussion of *2 Baruch*. He suggested that the Land would protect its sojourners, since God had drawn near to it again and surrounded it by his presence.[89] It is possible thus, that Mount Zion, the Land of 29:2, 40:2 and 71:1, shields its sojourners due to God's protective presence there.

We shall consider the agency of 'the holy land' (71:1) in this light. As we have seen above, 71:1 does not include any divine agent. On the contrary, it is 'the holy land' that protects its inhabitants in this passage. How can 'the holy land' be a vehicle of protection in the Messianic age? In Chapter Three I argued that the holiness of an area was an acquired, and thus not an inherent characteristic of any territory. Holiness derives first and foremost from the presence of God. The term 'the holy land' is therefore not another name for a given territory, but a term that may denote varying locations. However, the previous chapters have clearly shown that God's presence may easily abandon

---

[85] Smith, *Dictionary*, 73; Smith, *Thesaurus*, 742–744. *gn* also appears in 32:1 and 48:18. The other passages that discuss protection, e.g., 50:2; 6:8–10; 33:2; 44:3, apply forms of the root *ntr*, meaning "to guard," "to watch," "to keep," or "to preserve" (Smith, *Dictionary*, 337; Smith, *Thesaurus*, 2485–2487).

[86] Smith, *Dictionary*, 73.

[87] Similarly, Wis 19:8 in the Syriac applies forms of the root *gn* to describe how God's hand protects Israel when she crosses the Sea of Reeds.

[88] Smith, *Thesaurus*, 742–744.

[89] Davies, *Gospel and Land*, 51–52.

its earthly place of dwelling. The decisive precondition for preserving holiness on earth is the righteousness of Israel.[90] Righteousness is what retains God's presence, while wickedness in contrast makes the divine presence go away. In consequence, when 71:1 refers to Mount Zion as 'the holy land,' it basically tells us that the inhabitants of this area are living righteously and that the area they inhabit is therefore favoured by divine presence.[91]

This suggestion needs some further amplification in the context of 71:1. In fact, 71:1 does indeed say that the Holy Land, not any other agent, protects the inhabitants. To grasp how the Holy Land can protect its inhabitants, when its holiness in facts derives from the inhabitants it protects, it is crucial to note the dynamic relationship in the Apocalypse of the cloud between the moral of inhabitants and the character of the space they inhabit. In Chapter Three of this study, I pointed out that the acts of the inhabitants decided the character of time and space in the Apocalypse of the cloud. In general, wickedness creates chaos and makes the earth barren, whereas righteousness makes the earth fruitful and brings harmony.[92] In this sense, landscapes are always moral landscapes. In the description of the Apocalypse of the cloud, the condition of the world at the various stages of history reflects the moral state of humankind at those times.[93] During the end-time and its culmination (70:2–10), the perverted order of the wicked brings creation to a state of chaos (70:2–5). However, as I pointed out in Chapter Two, Creation cannot survive humankind's perversion and will necessarily react against it. Since the Law was meant to prescribe humankind's use of Creation, wickedness in fact becomes a way of abusing God's Creation.[94] Creation must therefore be healed through the extinction of the wicked (53:9). 70:6–10 describes Creation's response to wickedness as the tribulations that will kill the wicked at the culmination of the end-time (i.e., the Messianic pangs). The wicked die in war or in earthquakes, they burn by fire or perish by famine. And if those tribulations do not kill all the wicked, earth will finally swallow them up.[95] In this manner, Creation gets rid of the wicked: it kicks them

---

[90] Cf. pp. 49–54.
[91] For a different interpretation, cf. Harrington, "Holy Land," 669–670.
[92] Cf. Chapter Three.
[93] Cf. Chapter Four.
[94] Cf. Chapter Two.
[95] Cf. *L.A.B.* 16:3.

out, it swallows, shakes and burns them. So, the landscape the wicked created by their impious lifestyle in its turn strikes back and kills them.[96]

The Holy Land of 71:1 offers the remnant protection while Creation elsewhere kills its inhabitants. The reference to the protective Holy Land should thus be interpreted in that given context. In the context of the last black water of the Apocalypse of the cloud, it is evident that the protective force of 'the holy land' is decided by the lifestyle of the remnant. Since that particular land is not inhabited wickedly, there is no need to kill its inhabitants. The part of Creation where the righteous remnant sojourns therefore needed no healing. The Holy Land can protect its newly returned inhabitants because these inhabitants had not perverted it by impiety. The protective quality of the Holy Land is not a character of that country *per se*, but a quality which is derived from the pious lifestyle of the inhabitants. It is the piety of its inhabitants that attracts God's presence and makes it holy.[97] Holiness is thus the direct and indirect result of the remnant's piety. As a moral landscape, the Holy Land of 71:1 stands forth in contrast to the rest of Creation as an enclave of righteousness.

In light of the above considerations, I conclude that protection first and foremost is the result of righteous living in a place, and not the function of any given area as such. The Land indeed protects its sojourners in 29:2, 40:2 and 71:1, but it is not the territory itself that provides the necessary protection for the remnant. The Land at Mount Zion is protective because righteous people, and consequently divine presence, have returned.[98]

Messianic Space: Mount Zion, the Peak

The above discussion has established that the location of the Messianic Land in all probability is Mount Zion, and, further, that the righteous practice of Israel once again is the decisive element of the Land construction. It is the righteousness of Israel that enables protection to take place at Mount Zion in the Messianic era. Hence, in some respects the

---

[96] Cf. *2 Bar.* 48:29; 4QMMT; *1 En.* 7:6. This is a common topic, found for instance in various versions of the Flood-story.

[97] Cf. *Sib. Or.* 5.281–283.

[98] Cf. how *L.A.B.* 7:4 spares the land of Abraham during the Flood due to the righteousness of Abraham, and how *Jub.* 4:25–26 spares the Garden of Eden due to the righteousness of Enoch.

Messianic Land clearly resembles the Land of the period before the fall of the temple.

However, one important factor distinguishes the Messianic Land from prior versions of Israel's Land: the Land of the Messianic era does not have the temple at its centre. Unlike some other texts describing the Messianic era,[99] *2 Baruch* does not mention any rebuilding of the sanctuary in the Messianic age.[100] Therefore, in contrast to former variants of the Land in the area, the Land of the Messianic era is not 'the region of Zion' and not a temple environment.[101] Although the territorial extent of the Land overlaps more or less with the extent of the Land during the time of Josiah and the time of destruction, the conception of this territory differs: whereas the former Land was a temple surrounding city/Land, the Messianic Land is a mountain. As I pointed out above, the remnant climbs Mount Zion. It does not return to the temple, nor the temple-city, but to the top of the mountain.

2 Baruch thus suggests a restoration of Israel at Mount Zion, the peak, at the culmination of the end-time. Mount Zion is again the central place in *2 Baruch*'s cosmic scheme. This is not because it is the place of the temple,[102] or because it is the most distinguished mountain of the wilderness:[103] the return to Mount Zion must be important for other reasons. The following discussions will study how this localisation of the Land during the Messianic reign sets other connotations in motion.

---

[99] Cf. Laato, *Star*, 393. Cf. Tob 14:5; *Sib. Or.* 5.414–434; *Targum Jonathan to Isa* 52:5; 53:5.

[100] *2 Baruch* mentions two temples on earth, the First and the Second Temple, which both face destruction (32:2–3; 61:2; 68:5–7). 32:4 mentions a third temple, but that temple is in all likelihood heavenly, since it is perfected into eternity and is therefore everlasting. That description does not fit an earthly building of the temporary Messianic era (Cf. Bogaert, *Apocalypse de Baruch* I, 421–424 and Klijn, "Sources and Redaction," 69–71 for another point of view. Since *2 Baruch* uses the fall of the First Temple as a frame narrative to the fall of the Second Temple, it is sometimes difficult to determine what temple the author discusses (Cf. 32:2–5; 44:7)). Note also that although *2 Baruch* implies the presence of God in the Land by its use of *gn*, the above presentation of examples has shown that this usage does not presuppose the existence of the temple. Cf. further the discussion of the heavenly temple in Chapter Seven.

[101] Cf. Chapters Two and Three.

[102] Cf. Chapter Three.

[103] Cf. Chapter Four.

Summing up Time and Space

The above presentation showed that the Messianic reign terminates the wicked forces of the world. It marks the end of world history (39:7–40:3), or, alternatively, manifests itself immediately after the fulfilment of world history (29:3).[104] The discussion of the protective aspects of the Land also noted that the Messianic era sees the remnant's return to Mount Zion. In this manner, the Messianic reign ends Israel's suffering when the corruptible world enters its final phase and is about to give way to the other, incorruptible world. As a temporary era, the Messianic age thus ends one world and opens up another with Israel in power.

In the following discussion I will thematise the summarising functions 2 Baruch ascribes to the Messianic era: how does the Messianic era sum up this world and what is the function of spatial references in this description? I will focus on three topics: First, the role of judgement (36:6–11/40:1–4; 72:1–6), second, the function of the food imagery in 29:3–8, and third, the place of the references to the Garden of Eden and the Creation week in 29:4–8 and 73:1–74:1.

Re-establishing the Right Order: Judging All Nations at Mount Zion

Messianic judgement plays an important role both in the Apocalypse of the vine and the cedar and in the Apocalypse of the cloud.[105] The Apocalypse of the vine and the cedar gives the judgement scene considerable attention both in the vision (36:6–11) and in the interpretation context (40:1–4). Further, the spatial aspects are highlighted in this apocalypse. The spatial imagery is important in the definition of the crimes and the punishment of the wicked ruler. The Messiah's main accusation is that the reign of the wicked ruler knew no limits.[106] He

---

[104] 2 Bar. 70–72 may be interpreted both ways.

[105] Note that 2 Baruch describes two different kinds of judgement. The Messianic judgement is the Messiah's conviction of all men alive on earth at the time of his arrival. Messianic judgement is found in 36:6–10; 40:1–2 and 72:2–6. In addition, 2 Baruch describes a day of judgement. This is God's judgement of the resurrected dead. This judgement is described in 13:1–12; 30:4–5; 51:1–6 and 82–83 and is implied in passages like 36:11; 57:2; 75:6–8 and 85:13. Note that 29–30 does not describe Messianic judgement, but implies God's judgement in 30:2–5. 36:7–11 and 72–75 imply the existence of both in their apocalyptic schemes.

[106] Cf. further the Messiah as judge in Isa 11; 4 Ezra 12:31–34: 13:37; Pss. Sol. 20; Targum Jonathan to Isa 42:1–4; Targum Ps 45:7 and 110:4 (Laato, Star, 362).

extended his evil powers even to those who lived far from him, having no regard for the possessions or the birthrights of others (36:8). In other words, the Messiah accuses the wicked ruler of moving beyond his own realm and conquering peoples and countries he was not entitled to rule.[107] In addition, the wicked ruler even claimed that he could not be uprooted, implying that his reign would be everlasting. This enhanced the seriousness of his offence. In consequence of these crimes, the Messiah and his assistants eradicate the entire host of the wicked ruler before they kill the ruler himself. In the imagery of the vision, they uproot the entire forest and destroy its location to the extent that it could not be known any more (36:6; 39:7). Hence, they uproot those who thought they could not be uprooted.[108] In this manner the Messiah eliminates the universal reign of the wicked ruler entirely from the face of the earth. What was once a universal power becomes as if it had not been (36:6). The universal dominion of the Messiah replaces it and remains until the world ends (40:3).

In this context it is interesting to note how *2 Baruch* stresses the locality of the judgement scene. The vision and the interpretation both suggest that the wicked ruler is brought (36:6), and even brought *up* (40:1), to the place of the Messiah at Mount Zion. This upward movement underscores how Mount Zion stands out topographically as a peak (*ṭurā*) in the surrounding landscape.[109] This localisation not only makes the judgement and thus Israel's revenge visible for everyone to see. It also indicates that the judgement takes place on an elevated spot above the other parts of the earth. This pinpoints its universal authority. At this elevated spot, the wicked ruler must answer not only for his own deeds but also for all the impieties of his subordinates. In effect, all wickedness is punished when the Messiah kills the last wicked ruler at Mount Zion (40:2).[110]

It is generally acknowledged that the last wicked kingdom in the Apocalypse of the vine and the cedar must refer to the Roman Em-

---

[107] Cf. *2 Bar.* 12:3: 13:11. Cf. Mic 2:1–3.

[108] "Rooted out," from the root *'qr*. This is common imagery (Charles, *Apocalypse of Baruch*, 63). Cf., e.g., Isa 5:1; Ezek 19:10.

[109] *2 Bar.* 36:3–4 says that the vine rises over against or opposite the forest, before it moves towards it. This could perhaps allude to the description of the Mount of Olives and the mountain of the Lord in Ezek 14:3–5.

[110] Cf. the notion of Mount Zion as cosmic mountain and as the battleground of conflicting natural forces (Levenson, *Sinai and Zion*, 111).

pire.[111] The choice of Mount Zion as the locality of the judgement
and killing of the last wicked ruler is therefore particularly significant
in *2 Baruch*. Whereas *2 Baruch* certainly appeals to common notions of
Mount Zion as the place of judgement, this choice of location also fits
the scheme of *2 Baruch*'s frame story very well. Before the fall of the
temple and the surrender of Jerusalem to the Romans, Mount Zion
with its temple and its surrounding city was Israel's last bastion in
the world. The Messianic judgement on Mount Zion thus revenges
Israel's defeat by the Romans. Justice is stressed by the fact that the
fate of the wicked ruler in 36:10 parallels the fate of the temple in 35:5.
They both become dust and earth at Mount Zion. The last and most
glorious spot the Romans once conquered then becomes the place of
their final downfall during the Messianic era. By this choice of location
the Apocalypse of the vine and the cedar both reasserts the honour of
Zion, highlights the aspect of fair revenge and brings Mount Zion back
as the centre of the Messiah's worldwide power.

The Apocalypse of the cloud shares some of this spatial imagery
in its version of the judgement scene. Firstly, as suggested above, the
judgement scene of 72:2–6 in all probability also takes place at Mount
Zion. Secondly, the Apocalypse of the cloud ascribes universal range
both to the judgement and the following reign of the Messiah, just
like the Apocalypse of the vine and the cedar before it (53:8–10; 72:2–
4). The Apocalypse of the cloud implies universality by the call of the
Messiah to all nations (72:2), and by his judgement of each one of them
according to their deeds and misdeeds (72:3–4).

However, whereas the revenge of Israel and re-authorisation of
Mount Zion were highlighted in the former apocalypse, the Apocalypse of the cloud emphasises the healing of space as the outcome of
the judgement. According to Baruch's vision in 53:9–10, the lightning—
the Messiah—heals the regions where the last destructive black waters
had descended and takes control over the entire earth. In the interpretation section, the last bright waters that heal the earth (cf. 53:9) are
probably paralleled by the judgement that takes place during the ultimate bright waters (71:1–74:1).[112] In other words, the outcome of the
judgement is to bring healing to the earth. The logic should by now
be familiar: moral order brings cosmic order. When the Messiah erad-

---

[111] Rome is commonly referred to as the evil empire in Jewish texts of the first
centuries c.e. (Cf. *4 Ezra* 11–12; Dan 7; *b. Pesaḥ.* 54b; 118b. Cf. Laato, *Star*, 392).

[112] Cf. further the discussion below.

icates the wicked and only the righteous continue to inhabit the earth, Creation will again become healthy. The perversion of mankind that made the earth devour its inhabitants in 70:10 has been eliminated by the Messiah.

So, in what sense do these judgement scenes summarise the world? The Apocalypse of the vine and the cedar and the Apocalypse of the cloud both agree that Messianic judgement ends the dominion of the wicked.[113] Since the manifestation of the reign ensures the position of the righteous as masters of the world, it makes the world Israel's world at the very end of its existence.[114] The Messianic era therefore finally makes the world live up to the purpose of God's Creation. In addition, both apocalypses restore Mount Zion to the remnant, both as a place of judgement and, as we have already seen, as a continuing place of protection even after the judgement. In this manner, these apocalypses bring the remnant back to the central spot of the Davidic dynasty.[115] The promises implied by the Oracle of Nathan are fulfiled by the manifestation of the Messiah and the re-establishment of the remnant to Mount Zion.[116] Messianic power manifests itself universally and Israel's revenge is final.[117]

2 Bar. 29:4–8: Consuming Creation

According to 2 Bar. 29, the gradual revelation of the Messiah follows after the twelve periods of afflictions have filled their pre-appointed time. The ongoing manifestation of the Messianic reign thus corresponds to the final phase of mankind's life on earth. During this phase, Creation fulfils its potential again, since the earth is finally dominated

---

[113] The Messiah may also be considered a warrior, since he brings Israel triumph just like the kings did (Cf. Klausner, *Messianic Idea*, 343).

[114] Cf. pp. 52–54; 118. Cf. the notion of Mount Zion as the abode of the just in *1 En.* 25:4–7; 90:24–42. Cf. further Charles, *Apocalypse of Baruch*, liv.

[115] Cf. *4 Ezra* 7:30; 12:32. Ferch suggested that the 400 years of Messianic reign, attested in the Latin and one Arab manuscript, correspond to the period of Davidic kingship in Jerusalem ("Two Aeons," 143). Cf. additional Davidic expectations in *Pss. Sol.* 17:21–46.

[116] Cf. pp. 179–181. Cf. Jer 23:5–6; Amos 9:11–12; Ps 110:1–2; *4 Ezra* 9:7–8; 12:34; 13:48; 13:1–58. Cf. Levenson, *Sinai and Zion*, 56; 171; Harrington, "Holy Land," 666; Grelot, "Messie," 28–30.

[117] The universal extent of Messianic power can both be preceding judgement (36:6; 39:7) and a result of judgement (72:1–6). Cf. further Charles, *Apocalypse of Baruch*, 86–89; Bogaert, *Apocalypse de Baruch II*, 99–101. Cf. also Harrington who suggests that the Messianic Land is a strictly local kingdom ("Holy Land," 669).

by righteousness. This version of the Messianic era focuses primarily on the survival and nutrition of the righteous remnant. 29:4–8 says:

> And Behemoth will be revealed from his place and Leviathan will ascend from the sea, these two monsters, which I created on the fifth day of creation,[118] and I kept them until that time. Then they will be for food for all those who have been left. And the earth will give its fruit ten thousandfold. And on one[119] vine will be a thousand vine-shoots, and one vine-shoot will produce a thousand clusters, and one cluster will produce a thousand grapes, and one grape will produce a cor of wine. And those who have hungered will rejoice, and again, then, they will see marvels throughout the day. For winds will go out from before me, to bring fragrance of aromatic fruits every morning, and at the end of the day clouds to besprinkle dew of health. And it will happen at that time, that from on high the treasury of manna will again descend and they will eat from it in those years, because these are those who have arrived at the end of time.

According to this passage, the Messianic era presents the remnant with a wide range of food. Its diet includes meat, fruits of the earth, wine, water and bread, originating from numerous sources. An important concern of the passage is to ascertain the satisfaction and well-being of the remnant.[120] In 29:6 the positive effect of the abundance is neatly summed up in the exultation of the well-fed remnant.[121] But, why are

---

[118] Ceriani rendered *dbryt* (ms) into *dbryt'*. The rendering is generally accepted.

[119] Probably meaning "each" (Charles, *Apocalypse of Baruch*, 55).

[120] According to *Apoc. El. (H)* 3:66, Israel will eat and rejoice for 40 years. In contrast, Hos 4:10 describes lack of satisfaction as God's punishment: "They shall eat, but not be satisfied."

[121] A handful of scholars have suggested differing interpretations of this passage. Charles suggested that 29:4–8 presents three distinct diets: a flesh diet, a vegetarian diet and one consisting of heavenly food: manna (*Apocalypse of Baruch*, 54). However, Charles lists a selection of aspects only, and he does not provide any key to the composition of the elements within the passage. Bogaert, Nir and Harrington have understood *2 Bar.* 29 as a description of a Messianic meal (Bogaert, *Apocalypse de Baruch II*, 63; Harrington, "Holy Land," 669). Nir is however the only scholar who has elaborated on this topic. She understands *2 Bar.* 29 as a Christian Eucharist (Nir, *Destruction*, 132–151). Although she provides an interesting analysis of the elements involved in the passage, her conclusion is neither compelling, nor very likely. Nir's interpretation is based upon the hypothesis that *2 Baruch* is a Christian work. There are however no particular references to a Eucharist meal in *2 Bar.* 29. There is therefore no reason to disqualify other interpretations, since we cannot isolate the idea of the Messianic meal to a Christian context. The motif of the Messianic meal is found in Christian and Jewish texts alike (Cf. A.B. McGowan, *Ascetic Eucharists: Food and Drink in Early Christian Ritual Meals* (OECT; Oxford: Clarendon Press, 1999), 56–60). D.E. Smith says that the idea of a Messianic banquet was "a widespread motif found in various stages and forms of Jewish literature and constitutes a significant contribution to the banquet

these particular nutritional sources brought together in this passage? And what is the effect of bringing them together?

Creation Nurtures the Remnant: Spatial Implications

The first source of food that benefits the remnant is meat. Behemoth will be revealed "from his place" (*men atreh*) and Leviathan will emerge from the sea (29:4).[122] According to *2 Bar.* 29:4, these two monsters (*tanine*)[123] have been kept until the end to become food (*mekultā*) for the remnant.[124] *2 Baruch* thus describes Behemoth and Leviathan explicitly as sources of nutrition. *4 Ezra* 6:49–52, *1 En.* 60:7–9, 24–25, and the *Lev Rab.* 13:3 confirm the destiny of Behemoth and Leviathan.[125] These accounts all claim that the two primordial monsters were preserved for nutrition purposes.[126]

---

ideology of the Greco-Roman period" (*From Symposium to Eucharist: The Banquet in the Early Christian World* (Minneapolis: Fortress Press, 2003), 166). Cf. *1 En.* 62:15, *Fragmentary Targum to Deut* 32:14; *Jos. Asen.* 15–16; *Contempl.* 67–68. Cf. also D.E. Smith, "The Messianic Banquet Reconsidered," in *The Future of Early Christianity: Essays in Honor of Helmut Koester* (ed. B.A. Pearson; Minneapolis: Fortress Press, 1991), 64–73; P. Billerbeck, "Diese Welt, die Tage des Messias und die zukünftige Welt," in *Kommentar zum Neuen Testament aus Talmud und Midrasch* (ed. H.L. Strack and P. Billerbeck; vol. 4; München: Beck, 1928), 799–976 at 889; 951; H.J. de Jonge, "BOTRYC BOCHEI. The age of Kronos and the Millennium in Papias of Hierapolis," in *Studies in Hellenistic Religions* (ed. M.J. Vermaseren; EPRO 78; Leiden: E.J. Brill, 1979), 37–49; Rowland, *Open Heaven*, 171.

[122] The Genesis account does not identify the monsters by name or as a couple. Behemoth and Leviathan are paired as mythological monsters in Job 40:15–41:1 and presented as a pair by a number of texts of the first centuries C.E. Cf. Rev 13; *Jerusalem Targum to Gen* 1:24.

[123] *tanine* can also be translated "dragon" (Smith, *Dictionary*, 616).

[124] Cf. Gen 1:21; *4 Ezra* 6:49–52; *1 En.* 60:7–8; *Apoc. Ab.* 21:4; *Jub.* 2:11.

[125] Cf. *Jerusalem Targum to Genesis* 1:21. Cf. further C.A. Briggs, *A Critical and Exegetical Commentary on the Book of Psalms* (The International Critical Commentary on the Holy Scriptures of the Old and New Testaments; 2 vols.; Edinburgh: T & T Clark, 1906–1907), 155; J. Priest, "A Note on the Messianic Banquet," in *The Messiah: Developments in Earliest Judaism and Christianity* (ed. J.H. Charlesworth et al; The First Princeton Symposium on Judaism and Christian Origin; Minneapolis: Fortress, 1992), 222–238 at 235–236; Nir, *Destruction*, 134–135.

[126] Leviathan is described explicitly as food in Pss 74:12–14 and 104:26–27. Cf. Leviathan as nutrition for the righteous in *b. B. Bat.* 75a; *b. Pesah* 119b. Cf. also Gen 1:21; *Targum Ps* 50:10 and *Pirqe R. El.* 11 (Cf. J. Gutman, "Leviathan, Behemoth and Ziz: Jewish Messianic Symbols in Art," *HUCA* 38 (1968): 219–230 at 225; 229–230). Some sources present Leviathan as a big fish (Gutman, "Leviathan," 219–220). Although *2 Baruch* presents Leviathan primarily as a monster (*tnyn'*), he could also be understood as a fish due to his sea habitat. E.R. Goodenough has suggested a relationship between the Leviathan myths and fish symbolism (E.R. Goodenough, *Jewish Symbols in the Greco-*

Behemoth and Leviathan are both gathered from the wilderness. They both inhabited regions of Creation from which humans were normally excluded. Leviathan was imagined to be a sea monster, while Behemoth lived as cattle do on dry land.[127] Whereas *2 Baruch* says that Leviathan will ascend from the sea, it does not identify Behemoth's habitat (29:4). Different accounts place Behemoth in various parts of the earth's wilderness. *4 Ezra* locates him "where there are a thousand mountains" (6:49–52). This probably implies a desert location, since mountains are commonly understood to be dry areas.[128] *1 Enoch* puts Behemoth in an invisible desert called "Dundayin," lying east of Eden (*1 En.* 60:7–8). In that version, Behemoth lives in a wilderness located at the very end of the earth.[129] The two monsters were thus believed to dwell at the poles of their respective axes. Leviathan resided at the edge of a vertical axis, in the depth of the ocean,[130] whereas Behemoth sojourned at the edge of a horizontal axis, in the east at the end of the world.

The second nutritional source of the Messianic era results from the sudden fertility of the earth: wine and fruits of the earth are the produce of fertile soil. According to 29:5, the earth will give its fruits ten thousandfold.[131] In a similar manner, Ezek 47:12 and Rev 22:2 describe the abnormal frequency of the fruit harvests. Both texts describe trees that bear fruit every month.[132] The vine motif of *2 Bar.* 29:5 elaborates

---

Roman Period (vol. 6; Bollingen series 37; New York: Pantheon, 1953–1968), 3–61; Cf. C. Vogel, "Le repas sacré au poisson chez les chrétiens," *Revue des Sciences Religieuses* 40 (1966): 1–26 at 17–24, McGowan, *Ascetic Eucharists*, 131–132;137; K.W. Whitney, *Two Strange Beasts: Leviathan and Behemoth in Second Temple and Early Rabbinic Judaism* (HSM 63; Winona Lake, Ind.: Eisenbrauns, 2006). Is it possible that Leviathan is turned into a fish in rabbinic sources because he has a place in the coming Messianic meal (*Lev Rab.* 22:10)? According to Jewish dietary laws, sea-creatures could only be eaten if they had fins and scales. Consequently, Leviathan the seamonster could only be eaten if he were a fish.

[127] Cf. Klausner, *Messianic Idea*, 342; cf. 298–299. According to Nir, the Bible presents Leviathan as an antediluvian creature (Nir, *Destruction*, 134; Cf. Pss 74:14; 104:26; Job 3:8; 40:25; Isa 27:1). Cf. Collins, "Numerical Symbolism," 15; F.M. Cross, *Canaanite Myth and Hebrew Epic: Essays in the History of the Religion of Israel* (Cambridge, Mass.: Harvard University Press, 1973), 112–120. A.Y. Collins, *The Combat Myth in the Book of Revelation* (HDR 9; Missoula: Scholars Press, 1975), 76–79. Cf. *Apoc. Ab.* 10:10.

[128] Sources of water belong to the valleys.

[129] Cf. Gen 4:16; Ps. 50:10 (Nir, *Destruction*, 134–136).

[130] Cf. *1 En.* 60:7; *Apoc. Ab.* 21:4.

[131] Nir suggests that this is a reference to grain (*Destruction*, 136).

[132] Compare Hesiod (*Op.* 171–173) where the Isle of the blessed has three harvests a year. Cf. also Homer, *Od.* 4.86 concerning Libya.

further on the notion of abnormal fertility. This passage describes the vine and its super-naturally enhanced capacities in wine production. One single grape will yield as much as "one *cor* (*kurā*) of wine," estimated to about 230 litres.[133] Among the texts of the first centuries the combination of the motifs of vine and the fruits of the earth is frequent.[134] *2 Baruch*'s description of the fertile earth thus draws on well-known material to describe the fertility of the Messianic age. Within the context of 29:4–8, the purpose of the abundance of fruits and wine is clearly the good of the remnant. Thus, the remnant again consumes the best produce of the fertile earth.

A third source of sustenance is implied by the phrase "clouds to besprinkle dew of health": water (29:7). On a general basis, clouds, rain and dew are sources of water.[135] In the context of 29:7, dew is the water source of the remnant. In this passage, "clouds to besprinkle dew of health" will come at the end of the day. The spatial implications of the dew reference are double. On the one hand, dew was thought to come from clouds (29:7), or from heaven (10:11), and had affinities with rain (10:11).[136] On the other hand, since dew does not simply rain, but appears as moisture on the ground, dew also refers to the life giving humidity of the ground.[137] *Jubilees* states that dew was created on the third day along with the seas, the rivers, the waters and the ponds (*Jub.*

---

[133] From the Greek unit of measure *koros*; 230 litres (Bogaert, *Apocalypse de Baruch II*, 63–64. Cf. further Violet (*Apokalypsen*, 245) and Nir (*Destruction*, 149)). Cf. *Apoc. El. (H)* 3:66.

[134] Cf. *I En.* 10:19; 32:4; *Apoc. Ab.* 23:6–7; *Apoc. El. (H)* 3:66. Cf. Amos 9:13–14; Isa 5:10 and further *Apoc. Dan.* 10:1–7; 18 (Henze, *Syriac Apocalypse of Daniel*, 86–87; Nir, *Destruction*, 148). Another parallel description is Irenaeus *Haer.* V, 33.3 (interpreting Gen 27.28). Like *2 Baruch*, Irenaeus describes the abundant fruits of the earth. Moreover, Irenaeus applies the vine motif in a description of the fecundity of "those days" (*de temporibus illis*). Evidently, he makes use of the same material as *2 Baruch* does. The relation between *2 Baruch* and *Adversus haeresis* has gotten its fair share of attention (Charles, *Apocalypse of Baruch*, 54; L. Gry, "Hénoch 10,19 et les belles promesses de Papias," *RB* 53 (1946): 197–206; J. Jeremias, *Unbekannte Jesusworte* (Revised with O. Hofius; 3rd ed; Gütersloh: Mohn, 1963), 38; Bogaert, *Apocalypse de Baruch II*, 64; R. Hayward, "The Vine and Its Products as Theological Symbols in First Century Palestinian Judaism," *The Durham University Journal* 82 (1990): 9–18 at 16–17. Cf. Eusebius, *Hist. eccl.* 3.39; *Vis. Paul.* 21–22; *Ketub.* 111b; *Sipre Deut* 317, (Klausner, *Messianic Idea*, 343–344).

[135] According to Exod 16:14, 31, manna is "a fine flaky substance, as fine as frost on the ground" and with a taste of coriander seed and "wafers made with honey." Cf. *2 Bar.* 10:11; *I En.* 34:1–2; 36:1; 75:5; *Jub.* 12:4; 4Q157 XXXI, 5; 1QM XII, 9–10; XIX, 1–2; *Targum Ps* 68:10.

[136] Cf. *Jub.* 12:4; *L.A.B.* 23:12.

[137] Cf. *I En.* 39:5.

2:7). Dew is therefore also part of the water basins of the earth. Dew may thus be connected both to heavenly reservoirs and to the waters that irrigates the earth.

A fourth and last food source is manna, which descends from above to feed the remnant "in those years" (*bhāleyn šnayā*) (*2 Bar.* 29:8). According to Exod 16:4, manna is "bread from heaven."[138] Manna thus provides the remnant of *2 Baruch* with bread. According to 29:8, the treasury of manna will descend "from on high" (*men l'el*), from its place of storage in heaven.[139] Manna is far from the common bread made of earthly grain;[140] it is on the contrary made of "grain of heaven."[141] It is bread from the heavenly realm.[142]

What is the effect of this interplay of the various food motifs? The diet of 29:4–8 presents a collection of foods from all parts of Creation. Behemoth and Leviathan come from the sea and from the uninhabitable land. Fruits and wine are produced by the fertile earth. Dew provides water of heavenly and earthly origin. And manna descends from heavenly reservoirs. The effect of this combination of food motifs is a concentration of the most nutritious elements of Creation. The remnant drinks from the waters above and the waters below, they eat food from the uninhabited parts and the fertile areas of the earth. In addition, food rains down from heavenly reservoirs.[143] The whole of Creation is summed up and consumed at the very end. On the one hand then, 29:4–8 presents a deconstruction of Creation. The remnant's act of eating condenses and overcomes the distinctions between the constitutive parts that characterise Creation. On the other hand, since the

---

[138] Cf. Num 11:7; *Targum Jonathan to Ezek* 16:13.

[139] Cf. *Targum Ps* 71:19; 75:6; Job 25:2 and *L.A.B.* 19:10. (B.J. Malina, *The Palestinian Manna Tradition: The Manna Tradition in the Palestinian Targums and its Relationship to the New Testament Writings* (AGJU 7; Leiden: E.J. Brill, 1968), 59. *2 Bar.* 29:8 does not specify how manna descends, but the manna reference follows immediately after the mention of dew in 29:7. Exod 16:4, *Fragmentary Targum to Exod* 16:13–14, 21; *Sib. Or.* 7.145 and Josephus, *Ant.* 3.1.6 all connect manna with the fall of dew.

[140] According to P. Borgen, *Exod Rab.* 25:6 makes explicit comments to the change of the natural order in the Exodus story: water flows from a well in the ground, while bread comes from the sky (*Bread from Heaven: An Exegetical Study of the Concept of Manna in the Gospel of John and the Writings of Philo* (JSNTSup 10; Leiden: E.J. Brill, 1965), 7–8). Cf. *Mek. to Exod* 16:4 (cited by Malina, *Palestinian Manna*, 53); *Mos.* 12, 267.

[141] Ps 78:24.

[142] Manna is sometimes said to be the food of angels: Ps 78:25; LXX Ps 78:25: *b. Yoma* 75b, *L.A.B.* 19:6 (Borgen, *Bread*, 7–8).

[143] Manna and dew were the foods of the phoenix in *3 Bar.* 6:11 (Greek). This attests to the heavenly character of these foods.

food ensures the existence of a vital remnant, the eating brings revital-isation. The remnant is no longer hungry and marginalised. It is fully restored, and it rejoices. In this sense *2 Bar.* 29 becomes a perfect pre-lude to the description of resurrection to the other world in *2 Bar.* 30.[144] The remnant consumes the most nutritious elements of the world it will soon leave behind.

The Conflation of Beginning and End

Both *2 Bar.* 29 and 73:1–74:1 (in the Apocalypse of the cloud) allude to the very first days of Creation. 29:4–8 recalls creation week, whereas 73:1–74:1 describes the kingdom of the Messiah as a return to the Garden of Eden. What is the function of these descriptions in *2 Baruch?*

2 Bar. 29: Recalling Creation Week

In the preceding presentation of 29:4–8, I proposed that the remnant consumed foods from various parts of Creation both to overcome cre-ation and to gain vitality from its most nutritious components. Still, this excessive eating at the end of the world also includes elements that recall creation week (Gen 1:1–2:3). In fact, 29:4 makes the con-nection between beginning and end explicit, stating that Behemoth and Leviathan were made on the fifth day to become food for the remnant at the end of time.[145]

According to Gen 1:29, God gave man every plant and every tree with their fruits as food. Along with the dry land and the seas, these plants and trees were all created on the third day. *2 Baruch's* abundant harvest (29:5) is by implication the product of the third day of creation. There is however reason to believe that the dew and the fragrance of fruits described in 29:7 may be ascribed to the third day as well. *Jub.* 2:7 claims that dew was created on that day along with other sources of water. *Jubilees* also provides an interesting context of interpretation for the combination of the fruit and dew motifs in *2 Baruch.* *2 Bar.* 29:7 says: "For winds will go out from before me, to bring fragrance of aromatic

---

[144] Cf. *1 En.* 62:14: "(…); they shall eat and rest and rise with that Son of man forever and ever." Cf. also *Targum Pseudo-Jonathan to Deut* 32 and *Targum Song of Songs* 8:1–2.

[145] The common rendering of the Syriac word *behmut* is "hippopotamus" (Smith, *Thesaurus Syriacus*, 457). Thus, since Behemoth could also be classified as a beast living on dry land, he could be expected to be created on the sixth day (Cf. further Job 40:15).

fruits every morning, and the end of the day clouds to besprinkle
dew of health." The "fragrance of aromatic fruits" could of course
come from the lavish vegetation and the rich harvest of the earth.[146]
However, fragrance is more often ascribed to the fruit bearing trees of
the Garden of Eden. A similar passage in *Liber antiquitatum biblicarum*
points to the connotations at work. According to *L.A.B.* 32:8, the scents
of fruits are explicitly related to the Garden.[147] Moreover, *1 En.* 25:4
refers to the special tree in the Garden as "this fragrant tree." Thus,
the vegetal component of the remnant's fare brings allusions to the
Garden of Eden into play along with allusions to the lavish earth.[148]
Now, according to *Jub.* 2:7, God did four works of creation on the third
day: He created the earth, the seas, the flora and the Garden of Eden.[149]
So, according to this text, fruits, dew and the Garden of Eden are all
created on the same day. The combination of these motifs in *2 Bar.* 29:7
thus potentially revives the richness of the third day of creation.

My last point concerns the origin and storage of manna. Whereas
2 Baruch is silent on this matter, the contemporary *Jerusalem Targum*
includes manna in a list of ten items which were created on the Sabbath's eve of the creation week.[150] According to that account, manna
was created at twilight on the Sabbath at the very end of God's creational act.[151] According to the *Jerusalem Targum to Exod* 16:4 and 15, the
manna was hidden since the beginning only to descend again in the
Messianic era.[152] It is possible that *2 Baruch* alludes to these traditions in
its description of the "treasury of manna" (*awçre dmannā*) as something
stored in heaven. When the manna descends at the very end of time, it
thus both recalls the Sabbath's eve of creation week and signals that the
end has come.

---

[146] Cf. *Apoc. El. (H)* 3:66. Klausner quotes *Ketub.* 111b to interpret the reference to the
wind in *2 Bar.* 29:7: "Its fruits shall rustle like Lebanon (…); the Holy One, blessed be
He, will bring wind from His treasure house which he will cause to blow upon it."

[147] Cf. *Odes Sol.* 11:15–16; *1 En.* 24–25; *4 Bar.* 9:4; *Apoc. Mos.* 29 (Cf. Nir, *Destruction*,
138). *Apoc. Dan.* 32 relates the fragrance to the paradisiacal earth/land.

[148] Cf. Ezek 47. It is possible that the fruits are stored as well: Cf. *1 En.* 25:5; *Apoc. Ab.*
21:6; *Targum Neofiti to Gen* 3:22–24.

[149] Cf. *2 En.* 30:1.

[150] *The Jerusalem Targum to Num* 22:28.

[151] *The Jerusalem Targum to Num* 22:28 (Malina, *Palestinian Manna*, 57–58). Similar
references are found in several rabbinic lists (Cf. Nir, *Destruction*, 141). According to
Malina, these lists existed already in 100 c.e. (*Palestinian Manna*, 58).

[152] Cf. Rev 2:17.

The consummation of Creation in 29:4–8 not only contracts space, it also rounds off the *time* of this world.[153] The monsters which were created on the fifth day and stored until the end-time are finally eaten. The dew created on the third day descends during the Messianic era. Even the manna from the first Sabbath's eve rains down again. In addition, the goods of the Garden of Eden nurture those who are left at the consummation of time.[154] All these motifs thus recall the very beginning of the world.[155] When *2 Bar.* 29 applies them to describe the situation at the end they provide a sense of balance and symmetry to the presentation: they link creation to the end of the world.[156]

2 Bar. 73:1–74:1: Re-establishing the Conditions of Pre-transgression Man

73:1–5, cited earlier, describes the changes that will take place when the Messiah has come to the throne of the kingdom. It is likely that this passage answers the description of the first black waters of the apocalypse, the time of the transgression of Adam:

> For because of this transgression, untimely death came into being, and mourning was named, and grief was increased, and pain was created, and toil accomplished, and pride began to exist, and Sheol required to be renewed in blood and to take the children, and the passion of parents came into effect, and the greatness of mankind was humiliated and goodness faded (56:6).

When we compare these two passages, we see that the Messianic kingdom restores what Adam's transgression took away from mankind. Joy and rest will replace mourning, pain will be healed by the descending dew, untimely death ceases to disrupt the course of life,[157] and no one

---

[153] Implied in *2 Bar.* 3:7; Cf. *4 Ezra* 7:30.

[154] Gen 1:11, 29; Cf. *Jub.* 2:5–7. Compare also Gen 27:28, describing the blessing of Jacob: "May God give you of the dew of heaven, and of the fatness of the earth, and plenty of grain and wine."

[155] These 'first things' are reserved for the end of the world (Cf. N.A. Dahl, "Christ, Creation and the Church," in *The Background of the New Testament and It's Eschatology* (ed. W.D. Davies and D. Daube; Cambridge: Cambridge University Press, 1964) 422–443 at 427).

[156] Charles, *Apocalypse of Baruch*, 53; Bogaert, *Apocalypse de Baruch II*, 63, Nir, *Destruction*, 135.

[157] The discussion about the role of Adam's transgression in *2 Baruch* and *4 Ezra* is extensive. For my purpose, it suffices to note that *2 Baruch* does not hold Adam responsible for human death as such. His fall is responsible only for untimely death.

will suffer. In short, all the horrors of the corruptible world will come to
an end. 73:1–5 thus describes a situation that brings back the condition
of pre-transgression man.

73:7–74:1 elaborates further on this regained condition:

> And women will not again be in pain whenever they bear, nor will they
> be tormented when they give forth the fruit of the womb. And it will
> happen in those days: Reapers will not be weary by labour, nor will
> farmers toil. For of themselves the products will grow quickly, while they
> work on them in full rest.

The last part of this passage alludes quite openly to a restoration of
the pre-transgression conditions of Adam and Eve in the Genesis story,
since *2 Baruch* clearly revokes the curses of Gen 3:16–19. According to
Genesis, men and women were punished for eating the fruit of the
tree of life: women would endure painful pregnancies and childbirths
(Gen 3:16), whereas men would toil on the ground to produce enough
food to sustain life (Gen 3:17–19). *2 Baruch*'s Messianic era overcomes
this punishment of mankind. Procreation will no longer be painful, and
earth will again bring forth its produce without human labour.[158] In
effect, mankind will regain the same life conditions that Adam and Eve
enjoyed before God threw them out of the Garden of Eden (3:22–23).[159]

73:1–74:1 shows that the Messianic reign puts mankind back into the
position and habitat Adam and Eve once enjoyed. At the very end,
Creation is restored to its original condition.[160] The Garden of Eden is
in this sense re-established, possibly in an even better version than the
one that Adam and Eve enjoyed.[161]

Moreover, 54:14 suggests that Adam primarily was responsible for his own death, not
for the death of his successors.

[158] *2 Bar.* 74:1 seems to indicate that man will still work the soil, but he will no longer
toil.

[159] *2 Bar.* 73:6 may of course allude to Gen 3 as well, since it restores the relationship
between the serpent and the woman's offspring when asps will subject themselves to the
child instead of striking its heel (Gen 3:15). Still, the field of allusions is probably wider.
Several texts of the first centuries c.e. elaborate on the description of the coming of the
Messiah in Isa 11, among them *Sib. Or.* 3.367–395; 763–795; (Cf. further Ferch, "Two
Aeons," 148). Note, however, that the serpent is not forgiven in Isa 65:25.

[160] Cf. Grelot, "Messie," 29; Sayler, *Promises*, 71. A possible parallel is found in
4Q370. A. Feldman has suggested that 4Q370 says that the Flood generation got food
poured straight into their mouths (A. Feldman, "Mikra and Aggada in the Flood Story
according to 4Q370" (paper read at the First Graduate Enoch Seminar, Ann Arbor,
May 3rd 2006), 4). In other words, this generation did not have to toil. Cf. further
Virgil, *Ecl.* IV, 18–25, 39 and Hesiod, *Op.* 171–173.

[161] The return of the golden age is a classical topic. Cf. among others H. Gunkel with

Recapitulating Creation

The imagery of judgement, the theme of the revitalisation of the remnant by the most nutritious elements of Creation and the conflation of beginning and end all contribute to present the Messianic age as an era of restoration. The manifestation of the Messiah and the establishment of his reign bring Israel back to her entitled place at Mount Zion and ensure her triumph. In this manner *2 Baruch* proclaims Israel's victory over the nations and sees her as the master of the world. During the Messianic era, the world fulfils the purpose God assigned to it at the very beginning: it becomes Israel's world. Furthermore, the Messianic era ensures the revitalisation of the righteous remnant. Since all impiety has been removed by the Messianic judgement, the earth regains its immense productivity. And since the last days have arrived, the stored manna and the waiting primordial monsters finally fulfil their destiny and become sources of livelihood for the remnant. The members of the remnant draw from the most nutritious sources of Creation and in an act of eating encapsulates and condenses Creation in their bodies. The last image that contributes to the impression of the Messianic era as a time and place of restoration is that of a return to the pre-transgression condition of Adam and Eve. The reign of the Messiah makes the toils of procreation and food production, which distinguished life in the corruptible world, past history. The Messianic era brings men and women back to their original state by annulling the consequences of Adam's transgression during the first, black, waters. *2 Baruch*'s Messianic era thus reasserts the original, righteous, order.

Transforming the World: The Making of Liminal Space

This chapter has so far suggested that the Messianic era restores Mount Zion to Israel as a Land of protection during the final calamities of the corruptible world, that it restores the original order of the world and condenses Creation into livelihood for the remnant. In the next part of this chapter I will study another, related aspect of the Messianic

---

H. Zimmern, *Schöpfung und Chaos in Urzeit und Endzeit: eine religionsgeschichtliche Untersuchung über Gen 1 und Ap Joh 12* (Göttingen: Vandenhoeck und Ruprecht, 1895). Cf. also the reservations of Dahl, "Christ," 422–443 and the comments of Leuenberger, "Ort und Funktion," 226.

reign: the transition from the present, corruptible world to the other, incorruptible world. I will first discuss the function of the transitory Messianic era with particular attention to the process that transforms the spaces of the Messianic reign. I will then discuss how and in what regard the Land may be considered a liminal space during the Messianic era.

Transformation through Eating: 2 Bar. 29:4–8

What are the functions of the description of the remnant's excessive eating in 29:4–8? What does it tell us about spatial transformations?

Transforming Creation

The preceding chapters of this study have shown that the landscapes of the earth were turned into perversion and destruction during the history of mankind. During the end-time, the entire earth turned into wilderness. The fact that the remnant of the Messianic era is no longer hungry (29:6) proves that the Messianic era has caused a change to take place in Creation. The spatial implications of the abundance motif in 29:4–8 are therefore important. 29:5 depicts how the universal wilderness blossoms anew. The earth is no longer a barren wilderness, as it was during the end-time. On the contrary, it suddenly erupts in lavish vegetation and provides its lush produce anew.[162] This transformation of the earth necessitates the expulsion of the great monsters, at least Behemoth, from their place in the wilderness. The wilderness of Behemoth does not exist any more and causes the removal of the monster from his habitat. 29:5 thus accentuates how the Messianic era makes righteousness repossess the earth and eliminates the destructions of the end-time through the transformation of landscapes.[163] And most importantly, the remnant benefits from the transformation: the earth now provides for Israel as it was supposed to.[164]

The Eden allusions in 29:7 underscore the notion of blessing even more. Each morning, the fragrance of paradisiacal, aromatic, fruits

---

[162] Similar descriptions are found in, e.g., Isa 35:1–2; 41:18; Ezek 47:1–12; 1 En. 10:18; Rev 22:2.

[163] According to 4 Bar. 3:10–11, the fruitful season of the earth arrives when the Messiah manifests himself.

[164] Cf. Isa 35:1–2; 51:1–3; L.A.B. 23:12; Sib. Or. 3.620–624; 741–749; Eprem, Hymns on Paradise I.17; VII.18; IX.3–9; X.3 (Nir, Destruction, 139; 179).

fills the transformed earth of the Messianic reign and makes it similar
to the Garden. These allusions also suggest the marvelous aspects of
the change which has taken place, which the abnormal production of
wine and food already has suggested and which 29:6 claims explicitly.
The nature of the dew fall in 29:7 highlights this aspect even more.
According to this passage, clouds containing dew of health arrive each
evening. Exod 16:4, *L.A.B.* 13:7, the *Fragmentary Targum to Exod* 16:13–14,
Sib. Or. 7. 145 and Josephus, *Ant.* 3.1.6 all suggest that dew comes down
at night and covers the ground in the morning. Curiously, however, the
dew of *2 Bar.* 29 does not come at night. Instead, the clouds sprinkle
their dew in the evening. First of all, this changes the order of the
accounts above. Moreover, the evening dew of *2 Baruch* changes the
natural order as well. While dew normally falls at night and makes the
ground moist in the morning hours, *2 Baruch* turns this phenomenon of
nature into an evening event. Further, it is not common to see clouds
every evening in an Eastern Mediterranean environment. There are
on the contrary rainy seasons and dry seasons.[165] Thus, in a sense
2 Baruch turns climatic changes which normally occur during one year
into changes occurring in the course of one day.[166] The evening dew
thus clearly qualifies as one among the "marvels" (*tedmrātā*) of 29:6 and
implies that the extent of the transformation that takes place in the
Messianic era surpasses the ordinary circumstances of Creation.

Conquering the Land: Signs of Victory and Blessing

However, in light of the above discussion of the protective Land, it is
likely that *2 Bar.* 29 not only describes the transformation of the earth,
but also implies a parallel transformation of the Land.[167] Let us first
turn to the 29:1–3.

---

[165] Malina, *Palestinian Manna*, 34. Cf. H. Torczyner, "The Firmament and the
Clouds," *ST* 1 (1948): 188–196 at 190–191. Cf. Joel 2:23.

[166] Compare how *Targum Ps* 68:9 describes the dew of benevolence that fell when
God gave Moses the Law. The same passage asserts that the dew is a "dew of vivifica-
tion."

[167] Bogaert suggests that *2 Bar.* 29 describes Palestine (*Apocalypse de Baruch I*, 416). So
does A. Chester, "The Parting of the Ways: Eschatology and Messianic Hope," in *Jews
and Christians: The Parting of the Ways, A.D. 70 to 135. The Second Durham-Tübingen Research
Symposium on Earliest Christianity and Judaism (Durham, September, 1989)* (WUNT 66; Edited
by J.D.G. Dunn; Tübingen: J.C.B. Mohr, 1992), 239–313 at 250.

And he responded and said to me: That which will happen at that time concerns the whole earth. Therefore all who live will experience it. For at that time I will protect only those who are found in those days in this land. And it will happen after everything that was prepared to happen has come to an end in those parts, then the Messiah will begin to be revealed.

This passage first contrasts universal calamities with the special protection provided by the Land. Then, it claims that the Messiah, and his universal reign, will be revealed once history has been fulfiled "in those parts" (*bḥāleyn mnawātā*). The expression 'in those parts' may refer to the constituent parts of the world of calamities (29:1), to the periods of world history, or to the regions of the Land (29:2).[168] The inherent ambiguity of the Syriac word *arʿā* complicates the interpretation of the passage even further. The word *arʿā* in 29:2, and later in 29:5, can be translated both as "earth" and as "land." On the one hand, the translation of *arʿā*, "earth," is plausible, since the context of the apocalyptic sequence of *2 Bar.* 27–30 is the calamities and the subsequent transformation which befall the whole earth (27:15; 28:7; 29:1). On the other hand, the immediate context of *arʿā* in 29:5 is the description of the protective Land (29:2). The Land is thus the last space explicitly mentioned in this passage. In other words, the passage that follows 29:1–3 may refer either to the Land or to the earth, or the passage may possibly be meaningful in both contexts.

How does the use of narrative motifs in 29:4–8 fit the proposal that the passage describes the Land? The motifs of the vine and the fruits of the earth in 29:5 may allude to the Land-theme.[169] The vine and the fruits of the harvest are explicitly mentioned together in context of the Land in 10:9–10.[170] In general, the topos of the fertile Land enjoyed wide circulation both in biblical texts and in texts of the first centuries c.e.[171] The more specific vine motif provides more allusions to the Land.[172] The special relation of the vine to the Land appears for instance in Lev 26:4–5, Hos 10:1 and Amos 9:13–15.[173] Even the

---

[168] "In those parts" may refer either to parts of time or parts of space. *2 Bar.* 27 applies the Syriac word *mnawātā* (part) to the twelve parts of time, while 28:7 uses it to describe the parts of the earth (*mnawātāh d arc ā*). Cf. Bogaert, *Apocalypse de Baruch II*, 63.

[169] Nir interprets *2 Bar.* 29:5 in a Land-context (Nir, *Destruction*, 140).

[170] Cf. pp. 45–46.

[171] E.g., Lev 26:4–5; Deut 8:7–10; 11:14–15; Jer 2:7; Joel 2:18–26; 3:18; *Odes Sol.* 11:12.

[172] Cf. Lev 19:9–10.

[173] The vine motif may be used to describe the earth as well: Isa 24.

fragrance and the dew may relate to the Land-theme.[174] *2 Bar.* 10:11 explicitly describes God's irrigating dew in a Land-context (10:11). Like rain, the dew besprinkles the Land and makes it fruitful.[175] Deut 33:28 says: "So Israel lives in safety, untroubled is Jacob's abode in a land of grain and wine, where the heavens drop down dew."[176] Consequently, these narrative motifs may just as well allude to the fruitful Land as to the fertile earth of the Messianic era.[177] The motifs of the vine and the fruits of the earth, the fragrance and the dew are all part of the conventional semantic field of the Land-theme.

Moreover, according to a range of biblical texts a clear purpose of entering the Land is to eat sufficiently and be satisfied. The Land is to ensure the sustenance of the people.[178] One example is Deut 11:14–15:

> -then he will give the rain for your land in its season, the early rain and the later rain, and you will gather in your grain, your wine, and your oil: and he will give grass in your fields for your livestock, and you will eat your fill.

The combination of water (irrigation), a variety of produce of the earth and sometimes a reference to livestock as food is so commonly found in descriptions of the Land that we may consider them part of stereotype description of life in the Land.[179]

If *2 Bar.* 29 is indeed a description of Israel's life in the Messianic land, what would be the functions of this description? First, the passage can be read as a statement of triumph, since its food motifs may be understood as an imagery of victory and blessing. Descriptions of food and eating are plentiful in the texts of the first centuries C.E., also when the context of those texts or passages is the Messianic era. Scholars have taken particular interest in the so-called Messianic meals or banquets. This category of meals is common in both Jewish and Christian texts, often as a motif within an apocalyptic sequence. The Messianic meal may be understood specifically as an eschatological meal where the

---

[174] Hos 14:5–7.

[175] According to Deut 11:10–11, rain serves as a special blessing for the Land (Cf. Joel 2:23–24; *L.A.B.* 19:10; 23:12; *Targum Jonathan to Hosea* 6:3). The Land has direct access to the reservoirs of the heavens, in contrast to the archenemy Egypt, which gets water from a river (Cf. Philo, *Mos.* 1, 201–202; Cf. Borgen, *Bread*, 13.)

[176] Cf. *Odes Sol.* 11:13–18, 1QM IX–X; XIX, 1–2.

[177] Cf. *Apoc. Dan.* 10:7.

[178] Cf. pp. 45–47.

[179] Cf. similar accounts in Deut 8:10; 11:14–15; 32:10–15 Isa 65:13; Joel 2:18–26; 11Q14 (VI–X).

Messiah is present in one form or other. But according to D.E. Smith, the term may also be applied in a much broader sense as "the general symbolism of food and/or a festive meal to signify immortality and/or the joys of the end-time and afterlife."[180] Smith argues that a series of motifs came to be associated with the Messianic meal: "victory over the primordial enemies (…), eternal joyous celebration, abundance of food, the presence of the Messiah, judgement, and the pilgrimage of the nations."[181] This broad definition would thus apply to a passage like *2 Bar.* 29.[182]

What would the function of the meal motif in the Messianic era be? As Smith suggests, apocalyptic literature picks up the tradition of festive meals as celebrations of victory and deliverance.[183] Meals set in the end-time are typically celebrations of victory over eschatological enemies, beasts or men, and even over death.[184] In her study of combat myths, A.Y. Collins has proposed that, "These myths [of combat] involve a struggle between two divine beings for universal kingship. One combatant is often a monster representing the forces of chaos." She says further: "The bestial opponent is associated with disorder in society and sterility in nature, while the champion is linked with order and fertility."[185] *2 Bar.* 29's inclusion of the primordial monsters Behemoth and Leviathan may show how *2 Baruch* makes use of this mythic material. As we have already seen, the killing and eating of the two monsters lead to the restoration of order and fertility. The abundance of food, and the joy and satisfaction of the remnant do indeed close a section describing apocalyptic upheaval and Messianic revenge (26:1–29:4).[186] And in the broader context of *2 Bar.* 22–30, the eating scene in 29:2–9 shows how the world turns from wickedness to righteousness and from chaos to order. The function of the consumption thus corresponds well to the idea of the Messianic meal. In this sense, *2 Baruch* applies a com-

---

[180] Smith, *From Symposium to Eucharist*, 166.

[181] Smith, *From Symposium to Eucharist*, 169.

[182] The eating in *2 Bar.* 29 is not explicitly organised in the form of a meal. The passage neither refers to meal etiquette or procedures, nor to physical settings like the dining room or table (Cf. McGowan, *Ascetic Eucharists*, 52–60). Nor does the passage mention any liturgical aspects of the meal (Cf. *Fragmentary Targum to Deut* 32:14; *Jos. Asen.* 15–16; *Contempl.* 67–68). Still, the description is consonant with Smith's broad category of a Messianic meal.

[183] Cf. 1 Chr 12:38–40; 2 Macc 6:30–41; *L.A.B.* 27:9.

[184] Cf. Zech 9; Isa 25:6–8; 34:5–7; Joel 2:24–26, 3:18.

[185] Collins, *Combat*, 2. Cf. McGowan, *Ascetic Eucharists*, 137.

[186] Cf. *2 Bar.* 39–40; 70–73.

mon apocalyptic theme in the description of the joyous celebration of victory.

So, the Messianic era not only changes the world, as I argued above, it also brings about a radical redistribution of power. The reward of the triumphant party, the remnant, is the welfare and the protection provided by the Messianic realm. This would support the idea that 29:4–8 not only bears on imagery of creation and consummation. We can also read it as a comment on power relations in the very last phase of the world.

The link between victory, blessing and the diet of the Land is explicit in a number of texts. Neh 9:25, for instance, attests to the widespread idea that the Land of Promise, with all its delights, had to be conquered and possessed before it could be exploited.[187] Another example from the *Jerusalem Targum to Gen* 49:11–12 shows clearly how motifs of Messianic battle merge with imagery of Messianic abundance:

> How beautiful is the king Messiah who is to rise among those of the house of Judah! He girds his loins and goes forth to do battle against his foes, and he slaughters kings along with princes. He reddens the mountains with the blood of their slain and whitens the hills with the fat of their warriors. His garments drip with blood: he resembles a trampler of grapes. How beautiful, the eyes of the king Messiah: more so than pure wine! For he does not make use of them either to look upon illicit carnal commerce or to shed innocent blood. His teeth are whiter than milk, for he does not use them for that which comes from acts of violence and pillagings. The mountains shall be reddened with the wines and the vine-presses. The hills shall be whitened with an abundance of wheat and flocks of sheep and goats.[188]

These passages attest to the notion that eschatological victory restores Israel's access to the goods of the Land.[189] The steady supply of fruits of the Land in the Messianic era is in this sense an expression of Israel's ultimate triumph.

A second function of the meal motif is that the renewed fruitfulness of the Land in 29:5–7 answers Baruch's worries and laments over the lost Land in 10:9–11, cited in Chapter Two. Within the context of Baruch's lamentation (10:6–19), this passage questions the very purpose of harvests and wine production after the destruction of Zion.[190] Seen

---

[187] Cf. Zech 8:12; 9:13–17.
[188] Translation by Grelot, *Targums*, 36.
[189] Cf. also Isa 65:11–14; *Jub.* 22:8. Cf. *Targum Song of Songs* 7:12–14.
[190] Cf. pp. 45–47.

from this angle, the harvests of 29:5 must relieve Baruch's frustration, since they restore the fertility of the Land completely.

Likewise, the annihilation of the monsters in 29:4 may answer the threat of wicked forces to the Land. As I have already noted, the remnant's consummation of Leviathan and Behemoth on one level summons the outermost parts of the earth to serve the remnant. These uninhabited areas stop being threatening and submit to righteous rule.[191] On another level, the consummation also puts the symbolic enemies of Israel's to rest. Behemoth and Leviathan were symbols of the enemies Egypt and Assyria (Ezek 29:3; 32:2). Slaying them is therefore an additional expression of the defeat of the enemy and of the universal power of the Messianic reign.[192]

We may thus interpret *2 Bar.* 29:1–8 as a description of the victorious Israel in its restored Land. From this perspective, the description of the foods in 29:4–8 elaborates on the nurturing qualities of the protective Land, described in 29:2. Thus, the Messianic diet both assures victory and fulfils the Land promise in the very last times of this world.

A third function of the food motifs should be discussed. We should allow for the possibility that 29:4–8 argues the restoration of the Land for a specific purpose: the reintroduction of the temple offering. In Chapter Three I argued that the territorial extent of the Land corresponded to the extent of cultic responsibility, since only the ground tilled by the righteous could provide the temple with first fruits. Consequently, when no one was left to till and to live on the ground in the prescribed manner, there was no one left to present a temple offering. And, as the discussion of 10:9–11 showed, once the temple had fallen, there was no reason to sow again, no reason for the earth to bring forth its fruits, the vine might just as well cease its production, and the heaven might keep back its dew and rain, since no offering could be presented in Zion. In this light, the food categories of 29:4–8 may be read as proofs of the restored status of the Land, as the Land that provides offerings to the temple. The dew returns to water the fields, the vine increases its production again, the harvest is abundant and

---

[191] Cf. *Apoc. Ab.* 10:10; 21:4. Note also that the reference to the evil beasts that creep back into the forest in 39:6 may answer 10:8, where demonic forces enter the inhabitable world (Cf. pp. 112–114).

[192] Cf. Ginzberg, *Legends V*, 46; Gutman, "Leviathan," 220; 224; J. Priest, "A Note on the Messianic Banquet," in *The Messiah: Developments in Earliest Judaism and Christianity* (ed. J.H. Charlesworth et al; The First Princeton Symposium on Judaism and Christian Origins; Minneapolis: Fortress, 1992), 222–238 at 235; Nir, *Destruction*, 134.

even meat and bread are provided for. This means that the remnant has central ingredients of the food offerings available once more.[193] The new food available could indicate that the offering was in fact imagined to be restored, or that it should be restored in the near future.

Does 29:4–8 then still imply the rebuilding of the temple in the Messianic era? As I have argued above, 2 Baruch never mentions a rebuilding of the temple during the Messianic era. 40:1, for instance, describes a return to Mount Zion, but depicts Mount Zion as a place of rule and judgement, not as the place of the sanctuary. The return is not a return to Zion, but to Mount Zion. It is therefore more likely that 29:4–8 describes how the remnant has regained control over the Land where the offerings potentially could be taken from. 29:4–8 thus envisions a restoration of the Land, including its cultic capabilities, implying on the one hand that the remnant in Israel enjoys all the blessings of their Land, and on the other that they have prepared an offering for an already existing, but not yet visible other-worldly sanctuary.[194]

In conclusion, 29:4–8's description of the feeding of the remnant reveals that the Messianic era has transformed Creation. The heavens, the earth and the waters once again provide abundantly, and together nourish the remnant. It is also likely that the passage implies the transformation of the 'dust and earth' of Mount Zion. During the Messianic era the earth of is dominated by righteousness, and Mount Zion has turned into the Land.

Transforming the Remnant

One last point deserves some attention: the importance of the eating to the transformation of the remnant. The food 29:4–8 puts on the remnant's menu proves that its members are both strong and chosen by God. They are able to defeat primordial monsters, and they eat manna, the food which was predetermined to nourish only those who would survive until the end of the world (29:4, 8).

Now, the composition of the diet in the passage is far from coincidental, since its components are renowned for their special life giving qualities. The fruits of the Garden of Eden were considered particularly life enhancing. The fruits of the tree of life were believed to be essential

---

[193] Cf. b. B. Bat. 60 b. Cf. Murphy, Structure and Meaning, 99–100.
[194] Cf. further Chapter Seven.

for attaining life, in this world or the other, by several contemporary
texts.[195] According to *1 En.* 25:6, the fragrance of the tree will penetrate
the bones of the elect and assure life.[196] *2 Baruch*'s 'fragrance of aromatic fruits' thus relates to current ideas. A similar life-giving function
is ascribed to the cluster of grapes.[197] Isa 65:8 says: "As the wine is found
in the cluster, and they say, 'Do not destroy it, for there is blessing in it',
(...)." Wine is further associated with God's blessings in the *Targum Esth*
I 7:10, Aseneth drinks a cup of immortality in *Jos. Asen.* 16:16, and a
cluster of grapes gives life to all in Ephrem's *Hymns on Virginity* VI, 8.[198]

Manna and the dew add to the life providing diet. Because of the
miraculous character of the manna, several texts of the first centuries
C.E. regarded manna as the ultimate source of food for the survivors of
the Messianic era.[199] Manna is the "bread of angels" and the "bread
of life."[200] Since it comes from heaven, it brings a special blessing: it
does not require any labour.[201] Moreover, manna brings eternal life to
those who eat it.[202] Likewise, according to *2 Bar.* 29:7 and 73:2,[203] dew is
a health bringing wonder. Both biblical texts and later interpretations
ascribe a life giving power to the dew. Basically, dew irrigates dry land
and makes it blossom. But since dew, unlike rain, miraculously appears
on the ground, dew encourages further associations with life bringing

---

[195] Ezek 47:12; *1 En.* 25:5; *T. Levi* 18:10–11; Rev 22:14. Cf. Smith, *From Symposium to
Eucharist*, 167. Fruits from other trees in the Garden were life giving as well. The fruits
(*4 Ezra* 7:123), or, alternatively, the leaves of the fruit bearing trees bring healing in Rev
22:2. According to the Rev 22:2 this is the fruit bearing Tree of Life. *Hist. Rech.* 3:6; 11:4
locate fragrant fruits on the island of the blessed. These fruits sustain the blessed and
give them rest.

[196] Cf. *Odes Sol.* 11:12–19.

[197] Note that the tree is identified as a vine in, e.g., *Apoc. Ab.* 23:6; *3 Bar.* 4:8 and in
contemporary rabbinic debate (*b. Sanh.* 70a and *Gen Rab.* 15:7, according to H.E. Gaylord, "3 Baruch," in *Old Testament Pseudepigrapha I* (ed. J.H. Charlesworth; 2 vols; Garden
City, N.Y.: Doubleday, 1983–1985), 653–679 at 667).

[198] Cf. M. Smith, "On the Wine God in Palestine (Gen. 18, John 2, and Achilles
Tatius)," in *Salo Wittmayer Baron Jubilee Volume: On the Occasion of His Eightieth Birthday,
vol. 2* (ed. S. Lieberman; 3 vols; English section; Jerusalem: Central Press for the
American Academy for Jewish Research, 1974), 815–829.

[199] Manna is Messianic food in *Sib. Or.* 7.146–149; *Fragmentary Targum to Deut* 8:16,
Targum Eccles 12:11 and *Cant* 4:5; *b. Hag.* 12b (cf. Klausner, *Messianic Idea*, 354; Malina,
Palestinian Manna, 86–91; Davies, *Gospel and Land*, 332).

[200] *4 Ezra* 1:19; *Jos. Asen.* 16:16; John 6:34.

[201] Cf. the story about the life giving honeycomb in *Jos. Asen.* 15–16. The honeycomb
represents manna in this story (Smith, *From Symposium to Eucharist*, 167). Cf. Num 11:7;
Sib. Or. 3.746; *Targum Jonathan to Ezek* 16:13.

[202] *Jos. Asen.* 16:16. John 6 attests to this belief among Jews.

[203] Cf. *1 En.* 60–61; Wis 11:22.

humidity. In *2 En.* 60:20 and *b. Ḥag.* 12b the dew is an eschatological gift,[204] the dew of the *Odes Sol.* 11:14 promotes salvation, dew brings justice and blessings,[205] and the dew brings both earthly and eternal life in *L.A.B.* 23:12. Isa 26:19 shows the associative potential of the dew particularly well: "Your dead shall live, their corpses shall rise. O dwellers in the dust, awake and sing for joy! For your dew is a radiant dew, and the earth will give birth to those long dead." Possibly, this Isaiah passage considers dew an instrument of resurrection since it waters the earth that keeps the dead.[206] Thus, the mention of the dew in *2 Bar.* 29:7 adds a very potent motif to the description of the life enhancing diet of the remnant in the Land.

As I argued initially, the Messianic age is a temporary era. By means of its blessings, the remnant prepares for the next phase.[207] They have already conquered the Messianic Land, but the foods they eat signal that they prepare for resurrection and life in the other world.

Land, Garden, Mountian: The Ultimate Blend (2 Bar. 71–74)

The Apocalypse of the cloud presents *2 Baruch*'s most elaborate version of Messianic transformations (*2 Bar.* 72–74). The discussions in Chapter Three and the preliminary conclusions in the present chapter have shown that the Messianic era manifests itself at the end of the world or beyond world history. According to the Apocalypse of the cloud, the thirteenth waters (69:1–5) signaled the end of history. Since the intervention of the Messiah (70:9–10; 72:2) brings the end-time to an end, *2 Baruch* locates the Messianic era even beyond the end. It is thus not fully part of the world. But as 74:2 suggests, the Messianic age is not fully part of the other world either. In this manner, the definition of this era underscores the notion of an ultimate age: the Messianic era is both the end of the corruptible world and the beginning of the incorruptible one. The spaces of this period, thus, should not be expected to fall into the common order of spaces within history: they are liminal spaces.

The description of the spatial transformations of the Messianic era in the Apocalypse of the cloud is complex. These ultimate waters include the judgement scene at Mount Zion and the continued protection of

---

[204] Cf. Klijn, "2 Baruch," 631.
[205] 4Q157 XXXI, 5; 1QM XII, 9–10; XIX, 1–2; *Targum Ps* 110:3.
[206] Cf. *L.A.B.* 23:12–13 and the *Odes Sol.* 11; 35:1, 5 and 36:7.
[207] Cf. Neh 9:15.

the righteous in the Holy Land (71–72), the ascension of the Messiah
to the throne of the kingdom (73:1) and the restoration of a paradisiacal and Land-like, space (73:1–74:1). In this way the period of the ultimate bright waters presents the process of turning from a corruptible
to an incorruptible world (74:2). To describe the spaces where the end-
most transformation takes place, *2 Baruch* sets several spatial allusions
in motion. The ambiguous character of the Messianic era is reflected
in a special richness in the description of space. We have already seen
that the protective Holy Land keeps the righteous remnant safe from
destruction and lifts them out of the inferno of the end. We have also
seen that the Messianic judgement in 72:1–6 transforms the earth fundamentally. Judgement creates a world beyond corruption, which can
be described as a restoration of the Garden of Eden. In other words,
at this point we know that the spaces described in *2 Bar.* 71–74 are well
beyond history. They outlive the corruptible world order, while mirror-
ing the original condition of mankind.

71:1–74:1: Judgement and Enthronement

The first issue that demands attention is the relationship between the
description of the protective Holy Land (71) and the judgement scene
at mount Zion (72). It is not entirely clear whether the Apocalypse of
the cloud regards the protection provided by the Holy Land (71:1–2)
solely as a phenomenon of the end-time, or whether this protection
continues during the Messianic reign. On the one hand, 71:1 says that
the Holy Land will protect its inhabitants "at that time" (*bhaw zabnā*).
This expression could refer to the preceding description of the end-time
calamities in 70:6–10. If this is the case, the protection is limited to the
period that antecedes the Messianic era. On the other hand, keeping in
mind that the identity of 'at that time' cannot be fully determined, we
must take into account that the appearance of the Messiah is included
among the last calamities that afflict the wicked already in 70:9. The
coming of the Messiah in the Apocalypse of the cloud is thus described
twice; both in context of the last dark waters and as a feature of
the description of the ultimate bright waters. This may indicate that
70:9 is an interpolation, as Charles suggested.[208] However, the fact that
2 Baruch mentions the coming of the Messiah twice may just as well

---

[208] Charles, *Apocalypse of Baruch*, 114.

suggest that *2 Baruch* describes two different aspects of the same story. Whereas the coming of the Messiah is a catastrophe to the wicked, and thus properly belongs to their end-time afflictions, his appearance at the same time signals that Israel's redemption is imminent and is therefore a natural part of the ultimate bright period in Israel's history. If this is so, the repetition is accounted for. And since the protective Land is part of the Messianic era in both *2 Bar.* 29 and the Apocalypse of the cedar and the vine, it is likely that the Holy Land continues to protect the remnant during the Messianic era also in the Apocalypse of the cloud. Moreover, the above discussion of the location of the Land and the character of the Land's holiness showed that 71:1 and 72:2–4 in all probability describe the same locality. Thus, there is reason to believe that 71:1's description of the Holy Land is to be included in the presentation of the Messianic era in the Apocalypse of the cloud.

The second issue is the relationship between *2 Bar.* 71–72 and 73–74. Do these passages describe distinct phases and spaces, or can we regard the description of the Messianic era (71–74) as a single event? What, then, is the relationship between the protection and judgement that take place at Mount Zion in 71:1–72:6 and the description of the coming of the Messiah to the throne of the Messianic kingdom and the following paradisiacal condition in 73:1–74:1? One possible interpretation is that 73:1–74:1 describes a radically different situation from 71:1–72:6. 73:1–74:1 describes an entirely blissful state resembling the Garden of Eden, whereas 71:1–72:6 occupies itself with destruction, judgement, violent killing and perdition. If this interpretation is correct, the Messiah's seating at the throne in 73:1 would introduce a new tableau in the presentation of the era. Some aspects of 73:1–2 could indicate that this is a relevant reading of the text. According to this passage, the Messiah sits down in eternal peace (*bašlāmā l'ālam*) on the throne and as a result joy (*busāmā*) and rest (*nyāḥā*) appear. As I suggested in Chapters Two and Three, these concepts are often used to express the end of creative activity. God rested on the seventh day of creation week, and rest and peace filled the Land after the inauguration of the temple. The rest and peace of 73:1–2 could thus indicate that the world is recreated. This interpretation would make the space described in 73:1–74:1 a new, or a renewed, world.[209]

---

[209] Cf. Dahl, "Christ," 427; Laato, *Star*, 382.

However, the other possible interpretation is that 73:1–74:1 serves as the mirror image of 71:1–72:6. In other words, 73:1–74:1 may be seen as an elaboration as well as a parallel to 71:1–72:6. Firstly, as we have seen in Chapter Three, judging and ruling are commonly understood as the same activity. A king that rules, judges, and a king that judges, rules. And both are the responsibilities of the good king. The violent judgement of the Messiah in 72:1–6 is thus the counterpart of the peace that unfolds during the Messianic kingdom. 61:1–8 showed that as long as the judgement of the king is good, his reign is joyous and peaceful. Killing the enemy and living peacefully are not contradictions.[210] On the contrary, violence is beneficial and a necessary part of Israel's redemption. It is important to note that righteous judgement is regarded as a positive phenomenon in *2 Baruch*. The Day of Judgement is in fact one of God's promises to Abraham in 57:2, and as we have seen above, judgement is Israel's revenge and assures Israel's triumph during the Messianic era. Peace and rest may thus not only signal fulfilment of recreation. Peace may just as well result from judgement and annihilation of the enemy.[211]

The link between judging and ruling is also visible in the imagery of the throne (*trānāws*).[212] Several texts describe the one who sits on the throne as the one who performs judgement, such as for instance 1 Kgs 7:7: "He [Solomon] made the Hall of the Throne where he was to pronounce judgement, the Hall of Justice, covered with cedar from floor to floor."[213] When the Messiah sits down on the throne he is thus both ruler of the kingdom (*malkutā*) and eschatological judge.[214] 73:1 in fact points out this correlation between judgement and enthronement. It does not say that he sits down after he has fulfiled his duties as judge. Instead, it says that the world is in the process of being transformed by Messianic judgement *as well as* his enthronement. There is due reason, therefore, to argue that judgement and enthronement merge in the description of the Messianic era, and that the eruption of peace and rest in 73:1–74:1 equals the annihilation of the enemy in 72:2–6.[215]

---

[210] Cf. *2 Bar.* 61:2; 63:6–8; 66:3; Deut 13:9; Isa 11:14; Zech 9:13–17.

[211] Cf. *2 Bar.* 36:6; *Jub.* 23:30–31; 4Q246. In the Aramaic Enoch, the earth finds rest after the final judgement (4Q212 1 II, 13–17). Alternatively, the earth rests because it is cleansed from pollution (4Q204 5 I–II; *1 En.* 106–107).

[212] *Trwnws* (Ms. 14, 687).

[213] Cf. Dan 7:14; *1 En.* 45:3; 61:8; Rev 20:4, 11–12.

[214] Cf. *2 Bar.* 61:3–6.

[215] Cf. further Isa 11:1–5; Jer 23:5–6.

If this interpretation is correct, *2 Bar.* 71:1–74:1 serves as another example of how qualities of Land and Garden merge in *2 Baruch's* Messianic era. While 71:1–72:6 concentrates the Messianic era on the Mount Zion centred Holy Land and through this spatial focus draws on allusions to Davidic kingship, 73:1–74:1 applies Garden allusions to further enhance the authority and delight of Messianic spaces. In this sense, 71:1–74:1 blends Land and Garden allusions to describe the Messianic reign.

The Lofty Location of the Messianic Community

In the above discussion I have argued that the location of the Messianic Land in 71:1 is Mount Zion. Where is the rest of the passage 71:1–74:1 set? Earlier interpreters of 71:1–74:1 have suggested a variety of spatial settings for the Messianic reign. Some have suggested that 73:1 describes a heavenly, and even transcendent, locality. Bogaert, for instance, says that the Messiah enters the heavenly world, but suggests that the description of his transfer from earth is somewhat abrupt.[216] Others have understood the Messianic reign as predominantly earthly. Charles regards 73–74, as well as 29 and 39–40, as descriptions of Israel's well-being on earth. He says; "Since the kingdom is to be established in Palestine, (...) only those Jews who are found there are to share in it (...)." However, this interpretation is nevertheless troublesome to Charles. He goes on: "Again, since Palestine is the scene of the kingdom, Jerusalem must still be standing; for in case it had fallen, we should here be told of its restoration (...), or of setting up the new Jerusalem (...). The Messianic kingdom could not be set up over the ruins of the holy city."[217] These suggestions made Charles conclude that this part of *2 Baruch* must have been written before 70 C.E., a suggestion most scholars later have rejected. This diversity of interpretations shows that the spatiality of the Messianic reign is contested; at the same time, it attests to the ambiguity of the spatial description in the passage.

Can the above proposal that the judgement scene in 71:1–72:6 is the equivalent to the throne scene in 73:1–74:1 shed light on the spatial ambiguity of 71:1–74:1? Where does the Messianic Land take place?

---

[216] Bogaert, *Apocalypse de Baruch II*, 417. Ferch suggests that the passage presents "the transcendent view of the future age in *2 Baruch*" (Ferch, "Two Aeons," 146).

[217] Charles, *Apocalypse of Baruch*, 49; Cf. Klijn, "Sources and Redaction," 72; Chester, "Eschatology," 252; Rowland, *Open Heaven*, 174.

Let us start by looking closer at the throne imagery of 73:1, since enthronement, and thus judgement, has been shown to be essential to Messianic transformations. We need to address one question: where is the throne of 73:1? Is it set at Mount Zion or is the throne set in a more elevated location? To be sure, there is no clear answer to the question of the location of the throne in 73:1. Certainly, the imagery of the Messiah's coming to sit on his throne has broad connotations. A look at other texts may inform us about the possible range of interpretations. Several texts envision God's throne, the throne of the king and/or the Messiah on Mount Zion.[218] Descriptions of the throne at Mount Zion are probably related to the broader repertoire of thrones located on mountains, or thrones made similar to mountains, as for instance the throne of Moses on Mount Sinai.[219] Other descriptions locate the throne of God and the throne of the Messiah in heaven. Still, even the notions of heavenly thrones are far from fixed. Heaven, or one of the heavens, may itself be envisioned as God's throne, the throne may be elevated and mobile, or the throne may be located in the highest realms of heaven.[220] To complicate the picture even further, some thrones may reach from the mountain to heaven, or be set up in heaven with the earth as its footstool.[221] Moreover, differing locations may be advocated in the same text. *1 Enoch* describes the throne of the Messianic kingdom in two different passages, both in the Book of the Similitudes (*1 En.* 37–71). *1 En.* 69:29 seats the Son of Man on the throne of his glory in a world which has been freed from corruption. This passage probably locates the throne on earth in the Messianic age (69:28). *1 En.* 61:8, on the other hand, suggests that God places the Elect One on a heavenly throne of glory, where he will judge the holy ones in the heaven above. That passage implies a heavenly throne for the Messiah. *1 Enoch* thus envisions both an earthly and a heavenly location of the throne and there is no obvious tension between the two.

In light of these other accounts, the spatial allusions of *2 Bar.* 71:1–74:1 may be manifold when the Messiah sits down on the throne of the kingdom. The throne of the temple in Jerusalem may be envisioned, but so may a throne in heaven.[222] Another possibility is that the throne

---

[218] Exod 24:10; 1 Kgs 7:7: Pss 99; 110.

[219] *Ezek. Trag.* 1:68–69. Cf. *1 En.* 18:8; 24:3; 25:3.

[220] Cf. Ezek 1:26; 10:1; Isa 6:1; 66:1; Dan 7:9; Pss 11:4; 45:6; 103:19; *1 En.* 14:8–15; 84:2; *2 En.* 20–22.

[221] *Ezek. Trag.* 1:69.

[222] Bogaert, *Apocalypse de Baruch II*, 417.

is envisioned somewhere in between them, or that it connects heaven and Mount Zion. The connotations usually associated with the throne motif would anyhow tend to elevate the location of the throne.

Can the throne of the Messiah, as well as the surrounding kingdom be heavenly, or other-worldly?[223] A look at the description of the child-bearing women in 73:7 may shed some light on this issue. We have already seen that the last, bright, waters in general restore what the first, dark, waters destroyed. However, as 73:7 suggests, the production of children has not ceased. That implies that the realm of death still demands new blood and that erotic passion and child conception still prevails during the Messianic era (56:6). In fact, reproduction is joyful and possibly extensive during this period.[224] This implies that the Messianic kingdom does not belong to the heavenly other world. According to 21:19–23 and 51:9 and 16, earthly biological processes such as ageing and death, and by implication also birth, are overcome only in the other world. In this sense, the Messianic era still belongs to this world. The full transformation to a heavenly reality has not yet been effected.

The fact that the explanation part of the apocalypse (71:1–74:1) interprets its vision counterpart (53:1–11) may provide a possible answer to the question as to the location of the Messianic kingdom. The interpretation of the location should in other words reflect that the two

---

[223] In the preceding discussion I have presupposed that the one who ascends the throne is the Messiah. However, the identity of the enthroned figure in 73:1 may be God or the Messiah. *2 Baruch* mentions a throne in some other passages, most prominently in 51:11. In that passage, the throne is explicitly located in the heavenly Paradise and is the throne of God. However, the context of the Apocalypse of the cloud makes it unlikely that the throne in 73:1 is the throne of God (Cf. however 1 Cor 15:24–25; Rev 21:5; Cf. Charles, *Apocalypse of Baruch*, 115). The throne scenario in 51:11 belongs to the time after resurrection, whereas the kingdom of the Messiah in 73:1 takes place in a transformed world, but not yet fully in the age of incorruptibility (74:2). It is therefore more likely that the Messiah is the one who sits down on the throne of the eschatological, Messianic kingdom. Note that several texts are vague with regard to the identity of the figure at the throne (*Pss. Sol.* 17; *1 En.* 61:8). Cf. further Dan 7:14; *1 En.* 45:3, 61:8; 69:29; 11Q13; *Ezek. Trag.* 1:68–89; Eph 2:6. Cf. J.C. VanderKam, "Righteous One, Messiah, Chosen One, and Son of Man in *1 Enoch* 37–71," in *The Messiah: Developments in Earliest Judaism and Christianity* (ed. J.H. Charlesworth et.al; Minneapolis: Fortress Press, 1992), 169–191; J.J. Collins, and A.Y. Collins, *Daniel: A Commentary on the Book of Daniel* (ed. F.M. Cross; Hermeneia; Minneapolis: Fortress Press, 1993), 274–324; T. Eskola, *Messiah and the Throne: Jewish Merkabah Mysticism and Early Christian Exaltation Discourse* (WUNT 2; Tübingen: Mohr Siebeck, 2001), 91; K.J. Ruffatto, "Polemics with Enochic Traditions in the Exagoge of Ezekiel the Tragedian," *JSP* 15 (2006): 195–210.

[224] Cf. parallel notions in *1 En.* 10.17; *L.A.B.* 3.10; Cf. Klausner, *Messianic Idea*, 342; Sayler, *Promises*, 71; Boyarin, *Carnal Israel*, 45.

are meant to shed light upon each other. We must thus combine the
motifs of the vision and the interpretation to understand the location of
the Messianic kingdom. The imagery of 53:11 may suggest an elevated
location of the Messiah and the Messianic community:[225] "And I saw
after these things, behold, twelve rivers ascended from the sea, and they
surrounded the lightning and became subject to it." Certainly, this concluding phrase of the vision part of the Apocalypse of the cloud is not
explicit about locality.

Two conclusions may however be drawn: First, it is evident that
2 Baruch, as usual, does not primarily map territory: *2 Baruch* constructs
spaces by means of its constituent dwellers. The spatial construction
of this passage in this sense resembles the spatial constructions I have
identified in *2 Baruch*'s descriptions of the end-time. After the fall of
the temple, space is defined by the presence of a leader and his pious
group.[226] Thus, 53:11 primarily maps the Messiah and his subjects and
the main spatial reference of the passage is the presence of the Messianic community in an elevated position.[227] Second, the location of the
Messianic community could be understood as Mount Zion, but at the
same time so as to include the vertical continuum between Mount Zion
and the firmament. According to the 53:9, the lightning enlightens the
whole world. The imagery of this passage indicates that the lightening
spans the air[228] from the firmament to the earth. When 53:11 suggests
that the rivers[229] ascend from the sea to gather around the lightning,
this may mean that they rise to Mount Zion, but we should allow for
the idea that the rivers rise to the Messiah in a loftier location in the air.
Some texts of the first centuries C.E. imposed, as it were, a localisation
of the Messianic realm above or independent of the ground. Similar

---

[225] It is not obvious how the interpretation part reflects 53:11. My interpretation is
one of several options. Consequently, it is not certain that 53:11 is the vision equivalent
of 71:1–74:1 (Cf. Volz, *Eschatologie*, 44; Harnisch, *Verhängnis*, 261; Klijn, "Sources and
Redaction," 73; Leuenberger, "Ort und Funktion," 224; 227). The passage may also
refer to life in the heavenly realm of the other world beyond resurrection (cf. *2 Bar.* 30;
51).

[226] Cf. *1 En.* 71:16.

[227] Cf. *Targum Onkelos to Gen* 49:11.

[228] I understand the air (*āar*) as the space between the firmament and the earth (Cf.
2 Bar. 59:8).

[229] It is not evident what the rivers refer to. It may be the twelve tribes, but there is no
information in the interpretation part of the apocalypse to support this conclusion. The
other option is that it is the righteous: the remnant and those who escaped Messianic
judgement. This conclusion finds support in 72:3–5.

imagery appears in *4 Ezra* 13:1–13. Maybe 1 Thess 4:17 could also be read in this light: "Then we who are alive, who are left, will be caught up in the clouds together with them to meet the Lord in the air; and so we will be with the Lord for ever."[230]

If 53:8–11 and 71:1–74:1 are read together, we can conclude that *2 Baruch* envisions an elevated location of the Messianic reign, and pushes the connotations that go with Mount Zion to their limit. Possibly, the Messianic community may be located at the very summit of Mount Zion or the apocalypse may imply an even loftier location for the assembly. Maybe the location of the Messianic community on Mount Zion allows for both interpretations, seeing Mount Zion as the spot that embraces the vertical continuum between the summit and the firmament.[231]

The Land-Garden Blend

The blend of notions relating to Land, Garden and Mountain is not foreign to texts contemporaneous with *2 Baruch*. Blended imagery and connotational overlaps are widespread in literature stemming from the first centuries C.E., and also in descriptions of the Messianic era.[232] The Land may be envisioned as a mountain, as may the Garden, and in some accounts the differences between Land and Garden may be dissolved.[233] Examples of this trend are found for instance in *1 En.* 25,

---

[230] Cf. further *Vis. Paul* 21–22.

[231] Cf. discussions of Mount Zion as a cosmic mountain in Gunkel, *Schöpfung und Chaos*, 133 ff.; Clements, *God and Temple*, 63–67; Clifford, *Cosmic Mountain*, 98–181; Haran, "Temples," 255–257; Levenson, *Sinai and Zion*, 111–137; 145–176.

[232] Cf. Isa 51:3; *Odes Sol.* 11:18; *Targum Jonathan to Isa* 52:5, 10; *Sib. Or.* 5.238–285. Cf. further 1QapGen XXI, 8–14 (Cf. Moxnes, *Theology in Conflict*, 128–129; Nir, *Destruction*, 140).

[233] Several texts attest to a complex relationship between Land, Garden and Mountain. Cf. Isa 57:13; Ezek 28:13–14; 47:1–2; Gen 2:13 compared to 1 Kgs 1; Peshitta version of 4:8; *1 En.* 24–25; 32; 1QapGen XXI, 8; Ephrem, *Commentary on Genesis* VI; *Hymns on Paradise* I, 4 and possibly *L.A.B.* 7:4 and *Jub.* 4:23–26; 8:19. Cf. S. Brock, *St. Ephrem Syrus: Hymns on Paradise* (Crestwood, N.Y.: St. Vladimir's Seminary Press, 1990), 50; 52; P. Grelot, "La Géographie mythique d'Hénoch et ses sources orientales," *RB* 65 (1958): 33–69 at 43; R. Murray, *Symbols of Church and Kingdom: A Study in Early Syriac tradition* (London: Cambridge University Press, 1975), 306–310; J.C. VanderKam, *Enoch and the Growth of an Apocalyptic Tradition* (CBQ Monograph Series 16; Washington D.C.: Catholic Biblical Association of America, 1984), 184–187; Levenson, *Sinai and Zion*, 128–129; 131–132; Himmelfarb, *Ascent to Heaven*, 73–74; M., Himmelfarb, "The Temple and the Garden of Eden in Ezekiel, the Book of Watchers and the Wisdom of Ben Sira," in *Sacred Places and Profane Spaces: Essays in the Geographies of Judaism, Christianity and Islam* (ed.

Sib. Or. 5.348–349 and in *Hist. Rech.* 12; 14 and 15.[234] Descriptions of
Land and Garden may merge, or otherwise interchange. They may in
other words enter into metaphorical or metonymical relationships in
these texts. We cannot consistently distinguish one place from another,
nor is there reason to do so since it is exactly the comprehensive
character that authorises Messianic spaces.

In fact, several aspects of the description in *2 Bar.* 73:1–74:1 recall
both a Land and a Garden setting. Peace, joy (*ḥadutā*) and rest (73:1, 2),
for instance, are part of common descriptions of both spaces.[235] Dew
(73:2) can likewise be found to irrigate both.[236] And whereas the disappearance of sickness, lamentation and untimely death no doubt puts an
end to the troubles of this world and restores the condition of Adam,
the same imagery may also describe life in the Land.[237] Likewise, while
the motif of careless tilling of the ground recalls life in the Garden, it
may also be applied to describe the easy life in the Land during the
Messianic reign (Amos 9:13). In addition, whereas 73:7 indeed says that
pregnancy and birth will be painless and alludes to the situation before
Adam's transgression, this very passage also suggests that women will
bring forth several children. This is implied by the use of the expression *ma d*, "whenever."[238] As we have already seen in Chapter Two, the
Land is the perfect environment for bringing forth children and central in Israel's mission to become a great nation.[239] In Chapter Two
I also argued that barrenness became preferable to parenthood after
the fall of the temple and the loss of the Land (10:13). The afflictions
of the end-time became so severe that childbirth and procreation were
not advisable since it would only lead to pain and death. I also proposed that the barrenness meant the impossibility for Israel of becoming a great nation and thus from dominating the world which was in

---

J. Scott and P. Simpson-Housley; Contributions to the Study of Religion 30; New York:
Greenwood, 1991), 63–80 at 64–66; M., Ottosson, "Eden and the Land of Promise," in
Congress Volume: Jerusalem 1986 (ed. J.A. Emerton, Congress Volume Jerusalem (SVT 40);
Leiden: Brill, 1998): 177–188; Bautch, *Geography of 1 Enoch*, 61–65; 69; 188; 216–220.

[234] Note that some texts also describe the abundance of the antediluvian earth, not
the Garden, by using Land motifs (4Q370).

[235] Cf. *2 Bar.* 61; 63; Deut 12:12; Isa 65:18–19; *T. Levi* 18:9–14; *Sib. Or.* 3.770–786; *T. Ab.*
20:14. Cf. Ginzberg, *Legends* I, 306; Sayler, *Promises*, 71–72; Stordalen, *Eden*, 256–257.

[236] Cf. Deut 33:28; 11Q14.

[237] Cf. Isa 65:20; 11Q14.

[238] "Whenever," "as often as" (Smith, *Dictionary*, 246).

[239] Cf. Jer 23:3; Klausner, *Messianic Idea*, 342.

fact promised to her.[240] The Messianic reversal of this condition therefore implies that the life enhancing capabilities of the Land have been
restored. This extensive reproduction of offspring annuls the barrenness
that afflicted women during the end-time. Ambiguous spatial allusions
are thus present also in the use of this motif.

So, why does *2 Baruch* choose to blend Land and Garden allusions to
describe the Messianic reign on Mount Zion? When *2 Baruch* brings
Land and Garden allusions together, the text merges the only two
spaces in Creation that allowed for righteous living. Before Adam's
transgression, the Garden of Eden was the place where mankind could
live according to God's will. After the expulsion from the Garden,
the Land served as a righteous enclave in an otherwise wicked world.
Now, in the Messianic era, beyond history but still within the limits
of Creation, Land and Garden blend into a Paradisiacal Land. In
this manner *2 Baruch* shows how the Messianic kingdom protects the
remnant, epitomises the best elements of Creation and moves beyond
what had earlier been offered to the righteous in the corruptible world.

Transforming the World and the Remnant: Bridging Worlds

A main concern of the description of the Messianic era in *2 Baruch* is
that the remnant survives the last turmoil of the wicked world, that
it enjoys protection and revitalisation and even leaves the world tri-
umphantly. Land-imagery has proven important in all these regards.
The Land is Israel's most important protective enclave, it ensures won-
drous nutrition and it proves Israel's triumph over the enemy and the
wicked world order. At the very end of this world, Israel is finally
allowed to live in Creation as she was meant to and simultaneously
prepare for entering into the other, incorruptible world. The construction of Israel's Land in the Messianic era includes both the corruptible
and the incorruptible world and thus signals the transition from one
world to the next.

---

[240] Cf. Chapter Two, pp. 44–45.

CHAPTER SEVEN

FROM EGYPT TO LIFE:
THE HEAVENLY, PARADISIACAL, LAND

The reign of the Messiah finally made Israel master of the world. However, as the previous chapter pointed out, *2 Baruch*'s Messianic era is a temporary era. The Messianic Land at Mount Zion is therefore not the final redemptive space in *2 Baruch*'s story of Israel's salvation. Israel's safety and well-being are already secured, but she has still not attained her inheritance, the possession that God has promised her.

I concluded the preceding chapter by suggesting that the Messianic era prepared Israel for entering the other, incorruptible, world. The following chapter will study the last step on Israel's journey: the arrival in that other world. I will discuss what the other world is and does for Israel from the time of resurrection and until she is finally safe in God's heaven. Thus, the following study focuses on the incorruptible world in light of its relation to Israel and its function in Israel's history of redemption.

Of specific interest to my study is the relation between the Land and the other world. My previous analyses showed that Jerusalem and its temple have been destroyed and that Israel has lost her Land. However, the preceding chapter also showed that Israel returned to Mount Zion during the Messianic era and that the Land at Mount Zion again had an important protective and redemptive function throughout that period. The main question now is: does the Land belong only to the passing, corruptible, world as a place that goes to destruction, or does the Land-concept continue to define Israel's space in the other world? Given this important change of location, this chapter will also serve as the final check of the applicability of a praxis epistemology to the study of the Land in *2 Baruch*. We have arrived at the main question of this chapter's discussion and a major concern of the entire study: can the entry of Israel into the heavenly other world make that world into an ultimate Land of Israel?

Putting the Other World on 2 Baruch*'s Map of Redemption*

2 Baruch devotes several passages to the idea that Murphy has desig-
nated 'the two-world-concept.'[1] As I noted in Chapter One, it is safe to
say that the promotion of this two-world scheme is one of the main concerns of *2 Baruch*.[2] *2 Baruch* continually plays on the difference between
Israel's conditions of life in this world and the next, and constantly
argues for Israel's redemption on basis of that difference. And accordingly, the two-world concept of *2 Baruch* has been a popular topic of
research.[3] It is intriguing to note that *2 Baruch*'s actual descriptions of
the other world as space have not attracted corresponding interest.[4] My
first task is therefore to outline what *2 Baruch* actually says about the
spatiality of the other world, and to present my view in the context of
existing scholarly debates.

The Timing, the Cosmography and the Topography of the Other World

First of all, as I also pointed out in Chapter One, *2 Baruch*'s spaces are
always set in time. Even when the text moves beyond world history as
such, its spaces are never set in a void. In fact, the other world is a
time-space in a particular sense, since the Syriac word *'almā*, "world,"
may be understood both as a time and a space, and probably also
functioned as a merging of the two.[5] *2 Bar.* 44:8–13, for instance, shows
how closely "world" (*'almā*) and "time" (*zabnā*) are related in *2 Baruch*,

---

[1] Murphy, *Structure and Meaning*, 31–67.

[2] Cf. *2 Bar.* 4; 14–15; 21:4–25; 24:1; 30:1–5; 32:4; 37:1; 42:7–8; 43:2–3; 44; 48–51; 54:4, 13–16; 57:2; 59:4–12; 75:5–8; 78:6–7; 81; 83–85. Cf. also possible indications of a one-world scheme in 19:2; 32:6; 57:2; 85:14, and the possibility that there are more than two worlds in 59:9.

[3] Cf. Murphy, *Structure and Meaning*, 31–71; 135–142; Harnisch, *Verhängnis*, 89–106; Klausner, *Messianic Idea*, 408–420; Collins, "Apocalyptic Eschatology," 21–43; C. Barth, *Diesseits und Jenseits im Glauben des späten Israel* (SB 72; Stuttgart, KBW Verlag, 1974), 15–25.

[4] Harnisch's extensive study is typical in the sense that it is first and foremost preoccupied with the study of time (Harnisch, *Verhängnis*, 90–106; 131–141; 240–247). Cf. Münchow, *Ethik*, 106).

[5] This terminology probably reflects the meaning potential in the Greek word αἰών (Cf. Harnisch, *Verhängnis*, 95, but also Smith, *Dictionary*, 415; Smith, *Thesaurus*, 2898–2900). Cf. also H. Gressmann, *Der Ursprung der isrealitisch-jüdischen Eschatologie* (FRLANT 6; Göttingen: Vandenhoeck & Ruprecht, 1905); P. Billerbeck, "Diese Welt, die Tage des Messias und die zukünftige Welt," in *Kommentar zum Neuen Testament aus Talmud und Midrasch, vol. 4* (ed. H.L. Strack and P. Billerbeck; München: Beck, 1928), 799–976; Barth, *Diesseits*, 15; Murphy, *Structure and Meaning*, 32–33.

and similarly, passages like 14:13; 44:13 and 51:8 reveal that *zabnā* and *'almā* can be used interchangeably.[6] Other passages, like 21:24, attest to the spatial aspect of the concept. In that passage, *'almā* is God's Creation.[7] Similarly, 85:10 shows that *'almā* and *britā*, "Creation," can be used as synonyms.[8] 54:1 further shows that *'almā* has spatial dimensions, since it has "heights" (*mrawmay d'almā*) (Cf. 51:10). There is good reason, therefore, to allow for both meanings when we approach the concept of the other, incorruptible world: the other world denotes a time-space continuum.[9]

This notion of time-space is further complicated by the fact that whereas *2 Baruch* says that the other world is coming at a given time (15:7), it is imagined to be already existing. God knows it already (54:1), it is still generally hidden from mankind (51:8), but it will be revealed (55:8). This notion, which is clearly corroborated by contemporaneous texts, stresses on the one hand that the time of the coming of the other world is fixed in Israel's redemption history, but that nevertheless the other world is already there as a world that visionaries can catch a glimpse of.[10]

Murphy concluded his discussion of the two-world concept by saying that "the author of 2B places great emphasis upon the radical discontinuity between this world and the future one."[11] This conclu-

---

[6] Cf. Harnisch, *Verhängnis*, 95; Barth, *Diesseits*, 21–22. Note the use of *'alām*, "forever," in the text (5:2; 32:4; 40:3). *'alām* may in some instances describe the main quality of the new world, and stand alone as a reference to the new world (78:6). Cf. Charles, *Apocalypse of Baruch*, 8; Bogaert, *Apocalypse de Baruch I*, 465. Note that even though this world is determined by corruption, death and the existence of time (51:9), the other world, which in some passages is described as lasting forever, i.e., beyond time (51), may be described as a coming period. Ambiguities like these may attest to a sliding concept of time and space.

[7] Cf. *2 Bar.* 24:4; 56:3.

[8] In some passages, even "earth" (*ar'ā*) and "world" (*'almā*) may interchange. Barth has pointed out that the idea of 'the two cities' functions equivalently to the notions of the two worlds or the two periods. To distinguish between the two worlds is like separating between the two cities: Jerusalem and the heavenly city (Barth, *Diesseits*, 21). Cf. 4:1 and 25:4; *4 Ezra* 9:18–20.

[9] Many concepts share this inherit ambiguity. Cf., e.g., my discussion of "parts" (*mnātā*) at pp. 157–158. Further, *hārkā* may mean both "here" and "now" (Smith, *Dictionary*, 106). The other way around, *zabnā*, "period"/ "time," may have a spatial dimension to it (Cf. Violet, *Apokalypsen*, 313; Barth, *Diesseits*, 22).

[10] Cf. *2 Bar.* 4:1–7; 59:4–11; 76:3; Cf. Matt 12:32; Mark 10:30; Luke 18:30; Heb 11:5. According to Klausner, the New Testament uses the phrases 'the world to come' or 'the age to come,' where the Talmudic and other rabbinic literature have 'the world to come' (Klausner, *Messianic Idea*, 408–409).

[11] Murphy, *Structure and Meaning*, 67.

sion coincides with the interpretations of most scholars. Indeed, during the course of the present world, *2 Baruch* describes the two worlds as contrasting entities. Whereas this world is corruptible, sinful, transitory and characterised by mortality, the other world is incorruptible, glorious, eternal and beyond the biological processes of birth and death.[12] Murphy rightfully claims that: "The two worlds are being described in terms of a human quality—mortality. Baruch, and eventually all the righteous, are to escape from the sphere of mortality to one of immortality."[13] And as I suggested in the previous chapter, resurrection and God's judgement marks the transition from this world to the other, as well as a transition from death to life. In other words, the contrast between life and death, which is indeed a human quality, serves as a central metaphorical field to describe the divergence between the two worlds.[14]

So, at this point we know that *2 Baruch*'s other world is a merging of time and space, already existing alongside the corruptible world. We further know that the other world can be entered only at a given moment in time, through resurrection and judgement. But still, we do not know much about the spatiality of the other world. Murphy, who has indeed pointed out the central divergences between the two worlds, says very little about the geography and topography of that other world.

The Other World in the Heights

What can be said about the spatiality of the other, incorruptible world? Where is the other world, and what does it look like? First of all, it should be noted that *2 Baruch*, as usual, does not say exactly where the other world is. As we have seen several times already, *2 Baruch* does not provide its readers with exact spatial references. And with regard to a spatial entity like the other world, the references become even sparser.[15]

However, some information can be teased out of the text. Several passages indicate that the other world is in the heights of heaven.[16]

---

[12] Cf. Murphy, *Structure and Meaning*, 52–55.

[13] Murphy, *Structure and Meaning*, 56. Cf. Barth, *Diesseits*, 22–23.

[14] Cf. Chapter Four, pp. 120–121.

[15] Cf. Münchow, *Ethik*, 106.

[16] Cf. Stemberger, *Leib der Auferstehung*, 90; Murphy, *Structure and Meaning*, 35 and 135; Cf. Wright, *Early History*, 208. For a different opinion, cf. E. Puech, *La croyance des Esséniens en la vie future: Immortalité, réssurrection, vie éternelle? Histoire d'une croyance dans le Judaïsme Ancien* (2 vols; EBib Nouvelle série 21–22; Paris: Librairie Lecoffre, 1993), 142.

More specifically, the other world is in God's heaven.[17] According to 51:7–11, the sphere that contains God's throne and the beings just below it is the location of the other world. That place is in "the heights" (root *rwm*),[18] or in "the heights of heaven" (*rawmhun dašmayā*) (10:18).[19] As these references already indicate, 'the heights' is not a clearly delimited spatial entity. It is not explicit in the text exactly how the heights relate to the remaining heavenly realm: it may be located slightly beyond the heavenly realm, but it may also be its upper part. *2 Baruch* uses the term "heaven" (*šmayā*) in the singular throughout the text.[20] Moreover, *2 Baruch* does not differentiate between differing layers or spheres of heaven, and consequently does not convey any notion of multiple heavens, in the way that several other contemporaneous texts do.[21] *2 Baruch* thus operates within a one-heaven cosmography where the heavenly sphere is envisioned as one more or less united realm.[22] Thus, *2 Baruch* uses the word *šmayā* generously to denote heaven as part of God's Creation, for instance as the cosmological opposite to the earth and the abyss,[23] as well as to describe heaven as the container, or storehouse, of meteorological elements like dew, rain and winds (10:11; 59:6).[24]

Within this rather fuzzily defined heavenly realm, and although the spatial distinctions are never entirely clear, *2 Baruch* still maintains a certain distinction between the heights of heaven and the rest of the heavenly realm.[25] 21:4 says: "O hear me, you who created the earth,

---

[17] *2 Bar.* 10:18; 13:1: 22:1.

[18] *2 Bar.* 51:10; Cf. 13:1; 22:1.

[19] Cf. 10:18; 13:1; 21:4; 22:1; 48:5; 51:10; 54:1, 3. Cf. Smith, *Thesaurus*, 3857–3862.

[20] This fact alone does not necessarily indicate that *2 Baruch* envisions a singular heaven. In the Hebrew and the Greek, heaven is described by the singular and plural forms somewhat arbitrary (Cf. Wright, *Early History*, 124; 132; 186–187).

[21] Contemporaneous texts attest both to a single-heaven (*1 En.* 12, *Apoc. Zeph.*) and a multiple-heaven cosmography. Those texts most often describe three heavens (2 Cor 12:2–3; *T. Levi* 3) or seven heavens (*Apoc. Mos.* 35:2; *2 En.* 1–20; *Mart. Ascen. Isa* 7–9; *b. Hag* 12b). Some texts even attest to both schemes (Cf. *T. Levi* 3–5). Cf. Wright, *Early History*, 117–184; H. Bietenrand, *Die Himmlische Welt im Urchristentum und Spätjudentum* (WUNT 2; Tübingen: Verlag J.C.B. Mohr, 1951); A.Y. Collins, "The Seven Heavens in Jewish and Christian Apocalypses," in *Death, Ecstasy, and Other Worldly Journeys* (ed. J.J. Collins and M. Fishbane; Albany: SUNY Press, 1995), 59–93; Rowland, *Open Heaven*, 81–83; Himmelfarb, *Ascent to Heaven*, 31–33.

[22] Cf. Wright, *Early History*, 53; 137–138; 186.

[23] Cf. *2 Bar.* 10:9–10; 19:2; 21:4; 44:5; 48:5; 54:3; 84:2. Cf. Exod 20:4; Ps 139:8.

[24] These are common contents of heaven (Cf. Wright, *Early History*, 187; Cf. *1 En.* 69:23, 25).

[25] Cf. *1 En.* 71.

who fixed the firmament (*rqicā*) by the word, and made firm the heights
of heaven (*ramhun dašmayā*) by the spirit." This passage shows that
2 Baruch's cosmographic structure allows for some differentiation within
the heavenly realm. At least, the passage provides the reader with
the lower and higher limits of the realm. While the firmament is
the heavenly expanse visible from earth which marks the 'floor' of
the heavenly realm,[26] the "heights of heaven" denotes its uppermost
sphere.[27] Furthermore, 59:3 suggests a division between the highest
sphere of heaven as fixed and those spheres below it as shakable: "But
also heaven was shaken from its place at that time; those being under
the throne of the Most High where disturbed when he took Moses with
him." The Syriac of this sentence is unfortunately unclear. The entities
under the throne may refer to the angels and living beings beneath the
throne, or they may attest to the notion of lower heavens.[28] If the latter
interpretation is correct, this passage presents the sphere of heaven
where God abides as different from the rest of the heavenly realm.[29]
On the one hand, *2 Baruch* presents a God who, as omnipotent ruler,
is clearly beyond the corruptibility of the cosmos (54:13).[30] His location
in the heights should accordingly be immortal and everlasting (54:1),
and thus ontologically different from the cosmos. On the other hand,
though, the structure of *2 Baruch*'s universe allows for traffic between
the spheres of cosmos: from mountain tops Baruch communicates with
God (13:1; 22:1), angels may descend from heaven to earth (6:5; 80:1),
and at the end of his earthly existence Baruch ascends to heaven.[31] In
this view, 'the heights' lie on top of the heavenly realm, but do not
necessarily transcend the cosmos entirely.[32]

God's Throne and Its Surroundings

It has now been established that *2 Baruch* suggests that the heights of
heaven are the location of the other world. This leads to the following

---

[26] Cf. Gen 1:6–8; *Mart. Ascen. Isa.* 7:9; *Jos. Asen.* 12:2.

[27] Cf. *1 En.* 39:1.

[28] Cf. Charles, *Apocalypse of Baruch*, 100; Bogaert, *Apocalypse de Baruch I*, 507; Klijn,
"2 Baruch," 641.

[29] Cf. further *2 Bar.* 32:2; 54:1; Cf. *T. Job* 33:5; 9.

[30] Cf. Murphy, *Structure and Meaning*, 66; Wright, *Early History*, 139.

[31] *2 Bar.* 25:1; 46:7; 48:30; 76:2.

[32] Cf. further Deut 4:39; 26:15; 1 Kgs 8:23; Isa 63:15; Pss 11:4; 113:4; Job 11:8; 21:12;
Dan 2:28; Macc 2:15; Sir 16:18; *1 En.* 69:16; 71:5; 3; *Jos. Asen.* 22:13 (Cf. Wright, *Early
History*, 55; 141).

question: what objects are located in the heights, who populates the heights of heaven, and can we say anything about the spatiality of the heights on the basis of this? The focal point of the heights is undoubtedly God's throne.[33] The throne is central to the space of the heights in the sense that the heights and its population are several times described as surroundings of the throne. The holy beings (*ḥayātā qadištā*) of heaven stand *around* the throne (21:6), alternatively, the living beings (*ḥayātā daṯḥeyt*), the angels (*malake*) and the stars (*kawkbe*) dwell *under* the throne (51:11; possibly 59:3). In both instances, the throne is the centre of the heights. The throne and its relation to its surroundings form a spatial topography as well as a hierarchy among those who dwell in the heights. God and his throne are the peak of the heights, whereas hosts of angels and living beings, or holy ones equivalent to flame and fire (21:6; 48:8), stand below the throne, in accordance with their position (48:10) in the divine council.[34]

In addition to hosts of heavenly beings, *2 Baruch* also envisions treasuries (*awçre*) in the heights: repositories of important aspects of human acts.[35] 54:13 suggests that treasuries of wisdom are laid up under God's throne (44:14). Other passages locate treasuries of good works (14:12), righteousness (24:1), and insight (44:14) with God. These treasuries preserve the works of the righteous, already imagined to exist there.[36] In addition, treasuries of righteous souls are found with God (21:23; 30:2).[37]

---

[33] *2 Bar.* 21:6; 51:11; 54:13; 59.3.

[34] *2 Baruch* probably refers to the wide spread notion of the divine council (Cf. Cross, *Canaanite Myth*, 186–188; E.T. Mullen, Jr., *The Assembly of the Gods* (HSM 24; Chico, California: Scholars, 1980), 209–226; Himmelfarb, *Ascent to Heaven*, 13–14; G.W.E. Nickelsburg, *Resurrection, Immortality and Eternal Life in Intertestamental Judaism* (HTS 26; Cambridge: Harvard University Press, 1972), 12–14). *2 Baruch* says several times that that there are angels in the highest spheres of heaven (6:5; 48:10; 67:2; 80:1; Cf. *1 En.* 60:1–4; 61:8; 62:2–3). The living beings of 51:11 are not identified. Cf. the beings under the throne of God in Ezek 1:5; 10:20; the four living creatures of Rev 4:6–11; the souls under the throne in *b. Shab* 152b (Klijn, "2 Baruch," 638). The holy ones (*2 Bar.* 21:6) may possibly be the elders (Rev 4:4), possibly the patriarchs, or other holy men (*2 Bar.* 85:3; *Mart. Ascen. Isa.* 9:6–9, *Gk. Apoc. Ezra* 5:20–22; *T. Job* 33:2). Note, however, that *2 Baruch's* angels and holy ones are created (56:11), although from the very beginning (21:6). The heavenly beings have been discussed extensively (Cf. Charles, *Apocalypse of Baruch*, 75; Bogaert, *Apocalypse de Baruch I*, 425–438; and further, Wright, *Early History*, 190. Cf. also 1 Kgs 22:19–22; Isa 6; *1 En.* 14:22; 40:2; 71:7; *Apoc. Ab.* 18; 1QS IV, 12–13).

[35] Cf. Rowland, *Open Heaven*, 56.

[36] Cf. Nir, *Destruction*, 122.

[37] Cf. *4 Ezra* 7:32; Sir 3:19–22. Cf. A.F. Segal, *Life after Death: A History of the Afterlife in Western Religion* (New York: Doubleday, 2004), 142–145. Cf. alternative versions in *1 En.* 22; *4 Ezra* 7:32.

These treasuries gather and protect the souls of the righteous until the day of resurrection. The last objects that deserve attention are the books mentioned by 24:1. This passage mentions books (*sepre*) where all the sins of the wicked are written down. These books are described as the opposites of the treasuries of righteousness found in the heights.[38]

We see, thus, that *2 Baruch* utilises current ideas about the contents of God's heaven. God's throne stands in the centre and hosts of heavenly beings encircle it. In addition, *2 Baruch* mentions the existence of books and treasuries there that confirms God's omnipotence and memory of mankind's deeds.

Grasping the Spatiality of the Other World

So, what does *2 Baruch*'s other world look like? The above outline has shown that *2 Baruch* envisions the other world as being located in the heights of heaven. The discussion has also made it clear that the spatiality of the heavenly other world is complex. Since the other world is both a time and a place, it already exists but it can normally not be experienced until some future point in time. The spatiality of the other world is therefore particularly difficult to grasp.

As the above outline clearly conveys, a study of the other world's spatiality depends on the possibility of locating the presence of God and his host. It is their presence that ultimately defines the location of the other world. The other world in the heights is first and foremost recognisable as the place where God and his host dwell. Again, and more than ever, it is necessary to turn to its constitutive dwellers to identify the location of a place. Firstly, the throne of God, identified above as the focal point of the heights, is first and foremost important as the seat of God. Several passages show that God, his throne and the heights are interchangeable entities.[39] Likewise, being with God is equivalent to being in the heights of heaven: the good works stored in treasuries, are preserved "with you" (*lwātāk*)—with God (14:12)—and likewise, the building that will be revealed in 4:3 is "with me [God]" (*lwāty*). In addition, the common attribute of God as "Lord the Most High" (*māryā mraymā*, root *rwm*), used throughout *2 Baruch*, shows the near identification of God with the heights (root *rwm*). God is the

---

[38] Cf. Dan 7:10; *1 En.* 89:61–64; 98:6–8; *4 Ezra* 6:20; *Mart. Ascen. Isa.* 9:19–23; *T. Jud.* 20:3; Rev 20:11–12.

[39] Cf. for instance *2 Bar.* 21:6; 48:10; 67:2.

highest one: the one who dwells in the heights.[40] All in all, the notions of the throne, of God, and of the heights merge in the text. Secondly, it is the positions of the heavenly beings in relation to God and to each other that provide the reader with a sense of a heavenly topography. The heavenly beings encircle the throne of God and dwell under his throne. They constitute the surroundings of the throne. Distance in heavenly space is determined by the organisation of the heavenly hosts in relation to God and his throne. The attempt to map the heights thus becomes an attempt to map the heavenly population.

It is quite evident that *2 Baruch*'s description of the highest heaven does not seek to achieve spatial precision, in the territorial sense of the word.[41] The spaces of the other world rely more on the presence of God and his host than on a defined otherworldly geography. As I have already indicated, it would be a mistake to try to describe the other world only on the basis of its 'territorial' geography. The other world is indeed 'in the heights,' but it is so in more than the physical sense of the word. The other world is immortal, incorruptible and everlasting. It is elevated, it comes in the future and ultimately it is in the everlasting and constant place of divine presence.[42]

Several commentators have pointed out that God's heaven has the appearance of the throne room of a royal court or of a heavenly temple, or probably more correctly, a combination of the two. *2 Baruch*'s ideas on this point resemble those found in other contemporaneous literature.[43] Murphy has noted that God's heaven may also be interpreted as a description of the celestial city,[44] where God's throne stands in the middle and the heavenly beings encircle it in the heavenly city

---

[40] Cf. further Smith, *Thesaurus*, 3861; 3864.

[41] Cosmographical precision was probably not the main concern of *2 Baruch*. There is no consistent image of the heavenly realm in the text, nor does *2 Baruch* provide an accurate depiction of the universe. *2 Baruch* shares this tendency with most texts of the period (Cf. Wright, *Early History*, 118).

[42] Wright, *Early History*, 83.

[43] As Himmelfarb noted, "In biblical Hebrew *hekhal* serves for both the king's place and the temple. In relation to a god, the temple and palace are two aspects of the same dwelling place" (*Ascent to Heaven*, 14; Cf. 4; 14–23; 58–59; Wright, *Early History*, 75–78; 104; 135; 190; M. Haran, "The Divine Presence in the Israelite Cult and the Cultic Institutions," *Bib* 50 (1969): 251–267 at 259; M. Haran, "Temple and Community in Ancient Israel," in *Temple in Society* (ed. M.V. Fox; Winona Lake, Ind.: Eisenbrauns, 1988), 17–25 at 18; McKelvey, *New Temple*, 26; Rowland, *Open Heaven*, 78–79. Cf. Pss 11:4: 103:19; Jer 25:30; Amos 1:2. Cf. 1 Kgs 8; 22:19–22; Ps 29:10; Isa 6:1–7; *1 En.* 14–16; *T. Levi* 3–5; Rev 11:19 as well as the *Apocalypse of Zephaniah*.

[44] Cf. Murphy, *Structure and Meaning*, 89.

structure. These two interpretations are not mutually exclusive, but rather they complement each other. These spatial structures reflect the functions of God and his hosts in the heights. From the throne God rules both the heavenly host (21:6) and the entire Creation (54:13).[45] The throne stands in the centre, the hosts—the divine council—stand around God, seated on his throne, ready to carry out his commands (6:6–7; 48:8). In fact, everything is prepared for judgement in the heights:[46] there the books of sins are kept, which will be opened (24:1) to reveal all the wrongdoings of the wicked.[47] Likewise, the treasuries of righteous works in the heights will demonstrate the worthiness of the righteous for the future bliss. The scene of judgement is in a sense continually set, ready for the day of judgement.[48]

Transferal of Holiness: From Earth to the Heights of Heaven

Two more tendencies in *2 Baruch*'s description of heavenly spaces deserve our attention: *2 Baruch* envisions a heavenly model of the city and the sanctuary, and the text also describes an ongoing transfer of artefacts from earth to heaven. These important aspects broaden *2 Baruch*'s notion of the other world. *2 Bar.* 4:1–7 says:

> And the Lord said to me: "This city will be delivered up for a time, and the people will be chastened in that time, and the world will not be given over to oblivion. Or, do you think that this is that city (*mditā*) of which I said: 'On the palms of my hand I have engraved you'?[49] It is not this building (*benyānā*) which is now built in your midst. It is that which will be revealed with me, which was prepared here beforehand from when I decided to create Paradise.[50] And I showed it to Adam before he had transgressed, but when he transgressed the commandments he was deprived of it, as also Paradise. And after these things I showed it to my servant Abraham at night among the parts of the sacrifice. And again I also showed it to Moses at Mount Sinai when I showed him the shape

---

[45] Cf. similarly Mic 1:2–3; Wis 18:15; *T. Mos.* 4:2; 10:3. Cf. further *Apoc. Zeph.* 5:1–6.

[46] The divine council takes part in judgement (Cf. Ps 82; Zech 3:1–10; Job 1:6–12; Cf. Mullen, *Assembly*, 226–233).

[47] Cf. Dan 7:10; Rev 20:11–12.

[48] Cf. further Himmelfarb, *Ascent to Heaven*, vii; D.N. Freedman, "Temple Without Hands," in *Temples and High Places in Biblical Times* (ed. A. Biran; Jerusalem: Hebrew Union College—Jewish Institute of Religion, 1981), 21–30; Wright, *Early History*, 190–191.

[49] Isa 49:16.

[50] Note the alternative translation of Bogaert (*Apocalypse de Baruch I*, 464–465).

of the tabernacle and all its vessels. And now, behold, it is preserved with me, as also Paradise. Go, therefore, and do as I command you".[51]

4:2–3 shows that *2 Baruch* envisions a heavenly city and a heavenly sanctuary. Note that there is no distinction between that heavenly city and the sanctuary. The city and the sanctuary overlap in the heights, just like the city and temple on earth do.[52] According to 4:2, the heavenly city/sanctuary is the one God has engraved on the palms of his hands. *2 Baruch* here quotes Isa 49:16a, which refers to a discussion between Zion and God: "See, I have inscribed you [Zion] on the palms of my hands."[53] *2 Bar.* 4:2 thus reinterprets this Isaiah passage to pinpoint the fact that the real city/sanctuary is indeed the heavenly one. That is the one which will be revealed with God and which has been prepared "here," *hārkā*, beforehand (4:3).[54] In other words, the heavenly city/sanctuary was prepared before God created Paradise (4:3),[55] and it will be revealed again with God in the future. In the meantime, it is preserved with God, as is also the pattern of the tabernacle and all its vessels (4:5–6).[56] So, while the earthly city/sanctuary may be destroyed, there is an everlasting city/sanctuary in the heights of heaven which cannot be destroyed, but lasts forever. This passage conveys *2 Baruch*'s main argument as to why the destruction of Jerusalem and its sanctuary will not be devastating to the survival of Israel.[57] The passage attests to the widespread idea in this period of heavenly models and earthly copies of the city and its sanctuary. The destruction of the earthly Jerusalem and its temple, therefore, is not the catastrophe it may appear to be, since the real sanctuary and city, the patterns or models for the earthly copies, are preserved in heaven.

4:2–6 also claims that God showed the heavenly city/sanctuary to Adam, Abraham and Moses. He showed it to Adam before he trans-

---

[51] I.e., leave the city, since the destruction does not matter.

[52] Cf. pp. 35–36. Cf. *Apoc. Zeph.* 2:1–4.

[53] The Syriac of *2 Bar.* 4:2 is equivalent to the Syriac of the Peshitta version of Isa 49:16a. Cf. Charles, *Apocalypse of Baruch*, 6; Bogaert, *Apocalypse de Baruch I*, 362; McKelvey, *New Temple*, 40–41; Murphy, *Structure and Meaning*, 86.

[54] 'Here' refers either to the earthly sanctuary or to heaven. Since these are the words of God, it is probable that 'here' is in the heights of heaven.

[55] Maybe before creation week (Cf. *b. Pesaḥ* 54a; Klijn, "2 Baruch," 622).

[56] Cf. Exod 25:4, 40; *T. Dan.* 5; *4 Ezra* 7:26; 8:36, 52–53; 10:44–59; *4 Bar.* 3:10; Gal 4:26; Heb 8:5; 12:22; Rev 3:12; 21:2, 10.

[57] Cf. Chapter Two, pp. 41–47; 56–58.

gressed, he showed it to Abraham in the night of the so-called covenant between the pieces (Gen 15:7–21),[58] and he showed it to Moses at Mount Sinai (Exod 25:9, 40).[59] This means that God showed the heavenly city/sanctuary to Adam, Abraham and Moses while they were still on earth, possibly to comfort them (Cf. 54:4).[60]

So, in the heights, with God, there is the real heavenly sanctuary/city, complete with tabernacle and vessels, which is the pattern of its earthly copies. Although safely kept (root *nṭr*) with God, it has also been made visible to certain chosen men on earth. This proves that the city/sanctuary already exist in the heights. It has existed from before the creation of Paradise and it will remain safe there until God finally reveals it.

Where is Paradise?

In the previous chapter I proposed that *2 Baruch* used Land and Garden allusions to construct messianic spaces. These blended allusions to Land and Garden bring together the two spaces on earth which had served as enclaves of righteousness. Now, what is the relation between *2 Bar.* 29 and 73's Garden of Eden allusions and *2 Bar.* 4's Paradise? What is the relation between Paradise and the heavenly city/sanctuary in 4:1–7? And what does that tell us about the location of Paradise?

The main concern of 4:1–7 is to argue for the heavenly existence and perseverance of the city/sanctuary. However, alongside that argument the passage also tells us, in the form of additions, about the creation, the loss, and the preservation of Paradise (*pardaysā*) in the heights of heaven. This passage, thus, may provide information about the location and character of Paradise. 4:3 does not tell us when God created Paradise, but from the scarce information this passage gives us we know that *2 Baruch* imagined Paradise to have been created and that the city/sanctuary had already been prepared when God decided to make it.[61] *2 Baruch*'s Paradise is in other words not pre-existent, as the

---

[58] Cf. *L.A.B.* 23:6.

[59] Note the fluidity of the concept of the Jerusalem temple, the wilderness tabernacle, and the heavenly sanctuary (S. Bryan, *Jesus and Israel's Traditions of Judgement and Restoration* (Cambridge: Cambridge University Press, 2002), 192).

[60] Cf. Bogaert, *Apocalypse de Baruch II*, 16–17; Klijn, "2 Baruch," 622. Cf. further the *Fragmentary Targum to Gen* 15:12; *4 Ezra* 3:14; *L.A.B.* 19:10.

[61] Contemporaneous texts differs regarding the creation of Paradise. The previous chapter of this study suggested that *2 Baruch* might envision the creation of Paradise on

city/sanctuary may be. Still, as 4:6 tells us, Paradise is kept with God in the heights together with the city/sanctuary as are also the pattern (*dmutā*) of the tabernacle and its vessels.

However, the most interesting issue at this point is the description of the loss of Paradise in 4:3, since it gives crucial information about *2 Baruch*'s notion of Paradise and its relation to the heavenly city/sanctuary: "And I showed it to Adam before he had transgressed, but when he transgressed the commandments he was deprived of it, as also Paradise." This sentence states that God showed Adam the city/sanctuary and that it was taken away from him when he transgressed. Then it adds: "as also Paradise." It is not explicit here whether Paradise was just something that Adam lost, or whether it was also part of what God showed him. Grammatically the sentence is not complete, but the most likely suggestion is that God made Paradise manifest to Adam before he transgressed.[62] But, as a consequence of his transgression, Adam was deprived of[63] the city/sanctuary as well as of Paradise.[64] This means that in pre-transgression times God made both Paradise and the city/sanctuary manifest for Adam only to remove both of them when he transgressed.[65] This interpretation would place Paradise in the same category as the city/sanctuary as essentially heavenly entities, made visible or manifest to a select group of individuals at crucial points in the history of Israel.[66]

---

day three of creation week. Another option is that Paradise was created before creation week. Cf. further Stordalen, *Eden*, 268–270.

[62] Root *ḥw'*, "show"/ "to make manifest" (Smith, *Dictionary*, 129; Smith, *Thesaurus*, 1208–1209). Cf. Murphy, *Structure and Meaning*, 89–90. Cf., e.g., the reuse of Gen 15 in *Apoc. Ab.* 15–20.

[63] Alternatively "disinherited" (*etgalzat lāh meneh*) (Smith, *Dictionary*, 70).

[64] Cf. also Sayler, *Promises*, 66.

[65] According to the Apocalypse of the cloud, the pre-transgression period of Creation is not part of world history and therefore not part of the corruptible world: the first waters of the cloud, and thus the first period of the corruptible world, refer to the transgression of Adam (56:5). The pre-transgression reality belongs to a radically different world, equivalent to the Messianic world I described in the previous chapter. This also means that neither the city/sanctuary nor Paradise have ever been part of the corruptible world. They where part of Adam's pre-transgression world, but when Adam violated God's commands God removed them from him. Note how the place of Adam is defined by his righteousness, not its territoriality. Creation is righteous until his fall, but becomes corruptible as soon as Adam is no longer faithful. Note also that *2 Baruch* ascribes transgression to Adam, not to Eve (4:3; 48:42–43; 54:19; 56:5–6).

[66] Cf. further *2 En.* 31:2; *L.A.B.* 13:8; *QG* 3, 2. Cf. Charles, *Apocalypse of Baruch*, 7; Bogaert, *Apocalypse de Baruch II*, 15.

Now, where is the Paradise of *2 Bar.* 4?[67] 4:1–7 describes God's reaction to Baruch's worries about the imminent destruction of Jerusalem and its temple.[68] At this point in world history, well beyond pre-transgression times and at the threshold of the end-time, Paradise is clearly located in the heights of heaven, preserved with God. It is thus a heavenly reality and has been so throughout the history of the corruptible world.[69] Paradise, manifest as the Garden of Eden, benefited Adam before the transgression, but Adam's disobedient acts made the world turn wicked. The result of his deeds was the removal of the manifestation/vision of the heights of heaven.[70] When *2 Baruch*'s Messianic era recalls a paradisiacal condition, it recalls Paradise in a given time context: the Garden of Eden, the golden age of righteousness in the period before transgression made the world corruptible.[71] In the context of 4:1–7, however, Paradise is a spatial phenomenon of the heights, intimately connected to the heavenly city/sanctuary.[72] Throughout world history it is a heavenly entity preserved with God together with the heavenly city/sanctuary, and it is witnessed as such by Abraham and Moses, and ultimately by Baruch (51:11).[73]

---

[67] The following list records some important contributions to the discussion of the localisation of Paradise in Jewish and Christian literature: F. Delitzsch, *Wo lag das Paradies? Eine biblisch-assyrologische Studie* (Leipzig: Hinnrichs'sche Buchhandlung, 1881); H. Gunkel, *Genesis, übersetzt und erklärt* (3rd ed; Göttinger Handkommentar zum Alten Testament I/1; Göttingen: Vandenhoeck & Ruprecht, 1910); W.F. Albright, "The Location of the Garden of Eden," *AJSL* 39 (1922): 15–31; S. Mowinkel, "De fire Paradiselvene," *NTT* 39 (1938): 47–67; F. Stolz, "Paradiese und Gegenwelten," *Zeitschrift für Religionswissenschaft* 1 (1993): 5–24; Stordalen, *Eden,* 187–474.

[68] Cf. Chapter Two, pp. 31–32.

[69] It may possibly be located under God's throne, like the hosts of heavenly creatures. Cf. the various localisations of Paradise in lower heavens in, e.g., *2 Enoch* and *Aramaic Levi* (Cf. Collins, "Afterlife," 133).

[70] Note again how acts make space. In this sense the earthly Garden of Eden is the pre-transgression equivalent to the Land of Israel, and the question of where Paradise lies, is mistaken. It is not any given location that defines Paradise: it is the condition of pre-transgression righteousness (of all mankind) that defines it.

[71] Cf. Chapter Six, pp. 217–221.

[72] Cf. further Charles, *Apocalypse of Baruch,* 6–7; Harnisch, *Verhängnis,* 112; Bogaert, *Apocalypse de Baruch I,* 422. Note that *2 Baruch* reserves the use of the term 'Paradise' to the otherworldly, heavenly reality (*2 Bar.* 4:1–6; 51:11 and 59: 9; Cf. *4 Ezra* 7:36. Cf. Bogaert, *Apocalypse de Baruch I,* 422).

[73] Contemporaneous texts attest to an abundance of differing descriptions of Paradise(s). These paradises are sometimes manifest within Creation and at other times transcending it (Cf. e.g., *1 En.* 77:1–4; 2Q209 XXIII, 3–10; 4Q210 1 II, 14–20; 2 Cor 12:2; *Apoc. Mos.* 37:5). In the majority of accounts it is important to shield Paradise, for instance by locating it in an inaccessible place. In several accounts the Garden of

From Earth to Heaven: Keys, Vessels, Furniture, and Silk Fabrics with Gold of Ophir

Chapter Two of this study discussed *2 Baruch*'s presentation of the destruction of Jerusalem and its temple. A central concern in the account of *2 Baruch* was the protection of holiness. According to 7:1, it was not the enemy that destroyed Jerusalem. Angels did this. And, importantly, they did not destroy it until the righteous had left the city (5:5–6) and God's presence had been withdrawn from the temple (8:2). In addition, an angel was sent from heaven to bring all the furniture of the Holy of Holies and the vessels of the tabernacle to safety. The angel commanded the earth to swallow them up and protect them (6:5–10).[74]

6:8–9 explains why it was important to shield these objects:

> And he [the angel] said to the earth in a loud voice: earth, earth, earth,[75] hear the word of the mighty God, and receive the things that I entrust you and guard them until the last times, so that when you are commanded, you can give them back, so that strangers will not take possession of them. For the time comes when also Jerusalem will be surrendered for a time, until it is said that it again will return to be restored forever. And the earth opened up its mouth and swallowed them.

The angel commanded the earth to swallow up the furniture and the vessels of the Jerusalem temple to guard (root *nṭr*) them until the last times (*'damā lzabne ḥrāyā*) in order to keep strangers away from them. Then, when it is commanded to, the earth will give them back (root *ntl*). There are thus two reasons for the angel's command to the earth. Firstly, the furniture and the vessels need protection from Israel's enemies.[76] The earth, envisioned as a protective container,[77] ensures that the holy objects are hidden and kept safe. Secondly, since the earth will in fact guard these objects until the last times, they can be restored

---

Eden is in the east, and/or in the beginning, and/or at the end of the world (*1 En.* 32:2–6; *Jub.* 2:7). Several passages make it impossible to determine whether Paradise is earthly or heavenly (Cf. *T. Levi* 18:10). Several texts also mix and blend these versions (*L.A.E.* 1:1; 29:1; *Apoc. Mos.* 37:5; 40:1. Cf. Rowland, *Open Heaven*, 382; O.S. Wintermute, "Jubilees," in *Old Testament Pseudepigrapha, vol. 2* (ed. J.H. Charlesworth; 2 vols; Garden City, N.Y.: Doubleday, 1983–1985), 35–142 at 56; Laato, *Star*, 369; 393; Charles, *Apocalypse of Baruch*, 6–7.

[74] Cf. Chapter Two, pp. 32–34.
[75] Cf. Jer 22:29.
[76] Cf. Murphy, *Structure and Meaning*, 95.
[77] Cf. p. 34.

again when they are called for. 6:9 associates this restoration of the
vessels with the restoration of an everlasting Jerusalem. In other words,
the passage suggests that the vessels and the furniture will again be in
use in a restored city/sanctuary.[78]

10:18–19 adds more information:

> And you, priests, take the keys of the sanctuary and throw them into the
> heights of heaven, and take them to the Lord and say: guard your house
> yourself, for behold, we have been found to be false servants. And you,
> virgins, who spin fine white linen and silk with gold of Ophir, hasten
> and take all things and cast them into the fire to return them to him
> who made them. Flame, send them to him who made them so that the
> enemies will not take possession over them.

These events, like the events described in 6:8–9, are fictitiously set on
the eve of destruction. The false priests are commanded to throw the
keys of the temple up to the heights of heaven. They ask God to guard
his sanctuary himself, since they have proven incapable. Moreover, the
spinning virgins are told to take "all things" (*kulmedem*)—the white linen
(*buçā*)[79] and silk (*šrāye*) with gold of Ophir ('*am dahbā dawpir*)[80]—and
throw them into the fire. The fire then returns them to their creator.[81]

---

[78] The Syriac of this sentence is unclear. The passage may describe the earthly
or the heavenly sanctuary (Cf. Volz, *Eschatologie*, 373; Harnisch, *Verhängnis*, 112). Since
Jerusalem is explicitly described as everlasting (*lālam*) in the sentence, whereas the earth
is dying and the Messianic reign at Mount Zion is clearly temporary, the most likely
answer is that the vessels will be moved to the *heavenly* Jerusalem. The passage does
not, however, tell us when or where that event will take place. However, the restoration
of Jerusalem has been the topic of a long discussion. One group of scholars claims
that Jerusalem will be restored on earth (Cf. 1:4; 4:1; Cf. Charles, *Apocalypse of Baruch*,
5–6; 11; Klausner, *Messianic Idea*, 346; McKelvey, *New Temple*, 32–33; Klijn, "2 Baruch,"
617). Another group proposes that the restoration of Jerusalem is in heaven (Cf. 4:2–
7; 32:4; 43:1–3; 59:4; Rowland, *Open Heaven*, 133; Murphy, *Structure and Meaning*, 85–90;
114–116; Leuenberger, "Ort und Funktion," 238. Cf. also the discussion of Whitters,
Epistle, 120). These scholars argue that *2 Baruch*, firstly, envisions a destruction of the
earth which would make an earthly restoration improbable, and secondly, that *2 Baruch*
never describes a descent of the heavenly Jerusalem to the earth. Another possibility
would be that Jerusalem is restored during the Messianic era (Bogaert, *Apocalypse de
Baruch I*, 422). However, as the previous chapter showed, *2 Baruch* mentions neither the
restoration of Jerusalem nor the rebuilding of the temple during the Messianic era. We
should probably acknowledge the fact that *2 Baruch* provides no clear answer. Possibly,
the idea of a restored earthly sanctuary and the notion of a sanctuary in heaven may
have been blurred. Cf. further *1 En.* 90:28–29; *4 Ezra* 10:26; 13:36; Rev 21; *b. B. Bat.* 75b.
[79] Smith, *Dictionary*, 39; Cf. Bogaert, *Apocalypse de Baruch I*, 469.
[80] Ophir is famous for its high quality gold (2 Chr 8:18; *Targum Ps* 45:10; *Targum Esth I*
5:1; Josephus, *J.W.* 6.5.2).
[81] This scene could be described as a parallel to an offering scene. The smoke
ascends to the heights of heaven.

Probably, the items that the virgins made were either the veil of the Holy of Holies, or the garment of the High Priest, both important artefacts of the Jerusalem temple and its cult.[82] Note that the acts of casting the keys to God in the heights and throwing the fabrics into the fire are parallel actions. Both acts bring holy artefacts up into heaven and thus back to their rightful owner.[83] And like 6:8–9 above, these acts are done explicitly to assure the protection of the holy artefacts from the enemy (10:19).[84]

So, both 6:8–9 and 10:18–19 attest to the idea that before the destruction of Jerusalem and its temple, all holy objects were removed from the sanctuary to prevent attackers from getting hold of them. 6:8–9 says that the earth will protect the objects to restore them to the everlasting Jerusalem when they are called for. 10:18–19, on the other hand, states that the keys and the fabrics are sent directly to God and shielded there.

These passages reveal that the transfer and protection of holiness is a central concern of 2 Baruch. The transgression of Adam once led to the retraction of the city/sanctuary as well as of Paradise. The transgression of the two tribes in Judah led to the retraction of God's presence, the keys to the temple and the silk fabric made by the weaving virgins in the time of Baruch.[85] We have also seen how the vessels and the furniture are intended for the heavenly city/sanctuary, but are in the meantime kept by the earth.

In view of the above discussion, it seems correct to argue that 2 Baruch describes an ongoing transfer of holiness from earth to heaven.[86] 2 Ba-

---

[82] Cf. *Prot. Jas.* 10; *Targum Jonathan to Ezek* 16:10–13; *Targum Ps* 45:14–15; Cf. also Nir, *Destruction*, 100–109.

[83] Cf. God's garments in Lev 16:4; Exod 39:27–28; Ezek 9:2–3; Dan 7:9–10; 10:5; *1 En.* 14:20; 4Q405 XXIII, 2; *m. Yoma* 3:6 (Himmelfarb, *Ascent to Heaven*, 17–20; Cf. Haran, "Temple," 164).

[84] The idea that the boundary between the realms is permeable was widespread in the period. Cf. Himmelfarb, *Ascent to Heaven*, 4; Segal, "Heavenly Ascent," 1338–1340.

[85] Heaven was often described as God's true home (Himmelfarb, *Ascent to Heaven*, 12; Wright, *Early History*, 83; Murphy, *Structure and Meaning*, 96; 99; 114). The rapture/death of Baruch and the return of the Messiah to the heights, both exceptional figures in *2 Baruch*, could also be understood as part of *2 Baruch*'s withdrawal discourse.

[86] *2 Baruch* applies several common motifs to describe the relationship between the two worlds. Among them, the motif of the heavenly city/sanctuary (noting that the heavenly city/sanctuary does not descend but stays in the heights). *2 Baruch* also attests to the idea of a heavenly paradise (Cf. J. Jeremias, "Paradeisos," in *TDNT* 5 (ed. G. Friedrich; trans; G.W. Bromiley; Grand Rapids, Mich.: Eerdmans, 1967), 765–773; Rowland, *Open Heaven*, 382; Murphy, *Structure and Meaning*, 89). Further, *2 Baruch* pictures the existence of heavenly models or patterns and earthly copies. This idea is a commonplace in the ancient Near East (Cf. B. Meissner, *Die Kultur Babyloniens und*

ruch's eschatology advocates a shift from this world to the other world and the text's ongoing discourse about the relationship between the two worlds clearly points towards the future sole existence of the other world.[87] The corruptible world will however not be destroyed until all holiness has been collected from it. *2 Baruch*'s history of the world can therefore be read as a history about how holiness escaped this world. Adam's transgressions caused Paradise and the model city/ sanctuary to escape that world. When resurrection and judgement are imminent, there will be only two carriers of holiness left in the corruptible world: the righteous, both living and dead, and the vessels of the Jerusalem temple. As we shall see, the righteous and the temple vessels will both play important roles in the coming transformation of the heavenly world.

Resurrection and Judgement: The Transfer of Splendour

The following section will study the entrance of the righteous into the incorruptible world through the process of resurrection, judgement and transformations. I will discuss this entry into that world as the last incident of transfer of holiness from the corruptible world and study the connection of the entry to the restoration of the temple vessels.

Who Enters the Other World?

However, before I continue that discussion, one question needs to be answered: who enters the other, incorruptible world? The answer to the question should on the one hand be evident by now: we know already that the righteous, and only the righteous, will enter. However, the discussions of the preceding chapters suggested that the composition of that group is not entirely clear. *2 Baruch* gives several hints, but no definite answers. Chapter Six showed that the remnant was protected in the Land during the destruction of the world and that they led a joyful life during the Messianic era. According to 29:8, the members of the

---

Assyriens (Wissenschaft und Bildung 207; Leipzig: Quelle & Meyer, 1925); M. Eliade, *The Myth of the Eternal Return* (trans. W.R. Trask; Bollingen series 46; New York: Bollingen, 1954); Hamerton-Kelly, "Temple and Origin," 15; Himmelfarb, *Ascent to Heaven*, 12–13). These notions show that *2 Baruch* imagines two worlds apart during the course of history, the lower resembling the higher. The worlds are detached from each other, but sometimes 'converge' to allow for visions and communication.

[87] Cf. Murphy, *Structure and Meaning*, 87–88; Himmelfarb, *Ascent to Heaven*, 15–16.

Messianic remnant were indeed those who survived to the very end.[88] It is beyond reasonable doubt that the remnant group, the Messianic equivalent of Baruch's followers, will enter the bliss.

The fate of the other groups 2 Baruch mentions is uncertain. 2 Baruch is ambiguous about the destiny of the gentile nations. Several times 2 Baruch expresses that wickedness has become a universal phenomenon during the end-time. At other times, however, it is suggested that those nations that did not subdue Israel will be rescued (42:2; 72:4–6). These nations may possibly survive.

The fate of the exiled tribes is a major concern of 2 Baruch.[89] These tribes are the remnant's brothers, and their return to righteousness is pressing if all twelve tribes are to assemble.[90] Chapters Four and Five showed that 2 Baruch applies a web of allusions to authorise a return of the tribes. In fact, the entire Epistola Baruch (78–87) revolves around Baruch's concern for the dispersed tribes. It is important that the tribes choose the right path, and they need Baruch's instruction to make that choice. As we saw in Chapter Five, the exiles will only be able to return to the remnant if they turn to righteousness. Moreover, Chapter Four showed that Baruch and his followers atoned for the wickedness of the tribes and that Baruch instructed the remnant to help them survive in the Kidron valley. Possibly, 2 Baruch assumes that the righteous deeds of the remnant alone may lead the exiled tribes back to them (77:6).[91]

However, unlike 4 Ezra 13, 2 Baruch probably does not describe the return of the exiled tribes during the Messianic era. The only possibility is that Baruch's vision of twelve rivers ascending from the sea and surrounding the lightning in 53:11 may describe the return. Nevertheless, this proposal is uncertain and much debated.[92] If this passage in

---

[88] It is probable that righteous people who live at the time of judgement enter the other world alive (Bogaert, Apocalypse de Baruch I, 420 and II, 92; Stemberger, Leib der Auferstehung, 86). 2 Bar. 29–30 and 75, on the other hand, imply that death and resurrection are necessary to enter the other world. Cf. further Stemberger, Leib der Auferstehung, 86.

[89] Cf. Klijn, "Recent Developments," 9–10. The fate of the ten tribes was clearly a matter of discussion in the first centuries C.E. (Cf. 4 Ezra 13:39–50; m. Sanh. 10:3. Cf. Klausner, Messianic Idea, 462; Laato, Star, 389–390; Davies, Gospel and Land, 124).

[90] Cf. 2 Sam 19:40–44.

[91] Cf. Chapter Four, pp. 127–129.

[92] Scholars have reached no general agreement regarding the identification of the rivers in 53:11. Cf. Charles, Apocalypse of Baruch, 89; Klausner, Messianic Idea, 348. Cf. 2 Bar. 72:3–4; 41:4; Cf. Isa 11; 48:4; Jer 23:5–8; 30:8–11; Zech 9:10; 14:16–19; 1 En. 48:4; 10:21; 90:38; Pss. Sol. 17:26–28; Targum Jonathan to Isa 42:5–7 and Deut 1:1.

fact describes a return, in light of the explanation part of the apocalypse (71:1–74:1) it is more probable that the ascension of the twelve
rivers refers to the gathering of the righteous, regardless of their former
status.

This means that if *2 Baruch* envisions an explicit return of the tribes,
it must therefore take place in the other world. The *Epistola Baruch*
provides the most optimistic assessment of the destiny of the tribes.
78:7 opens up the possibility that the exiled tribes, as well as righteous
gentiles, may enter the other world.[93] However, on several occasions
2 Baruch emphasises that the destiny of the tribes depends on their
return to righteousness in the present life. They must choose the right
path in life now: there is no room for regrets after death.[94] In a way,
the lack of emphasis regarding the fate of the tribes after resurrection
stands in contrast to the stress of Baruch's efforts to help the tribes
return. It is possible that *2 Baruch*'s silence concerning the final fate of
the tribes may be approached as a didactic point in the text: Baruch
and the remnant have done whatever they can to bring about the
return, but the actual inclusion into the ultimate bliss relies on the
choices of the tribes. Righteousness remains the main prerequisite for
entering the other world.[95]

2 Bar. 48:48–51:16: The Survival of Splendour

The previous chapter's discussion of the Messianic era pointed out that
the process of resurrection and the final judgement signaled the end of
the intermediary Messianic period and the entry into the other world.[96]
Each of the three major apocalyptic sections of *2 Baruch* discussed in
that chapter refers implicitly or explicitly to the resurrection and to
God's judgement as the main events in the whole history of Israel and

---

[93] In light of the idea that nourishment of the faithful few ensures nourishment for a
great people in *Targum Jonathan to Zech* 2:14 and *Sib. Or.* 4.45–46, it is possible that *2 Bar.*
29:4–8 may allude to the survival of all tribes. In addition, the enhanced fertility of the
wives and easiness of childbirth in 73:7 also suggest that the group is at least expanding.
The childbirths may also allude to the coming resurrection, since several texts imagine
a link between birth and rebirth to new life (Cf. *1 En.* 62:4; *4 Ezra* 4:33–43: 4 Macc 17;
1QH 11; Gal 4; Rom 8:22–23). Anyhow, *2 Bar.* 29:4–8 adds to the impression that the
group that experience the final bliss is larger than the small remnant that survived in
the Messianic Land.

[94] *2 Bar.* 14:13; 30:1; 51:3. Cf. *4 Ezra* 7:60, 129; 8:3. Cf. Harnisch, *Verhängnis*, 180–188.

[95] Harnisch, *Verhängnis*, 222–229.

[96] Cf. Chapter Six (cf. further Bogaert, *Apocalypse de Baruch I*, 419–420).

the world at large (*2 Bar.* 30; 75 and 36:10–11). Whereas the Messiah judged the living and transformed the present world, the process of resurrection and God's judgement mark the ultimate separation between the righteous who will enter into the other world, and the wicked who face punishment.

2 Baruch presents general resurrection as a necessary condition for God's judgement.[97] In other words, resurrection has a judicial function.[98] The text mentions or alludes to resurrection in a series of passages, including 14:1–15:8 and 21:1–26. The most explicit and detailed account of the redemption process is 48:48–52:7. This passage is a central part of the so-called Prayer of Baruch, and describes resurrection (50:2–4), God's judgement (50:4) and the resulting fate of the wicked and the pious (51:1–16). 50:2–4 says:

> For the earth will then surely give back the dead, which it receives now to keep, although transforming nothing in their appearance, but as it received [them], so it gives them back. And as I delivered them to it, so also it will raise them. For then it is needed to show those who live that the dead have come to life and that those who went [away] have come [back]. And it will happen after they have recognised one another, those who know now, then judgement will become strong, and these [things] will come, which were spoken of.

This passage states that when the time has come, the earth (*ar'ā*) will give back (root *pn'*) the dead (*mite*) in exactly the same appearance (*ṣurtā*) as they had when the earth received (root *qbl*) them.[99] The earth will in other words keep (root *nṭr*) the dead without transforming (root *ḥlp*) them. According to 50:3, it is important to preserve the appearance of the dead in order to show (root *ḥw'*) the living that God has in fact made the dead come back (root *'t'*). The passage ends with an important, yet brief description of the day of judgement: when "those

---

[97] The Apocalypse of the vine and the cedar does not mention resurrection explicitly. However, resurrection is probably implied in 36:10–11. The wicked ruler will become ashes and blend with the ashes of the forest. The wicked ruler will experience no afterlife, since his remains are mixed with the remains of others. This apocalypse may thus suggest a resurrection of the righteous dead, not of the wicked. Cf. further Dan 12:2–4; *1 En.* 22; *4 Ezra* 7:32–38. Cf. Bogaert, *Apocalypse de Baruch, I*, 420; Nickelsburg, *Resurrection*, 171–174; Segal, *Life after Death*, 495–497.

[98] Cf. Nickelsburg, *Resurrection*, 23.

[99] Cf. *4 Ezra* 7:30–33; *Sib. Or.* 4.179–182. Cf. related ideas in *1 En.* 51:1; 61:5; *L.A.B.* 3:10; *Targum Neofitti to Exod* 15:12; Rev 20:13. Cf. further Charles, *Apocalypse of Baruch*, 82; Bogaert, *Apocalypse de Baruch II*, 92.

who know now"—the righteous who are knowledgeable (cf. 48:33)[100]—
have recognised one another (*eštada'w*[101] *ḥad lḥad*), then God's judgement
will come in its predicted form.

To comprehend this small, but complex passage it is necessary to
read a bit further:

> And it will happen when that appointed day has passed on, then after
> that the [elevated] pride[102] of those found guilty will soon be trans-
> formed, and also the glory (*tešbuḥtā*) of those found righteous. For the
> shape of those who now act wickedly will be made more evil than it is,
> like those who endure torment. Also the glory of those who now have
> been declared justified in my Law, those in whom there has been under-
> standing in their lives, those who planted the root of wisdom in their
> heart, then their splendour will be glorified (root *šbḥ*) in transformations,
> and the shape of their faces[103] will be changed (root *hpk*) in the light of
> their beauty, to enable them to acquire and receive the world that does
> not die, which then is promised to them (51:1–3).

This passage describes the transformations (root *ḥlp*) that occur as the
result of the judgement. Whereas the shape of the wicked will become
more evil, the righteous ones, those who lived by the Law and were wise
and had understanding on earth, will experience that their splendour
(*ziwā*) and beauty (*yayutā*)[104] will be enhanced and transformed. This
passage answers Baruch's questions about the fate of the righteous in
49:2–3:[105]

> In what shape will they live, those who live in your day? Or, how will
> their splendour remain (root *qw'*), [the splendour] which will be after
> that time? Will they then take this appearance of today and put on these
> limbs of bondage which are now in evils and in which evils are fulfiled?
> Or will you perhaps transform these things which are in the world, as
> also the world?

One element of Baruch's communication with God is central to the
ongoing discussion of transfer of holiness from earth to heaven. The

---

[100] Cf. L.I. Lied, "Recognizing the Righteous Remnant? Resurrection, Recognition
and Transformation in *2 Baruch* 49–51," in *Metamorphoses: Resurrection, Body and Transformative Practices in Early Christianity* (Eds. T.K. Seim and J. Økland; Berlin, Walter
DeGruyter, forthcoming 2009).

[101] In the Eshtaph'el form *eštada'w* the Syriac word *yd'*, "to know," is commonly
translated "to know, recognise, understand, to see, perceive" (Smith, *Dictionary*, 188;
Smith, *Thesaurus*, 1558). Cf. Gen 27:23; 31:32; 37:32–33; 38:26; 42:7–8; Deut 33:9.

[102] The ms. has *rmwthwn*. Ceriani rendered it to *dmwthwn*, in compliance with 51:2.

[103] *Ape*: "face," or "presence" (Smith, *Dictionary*, 25).

[104] And/ or, "honourableness" (Smith, *Dictionary*, 184).

[105] Cf. 1 Cor 15:35 and *b. Sanh.* 90b.

topic of the discussion in *2 Baruch* is the appearance (*ṣurtā*) of the resurrected and those who still are alive on that day, with a special regard for the splendour (*ziwā*) of the righteous.[106] We have already seen that *2 Baruch* suggests general resurrection. This means that resurrection is by no means positive for everyone. For the wicked majority, in fact, resurrection leads to more suffering. We have also noted that no appearances have been changed by the earth. The dead, both the righteous and the wicked, will rise (root *qwm*) in the shapes they had when they died (50:2–4). Now, 50:3 states that the resurrection of the dead is necessary since the living need to understand that the dead have come back to life, as a miracle of God. 50:4 says further that the living and the dead who were wise and righteous will recognise one another. But what is it that they recognise in each other? It is possible that they first and foremost recognise aspects of a person's physical appearance that signal his moral standing, since 49:2 suggests that splendour is already a characteristic of the righteous on earth. *2 Baruch* suggests that the appearance of a person even now reveals his moral standing. The righteous already possess splendour (49:2; 51:3), whereas the wicked look evil (51:2). Evil and splendour are in other words recognisable traits both of the earthly and the resurrected physiognomy.[107] The earth needs to protect the forms of the dead until the day of judgement so that it may then become revealed who is wicked and who is righteous.[108] There is no possibility of escape on the day of judgement since even their appearance will give the guilty away.[109]

---

[106] Cf. Puech, *Croyance*, 140.

[107] Cf. further Dan 12:2–4; *1 En.* 22, *4 Ezra* 7:32–38 and possibly 1QS IV. Cf. Segal, *Life after Death*, 495–497.

[108] Possibly, human physiognomy may serve as documentation, together with the information stored in the books and the treasuries in the heights, and witnesses such as Baruch (13:3; 25:1. Cf. also 83:3). Cf. Zweip, *Ascension*, 75. Unlike *L.A.B.* 61:9, *2 Bar.* 51 does not say that transformation makes the righteous unrecognisable. Cf. Charles, *Apocalypse of Baruch*, 82–83; Stemberger, *Leib der Auferstehung*, 88; Harnisch, *Verhängnis*, 188–194.

[109] The link between physiognomy and moral standing can be seen in some texts. Cf., e.g., Ps 45:2; 4Q186. Cf. Ml. Popovic, "4QZodical Physiognomy (4Q186) and the Cultural Locus of Physiognomics and Astrology in Second Temple Period Judaism" (paper presented at the First Graduate Enoch Seminar, Ann Arbor, May 3, 2006); Ml. Popovic, *Reading the Human Body: Physiognomics and Astrology in the Dead Sea Scrolls and Hellenistic-Early Roman Period Judaism* (STDJ 67; Leiden, E.J. Brill, 2007). Cf. further discussions of this passage by Klijn, "Sources and Redaction," 76; Segal, *Life after Death*, 496; Puech, *Croyance*, 140.

So, Baruch's special concern for the splendour of the righteous on earth thus gets a satisfactory answer in 51:3. Those who already shone with righteousness on earth will also be the ones who shine in the other world. Their splendour will survive and become even more radiant after the day of judgement. Finally, the righteous will get their revenge over the wicked, and this time their triumph will be everlasting.

The Resurrection of the Dead and the Restoration of the Temple Vessels

In her discussion of 50:2, Sayler has pointed out the connection between the resurrected dead and the temple vessels. She says: "The terminology previously used to describe the burial and ultimate restoration of the Temple vessels (...) here is used to describe the burial and resurrection of the dead." For instance, we find that both 50:2 and 6:8–9 apply forms of the roots *nṭr* ("keep"), *qbl* ("receive") and *šlm* ("deliver"). According to Sayler, this is a fixed vocabulary which several contemporaneous texts, such as *1 En.* 51:1; *L.A.B.* 3:10 and *4 Ezra* 7:26–38, use to describe resurrection.[110] But, as she says: "Interestingly, only *2 Baruch* uses this terminology to establish a parallel between the restoration of the Temple vessels and the resurrection of the dead."[111]

As I have suggested above, *2 Baruch* describes an ongoing process of the transfer of holiness. With the exception of the remnant still living in the Land, the vessels of the Jerusalem temple and the righteous dead were the only carriers of holiness left on earth on the day of resurrection. Until that day, both were protected by the ground (6:8–9; 50:2).[112] The above discussion of 48:48–51:16 showed that the earth gave up the dead on the day of resurrection. The use of resurrection language in 6:8–9 and the statement that the vessels will be restored to the everlasting Jerusalem in the last times makes it likely that *2 Baruch* implies a parallel restoration of the vessels of the Jerusalem temple to the other world. In other words, *2 Baruch* suggests resurrection and

---

[110] Cf. H.C.C. Cavalin, *Life after Death: Paul's Argument for the Resurrection of the Dead in 1 Cor 15. Part I: An Enquiry into the Jewish Background (ConBNT* 7:1; Lund: CWK Gleerup, 1974), 44; 74–80.

[111] Sayler, *Promises*, 65. Cf. G.B. Sayler, "*2 Baruch*: A Story of Grief and Consolation," in *Society of Biblical Literature 1982 Seminar Papers* (SBLSP 21; Chico, Calif.: Scholars Press, 1982), 485–500 at 494.

[112] *2 Baruch* describes the protective quality of the ground on several occasions (6:8–9; 42:8; 50:2). Cf. *4 Ezra* 7:32; *L.A.B.* 3:10–11 and *Apoc. Dan.* 35. Cf. also Isa 26:19.

restoration both of the righteous dead and of the vessels. They escape
to the heavenly other world as the very last carriers of holiness before
the final elimination of the corruptible world.

In this light, the resurrection, judgement and transformation of the
righteous dead and the equivalent restoration of the temple vessels
can be understood as concluding a continuing process of transferal of
holiness from earth to heaven. The divine presence, the people and
the artefacts that shaped holy space on earth are all transferred into
the heavenly other world. From this point onwards, there will be only
one world: the heavenly, incorruptible world. The destruction of the
corruptible world can now begin.

Approaching the Promised, Undying, World

The preceding discussion has pointed out that _2 Baruch_ indeed envisions the existence of two worlds, one corruptible world on earth and
another, incorruptible, and everlasting world in the heights of heaven.
At the same time, _2 Baruch_ attests to the idea that the boundary between
the realms is permeable. Throughout world history carriers of holiness
have escaped to the heavenly world, away from human wickedness.
Resurrection and judgement become a turning point in this regard,
since these events finally evacuate the righteous from the corruptible
world as the last carriers of holiness and righteousness on earth. In
addition, resurrection and judgement introduce a series of transformations that enable Israel to acquire the eternal world which has been
promised to her (51:3).

Redirecting the Promise

The following section will further the analysis of _2 Baruch_'s description
of the final destiny of Israel in the heavenly other world. I will attempt
to detect the narratives to which _2 Baruch_ alludes, to isolate imageries
and metaphors applied by the text, and to discuss how they are used
in the description of the heights as a world of promise. Three sets
of imageries are of central importance in this context: allusions and
explicit references to the Exodus narrative, references to the Abraham
story, and a reused (probably Deuteronomic) terminology of planting
and possessing. What does _2 Baruch_'s use of this imagery tell us about
the role of the other world in Israel's redemptive history?

Exodus—Resurrection: From Egypt to Life

The first set of narratives and imageries I will discuss are those related to the Exodus-story. 75:7 shows that *2 Baruch* uses Exodus imagery explicitly to describe resurrection and the change of dwelling place:

> But we who are existing, if we know now why we have come, and subject ourselves to him who brought (root *'t'*) us from Egypt, again we will come (root *'t'*),[113] and we will remember those things that passed away, and rejoice because of that which has been.

Scholars generally agree that this passage equates being brought from Egypt and into the Land with the process of being resurrected and brought into the final abode of the righteous.[114] *2 Baruch* uses covenant rhetoric and alludes to the Exodus story to argue for the final redemption of those who have remained righteous. In the same way that God once led the Exodus generation out of Egypt and into the Promised Land, he will again lead the righteous from the corruptible world and into the incorruptible world.

Walking through the Wilderness: The Promises of the Desolate Landscape

Chapters Four and Five above showed the importance of the wilderness as an anti-place or non-place of the end-time. However, in view of the discussion of 75:5 it is evident that *2 Baruch* also alludes to the wilderness as a promising place. *2 Baruch* alludes to the setting of the Exodus story to justify its hopes for the future. In this way, the wilderness of the Exodus story is projected onto the wilderness of the end-time. In 84:2–7 the Exodus generation and the generation that has reached the end of time are again equated:

> Remember that in that time Moses called heaven and earth to witness against you and said: If you trespass the law you will be scattered, but if you keep it, you shall be kept. And he also said other things when

---

[113] Or "we are coming." Cf. Bogaert on the use of *'t'* in the context of resurrection (*Apocalypse de Baruch II*, 92–93).

[114] Charles, *Apocalypse of Baruch*, 117; Collins, "Apocalyptic Eschatology," 18; Sayler, *Promises*, 73; 97; Murphy, *Structure and Meaning*, 113; Nir, *Destruction*, 151. Cf. Himmelfarb, *Ascent to Heaven*, 75. Cf. *L.A.B.* 19:12, and note the reference to the phoenix in *Ezekiel the Tragedian* in the context of the Exodus. This may allude to the idea that the phoenix is a bird that dies and resurrects, making the Exodus both a journey and an ascent (cf. *2 En.* 12:3; 15:1).

you the twelve tribes were in the desert (*madbārā*) together. And after his death you cast them away from you and, therefore, that which has been predicted has come upon you. And now, Moses spoke to you before it happened to you and, behold, it has occurred, for you have forsaken the law. Also I, behold, I say to you after you suffered that if you obey the things that I have said to you, you shall receive from the Mighty One everything which has been laid up and preserved for you.

In this passage from the *Epistola Baruch*, Baruch refers to Moses, to the twelve tribes, to the Law and the polarity between the exiled and the settled in order to recall the situation of the wilderness generation, thus adding its atmosphere to the circumstances of the people in the end-time. In this sense, the current situation is seen as a re-enactment of the Exodus story.[115] This is a much-utilised literary device in the eschatological oriented texts of the Pseudepigrapha.

What does *2 Baruch* gain by applying the Exodus story to the narrative of the end of the corruptible world? Above all, references to the Exodus serve to describe the general deconstruction of the corruptible world and the reconstruction of Israel as a people belonging to the incorruptible world. The Exodus story conveys a general aura of *mobility* to the people, the Law, and to the presence of God.[116] The use of the Exodus story underlines the fact that Israel does not depend on a particular spot, be it the temple, the city or a specific territory to survive and attain her redemption.[117] The Exodus story is often considered the national founding myth of Israel. The constitution of Israel as a people took place in the wilderness while Israel was on the move. Consequently, Israel was never dependent on life in Palestine to be considered a people (Deut 7:6–16). Rather, Israel can be remade as a people by walking through the wilderness again. *2 Baruch* thus questions the notion that Israel is dependent on the region of Palestine for her survival.[118]

Moreover, 85:3, discussed in Chapter Four, shows that the mobility also applies to the Law and to the presence of God. This assertion of the independence of the Law from life in Palestine underlines the freedom of Israel from any fixed location.[119] As I have already noted

---

[115] Burden, *Kerygma*, 4.
[116] Koester, *Dwelling of God*, 10; Lied, "Frå Palestina," 57; 66; 80–81.
[117] Cf. Chapters Three, Four and Five. Cf. Murphy, *Structure and Meaning*, 113.
[118] Cf. Chapter Three.
[119] Cf. Davies, *Gospel and Land*, 354. Cf. *Apoc. Ab.* 10:15, where the Law is still "the way of the land."

several times, divine presence was never restricted to the temple of Jerusalem. And even before the temple fell, *2 Baruch* disengages the presence of God from the Jerusalem temple, stressing the connection between Israel and God, at the expense of the relation of God to the temple.[120] Thus, all territorial landmarks central to Israel in the corruptible world are now rejected. In the end-time, the remnant of the people resides in the wilderness, just like the generation of the Exodus story did.

In addition, the learned reader of *2 Baruch* would recall that the generation of the Exodus story spent only 40 years in the wilderness. The sojourn in the wilderness should thus to be considered no more than an intermezzo (52:6).[121] The temporary stay in the wilderness necessarily points to an *eisodus*, an entrance, and thereby gives the narrative a geographical direction. Eventually, Egypt and Babylon were not only places of exile, they were also places Israel finally left (75:7–8).[122]

In this context we can understand why the period of the Exodus generation can be labelled a bright water by the Apocalypse of the cloud (59:1–12). The wilderness is by no means only a terrifying place that brings death. It is also a life giving and constructive space that points to a new beginning.[123] The wilderness will soon be left behind for a Land of Promise.

Manna at the Threshold (*2 Bar.* 29)

In the previous chapter I interpreted the eating scene in 29:4–8 as a condensation of creation and a transformation of the remnant during the Messianic era. There are, however, still intriguing aspects in this passage that demand additional attention. We shall look more specifically at the manna reference in 29:8: "And it will happen at that time, that from on high the treasury of manna will again descend and they will eat from it in those years, because these are those who have arrived at the end of time." What is the function of the manna reference in *2 Bar.* 29?

---

[120] Compare 25:4, 64:7 and 77:13–14, as well as Exod 29:45–46, 1 Kgs 6:13, Zak 2:9, *Jub.* 1:17; *T. Mos.* 4:7; Acts 7:9. Cf. further Davies, *Gospel and Land*, 270.

[121] Cf. *Liber antiquitatum biblicarum*, the *Testament of Moses* and the *Testaments of the Twelve Patriarchs*.

[122] Cf. Volz, *Escatologie*, 320.

[123] The Exodus story is commonly acknowledged to be influenced by the motif of the battle against chaos (Exod 15:8–10; Pss 77:16–21; 106:7–12).

The manna motif comes with a set of connotations that have roots in a specific narrative setting. In several biblical accounts, manna is identified as the extraordinary nutritional source of the Exodus story.[124] The manna reference of 29:8 alludes to the provision of heavenly bread which sustained the tribes of Israel during their forty year journey through the wilderness. This indicates that manna belongs within a special geographical setting and a specific interim situation.

Exod 16:35 says: "The Israelites ate manna for forty years, until they came to a habitable land; they ate manna, until they came to the border of the land of Canaan." Josh 5:12 describes the end of the manna period: "The manna ceased on the day they ate the produce of the land, and the Israelites no longer had manna; they ate the crops of the land of Canaan that year."[125] Likewise, Josephus understands manna as a source of sustenance in the wilderness: "Now they made use of the food for forty years, or as long as they were in the wilderness" (*Ant.* 3.1.6).[126] The drizzle of manna thus came to an end on the day the people first ate the produce of the Land.[127] When the people crossed the Jordan, the manna was no longer needed and this miraculous source of food was withdrawn.

Let us take a closer look at the wording of *2 Bar.* 29:8. First, the passage states that the treasury of manna will descend "again" (*tub*) at the end of time. This use of *tub* implies that the treasury of manna has descended before. The descent of manna in the Messianic world alludes to the first opening of the heavenly reservoirs that took place in the wilderness of the Exodus story.[128] Then, the passage describes those who have arrived (root *mt'*) at the end of time. This last sentence of the passage indicates movement. The remnant has covered a wide distance and reached the limits of its journey. Hence, the descent of manna in 29:8 frames the years of wandering towards the final consummation of

---

[124] Cf. Exod 16; Num 11:6–9; 21:5; Deut 8:3; 16; Josh 5:12; Ps 78:23–25; 105:40; Nah 9:15–20; Wis 16:20–29; 19:21; 1 Cor 10:3; Rev 2:17; John 6:25–65; Heb 9:4; Cf. further *Targum Jonathan to Deut* 1:1–2.

[125] Malina suggests a link between the two passages (Malina, *Palestinian Manna*, 30).

[126] Translated by W. Whiston, Josephus. *The Antiquities of the Jews II* (McLean, Virg.: IndyPublish, (Year of publication: not specified)).

[127] Josephus, *Ant.* 3.1.6; 5.1.4. Cf. *L.A.B.* 19:5; 20:8; *Fragmentary Targum to Exod* 16:35 and *Jerusalem Targum to Exod* 16:35.

[128] According to Exod 16:32–34, Aaron collected an omer of manna in a jar. It was placed "before the covenant for safe keeping" (Cf. Heb 9:4 and possibly Rev 2:17). Thus, the stored manna may come from the same source as the manna of the wilderness. However, it may also be imagined to stem from a jar in the tabernacle.

time. At the threshold of time, manna still sustains the remnant. While
the Messianic reign ensures that the victorious remnant consumes vital
foods during its sojourn in the Land, the allusions to the Exodus diet
hint at the coming evacuation of the world. The diet thus elaborates on
the condensing *and* regenerating role of the Messianic era.

Now, *where is* the remnant in *2 Bar.* 29? The remnant is surely in
the superabundant world of the Messianic era. And, as I suggested
in Chapter Six, the remnant is already in the Messianic Land. Still,
the remnant is in a sense still at the threshold, due to the allusions
to the setting of the Exodus story and the sense of temporality of the
Messianic era.[129] The analysis thus brings us to the conclusion that the
remnant is in the Land, but still not yet there.

This apparent paradox should however not surprise us this time,
since it agrees with the ambiguous placing of Baruch and his followers
in *2 Bar.* 76–85, discussed in Chapter Five. We have already seen that
the location and whereabouts of Baruch in the wilderness of the southern parts of Palestine is somewhat paradoxical due to Baruch's function
as a *Moses redivivus* of the end-time. Baruch, however, never left Palestine, and the mountain he ascends in 76:3–5 lies in the Hebron area.
The wilderness of the Exodus narrative and the wilderness of Palestine thus merge. Moreover, while Baruch and his followers state that
they have left the Land, just as their brothers in exile did (85:3), they
are clearly still in the wilderness of Palestine (77:5; 78:6). So, although
Baruch and his group sojourn within Palestine, *2 Baruch* still ascribes a
status of exodus to their stay there. Baruch and his group are thus at
the threshold, as is the remnant in 29:8. In this sense the paradoxical
placing of the remnant during the Messianic reign serves as a parallel
to the location of Baruch and his followers in the wilderness of Palestine
(*2 Bar.* 77).

In *2 Bar.* 29 there are two aspects to this paradoxical localisation:
Firstly, the remnant has already arrived and already has a part in
redemption, since they sojourn in the protective Land of the Messianic
reign. As shown in Chapter Six, the significant turn in the ways of
the world comes with the reign of the Messiah (29:3; 39:7; 70:10). The
Messianic reign is therefore the starting point and the first phase of

---

[129] As several scholars have suggested, Isa 11 probably is an important intertext to
2 Bar. 29 as well as to 73:1–7 (Cf., e.g., Chester, "Eschatology," 251). Cf. *Sib. Or.* 3.367–
395, 787–795; and Ferch, "Two Aeons," 148).

the redemptive period,[130] but it unfolds gradually and advances unto subsequent stages.[131]

Secondly, the other aspect to the paradox is that the stay in the Messianic Land is not final. That Land is part of a temporary reign in the corruptible world and therefore it is doomed to be left behind. A final *eisodus* on the one hand evacuates the people from the world and consequently also from the earthly Land. On the other hand, by means of allusion the *eisodus* necessarily points towards a Land of Promise. Although the remnant is already in the Land, it is nevertheless not yet in the ultimate Land.[132] The Land implied in *2 Bar.* 29 is not enough—a comprehensive Land is needed.

Consequently, the exodus of *2 Bar.* 29 will bring the remnant out of the Messianic Land on earth. The remnant is on its way, moving from a provisional to a final redemption, walking through the changing world until the consummation of time. In 29:8 we find the remnant at the threshold. It has arrived at the border of the corruptible world. It still feeds on provisions of manna, a fact that indicates that it has still not crossed the border.[133]

The Redemptive Eschatological Exodus

This outline suggests that *2 Baruch* uses the relatively common notion of an eschatological exodus. To *2 Baruch*, resurrection and ascension to the other world becomes an exodus out of Egypt and an *eisodus* into the Promised Land. The web of allusions to the wilderness and its sites, as well as to the manna in 29:8, supports this idea.

God's Promises to Abraham

Now, where is the place of promise according to *2 Baruch*? A closer examination of the text reveals that *2 Baruch* never explicitly suggests

---

[130] *2 Baruch* probably integrates the eschatological model of Isaiah, where the earthly Land is the final goal for Israel (Isa 26–27; 35). *2 Baruch* makes the Messianic Land on earth the first, but not the final, goal. In this manner, *2 Baruch* combines different eschatological traditions.

[131] This model is also found in *2 Bar.* 49–51 and 72–75.

[132] This blend of temporary redemption and continued movement is not uncommon. Both *4 Ezra* (7:27; 13:50) and the *Fragmentary Targum to Deut* 8:16 include an exodus scenario in the description of the last times (Cf. Malina, *Palestinian Manna*, 91).

[133] Cf. Neh 9:15 and Josephus, *Ant.* 7.2.2.

that God's promises refer to any earthly location. Neither Palestine, nor
Judah, nor Jerusalem is ever mentioned explicitly as the target area of
God's promise.[134] In *2 Baruch* promises apply to the other world (14:13;
21:25; 51:3; 83:4), to future life (57:2), to a coming period (44:13; 83:6) or
to an undefined future space, situation or reward (3:9; 22:4; 48:34; 54:9;
59:2; 78:7).[135] In other words, *2 Baruch* reserves the promise terminology
for the future, otherworldly reality, described by either its time or its
space aspect.[136] The other world is thus what the righteous Israel can
hope for, since that is what has been promised her by God.[137]

  2 Baruch associates the notion of the promised other world with the
ideas that the other world was created for Israel and that it is the
inheritance of Israel.[138] On several occasions *2 Baruch* says that the
other, incorruptible world, as well as the present corruptible world, was
originally created for the righteous (14:19; 15:7–8), or for the patriarchs,
that is, Israel (21:24–25).[139] This notion focuses God's creational act on
the well-being of Israel, underscores the corruption of the present world
order and redirects hope to the other world. While the present world
has been a struggle for Israel, and thus did not live up to its intentions,
the other world will not fail to redeem Israel (15:1–8). The idea that
the other, future, world is also the inheritance (root *yrt*) of the righteous
(16:1; 44:13) strengthens Israel's claim on that world.[140]

  The second, bright, waters of the Apocalypse of the cloud (57:1–3)
demand attention in this context:

---

[134] Cf. Murphy, *Structure and Meaning*, 88.

[135] Forms of the root *mlk*, "promise," is applied throughout *2 Baruch* (with the exception of 48:34) to describe the space/time of promise (Smith, *Dictionary*, 277; Smith, *Thesaurus*, 2139–2140). Note that *2 Baruch* frequently describes promise, hope, and belief for
the other world together (Cf. 2 Bar. 14:11–19; 15:7–8; 42–44; 57; 59; 78:6–7; 84; 85).

[136] As I have pointed out at several occasions, *2 Baruch* describes time and space
interchangeably. Cf. further Sir 44:19–21; *4 Ezra* 6:59; 7:26; 8:52–53; *L.A.B.* 32:3; Rom
4:13. Cf. G. Delling, "Die Weise, von der Zeit zu reden, im Lieber Antiquitatum
Biblicarum," *NovT* 13 (1971): 305–321 at 306–308; G. Delling, "Von Morija zum Sinai
(Pseudo-Philo, Liber Anitquitatum Biblicarum 32.1–10)," *JSJ* 2 (1971): 1–18 at 14–15;
Davies, *Gospel and Land*, 145–148; Moxnes, *Theology in Conflict*, 247–248.

[137] Cf. p. 53. Cf. further *T. Mos.* 1:12; *4 Ezra* 6:55.

[138] Cf. *4 Ezra* 7:1–25. Note that the Land is commonly understood as 'the inheritance'
(Sir 46:1; 2 Macc 2:4).

[139] Cf. *4 Ezra* 7:9. Note also the idea that both worlds were originally created for man
(or for Adam) (14:18). Several contemporary sources claim that the world was created
either for Abraham, Moses, David, or the Messiah (*Apoc. Ab.* 13:8; *Mos.* 1, 155; *Targum
Jonathan to Isa* 33:7; *Targum Esth I* 5:1; *b. Sanh.* 98b; cf. Ginzberg, *Legends VI*, 272).

[140] Cf. *4 Ezra* 7:96.

And after these things you saw bright waters. That was the fountain of Abraham, and also his generation, and the coming of his son and his son's son and of those like them. Because at that time the unwritten law was obeyed among them, and the works of the commandments were then fulfiled, and belief (root *'mn*) in the coming judgement was then begotten, and hope (root *sbr*) of the renewed world was then founded, and the promise (root *mlk*) of the life that will come afterwards was planted. These are the bright waters you have seen.

The second, bright, waters are the period of Abraham, his generation and descendants. *2 Baruch* describes this period, the first bright waters of world history, as a founding period for the hope, belief and promise of Israel's redemption. It was the first time the Law—the unwritten Law[141]—and the commandments were fulfiled, and it was when the belief in the coming judgement was begotten (root *yld*), the founding (root *bn'*) of hope in the renewed world and the planting (root *nçb*) of the promise of the life hereafter.

How can we understand this interpretation of the Abraham story? On the one hand, the period of Abraham and his descendants, the second, bright, waters (57:1–3), contrasts with the period of Adam, the first, dark waters (56:5–16). It thus points backwards in history. The time of Abraham brought righteousness and obedience where Adam transgressed, and it restored hope in life where the period of Adam brought death. On the other hand, the period of Abraham also points forwards in time: it promises a new world, since the present world turned to corruption when Adam transgressed. Hence, the direction of Israel's hope towards the other world is set at this point.[142] *2 Baruch* clearly takes a radical interpretation of the well-known Abraham narratives of Genesis. We recognise the stress on Abraham's righteousness and obedience from the Genesis account (Gen 12:1–4; 15:6), but *2 Baruch* does not mention the promise of descendants, the promise of the Land and the promise of blessing we find in Gen 12 and 15. The mention of judgement (*dinā*), the renewed world (*'almā dmethadat*) and the promise of life (*haye*) in 57:1–3 therefore needs some exploration.

2 Bar. 4:4 probably gives an important lead: "And after these things I showed it to my servant Abraham at night among the parts of the sacrifice." This passage states that God showed the heavenly city/sanctuary to Abraham in the night of the covenant between the pieces (Gen 15:7–

141 Cf. Charles, *Apocalypse of Baruch*, 99.
142 Cf. Sayler, *Promises*, 70.

21). According to this Genesis passage, Abraham (Abram) asks God how he can be sure that he will in fact possess the Land God brought him out of Ur to possess. God commands Abraham to bring him a heifer, a goat, a ram and a pigeon. Abraham cuts the animals, not the birds,[143] in two, and lays each half over against the other (15:9–11). When the night comes, darkness descends on Abraham and God speaks:

> 'Know this for certain, that your offspring shall be aliens in a land that is not theirs, and shall be slaves there, and they shall be oppressed for four hundred years; but I will bring judgement on the nation that they serve, and afterwards they shall come out with great possessions. (…). And they shall come back here in the fourth generation; for the iniquity of the Amorites is not yet complete' (Gen 15:13–16).

The story continues as "a smoking fire-pot and a flaming torch passed between these pieces" (15:17):

> On that day the LORD made a covenant with Abram, saying, 'To your descendants I give this land, from the river of Egypt to the great river, the river Euphrates, the land of the Kenites, the Kenizzites, the Kadmonites, the Hittites, the Perizzites, the Rephaim, the Amorites, the Canaanites, the Girgashites, and the Jebusites' (15:18–21).

During this night, Abraham is thus granted a vision of Israel's slavery in Egypt, God's judgement of the nation that oppressed her and Israel's triumphant return to the country where Abraham lived as a foreigner. The night culminates with God's promise to give Abraham's descendants the Land. *2 Bar.* 4:4 thus places Abraham's vision of the heavenly city/sanctuary in the context of God's promise of the Land to Abraham in Gen 15.[144] According to *2 Bar.* 4:4, then, the vision of the heavenly city/sanctuary parallels the return to and conquest of the country between the rivers in Gen 15:17.

In the light of the above discussion of *2 Bar.* 48:48–52:7, it is quite evident that both 4:4 and 57:1–3 link the period of Abraham to the other world as the world promised to Israel (51:3). That is where God's promises of judgement, a renewed world and a new life will be fulfiled. God will judge mankind, just as he once judged Egypt (Gen 15:14),[145]

---

[143] Cf. *L.A.B.* 23:7.
[144] Cf. McKelvey, *New Temple*, 32.
[145] Cf. *Apoc. Ab.* 31–32 for a similar interpretation. Cf. also the notion of the judgement as a positive and promised event in *4 Ezra* 7:60; 11:46. Judgement also plays a part in covenant rhetoric: God promises blessings to the righteous and curses to the wicked

whilst the righteous will escape the struggles of the corruptible world (15:8) and be resurrected to new life. When we read 57:2's promise of life in light of the suggestion of an exodus from Egypt to life (75:7) and 51:3's description of the fulfilment of that promise, we see that *2 Baruch* equates life, the heavenly world and the Land. As Davies has pointed out, 'life' is part of the Land-vocabulary.[146] The promise of life, particularly resurrected life, may thus play on allusions to the promise of Land and the terms may also interchange. So, *2 Baruch*'s Israel will enter the other world, which will be renewed, and Israel will be transformed, just as Israel escaped from slavery in Egypt, transformed the territory between the rivers into the Land promised to them by God and thus turned from being slaves into landowners. Thus, 57:1–3 redirects hope, promise and belief towards the other world. That is where Israel will become a great people, and life there is the content of God's blessing.[147]

These references and allusions to the Abraham narrative must have been particularly apt for promoting the other world as the place of promise, due to that narrative's richness of allusions to a shift of place and the creation of a new beginning. On God's command, Abraham obediently left the country of his family due to the idolatry there, and walked towards a country he did not know, trusting God's promise (Gen 12). The story of Israel's progenitor thus implies both a radical change of place and a firm belief in God's promise. *2 Baruch* presents the move from the corruptible world to the incorruptible world in the same terms. The righteous must trust God's promise, leave the world and look to the world God promises them. Likewise, just as Abraham was always a stranger in Palestine (23:4), so the righteous are strangers in the corruptible world. They do not belong there, even though the world was once made for them and was promised to them to live in.[148]

(Cf. Deut 28–31). Cf. G.W.E. Nickelsburg, "Judgement, Life-After-Death, and Resurrection in the Apocrypha and the Non-Apocalyptic Pseudepigrapha," in *Judaism in Late Antiquity, Part 4: Death, Life-After-Death, Resurrection and the World-to-Come in the Judaisms of Antiquity* (HO 49; ed. A.J. Avery-Peck and J. Neusner; Leiden: Brill, 2000), 142.

[146] Davies, *Gospel and Land*, 331–333. Cf., e.g., John 5:29 in comparison with Dan 12:2 and the differing manuscript witnesses to *T. Job* 33:5. Cf. also *1 En.* 40:9.

[147] It is possible that the description of Israel as stars in the other world (*2 Bar.* 51) may also allude to the star-vision of Gen 15. According to Gen 15:5, God commands Abraham to count the stars to get an impression of the number of his descendants. Cf., e.g., *Apoc. Ab.* 20's interpretation of the scene.

[148] Several texts advocate a similar shift towards heavenly realities in the Abraham narrative, among them *Abr.* 4 and 68; *Her.* 96–99; Heb 11:8–10; *Ep. Barn.* 6:8–19; 15:7. Cf. A.P. O'Hagan, *Material Re-Creation in the Apostolic Fathers* (TU 100; Berlin: Akademie-

What God Promised Moses

Intriguingly, *2 Baruch* reorients the promises God made to Moses in a
similar manner. In 84:2–7, cited above, Baruch, in the role of *Moses
redivivus*, commands the tribes to remember that the promises and the
demands of the covenant are valid for them just as they were for the
Exodus generation. So, if the tribes obey Baruch's words, they will
receive what God has preserved for them. This passage thus equates
the Exodus generation with the followers of Baruch: the promises God
made to Moses will ultimately be fulfiled in the heights for those who
listen to Baruch's words.

2 Bar. 59–60 presents an even more radical reading: it skips the Palestine interlude and makes the promises apply directly to the other world.
The fourth, bright, waters of the Apocalypse of the cloud concern
the Exodus generation (59). 59:1–12 devotes much space to the cosmic
visions Moses received before his death (59:3–12). This vision scene is
followed by the fifth, black, waters which describes the mingling of the
tribes with the Amorites (60). As I pointed out in Chapter Three, there
is thus no description of any entry into Palestine in the Apocalypse of
the cloud.[149] It moves directly from the final vision of Moses to the sins
that took place in that country. Moreover, while 59:4–12 grants Moses
a vision of the entire cosmos, and particularly of the other world with
its city/sanctuary and its Paradise in the heights, Moses does not get to
see the landscapes of Palestine, as he did in the equivalent Deuteronomy scene (Deut 34). In contrast to its parallel in Deuteronomy, *2 Bar.*
59–60 thus excludes both the crossing of the Jordan and the conquest of
Palestine and thereby changes the target of Moses' vision. Palestine was
never seen by Moses. He looked directly at the other world. The entry
into Palestine is no longer a landmark in Israel's history: it is passed
over in silence. *2 Baruch* thus applies the same strategy to the story of
Moses as it did to the Abraham narrative: while playing on a notion of
parallel exoduses, it moves expectations directly to the other, incorruptible world.[150]

Verlag, 1968), 45–50; Moxnes, *Theology in Conflict*, 181–182; Sandmel, *Philo's Place*, 88;
Chester, "Eschatology," 273–274; Brueggemann, *Land*, 67.

[149] Cf. Chapter Three, pp. 74–75.

[150] Cf. also the interpretation of Gen 15 in *L.A.B.* 23:6.

2 Bar. 36–40 and 84–85: Planting Israel and Possessing the Land

I have discussed *2 Baruch*'s use of vegetation imagery on several occasions in this study.[151] An important part of this imagery is the idea that Israel is a plant, most often a vine, which God may tend to or discard, plant or uproot.[152] Several texts link vine imagery explicitly to the Land. Ps 80:8–9 says for instance: "You brought a vine out of Egypt; you drove out the nations and planted it. You cleared the ground for it; it took deep root and filled the land."[153] According to Davies, the vine is "the symbol of what attaches a man to the land."[154] The notion of planting and uprooting Israel in the Land also extends beyond the specific notion of Israel as a vine. For instance, Exod 15:17 says: "You brought them in and planted them on the mountain of your own possession (…)," referring to the planting of Israel in a Mount Zion-centred Land.[155] The concept of planting and uprooting can also be applied to other nations than Israel in many texts. Jer 1:10, for example, applies it to describe the uprooting of foreign empires. This uprooting is the consequence of their wickedness towards Israel and their abuse of power.[156]

Above all, though, the image of the luxuriant, thriving plant of Israel serves as a sign of God's care for his people. As long as Israel lives according to the regulations of the covenant, the plant will remain rooted in the Land. However, if Israel turns wicked, the plant will be rejected by God and uprooted from its soil.[157] Uprooting is thus

---

[151] Cf. Chapter Six, p. 194, in particular.

[152] Cf. *2 Bar.* 22:6; 36–37; Cf. Ps 80:8–16; Isa 5:1–7; 16:6–11; 27:2–6; Jer 1:10; 2:21; 6:9; Ezek 15:1–6; 17:5–10; 19:10–14; Hos 10:1; 14:5–7; *Targum Jonathan to Isa* 5:1; *Targum Esth I* 7:10 (Cf. Hayward, "Vine," 9; Stordalen, *Eden*, 91; 171–172). 2 Sam 7:10 describes David's accomplishments as a 'planting' of Israel (cf. 1 Chr 17:9; Ps 44:2; *Jub.* 16:26; Cf. 2 Sam 20:1). Note how tree metaphors are commonly applied to persons and groups: Ps 92:12–15; Isa 61:3; Prov 3:18; 11:30; 13:12; 15:4; *Pss. Sol.* 14:3–4; *1 En.* 93:2–5 (Hayward, "Vine," 9–10; Stordalen, *Eden*, 86–89).

[153] Cf. *L.A.B.* 12:11–12; 4Q378 Fragment 11, 1–6; *Targum Song of Songs* 7:12–13; *Targum Esth I* 7:10.

[154] Davies, *Gospel and Land*, 332; Murphy, *Structure and Meaning*, 83.

[155] Cf. Deut 6:10–11; Ezek 17:22–23. Cf. Stordalen, *Eden*, 91; Wright, *Baruch ben Neriah*, 30.

[156] Cf. further *Jub.* 7.

[157] Cf. the use of this imagery in connection to the Baruch figure in Jer 45:4 (Cf. Wright, *Baruch ben Neriah*, 28–31).

the consequence of Israel's wickedness and displays the vulnerability of Israel, the plant, in the face of God, who tends it.[158]

"Flowers that do not fade" (37:1)

The motif of uprooting and planting is the key motif of the Apocalypse of the vine and the cedar (35–40). The previous chapter sketched the storyline of this apocalypse.[159] The vine (the Messiah) and the fountain (his forces) uproot the wicked forest, destroy the plain where it grows and convict and kill the cedar (the last wicked ruler). 37:1 describes the grand finale of the vision: "And after these things I saw that cedar set on fire, and the vine was growing, it and all surrounding it, the plain filled with flowers that do not fade." This apocalypse applies the imagery of uprooting to describe how the Messiah and his followers finally destroy the world's impiety (36:4).[160] The Messiah and his men uproot the forest of wickedness, convict the cedar and turn them into ashes (36:10). However, the apocalypse also adds a new element to the relatively common imagery of the new planting. The vine and its surroundings transform into a valley of *unfading* flowers. The Apocalypse of the vine and the cedar thus combines the idea of uprooting and planting with the metaphor of an un-withering plant. What is the function of this combination of images in the apocalypse?

Flowers fade. That is a fact of nature, as well as a central aspect of biblical metaphorical imagery concerning flowers. Job 14:1, for instance, reflects the common usage of the fading flower metaphor: "'A mortal, born of woman, few of days and full of trouble, comes up like a flower and withers, flees like a shadow and does not last."[161] This Job passage displays the most common usage of the metaphor: the life of mankind is likened to the withering flower, being short and transitory. The fact that the wicked forest of *2 Bar.* 36 can be uprooted proves that the forces of wickedness are slaves to the laws of nature and thus transitory and mortal.[162] In contrast, unfading flowers are everlasting[163]

---

[158] Cf. *1 En.* 62:8; *Odes Sol.* 11:18; *Pss. Sol.* 114:3–4; *Targum Jonathan to Isa* 5:1 (Cf. Stordalen, *Eden*, 91; Wright, *Baruch ben Neriah*, 31).

[159] Cf. pp. 189–191.

[160] Cf. pp. 208–210.

[161] Cf. further *2 Bar.* 82:7 as well as Ps 103:15–16; Wis 2:7–8; Matt 6:28–30. Cf. Stordalen, *Eden*, 87–90.

[162] Cf. pp. 208–210.

[163] Cf. *2 Bar.* 44:11; 48:50; 51:16; 85:5.

and cannot therefore be uprooted again. In this way, *2 Baruch* both turns the biblical metaphor of the withering plant upside down and shows how the cycle of alternating planting and uprooting will come to en end in the description of the ultimate redemption of Israel: Israel will be a flower that does not fade, and she will be planted forever.[164]

"Possess, not be taken possession of" (85:9)

According to 36:7–8, the main crime of the wicked cedar was that he took possession of territories and peoples that did not belong to him. In other words, he extended his evil powers beyond the extent of his birthright.[165] To put it in the terminology of *2 Baruch*, the cedar trampled and trod down the possessions of others, he did not limit himself to his own country and by his impious way of life he used Creation unrighteously.[166] Evidently, the focus of the apocalypse is Rome's subjection of areas belonging to Israel by birthright. Rome destroyed the temple and Jerusalem and thus subdued their Land.

Chapter Two of this study showed that dispossession of the Land was one of the elements that lead to the disaster of Israel in the end-time.[167] Klijn has argued that the dispossession of the area of Zion and the subsequent dispersion of the tribes, not the destruction of the earthly temple, were the core elements of that disaster and the main concern of the author. Indeed, the exile of the tribes and the fact that no-one any longer inhabits Zion (80:7) are important worries in *2 Baruch*, much more so than the concern about the earthly temple.

---

[164] The idea of a field of everlasting flowers is common goods to several Greek and Roman authors, and is attested in *Jos. Asen.* 16:16. During the first centuries C.E. several texts applied the imagery in descriptions of paradisiacal spaces, or to indicate immortality, or new life (Cf. *1 En.* 10:16; 84:6. Cf. further M.E. Irwin, "Fair flowers of paradise in Clement of Alexandria and others," www.odu.edu/webroot/instr/sci/plant.nsf/pages/wreaths#N_1_ (April 1st 2006)). Thus, in the context of *2 Baruch*, the imagery of unfading flowers could probably *both* be considered a familiar ingredient of a well known redemptive scheme *and* as a paradoxical metaphor.

[165] Cf. pp. 208–210. Note that Israel's 'possession' of the Land does not mean that the Land should be understood as Israel's private property. The Land is Israel's to administer and inhabit as God's gift to her. Brueggemann has pointed out the tension between the concepts of inheriting and possessing in this context (*Land*, 89–90). That tension is however not pressing to *2 Baruch*, since the Syriac word *yrt* means both "to inherit" and "to possess" (Smith, *Dictionary*, 197–198). The notion of Israel as heir or landlord may possibly be blurred in *2 Baruch*.

[166] Cf. Chapter Two, p. 53.

[167] Cf. Chapter Two, pp. 52–55.

85:1–11 describes the future repossession of the area that belongs to Israel by birthright. Now, what area is in fact restored to Israel? Does Israel return to Jerusalem and its surroundings, or does the repossession of Israel's birthright take place in another location? As the preceding chapter showed, the remnant indeed returns to Mount Zion in the Messianic era. However, that chapter also made it clear that its stay was temporary. 85:1–11 answers the question as to Israel's final possessions, even including the concern for the dispersed tribes in relation to this:

> Further, know that in the times of former generations, our fathers had righteous helpers, prophets and pious men. But then we were also in our land, and they helped us when we sinned, and they prayed for us to him who created us, because they trusted their works, and the Mighty One heard their prayers and absolved us. But now, the righteous have been gathered and the prophets are sleeping, and we have also left the land, and Zion has been taken away from us, and now we have nothing except the Mighty One and his law. If now we direct our hearts and make them firm, we will receive (root *nsb*) everything that we lost—much better than that we lost, greatly increased. For what we lost was part of corruption and what we will receive will not be corruptible. Also, I have written this to our brothers to Babylon, so that also to them I may bear witness to these things (85:1–6)

This passage asserts that at the time of Baruch both the remnant and the dispersed tribes have left the Land and lost Zion.[168] In contrast to former generations who dwelled in the Land and benefited from the constant help of prophets and pious men, Baruch and his generation have only God and the Law (85:3).[169] In this situation, Baruch encourages the tribes to remain righteous, or alternatively embrace righteousness again, and to remember that what they lost, in other words the temple and its surrounding region,[170] was part of the corruptible world. If they do in fact choose the right path they will receive an incorruptible, increased and better version of what they lost. 85:9–11 continues:

> Now, before judgement demands its own, and truth that which is its right, we shall prepare our souls to possess and not be taken possession of, and that we shall hope (root *sbr*) and not be dishonoured and that we

---

[168] Cf. Chapter Five, p. 169.

[169] According to Deut 18:15–22, there will always be prophets in Israel. Since 85:9–11 states that they are all gone, this indicates, again, that the end is near (Cf. Wright, *Baruch ben Neriah*, 89–90; H. Ulfgard, "…nu har vi inget annat än den Mektiga och hans Lag": Kris, kontinuitet och apokalyptik i *2 Baruk*," *Det gamle testamente i jødedom og kristendom* (FBE 4; København: Museum Tusculanum Forlag, 1993), 79–122).

[170] Cf. *2 Bar.* 43:1–3; 75:7–8.

shall rest with our fathers and not be punished with those who hate us. For the youth of the world has passed away, and the strength of Creation is sufficiently exhausted, and the advent of the times decreases rapidly and passes by, and the pitcher is near the well, and the ship to the port, and the course of the journey to the city, and life to completion. And again prepare your souls, so that when you go and ascend from the ship, you will rest and not be brought low when you go away (root *'zl*) (85:9–11).

Baruch then instructs the tribes to prepare their hearts before the coming judgement. But time is short: the end of the world is near. In this situation the tribes should make ready to possess, to hope and to rest, and thus not be taken possession of, not to be dishonoured (root *bht*) and not to be punished.

85:1–11 triggers a wide range of allusions. Firstly, we recognise that this passage, like several other sequences of *2 Baruch*, draws on a journey motif with affinities to Exodus imagery to describe death and resurrection to the other world: the ship is close to the port, the journey to the city and life to an end (85:10).[171] These motifs are commonly used to describe the New Exodus and the voyage to the celestial city.[172] Israel will ascend from (root *slq*) the ship, that is, she will traverse the distance from earth to heaven and attain rest there (85:11). The passage combines this imagery with the widespread metaphor of (Sabbath-) rest in the Land.[173] However, the metaphor is not applied to describe a return to Palestine as the ideal location of rest in life, or to the reassembly of the dead, but to describe resurrection with the fathers in the other world (85:9).[174] The opposite of ascending from the ship and finding rest in 85:11 is to be brought low (root *thb*). Note that 85:9 in all probability urges the tribes to prepare for the situation described in 51:1–13: after God's judgement, the righteous will enjoy reunion with the fathers, probably implied in 51:13, and not suffer the torment of the wicked (51:4–6).[175]

Secondly, like the Apocalypse of the vine and the cedar, 85:1–11 plays on the contrast between possessing and being possessed (root *nsb*).[176] We should note that 85:9 in a sense answers 36:8: the Roman emperor

---

[171] Cf. the double meaning of *'zl*: "to die"/ "to journey" (Smith, *Dictionary*, 9; Smith, *Thesaurus*, 106–107).

[172] Cf. 1QH XI. Cf. *2 Bar.* 22:3.

[173] The passage may refer to death and afterlife as rest as well.

[174] Cf. further 4 Macc 6:17, 23; 7:20; 13:17; 18:23; Heb 3:11–4.11.

[175] Cf. also *2 Bar.* 83:8.

[176] Cf. also Smith, *Map*, 110–111.

once subdued Israel and took possession of her birthright, but now Israel gains revenge and enters into her real possession in the other world. 85:1–11 highlights this contrast by its choice of words. *2 Baruch* uses forms of the root *nsb*, "to receive," "to possess," on the one hand to describe God's gift to Israel (85:4), and on the other to describe Israel's more active role of taking possession as a result of steadfast belief (85:9).[177] This usage underlines both the firmness and strength of Israel and the legitimacy of Israel's possession of the other world. Further, 85:9 likens the contrast between possessing and being possessed to the contrast between hoping (root *sbr*) and being dishonoured (root *bht*). Thus, the opposite of hope and possession is the humiliation of dispossession by foreigners. The hope (*sabrā*) of the other world, which was born during the time of Abraham (57:2) and fulfiled in 51:1–13, is thus a hope of revenge as well as of the triumphant possession of the promised world in the heights.

This web of metaphors is an important part of the argument pursued by *2 Baruch* in this passage: it does not matter that Israel lost the temple, the city and the Land on earth, since what awaits her outdoes the loss many times over. Thus, on the one hand 85:1–11 plays on the contrast between the earthly versions of the Land—the regions of Palestine, Judah or Jerusalem—and the heavenly world that awaits Israel. These regions belonged to the order of corruption and are therefore not worthy of grief (85:5).[178] *2 Baruch* directs all hope to the other world and moves Israel's bliss to that heavenly location. On the other hand, this passage also draws a parallel between the golden age of the Land on earth and the heavenly realities above. As we have seen in previous chapters, the entire earth, including even Jerusalem, had turned wicked by the time of Baruch. At that time, all former localities of the Land were indeed part of the corruptible world, as 85:5 asserts. But as Chapters Two and Three showed us, and as 85:1–2 proposes, those earthly versions of the Land had also been a place of bliss that for a long time secured Israel's survival. In their time, Israel's fathers had helpers who assisted them in maintaining a righteous way of life, interceded on their behalf with God and thus ensured former generations' survival in the Land.[179] When 85:9 foresees that Israel will be reunited with the fathers after resurrection, it lends the atmosphere

---

[177] Smith, *Dictionary*, 341.
[178] Cf. *2 Bar.* 75:7–8.
[179] Klijn, "Recent Developments," 9–10.

of the life of the fathers on earth to the resurrected life of a united Israel in the heights. In other words, while the other world is the contrast to the wicked Jerusalem and its surroundings in the generation of Baruch, it is also the equivalent to the Land the fathers once enjoyed in Palestine.

Some further indications support this conclusion. Most importantly, *2 Baruch* sets this equation between the earthly Land and the heavenly other world in the broader context of the renewal and revival of the Mosaic covenant and its promises.[180] As several scholars have pointed out, the entire *Epistola Baruch* can be read as a parallel to the testament of Moses in Deut 33.[181] As I have already argued, 84:2–7 makes Baruch's instruction parallel the instructions of Moses to the tribes in the desert. Basically, this mechanism is the central rhetorical device of the *Epistola Baruch*.

78:6–7 and 83:8 both give examples of Baruch's exhortation of the dispersed tribes. In 83:8 Baruch equates their present captivity with the future torment, arguing that their transgressions will exclude them from both worlds if they do not return to righteousness. Exile, the opposite of life in the Land in the corruptible world, is thus paralleled with punishment, the opposite to life in the heights in the future, incorruptible world. A similar argument appears in 78:6–7, where Baruch claims that the dispersed tribes will again receive everlasting hope (root *sbr*) if they turn away from the wickedness that caused their exile. In the event of such a conversion, God's promise to the fathers will still be valid for them, and God will again assemble the dispersed offspring. Thus, like 85:1–11 above, both 78:6–7 and 83:8 make explicit use of the logic and the terminology of the Mosaic covenant to argue the fulfilment of promises and the return to the Land in the heights of heaven.

The Real and Everlasting Place of Promise

2 Bar. 85 confirms a tendency that permeates *2 Baruch* in general: *2 Baruch* replaces Palestine with the other world, but at the same time retains the idea of the Promised Land and uses it to develop the notion

---

[180] Cf. Wright, *Baruch ben Neriah*, 88.

[181] Cf. further Whitters, *Epistle*, 156–158; M.F. Whitters, "Testament and Canon in the Letter of Second Baruch (*2 Baruch* 78–87)," *JSP* 12 (2001): 149–163; L. Hartmann, *Asking for a Meaning: A Study of 1 Enoch 1–5* (ConBNT 12; Lund: CWK Gleerup, 1979), 22–26.

of the other world as the place of the real promise. *2 Baruch* creates an intricate web of allusions and references that build up the other world as the space promised to Israel by God through the covenant. In some passages of the text, such as 84:2–7, Palestine and the other world become equivalents: as Israel once entered Palestine, she will now enter the other world. Other passages, like 57:1–3; 59:1–12 and 75:7, put it more radically. They skip all mention of Palestine and point directly to the other world as the sole place promised to Israel by God. This overall inclination to prefer the heavenly sphere to Palestine further strengthens the tendency to renounce the world that I have already pointed out in previous chapters. In addition, it contributes to the identification of the other world as the real and original Land of Promise. That Land of Promise does not lead to corruption. Rather, it is a glorious and everlasting alternative that waits in the heights, waiting to be realised by Israel's entry. In keeping with the covenant ideology that permeates *2 Baruch*, the other world thus becomes Israel's ultimate Promised Land.

The Final Fulfilment of Promises: Transforming the Heavenly World

The first of the two preceding sections of this chapter showed that *2 Baruch* describes another world in the heights, and that this heavenly other world throughout history has attracted all earthly carriers of holiness. The last carriers to enter the other world were the temple vessels and the righteous Israel. In the second section of the chapter I argued that *2 Baruch* redirects expectations and promises to the other world, in order to underscore that the other world is the real place of promise, at the expense of the earthly locations Palestine, Judah and Jerusalem.

Below I will argue that the transfer of Israel and the temple vessels transforms the other world in heaven. My hypothesis is that the other world is transformed into an extraordinary Land when Israel settles in it and the temple vessels are restored to the heavenly temple.

Transforming the Heavenly World

In the discussion of 51:1–3 above, I pointed out that the splendour that characterised the righteous on earth was retained after resurrection and was further enhanced and perfected after judgement to enable them to receive, or alternatively possess (root *nsb*), the world which had been promised to them.[182] 51:1–3 describes only the first phase of what 51:1–13 presents as a transformation process.[183] The transformation of splendour and the shape of their faces into "the light of their beauty" (51:3) is thus only the first part of that process.[184]

The Angelic Transformation of Israel

51:7–12 describes the continuation of the transformation process:

> For those who have been delivered by their deeds, and for whom the law is now a hope, and understanding an expectation, and wisdom a firmness, wonders will appear to them in their time. For they will see that world (*haw 'almā*) which is invisible to them now, and they will see the time (*zabnā*) which is now hidden from them. And again time will not make them old. For they will dwell in the heights of that world, and they will be like angels, and they will equal stars. And they will be transformed into every form they desire, from fairness to beauty, and from light into the splendour of glory. For the extent (*patyutā*) of Paradise will spread out before them, and to them will be shown (root *ḥw'*) the fairness of the greatness of the living beings under the throne, and the hosts of the angels, who are now held by my word, so that they do not show themselves, and who are held fast by the command so that they will stand in their places until their advent has arrived. And then the excellence in the righteous will become greater than in the angels. For the first will receive the last, the ones they were expecting, and the last those they used to hear had passed away.

This intriguing passage describes how Israel and her surroundings will be transformed in the heavenly world. To match their new place of dwelling in the heights, the righteous become like angels (*malake*) and stars (*kawkbe*).[185] Still, the transformation process does not end there. The righteous are changed from fairness to beauty, and even from

---

[182] Cf. *Mart. Ascen. Isa.* 7:25; Matt 13:43.

[183] Cf. Charles, *Apocalypse of Baruch*, 83; Nickelsburg, *Resurrection*, 174; Cavallin, Life after Death, 80–89; Puech, *Croyance*, 139–141; Cf. T.K. Seim, "Udødelig og Kjønnsløs? Oppstandelseskroppen i lys av Lukas," in *Kropp og oppstandelse* (eds. T. Engberg-Pedersen and I.S. Gilhus; Oslo: Pax Forlag as, 2001), 80–98 at 98.

[184] Cf. in particular 1 Cor 15:35–38.

[185] The heavenly hosts were often equated with stars. The two categories of heavenly phenomena interchanged and stars may therefore have been understood as angelic creatures (Cf. Judg 5:20; Job 38:7; *1 En.* 39:4–7; 104:2–6; *L.A.B.* 33:5). Cf. Himmelfarb, *Ascent to Heaven*, 50; Segal, *Life after Death*, 265; Puech, *Croyance*, 141; Collins, "Afterlife," 126.

light into the splendour of glory (*ziwā dtešbuḥtā*). 51:12 states that Israel's excellence at that point will be even greater than the excellence of angels. Then, the first and the last meet again, probably a reference to the reunion of the generations of 'fathers' (85:9) with the generation of Baruch's time.[186]

The theme of angelic transformation is quite common in contemporaneous texts of *2 Baruch*.[187] According to M. Himmelfarb, a series of apocalypses include this motif. They either apply it to prominent figures like Enoch, Moses, Isaiah and Abraham, or they alternatively propose that the righteous in general become angel-like.[188] In these cases, as in *2 Baruch*, the transformation of Israel into angels is most commonly described as the reward of the righteous after death.[189] Some texts, like *Mart. Ascen. Isa.* 8–9, also share *2 Baruch*'s notion that the righteous may surpass the angels in rank in the heavenly hierarchy.[190] In the case of *2 Bar.* 51:12–13, the upper part of the heavenly hierarchy is the place where the generations of Israel reunite. So, during the first centuries C.E., *2 Bar.* 51's description of Israel's destiny was not unusual in this regard. The idea that Israel would ascend to heaven and become like stars and angels, and even excel them, was a common one at the time.[191]

---

[186] This may refer to the exiled tribes, but the patriarchs are more likely (14.8; 85.3). Cf. Puech, *Croyance*, 141.

[187] Cf. Dan 12:2–4; Matt 22:30; Luke 20:36; *T. Mos.* 10; *1 En.* 104; *2 En.* 9:17–19; *4 Ezra* 7:97; 1QSb IV, 24–28; *Her.* 88.

[188] Cf. *1 En.* 14; 71:11; *2 En.* 21:3; 22:6, 10; 46:2; *Ezek. Trag.* 1.68–82; *Mos.* 1, 158; *Mart. Ascen. Isa.* 8–9; *Apoc. Ab.* 17:1–6; 1QH III, 21–22; *Sacr.* 5; *T. Mos.* 10.

[189] Cf. Dan 12:3; *T. Mos.* 10; *Apoc. Zeph.* 2:7; 11:5–6. Cf. Nickelsburg, *Resurrection*, 85. Cf. further W. Bousset, "Die Himmelreise der Seele," *ARW* 4 (1901): 136–169; 229–273; J.J. Collins, "A Throne in the Heavens: Apotheosis in pre-Christian Judaism," in *Death, Ecstasy, and Other Worldly Journeys* (ed. J.J. Collins and M. Fishbane; Albany: SUNY Press, 1995), 41–58; Collins, "Apocalyptic Eschatology," 21–48; C.R.A. Morray-Jones, "Transformational Mysticism in the Apocalyptic-Merkabah Tradition," *JJS* 43 (1992): 1–31; Himmelfarb, *Ascent to Heaven*, 4; 114; Segal, *Life after Death*, 303–308.

[190] Cf. Stemberger, *Leib der Auferstehung*, 89; Himmelfarb, *Ascent to Heaven*, 56–57; 71; Puech, *Croyance*, 141. *1 En.* 62:15–16 argues that Enoch became second only to God (Cf. Himmelfarb, *Ascent to Heaven*, 61; 71). Cf. further Bogaert for a list of relevant rabbinic parallels (*Apocalypse de Baruch II*, 95).

[191] Cf. Bogaert, *Apocalypse de Baruch II*, 93–95; Stemberger, *Leib der Auferstehung*, 88–89; Himmelfarb, *Ascent to Heaven*, 70; Collins, "Afterlife," 125. Cf. further F. Cumont, *Lux Perpetua* (Paris: P. Geuthner, 1949), 142–288.

Can Israel Transform the Heavenly World?

As a series of commentators have already noted, 51:1–13 makes an explicit link between anthropology and geography/cosmology.[192] The passage underscores that the shape of a person corresponds to the nature of his location: people are transformed to fit the natures of their destinations. The righteous become more glorious and shining in order to qualify them to enter the undying, promised world, and they become like stars and angels to make them fit for the heavenly world into which they enter. In fact, several contemporaneous texts associate a transformation of human form with a change of place. This is particularly common in descriptions of ascent into heaven.[193] And as G.W.E. Nickelsburg has pointed out, a series of texts attests to the notion that judgement and exaltation are intimately connected, and that judgement commonly leads to the exaltation of the righteous, also in the spatial meaning of the word.[194]

However, is it possible the transformation process described in *2 Bar.* 51:1–13 not only changes human shapes, but changes the spaces Israel enters as well (Cf. 49:3)? Is this not only an adjustment of human form, but also and adjustment of space? I started this chapter by trying to isolate the other world as a spatial entity *in se*. I argued that *2 Baruch's* other world was a heavenly reality hidden from mankind. That reality remained unapproachable during the course of the corruptible world and was only seen on special occasions by high profiled individuals. The heavenly world indeed exists before Israel enters it, but it is not yet a lived reality to Israel. In the following I will look at how the entrance of the righteous into the other world changes that heavenly space: how does 51:1–13 describe this spatial transformation, and how does the entry of Israel transform the heavenly world?

---

[192] Cf. in particular Charles, *Apocalypse of Baruch*, 81–83; Harnisch, *Verhängnis*, 228; Stemberger, *Leib der Auferstehung*, 89. This notion is particularly evident in 48:48–52.7, but as the present study has argued, this is a general tendency in *2 Baruch*.

[193] Cf. *1 En.* 62:14–16; 108; *Mart. Ascen. Isa.* 7:25; 11; *Apoc. Ab.* 15:4; *Jos. Asen.* 18:7; 1 Cor 15. Scholars generally accept that *2 Bar.* 49–51 describes a resurrection of the body. Possibly, this passage, in contrast to other passages in *2 Baruch* (30:1–4; 36:10–11. Cf. *4 Ezra* 5:25–28; 7:88; *Jub.* 23:26–31; *T. Ab.* B 7), envisions a resurrection of the *dead*, i.e., the entire human being, body and soul (Stemberger, *Leib der Auferstehung*, 87; 90–96). Cf. further Charles, *Apocalypse of Baruch*, 82; Collins, "Afterlife," 124–125; 131; Lied, "Recognizing the Righteous Remnant?"

[194] Cf. Nickelsburg, *Resurrection*, 27; 39–40; 85–86; 171; 174; Himmelfarb, *Ascension to Heaven*, 58. Cf. Isa 24; Dan 12, *T. Mos.* 10; *1 En.* 104.

An initial, implicit, change consists of the transformation of heavenly space *from* a place of judgement (51:1–3). As we have seen in the above presentation, *2 Baruch* described the other world before Israel's entry as a heavenly court set for the day of judgement. When the judgement is over, however, the text presents that world as a space that is transformed together with those who enter it. 51:3 reminds us that the heights are not only the location of the divine council, but that the undying world is also Israel's promised world. However, that promise has not yet been fulfiled, and that world is therefore not yet manifest to Israel: it still remains a place of future promise.

The explicit transformation of the heavenly world starts when Israel enters it in 51:7–13. The passage describes two phases of transformation: the world which until then had been invisible at this moment becomes visible to Israel (51:7–8), and then, after a new phase of anthropological transformation, the extent[195] of Paradise spreads out before Israel's eyes, as do also the spaces of the hosts of heaven (51:11). There, the righteous enter into the heavenly topography constituted by the angelic hierarchy and meet their forefathers (51:12–13).

The first spatial transformation that takes place when the righteous enter the heights is thus that that world becomes visible to those who enter. 51:7–8 expresses this twice: 51:7 states that wonders will appear to them, or more precisely: wonders will be seen by them (*nethazyān lhun*, root *ḥz'*). 51:8 develops this theme: the world which was invisible (*lā methze*, root *ḥz'*), and hidden (root *ks'*) appears to the righteous (*lhun*). Two points deserve attention. Firstly, it is this sudden visibility that makes the heavenly world manifest to Israel. Although *2 Baruch* argues that the other world has been there throughout history, it becomes a reality to Israel only when it becomes visible to her.[196] Secondly, this manifestation of the world is dependent on Israel's act of seeing. The manifestation is relative to Israel's perception.[197] The same two points are repeated in the subsequent spatial transformation in 51:11: Par-

---

[195] Cf. Charles, *Apocalypse of Baruch*, 85; Klijn, "2 Baruch," 638. *2 Bar.* 59:8, "the extent of Paradise", may also be translated "the greatness of Paradise," or "the abundance of Paradise" (Cf. Smith, *Dictionary*, 470; Cf. Smith, *Thesaurus*, 3787).

[196] On the importance of seeing and being seen, cf. *2 Bar.* 51:6; *4 Ezra* 7:37–38; *1 En.* 104:2. Cf. further Nickelsburg, *Resurrection*, 84.

[197] It is probably not insignificant that the other world manifests itself to Israel in an act of seeing. *2 Bar.* 51 describes Baruch's vision, which is part of the instruction to his followers. The passage describes how the other world, which currently is visible only for visionaries at special occasions, later will be seen by all. At that moment only, the other world turns into a reality the followers can *see*. In the present, they can only *hear*

adise spreads out to its full extents in front of the righteous (*netpašṭun*[198] *qdāmayhun*), and the space of the heavenly hosts is shown to them as they arrive (root *'t*). Israel sees the heavenly hosts, just as she saw the heavenly world in 51:7–8. Similarly, the Paradise of this passage is not described as a fixed location, but as a place that expands in the presence of, or "in front of" (*qdām*), Israel. This relative perspective is again applied to describe how these spaces come into being for Israel. Thus, 51:7–12 gives no static description of these otherworldly spaces. Instead, these spaces turn into reality for the righteous when they perceive them and enter them. The heavenly world thus becomes a manifest reality for Israel.

In addition to these acts of seeing, the arrival of the righteous destabilises the hierarchy of the heights. Consequently, as the above discussion of heavenly topography has pointed out, the newly arrived inevitably transform the socially conceived spatial structure of the heights. 51:12–13 states explicitly that the righteous will be more excellent than the angels and that this elevated location is the place where the generations of Israel will meet again. However, the choice of words in 51:10–11 suggests that the righteous will not only surpass the angels, but will also excel the other living creatures under the throne. The greatness of the living creatures is described as "fair" (*šuprā*), whereas the righteous are transformed from mere fairness to beauty (*yayutā*). Similarly, 51:10 says that the righteous will turn "from light into the splendour of beauty." The word *nuhrā*, "light," is commonly applied to describe the lights of the firmament.[199] The righteous thus move beyond the light of the stars and into the enhanced brightness of beauty. The righteous, potentially 'all Israel', intrude in the heavenly hierarchy that constitute the topography and social geography of the heights, and establish themselves as an assembly next to God's throne.[200]

It is not entirely clear how these phases of transformation and the spaces they shape relate to each other. Probably, 51:10–13 describe two phases, as has been suggested here. Paradise and the spaces of the hosts can thus be localised in the loftier part of heaven. It is however also

---

about it in Baruch's instruction. Cf. further the function of seeing in Gen 12:1; 13:4–5; Deut 34:2.

[198] Root *pšṭ*.

[199] Cf. *2 Bar.* 10:11–12. Cf. Smith, *Dictionary*, 330; Smith, *Thesaurus*, 2302. Cf. Dan 12:3 and *b. Ber.* 17a.

[200] Cf. Nickelsburg for another point of view (*Resurrection*, 85).

possible that the passage is meant to describe overlapping processes and that the spaces may therefore interchange.[201] Heaven and Paradise are used interchangeably both in biblical texts and in later exegesis, and the same tendency appears in descriptions of Paradise and the city.[202] Both options are possible and they are not necessarily mutually exclusive. As I have pointed out in earlier chapters, 2 Baruch tolerates considerable spatial overlap.

Based on these tendencies in the text, I will suggest that the establishment of Israel in the heavenly world is a space-shaping act. This passage of 2 Baruch does not describe how Israel enters a static space. On the contrary, the heavenly world is transformed at Israel's arrival. Moreover, we see that the righteous, both the fathers and the generations of Baruch's time, themselves become components of that space as they assemble. And if 2 Baruch in fact envisions an assembly of the tribes, this is where and when it happens. In any case, the righteous become part of the heavenly topography.

51:1–13 is not unique in its emphasis on Israel's space-shaping acts. Interestingly, 37:1, describing the place of the grand finale of the Apocalypse of the vine and the cedar as a plain of unfading flowers, bases otherworldly space on the establishment of the resurrected in that space. The Syriac of the passage literally reads that "it," the vine, "and all surrounding it"—"the plain filled with flowers that do not fade"— expands, while the cedar burns.[203] The Syriac, then, suggests that it is the Messiah, his followers and their surroundings that expand into a plain of un-withering flowers. In other words, the space 37:1 describes is constituted by the Messiah and his followers into that space.

As I have already suggested, the Apocalypse of the vine and the cedar describes how the Messiah and his forces destroy the cedar, the forest as well as their surroundings. The destruction is first described as an uprooting and extinction of the forest and the chief cedar. However, 36:6 adds that the location where the forest and the cedar had grown would not even be known any more after the destruction. As we saw in Chapter Two, the suggestion that a place is no longer known to anyone implies that the location ceases to exist.[204] The restoration and

---

[201] Cf. Bogaert, *Apocalypse de Baruch I*, 422; K.L. Schmidt, "Jerusalem als Urbild und Abbild," *Eranos-Jahrbuch* 18 (1950): 207–248; Stemberger, *Leib der Auferstehung*, 90.

[202] Cf. Harnisch, *Verhängnis*, 111; Laato, *Star*, 382.

[203] Cf. the suggestions of Charles, *Apocalypse of Baruch*, 63; Violet, *Apokalypsen*, 254; Bogaert, *Apocalypse de Baruch I*, 487; Klijn, "2 Baruch," 632.

[204] Cf. pp. 41–42.

expansion of the plain of unfading flowers in 37:1 is thus not only a restoration of righteousness to power, it is also a recreation of its space. Thus, the righteous do not simply reoccupy the plain of the forest; they are themselves constitutive in the making of the new plain, that is, the other paradisiacal world.[205] In contemporaneous literature, the imagery of unfading flowers is commonly applied to describe immortality, resurrection and new life in a paradisiacal world. The plain of unfading flowers in 37:1 is thus a description of the otherworldly existence of the Messiah and the resurrected Israel following the universal triumph of the Messianic reign.[206]

We see, thus, that the establishment of the righteous in the heavenly world is fundamental to the transformation of that space into a redemptive place. Like 51:1–13 above, the spatiality of the transformed plain is fully dependent on the existence of the righteous in it. Probably, we could also ascribe the same quality to 85:9's concept 'rest with the fathers' as the goal of Israel's journey, as well as to 'come to you' in 77:6. The reassembly of the dispersed righteous and the meeting with past generations is therefore what constitutes redemption in the heavenly world.[207] Quite literally, the righteous become part of the space of the world into which they enter.

Actualising the Model City/Sanctuary

The advent and the establishment of Israel in the other world in 51:1–13 transform that heavenly world into the place of Israel's ultimate redemption. In other words, the other world changes into a place-for-Israel. Does the transformed heavenly world turn into an ultimate Land of Israel?

---

[205] Note also, that 37:1, like 51:7–12, describes the making of the plain as a process: the plain comes into being.

[206] It is not clear whether 37:1 describes the Messianic reign in-between worlds in these terms (Cf. pp. 189–191), or whether this is a description of the other world. I understand it as a description of the other world. Firstly, since the imagery 37:1 applies is commonly used to the place of the resurrected, and secondly, because the passage that precedes it (36:10–11) suggests resurrection. Still, the Apocalypse of the vine and the cedar does not suggest clear cut divides between the Messianic era and the life of Israel in the other world. The divide is much more fuzzy, not the least because the vision alludes to a possible resurrection (36:10–37–31), whereas the explanation part ends at Mount Zion (40:1–4), suggesting a correspondence between the two.

[207] Cf. 2 Bar. 30:2.

In the preceding analysis I have pointed out that *2 Baruch* attests
to the widespread notion of the heavenly model city/sanctuary and
the earthly copy in Jerusalem. One of the central arguments of the
text is that the loss of the temple in Jerusalem is of no importance,
since the real, everlasting model of the city/sanctuary exists safe and
sound under God's protection in heaven. Now, my discussion of heavenly spatiality above displayed how *2 Baruch* envisions the basic layout
of that model. God's throne is a summit and a focal point, whereas
the heavenly hosts dwell under it. As some scholars have pointed out,
this heavenly layout has the appearance of a royal throne room and
a heavenly temple, or possibly a celestial city. In light of the topography 4:1–7 describes, it would be wrong to separate these images.
There is no clear divide between temple and palace. Neither can
we fruitfully separate the city and the sanctuary in the text. Hence,
there is good reason to believe that the imagery of the heavenly host
and the imagery of the celestial city/sanctuary are interchangeable in
2 Baruch. Given this relation we might say that Israel arrives at the
heavenly city/sanctuary when she enters into the heavenly hierarchy
in 51:11–13. Israel thus both returns to 'the mother'[208] *and* joins with the
fathers.[209]

In the present chapter I have shown that *2 Baruch* envisions an ongoing transferal of persons as well as artefacts from earth to heaven.
Throughout history vehicles of holiness have escaped the earth, until all
holiness becomes gathered in heaven. The imminent destruction of the
Jerusalem temple made this transferal urgent. The virgins in the temple
cast the white linen fabrics they spin, either the veil or the high priest's
garment (or both), into the fire to transport them to heaven, and the
false priests of the Jerusalem temple threw the temple keys up to God
(10:18–19). The virgins and the false priests thus handed over central
cultic objects to heaven. As a result, they add, or possibly reintegrate,
earthly artefacts of cultic importance into the heavenly model.

As we have seen, however, the temple vessels seem to occupy a
special role in *2 Baruch*. *2 Baruch* seemingly ascribes a process of death
and resurrection to the vessels and makes their restoration equivalent
to the reestablishment of Israel in the heavenly world. As 6:9 points
out, once the vessels are restored, they are restored to the everlasting

---

[208] Cf. Chapter Four, pp. 119–120.
[209] Cf. Chapter Five, pp. 156–159. Note also how Baruch's dilemma in 3:2–3 is
overcome.

sanctuary in the heavenly Jerusalem. It is possible therefore, that *2 Baruch* implies a restoration of the temple cult in the heavenly temple.[210]

Both 4:2–3 and 32:4 assert that there already is a sanctuary in heaven: the real, model sanctuary. To be precise, 4:2–3 states that there is a *building (benyānā)* in the heights, complete with the shape of the tabernacle and its vessels (4:5). But, according to 32:4, this building must be renewed (root *ḥdt*), and perfected into eternity. However, since *2 Baruch* never actually describes this act of renewal, but only presents it as a prediction, it is not clear what is implied by the term. Still, since the use of forms of the root *ḥdt* may indicate that the renewal of the temple is in fact a rededication of an existing temple,[211] and since *2 Baruch* stresses the transportation of cultic artefacts to the heavenly realm, it is likely that the renewal of the sanctuary consists of a rededication of the building (4:2) and an active restoration of Israel's service to God in the heavenly temple. In other words, the temple edifice has remained ready and waiting in the heights, and now it is realised for Israel through the transfer of the cultic artefacts and the restoration of the cult. Thus Israel re-enters God's presence.

This interpretation also makes other passages more meaningful. Firstly, the rest attained by the righteous in the other world according to 85:9 may be likened to the Sabbath rest, as was the rest that followed the inauguration of the temple in Jerusalem in 61:3. Secondly, this reading supports the idea of the previous chapter that the selection of foods in 29:4–8 may be read as a preparation for the reintroduction of the temple service. The finest foods have been gathered from the passing world to be offered up in the heavenly sanctuary. And thirdly, as Klijn has pointed out, *2 Baruch* proposes a clear correlation between the devastation of Zion and its following depopulation.[212] The restoration of the heavenly sanctuary would logically add authority to Baruch's claim that the dispersed tribes still have a chance to return. Once the cult is restored, and if they return to righteousness, they may repossess their inheritance. The link *2 Baruch* suggests between the resurrection of the righteous and the restoration of the temple vessels to the heavenly temple further confirms that the re-inauguration of the temple cult is connected to the establishment of Israel in the heavenly world. Thus, an

---

[210] Cf. Bogaert, *Apocalypse de Baruch I*, 422–425.
[211] Smith, *Dictionary*, 128; Smith, *Thesaurus*, 1206–1207.
[212] Klijn, "Recent Developments," 9–10.

important part of Israel's space-transforming act is her renewed service to God in the real and everlasting heavenly temple.

Consequently, one might say that when the generations of Israel assemble and establish themselves at the highest level of the heavenly hierarchy, they replace the false priests of the Jerusalem temple and establish themselves as the real priests of the heavenly sanctuary. They thus dwell in the central, lofty, part of the heavenly city/sanctuary above the other inhabitants of the heavenly city.

The Realisation of Paradise

According to 51:11, Israel did not only see and arrive at the heavenly hosts. Paradise also spread out in front of her. How do we understand this notion of the heavenly Paradise and its relation to the city/sanctuary?

In the above discussion I suggested that 4:1–7 was particularly important to this study, since that passage presents God's answer to Baruch's worries in 3:4–9.[213] 4:1–7 shows that Baruch's concerns about the earthly Land, city, and sanctuary, analysed in Chapter Two of this study, were groundless, since the real city/sanctuary is the heavenly one, not the earthly copy in Jerusalem. The passage further states that the real city/sanctuary is preserved with God along with Paradise until the day they will be revealed (4:3). Thus, there is a heavenly model of the city/sanctuary and a Paradise that no enemies can destroy.

Now, as I noted in passing in the preceding discussion of 4:1–7, 4:2 makes a quite radical interpretation of Isa 49:16. This has been pointed out by several scholars.[214] Murphy says:

> The verse in its original context promises a rebuilding of the ruined city of Jerusalem and assures that God will never forget Zion (...). Given that context, the author makes an astounding assertion. That verse did not apply to "this building now built in your midst" at all! Rather, it applied to the building which is 'preserved' (root *ntr*) with God, and this building is presumably in heaven with God. The earthly Temple is not the one God has promised to remember forever. One can only conclude that all

---

[213] Cf. Chapter Two. Cf. Murphy, *Structure and Meaning*, 85–92; Wright, *Baruch ben Neriah*, 78.

[214] Charles, *Apocalypse of Baruch*, 6; Bogaert, *Apocalypse de Baruch* I, 362; II, 14; Harnisch, *Verhängnis*, 111.

similar promises concerning Zion also refer to the heavenly one and not to the earthly one.[215]

In this excerpt Murphy correctly proposes that 4:2 creates a shift in expectations from the earthly reality to the heavenly world. However, Murphy limits his interpretation to the destiny of Zion. It is my opinion that 4:1–7 also answers the more general concerns expressed in 3:9: "And where is all that which you said to Moses regarding us." Given this, the promises God made to Moses regarding the Land will therefore also be fulfiled in the other world.

As Chapter Two pointed out, Baruch's concern for the Land plays an important role in 3:4–9. The Land, be it Palestine, Judah, or Jerusalem, was vital to Israel throughout history, and Baruch worries that the dispossession of Jerusalem will lead to the extinction of Israel. As the promises to Moses are transferred to the heavenly model, Paradise takes the position Palestine, Judah, and Jerusalem once had in relation to Jerusalem, the city, and the temple on earth. In other words, the earthly triad consisting of temple, Jerusalem, and Palestine, is replaced by the heavenly triad temple, city, and Paradise. Thus, the heavenly triad can be grasped as the model Land awaiting Israel in heaven. This suggestion would also answer Murphy's concern about the relationship between the heavenly city and the heavenly Paradise: "The placing of these two ideas [the heavenly Jerusalem and the heavenly Paradise] in proximity here, though it is somewhat awkward, helps in this redirection of hopes."[216] If Paradise is the location of Israel's Land this combination is not awkward: Paradise can be understood as the city's surrounding, or alternatively the territorial extension of the city.[217]

We have now seen that 51:11–13 can be read as an occupation and actualisation of the heavenly city/sanctuary through the reestablishment of the cult. What, then, about Paradise? What happens when Israel enters it? In the introductory discussion of 4:3–5's Paradise, I stressed the temporary character of Adam's Paradise. In contrast, in 51:11 Israel turns the heavenly Paradise into a permanent place of dwelling by her entry. Paradise also existed in heaven before the arrival

---

[215] Murphy, *Structure and Meaning*, 86.

[216] Murphy, *Structure and Meaning*, 89.

[217] The notion of Paradise and New Jerusalem combined is not uncommon (Cf. Dan 5:12; Rev 21; *Jub.* 8:19). Cf. Levenson, *Sinai and Zion*, 128–133. Volz and Harnisch have both underscored that Paradise and Jerusalem tend to merge (Volz, *Eschatologie*, 412; Harnisch, *Verhängis*, 111).

of Israel, but to Israel it is her advent and establishment that turn Paradise into a manifest place.[218]

In Chapter Three I argued that the Land is not a territory that passively lies there. Two interrelated factors transform a territory into the Land: the righteous dwelling of Israel and the residency of the divine presence there. In the case of the Lands of the Davidic kings, the region of Palestine had to be settled by the righteous and administered according to the Law to become the Land. In addition, the realisation of the Land demanded the proximity of God's presence. The inauguration of the Jerusalem temple secured God's dwelling in the sanctuary under the reigns of David and Solomon. Chapter Two underscored the importance of God's presence on earth, the vital cultic role of Israel on earth, and the seeming catastrophe that followed the withdrawal of the divine presence to heaven. From that point onwards, God could only be approached through visions, and importantly, through his Law.[219] The general idea is thus that an area must be inhabited righteously in the presence of God to become Israel's Land. Until that point it remains a place of promise, a place that awaits fulfilment. Chapter Three also pointed out that the inauguration of the temple is commonly connected to the fulfilment of God's creational act. An act of temple dedication also implies that a process of creation is completed. As I also pointed out in that chapter, the inauguration of the temple not only signals the completion of creation, it marks the fulfilment of the Land promise and in effect connects the two. The inauguration of the temple thus creates a world for Israel. *2 Baruch* stresses that the purpose of God's creative act is to make a world for Israel, since the surrounding world was inaccessible to Israel due to its corruption. It is quite possible that the same logic applies to the dedication of the heavenly temple in 32:1–6. Although that passage is not entirely clear, it probably makes a connection between the dedication of the heavenly temple and the renewal of God's creational act, since the passage links these two events, and only these, with the other world. In effect, the realisation of Paradise and the restoration of the temple cult in the heavenly temple becomes both a Land-shaping and a world-transforming activity (Cf. 57:2).

Given the above interpretation of Israel's arrival in the heavenly world, 51:11–13 can be read as an actualisation of Paradise and the

---

[218] Cf. Stemberger's discussion of Paradise and Land in *4 Ezra* 7.26 (*Leib der Auferstehung*, 83).

[219] Cf. Chapter Four, pp. 132–138.

heavenly city/sanctuary as a place for Israel. Israel has resumed the cult and established herself in the celestial city. And, importantly, this is the place where the generations of Israel reassemble. As some scholars have already pointed out, the topography of this place resembles Israel's Land on earth.[220] 51:10 may indicate that Israel will inhabit the most elevated part of the heavenly world.[221] This lofty, paradisiacal region of immeasurable size spreads out in front of Israel, while she dwells under the throne in the heavenly city. Since Israel in fact appropriates the heavenly model and makes it manifest as her space, this can be read as describing the establishment of Israel in the heavenly Land. This is a Land that will never fail her and that surpasses its predecessors in excellence.

Shared Imagery and Collocations: Beauty, Fairness, Glory and Light

The hypothesis that the heavenly model becomes realised as Israel's Land is strengthened by the collocations of 2 Bar. 4; 10 and 51. Sayler first called attention to the link between 4:2–6; 10:17 and 51:7–14. She pointed out that these three passages apply the same terminology and motifs.[222] Her example was the use of the Syriac term šuprā ("fairness") and yayutā ("beauty") in the passages. After the fall of Zion, Baruch saw no meaning in talking about fairness and beauty any more (10:17). But, in 51:10 fairness and beauty reappear as central characteristics of the righteous in their heavenly dwelling. As Murphy has pointed out, fairness and beauty first and foremost belong to the other world in 2 Baruch. 2 Baruch applies them to describe qualities of God (21:23; 54:8) and the status of the righteous in the other world (51:3, 10).[223] This is interesting, since aspects of beauty are commonly associated with the Land and Mount Zion.[224]

---

[220] Cf. Grelot, "Géographie mythique," 33–69; J. Danielou, "Terre et Paradis chez les Pères de l'Église," *Eranos-Jahrbuch* 22 (1953): 433–472; Bogaert, *Apocalypse de Baruch II*, 94; Stemberger, *Leib der Auferstehung*, 90; Murphy, *Structure and Meaning*, 89; Puech, *Croyance*, 142, Barth, *Diesseits*, 21.

[221] According to 51:10, the righteous will live in the heights of "that world" (*haw ʿalmā*). It is not clear, however, whether the passage describes heaven in these terms or whether it implies additional topographical distinction in the heavenly world (Cf. Bogaert, *Apocalypse de Baruch II*, 94).

[222] Sayler, *Promises*, 66.

[223] Murphy, *Structure and Meaning*, 101.

[224] Cf. Dan 11:16, 41; *1 En.* 89:40; Cf. Levenson, *Sinai and Zion*, 129. The beauty of the heavenly city is also expressed in *Apoc. Zeph.* 2; *4 Ezra* 10:50; *Jos. Asen.* 6:3–4; 16:16.

In my opinion, beauty and fairness are part of a group of concepts that often appear together to describe first the earthly versions of the Land and then its otherworldly equivalent: light (*nuhrā*) and glory (*tešbuḥtā*) tend to be added to beauty and fairness in both contexts.[225] According to 10:12, Baruch urges the sun and the moon to extinguish their light since the light of Zion is darkened.[226] In the heights, on the other hand, there is a fountain of light (54:13) and there are treasuries of light (59:11). 51:3 and 10 show that in the heavenly world the faces of the righteous shine with light, in correspondence with their heavenly surroundings. There is thus no doubt that the lights are relit in the heavenly life of the righteous.[227] Likewise, 'glory' is first and foremost reserved for the heavenly world.[228] 51:16 describes the heavenly world as a world that provides glory to those who choose righteousness on earth. Interestingly, 61:7, depicting the Land during the reign of David and Solomon, ascribe the same quality to the Land which was free of sin at that time. Thus, the concepts of fairness, beauty, light and glory tend to appear together, or in various combinations, in *2 Baruch*'s descriptions of life both in the region of Palestine and in the heavenly world. This underscores the fact that *2 Baruch* connects these qualities to the earthly as well as the heavenly realisation of Israel's Land.

The Postponed Consequence of Righteousness

As many scholars have already pointed out, the Law is the key both to survival in the corruptible world and the ticket to the other world. The ones who followed the commandments and lived according to the Law on earth will survive God's judgement and qualify for life in the heavenly world after resurrection.[229]

---

[225] Cf. *2 Bar.* 21:23; 82:6–7.

[226] In addition, we have seen that the Law, alternatively Baruch as the interpreter of the Law, has served as a light throughout the end-time (*2 Bar.* 17:4; 46:2; 54:5; 59:2; 77:16). Note also that the concepts of light and life may interchange (Job 3:20).

[227] Cf. further *2 Bar.* 34:1; 48:50 and related notions in Isa 60:1, 3, 19; Dan 12:3; *4 Ezra* 7:97; *L.A.B.* 19:12; 23:6; *2 En.* 31:2. Cf. Nickelsburg, *Resurrection*, 26.

[228] Cf., e.g., *2 Bar.* 5:2; 15:8; 21:23–25; 32:4; 54:8; 82:6. Note that 'glory' is a wide concept. Glory may appear as a place, and glory may be a hypostasis of God's attribute (Cf. L.W. Hurtado, *One God, One Lord: Early Christian Devotion and Ancient Jewish Monotheism* (Philadelphia: Fortress Press, 1988), 17–18; Himmelfarb, *Ascent to Heaven*, 58). Cf. Tob 14:5; Phil 2; 1 Cor 15:40.

[229] Cf. *2 Bar.* 54:15; Cf. Charles, *Apocalypse of Baruch*, 26; Kolenkow, "Introduction,"

Throughout this study I have argued that the righteous practices of Israel shape space. I have argued that the Land in *2 Baruch* is first and foremost recognisable as the spatial function of Israel's righteousness. Life according to the Law should therefore be a factor 51:1–13 should single out. But, where are Israel's acts of righteousness in 51:1–13? Israel sees the heights, Paradise expands in front of her and the hosts are shown to her as she arrives. These acts are however not specifically related to fulfiling the Law. 51:7–8 provides us with an answer:

> For those who have been delivered by their deeds, and for whom the law is now a hope, and understanding an expectation, and wisdom a firmness, wonders will appear to them in their time. For they will see that world which is invisible to them now, and they will see the time which is now hidden from them.

This passage makes it clear that the other world is the reward for those who act righteously now (*hāšā*) on earth. The consequences of their righteous acts are in other words postponed until the heavenly world.[230] Thus the heavenly Land is the spatial function of the acts of the righteous generations of Israel on earth. The same mechanism operates in 75:7–8: the one who brought Israel out of Egypt will bring her to resurrected life again if she acknowledges here and now the sovereignty of God. In light of my former discussion of this passage, the choice Israel makes *here and now* therefore creates Land in the afterlife.[231]

This point adds importance to Baruch's struggle to instruct the dispersed tribes. Their choice in this life is vital to the further existence of a Land in the other world. Since Land is dependent on righteous acts, Israel's righteousness will decide whether there will be Land or not. Someone must have been righteous for the Land to become manifest. The way the tribes behave thus decides their own eschatological destiny, but it also affects Israel's redemption as a people. If no group remains righteous, there will be no Land.

The logic of this argument also explains why *2 Baruch* pays so much attention to the reversed nature of the world of the end-time. *2 Baruch* tries to justify why righteousness does not pay off here and now (14:1–15:8). Life in accordance with the Law clearly brought Israel protection, but the forces of the corruptible world were still triumphant and con-

---

128; Harnisch, *Verhängnis*, 182–193; Sayler, *Promises*, 65–66; Murphy, *Structure and Meaning*, 36; Münchow, *Ethik*, 110–111.

[230] Cf. *T. Levi* 13:5.

[231] Note also how the terminology resembles the terminology of 61:2–7.

tinued to challenge Israel's survival. The solution to this problem is that
the consequence of earthly righteousness belongs to the other, heavenly
world. Münchow has put this particularly well in German:

> Die Bedeutung der Ethik liegt darin, dass sie die voneinander getren-
> nten Äonen zu einer dem Menschen erfahrbaren Einheit zwingt. Daher
> betont der 2. Bar. das Gesetz, das nicht eine die Lage der Gegenwart
> verbessernde, sondern eine ins heilvolle Eschaton führende Grösse ist.
> Das Gesetz ist die Norm des Gerichts. Seine Heilswirksamkeit wird in
> 2. Bar. nicht bezweifelt denn die Teilhabe am künftigen Heil ist von der
> (möglichen) Erfüllung des Gesetzes abhängig.[232]

Münchow emphasises the relationship between the two worlds. They
are connected through the logic of the Law. Acts in accordance with
the Law in this world are rewarded in the other world.[233]

Thus, the heavenly Land is the spatial outcome, the reward, of
Israel's righteous acts on earth. This spatial manifestation is therefore
the final fulfilment of the postponed hope and promise and the ultimate
consequence of Israel's righteousness on earth.

The Comprehensive Land of Israel

The question now is: does *2 Baruch* discard the Land and replace it with
the heavenly other world, or is the heavenly world transformed into
the Land? One of Murphy's main arguments in *The Structure and Meaning of Second Baruch* is that *2 Baruch* creates new hope in a situation of
despair through rejecting the Land, Jerusalem and its temple, and redi-
recting the promises to the other world.[234] Murphy thus sees the change
of eschatological place implied in the shift between two inherently different worlds, as the main device for keeping hopes up. Murphy is no
doubt correct that *2 Baruch* redirects hope towards the heavenly world,
and that Palestine, Jerusalem and the earthly temple are rejected as
objects of hope. However, I am not convinced that *2 Baruch* describes
the manifest heavenly reality as a radically different place in a radically
different world. Rather, we may bring some nuances to Murphy's clear
division between worlds on the basis of the epistemological shift implied
by a praxis epistemology.

---

[232] Münchow, *Ethik*, 111; Leunberger, "Ort und Funktion," 228–229; 235; 237.
[233] Cf. also Charles, *Apocalypse of Baruch*, 25; 83; Harnisch, *Verhängnis*, 185; T.W. Willet,
Eschatology in the Theodicies of 2 Baruch and 4 Ezra (JSPSup 4; Sheffield, JSOT Press, 1989),
127.
[234] Cf. Murphy, *Structure and Meaning*, 28; 125–126.

This chapter has pointed out that *2 Baruch* subscribes to the widespread idea of a heavenly model and an earthly copy. In addition, *2 Baruch* describes the heavenly realm of the model and the earthly world of the copy in terms of two worlds set apart in space and time. I have argued that earth and heaven are nevertheless connected. *2 Baruch* describes a transportation of artefacts and people from earth to heaven during the course of the corruptible world. Thus, when the corruptible world and its proponents are destroyed, there are earthly objects in heaven. I have shown these objects to be vital to the realisation of the heavenly world as a manifest place for Israel. Moreover, once the corruptible world dies, there will only be one world; the heavenly, incorruptible one. From this point onwards there is no dichotomy between the worlds. Rather, it is my opinion that aspects of the earthly copy become integrated into the heavenly model through a process of transformation, and that this process shapes the heavenly model into a manifest, comprehensive place. It is also my opinion that the focus on the difference between the two worlds has overshadowed the similarity between the copy and the model: although they exist in worlds set apart, to Israel the copy and the actualised model serve as the same place in their history of redemption. In other words, as spatial constructions and outcome of Israel's practices, they overlap.

I have argued above that the Land-making righteousness of Israel on earth is rewarded only in heaven. This means, as Münchow has pointed out, that the heavenly and earthly realities connect, in Israel's experience of cause and effect. The heavenly Land, the spatial function of her righteousness on earth, thus links the spaces and makes the divide above all a postponement in time.

The description of Israel's future reward in 85:1–11 shows this phenomenon particularly well. Note how 85:4 describes the connection between what Israel lost and what she will receive: "If now we direct our hearts and make them firm, we will receive everything (*kulmedem*) that we lost (root *'br*)—much better (*myatrān sagi*) than that we lost, greatly increased." This passage does not refer to the former earthly possession and the future heavenly possession as contrasting. Instead, it describes the heavenly possession as a refined and magnified version of what Israel had during the generations of the fathers. Israel regains what she lost, but in a transformed, perfected version. This may indicate that the Land of the fathers will once more be the possession of Israel, only immensely better and larger, when Israel establishes herself in the heavenly world.

This conclusion is supported by the way 85:1–2 constantly compares the tribes—both the remnant and the dispersed tribes—with former generations by appealing to their common descent. In fact, the passage eliminates the divide between the fathers and the generations of Baruch's time. This rhetorical device is particularly noticeable in 85:1–2: "(…) our fathers had righteous helpers, prophets and pious men. But then *we* were also in our land, and they helped us when we sinned (…)."[235] Baruch refers to the collective *we*, the righteous Israel, as the inhabitants of the Land at the time of the fathers. So, what Israel once had, Israel will soon repossess. On the level of allusions, Deut 30:5 comes to mind: "The LORD your God will bring you into the land that your ancestors possessed, and you will possess it; he will make you more prosperous and numerous than your ancestors."

The connection between earthly and heavenly realities is further enhanced by the reference to the terminology of remembrance in 84:6–8, a passage immediately preceding 85:1–11 and contextualised by the description of Baruch as *Moses redivivus*. In this passage, Baruch assures the tribes, as he has done so many times before, that they will receive what has been preserved and prepared for them (cf. 4:1–6; 51:7–12), if they obey the Law. Baruch instructs them to remember two things: firstly, God's commandments and secondly: "the law and Zion, and the holy land and your brothers, and the covenant of your fathers, and do not forget the festivals and the Sabbath" (84:8).[236] This passage neatly summarises the main aspects of life in the earthly Land, recognisable from passages like *2 Bar.* 61; 63 and 66. As I pointed out in Chapter Two, the terminology of remembrance conveys the idea of continued life in contrast to oblivion which equals extinction. Baruch thus urges his audience to keep the Land with its important institutions alive in their memories until it manifests itself in the heavenly sphere. Through Israel's remembrance, the Land may be revived in heaven.

32:6 extends this notion of connection between the earthly copy and heavenly model, also with regard to the temple. The earthly temple edifice has of course been destroyed, but the heavenly sanctuary is re-inaugurated when Israel restores the temple cult. So, although the earthly temple and the heavenly sanctuary are different buildings, they

---

[235] My emphasis.
[236] Cf. Whitters, *Epistle*, 163–164.

both become the sites of God's cult through Israel's transformational cultic activity.

According to these passages, the heavenly Land of Israel is connected to its earthly predecessors in the sense that it provides a perfected and comprehensive version of what already existed for Israel on earth. The Land is characterised by beauty, fairness, light and glory in both realms. The importance of the shift from earth to heaven lies in the incorruptibility and everlasting character of the heavenly realm. In other words, the shift of realm makes it possible for *2 Baruch* to blend the model's flawlessness and heaven's shining loftiness with the covenantal promise of the Land.[237] And importantly, the righteous finally receives their award. Their present lives in accordance with the Law have made the most glorious Land imaginable manifest to them in God's everlasting presence.[238]

---

[237] In this manner *2 Baruch* combines the contemporary heavenward trend with the insistence of the covenant and the promise of the Land. Cf. Charles, *Apocalypse of Baruch*, 46; Lieu, *Christian Identity*, 224–225; Klausner, *Messianic Idea*, 409; R. Bauckham, "The Messianic Interpretation of Isaiah 10.34 in the Dead Sea Scrolls, *2 Baruch* and the Preaching of John the Baptist," *DSD* 2 (1995): 202–216 at 206–210; H. Braun, "Das himmlische Vaterland bei Philo und im Hebräerbrief," in *Verborum Veritas. Festschrift für C. Stählin zum 70. Geburtstag* (ed. O. Böcher and K. Haacker; Wuppertal: Brockhaus, 1970), 319–327.

[238] Compare *T. Job* 33:3–7; *T. Mos.* 10; *L.A.B.* 19:12; *Vis. Paul* 21–22.

THE OTHER LANDS OF ISRAEL

This study has discussed the commonly held notion that the Land is of minor importance in *2 Baruch*. In this study I have attempted to establish an alternative approach to the spatiality of the text, studying the Land in light of a praxis epistemology.

The Lands of 2 Baruch

The previous chapters of this study have suggested that *2 Baruch* presents several versions of the Land, or several Lands. In the description of the period of the First Temple, the Land appeared in the form of the various Lands of the law-abiding kings. These Lands were all Temple-centered and constituted by righteous kingship, but they comprised different areas: first, all Palestine, then only Judah, and then, in the period of the last righteous king, the extent of the Land did not extend beyond the city of Jerusalem.

During the end-time, ambiguous and hybrid spatial constructions were located in the wilderness of the Kidron valley. The end-time city of the pillar and the wall (Chapter Four) and the spatial construction 'here with me' (Chapter Five) were both constituted by the social space of the righteous community. These mobile righteous spaces were set in non-place—the wilderness—and were described by means of multivalent allusions to authoritative stories and their spaces. While clearly referring to a city/temple structure, these spaces could also be described in terms of the camp of the Exodus story and as exilic spaces. Baruch's move to Hebron opened up a new and wider field of connotations for these spaces. The Hebron reference supplied the spatiality of the community with elements of hope and expectation, both for the remnant and for the dispersed tribes.

At the breakthrough of Messianic power, the remnant re-entered Mount Zion, the Land of the Messianic era. The Messianic era made the world into a space of liminal character and bridged the corruptible and the incorruptible world. As I finally pointed out in Chapter Seven, at the very end—after resurrection and God's judgment—the heavenly other world was transformed into the ultimate and everlasting Land.

Here I show that the common denominator of all these versions of the Land was Israel's righteous praxis. The Land was always constituted by the localised, law-abiding, and cult-observing praxis of the righteous. However, I also pointed out that *2 Baruch* describes Israel as a flexible entity that lost members during the course of history. At the time of the destruction of the temple, the ten tribes were long gone, and the two tribes were already doomed. The righteous remnant, equivalent to the followers of Baruch, constituted the last survivors of the corruptible world who had to achieve the task of saving themselves, possibly the lost tribes, and hence the Land, in order to continue onto the other world.

While giving praxis priority as the defining aspect of the Land, one of my main concerns has been to show *how* the territorial aspect is still relevant to *2 Baruch*'s conception of Land. The decrease in territory during the reigns of the Davidic kings, for instance, clearly signaled that Israel's position in the corruptible world was deteriorating. The extent of territory inhabited and maintained by the righteous shrank throughout *2 Baruch*'s history of the corruptible world. The spacious Davidic Land, universal in its potentials, was reduced to include only Judah, which itself was decreased to its core area: Jerusalem and its temple. When the end-time set in, Israel was left without territory. She was marginalised. To stress this point, *2 Baruch* states that Israel dwelled in the Kidron valley, the spatial counterpart to Jerusalem at that time. Thus, the community itself became the center and territorial base of the imagined spaces of the end-time, a fact that highlights the idea that Israel had become different from the corruptible world. So, while becoming territorially marginalised, Israel simultaneously became powerful through that very mobility—through her access to the Law and to God, and through her estrangement from the world. Furthermore, the territorial aspects of the Messianic Land stressed the elevated character of the Land on Mount Zion and the universal dominion of righteousness. And finally, Israel's entry into the heavenly, incorruptible, world led Israel into the space of God's constant and everlasting presence: the Land was finally set in the perfect location. Thus, it is clear that the territorial aspect of the Land is important, in the sense that the qualities of the various locations tell us how *2 Baruch* wanted to present the Land in different time periods. The extent of David and Solomon's Land signaled that Israel was in its golden age of kingship, the total destruction and estrangement of territory at the fall of Jerusalem told us about Israel's despair, and the entrance into the incorruptible world proved that Israel was finally safe, triumphant and happy.

In this study I have also indicated that 2 Baruch refers to a reservoir of commonplace notions about what the Land should look like and what it should do for Israel. 2 Baruch actively plays with motifs and metaphors, recombining them and blending them with motifs related to other high-profiled redemptive spaces of the contemporary era in order to create authoritative and alternative Lands for Israel. 2 Baruch introduces familiar stories and motifs and applies them in the presentation of the Land to make that presentation recognisable, meaningful, and a source of comfort to its audience. The Land becomes the Land of the good kings, with all the connotations implied therein; the Land becomes the Land of the functioning sanctuary and is thereby blessed with holiness and divine presence; the Land is lush, protective and secures the reproduction of descendants, it is the arena where the enemy falls or bows down to Israel. 2 Baruch further recalls the covenants of Moses and Abraham and introduces the stories and the places of these patriarchs.

The use of conventional images like these are crucial to secure recognition of the Land in new locations. The fact that the metaphors and the images used in 2 Baruch are common, and sometimes almost clichés, helps the process of imagining alternative spaces: they let the mind wander from one location to the other, while identifying them as equivalent spaces.

The Land in Israel's History of Redemption

In this study, I have proposed that 2 Baruch employs the Land-concept throughout its description of Israel's history of redemption, although to a varying degree. Moreover, I have argued that the description of the Land varies with regard to its composition. The three time-categories in 2 Baruch, which were established in Chapter One, influence the shape of these Land-constructions. In the period of the First Temple the Land was temple-oriented and blissful, yet always a threatened enclave of protection. The spaces of the end-time were ambiguous, mobile, ungrounded, but served redemption by promoting future access to the Land. Finally, the Land-constructions of the time of redemption were beyond worldly afflictions and they were comprehensive in character. These various imaginations of the Land were adapted to their time contexts, while simultaneously always representing an environment of survival for Israel.

In what sense, and why, is the Land a central place of redemption in *2 Baruch*? Firstly, as scholars have already pointed out, an important concern of *2 Baruch* is to reassert the ultimate redemption of Israel, despite the destruction of Jerusalem and the temple. *2 Baruch* upholds that the covenant is still valid and that God's promises will therefore be fulfilled. Covenant obedience will ultimately lead to the fulfillment of promises, some during the Messianic era and others in the other world. This reorientation in time parallels a reorientation in space. *2 Baruch* turns attention away from Jerusalem and its temple, towards the Messianic reign and the other world. The text argues that the loss of the temple and its surroundings was part of God's plan for Israel and a sign of future hope. The catastrophe showed that Israel should look for salvation elsewhere. However, this spatial reorientation is not a turning away from the Land-concept, as has often been argued. In my view, the change of location is rather a part of the creative redefinition of what the Land can be. The loss of territory is not fatal, since covenant obedience continues to be the key of access to covenantal space. By redefining Messianic spaces and heavenly spaces as the Land, *2 Baruch* is both able to prove that the covenant still is valid, and that righteousness assures redemption.

Secondly, *2 Baruch* strengthens this argument by pointing to the fact that the Land was available to the righteous in former generations. Those who lived according to the Law and the commandments consequently lived in a blessed space. At least the righteous always were protected from extinction, even in times of turmoil. *2 Baruch*'s description of the transition from the end-time to the Messianic era shows its audience that an obedient lifestyle protected Israel even when Jerusalem fell and when the entire earth was shaking. The end-time city of the pillar and the wall assured survival in the Kidron valley and the protective Land safeguarded Israel when the earth swallowed its inhabitants. Thus, *2 Baruch* is able to point to history as proof of the redemptive effect of obedience to God and his Law.

Thus, in my view, *2 Baruch* constructs the history of Israel and its corresponding spaces to argue for the final redemption of the righteous. A main concern of the text is the history of Israel, and its spaces, and the proof it affords that God never forgot the righteous and his promise to them. The Land, in one version or another, assured the survival of the righteous in the past. The Land will therefore also secure Israel's redemption in the future. *2 Baruch* constructs Lands in Israel's history in order to guarantee her ultimate redemption, creating alternative Lands and possible Lands: Lands to remember, to hope for, and to trust. These 'other Lands' play an important role in *2 Baruch*'s effort to create authoritative, alternative spaces to promote hope of Israel's redemption in the time of crisis.

Discussing Land: Spatial Epistemologies

In many regards, my analysis of the Land-theme builds on conclusions from previous studies of *2 Baruch*. Above all, I support the general agreement of earlier studies concerning the importance of the Law in *2 Baruch*. In addition, the works of Murphy and Sayler have been particularly useful to my discussion. I agree with Sayler that consolation and hope are among the most important issues of *2 Baruch* and that *2 Baruch* attempts to reassure its audience that God's promises to Israel have not failed. Further, I agree with Murphy that *2 Baruch* turns the attention of its audience away from the present world and the Jerusalem temple, and that the text instead argues the importance of the other world.[1] In addition, my analysis concurs with Charles and Kolenkow's emphasis on the importance of works in *2 Baruch*.[2] Moreover, I also extend some of the insights presented by Whitters, who rightfully regards *2 Baruch*'s description of geography as an integrated, and important aspect of how the text communicates with its audience.[3] In other words, my conclusions build on the presumptions of the current state of research regarding the importance of the covenant and its promises, Israel's righteous praxis, the otherworldly focus and to some extent the meaning bearing function of geography in *2 Baruch*.

However, my interpretation also provides fresh insights into—and an alternative reading of—some issues in *2 Baruch*. First, this study has proposed that a praxis epistemology may allow for other interpretations of *2 Baruch*'s spatial descriptions. One of the benefits of studying space from a praxis perspective is that this approach provides a key to the frequent spatial overlaps and ambiguity, as well as to the recycling and blending of metaphors and imagery. When we assume that space is defined by acts and presence and not by territory, the

---

[1] Cf. Chapter One, p. 4.
[2] Cf. Charles, *Apocalypse of Baruch*, 25–26; Kolenkow, "Introduction," 128–137.
[3] Whitters, *Epistle*, 35.

fact that concepts such as 'Zion' may refer to an imprecisely defined territory is no longer problematic. A praxis epistemology acknowledges that territories are fuzzily defined, since the primary interest of texts like *2 Baruch* lies in people and their localised acts. *2 Baruch* therefore creates moral spaces—spaces as inhabited spaces. Likewise, when we consider the well of allusions and references to authoritative texts and stories as a means of enhancing the legitimacy of a place, the frequently-occurring descriptions of compiled allusions to redemptive spaces become meaningful. When *2 Baruch*, for example, describes Messianic space in terms of both Garden and Land, it creates a comprehensive place of bliss.

Second, a praxis epistemology also provides other angles on the study of the Land-concept. In previous research, the Land in *2 Baruch* has only been studied in the context of the period before the fall of Zion, and scholars have treated the Land of *2 Baruch* as a geographically fixed place within the corruptible world. In my view, this scope has resulted in too narrow an approach to the Land, which has left out most of the creative use of the Land-theme in *2 Baruch* and shaped the Land as a rather uniform and monolithic spatial entity. A benefit of the epistemological shift is therefore that it denies that a description of the region of Palestine is the only possible description of the Land in the text. Rather, it allows the concept of the Land to be broader and more multivalent.

Studies having a territorial epistemology as their point of departure have produced some interpretational knots that may be resolved by the proposed shift of spatial epistemology. As suggested in Chapter One, Harrington's study of the Holy Land presupposed that the various uses of the expression 'the holy land' were uniform with regard to their territorial reference. However, here I propose that the territory of 'the holy land' may vary. The passages that refer to 'the holy land' describe Judah (63:10), Mount Zion (71:1) and Land as remembered (84:8), with the latter passage referring to either Palestine, Judah, or Jerusalem. The common denominator of the three passages is the practice of correct cultic behavior that ensures God's presence in the Land. In the situations when God's presence has drawn near to Israel in the Land, *2 Baruch* may describe these locations as the Holy Land. So, although I agree with Harrington that the expression 'the holy land' should be discussed in the context of the broader Land-theme, I find it difficult to accept that the common denominator of the Land is its assumed territorial reference.

Moreover, this study, which assumes a praxis epistemology, also challenges the idea that texts should somehow passively reflect real geo-historical places, as implied by Bogaert.[4] The present study points out that texts create and recreate imagined spaces. It is clearly possible—and even likely—that texts *discuss* perceived real-life places or that the imagined spaces of texts may be part of a wider discussion of what a reality *should* be and should have been. Still, imagined spaces are part of the rhetoric and the narratives of texts. They are alternative spaces, counter-spaces and comprehensive, excellent spaces to hope and long for.

Last, my study suggests that there is continuity between the two worlds of *2 Baruch*. In Chapter Seven, I argued that Israel shapes the Land in the heavenly world, in the same manner as she shaped Land in earthly locations that preceded it. In Israel's history of redemption, the heavenly world is consequently the last in a series of locations that are transformed into her Land. From the point of view of praxis epistemology, I therefore argue for the perspective of continuity between the two worlds. Being the heavenly Land, shaped by Israel's righteous action while still on earth, the incorruptible world is analogous to—whilst also much better than—its earthly counterparts. Consequently, my interpretation of the relationship between the worlds and between the notion of the Land and the other world differs from the interpretations of Sayler, Murphy and Whitters. I question Murphy's contention that the two worlds are ontologically distinct. Although I agree that the worlds are distinct during the course of the corruptible world, *2 Baruch* implies that the realms are mutually penetrable, and once the corruptible world has died and Israel has entered into the incorruptible, heavenly world, *2 Baruch* emphasises the active role of Israel, who transforms that world into her Land. In my view, the Heavenly Land of Israel is the perfected and greatly enhanced version of the Land, similar to but better than its earthly counterparts.

In this study of the Land-concept in *2 Baruch* I propose that *2 Baruch's* reorientation in space includes a transformation of the notion of the Land as the redemptive space of Israel. The epistemological shift proposed here adds a new emphasis to the role of the Land-theme in *2 Baruch's* descriptions of the end-time and the time of redemption. Instead of approaching an eschatological text like *2 Baruch* as a text that

---

[4] Cf. Chapter One, pp. 8–10.

disqualifies the Land, I propose that the Land-concept is renewed as a central spatial category in *2 Baruch*'s eschatology. It is my view that *2 Baruch* does not reject the Land in order to look to the other world. It solely points away from a former location on earth towards new, excellent opportunities in the other, heavenly world. This interpretation of the Land shows the ability of the Land-concept to adapt to new situations and displays how *2 Baruch* brings the idea of the covenant and its promises into new redemptive scenarios. So, while I agree with earlier interpreters that Jerusalem, its temple, and the region of Palestine are destroyed together with the rest of the corruptible world, I argue that the Land continues to be an important place for Israel even after the destruction of Jerusalem and the escape of the righteous to the other world: the other world becomes the Land *par excellence*.

The creative redefinitions undertaken by *2 Baruch* have thus been obscured by the spatial epistemology that has dominated previous scholarship. Instead of studying the concept of the Land as a broad, inclusive, flexible and changing space in the first centuries C.E., the study of the Land has been confined to a study of Palestine. I do not claim that a praxis approach to space is the only way to grasp the Land-concept in *2 Baruch*. However, I do suggest that it provides a novel and fruitful reading.

Recontextualising the Land

In this section I specifically address the following questions: how can an epistemology that gives priority to praxis shed new light on conceptions of redemptive spaces in texts dating from the turn of the era and the first centuries C.E., how does my interpretation of the Land in *2 Baruch* accord with other descriptions of Israel's Land in this period, and how does this approach relate the Land to other contemporaneous notions of redemptive spaces?

Several studies of texts of late antiquity have pointed out tendencies that are concurrent with the findings presented here. These studies have shown that the idea that people shape the character of space was not alien to early Jewish and early Christian thought. In particular, the well-known studies of J.Z. Smith deserve to be mentioned in this context. Smith emphasised the human role in shaping space, saying that people are not placed, but rather bring space into being.[5] A number

---

[5] Smith, *To Take Place*, 28; Smith, *Map*, 110–111.

of scholars have made similar observations and discussed issues relating
to them in early Christian texts, among them B. Malina, H. Moxnes,
J. Økland and, recently, K. Wenell.[6] Likewise, in the field of Qumran
studies, discussions of the liturgy and 'the temple of men' in the Dead
Sea Scrolls revolve around related issues.[7] The notion that people and
their righteous living can create space is also found in rabbinic thought.
J. Neusner remarks: "The equation between the kingdom [The kingdom of God] and accepting the Torah (...) implies that the human act
of obedience creates space, the realm in which the rule of God prevails."[8]

With regard to the conception of the Land, a handful of studies of
the Mishnah and the Babylonian Talmud have reached conclusions
which are indicative of spatial constructions equivalent to those I have
isolated in 2 Baruch. Most prominently, I.M. Gafni discussed overlaps
and tensions between local patriotism and devotion for the Land in
the Babylonian diaspora. He summarises one of the tendencies in the
material as follows:

> In sum, there emerges over the years a Babylonia enjoying all the at-
> tributes of the historically central Land of Israel: Davidic leadership,
> remnants of the Jerusalem Temple, links with the Patriarchs, and even
> hallowed earth and sacred boundaries. (...) If the decisive factor in main-
> taining the subservience of the diaspora to Eretz Israel was considered to
> be the very essence of "the Land" and its position in Jewish minds, the
> one way of overcoming this dependence was by refashioning the Babylo-

---

[6] B.J. Malina, *The Social Gospel of Jesus: the Kingdom of God in Mediterranean Perspective*
(Minneapolis, Minn.: Fortress Press, 2001), 77; 90–91; Moxnes, "Kingdom takes Place";
Moxnes, *Jesus in His Place*; Økland, *Women in Their Place*; Wenell, *Jesus and Land*. Cf.
also Ward, *Postmodern God*, xv–xlvii; Davies, *Gospel and Land*, 367. A series of scholars
have studied Christian interpretations of the Land and related spaces. The following
list presents only a small selection: R.H. Lightfoot, *Locality and Doctrine in the Gospels*
(London: Hodder and Stoughton, 1938); H. Conzelmann, *Die Mitte der Zeit: Studien
zur Theologie des Lukas* (BHT 17; Tübingen: Mohr, 1954); E. Lohmeyer, *Galiläa und
Jerusalem* (FRLANT 52; Göttingen: Vandenhoeck & Ruprecht, 1959); H. Conzelmann,
The Theology of St. Luke (London: Faber and Faber, 1961); G. Stemberger, "Galilee—
Land of Salvation?" appendix IV in *The Gospel and the Land: Early Christianity and Jewish
Territorial Doctrine* (by W.D. Davies; BSem 25; Berkeley: University of California Press,
1974; Repr., Sheffield: JSOT Press, 1994); Lieu, *Christian Identity*, 220–230.

[7] The discussion is longstanding. T. Elgvin summarises it in the article "Temple
Mysticism and the Temple of Men," in *The Dead Sea Scrolls: Texts and Contexts* (ed.
C. Hempel; Leiden: E.J. Brill, forthcoming). Cf. also C.A. Newsom, *The Self as Symbolic
Space: Constructing Identity and Community at Qumran* (STDJ 52; Leiden: Brill, 2004).

[8] J. Neusner and B. Chilton, *Jewish-Christian Debates: God, Kingdom, Messiah* (Minneapolis: Fortress Press, 1998), 127.

nian community to be a precise copy of the original "Land," inasmuch
as all the criteria for the historical centrality of the Holy Land could now
be located in Jewish Babylonia as well. (...) In our case it appears that
the "agent" has now rendered himself literally a clone or exact copy of
the original Land of Israel.[9]

Here, Gafni suggests that the Babylonian diaspora may have interpreted their situation there as being in the Land.

R.S. Sarason has identified the same phenomenon in the Mishnah,
in particular in *m. Yad.* 4.3. This tractate illustrates how Jewish settlements outside Palestine—in Egypt and Babylonia—may have given
tithes. Although Sarason assures the reader that this phenomenon does
not represent a major trend in the Mishnah, he nevertheless discusses
whether "this scenario also supposes a symbolic transfer of attributes of
the Land of Israel to large Jewish settlements outside the Land ('new
Jerusalems')."[10] Of particular interest to my study of *2 Baruch* is Sarason's discussion of the Mishnah's ideas about the community of Jews in
Syria. According to Sarason, Syria occupied an intriguing middle position at the time of the composition of the Mishnah, both because Syria
was contingent with the commonly-accepted northern borders of the
biblical Land and because many Jews lived there. Thus, according to
Sarason, "in some ways Syria is deemed to be like the Land of Israel
and in some ways not."[11]

In his article "The Link to the Land of Israel in Jewish Thought,"
S. Rosenberg similarly suggests that the notion of the Land continued to legitimise diaspora communities during the Middle Ages. These
communities could be described as Jerusalem and/or the Land, and
their gates could be 'gates distinguished by Halakah,' while simultaneously not denying the special role of Jerusalem 'of dust and stone.'
According to Rosenberg, these communities could operate with several
notions of the Land at the same time.[12] All these examples thus attest
to the flexibility and the mobility of the notion of the Land. They show
righteous praxis, or the presence of communities of Jews, may have
been conceived as the defining principle of the Land.[13]

---

[9] Gafni, *Land*, 116.

[10] Sarason, "Significance of Land," 119.

[11] Sarason, "Significance of Land," 121; 122–124.

[12] Rosenberg, "Link to the Land," 157–161.

[13] Cf. Smith, *Map*, 110, and my discussion of these articles in "Land *and* Diaspora: Spatial Perspectives," in *Complexity: Interdisciplinary Communications 2006/2007* (Ed.

In light of this short overview of other studies, as well as the conclusions of my own study, it is my opinion that the understanding of the Land of Israel in the first centuries C.E., and particularly in the centuries after the fall of the temple, covered a wide spectrum of interpretations. The interpretation of the Land as a flexible, spatial construction that was shaped by the righteous acts of a community is one among several options that coexisted during this period. The studies mentioned above show how other localities and other communities of Jews could understand themselves and their place as the Land; other studies again suggest that the Torah could be the Land, or that the redeemed themselves could be the Land.[14] At the same time, the Jerusalem 'of dust and stone' continued to be the Land for many. In this manner, the notion of the Land became a broad redemptive category, lending its authority to other places and groups, to ritual experiences, and to future hope.

These reflections make it reasonable to break the interpretational isolation that has dominated most studies of the Land—my own included. Rather than treating the Land of Israel as a unique spatial concept due its assumedly fixed relation to the region of Palestine, it may be fruitful to understand the Land in the context of other high-profiled redemptive spaces of the first centuries C.E. As a space of redemption, the Land shares several traits with spaces such as Paradise, Heaven and the Kingdom of God. Scholars most often study these redemptive spaces as flexible and dynamic spaces. None of these spaces is attached solely to one fixed location: some may be located on earth or in heaven, or both, and others may exist somewhere in the east or in the west. Nor do these redemptive spaces have only spatial connotations: they bring along with them connotations of time and condition as well as space. Accordingly, these spaces may prove to be an interesting context to the study of the Land. It is possible that a spatial epistemology that has been giving priority to territory has prevented scholars from noticing the similarities—and the interconnections—among these spaces. Still, the Land may appear just as imprecise, ungraspable and unplaced as for example Paradise, Heaven and the Kingdom of God. Consequently,

---

W. Østereng; Oslo: Centre for Advanced Study, 2008. Online: http://www.cas.uio.no/Publications/Seminar/Complexity_Lied.pdf).

[14] Cf. Vermes, *Scripture and Tradition*, 45–46; Davies, *Gospel and Land*, 367; Lied, "Damascus," 122–125.

I propose that we should interpret the various conceptions of the Land in the same manner as we interpret other spaces of redemption in eschatological texts of this period.

Concluding Remarks

This study has proposed that *2 Baruch* does not reject the Land of Israel as a redemptive category. Instead, I conclude that *2 Baruch* transforms this important covenantal space to address the crisis caused by the fall of the Jerusalem temple and the dispossession of Palestine in 70 C.E., and to argue for Israel's survival and ultimate redemption in the other world. The imagined Lands of *2 Baruch* may have offered hope and consolation to marginalised groups at a time when the traditional center in Jerusalem and Palestine was already lost.

BIBLIOGRAPHY

Ackroyd, P.R. "The Temple Vessels—A Continuity Theme." *VT* 23 (1972): 166–181.

Albright, W.F. "The Location of the Garden of Eden." *AJSL* 39 (1922): 15–31.

Alt, A. "The God of the Fathers." Pages 3–77 in *Essays on Old Testament History and Religion*. Translated by R.A. Wilson. Oxford: Blackwell, 1966.

Arbeitman, Y.L. "Mamre." Pages 492–493 in vol. 4 of *ABD*. Edited by D.N. Freedman. 6 vols. Garden City: Doubleday, 1992.

Baars, W. "Neue Textzeugen der syrischen Baruchapokalypse." *VT* 13 (1963): 476–478.

Bakhtin, M.M. *Dialogic Imagination: Four Essays*. Edited by M. Holquist. Translated by C. Emerson and M. Holquist. Austin: University of Texas Press, 1981.

Barth, C. *Diesseits und Jenseits im Glauben des späten Israel*. SBS 72. Stuttgart: KBW Verlag, 1974.

Bauckham, R. "The Messianic Interpretation of Isaiah 10:34 in the Dead Sea Scrolls, *2 Baruch* and the Preaching of John the Baptist." *DSD* 2 (1995): 202–216.

Bautch, K.C. *A Study of the Geography of 1 Enoch 17–19: 'No One Has Seen What I Have Seen'*. JSJSup 81. Leiden: E.J. Brill, 2003.

Berquist, J.L. "Critical Spatiality and the Uses of Theory." No pages. Online: http://www.cwru.edu/affil/GAIR/papers/2002papers/berquist.html.

Bhabha, H.K. "The Third Space: Interview with Homi Bhabha." *Identity, Community, Culture, Difference*. Edited by J. Rutherford. London: Lawrence and Wishart, 1990.

Bietenrand, H. *Die Himmlische Welt im Urchristentum und Spätjudentum*. WUNT 2. Tübingen: J.C.B. Mohr, 1951.

Billerbeck, P. "Diese Welt, die Tage des Messias und die zukünftige Welt." Pages 799–976 in vol. 4 of *Kommentar zum Neuen Testament aus Talmud und Midrasch*. Edited by H.L. Strack and P. Billerbeck. München: Beck, 1928.

Black, M. and A.-M. Denis. *Apocalypsis henochi graece: fragmenta pseudepigraphorum quae supersunt graeca*. Pseudepigrapha veteris testamenti graeca 3. Leiden: E.J. Brill, 1970.

Blackman, P. *Mishnayoth*. 7 vols. 2nd ed. New York: Judaica Press, 1963–1964.

Blenkinsopp, J. *Prophecy and Canon: A Contribution to the Study of Jewish Origins*. Notre Dame, Ind.: University of Notre Dame Press, 1977.

———. "The Structure of P." *CBQ* 38 (1976): 275–292.

———. *Treasuries Old and New. Essays in the Theology of the Pentateuch*. Grand Rapids, Mich.: Eerdmans, 2004.

Bloch-Smith, E. "'Who is the King of Glory?' Solomon's Temple and Its

Symbolism." Pages 18–31 in *Scripture and Other Artifacts. Essays on the Bible and Archeology in Honor of Philip J. King.* Edited by M.D. Coogan, J.C. Exum and L.E. Lawrence. Louisville, KY: Westminster/John Knox, 1994.

Boccaccini, G. *Beyond the Essene Hypothesis: The Parting of the Ways Between Qumran and Enochic Judaism.* Grand Rapids, Mich.: Eerdmans, 1998.

Boer, M.C. de. "Paul's Quotation of Isaiah 54.1 in Galatians 4.27." *NTS* 50 (2004): 370–389.

Bogaert, P.-M. *Apocalypse de Baruch, Introduction, Traduction du Syriaque et Commentaire.* 2 vols. SC 144–145. Paris: Les Éditions du cerf, 1969.

———. "Les réactions juives après la ruine de Jérusalem: L'apocalypse de Baruch." *MdB* 29 (1983): 19–20.

———. "La ruine Jérusalem et les apocalypses juives après 70." Pages 123–141 in *Apocalypses et théologie de l'èspérance. Congrès de Toulouse 1975.* Edited by L. Monloubou. Lectio Divina 95. Paris: Latour-Maubourg, 1977.

Bokser, B.M. "Approaching Sacred Space." *HTR* 78 (1985): 279–299.

Boorer, S. "The Earth/Land in the Priestly Material: The Preservation of the 'Good' Earth and the Promised Land of Canaan throughout the Generations." *Australian Biblical Review* 49 (2001): 19–33.

———. "The Kerygmatic Intention of the Priestly Document." *ABR* 24 (1976): 12–20.

Borgen, P. *Bread from Heaven: An Exegetical Study of the Concept of Manna in the Gospel of John and the Writings of Philo.* NovTSup10. Leiden: E.J. Brill, 1965.

Bousset, W. "Die Himmelreise der Seele." *ARW* 4 (1901): 136–169, 229–273.

Boyarin, D. *Carnal Israel: Reading Sex in Talmudic Culture.* The New Historicism 25. University of California Press: Berkeley, 1993.

Branham, J.R. "Sacred Space under Erasure in Ancient Synagogues and Early Churches." *ArtB* 74 (1992): 374–394.

Braude, W.G. and I.J. Kapstein, eds. *Pesikta De-Rab Kahana: R. Kahana's Compilation of Discourses for Sabbaths and Festal Days.* The Littman Library of Jewish Civilization. London: Routledge & Kegan Paul, 1975.

Braulik, G. *Deuteronomium II 16,18–34,12.* NechtB 28. Würzburg: Echter verlag, 1992

Braun, H. "Das himmlische Vaterland bei Philo und im Hebräerbrief." Pages 319–327 in *Verborum Veritas. Festschrift für C. Stälin zum 70. Geburtstag.* Edited by O. Böcher and K. Haacker. Wuppertal: Brockhaus, 1970.

Briggs, C.A. *A Critical and Exegetical Commentary on the Book of Psalms.* The International Critical Commentary on the Holy Scriptures of the Old and New Testaments. 2 vols. Edinburgh: T & T Clark, 1906–1907.

Brooke, G. "The Significance of the Kings in 4QMMT." Pages 109–113 in *Qumran Cave IV and MMT. Special Report.* Edited by Z.J. Kaspera. Krakow: Enigma Press, 1991.

The Brown-Driver-Briggs Hebrew and English Lexicon. Edited by F. Brown, C. Briggs and S.R. Driver. Peabody, Mass.: Hendrickson, 1996.

Brueggemann, W. "From Dust to Kingship." *ZAW* 84 (1972): 1–18.

———. "Kingship and Chaos: A Study in Tenth Century Theology." *The CBQ* 33 (1971): 317–332.

———. *The Land: Place as Gift, Promise, and Challenge in Biblical Faith*. 2nd ed. OBT. Minneapolis: Fortress Press, 2002.

Bryan, S. *Jesus and Israel's Traditions of Judgement and Restoration*. Cambridge: Cambridge University Press, 2002.

Bultmann, R. "History and Eschatology in the New Testament." *NTS* 1 (1954): 5–16.

Burden T.L. *The Kerygma of the Wilderness Traditions in the Hebrew Bible*. American University Studies Series 7: Theology and Religion 163. New York: Peter Lang, 1994.

Burkes, S. "'Life' Redefined: Wisdom and Law in Fourth Ezra and Second Baruch." *CBQ* 63 (2001): 55–71.

Butcher, K. *Roman Syria and the Near East*. London: British Museum Press, 2003.

Camp, C.V. "Storied Space, or, Ben Sira 'Tells' a Temple." Pages 64–80 in *'Imagining' Biblical Worlds. Studies in Spatial, Social and Historical Constructs in Honor of James W. Flanagan*. Edited by D.M. Gunn and P.M. McNutt. Sheffield: Sheffield Academic Press, 2002. Online: http://www.gunnzone .org/BenSira_Space.html.

Casey, E.S. *The Fate of Place: A Philosophical History*. Berkeley: University of California Press, 1997.

———. *Getting Back into Place: Toward a Renewed Understanding of the Place-World*. Studies in Continental Thought. Bloomington, Ind.: Indiana University Press, 1993.

Cavallin, H.C.C. *Life after Death: Paul's Argument for the Resurrection of the Dead in 1 Cor 15. Part I: An Enquiry into the Jewish Background*. ConBNT 7. Lund: CWK Gleerup, 1974.

Ceriani, A.M. "Translatio syra pescitto Veteris Testamenti ex codice Ambrosiano sec. fere VI photolithographice edita." Pages 533–553 in *Monumenta sacra et profana 6*. Milano, 1876. Photolithographic reproduction of the Syriac text, with translation.

Charles, R.H. *The Apocalypse of Baruch, Translated from the Syriac, Chapters I–LXXVII from the Sixth Cent. MS in the Ambrosian Library of Milan, and Chapters LXXVIII–LXXXVII—the Epistle of Baruch—from a New and Critical Text Based on Ten MSS and Published Herewith. Edited, with Introduction, Notes, and Indices*. London: Black, 1896.

———. "The Apocalypse of Baruch Translated from the Syriac." Pages 470–526 in vol. 2 of *The Apocrypha and Pseudepigrapha of the Old Testament in English, with Introductions and Critical and Explanatory Notes to the Several Books, Edited in Conjunction with Many Scholars*. Edited by R.H. Charles. 2 vols. Oxford: Clarendon, 1913.

———. *The Assumption of Moses: Translated from the Latin Sixth Century MS*. London: Black, 1897.

———. *The Book of Enoch or 1 Enoch*. Oxford: Clarendon, 1912.

Charlesworth, J.H. "From Jewish Messianology to Christian Christology: Some Caveats and Perspectives." Pages 225–264 in *Judaisms and their Messiahs at the Turn of the Christian Era*. Edited by J. Neusner, W.S. Green and E.S. Frerichs. Cambridge: Cambridge University Press, 1987.

Charlesworth, J.H., ed. *OTP*. 2 vols. Garden City, NY: Doubleday, 1983, 1985.

Chester, A. "The Parting of the Ways: Eschatology and Messianic Hope." Pages 239–313 in *Jews and Christians: The Parting of the Ways, A.D. 70 to 135. The Second Durham-Tübingen Research Symposium on Earliest Christianity and Judaism (Durham, September, 1989)*. WUNT 66. Edited by J.D.G. Dunn. Tübingen: J.C.B. Mohr, 1992.

Chilton, B.D. *The Isaiah Targum: Introduction, Translation, Apparatus and Notes*. ArBib 11. Collegeville, Minn.: The Liturgical Press, 1987.

Clark, E.A. *History, Theory, Text: Historians and the Linguistic Turn*. Cambridge, Mass.: Harvard University Press, 2004.

Clemen, C. "Die Zusammensetzung des Buches Henoch, der Apokalypse des Baruch und des vierten Buches Esra." *TSK* 71 (1898): 211–246.

Clements, R.E. *Abraham and David: Genesis XV and Its Meaning for Israelite tradition*. SBT 5. London: SCM, 1967.

———. "Temple and Land: A Significant Aspect of Israel's Worship." *TGUOS* 19 (1963): 16–28.

Clifford, R.J. *The Cosmic Mountain in Canaan and the Old Testament*. Cambridge, Mass.: Harvard University Press, 1972.

Cohen, H.D. "The Destruction: From Scripture to Midrash." *Prooftexts* 2 (1982): 22.

Collins, A.Y. "Aristobulus." Pages 831–842 in vol. 2 of *OTP*. Edited by J.H. Charlesworth. 2 vols. Garden City, NY: Doubleday, 1985.

———. *The Combat Myth in the Book of Revelation*. HDR 9. Missoula: Scholars Press, 1975.

———. *Cosmology and Eschatology in Jewish and Christian Apocalypticism*. JSJSup 50. Leiden: E.J. Brill, 1996.

———. "Numerical Symbolism in Jewish and Early Christian Apocalyptic Literature." *ANRW* 21.2:1221–1287. Part 2, *Principat*, 21.2. Edited by W. Haase. New York: Walter de Gruyter, 1984.

———. "The Seven Heavens in Jewish and Christian Apocalypses." Pages 59–93 in *Death, Ecstasy, and Other Worldly Journeys*. Edited by J.J. Collins and M. Fishbane. Albany: SUNY Press, 1995.

Collins, J.J. "The Afterlife in Apocalyptic Literature." Pages 119–139 in *Judaism in Late Antiquity: Part 4: Death, Life-After-Death, Resurrection and the World-to-Come in the Judaisms of Antiquity*. HO 49. Edited by A.J. Avery-Peck and J. Neusner. Leiden: E.J. Brill, 2000.

Collins, J.J., ed. *Apocalypse: The Morphology of a Genre*. Semeia 14. Missoula: Scholars Press, 1979.

Collins, J.J. "Apocalyptic Eschatology as the Transcendence of Death." *CBQ* 36 (1974): 21–48.

———. *The Apocalyptic Imagination. An Introduction to the Jewish Matrix of Christianity*. New York: Crossroad, 1984.

———. *The Scepter and the Star: The Messiahs of the Dead Sea Scrolls and Other Ancient Literature*. ABRL. New York: Doubleday, 1995.

———. "Testaments." Pages 325–356 in *Jewish Writings of the Second Temple Period: Apocrypha, Pseudepigrapha, Qumran Sectarian Writings, Philo, Josephus*. Vol. 2 of The Literature of the Jewish People in the Period of the Second Temple and the Talmud. Edited by M.E. Stone. CRINT 2. Assen: Van Gorcum, 1984.

———. "A Throne in the Heavens: Apotheosis in pre-Christian Judaism." Pages 41–58 in *Death, Ecstasy, and Other Worldly Journeys*. Edited by J.J. Collins and M. Fishbane. Albany: SUNY Press, 1995.

Collins, J.J. and A.Y. Collins. *Daniel: A Commentary on the Book of Daniel*. Edited by F.M. Cross. Hermeneia. Minneapolis: Fortress Press, 1993.

Collins, M.F. "The Hidden Vessels in Samaritan Traditions." *JSJ* 3 (1972): 97–119.

Conzelmann, H. *Die Mitte der Zeit: Studien zur Theologie des Lukas*. BHT 17. Tübingen: Mohr, 1954.

———. *The Theology of St. Luke*. London: Faber and Faber, 1961.

Cresswell, T. *In Place, Out of Place: Geography, Ideology and Transgression*. Minneapolis: University of Minnesota Press, 1996.

Cross, F.M. *Canaanite Myth and Hebrew Epic: Essays in the History of the Religion of Israel*. Cambridge, Mass.: Harvard University Press, 1973.

Cumont, F. *Lux Perpetua*. Paris: P. Geuthner, 1949.

Dahl, N.A. "Christ, Creation and the Church." Pages 422–443 in *The Background of the New Testament and It's Eschatology*. Edited by W.D. Davies and D. Daube. Cambridge: Cambridge University Press, 1964.

Daniélou, J. *The Presence of God*. Baltimore: Helicon Press, 1959.

———. "Terre et Paradis chez les Pères de l'Église." *ErJb* 22 (1953): 433–472.

Davies, W.D. *The Gospel and the Land: Early Christianity and Jewish Territorial Doctrine*. BSem 25. Berkeley: University of California Press, 1974. Repr., Sheffield: JSOT Press, 1994.

———. *The Territorial Dimension of Judaism*. Berkeley: University of California Press, 1982.

Davila, J.R. *The Provenance of the Pseudepigrapha: Jewish, Christian or Other?* JSJSup 105. Leiden: E.J. Brill, 2005.

Dean-Otting, M. *Heavenly Journeys: A Study of the Motif in Hellenistic Jewish Literature*. Judentum und Umwelt 8. Frankfurt am Main: Peter Lang, 1984.

Dedering, S. "Apocalypse of Baruch." in *The Old Testament in Syriac, According to the Peshitta Version*. Part IV, fasc. iii. Edited by S.P. Brock. Leiden: E.J. Brill, 1973.

Delitzsch, F. *Wo lag das Paradies? Eine biblisch-assyrologische Studie*. Leipzig: Hinrichs'sche Buchhandlung, 1881.

Delling, G. "Von Morija zum Sinai (Pseudo-Philo Liber Antiquitatum Biblicarum 32, 1–10)." *JSJ* 2 (1971): 1–18.

———. "Die Weise, von der Zeit zu reden, im Lieber Antiquitatum Biblicarum." *NovT* (1971): 305–321.

Desjardins, M. "Law in *2 Baruch* and *4 Ezra*." *SR* 14 (1985): 25–37.

Diepold, P. *Israel's Land*. BWANT 95. Stuttgart: Kohlhammer, 1972.

Diez Macho, A. *Neophyti I. Targum Palestinense ms. de la Biblioteca Vaticana*. Vols I–VI. Madrid: Consejo Superior de Investigaciones Científicas, 1968–1979.

Dimant, D. "The Testament as a Literary Form in Early Jewish Pseudepigraphic Literature." *World Congress of Jewish Studies* 8 (1982): 79–83.

Duncan, J. and D. Ley, eds. *Place, Culture, Representation*. London: Routledge, 1993.

Dunn, J.D.G. *The Parting of the Ways: Between Christianity and Judaism and Their Significance for the Character of Christianity*. London: SCM Press, 1991.

Eckert, W.P. and M. Sohr Levinson, eds. *Jüdische Volk, gelobtes Land*. München: Kaiser, 1970.

Edmunds, L. *Intertextuality and the Reading of Roman Poetry*. Baltimore: John Hopkins University Press, 2001.

Ehrman, B.D., ed. and trans. *The Apostolic Fathers: Epistle of Barnabas, Papias and Quadratus, Epistle to Diognetus, The Shepherd of Hermas*. LCL 25.2. Cambridge, Mass.: Harvard University Press, 2003.

Elgvin, T. "Temple Mysticism and the Temple of Men." In *The Dead Sea Scrolls: Texts and Contexts*. Edited by C. Hempel. Leiden: E.J. Brill, forthcoming.

Eliade, M. *The Myth of the Eternal Return*. Translated by W.R. Trask. Bollingen Series 46. New York: Bollingen, 1954.

——. *Patterns in Comparative Religion*. New York: Sheed & Ward, 1958.

——. *The Sacred and the Profane: The Nature of Religion*. New York: Harcourt, Brace & Company, 1959.

Elliger, K. and W. Rudolph, eds. *Biblia Hebraica Stuttgartensia*. 4th ed. Stuttgart: Deutsche Bibelgesellschaft, 1990.

Endsjø, D.Ø. "Parfyme, død og udødlighet." *Chaos 39* (2003): 91–98.

Ephrem Syrus. *Hymns*. Translated by K.E. McVey. CWS. New York: Paulist Press, 1989.

——. *Hymns on Paradise*. Translated by S.P. Brock. Crestwood, N.Y.: St. Vladimir's Seminary Press, 1990.

Eshel, E. "The Dream Vision in the Noah Story of the Genesis Apocryphon and Related Texts." Paper presented at the 4th annual symposium of the Nordic Network in Qumran Studies. Copenhagen, August 25, 2006.

Eskola, T. *Messiah and the Throne: Jewish Merkabah Mysticism and Early Christian Exaltation Discourse*. WUNT 142. Tübingen: Mohr Siebeck, 2001.

Esler, P.F. "God's Honor and Rome's Triumph. Responses to the Fall of Jerusalem in 70 CE in Three Jewish Apocalypses." Pages 239–258 in *Modelling Early Christianity: Social-Scientific Studies of the New Testament in Its Context*. Edited by P.F. Esler. London: Routledge, 1995.

Etheridge, J.W., ed. and trans. *The Targums of Onkelos and Jonathan ben Uzziel on the Pentateuch: with Fragments of the Jerusalem Targum*. New York: Ktav Publishing House, 1968.

Eusebius. *The Ecclesiastical History*. Translated by D.D. Kirsopp Lake. 2 vols. LCL. Cambridge, Mass.: Harvard University Press, 1965.

Farmer, W. *Maccabees, Zealots and Josephus*. New York: Columbia, 1956.

Faye, E. de. *Les apocalypses juives. Essai de critique littéraire et théologique*. Lausanne: G. Bridel, 1892.

Feldman, A. "Mikra and Aggada in the Flod Story According to 4Q370." Paper presented at the First Graduate Enoch Seminar, Ann Arbor, May 3, 2006.

Ferch, A.J. "The Two Aeons and the Messiah in *Pseudo-Philo*, *4 Ezra*, and *2 Baruch*." *AUSS* 15 (1977): 135–151.

Fischer, A.A. *Von Hebron nach Jerusalem*. BZAW. Berlin: Walter de Gruyter, 2004.

Fishbane, M. "Jeremiah 4.23–26 and Job 3.13: A Recovered Use of the Creation Pattern." *VT* 21 (1971): 151–167.

———. "The Sacred Center: The Symbolic Structure of the Bible." Pages 6–27 in *Texts and Responses: Studies Presented to Nahum N. Glatzer on the Occasion of his Seventieth Birthday by his Students*. Edited by M. Fishbane and P.R. Mendes-Flohr. Leiden: E.J. Brill, 1975.

Fisher, C.D., ed. *Tacitii Historiarum Libri*. OCT. Oxford: Oxford University Press, 1952.

Fisher, L. "The Temple Quarter." *JSS* 8 (1963): 34–41.

Flanagan, J.W. "Mapping the Biblical World: Perceptions of Space in Ancient Southwestern Asia." Pages 1–18 in *Humanities Group Working Papers 5*. Edited by J. Murray. Windsor, Ont.: University of Windsor, 1999. Online: http://www.cwru.edu./affil/GAIR/canada/Windsor/Windsor.html.

Foucault, M. "Other Spaces: The Principles of Heterotopia." *Lotus 48/49* (1986): 9–17.

———. "Of Other Spaces." Translated by J. Miskowiec. *Diacritics* 16 (1986): 22–27.

———. *Power/Knowledge: Selected Interviews and Other Writings 1972–1977*. Edited by C. Gordon. Translated by Colin Gordon et al. Brighton: Harvester Press, 1980.

Freedman, D.N. "Temple without Hands." Pages 21–30 in *Temples and High Places in Biblical Times*. Edited by A. Biran. Jerusalem: Hebrew Union College—Jewish Institute of Religion, 1981.

Fretheim, T.E. "'Because the Whole Earth is Mine': Theme and Narrative in Exodus." *Int* 50/3 (1996): 229–239.

———. "The Plagues as Ecological Signs of Historical Disaster." *JBL* 110 (1991): 385–396.

Fretz, M.J. and R.I. Panitz. "Caleb." Pages 808–810 in vol. 1 of *ABD*. Edited by D.N. Freedman. 6 vols. Garden City: Doubleday, 1992.

Friedman, R.E. "Tabernacle." Pages 292–300 in vol. 6 of *ABD*. Edited by D.N. Freedman. 6 vols. Garden City: Doubleday, 1992.

Gaca, K.L. *The Making of Fornication: Eros, Ethics, and Political Reform in Greek Philosophy and Early Christianity*. Berkeley: University of California Press, 2003.

Gafni, I. *Land, Center and Diaspora: Jewish Constructs in Late Antiquity*. JSPSup 21. Sheffield: Sheffield Academic Press, 1997.

Galil, G. and M. Weinfeld. Preface to *Studies in Historical Geography and Biblical Historiography*. Edited by G. Galil and M. Weinfeld. Leiden: E.J. Brill, 2000.

Gammie, J.G. "Spatial and Ethical Dualism in Jewish Wisdom and Apocalyptic Literature." *JBL* 93 (1974): 356–385.

García Martínéz, F. and E.J.C. Tigchelaar, eds. *The Dead Sea Scrolls: Study Edition*. 2 vols. Grand Rapids, Mich.: Eerdmans; 1997–1998.

Gärtner, B. *The Temple and Community in Qumran and the New Testament: A Comparative Study in the Temple Symbolism of the Qumran texts and the New Testament*. SNTSMS1. Cambridge: Cambridge University Press, 1965.

Gaston, L. *No Stone on Another: Studies in the Significance of the Fall of Jerusalem in the Synoptic Gospels*. NovTSup 23. Leiden: E.J. Brill, 1970.

Gaylord, H.E. "3 Baruch." Pages 653–679 in vol. 1 of *Old Testament Pseude-*

pigrapha. Edited by J.H. Charlesworth. 2 vols. Garden City, N.Y.: Doubleday, 1983–1985.

Geus, C.H.J. de. *The Tribes of Israel: An Investigation into some of the Presuppositions of Martin Noth's Amphictyony Hypothesis*. SSN 18. Assen: Van Gorcum, 1976.

Ginzberg, L. "Apocalypse of Baruch (Syriac)." Pages 551–556 in vol. 2 of *The Jewish Encyclopedia: A Descriptive Record of the History, Literature, and Customs of the Jewish People from the Earliest Time to the Present Day*. Edited by I. Singer, A. Cyrus et al. 12 vols. New York: Funk and Wagnalls, 1901–1905. Repr. 1925.

———. *The Legends of the Jews*. 7 vols. Philadelphia: Jewish Publication Society of America, 1909–1938. Repr., 1998.

Goodenough, E.R. *Jewish Symbols in the Greco-Roman Period*. 13 vols. Bollingen Series 37. New York: Pantheon, 1953–1968.

Grabbe, L.L. "Chronology in *4 Ezra* and *2 Baruch*." Pages 49–63 in *Society of Biblical Literature 1981 Seminar Papers*. SBLSP 20. Chico, Calif.: Scholars Press, 1981.

Grelot, P. "La Géographie mythique d'Hénoch et ses sources orientales." *RB* 65 (1958): 33–69.

———. "Le Messie dans les Apocryphes de l'Ancien Testament, état de la question." Pages 19–50 in *La Venue du Messie: Messianisme et eschatologie*. Edited by E. Massaux. RechBib 6. Bruges: Descleé de Brouwer, 1962.

———. *What are the Targums? Selected Texts*. Translated by S. Attanasio. OTS 7. Collegeville, Minn.: Liturgical Press, 1992.

Grenfell, B.P. and A.S. Hunt. "Apocalypse of Baruch xii–xiv." Pages 4–7 in *The Oxyrhynchus Papyri III*. No. 403. London, 1903.

Gressmann, H. *Der Ursprung der israelitisch-jüdischen Eschatologie*. FRLANT 6. Göttingen: Vandenhoeck & Ruprecht, 1905.

———. "Vorschläge von Hugo Gressmann. Zur Esra-Apokalypse." Pages 337–350 in *Die Apokalypsen des Esra und des Baruch in deutscher Gestalt*. GCS 32. By B. Violet. Leipzig: J.C. Hinrichs'sche Buchhandlung, 1924.

Grossfeld, B. *The First Targum to Esther According to the MS Paris Hebrew 110 of the Bibliotheque Nationale*. New York: Sepher-Hermon Press, 1983.

———. *The Targum Sheni to the Book of Esther: A Critical Edition Based on MS. Sassoon 282 with Critical Apparatus*. New York: Sepher-Hermon Press, 1994.

Gry, L. "La date de la fin des temps selon les révélations ou les calculs du Pseudo-Philon et de Baruch (Apocalypse syriaque)." *RB* 48 (1939): 336–356.

———. "Hénoch 10,19 et les belles promesses de Papias." *RB* 53 (1946): 197–206.

———. "La Mort du Messie en IV Esdras, VII, 29 [III, v. 4]." Pages 133–139 in *Mémorial Lagrange: Cinquantenaire de l'École biblique et archéologique française de Jérusalem, 15 novembre 1890 – 15 novembre 1940*. Edited by L.-H. Vincent. Paris: J. Gabalda, 1940.

Guian, D. "Davidic Covenant." Pages 69–72 in vol. 2 of *ABD*. Edited by D.N. Freedman. 6 vols. Garden City: Doubleday, 1992.

Gunkel, H. *Genesis, übersetzt und erklärt*. 3rd ed. Göttinger Handkommentar zum Alten Testament I/1. Göttingen: Vandenhoeck & Ruprecht, 1910.

Gunkel, H. with H. Zimmern. *Schöpfung und Chaos in Urzeit und Endzeit: eine religionsgeschichtliche Untersuchung über Gen 1 und Ap Joh 12.* Göttingen: Vandenhoeck und Ruprecht, 1895.

Gunn, D.M. "David and the Gift of the Kingdom." *Semeia* 3 (1975): 14–45.

Gurevitch, Z. "The Double Site of Israel." Pages 203–216 in *Grasping Land: Space and Place in Contemporary Israeli Discourse and Experience.* Edited by E. Ben-Ari and Y. Bilu. Albany, NY: State University of New York Press, 1997.

Gurevitch, Z. and G. Aran. "The Land of Israel: Myth and Phenomenon." Pages 195–209 in *Reshaping the Past: Jewish History and the Historians.* Edited by J. Frankel. New York: Oxford University Press, 1994.

Gutman, J. "Leviathan, Behemoth and Ziz: Jewish Messianic Symbols in Art." *HUCA* 38 (1968): 219–230.

Habel, N.C. *The Land is Mine: Six Biblical Land Ideologies.* OBT. Minneapolis: Fortress Press, 1995.

Halpern-Amaru, B. *Rewriting the Bible: Land and Covenant in Postbiblical Jewish Literature.* Valley Forge, Penn.: Trinity Press International, 1994.

Hamerton-Kelly, R.G. "The Temple and the Origins of Jewish Apocalyptic." *VT* 20 (1970): 1–15.

Haran, M. "The Divine Presence in the Israelite Cult and the Cultic Institutions." *Biblica. Commentarii editi cura Pontificii Instituti Biblici* 50 (1969): 251–267.

———. "Temple and Community in Ancient Israel." Pages 17–25 in *Temple in Society.* Edited by M.V. Fox. Winona Lake, Ind.: Eisenbrauns, 1988.

Hare, D.R.A. "The Lives of the Prophets." Pages 379–399 in vol. 2 of *OTP.* Edited by J.H. Charlesworth. 2 vols. Garden City, NY: Doubleday, 1985.

Harnisch, W. *Verhängnis und Verheissung der Geschichte. Untersuchungen zum Zeit- und Geschichtsverständnis im 4. Buch Esra und in der syr. Baruchapokalypse.* FRLANT 97. Göttingen: Vandenhoeck and Ruprecht, 1969.

Harrington, D.J. "'The Holy Land' in *Pseudo-Philo, 4 Ezra,* and *2 Baruch.*" Pages 661–672 in *Emanuel: Studies in Hebrew Bible, Septuagint, and Dead Sea Scrolls in Honor of Emanuel Tov.* Edited by S.M. Paul, R.A. Kraft, L.H. Schiffman and W.W. Fields with the assistance of E. Ben-David. VTSup 94. Leiden: E.J. Brill, 2003.

———. "Interpreting Israel's History: The Testament of Moses as a Rewriting of Deut 31–34 [Summary of G. Reese, *Die Geschichte Israels in der Auffassung des frühen Judentums,* chapter 3]." Pages 59–70 in *Studies on the Testament of Moses: Seminar Papers.* Edited by G.W.E. Nickelsburg. Septuagint and Cognate Studies 4. Cambridge, Mass.: Society of Biblical Literature, 1973.

Hartman, L. *Asking for a Meaning: A Study of 1 Enoch 1–5.* ConBNT 12. Lund: CWK Gleerup, 1979.

———. "An Early Example of Jewish Exegesis: 1 Enoch 10.6–11.2." *Neot* 17 (1983): 16–26.

———. *Prophecy Interpreted: The Formation of Some Jewish Apocalyptic Texts and of the Eschatological Discourse in Mark 13 par.* ConBNT 1. Lund: CWK Gleerup, 1966.

Harvey, D. *The Condition of Postmodernity: An Enquiry into the Origins of Cultural Change.* Oxford: Blackwell, 1989.

Harvey, S.A. *Scenting Salvation: Ancient Christianity and the Olfactory Imagination.* The

Transformation of the Classical Heritage 2. Berkley, Calif.: University of California Press, 2006.

Hasel, G.F. "Sabbath." Pages 849–856 in vol. 5 of *ABD*. Edited by D.N. Freedman. 6 vols. Garden City: Doubleday, 1992.

Hayward, R. "The Vine and Its Products as Theological Symbols in First Century Palestinian Judaism." *The Durham University Journal* 82 (1990): 9–18.

Hengel, M. *Die Zeloten*. Leiden: E.J. Brill, 1961.

Henze, M. "From Jeremiah to Baruch: Pseudepigraphy in the *Syriac Apocalypse of Baruch*." Pages 157–177 in *Biblical Traditions in Transmission: Essays in Honour of Michael A. Knibb*. Edited by C. Hempel and J. Lieu. Leiden: E.J. Brill 2006.

——. Review of R. Nir, *The Destruction of Jerusalem and the Idea of Redemption in the Syriac Apocalypse*. *RBL* (June 2004). No pages. Online: http://www.bookreviews.org/bookdetail.asp?TitleId=3410.

——. *The Syriac Apocalypse of Daniel: Introduction, Text and Commentary*. Tübingen: Mohr Siebeck, 2001.

Herodotus. *Historiae*. Translated by A.D. Godley. 4 vols. LCL. Cambridge, Mass.: Harvard University Press, 1966.

Hesiod. *Works & Days*. Edited with prolegomena and commentary by M.L. West. Oxford: Clarendon Press, 1978.

Himmelfarb, M. *Ascent to Heaven in Jewish and Christian Apocalypses*. New York: Oxford University Press, 1993.

——. "The Temple and the Garden of Eden in Ezekiel, the Book of Watchers and the Wisdom of Ben Sira." Pages 63–80 in *Sacred Places and Profane Spaces: Essays in the Geographies of Judaism, Christianity and Islam*. Edited by J. Scott and P. Simpson-Housley. Contributions to the Study of Religion 30. New York: Greenwood, 1991.

Hirshman, M. "Rabbinic Universalism in the Second and Third Centuries." *HTR* 93 (2000): 101–115.

Hock, R.F. *The Infancy Gospel of James and Thomas*. The Scholars Bible vol. 2. Santa Rosa, Cal.: Polebridge Press, 1995.

Hoffman, L.A., ed. *The Land of Israel: Jewish Perspectives*. University of Notre Dame Center for the Study of Judaism and Christianity in Antiquity 6. Notre Dame, Ind.: University of Notre Dame Press, 1986.

Høgenhaven, J. "Geography and Ideology in the Copper Scroll." Paper presented at the 4th annual symposium of the Nordic Network in Qumran Studies. Copenhagen, August 25, 2006.

Holy Bible: New Revised Standard Version: Anglicized Edition. Oxford: Oxford University Press, 1995.

Homer. *The Odyssey*. Translated by A.T. Murray. 2 vols. LCL. Cambridge, Mass.: Harvard University Press, 1966.

Howard, D.M. "David." Pages 41–49 in vol. 2 of *ABD*. Edited by D.N. Freedman. 6 vols. Garden City: Doubleday, 1992.

Hultgård, A. *L'eschatologie des Testaments des douze patriarches*. 2 vols. Acta Universitatis Upsaliensis. Historia religionum 6–7. Uppsala: Almqvist & Wiksell, 1977–1981.

Hurtado, L.W. *One God, One Lord: Early Christian Devotion and Ancient Jewish Monotheism*. Philadelphia: Fortress Press, 1988.

Irwin, M.E. "Fair Flowers of Paradise in Clement of Alexandria and Others." No pages. Cited 1 April 2006. Online: http://www.odu.edu/webroot/instr/ sci/plant.nsf/pages/wreaths#N_1_.

Isaac, E. "1 (Ethiopic Apocalypse of) Enoch." Pages 5–89 in vol. 1 of *Old Testament Pseudepigrapha*. Edited by J.H. Charlesworth. 2 vols. Garden City, N.Y.: Doubleday, 1983–1985.

Jacob, I. and W. Jacob. "Flora." Pages 803–817 in vol. 2 of *ABD*. Edited by D.N. Freedman. 6 vols. Garden City: Doubleday, 1992.

Jacobs, A.S. *Remains of the Jews: The Holy Land and Christian Empire in Late Antiquity*. Stanford: Stanford University Press, 2004.

Japhet, S. *The Ideology of the Book of Chronicles and Its Place in Biblical Thought*. BEATAJ 9. Frankfurt am Main: Peter Lang, 1989.

———. "'Lebanon' in the Transition from Derash to Peshat: Sources, Etymology and Meaning (with Special Attention to the Song of Songs)." Pages 707–724 in *Emanuel: Studies in Hebrew Bible, Septuagint, and Dead Sea Scrolls in Honor of Emanuel Tov*. Edited by S.M. Paul, R.A. Kraft, L.H. Schiffman and W.W. Fields with the assistance of E. Ben-David. VTSup 94. Leiden: E.J. Brill, 2003.

Jeremias, J. *Heiligengräber in Jesu Umwelt (Mt.23,29; Lk. 11,47): eine Untersuchung zur Volksreligion der Zeit Jesu*. Göttingen: Vandenhoeck & Ruprecht, 1958.

———. "Paradeisos." Pages 765–773 in vol. 5 of *TDNT*. Edited by G. Friedrich. Translated by G.W. Bromiley. Grand Rapids, Mich.: Eerdmans, 1967.

———. *Unbekannte Jesusworte*. Revised with O. Hofius. 3rd ed. Gütersloh: Mohn, 1963.

Johnson, A.R. "The Role of the King in the Jerusalem Cultus." Pages 73–111 in *The Labyrinth: Further Studies in the Relation between Myth and Ritual in the Ancient World*. Edited by S.H. Hooke. London: Society for Promoting Christian Knowledge, 1935.

Jonge, H.J. de. "ΒΟΤΡΥΣ ΒΟΗCΕΙ. The age of Kronos and the Millenium in Papias of Hierapolis." Pages 37–49 in *Studies in Hellenistic Religions*. Edited by M.J. Vermaseren. EPRO 78. Leiden: E.J. Brill, 1979.

Jonge, M. de. *Pseudepigrapha of the Old Testament as Part of Christian Literature: The Case of the Testaments of the Twelve Patriarchs and the Greek Life of Adam and Eve*. SVTP 18. Leiden: E.J. Brill, 2003.

———. *The Testaments of the Twelve Patriarchs: A Study of Their Text, Composition and Origin*. Van Gorcum's Theologische Bibliotheek 25. Assen: Van Gorcum & comp., 1953.

Joosten, J. *People and Land in the Holiness Code: An Exegetical Study of the Ideational Framework of the Law in Leviticus 17–26*. VTSup 67. Leiden: E.J. Brill, 1996.

Josephus. *The Antiquities of the Jews*. Translated by W. Whiston. *2 vols*. McLean, Virg.: IndyPublish (Year of publication: not specified).

Josephus. Translated by H. St. J. Thackeray et al. 9 vols. LCL. Cambridge, Mass.: Harvard University Press, 1961.

Kabisch, R. "Die Quellen der Apokalypse Baruchs." *JbPT* 18 (1892): 66–107.

Kalimi, I. and D.J. Purvis. "The Hiding of the Temple Vessels in Jewish and Samaritan Literature." *CBQ* 56 (1994): 679–685.

Kallai, Z. *Historical Geography of the Bible: The Tribal Territories of Israel.* Jerusalem: The Magnes Press, 1986.

Kearney, P.J. "Creation and Liturgy; The P Redaction of Ex 25–40." *ZAW* 89 (1977): 375–387.

Kieffer, R. *Le Monde symbolique de Saint Jean.* LD 137. Paris: Les Éditions du cerf, 1989.

Kirschner, R. "Apocalyptic and Rabbinic Responses to the Destruction of 70." *HTR* 78 (1985): 27–46.

Klausner, J. *The Messianic Idea in Israel: From Its Beginning to the Completion of the Mishnah.* Translated by W.F. Stinespring. New York: Macmillan, 1955.

Klijn, A.F.J. "Recent Developments in the Study of the Syriac Apocalypse of Baruch." *JSP* 4(1989): 3–17.

———. "The Sources and Redaction of the Syriac Apocalypse of Baruch." *JSJ* 1 (1970): 65–76.

———. "2 (Syriac Apocalypse of) Baruch." Pages 615–652 in vol. 1 of *OTP*. Edited by J.H. Charlesworth. 2 vols. Garden City, NY: Doubleday, 1983.

Kmosko, M. "Apocalypsis Baruch filii Neriae, translatus de graeco in syriacum." Pages 1068–1207 in vol. 2 of *Patrologia syriaca*. Edited by R. Graffin. 3 vols. Paris: Firmin-Didot et Socli, 1894–1926.

Knot, K. *The Location of Religion: A Spatial Analysis.* London: Equinox, 2005.

Koester, C.R. *The Dwelling of God: The Tabernacle in the Old Testament, Intertestamental Literature, and the New Testament.* CBQMS 22. Washington: The Catholic Biblical Association of America, 1989.

Koester, H. *History, culture, and religion of the Hellenistic Age.* Vol. 1 of *Introduction to the New Testament*. By H. Koester. 2 vols. Berlin: Walter de Gruyter, 1982.

Kolenkow, A.B. "The Fall of the Temple and the Coming of the End: The Spectrum and Process of Apocalyptic Argumentation in *2 Baruch* and Other Authors." Pages 243–250 in *Society of Biblical Literature 1982 Seminar Papers*. SBLSP 21. Chico, Calif.: Scholars Press, 1982.

———. "An Introduction to *2 Baruch* 53, 56–77: Structure and Substance." PhD diss., Harvard, 1972.

———. "The Literary Genre 'Testament.'" Pages 259–267 in *Early Judaism and Its Modern Interpreters*. Edited by R.A. Kraft and G.W.E. Nickelsburg. BMI 2. Atlanta: Scholars Press, 1986.

Koningsveld, P.S. van. "An Arabic Manuscript of the Apocalypse of Baruch." *JSJ* 6 (1975): 205–207.

Kort, W.A. "Sacred/Profane and an Adequate Theory of Human Place-Relations." No pages. Online: http://www.cwru.edu/affil/GAIR/papers/2001papers/kort.html.

Kraft, R.A. "The Pseudepigrapha and Christianity Revisited: Setting the Stage and Framing Some Central Questions." *JSJ* 32 (2001): 371–385.

———. "The Pseudpigrapha in Christianity." Pages 55–86 in *Tracing the Threads: Studies in the Vitality of the Jewish Pseudpigrapha*. SBLEJL 6. Edited by J.C. Reeves. Atlanta: Scholars Press, 1994.

Kugel, J.L. *Traditions of the Bible: A Guide to the Bible as it Was at the Start of the Common Era.* Cambridge, Mass.: Harvard University Press, 1998.

Kunin, S. *God's Place in the World: Sacred Space and Sacred Place in Judaism*. London: Cassell, 1998.

Laato, A. *A Star is Rising: The Historical Development of the Old Testament Royal Ideology and the Rise of the Jewish Messianic Expectations*. University of South Florida International Studies in Formative Christianity and Judaism 5. Atlanta, Ga.: Scholars Press, 1998.

Lane, W. "Times of Refreshment: A Study of Eschatological Periodization in Judaism and Christianity." PhD diss., Harvard, 1962.

Lefebvre, H. *La production de l'espace*. Paris: Anthropos, 1974.

———. *The Production of Space*. Translated by D. Nicholson-Smith. Oxford: Blackwell, 1991.

Leemhuis, F., A.F.J. Klijn and G.H.J. van Gelder. *The Arabic Text of the Apocalypse of Baruch: Edited and Translated with a Parallel Translation of the Syriac Text*. Leiden: E.J. Brill, 1986.

Leuenberger, M. "Ort und Funktion der Wolkenvsion und ihrer Deutung in der Syrischen *Baruchapokalypse*." *JSJ* 36 (2005): 206–246.

Levenson, J.D. *Sinai and Zion: An Entry into the Jewish Bible*. New Voices in Biblical Studies. Minneapolis: Winston Press, 1985.

———. "The Temple and the World." *JR* 64 (1984): 275–298.

Levine, E., intro and trans. *The Targum to the Five Megillot: Ruth, Ecclesiastes, Canticles, Lamentations, Esther*. Jerusalem: Makor, 1977.

Lied, L.I. "Another Look at the Land of Damascus: The Spaces of the Damascus Document in Light of Edward W. Soja's Thirdspace Approach." Pages 101–125 in *New Directions in Qumran Studies: Proceedings of the Bristol Colloquium on the Dead Sea Scrolls, 8–10th September 2003*. Edited by J.G. Campbell, W.J. Lyons and L.K. Pietersen. LSTS 52. London: T&T Clark International, 2005.

———. "Døde, jordiske bein i Guds himmel? Det lova landet og dødens geografi." *Chaos* 39 (2003): 71–90.

———. "Frå Palestina til himmelen: Forestillingane om Landet i Testamentet til Moses." Masters thesis, University of Bergen, 2000.

———. "Land *and* Diaspora: Spatial Perspectives." *Complexity: Interdisciplinary Communications 2006/2007*. Edited by W. Østereng. Oslo: Centre for Advanced Study, 2008. Online: http://www.cas.uio.no/Publications/Seminar/Complexity_Lied.pdf.

———. "Recognizing the Righteous Remnant? Resurrection, Recognition and Transformation in *2 Baruch* 49–51". In *Metamorphoses: Resurrection, Body and Transformative Practices in Early Christianity*. Edited by T.K. Seim and J. Økland. Berlin, Walter de Gruyter, forthcoming 2009.

———. Review of Rivka Nir, *The Destruction of Jerusalem and the Idea of Redemption in the Syriac Apocalypse of Baruch*. *JSS* 50 no. 2 (2005): 403–405.

Lieu, J.M. *Christian Identity in the Jewish and Graeco-Roman World*. Oxford: Oxford University Press, 2004.

Lightfoot, R.H. *Locality and Doctrine in the Gospels*. London: Hodder and Stoughton, 1938.

Lohfink, N. *Die Landverheißung als Eid: Eine Studie zu Gn 15*. SBS 28. Stuttgart: Katholisches Bibelwerk, 1967.

———. *The Theology of the Pentateuch: Themes of the Priestly Narrative and Deuteronomy.* Translated by L.M. Maloney. Minneapolis: Fortress Press, 1994.

Lohmeyer, E. *Galiläa und Jerusalem.* FRLANT 52. Göttingen: Vandenhoeck & Ruprecht, 1959.

Mader, E. *Mambre: Die Ergebnisse der Ausgrabungen im heiligen Bezirk Râmet El-Halîl in Südpälestina 1926–1928.* Freiburg im Breisgau: Erich Wewel, 1957.

Malina, B.J. *The Palestinian Manna Tradition: The Manna Tradition in the Palestinian Targums and Its Relationship to the New Testament Writings.* AGJU 7. Leiden: E.J. Brill, 1968.

———. *The Social Gospel of Jesus: The Kingdom of God in Mediterranean Perspective.* Minneapolis, Minn.: Fortress Press, 2001.

Mare, W.H. "Kidron." Pages 37–38 in vol. 4 of *ABD.* Edited by D.N. Freedman. 6 vols. Garden City: Doubleday, 1992.

Massey, D. *Space, Place and Gender.* Cambridge: Polity Press, 1994.

McGowan, A.B. *Ascetic Eucharists: Food and Drink in Early Christian Ritual Meals.* Oxford Early Christian Studies. Oxford: Clarendon Press, 1999.

McKelvey, R.J. *The New Temple: The Church in the New Testament.* Oxford: Oxford University Press, 1969.

Meeks, W.A. *The First Urban Christians: the Social World of the Apostle Paul.* New Haven, Conn.: Yale University Press, 1983.

Meeks, W.A., J.M. Bassler, W.E. Lemke, S. Niditch, and E M. Schuller, eds. *The HarperCollins Study Bible: New Revised Standard Version, with the Apocryphal/Deuterocanonical books.* San Francisco: Harper, 1993.

Meissner, B. *Die Kultur Babyloniens und Assyriens.* Wissenschaft und Bildung 207. Leipzig: Quelle & Meyer, 1925.

Mendels, D. *The Land of Israel as a Political Concept in Hasmonean Literature: Recourse to History in 2. Century BC Claims to the Holy Land.* Tübingen: J.C.B. Mohr, 1987.

———. *The Rise and Fall of Jewish Nationalism: The History of Jewish and Christian Ethnicity in Palestine within the Greco-Roman Period (200 B.C.E. – 135 C.E.).* ABRL. New York: Doubleday, 1992.

Mendenhall, G.E. "The Monarchy." *Int* 29 (1975): 155–170.

———. "Samuel's 'Broken Rib': Deuteronomy 32." Pages 63–74 in *No Famine in the Land: Studies in Honor of John L. McKenzie.* Edited by J.W. Flanagan and A. Weisbrod Robinson. Missoula: Scholars Press, 1975.

Menzies, A., ed. *The Gospel of Peter, the Diatessaron of Tatian, the Apocalypse of Peter, the Visio Pauli, the Apocalypses of the Virgin and Sedrach, the Testament of Abraham, the Acts of Xanthippe and Polyxena, the Narrative of Zosimus, the Apology of Aristides, the Epistles of Clement (Complete Text), Origen's Commentary on John, Books 1–10, and Commentary on Matthew, Books 1, 2, and 10–14.* 10 vols. 5th ed. The Ante-Nicene Fathers: Translations of the Writings of the Fathers down to A.D. 325. Grand Rapids, Mich.: Eerdmans, 1971–1986.

Metzger, B.M. "The Fourth Book of Ezra: A New Translation and Introduction." Pages 516–559 in vol. 1 of *OTP.* Edited by J.H. Charlesworth. 2 vols. Garden City, N.Y.: Doubleday, 1983.

Meyers, C.L. "Jachin and Boaz in Religious and Political Perspective." *CBQ* 45 (1983): 167–178.

Meyers, E.M. *Jewish Ossuaries: Reburial and Rebirth*. BibOr 24. Rome: Biblical Institute Press, 1971.

Milik, J.T. "Notes d'épigraphie et de topographie palestiennes." *RB* 66 (1959): 550–575.

Morray-Jones, C.R.A. "Transformational Mysticism in the Apocalyptic-Merkabah Tradition." *JJS* 43 (1992): 1–31.

Moss, C. *Catalogue of Syriac Printed Books and Related Literature in the British Museum*. Gorgias Historical Catalogues 2. Gorgias Press, forthcomming.

Mowinkel, S. "De fire Paradiselvene." *NTT* 39 (1938): 47–67.

Moxnes, H. "Kingdom Takes Place: Transformations of Place and Power in the Kingdom of God in the Gospel of Luke." In *Social Scientific Models for Interpreting the Bible: Essays by the Context Group in Honor of Bruce J. Malina*. Edited by J.J. Pilch. BibInt 53. Boston: E.J. Brill, 2001.

———. *Putting Jesus in His Place. A Radical Vision of Household and Kingdom*. Louisville: Westminster John Knox, 2003.

———. *Theology in Conflict: Studies in Paul's Understanding of God in Romans*. NovTSup 53. Leiden: E.J. Brill, 1980.

Muddiman, J. "Fast, Fasting." Pages 773–776 in vol. 2 of *ABD*. Edited by D.N. Freedman. 6 vols. Garden City: Doubleday, 1992.

Mueller, J.R. "The Apocalypse of Abraham and the Destruction of the Second Jewish Temple." Pages 341–349 in *Society of Biblical Literature 1982 Seminar Papers*. SBLSP 21. Chico, Calif.: Scholars Press, 1982.

Mullen, E.T., Jr. *The Assembly of the Gods*. HSM 24. Chico, Calif.: Scholars Press, 1980.

Münchow, C. *Ethik und Eschatologie. Ein Beitrag zum Verständnis der frühjüdischen Apokalyptik mit einem Ausblick auf das Neue Testament*. Göttingen: Vandenhoeck & Ruprecht, 1981.

Murphy, F.J. Review of R. Nir, *The Destruction of Jerusalem and the Idea of Redemption in the Syriac Apocalypse of Baruch*. *CBQ* 66 (2004): 326–327.

———. *The Structure and Meaning of Second Baruch*. SBLDS 78. Atlanta: Scholars Press, 1985.

Murray, R. *Symbols of Church and Kingdom: A Study in Early Syriac Tradition*. London: Cambridge University Press, 1975.

Mynors, R.A.B., ed. *Vergili opera*. OCT. Oxford: Oxford University Press, 1969.

Neusner, J. *Ancient Judaism and Modern Category Formation: 'Judaism,' 'Midrash,' 'Messianism,' and Canon in the Past Quarter-Century*. Lanham, Md.: University Press of America, 1986.

———. "History and Purity in First-Century Judaism." *HR* 18 (1978): 1–17.

———. *The Idea of Purity in Ancient Judaism*. Leiden: E.J. Brill, 1973.

———. *Judaism: The Evidence of the Mishnah*. Chicago: University of Chicago Press, 1981.

Neusner, J., E.S. Frerichs and C. McCracken-Flesher, eds. *"To See Ourselves as Others See Us": Christians, Jews, "Others" in Late Antiquity*. SPSHS. Chico, Calif.: Scholars Press, 1985.

Newsom, C.A. *The Self as Symbolic Space: Constructing Identity and Community at Qumran*. STDJ 52. Leiden: E.J. Brill, 2004.

Nickelsburg, G.W.E. *1 Enoch 1: A Commentary on the Book of 1 Enoch, Chapters 1–36;*

81–108. Edited by G.W.E. Nickelsburg. Hermeneia. Minneapolis: Fortress Press, 2001.

———. "Judgement, Life-After-Death, and Resurrection in the Apocrypha and the Non-Apocalyptic Pseudepigrapha." Pages 141–162 in *Judaism in Late Antiquity: Part 4: Death, Life-After-Death, Resurrection and the World-to-Come in the Judaisms of Antiquity*. HO 49. Edited by A.J. Avery-Peck and J. Neusner. Leiden: E.J. Brill, 2000.

———. *Resurrection, Immortality and Eternal Life in Intertestamental Judaism*. Harvard Theological Studies 26. Cambridge, Mass.: Harvard University Press, 1972.

Nir, R. "The Aromatic Fragrances of Paradise in the Greek Life of Adam and Eve and the Christian Origin of the Composition." *NovT* 46 (2004): 20–45.

———. *The Destruction of Jerusalem and the Idea of Redemption in the Syriac Apocalypse of Baruch*. SBLEJL 20. Atlanta: Society of Biblical Literature, 2003.

Nordheim, E. von. *Das Testament als Literaturgattung im Judentum der hellenistisch-römischen Zeit*. Vol. 1 of *Die Lehre der Alten*. ALGHJ 131. Leiden: E.J. Brill, 1980.

O'Hagan, A.P. *Material Re-Creation in the Apostolic Fathers*. TUGAL 100. Berlin: Akademie-Verlag, 1968.

Økland, J. "The Language of Gates and Entering: On Sacred Space in the Temple Scroll." Pages 149–165 in *New Directions in Qumran Studies: Proceedings of the Bristol Colloquium on the Dead Sea Scrolls, 8–10th September 2003*. Edited by J.G. Campbell, W.J. Lyons and L.K. Pietersen. LSTS 52. London: T&T Clark International, 2005.

———. *Women in their Place: Paul and the Corinthian Discourse of Gender and Sanctuary Space*. JSNTSup 269. London: T&T Clark, 2004.

The Old Testament in Syriac: According to the Peshitta Version. Edited on behalf of the International Organization for the Study of the Old Testament by the Peshitta Institute. Leiden: E.J. Brill, 1972–.

Ottosson, M. "Eden and the Land of Promise." Pages 177–188 in *Congress Volume: Jerusalem 1986*. Edited by J.A. Emerton. VTSup 40. Leiden: E.J. Brill, 1988.

Penas Ibánez, B., ed. *The Intertextual Dimension of Discourse: Pragmalinguistic-Cognitive-Hermeneutic Approaches*. Zaragoza: Universidad de Zaragoza, 1996.

Perles, F. "Notes sur les Apocryphes et les Pseudépigraphes I: Traces des Apocryphes et des Pseudépigraphes dans la Liturgie juive." *REJ* 73 (1921): 173–185.

Philo. Translated by F.H. Colson and G.H. Whitaker. 10 vols. LCL. Cambridge, Mass.: Harvard University Press, 1958.

Popovic, Ml. "4QZodical Physiognomy (4Q186) and the Cultural Locus of Physiognomics and Astrology in Second Temple Period Judaism." Paper presented at the First Graduate Enoch Seminar, Ann Arbor, May 3, 2006.

———. *Reading the Human Body: Physiognomics and Astrology in the Dead Sea Scrolls and Hellenistic—Early Roman Period Judaism*. STDJ 67. Leiden: E.J. Brill, 2007.

Priest, J. "A Note on the Messianic Banquet." Pages 222–238 in *The Messiah: Developments in Earliest Judaism and Christianity*. Edited by J.H. Charlesworth et al. *The First Princeton Symposium on Judaism and Christian Origins*. Minneapolis: Fortress Press, 1992.

Propp, W.H.C. "A Land of Milk and Honey—Biblical Comfort Food." *BRev* 15/3 (1999): 16–17.

Puech, E. *La croyance des Esséniens en la vie future: Immortalité, réssurrection, vie éternelle? Histoire d'une croyance dans le Judaïsme Ancien*. 2 vols. Ebib 21–22. Paris: Librairie Lecoffre, 1993.

Rad, G. von. *Das fünfte Buch Mose: Deuteronomium*. ATD 8. Göttingen: Vandenhoeck & Ruprecht, 1983.

———. *The Problem of the Hexateuch and Other Essays*. Translated by E.W.T. Dicken. New York: McGraw-Hill, 1966.

———. *Studies in Deuteronomy*. London: SCM Press, 1953.

———. "Verheissenes Land und Jahwes Land im Hexateuch." ZDPV 66 (1943): 191–204.

Rahlfs, A., ed. *Septuaginta*. Stuttgart: Deutsche Bibelgesellschaft, 1979.

Rendtorff, R. *The Covenant Formula: An Exegetical and Theological Investigation*. Translated by M. Kohl. OTS. Edinburgh: T&T Clark, 1998.

Rigsby, R.O. "First Fruits." Pages 796–797 in vol. 2 of *ABD*. Edited by D.N. Freedman. 6 vols. Garden City: Doubleday, 1992.

Roberts, A. and J. Donaldson, eds. *The Apostolic Fathers with Justin Martyr and Irenaeus*. The Ante-Nicene Fathers: Translations of the Writings of the Fathers down to A.D. 325. Ann Arbor, Mich.: 1969.

Roberts, J.J.M. "Zion in the Theology of the Davidic-Solomonic Empire." Pages 93–108 in *Studies in the Periods of David and Solomon and Other Essays: Papers Read at the International Symposium for Biblical Studies, Tokyo, 5–7 December 1979*. Edited by T. Ishida. Winona Lake, Ind.: Eisenbrauns, 1982.

Robinson, J.A., ed. *Texts and Studies, No. 2: The Testament of Abraham*. Contributions to Biblical and Patristic Literature. Cambridge: University Press, 1892.

Robinson, T.H. *Paradigms and Exercises in Syriac Grammar*. 4th Edition. Oxford: Clarendon Press, 1962.

Romm, J.S. *The Edges of the Earth in Ancient Thought: Geography, Exploration and Fiction*. Princeton, N.J.: Princeton University Press, 1992.

Rosenberg, S. "The Link to the Land of Israel in Jewish Thought: A Clash of Perspectives." Pages 139–169 in *The Land of Israel: Jewish Perspectives*. Edited by L.A. Hoffman. University of Notre Dame Center for the Study of Judaism and Christianity in Antiquity 6. Notre Dame, Ind.: University of Notre Dame Press, 1986.

Rosenkranz, S. "Vom Paradies zum Tempel." Pages 27–131 in *Tempelkult und Tempelzerstörung (70 n.Chr). Festschrift für Clemens Thoma zum 60. Geburtstag*. Edited by S. Lauer and H. Ernst. JudCh 15. Bern: Peter Lang, 1995.

Rosenthal, F. *Vier apokryphische Bücher aus der Zeit und Schule R. Akiba's: Assumptio Mosis, Das vierte Buch Esra, Die Apokalypse Baruch, Das Buch Tobi*. Leipzig, Otto Schulze, 1885.

Rost, L. *Das kleine Credo und andere Studien zum Alten Testament*. Heidelberg: Quelle und Meyer, 1965.

Rowland, C. *The Open Heaven. A Study of Apocalyptic in Judaism and Early Christianity*. London: SPCK, 1982.

Ruffatto, K.J. "Polemics with Enochic Traditions in the Exagoge of Ezekiel the Tragedian." *JSP* 15 (2006): 195–210.

Russell, D.M. *The Method and Message of Jewish Apocalyptic 200 BC–AD 100*. London: SCM Press, 1964.

Ryssel, V. "Die Apokalypsen des Baruch: Die syrische Baruchapokalypse." Pages 402–457 in vol. 2 of *Die Apokryphen und Pseudepigraphen des Alten Testaments*. Edited by E. Kautzsch. 2 vols. Tübingen: Wissenschaftliche Buchgesellschaft, 1900.

Safrai, S. "Jerusalem in the Halakah." Pages 94–113 in *The Centrality of Jerusalem*. Edited by M. Poorthuius and C.H. Safrai. Kampen: Kok Phaors, 1996.

Saldarini, A.J. "Apocalyptic and Rabbinic Literature." *CBQ* 37 (1975): 348–358.

Sancti Cypriani Episcopi opera: Ad Quirinum: Ad Fortunatum. Edited by R. Weber. Pars 1 Corpus Christianorum: Series Latina 3, 1972. Reprint in A.-M. Denis, ed., *Concordance latine des pseudépigraphes d'Ancien Testament: Concordance, corpus des textes, indices*. Corpus christianorum. Thesaurus patrum latinorum. Supplementum. Turnhout: Brepols, 1993.

Sanders, E.P. *Judaism: Practice and Belief, 63 BCE – 66 CE*. London: SCM Press, 1992.

———. "Testaments of the Three Patriarchs." Pages 869–918 in vol. 1 of *OTP*. Edited by J.H. Charlesworth. 2 vols. Garden City, NY: Doubleday, 1983.

Sandmel, S. *Philo's Place in Judaism: A Study of Conceptions of Abraham in Jewish Literature*. Oxford: Oxford University Press, 1971.

Sarason, R.S. "The Significance of the Land of Israel in the Mishnah." Pages 109–137 in *The Land of Israel: Jewish Perspectives*. Edited by L.A. Hoffman. University of Notre Dame Center for the Study of Judaism and Christianity in Antiquity 6. Notre Dame, Indiana: University of Notre Dame Press, 1986.

Sayler, G.B. "*2 Baruch*: A Story of Grief and Consolation." Pages 485–500 in *Society of Biblical Literature 1982 Seminar Papers*. SBLSP 21. Chico, Calif.: Scholars Press, 1982.

———. *Have the Promises Failed? A Literary Analysis of 2 Baruch*. SBLDS 72. Chico, Calif.: Scholars Press, 1984.

The SBL Handbook of Style: For Ancient Near Eastern, Biblical, and Early Christian Studies. Edited by P.H. Alexander *et alii*. 4th reprint. Peabody, Ma., Hendrickson Publ., 2004.

Schmidt, K.L. "Jerusalem als Urbild und Abbild." *ErJb* 18 (1950): 207–248.

Segal, A.F. "Heavenly Ascent in Hellenistic Judaism, Early Christianity and Their Environment." *Aufstieg und Niedergang der römischen Welt: Geschichte und Kultur Roms im Spiegel der neueren Forschung* 23.2:1333–1394. Part 2, Principat, 23.2. Edited by W. Haase. New York: Walter de Gruyter, 1980.

———. *Life after Death: A History of the Afterlife in Western Religion*. New York: Doubleday, 2004.

Seim, T.K. "Udødelig og kjønnsløs? Oppstandelseskroppen i lys av Lukas." Pages 80–98 in *Kropp og oppstandelse*. Edited by T. Engberg-Pedersen and I.S. Gilhus. Oslo: Pax Forlag As, 2001.

Shiner, L.E. "Sacred Space, Profane Space, Human Space." *JAAR* 40 (1972): 425–436.

Siker, J.S. *Disinheriting the Jews: Abraham in Early Christian Controversy*. Louisville, Ky.: Westminster/John Knox Press, 1991.

Simon, M. "La Prophétie de Nathan et le Temple," *RHPR* 32 (1952): 44–58.

Simon, M. and I.W. Slotki, trans. *Baba Bathra: Translated into English with Notes and Glossary*. 2 vols. Seder Nezikin. Hebrew-English Edition of the Babylonian Talmud 4. London: The Soncino Press, 1976.

Smith, D.E. *From Symposium to Eucharist: The Banquet in the Early Christian World*. Minneapolis: Fortress Press, 2003.

———. "Messianic Banquet." Page 788–791 in vol. 4 of *ABD*. Edited by D.N. Freedman. 6 vols. Garden City: Doubleday, 1992.

———. "The Messianic Banquet Reconsidered." Pages 64–73 in *The Future of Early Christianity: Essays in Honor of Helmut Koester*. Edited by B.A. Pearson. Minneapolis: Fortress Press, 1991.

Smith, J.P. *A Compendious Syriac Dictionary. Founded upon the Thesaurus Syriacus of R. Payne Smith*. Oxford: Oxford University Press, 1902. Repr., Eugene, Or.: Wipf and Stock, 1999.

Smith, J.Z. *Imagining Religion: From Babylon to Jonestown*. CSJH. Chicago: University of Chicago Press, 1982.

———. *Map is not Territory: Studies in the History of Religions*. SJLA 23. Leiden: E.J. Brill, 1978.

———. *To Take Place. Toward Theory in Ritual*. Chicago: University of Chicago Press, 1987.

Smith, M. "On the Wine God in Palestine (Gen. 18, John 2, and Achilles Tatius)." Pages 815–829 in vol. 2, English section, of *Salo Wittmayer Baron Jubilee Volume: On the Occasion of His Eightieth Birthday*. Edited by S. Lieberman. 3 vols. Jerusalem: Central Press for the American Academy for Jewish Research, 1974.

Smith, R.P. *Thesaurus Syriacus*. 2 vols. Oxford, 1879–1901. Repr., 4. Nachdruck der Ausgabe Oxford 1879–1901. Hildesheim: Georg Olms, 2006.

Soja, E.W. *Postmetropolis: Critical Studies of Cities and Religions*. Oxford: Blackwell, 2000.

———. *Postmodern Geographies*. London: Verso, 1989.

———. "Thirdspace: Expanding the Scope of the Geographical Imagination." Pages 13–30 in *Architecturally Speaking. Practices of Art, Architecture and the Everyday*. Edited by A. Read. London: Routledge, 2000.

———. *Thirdspace: Journeys to Los Angeles and Other Real-and-Imagined Places*. Cambridge, Mass.: Blackwell, 1996.

Sperber, A., ed. *The Former Prophets according to Targum Jonathan*. Vol. 2 of The Bible in Aramaic: Based on Old Manuscripts and Printed Texts. Leiden: E.J. Brill, 1959.

Steck, O.H. *Israel und das gewaltsame Geschick der Propheten: Untersuchungen zur Überlieferung des deuteronomistischen Geschichtsbildes im alten Testament, Spätjudentum und Urchristentum*. WMANT 23. Tübingen: J.C.B. Mohr, 1992.

Stegemann, H. "'Das Land' in der Tempelrolle und in anderen Texten aus den Qumranfunden." Pages 154–171 in *Das Land Israel in biblischer Zeit. Jerusalem-Symposium 1981 der Hebräischen Universität und der Georg-August-Universität.* Edited by G. Strecker. GTA 25. Göttingen: Vandenhoeck & Ruprecht, 1983.

Stemberger, G. "Galilee—Land of Salvation?" Appendix IV. Pages 409–438 in *The Gospel and the Land: Early Christianity and Jewish Territorial Doctrine.* BSem 25. By W.D. Davies. Berkeley: University of California Press, 1974. Repr., Sheffield: JSOT Press, 1994.

———. *Der Leib der Auferstehung. Studien zur Anthropologie und Eschatologie des palästinischen Judentums im neutestamentlichen Zeitalter (ca. 170 v.Chr – 100 n. Chr).* AnBib 56. Rome: Biblical Institute Press, 1972.

Stolz, F. "Paradiese und Gegenwelten." *Zeitschrift für Religionswissenschaft* 1 (1993): 5–24.

———. "Sea." Pages 740–742 in *DDD.* Edited by K. van der Toorn, B. Becking, and P.W. van der Horst. Leiden: E.J. Brill, 1995.

Stone, M.E. *Fourth Ezra: A Commentary on the Book of Fourth Ezra.* Hermeneia. Minneapolis: Fortress Press, 1990.

———. "Reactions to Destruction of the Second Temple." *JSJ* 12 (1981): 195–204.

Stordalen, T. *Echoes of Eden: Genesis 2–3 and Symbolism of the Eden Garden in Biblical Hebrew Literature.* CBET 25. Leuven: Peeters, 2000.

Struthers Malbon, E. *Narrative Space and Mythic Meaning in Mark.* New York: Harper & Row, 1986.

Sulzbach, C. "The Function of the Sacred Geography in the Book of Jubilees." *JSem* 14/2 (2005): 283–305.

Tacitus. *The Histories.* Translated by A.D. Godley. 2 vols. London, 1942–1949.

Temporini, H. and W. Haase, eds. *Aufstieg und Niedergang der römischen Welt: Geschichte und Kultur Roms im Spiegel der neueren Forschung.* Part 2, Principat. Edited by W. Haase. New York: Walter de Gruyter, 1975.

Thackston, W.M. *Introduction to Syriac: An Elementray Grammar with Readings from Syriac Literature.* Bethesda, Maryland: IBEX Publishers, 1999.

Thompson, A.L. *Responsibility For Evil in the Theodicy of IV Ezra.* Missoula, MT: Scholars Press, 1977.

Torczyner, H. "The Firmament and the Clouds." *Studia theologica* 1 (1948): 188–196.

Torrey, C.C. "The Messiah Son of Ephraim." *JBL* 66 (1947): 253–277.

Tromp, J. *The Assumption of Moses: Critical Edition with Commentary.* SVTP 10. Leiden: E.J. Brill, 1993.

Tunyogi, A.C. *The Rebellions of Israel.* Richmond: John Knox, 1969.

Ulfgard, H. "'…nu har vi inget annat än den Mektiga och hans Lag': Kris, kontinuitet och apokalyptik i *2 Baruk*." Pages 79–122 in *Det gamle testamente i jødedom og kristendom.* FBE 4. Edited by M. Müller and J. Strange. København: Museum Tusculanum Forlag, 1993.

Ulmer, R. *Pesiqta rabbati: A Synoptic Edition of Pesiqta rabbati Based upon All Extant Manuscripts and the editio princeps.* South Florida Studies in the History of Judaism 155. Atlanta: Scholars Press, 1997.

VanderKam, J.C. *The Book of Jubilees.* Guides to Apocrypha and Pseudepigrapha. Sheffield: Sheffield Academic Press, 2001.

——. *Enoch and the Growth of an Apocalyptic Tradition*. CBQMS 16. Washington D.C.: Catholic Biblical Association of America, 1984.

——. "Righteous One, Messiah, Chosen One, and Son of Man in 1 Enoch 37–71." Pages 169–191 in *The Messiah: Developments in Earliest Judaism and Christianity*. Edited by J.H. Charlesworth et al. The First Princeton Symposium on Judaism and Christian Origins. Minneapolis: Fortress, 1992.

Vermes, G. *Scripture and Tradition in Judaism*. StPB 4. Leiden: E.J. Brill, 1973.

——. "The Symbolic Interpretation of Lebanon in the Targums: The Origin and Development of an Exegetical Tradition." *JTS* 9 (1958): 1–12.

Violet, B. *Die Apokalypsen des Esra und des Baruch in deutscher Gestalt*. GCS 32. Leipzig: J.C. Hinrichs'sche Buchhandlung, 1924.

Vogel, C. "Le repas sacré au poisson chez les chrétiens." *RevScRel* 40 (1966): 1–26.

Volz, P. *Eschatologie der jüdischen Gemeinde im neutestamentlichen Zeitalter. Nach den Quellen der rabbinischen, apokalyptischen und apokryphen Literatur*. Tübingen: J.C.B. Mohr, 1934. Repr. Hildesheim: Georg Olms, 1966.

——. *Jüdische Eschatologie: Von Daniel bis Akiba*. Tübingen: J.C.B. Mohr, 1903.

Ward, G. *The Postmodern God: A Theological Reader*. Blackwell Readings in Modern Theology. Malden, Mass.: Blackwell, 1997.

Weinfeld, M. *Deuteronomy and the Deuteronomic School*. Oxford: Clarendon, 1972.

——. "Inheritance of the Land—Privilege versus Obligation: The Concept of the 'Promise of the Land' in the Sources of the First and Second Temple Periods" (in Hebrew). *Zion* 49 (1984): 115–137.

——. "Sabbat, Miqdas, Wehamlakat H" (in Hebrew). *Bet Miqra* (1977).

Weissenberg, H. von. "Covenantal Motifs in 4QMMT." Paper presented at the First Graduate Enoch Seminar, Ann Arbor, May 3, 2006.

——. "4QMMT—The Problem of the Epilogue." PhD diss., University of Helsinki, 2006.

Wenell, K.J. *Jesus and Land: Sacred and Social Space in Second Temple Judaism*. LNTS 334. London: T&T Clark, 2007.

Wewers, G.A., trans. *Hagiga = Festopfer*. Der Jerusalemer Talmud in deutscher Übersetzung: herausgegeben vom Institutum Judaicum der Universität Tübingen 2. Tübingen: Mohr, 1983.

Wharton, A. "Erasure: Eliminating the Space of Late Ancient Judaism." Pages 195–214 in *From Dura to Sepphoris: Studies in Jewish Art and Society in Late Antiquity*. Journal of Roman Archaeology Supplement Series 40. Edited by L.I. Levine and Z. Weiss. Portsmouth, RI: JRA, 2000.

Whitelam, K.W. *The Invention of Ancient Israel: The Silencing of Palestinian History*. London: Routledge, 1996.

——. *The Just King: Monarchical Judicial Authority in Ancient Israel*. Sheffield: Journal for the Study of the Old Testament Press, 1979.

Whitney, K.W. *Two Strange Beasts: Leviathan and Behemoth in Second Temple and Early Rabbinic Judaism*. HSM 63. Winona Lake, Ind.: Eisenbrauns, 2006.

Whitters, M. *The Epistle of Second Baruch: A Study of Form and Message*. LSTS 42. Sheffield: Sheffield Academic Press, 2003.

——. "Testament and Canon in the Letter of Second Baruch (2 Baruch 78–87)." *JSP* 12 (2001): 149–163.

Widengren, G. *The King and the Tree of Life in Ancient Near Eastern Religion.* King and Saviour 4. UUA 4. Uppsala: Lundquistska Bokhandeln, 1951.

———. *Sakrales Königtum im Alten Testament und im Judentum.* Franz Delitzsch-Vorlesungen 1952. Stuttgart: Kohlhammer, 1955.

Wilcke, H.A. *Das Problem eines messianischen Zwischenreichs bei Paulus.* ATANT 51. Zürich: Zwingli Verlag, 1967.

Wilken, R.L. *The Land Called Holy: Palestine in Christian History and Thought.* New Haven: Yale University Press, 1992.

Willet, T.W. *Eschatology in the Theodicies of* 2 Baruch *and* 4 Ezra. JSPSup 4. Sheffield: JSOT Press, 1989.

Wintermute, O.S. "Jubilees." Pages 35–142 in vol. 2 of *Old Testament Pseudepigrapha.* Edited by J.H. Charlesworth. 2 vols. Garden City, N.Y.: Doubleday, 1983–1985.

Wright, J.E. *Baruch ben Neriah: From Biblical Scribe to Apocalyptic Seer.* Colombia, SC: University of South Carolina Press, 2003.

———. *The Early History of Heaven.* Oxford: Oxford University Press, 2000.

Wright, W. *Catalogue of the Syriac Manuscripts in the British Museum.* 3 vols. London: The British Museum, 1870–1872.

Zahn, Th. *Die Offenbarung des Johannes.* Vol. 18 of Kommentar zum Neuen Testament. Edited by Th. Zahn. Leipzig: A. Deichertsche Verlagsbuchhandlung, 1924.

Zimmerli, W. *Man and His Hope in the Old Testament.* SBT. Naperville, Ill.: Allenson, 1968.

———. *The Old Testament and the World.* London: SPCK, 1976.

Zimmermann, F. "Translation and Mistranslation in the Apocalypse of Baruch." Pages 580–587 in *Studies and Essays in Honor of Abraham A. Neuman.* Edited by M. Ben-Horin, B.D. Weinryb and Z. Zeitlin. Leiden: E.J. Brill, 1962.

Zimmermann, J. *Messianische Texte aus Qumran: köngliche, priesterliche und prophetiche Messiasvorstellungen in den Schriftfunden von Qumran.* WUNT 104. Tübingen: Mohr Siebeck, 1998.

Zweip, A.W. *The Ascension of the Messiah in Lukan Christology.* Leiden: E.J. Brill, 1997.

INDEX OF REFERENCES